# COLONIAL VIRGINIA'S COOKING DYNASTY

Archaeological excavation at Curles Plantation, 1988.

# COLONIAL VIRGINIA'S COOKING DYNASTY

KATHARINE E. HARBURY

University of South Carolina Press

Published in Columbia, South Carolina, by the
University of South Carolina Press

Manufactured in the United States of America

08 07 06 05 04 5 4 3 2 1

Library of Congress Cataloging-in-Publication Data

Harbury, Katharine E., 1950–
Colonial Virginia's cooking dynasty / Katharine E. Harbury.
p. cm.
Includes bibliographical references and index.
ISBN 1-57003-513-X (cloth : alk. paper)
1. Cookery—Virginia—History. 2. Food habits—Virginia. 3. United States—History—Colonial period, ca. 1600–1775. I. Title.
TX715 .H258 2003
394.1'09755—dc22

2003016363

*Frontispiece:* Archaeological excavation at Curles Plantation, 1988. The white brick foundation near the center of the photograph represents Jane (Bolling) Randolph's kitchen. The square hole in the foreground is the remnant of Nathaniel Bacon the Rebel's house. A well is on the right. On the left side between the kitchen and Bacon's house is the site of Thomas Harris's house, yet to be discovered. Courtesy of Katharine E. Harbury

Cookery means the knowledge of Medea, and of
Circe, and of Calypso, and of Helen, and of Rebekah,
and of the Queen of Sheba . . . of all herbs, and fruits,
and balms and spices; and all that is healing and
sweet in the fields and groves, and savoury in meats. . . .

—John Ruskin

Madam Turner . . . and Mrs. Morrice . . . I carried them on board the King's Pleasure-boat—all the way reading in a book of Receipts of making fine meats and sweetmeats; among others, one "To make my own sweet water"—which made us good sport.

—Samuel Pepys

# CONTENTS

# ILLUSTRATIONS

# ACKNOWLEDGMENTS

I am greatly indebted to my parents, brothers, and sister for their personal encouragement, advice, and support; Dr. L. Daniel Mouer and Dr. Joanne Bowen for wise and helpful guidance; Mr. Polk Lafoon, Mr. E. Lee Shepard, and Mr. Brad Rauschenburg for their gracious permission to include material from the three culinary manuscripts; the staff of the Rare Book and Special Collections Division of the Library of Congress and the staffs of the Library of Virginia, the Virginia Historical Society, and the Earl Gregg Swem Library at the College of William and Mary for generously sharing their knowledge and expertise; Mrs. Marion E. Briggs of Briggs and Associates, Inc., for her analysis of handwriting; Dr. Helen Rountree for her assistance with the term "Kipscacuanna"; Mr. Roger Goodburn for his assistance in matters of chemistry and terminology; and Mrs. Annie Goodburn for her help with the "chawdron" recipes.

I wish as well to express my appreciation to the anonymous reader of a draft of this book for directing me to the 1744 manuscript; Ms. Donna Rothrock and the staff of the Museum of Early Southern Decorative Arts for facilitating my examination of this cookbook; and Mr. E. Lee Shepard and Ms. Stacy Rusch of the Virginia Historical Society for their assessment of the dating analysis of the "c. 1700" manuscript.

I thank them all.

### Editorial Note

Bibliographic references for each chapter's epigraphs are found in an unnumbered note at the beginning of the chapter's citations.

# INTRODUCTION

I had for them, after oysters—at the first course, a hash of rabbits and lamb, and a rare chine of beef—next, a great dish of roasted fowl, cost me about 30s, and a tart; and then fruit and cheese. My dinner was noble and enough . . . both them and myself highly pleased.

—Samuel Pepys

Mrs. Blackburn . . . who did treat my wife and I with a great deal of civility . . . did give us a fine collation of collar of beef, &c.

—Samuel Pepys

We were now shown into the drawing room and there had the pleasure of seeing Miss [Maria] Beverley and Mr. [Richard] Randolph joined in holy matrimony.

The ceremony was really affecting and awful [awe-inspiring]. The sweet bride could not help shedding tears, which affected her mother and the whole company. She was most elegantly dressed in white satin, and the bridegroom in a lead color, lined with pink satin. After the ceremony of saluting, the ladies retired.

At four we joined them to a most sumptuous and elegant dinner that would have done honor to any nobleman's house in England. We were about a hundred in company. . . . Those I recollect . . . Miss Carey, Mrs. Bird, Miss Betsy Randolph. . . . After dinner we danced cotillions, minuets, Virginia and Scotch reels, country dances, jigs, etc. till ten o'clock. . . . After supper, which was as elegant as the dinner—it's vain to attempt describing it—we continued dancing until twelve.

We rose to an elegant breakfast, at ten, consisting of tea, coffee, chocolate, cold ham, fowls, hashed mutton, and other dishes. The bride came, beautifully blushing, into the room soon after in an elegant undress, and looked more amiable than ever. The fright of yesterday had taken away all her color, which now returned with a double glow.

The bridegroom looked completely happy. I think him a most agreeable young man. He with several of the gentlemen took a ride after breakfast.

—Robert Hunter

In 1988, while examining historical documents, I came across "Unidentified cookbook, c. 1700" by Anonymous and "Jane Randolph her Cookery Book, 1743" by Jane (Bolling) Randolph. It was recognized that these two documents were related not only to each other but also to the 1824 classic *The Virginia Housewife* by Mary Randolph. Not only was the discovery of such an unusually early and historically significant collection of cookbooks an exciting one for Chesapeake studies, but it also formed the basis of my master's thesis, "Colonial Virginia's Cooking Dynasty: Women's Spheres and Culinary Arts," which was completed in 1994. This book carries the research project further by publishing the recipes from the c. 1700 and 1743 historical cookery manuscripts, a 1744 manuscript arranged by "The Compiler," and Mary Randolph's published recipes. The format has been designed for the purpose of comparison and ease of reference for anthropologists, archaeologists, food historians, and the general public.

Cookery manuscripts were traditionally handed down from mother to daughter and were treasured compilations of recipes from family and friends. In 1738 Zachariah Brook(e) of Henrico County bequeathed his daughter Sarah Brook "my first wife's receipts of cookery in manuscript."[1] Although most surviving examples date from the latter part of the eighteenth century, the intergenerational cookbooks written by Anonymous (1700) and Jane (Bolling) Randolph are substantially older and therefore of great historical interest. The significance of the two cookbooks is threefold: (1) they offer views into the everyday lives of Virginia women of this era as Chesapeake society evolved; (2) they reveal the customs and traditions surrounding the preparation of food and the duties of a hostess; and (3) the provenance of the cookbooks (in or near Henrico County) and the social prominence of the cooks outline the lives and customs of the colonial gentry.

The original endpapers (and thus the author's name) of the fascinating culinary work by Anonymous (1700) have unfortunately been pasted over and written on by successive hands. Anonymous (1700) appears to have been a well-educated woman of respectable standing who interacted with various members of the Randolph family, among others. She may have been a Randolph or connected to them by marriage or social network. It is not known if the initials M. B. found among her pages apply to her, but they do not refer to a seventeenth-century author who used identical initials. M. B. could be the initials of Anonymous (1700) or of one of the following candidates: Mary (Kennon) Bolling, mother of Jane (Bolling) Randolph; Mary (Cocke) Bolling, wife of Col. John Bolling; Maria (Taylor) Byrd, wife of William Byrd II; or Mary (Chiswell) Barrett, who provided food "on the table" for staff and students at the College of William and Mary. It may be no coincidence that Mary (Chiswell) Barrett's descendant Lewis Barrett married Jane Price, daughter of John Price and Mary Randolph, before their move to Georgia.[2] This latter fact may or may not explain the presence of the surname Price printed in block letters in the interior back cover of the c. 1700 manuscript. It is also possible that M. B. was one of the contributors to a manuscript belonging to Mary (Isham) Randolph, who apparently had a manuscript, since she shared a recipe for metheglin, which was found in Jane (Bolling) Randolph's manuscript. Possibly, Anonymous (1700)'s identity will come to light in the future.

The upper corners of the cookbook's pages were deeply scorched from some fire, and it appears that an unknown number of pages after the title page have been lost, as there is a remnant of a recipe at the top of the first page now available. It is assumed that the recipes in the first, missing group were the oldest ones of all. The recipes in the manuscript by Anonymous (1700) show an unmistakable overall progression from "old" recipes of the seventeenth century to those penned during the second quarter of the eighteenth century. According to Marion Briggs, a handwriting expert in the judicial and legal field for Briggs and Associates, Inc., in Troy, Michigan, there were at least four additional hands over a period of time; she also confirmed that two submitted recipes did indeed contain two different handwritings.[3] This was also true of Jane (Bolling) Randolph's manuscript, which was begun in 1739 and completed in 1743.

Regardless of its origins, there are indications that Anonymous (1700)'s manuscript ended up at Ampthill Plantation in Richmond, Virginia. It appears to have been quickly hidden there at one time in response to the threat of a raid by Benedict Arnold during the Revolutionary War. In April 1781 Mary (Randolph) Cary barely fled Ampthill in time. Benedict Arnold's arrival on the next day led to the destruction of her husband Archibald Cary's flour mill complex at nearby Warwick.[4] Anonymous (1700)'s cookbook continued to lie undisturbed until it was briefly perused around the turn of the century by the Pleasants girls, as evidenced by their signatures and drawings by a young child of a horse, a lighthouse, and Napoleon in his classic pose. It was briefly used again during the 1830s and the Civil War.

Although dating of Anonymous (1700)'s manuscript is difficult, the Virginia Historical Society has applied the "c. 1700" date as a best estimate. Ms. Stacy Rusch, a conservator at the Virginia Historical Society, dates the bound manuscript to the late seventeenth century. She bases her conclusion on the following characteristics: the type of cording and binding of the book, the thickness of the cover boards, the blind design motif on the covers, and the remains of metal hasps or latches. The latter show a Germanic influence and were in widespread use during the late seventeenth century. Her conclusion is supported by a similar book, *The Way to Get Wealth* by Thomas Tryon, which I personally examined at the Library of Congress in Washington, D.C. This book, in pristine condition, has an intact title page dated 1702.

After some study it was concluded that the earliest handwriting in the c. 1700 manuscript could date to the late seventeenth century but would be consistent as well with dates in the early eighteenth century. Since a number of the recipes in this manuscript appear to have been copied from British cookbooks that appeared in 1705 and 1714, it seems likely that the handwriting by Anonymous (1700) was begun approximately in the period 1706–15. Mr. E. Lee Shepard, archivist of the Virginia Historical Society, examined the papers and concurs with this assessment.

A careful examination of several published seventeenth- and eighteenth-century English cookbooks suggests that the majority of the recipes in Anonymous (1700)'s manuscript were based on recipes that dated from no later than the last half of the seventeenth century to approximately 1740. The language that most closely resembles the wording found in the earliest recipes in Anonymous (1700)'s manuscript can be found in the works of John Murrell published during the 1630–40 decade. It is also clear that Anonymous (1700) had recopied the earliest recipes from a treasured but tattered family manuscript now nonexistent but perhaps once in the possession of her mother or grandmother. She then proceeded to copy the latest fashionable recipes beginning around 1706–15, including Edward Kidder's *Receipts of Pastry and Cookery,* which was published at least twice: in 1720 and 1740. After a careful assessment of one of the three "1740" editions of Kidder at the Library of Congress in Washington, D.C., the bibliographic experts at Maggs Brothers of London concluded that the 1740 date was too late for the book in question; they dated it to the 1720s.[5] Works by Robert Smith (1723–25), John Nott (1724), Charles Carter (1732), and Sarah Harrison (1733) not only show how heavily Edward Kidder's work was plagiarized but make use of language that is already more modern. According to Sandra Oliver of Isleboro, Maine, this was commonly done in both America and Europe.[6]

In addition to location and the mention of Randolph women in both "Unidentified cookbook, c. 1700" and "Jane Randolph her Cookery Book, 1743," a third consideration suggests these works may be related to one another through family or close social ties. Both manuscripts had at least one contributor who made odd choices of letters, such as *T* for *Ph* in the word *Pheasant, W* for *L* in the word *Leaven,* and in a number of instances the letter *p* was substituted for *b* and vice versa: for example, *botts* instead of *potts* (perhaps an indication of dyslexia?). At times, too, letters appear in an incorrect sequence: for instance, *smallage* written neatly as *samllage.* When shown some examples such as these, Dr. Thomas B. King of the Child Neurology Department at the Medical College of Virginia confirmed that some kind of cognitive-auditory difficulty was likely involved, although this could not be officially confirmed without testing the individual in person.[7]

Cooking is "a tradition with social associations . . . recipes are abstracted from meteorological, political, technical and social environments, past and present"; recipes are not static but rather change and evolve, and over a period of time and at different locations, "certain procedures and ingredients have been preferred to others . . . collections whose pieces change from period to period."[8] The cookbooks belonging to Anonymous (1700), Jane (Bolling) Randolph, and Mary Randolph were no exception.

As the wife of socially prominent Richard Randolph of Curles Plantation, Jane was fully aware of her obligations as a proper hostess. Her manuscript collection was carefully hand-sewn together and signed "Jane Randolph Her Cook Book 1743." Although absolute proof is lacking, the 1743 date is believed to represent the completion of her compilation, because her accounts, dated 1739, were an integral part of this manuscript.

Jane was spontaneous in her manner and outlook, as if she wrote down a mixture of recipes, elegant and plain, whenever they were available—sometimes in haste. While some of her recipes were more practical and intended for everyday use yet acceptable for guests, they were not always arranged in order. Recipes for soap-making and lye were penned next to one for Mrs. Cary's plum cake, while a pickled sturgeon recipe was listed beside instructions to remove grease from silk. In addition she exhibited a great interest in medical cures.

Jane (Bolling) Randolph wanted to make sure her daughters were well trained in the domestic arts, which included culinary skills. She apparently cherished her cookbook, because it was given first as an heirloom to her daughter Jane ("Jenny") Walke and then to her designated granddaughter and namesake, Jane Randolph. They also added their recipes to the manuscript. The cookbook was indeed treasured over the years, if the missing meat recipes and recopying of her worn and now sometimes lost recipes are any indication. Recipes such as "Mrs. Dudley's Cake" and "Dr. Butler's Oyl" were copied twice over time. Jane's personally penned recipe for wafers is still extant, and yet someone recopied it on an earlier page. It is, however, often difficult to distinguish her penmanship from one other possible hand—if it was not her handwriting later in life.

Portrait of Mary (Isham) Randolph, wife of William Randolph. Courtesy of the Virginia Historical Society, Richmond, Virginia.

Portrait of Richard Randolph Sr. of Curles Plantation. Courtesy of Muscarelle Museum of Art, College of William and Mary. Gift of Mrs. Robert Malcolm Littlejohn. 1940.011.

Portrait of Jane (Bolling) Randolph. Courtesy of Muscarelle Museum of Art, College of William and Mary. Gift of Mrs. Robert Malcolm Littlejohn. 1940.010.

A nonaccretive type of cookbook arranged by The Compiler (1744) serves as a contrasting yet supportive model. Initiated in 1744, all of her recipes were copied more or less at one time from the latest available sources. In spite of water and probable smoke stains, her pages remained clean and crisp, with almost no signs of wear. In addition, it is clear from the handwriting that, with perhaps a few exceptions, the recipes were penned by a single person. The lack of other hands suggests that The Compiler (1744) may not have lived long after her manuscript was finished. (It would not be rediscovered until 1864 when a Civil War soldier found and removed it from "Mr. Lumkins" [*sic*] house at Mechanicsville, Hanover County, Virginia, not far from colonial Meadowbridge Plantation.[9] The cookbook's possible link to this plantation has not yet been verified.)

While Jane (Bolling) Randolph and The Compiler (1744) may well have utilized a common source, I doubt that any of the recipes in Jane (Bolling) Randolph's manuscript were taken from the work of The Compiler (1744). Rather, the reverse appears to be the case. The Compiler (1744) received some recipes from Jane (Bolling) Randolph, who started her manuscript in 1739 and signed her name and date when she completed it in 1743. The additional significance of The Compiler (1744)'s cookbook is that it lacks some of the recipes Jane (Bolling) Randolph penned in her manuscript. It is interesting to note that the Compiler inaccurately attributes the liquid soap formula to Jane instead of Jane's attributed source, "Dr. Tscheffiely." However, we know Jane (Bolling) Randolph did not include all of her recipes in her manuscript, since Elizabeth Tucker Coalter attributes a yellow pickle recipe in her cookbook to "Mrs. J. Randolph."[10]

Anonymous (1700)'s inclusion of "affrecan skarlit=beans" (however wrongly attributed) and Jane (Bolling) Randolph's kipscacuanna and persimmon beer indicate that foodways among the Virginia gentry were no longer "purely British." The presence of these ingredients may point to early signs of "creolization of colonial foodways" as defined by Dr. L. Daniel Mouer of Virginia Commonwealth University in Richmond.[11] Just as important, however, their culinary creations served as an influential background and foundation for Mary Randolph and consequently her published classic, *The Virginia Housewife,* in 1824. Anonymous (1700), Jane (Bolling) Randolph, and Mary Randolph participated in a colonial cooking dynasty in the best Virginia tradition.

# GENEALOGY

I. William Randolph I m. Mary Isham and had two sons among others:

IA. Col. William Randolph (1681–1742) m. Elizabeth Beverley (1691–1723).

A. Elizabeth "Betty" Randolph (1715–1776) m. Col. John Chiswell (1726–?) of Scotchtown, Hanover County.

B. Peter Randolph (1717–1767) of Chatsworth m. Lucy Bolling (1719–?).

C. Mary "Molly" Randolph (1719–?) m. John Price of Coolwater, located next to Scotchtown, Hanover County.

IB. Richard Randolph I (1691–1748) m. Jane Bolling (1703–1766/7), author of "Jane Randolph her Cookery Book, 1743," and daughter of Col. John Bolling I and Mary Kennon. (Jane was a descendant of John Rolfe and Pocahontas.) They had the following children among others:

B1. Richard Randolph II (1725–1786) m. Anne Meade (1731–1814). Among other children:

B1a. Jane Randolph (19 Nov. 1755–March 1796) m. Archibald Bolling, 1 Oct. 1774.

Blb. David Meade Randolph (b. 14 Mar. 1759) m. Mary Randolph, author.

B2. Mary Randolph (1727–1781) m. Archibald Cary (1721–1787) of Ampthill, Chesterfield County, 1744.

B2a. Anne Cary m. Thomas Mann Randolph (1741–1793) of Tuckahoe.

B2a1. Mary "Molly" Randolph m. David Meade Randolph of Moldavia, 9 Dec. 1780. Mary was author of *The Virginia Housewife.*

B3. Jane "Jenny" Randolph (1729/30–before 1757) m. Anthony Walke.

Sources: J. Daniels, *The Randolphs of Virginia* (Garden City, N.Y.: Doubleday, 1972), genealogical tables; Gerald Steffan Cowden, "The Randolphs of Turkey Island: A Prosography of the First Three Generations, 1650–1806" (Ph.D. diss., College of William and Mary, 1980), 165, 167, 190.

# PART ONE

# Tidewater Society in Colonial Virginia

In the evening I begun to look over my accounts; and upon the whole, I do find myself . . . worth near 600 *l*; for which God be blessed.

—Samuel Pepys

To Capt. Wm Randolph for doeing the County's businees as Clerke. . . . To Richard Randolph p account 1.12.9. . . . July 8, 1731.

—Henrico County Record Book No. 1

If you could send me Six, Eight or Ten Servants (Men or Lusty boys) by the first Ship, and the procuration might not bee too dear, they would much assist in purchasing some of our best crops they seldome being to bee brought without servants.

—William Byrd

About 4 o'clock Isham Randolph came to see me. I gave him a letter to the Governor in his favor and sent a squirrel to Mrs. Russell.

I thanked them all for the honor they had done me.

About 12 o'clock I went to the Governor's. In the afternoon we drank two bottles of the best claret I ever drank in the country.

—William Byrd

I sent John G-r-l with orders to Colonel Randolph and Colonel Eppes to summon the militia of the two counties for the Governor to review. . . . We fired several pistols to teach my horse to stand fire. Captain Randolph came over to give notes for more tobacco for my sloop to fetch and went away in the evening again.

—William Byrd

Then the French company was exercised and performed very well and the Governor made out of them a troop of dragoons with orders that Mr. Salle should command them as well as the foot. About 3 o'clock we went from hence to Colonel Hill's where we supped and I ate roast beef.

Everybody showed me abundance of respect. . . . Everybody respected me like a king.

—William Byrd

Although the settlers did bring a degree of class consciousness with them to Virginia, it was less permanent and obvious than it had been in England. The harsh realities of the frontier quickly made a mockery of any social pretensions. What mattered was a settler's ability to achieve his goals in the New World, which were defined as success and prosperity. Unlike their British peers, citizens did not look "down on trade" but seized all opportunities to improve their financial status.[1] As in England, prosperous small planters could marry daughters of more socially prominent planters who had fallen on hard times.[2] The frontier was a great social leveler.

All settlers had opportunities to achieve wealth with great tracts of land through either hard labor or capital. Tobacco fields were quickly perceived by many as a "potential source of enrichment."[3] The more acreage an owner possessed, the greater his prestige and power.[4] Capital was essential for the employment of servants to help planters convert the wilderness into cultivated tobacco fields. Having immediate capital, Henry and William Randolph were among the more fortunate newcomers who took advantage of Virginia's raw resources and quickly became financially successful planters. Being educated as well, they soon became leaders in their community.

Henry Randolph (1623–73) served as a county clerk and clerk of the Virginia General Assembly.[5] His civic-minded nephew William Randolph (1650–1711) of Turkey Island owned 16,095 acres and became the founder of one of Virginia's most distinguished families. In contrast, William Byrd I, Robert Bolling, and Miles Cary achieved success through trade and joined the Randolphs as "planter-aristocrats."[6] Such families became dominant in "politics and society."[7]

There was, however, an important distinction between the seventeenth and eighteenth centuries in terms of cultural refinement. The conditions of everyday life in the seventeenth century continued to be extraordinarily harsh and uncertain until after the Restoration of 1660.[8] By the 1680s a small but steadily growing number of planters possessed respectable items, but these household items were generally old, broken, "unfixt," full of holes, or, like one kettle, "short on one leg."[9] Assets remained exclusively stock, simple household furnishings and requisite kitchen utensils to make basic stews and potages. It would take another generation before the majority of Virginia's settlers showed substantial financial improvement.

With the exception of a small and exclusive number of merchant-planters including William Byrd, Robert "King" Carter, and Edward Hill, the rural gentry such as Henry Randolph lived in more modest but respectable houses typical of the period. So did Richard Randolph and his wife Jane Bolling when they inhabited their first domicile at Curles Plantation. This two-room, one-story brick house contained a stairway leading to the garret. Only later did this relatively simple abode become Jane's kitchen and living quarters for her enslaved cook.[10]

These emerging planter-aristocrats both imitated and differed from their British peers. The main ambition of a successful planter was to live the life of an English country squire in the Virginia wilderness.[11] A French visitor to Virginia in 1686–87 observed, "There are no lords, but each is a sovereign on his own plantation."[12] With this new hierarchical social order concentrated in the hands of a few, these powerful planters soon monopolized trade. Ultimately the "political and social control" they exerted and the "American ideas and social concepts" they developed would determine the course of Virginia's culture and history.[13] This was made possible with the vital participation of the women in their lives and the adoption of Britain's social prescriptions.

The Virginia-born planters were sensitive to England's perception of them as country yokels or inferiors in terms of cultural refinement.[14] By the 1680s the majority of the population was native-born and determined to be just as civilized as its British counterparts. Robert Beverley commented in 1705 that the "gentry pretend to have their Victuals drest, and serv'd up as Nicely, as at the best Tables in London."[15] This sensitivity about their public image persisted into the nineteenth century. First Lady Elizabeth (Kortright) Monroe served French cuisine and had a thirteen-foot-long mirrored gilt bronze centerpiece, which impressed her British and French guests who had expected "gawky colonials."[16]

Wealth alone did not qualify the planters as gentlemen, however. An awareness of social and civic obligations and the adoption of social graces were also required. These Virginians sought and kept various offices not only for personal advancement and status but also because of their sense of noblesse oblige. Conscious of "the gentleman's code to attend to the welfare of his social inferiors,"[17] each made certain that he was active in the public eye, even if this was no more than serving as vestryman in the local church.[18] To prevent their sons and grandsons from being guilty of "boorishness" and to help them make judicious use of their "prerogatives," these fathers took pains to have their sons well educated.[19] They had the choice of the few local schools, professional tutors, or educational institutions in England. Martha Stratton desired educational opportunities for her son, a boarder of John Steward, c. 1698–99. When Steward complained in court that she owed him six pounds for her son's board for six months, a fact which she affirmed, she agreed to pay three pounds and then credit it further with "two flitches of Bacon which she already sent him . . . 69 pounds bacon . . . at 5 p per pound . . . a total of 28 shillings and 9 pence" and vowed to deliver the remaining debt of thirty-one shillings and three pence shortly to complete her payment.[20] William Randolph hired a French Huguenot refugee at Manakintown as a tutor to one of his sons.[21] Richard Randolph made clear in his 1742 will that his sons would "not be Useless members of their Country, or . . . become Burthensome to it by taking Such courses as are Generally the Companions of Idleness."[22] Sons were to be as polished as Mr. Hadfield, who incited admiration from a British traveler, Robert Hunter: "My friend Hadfield the most agreeable, elegant, sensible, and polite young man I am acquainted with. He is everything . . . that Lord Chesterfield could have wished his son to have been."[23]

Daughters of these planters were also educated, but to varying degrees. Most received only a year's worth of schooling, just enough to read the Bible. Writing skills were usually omitted.[24] A fortunate few (usually wealthy) women,[25] such as Jane (Bolling) Randolph and Elizabeth (Bray) Allen-Smith, were well educated, but in most instances daughters were mainly schooled in the "social graces" and to function as capable home managers.[26] In 1753 Elizabeth (Bray) Allen-Smith of Bacon's Castle stipulated that poor boys and girls were to learn to read and write at the free school she established at Smithfield. After three years of schooling, the boys were to be apprenticed out to "some honest Calling," while the girls were to be bound to "some Honest Woman, to be taught Household affairs."[27] In contrast, the will of William Randolph of Tuckahoe stipulated that his daughters Judith and Mary were to be educated "suitable to their Quality and Circumstances."[28] Many sisters understood the importance of their brothers' education, even if not all of them agreed with it. Little Sally Cary Fairfax wistfully wrote to her father that she hoped her brother "will acquire the polite assurance & affable cheerfulness of a gentleman, yet not forget the incidents of Fairfax Co."[29]

Such education, however limited, was part of women's contributions to the development of Tidewater Virginia society. Their fascinating insights into that society are well illustrated in the "c. 1700" and 1739–43 manuscripts, which contain not only recipes from the mid–seventeenth and eighteenth centuries, but also the domestic "prescription" that determined the social role of these women. The significance of these manuscripts is enhanced by their historical provenance and the social prominence of the cooks: Anonymous (1700); Jane (Bolling) Randolph, the wife of Richard Randolph of Curles Plantation; and completing the circle, Jane's great-granddaughter, Mary "Molly" Randolph, author of *The Virginia Housewife,* a timeless classic.

In order to understand fully the background of the English culture and frontier conditions in Virginia, the next few chapters are devoted to the factors with greatest influence. These include society's prescriptions, the frontier, social power and networks, and, last, the plentiful foods that replaced the English emphasis on the rarity of an item. The critical roles of women, in terms of food preparation, were all entwined with these elements into one smoothly running machine. No single component could function independently.

# Men's Public Sphere in the Chesapeake

[The captain] . . . giving me a barrel of pickled oysters, and opened another for me, and a bottle of wine, which was a very great favour.

—Samuel Pepys

Capt. Robt. Blake . . . Sir W. Pen . . . took them home to my house (having by chance a good piece of roaste beef at the fire for dinner); and there they dine with me.

—Samuel Pepys

With my wife looked over our plate and picked out 40*l* worth I believe, to change for more useful plates to our great content; and then we shall have a very handsome cupboard of plate.

—Samuel Pepys

Worthy Captain Matthews an old planter . . . hath a fine house, and all things answerable to it; he sows yearly store of hemp and flax, and cause it to be spun; he keeps weavers, and hath a tan house, causes leather to be dressed, hath eight shoemakers employed in their trade, hath forty negro servants, brings them up to trades in his house; he yearly sows abundance of wheat, barley, &c. the wheat he selleth at four shillings the bushel, kills store of beeves, and sells them to victual the ships when they come thither: hath abundance of kine, a brave dairy, swine great store, and poultry; he married the daughter of Sir Thomas Hinton, and in a word, keeps a good house, lives bravely, and a true lover of Virginia; he is worthy of much honor.

—William Maxwell

I began to read geometry but was interrupted by the coming of Mr. Will Randolph and his wife and Mrs. Cocke. I was as courteous as possible to them to give Mrs. Randolph a good impression of this part of the country. They dined with us and I ate blue wing for dinner.

—William Byrd

Colonel Randolph with a troop met us at Pleasant's mill and conducted us to his plantation, where all the men were drawn up in good order. The Governor was pleased with them and exercised them for two or three hours together. He presented me likewise

> to them to be their commander-in-chief [who] received me with an huzzah. About 3 o'clock we went to Colonel Randolph's house and had a dinner and several of the officers dined with us and my hogshead of punch entertained all the people and made them drunk and fighting all the evening but without much mischief.
>
> —William Byrd

> Rode to Mr. Samuel Bourk's where Jonas very kindly entertaind, lodged all Night, very warm.
>
> Rode to Richard Rennolds where met with a very Rude guest.
>
> —Robert Rose

Englishmen brought with them to Virginia their traditional definitions of their roles in society, roles they enacted not only on their plantations but also in the public arena. Their functions were further emphasized by evidence of success or power, be it material goods or political office. These elements were crucial to the maintenance of their status in society, and such social criteria were to remain influential for more than three hundred years.

Men earned their fortunes in the tobacco economy, built fine homes along the riverways, and secured "extensive power" through "the control of credit."[1] However, the more widespread cultural refinement of the colonies did not begin until approximately the last quarter of the seventeenth century, a time when the effects of Bacon's Rebellion were fading. The emerging middle class could afford more visible tokens of success, such as handsome houses, stylish silverware and tea sets, books, and lessons in polished manners.[2] While Richard Bushman did not discuss the events leading up to the adoption of Georgian thought so prevalent in Britain, it is likely that other factors played roles as well. More settled conditions, reduced Native American warfare, improved mortality rates, and inexpensive land contributed to the upward mobility of the settlers.

By 1730 a boom in terms of cultural refinement throughout the colonies was well under way. Wealth and position enabled a number of colonists to build "the great house" that was society's "elaborate, overt expression of social values."[3] They took "pleasure from their estates" and held an "air of great satisfaction," in part at least, because the "acquisition of acreage and luxury items" served as "declarations of the owner's status," and "they compared their current circumstances with what they had in the beginning."[4] As was the case with Henry Randolph, their achievements paved the way to other "high-status" opportunities.

While goods could "be cherished or judged inappropriate, discarded and replaced" over time,[5] the attributes of high-status items remained constant. Good breeding and family pedigree were now essential to enhancing a man's position as the "head of the household."[6] Deferential treatment by peers was carefully noticed and measured as an indication of respect for one's niche in society. Samuel Pepys of London spoke for many Virginians when he wrote: "It was a great pleasure all the time I stayed here, to see how I am respected and honoured by all the people."[7] Social courtesies, such as gifts, were either received or sent as a mark of respect. Pepys wrote: "Mrs. Gawden sent me a great Chine of beef and half a dozen Toungs" and "This day I lent . . . my chine of beef for to serve at dinner tomorrow at Trinity-House, the Duke of Albemarle being . . . there."[8]

Like his British counterpart Samuel Pepys, William Byrd was supersensitive to any negative reflections on his status. In his diaries he made note not only of what gifts he sent but also what gifts were sent to him. Both men were excessively critical of the manner in which their wives carried out their duties in the private sphere, a fact they themselves secretly acknowledged. Often closely involved with domestic matters, Pepys took pains to ensure that his notions of what was proper or correct were adhered to, as evidenced in his revealing entries: "Hanging up pictures and seeing how my pewter Sconces . . . become my stayres and entry"; "Got most things ready against tomorrow, as fires and laying the cloth, and my wife was the making of her tarts and larding her pullets till 11 a-clock"; "I was not well contented with the littleness of the room and my wife's want of preparing things ready as they should be for supper"; and "Mr. Coventry . . . inviting himself to my house to dinner, of which I was proud; but my dinner being a leg of mutton and two capons, they were not done enough; which did vex me, but we made shift to please him I think; but I was, when he was gone, very angry with my wife and people."[9]

The men as well as their wives knew that the house, goods, plentiful food, and family relationships stood as public and social status codes for neighbors to read. Samuel Pepys's acute self-consciousness in this regard could not be more vivid than in his March 1666 entry: "I find my Lord Brucher and Mrs. Williams . . . see my house and my wife; which I showed them, and made them welcome."[10] The achievement of high status was also a source of pride in Virginia, as attested by William Byrd: "I have a large Family of my own, and my Doors are open to every Body, yet I have no Bills to pay, and half-a-Crown will rest undisturbed in my Pocket for many Moons together. Like one of the Patriarchs, I have my flocks and my Herds, my Bond-men and Bond-women, and every Soart of trade amongst my own Servants, so that I live in a kind of Independence on every one by Providence. However this Soart of Life is without expence, yet it is attended with a great deal of trouble. I must take care to keep all my people to their Duty, to set all the Springs in motion and to make every one draw his equal Share to carry the Machine forward."[11] However, they did not tolerate excessive or tasteless ambitions beyond a person's natural abilities. As Gen. Nathanael Greene noted in his diary one September day in 1783, he and his friend Mr. Edwards fooled Mr. John Baylor with their exaggerated tales of wealth found in South Carolina, and Mr. Baylor was mortified by the comparison, not realizing they were "a humming of him."[12]

Each planter was indeed king of his turf, while his wife provided essential food and medical services behind the scenes. As Randall Collins and Richard Bushman state in their studies, husbands and wives were teams of actors and actresses performing their requisite roles onstage in front of the public.[13]

# Women's Private Sphere
## *The English and Colonial Virginia Prescription*

Dined at home in the garret, where my wife dressed the remains of a turkey, and in the doing of it she burned her hand.

Where I find my wife making of pyes and tarts to try her oven with (which she hath never yet done); but not knowing the nature of it, did heat it too hot and so did a little overbake her things, but knows how to do better another time.

—Samuel Pepys

And then rise, leaving my wife desirous to sleep, having sat up till 4 this morning seeing her maids make mince pies.

My wife . . . home to see how the wash goes on.

—Samuel Pepys

I was out of humor with my wife for trusting Anaka with rum to steal when she was so given to drinking, but it was soon over.

I had a quarrel with my wife about her servants who did little work.

I was out of humor with my wife for her foolish passions, of which she is often guilty, for which God forgive her and make her repent and amend.

—William Byrd

I like the idea of your keeping house; the sentiment of limiting your expenses until Mr. Taylor and you are in a way to make money, I approve; not that I would anything in my power to give you . . . it is a sentiment of pride and independence that I like to see cherished. . . . Learn to limit your expenses to your income; it is the sure foundation of domestic happiness and enjoyment.

You will have to study housekeeping,—you are too young to have learnt much of it; but you have been an apt scholar in other branches, and I hope will prove so in this. It is a fault in female education that house-keeping is not made more a part of it; book learning is not sufficient; the kitchen and dairy must be attended to as well as the drawing room.

The perfection of female character unites the domestic virtues of Penelope and Andromache, with the intellect of Madame De Staeil [*sic*] and Lady Morgan. Women should be made fit companions for their husbands, and not their slaves or idols. But I must cease lecturing.

—William T. Barry

Two published multipurpose cookbooks ("prescriptions") that would shape women's roles for centuries to come came off the press in the seventeenth century. Sir Hugh Platt's *Delightes for Ladies* (1609) focused on utilizing produce grown at home. Mixed among the recipes were lectures about what constituted women's duties: "Our English housewife, who is the mother and mistress of the family, and hath her most general employment within the house—where from the general examples of her virtues, and the most approved skill of her knowledge, those of her family may both learn to serve God, and sustain men in that goodly and profitable sort which is required of every true Christian."[1]

The second classic, *The English Hus-Wife* by Gervase Markham, appeared in 1615. Unlike previous publications used solely by nobility or professional cooks in aristocratic households, Gervase Markham's cookbook was geared toward gentlewomen and housewives, and it had considerable impact. His concept of the duties of women was just as demanding: "The inward and outward vertues which *ought to be in a compleat woman.* As, her skill in Physicke, Cookery, Banqueting-stuffe, Distillation, Perfumes, VVool, Hemp, Flax, Dayries, Brewing, Baking, *and all other things belonging to an Household.*"[2]

Wives played an important role in food sustenance, since they were expected to know all about herbs, planting vegetables, and conserving seed for future planting. Gardens were an essential part of the household plan.[3] Each year English ladies were busy "preserving, conserving, candying, making syrup, jellies, and pickles."[4] Lady Gardner apologized to Sir Ralph Verney, excusing herself for not writing a proper epistle since she was "almost melted with the double heat of the weather and her hotter employment, because the fruit is suddenly ripe and she is so busy preserving."[5]

Markham's additional emphasis concerned cleanliness. The dairy was to be sweet-smelling and as spotless as a prince's bedchamber.[6] His confident advice and influence lasted up to the early nineteenth century. Even Hannah Woolley, the first female cookbook publisher, reiterated women's roles along the same lines as Markham had: "Responsibilities for cleanliness in the dairy, brew-house, bake-house, and kitchen. . . . [Don't let] the smallness of your Beer become a disparagement to your Family."[7] Not all women were in full agreement with the dictum, however. One woman complained that men undervalued their work and asked where men would be if not for women's careful domestic management.[8] Samuel Pepys wrote that his "wife . . . doth mightily complain of her want of money and liberty, which I will rather hear and bear the complaint of then grant the contrary, and so we had very hot work a great while."[9]

The definition of a woman's duty in the domestic sphere was extended to include her personal conduct as a wife, hostess, and friend to her neighbors.[10] Religion played an extensive part in people's lives to a degree that is difficult for the modern reader to grasp.[11] All cookbooks also held the common double view of women as simultaneously emblems of divinity through moral instruction and emblems of sin. It was imperative for a woman to know "the law of God; without her Bible and small prayer book, she would not be an exemplary role model for her family and community."[12] Elizabeth Pepys took notice of her drunk spouse's lapse by way of prayers when he came home "so out of order" that he "was loath to say prayers tonight"; not only did his wife notice, but so did "the people of my house," which he "was sorry for."[13] This prescription was carried over to the American colonies. The inventory of Edward Jones in 1696 listed "1 book called ye Mothers Blessing."[14] This outlook continued into the eighteenth and nineteenth centuries with similar books emphasizing such feminine Christian virtues.[15]

In addition to being pious, a woman was expected to show compassion, meekness, humility, and patience[16] toward her family, neighbors, and work force, a dictum often stressed in cookery books.[17] In a 21 February 1677 court session John and Susan Greenway testified that Benjamin Hatcher requested Margaret Good to try to cure his head sore. She consented to his treatment and would accept whatever recompense Benjamin Hatcher could give for her trouble. In return he promised Margaret Good that if she were successful, he would give her his "honest satisfaccon."[18] Margaret Good's example of Christian virtue and charity shows that she was fully aware of society's prescriptions.

Women were also expected to be skilled in "physick," since this art was closely related to acts of charity and compassion. Expected to care not only for her family but also for her friends, indigent neighbors, and the labor force, women learned to diagnose medical disorders, select appropriate remedies, and concoct salves, ointments, potions, and plasters.[19] Jane (Bolling) Randolph and probably one of her namesakes followed the custom of incorporating into the cookery book a large collection of medical remedies. "Lady Allen's Water," "For the Bite of a Mad Dog," her tobacco ointment, and "Lady Arundel's" recipe for cancer were included among the treasured "receipts."

Many a cookbook drummed home to its audience the necessity of correct deportment and untarnished reputations. Qualities such as chastity,[20] civility, modesty, humility, affability, courtesy,[21] and silence[22] were encouraged. "Handsome decorum" and proper carriage, preferably with "a bonne grace and a neat becoming air," were also highly desirable.[23] The social skills and conduct of women such as Catherine McCall and Mrs. Tucker inspired great admiration from Robert Hunter, a traveling Englishman: "We were all extremely happy in each other's company, the ladies being perfectly free and easy and at the same [time] elegant in their manners. They would grace any country whatsoever."[24]

Acceptable recreation meant the arts, music, dance, and ladylike literature such as poetry or history. It was unthinkable for a properly brought up lady to be informed about or meddle in politics, jurisprudence, war, or other masculine matters. In short, women were modeled after an ancient classical figure, Antiope, who excelled in both the domestic arts and "feminine accomplishments."[25]

While a woman was responsible for everything that had to do with the home,[26] her husband was in control of everything "without doors,"[27] i.e., the cultivated fields, the workmen, profitable opportunities, and official positions. Above all, he was an upholder of the social hierarchy.[28] While male vices such as drunkenness or infidelity were generally overlooked, a woman was not permitted to possess any such flaws; the wife was to rise above her spouse's indiscretions and be the woman running a perfect household. Jane (Bolling)

Randolph may have followed this dictum implicitly but perhaps tongue in cheek, since her cookery book included a recipe for "the stone [gallstones] and drunkeness."[29]

A woman had to be an excellent wife and mother.[30] Hannah Woolley pointed out how carefully daughters should be raised in any respectable home: "As you are a kind Mother to them be a careful Monitor about them; and if your business will permit, teach them your self, with their letters, good manners."[31] William Byrd, who may have been unduly critical, apparently did not feel that his wife Lucy was following this prescription. He made clear his dissatisfaction: "This morning I quarreld with her about her neglect of the family."[32]

Reading, writing, and arithmetic were desirable but were not well followed. Females preferably were to learn the domestic arts, and such training was viewed as crucially important to the success of daughters in the private sphere once they married. Samuel Pepys was twice highly pleased with his wife Elizabeth for embroidering bed hangings, one of which she had sewn on diligently for two weeks: "My poor wife, who works all day at home like a horse. . . . But pleased with my wife's minding her work so well and busying herself about her house."[33] She was adhering to an aspect of Gervase Markham's prescription. Similarly, Jane (Bolling) Randolph was following this prescription when she made note of her order for sampler material in her accounts for her daughters. One daughter, Jane (Jenny) Randolph-Walke, later took "great pains" making embroidered curtains during her marriage.[34] Jane's daughter Mary loaned to her sister-in-law four pairs of knitting needles.[35]

One of the most vital responsibilities of women was the preparation and presentation of food. They were expected to be able to prepare delicious and yet thrifty courses that would elevate their husbands' social status. Markham informed his readers that they could strike a balance between "the royal feast" and "the shearer's festival"; for the creation of a truly respectable banquet, he suggested that sixteen "full dishes" were sufficient, with the addition of "sixteen more fanciful concoctions," totaling thirty-two dishes in all, constituting a meal "which will be both frugal in the spender, contentment to the guest, and much pleasure and delight to the beholders."[36] Samuel Pepys managed to get away with seven "neat" dishes in plate, which greatly pleased his guests.[37] In Markham's view, the housewife who was ignorant of the "pretty and curious secrets" of preparing food for a banquet was "but the half part of a compleat Hous-wife."[38]

At an appropriate age daughters were to be schooled in the art of cookery: "In due time let them know how to Preserve, Conserve, Distil; with all those laudable Sciences which adorn a compleat Gentlewoman."[39] Either these skills were passed from mother to daughter or daughters were sent to fashionable cooking schools such as Mrs. Bathseba Makin's at Tottenham High Cross in London.[40] According to Sandra Oliver, such cooking traditions are "cooking habits" that "are part of an evolution."[41] Women such as Elizabeth Pepys and Mrs. Turner had been trained in this manner, much to the pleasure of the men in their lives: "My wife hath been busy all the day making of pies"; and "Some spirits of her making (in which she hath great judgment), very good."[42] In Virginia, Jane (Bolling) Randolph followed the same pattern, teaching her ten-year-old daughter Jane (Jenny) the fine art of cookery, as shown by a childish script interspersed among the pages of her cookery book.

Markham also stressed frugality, industriousness, and thriftiness to his readers: "to keep their accounts carefully . . . sometimes [housewives] took over the arrangement of the

Portrait of Jane (Randolph) Walke. Courtesy of Muscarelle Museum of Art, College of William and Mary. Gift of Mr. and Mrs. O. W. June 1963.005.

Portrait of Mary (Randolph) Cary. Courtesy of the Library of Virginia, Richmond, Virginia.

whole estate, either because of her skill or because her husband was absent or dead."[43] Concerning the kitchen, there were to be "no necessaries wanting, nor waste or spoil made, but that the Meat be salted, and spent in due time," and the wife was not to "squander away without credit the Wine, Ale and Beer in the buttery or cellars"; she was to check "once a month an account of all the expenses of the whole House."[44]

In England it was not unheard of for wives to take part in their husbands' business affairs. Some wives participated out of necessity, while others were active partners because of their knowledge. In contrast to English women, most women in Virginia did not keep accounts since these were largely taken care of by husbands, overseers, or accountants. This work was almost exclusively done by males, both because it was part of their civic duty, i.e., public sphere; and because women in general did not have the requisite educational skills. Even if an unusual woman knew how to manage business matters, society's sharp definition of male vs. female roles usually would not have permitted her to do so. There were indeed few exceptions. William Byrd mentioned that he went to visit Colonel Randolph but spoke with Mrs. Randolph about "the debt which the Colonel owes to Mr. Perry."[45] Jane (Bolling) Randolph was an outstanding exception by virtue of some of her husband's absences and made careful notes in 1739 of how much was spent on each ordered item. According to Dr. L. Daniel Mouer, she treated each class of subjects differently in terms of repayment.[46] The slaves, servants, and hired hands had to pay their debts in cash, while members of her family settled their IOUs in private with her husband Richard Randolph. It was a matter of ages-old social honor and obligation. Having encountered precisely the opposite problem, William Byrd noted crossly in his diary that he had received "letters for me from England, with an invoice of things sent [for] by my wife which are enough to make a man mad."[47]

A woman's domestic niche in Virginia was therefore based on the English ideal. Besides the never-ending tasks of running the household and laborers, managing poultry and livestock, gardening, food preparation and preservation, distilling, making family clothing, and nursing the ill, women had to contend with regular childbearing and the care of a growing brood. It was a woman's duty to produce children, and surviving children as adults made "direct and essential contributions to Virginia's economic development."[48] The latter fact made women important to the public sphere, but this generally remained unacknowledged. Men continued to focus on women's duties within their domestic circles, with women's lives still centered upon the motif of the home and family name. Frances, wife of Robert Carter of Nomini Hall, was judged by an admirer to be the perfect embodiment of a woman in her private sphere: "I am daily more charmed & astonished with Mrs. Carter, I think indeed she is to be placed in the place with Ladies of the first Degree. . . . prudent, always cheerful, never without Something pleasant, a remarkable Economist, perfectly acquainted (in my Opinion) with the good-management of Children, intirely free from all foolish and unnecessary fondness . . . also well acquainted (for She has always been used) with the formality and Ceremony which we find commonly in high Life."[49]

Socially prominent men often took the trouble of double-checking their wives and were not always pleased with their domestic performances. It is perhaps significant that diaries and other documentary records show a far more disproportionate ratio of criticism to praise. William Byrd, who was perhaps excessively critical, found that his wife was not applying herself. He complained that he ate little of the undercooked beef she prepared and that during her walk with Mrs. Dunn his wife had forgotten about dinner. This led to a quarrel. He also vented his "passion against Moll for doing everything wrong" and chastised her for spoiling "a good plum puding."[50]

Samuel Pepys found fault with his wife and servants. Over the "blackness of the meat," he "fell out" with his wife and the maids for their "sluttery" and left the table. He was annoyed that his wife paid more attention to her new gown than making sure all was ready for tomorrow's feast, and "in that passion [he] sat up long and went discontented to bed." He even came to blows with his wife over the "ill serving up of our victuals yesterday; but all ended in love."[51]

Management of house servants and slaves were also a concern and received complaints. Samuel Pepys further berated his wife for "not commanding her servants as she ought" and "neglecting the keeping of the house clean"; he even threatened to throw her dog out the window "if he pissed the house any more."[52] Landon Carter of Nomini Hall took umbrage with his staff: "My cook wench cannot dress a dish of beans or Peas but they come in quite raw."[53] William Byrd complained: "I ate nothing at dinner but pork and peas which were salty and made me dry all the afternoon."[54] Praises were few and far between: "We having a good dish of stewed beef of Jane's own dressing, which was well done"; "Home to bed, and find, to my infinite joy, many rooms clean."[55]

While demanding husbands must have tried the patience of overworked women, the excessively critical male responses reveal that they were ever conscious of the prescriptive role of women. Possessing great sensitivity about how they might appear to the public, they believed it was their duty to inspect their wives' adherence to the social prescription. A man's public image, hospitality, and reputation were everything.

While some women must have rebelled, their viewpoints unfortunately are largely lost to history. Some were trained not to complain, while others feared listening ears. Sally Cary Fairfax expressed it well: "I wish I could write free and unreserved, for I have many things I would say . . . that I don't like the curious should see. I will endeavour to act in the department I am in as well as circumstance will permit."[56] The following two statements, however, probably indicate the feelings of many:

> She is confirmed in it that all that I do is by design, and that my very keeping of the house in dirt, and the doing of this and anything else in the house, is but to find her employment to keep her within and from minding her own pleasure. In which, though I am sorry to see she minds it, is true enough in a great degree.[57]

> Apparently the Custis marital squabbles stemmed from disagreements about the living arrangements and finances. He wanted to live at Arlington and thought her extravagant; she preferred Queen's Creek and thought him stingy. Their famous marriage agreement of 1714 supports this view. In it he promised to allow her adequate household supplies from the produces of the estate; wheat, corn, meat, cider, and brandy were specifically mentioned. She in turn promised not to exceed her allowance or to interfere in his if he would not intermeddle in her domestic affairs.[58]

Women who resisted the confinement of the home place often paid the price. As Dolley Madison wistfully wrote: "Our sex are ever losers, when they stem the torrent of public opinion."[59] Nevertheless, there were several Chesapeake women who did not hesitate to break out of their circumscribed circle when opportunities to do so presented themselves.

# Women's Public Sphere in the Chesapeake

You must know that there is a great scarcity of sugar and coffee, articles which the female part of the State is very loath to give up, especially whilst they consider the scarcity occasioned by the merchants having secreted a large quantity. . . . It was rumored that an eminent, wealthy, stingy merchant (who is a bachelor) had a hogshead of coffee in his store, which he refused to sell to the committee under six shillings per pound. A number of females, some say a hundred, some say more, assembled with a cart and trucks, marched down to the warehouse, and demanded the keys, which he refused to deliver. Upon which one of them seized him by his neck, and tossed him into the cart. Upon his finding no quarter, he delivered the keys, when they tipped up the cart and discharged him; then opened the warehouse, hoisted out the coffee themselves, put into the trucks, and drove off. It was reported that he had personal chastisement among them; but this, I believe, was not true. A large concourse of men stood amazed, silent spectators of the whole transaction.

—Abigail Adams

Patriotism in the female Sex is the most disinterested of all virtues. . . . Even in freest countrys our property is subject to the controul and disposal of our partners, to whom the laws have given a sovereign Authority. Deprived of a voice in Legislation, oblige to submit to those Laws which are imposed on us, it is not suficient to make us indifferent to the publick Welfare? Yet all history and every age exhibit Instances of patriotic virtue in the female Sex; which considering our situation equals the most Heroick.

—Abigail Adams

Then the Governor and I went to church in the coach and my wife was terribly out of humor because she could not go likewise. . . . After church I invited abundance of gentlemen home where we had a good dinner. My wife after much persuasion came to dinner with us.

—William Byrd

Social prescriptions concerning the traditional concepts of men and women's separate spheres in colonial Virginia included the taboo against the involvement of women in political or public affairs. The public sector was allocated to men, while the private sector (still under men's control) was relegated to women.[1] While this was a separation that both denigrated and subordinated women, it reflected "long standing Western assumptions about the women's separate world."[2] Under the British model of patriarchal authority that the settlers brought with them,[3] the male head of the household was responsible for his family's conduct and welfare. His word was "unquestioned law."[4]

Forbidden to vote, sell land, conduct deeds, argue in court except through a male representative, hold a public office, or write a will without their spouses' consent,[5] women had few choices. Widow Mary (Isham) Randolph oversaw the protection of her property through William Byrd II, whose official capacity in a lawsuit involved her husband's debts and a creditor.[6] In August 1691 Thomas Branch chose his "well beloved wife Eliza. Branch" as his "true & lawfull Attourney in a Cause depending between me" and "Xtopher Branch, deft."[7] While Elizabeth Branch could not stand in court as an "attourney" in her own right, her male counterparts would have to respect her decisions.

Females did possess a few rights. A woman could state her wishes in private concerning her dower rights if the family property were to be sold. Some managed to draw up wills of their own. Jane (Bolling) Randolph's will gives an invaluable insight into what society of the day viewed as status symbols: silver sweetmeat spoons, silver salvers, a silver waiter, and a chased-silver milk pot (see the appendix).

The sociopolitical restrictions left women with the ubiquitous church and church-related activities, the county court, village trips, and visits to friends as the only means of alleviating the tedium of their private lives. For Virginia women isolated on their far-flung plantations, the church was an important focus of their lives because, in addition to religious support, it provided them social contacts and a sense of community.[8] This did not always please Maria Byrd, the second wife of William Byrd, since she, as a prominent hostess, was expected to entertain various church members after services every Sunday. It is reputed that she determined the location of the new Westover church two miles away, thereby greatly reducing the number of her guests. As William Byrd noted, "Nobody came from church to dinner. I ate roast beef."[9]

The belief was that if women were permitted to participate more fully in the public sphere, they would then be less willing to remain in their allotted private spheres. Unacknowledged were men's concerns of further political or civil competition, since in the seventeenth century public office was one of the best means for males to gain public esteem and social influence. Women were "relegated to a more clearly articulated subordinate status."[10] This purpose may have been twofold: an unacknowledged emphasis on male status support and control of any moves against male authority. Samuel Pepys and William Byrd reflected such patriarchal attitudes. When Pepys did not like what he perceived as his wife's impertinent response, he "pulled her by the nose"; although they later "made up," he firmly believed in keeping his "wife within bounds."[11] William Byrd quarreled with and prevented his wife from plucking her eyebrows; he "got the better of her and maintained my authority."[12]

There was "nothing in English law or thought" in the seventeenth century that encouraged women's participation in public or political affairs.[13] As an "ancient planter" who could patent land in her own right, Mary Bouldin patented one hundred acres at "Strawberry Banke" under her name in 1624.[14] In 1650 Virginia Ferrar, well aware that an educated or elite woman could influence the destiny of a colony (public sphere), encouraged her friend

Lady Berkeley to take advantage of her position: "Nay Madame h[appy] Virginias good Genious Calls upon you and you designed to be a happy promoter of this Heroyicke Interprize. . . . a woman to have a Share of Honor in this Incomparable happiness to the Colony if not as a Leader then as a Cheife promoter of the bussines . . . me to pray and wish Virginias prosperity."[15]

Circumstances in colonial Virginia provided a reality check to patriarchal attitudes and modified Markham's prescription. At this time the roles and opportunities for women were greater in Virginia than they had been in the eighteenth and nineteenth centuries. High mortality rates, marriage patterns, economic opportunities, and increased life spans for the lucky few[16] determined "new life courses for women."[17] Most seventeenth-century women immigrants were young, were willing to take risks in the New World, and were seeking opportunities to improve life through marriage: "Marriage still offered almost the only way for a woman to enhance her status and make her future secure."[18] This belief remained in force up to the nineteenth century. Once married, a woman was a mistress with authority in her own household,[19] even though that meant that she was busy fulfilling the requisites of her private sphere. She was part of a system, not a truly autonomous person in her own right,[20] and her social standing depended on her husband's social position in society. May-December romances were commonplace but frequently led to brief marriages and numerous remarriages.[21] New husbands often were financially better-off and provided a further step up in status and income for widows with or without young children. The combination of all these factors resulted in family dynamics normally not seen in England. These wives, working to hold their families together, recognized that they had better "bargaining power" than they would ordinarily have achieved elsewhere.[22] Many women negotiated premarital contracts in cases of remarriage to ensure that their possessions or property remained under their control. Although the husband's word was theoretically to be "taken as law," the wife's wishes (unless the family was wealthy) were taken into account, since she "was of critical importance to the household economy."[23]

The unique needs of the frontier and unsettled conditions made it possible for women to take advantage of opportunities that presented themselves, take matters into their own hands, or circumvent restrictive laws. Besides childbirth, men and women had to deal with numerous other life-threatening factors: accidents, epidemics, and Indian warfare all took their appalling toll. The harsh frontier life made men more aware of their women's abilities and resilience, which made enforcing the ideal of "domestic patriarchalism" difficult[24] and often unrealistic. Collectively these "demographic accidents"[25] challenged the English concept of an exclusively male authority and led to a "major step forward for women."[26] The ways these women perceived themselves, their families, and their roles in life were determined by "their daily experiences and by society's expectations."[27]

Aware of their mortality and the economic participation of their wives, men quickly learned to be more generous and respectful to their families when they drew up wills.[28] Wives usually received more than the requisite widow's one-third of the estate and were often made executrixes, even when they were illiterate. There was an uneven level of education since women were still mainly viewed as their spouses' helpmates, and men felt that women needed little education as managers of domestic matters.[29] (William Byrd refused to let his wife Lucy take a book out of his sacred library.[30]) Daughters often received bequests equal in value to those of sons or brothers. During his fatal sickness in 1655 William Grimes gave his daughter Ann five cows (named Captaine, Lieutenant, Yellowlocks, Golden-Locks, and Tapp), four pewter dishes, a trunk, some other items, and 280 acres of land. His wife received the rest of the estate and was to be his "full and sole executrix."[31]

In spite of these social limitations, seventeenth-century Chesapeake women from the illiterate to the elite managed to enter the public sphere without consulting their men. During the time of Bacon's Rebellion in 1676, Anthony Haviland's wife acted as "Bacon's emissary," carrying his "declaration papers."[32] Sarah Drummond, a Berkeley foe who informed soldiers that "they need not fear the King, nor any force out of England, no more than a broken straw for the King was dead," subsequently was described as "a notorious & wicked rebel, in inciting & incouraging the people to the last rebellion."[33] Sarah Grendon gained a similar reputation for being a "great encourager and assister in the late horrid Rebellion," and she was the only woman refused a pardon in an act of indemnity and free pardon during an assembly in February 1677.[34] Other women made their mark through different activities. Ann Cotton of Queen's Creek became the first female historian in Virginia, writing an account of Bacon's Rebellion in 1676: "An Account of Our Late Troubles in Virginia."[35] Still other women acted out of personal convictions. Sarah Harrison became famous in Virginia history for her refusal to say *obey* during her marriage ceremony to James Blair in 1687.[36]

Illiterate women resorted to "name calling," resistance, and disobedience as means of drawing attention to unsatisfactorily solved problems and to show that they could not be "pushed around."[37] By doing so, they made their own "political statement[s]."[38] One wonders if William Byrd's enslaved cook Moll may have made her own "statement" by exerting revenge for the punishments she suffered at his hand. Did she retaliate by deliberately spoiling some culinary dish or other, even though she must have known she would suffer further consequences?

Although women's public activities became somewhat more restricted in scope during the eighteenth century, the constraints were not as severe as those of the nineteenth century. Life became less precarious. Life spans increased, and women no longer were fewer in number than men.[39] The power and authority of males "expanded and stabilized,"[40] while increasing scarcity of land resulted in reduced legacies for daughters.[41] Increased life spans did mean that more daughters learned about cookery and other household management skills directly from their own mothers, and families could afford servants or slaves to perform the arduous household tasks.[42]

However, this greater life expectancy led to the loss of women's unusual powers.[43] By the third quarter of the eighteenth century in Virginia there was further reestablishment of men's patriarchal attitudes reflecting English prescriptions.[44] This "increasingly sharp differentiation of male and female roles permitted a very limited sphere in which girls could exercise their new skills and learning."[45] Thomas Jefferson firmly stated that the only political role women possessed was "to soothe and calm the minds of their husbands returning ruffled from political debate."[46] In 1785 a wishful Judith Randolph expressed her wish to her luckier cousin Martha Jefferson that she could receive a similar education: "I wish I was as fortunate as you are, for at present I am deprived of a tutor, consequently, my prospect for a tolerable education, is but a bad one, which in my opinion is one of the greatest disadvantages which the Virginia Girles are attended with: unless some few, who are more lucky than others."[47] Only traditional activities remained acceptable: the church, the nursing of the sick, hostessing, and needlework. Women's goal in life was to be "notable women," which "almost universally meant no more than that they intended to become exemplary household managers" and excellent mothers.[48]

It is no accident that well-educated or elite women with remaining clout still participated in the public sphere during the eighteenth century. But illiterate or middling-class women, held back by the demands of everyday tasks, had faded from the scene. Indigent women and widows could partake of socially acceptable public and nonpolitical occupations that would keep them from being on "public relief."[49] Occupations such as seamstress, cook, governess, milliner, and instructor of the arts or needlework[50] were found appropriate. Mrs. Barrett, one of the contributors to Jane (Bolling) Randolph's culinary manuscript, kept "the table at the College of William and Mary" before she moved to Hanover County.[51]

Although widows had operated taverns or boardinghouses for the last few hundred years in England,[52] they were not perceived in the same light as genteel women. As members of the working class, such women were exempt from society's higher expectations. The exception was Mary Randolph, author of *The Virginia Housewife,* because she was in a class by herself. Most of these widows behind tavern operations focused on strictly economical menus that ranged from plainly cooked to nondescript. Status was not high on their list of priorities. Although these women and Mary Randolph were trying to make ends meet, Mary Randolph elevated her menus and service to genteel form. Her meals were delicious and tastefully presented, and their variety reflected her social status and training.

It took extraordinary conditions of the Revolutionary War to enable Chesapeake women to engage themselves in the public sphere on a truly large scale and determine their public role.[53] Having previously "experienced" politics only through "their husbands, fathers, and sons,"[54] women quickly entered the public sphere from which they had previously been excluded. Possessing a sense of autonomy, they were determined to help shape the future of the government. Even if the theme of domesticity was still emphasized, a new (and republican) ideology was born.

Equally important was the fact that education available to women had improved significantly. It is no coincidence that many of Virginia's most outstanding women belonged to the Cary-Bolling-Randolph group. The available resources and outlook of these families resulted in the encouragement of women's education. The ways these women perceived themselves, their families, and their roles in life were determined by "their daily experiences and by society's expectations."[55]

Mary Randolph, who would become the wife of David Meade Randolph (cousin), received her first taste of involvement in the public sphere when she was active as one of the "Immortal Eleven" who risked a charge of treason for the sake of liberty during the Revolutionary War.[56] Her kinswoman Lucy (Bolling) Randolph not only provided much-needed supplies for the Revolutionary War army,[57] but she also joined four other prominent Virginian women to sign a nonimportation agreement against England in 1769: "Widow Ladies who have acceded to the Association: Mrs. Lucy Randolph . . . Mrs. Anne Randolph

. . . Mrs. Mary Starke . . . Mrs. Christian Burwell, & Mrs. Rebecca Watson of Richmond City."[58] Fifty-one educated women in North Carolina signed an edict in 1774 in what subsequently became the famous Edenton Tea Party: "As we cannot be indifferent on any Occasion that appears nearly to affect the Peace and Happiness of our Country . . . to do every Thing as far as lies in our Power to testify our sincere Adherence to the same."[59] Women indicated that they would refuse to "receive" young men who were derelict in signing up for their "military duties" and do "everything as far as lies in our power" to share the public burdens of a forming nation.[60] As Rachel Wells put it, "I have Don as much to Carrey on the warr as maney that Sett Now at the healm of government."[61]

In spite of women's active and public participation during the Revolutionary War, men's perceptions concerning them remained relatively intact. The efforts of women in the public sphere were often ridiculed, and men refused to "recognize the ways in which their concept of their role was changing . . . did not approve . . . signs of feminine autonomy."[62]

The only somewhat rueful voice among such resistance was John Adams, who wrote in response to his wife Abigail's famous request that he do "in the new Code of Laws . . . Remember the Ladies, and be more generous and favourable to them than your ancestors." He responded that this was the first indication that women were not happy with their circumstances and that: "You are so saucy. . . . Depend on it, We know better than to repeal our Masculine systems. . . . Altho they are in full Force, you know they are little more than Theory. We dare not exert our Powers in its full Latitude. We are the subjects. We have only the Name of Masters, and rather than give up this, which would compleatly subject Us to the Despotism of the Peticoat."[63]

The diminution of women's participation in the public sphere became more pronounced in the nineteenth century. Several factors contributed to this change. First, soil exhaustion caused the more ambitious inhabitants to migrate west for newer opportunities, and as a consequence the state no longer maintained its position of national leadership.[64] Next, slave unrest such as Gabriel's Rebellion and related new laws caused Virginian society, especially the elite, to become more structurally rigid.[65]

Women did what they could to rise above these restrictions by expressing their political views in a subtle manner, such as through their involvement in activities such as quilting and cookery. "Charter Oak," "Whig's Defeat," "Burgoyne Surrounded," and "Dolley Madison's Star"[66] were some of the quilts' names, while cakes were christened, for example, "Election Cake," "Independence Cake," and "Federal Pan Cake."[67] Election cakes, richly studded with raisins and sweet spices, were served on election days throughout the nineteenth century.[68] There were "Ratification," "Inauguration," and "Columbia" cakes as well as "Lady Baltimore," "Dolley Madison's Layer Cake," "Washington Cake," "Lafayette Cake," and "Robert E. Lee Cake."[69] Mary Randolph reflected the new democratic and patriotic feeling with her "Plebeian Ginger Bread."[70]

The independent spirit of seventeenth- and eighteenth-century women was not forgotten, however. There were still intrepid women who ventured against the social grain, among them two Randolph women. During her widowhood Ann Randolph (Meade) Page took an exceptional interest in the health and well-being of her family slaves. She freed them and arranged for their return to Liberia (Africa) in 1822 at her personal expense.[71]

The second woman was the multitalented Mary Randolph, who did not hesitate to state her decided political views and participate in the public sphere in the true sense of the word. After David Meade Randolph lost his position as marshall of Virginia in an 1800 political election fiasco, financial problems arose. Like her predecessors, Mary Randolph understood the importance of upholding her husband's status. The solution was to sell their Richmond home known as Moldavia, where "there were few more festive boards. . . . Wit, humor and good fellowship prevailed, and excess rarely."[72] The family set up a boarding-house on Cary Street with genteel accommodations. Mary continued her famed cooking with great elan and enjoyed immediate success. According to Henry Heth, her "enviable board" plus her wit and charm attracted customers "who treat[ed] her more like a Queen than a keeper of a Boarding House."[73] A shocked guest named Mr. Blennerhassett wrote in a letter that during one of her parties in 1807 she "uttered more treason than my wife ever dreamed of . . . she ridiculed the experiment of a Republic in this country . . . talked much of Thomas Moore, with whom she was highly pleased."[74]

Striving to be the perfect hostess, Mary Randolph paid close attention to every detail. All aspects of cookery were examined. She wrote that a "puddle of greasy water in the bottom of every vegetable dish is a disgusting sight . . . it is a certain indication of a bad cook or an inefficient mistress, or both."[75] Her cooking became so famed that the slave Gabriel, leader of Gabriel's Insurrection in 1800, had planned to have her serve as his personal cook if his rebellion were successful.[76]

Mary Randolph's life included other achievements as well. She invented two household items, the tub and the refrigerator. Mary made no move to patent her refrigerator. It was a working model, but she realized that to patent it would be to enter the business world. This would have been unacceptable, and she was wise enough to know it. (Her invention was patented by a Yankee guest.[77]) She authored *The Virginia Housewife,* which was published in 1824. In so doing, she became even more public in the eyes of the world. Society found her activities appropriate, however, because her "career" was based on cooking, an activity considered to be in the domestic category.

These women participated in the public arena without consulting their men. They believed in their own personal capabilities to achieve desired results. The perceptions of women about themselves, their families, and their roles in life were shaped and determined by "their daily experiences and by society's expectations."[78] Some were strong-willed and made themselves heard by assuming "positions of power" and "authority or trust."[79] Their very characters had been molded by these historical events and therefore colored their approaches to their roles in life. Jane (Bolling) Randolph, like her great-granddaughter, managed to keep her husband's approval when she was pretty much in a position of power within her private life. From within their restricted domains the influences of such women not only touched their families but also extended their reach far beyond to their local communities and, ultimately, the colony as well.[80] This was achieved through cookery and entertainment, their mediums.

# Status and the Cookbook Authors

So my poor wife rose by 5 a'clock in the morning, before day, and went to market and bought fowle and many other things for dinner—with which I was highly pleased. And the chine of beef was done also before 6 a'clock.

—Samuel Pepys

Mr. Creed . . . where he and I and my Will had a good udder to dinner.

At noon home to dinner to a sheep's head.

At noon dined at home alone—a good calf's head boiled and dumplings, an excellent dinner methought it was.

To Wilkinson's to dinner, where we had some base rost beefe and a mutton-pie and a mince-pie, but none of them pleased me.

We had a good pie, baked of a leg of mutton.

Dined at home upon a Hare=py, very good meat.

Mrs. Turner came in and did bring us an Umble-pie hot out of her oven, extraordinary good.

—Samuel Pepys

About one we went to dinner and I ate fish. Mrs. [Ware] managed with great [order].

—William Byrd

I . . . took leave of Mrs. Randolph and went to Will Randolph's where I drank more persico.

Then we returned to Will Randolph's to dine, and I ate some mutton. . . . In the afternoon we . . . returned home where we found all well, thank God. I ate some cold roast beef for supper. The women were tired very much and I myself a little.

—William Byrd

The Doctor and me . . . to Colonel Hill's. When we came there nobody was at home but the ladies but about 2 o'clock the Colonel came home and we went to dinner and I ate sheep's head and bacon for dinner.

—William Byrd

My wife wished to seal an instrument before two justices and she did it before them.

—William Byrd

. . . the freely extended hospitality of the delightful mansion over which she presided.

—Epitaph of Ann M. Eyre

The majority of Chesapeake women were neither passive nor accepting concerning their roles. Gervase Markham's cultural prescriptions were in effect but not always enforced. Although confined to the private sphere in accordance with his cultural prescriptions, women shaped their attitudes by the realities Virginia provided. Such demographic accidents and historical events required adaptability to survive, and Markham's rigid gender roles could not survive intact. By assuming positions of trust or power, women had taken advantage of any opportunities to manipulate the reality around them, often without their spouses' consent.

Many more families now could afford to imitate the life of the English squire, down to the silver tea set on the dining room sideboard. The more polished the family, the higher the status. Women were expected to uphold and preserve this status by observing Markham's prescriptions to a more marked degree. This ranged from the elevation of their husbands' positions to the preservation of fruits and correct deportment. Men remained conscious of women as partners in maintaining their status and public image.

With such heavy emphasis on familial status, there was a "strong admixture of status display."[1] Regardless of her feelings, a wife usually conformed to established norms because she was her husband's representative.[2] Her household work primarily (status production) consisted of tasks that identified the place and position of her family in the public world. Such household status production could be revealed through the "style and orderliness of its furnishings and the presentation of food."[3] Although Randall Collins goes on to state that women were in charge of status display, this author somewhat disagrees. While women were largely responsible for such social codes, men were also responsible for status display by their very ability to purchase expensive household items such as exotic foods, elegant furnishings, and silverware. Men knew that such goods stood as public symbols, while the wives elevated and supported their status through cooking and entertainment. We think of this as hospitality.

There was the "ritual setting" of cuisine to guests, the most satisfying kind of cooking. There was "proper group behavior," which was characterized by the correct placement of dishes and carving of meat. In addition, food preparation was a form of crucial teamwork and an integral part of women's social network as they shared their recipes. Cooking is "the most ceremonial form of household work," according to Mary Douglas, and therefore the presentation of food to outside guests "is a Goffmanian ritual par excellence."[4] The preparation of food in the kitchens was backstage activity, while entertainment and conversation were out front in terms of image. Wives specialized in initial impression management whenever they greeted visitors. Their performances were critical because they could either enhance or detract from their husbands' standing and effectiveness in the public sphere. Dolley Madison excelled at both management and hostess skills.

Men and women's spheres were therefore not as separate as was commonly stated in anthropological literature. The degree of separation of their spheres had actually diminished as a result of women's increasing responsibilities in formal entertaining. Although the prescriptions clearly defined male and female roles in exclusive terms, their spheres actually overlapped in function[5] and were also interdependent. This was a fact not recognized by men. As representatives of their husbands,[6] women were not viewed by men as having standings in their own right but as supporters of males' status as well as family honor. Women served as "a counterpoint to men's forceful public character."[7]

Anonymous (1700), Jane (Bolling) Randolph, and Mary Randolph were well aware of these subtle but powerful changes concerning their domestic roles and personal self-respect. All three adapted their culinary skills to their local circumstances, but each also chose to entertain with her unique personal flair. What kind of women were these three who took such an active role in Chesapeake society from within or outside their domestic boundaries? How were they influenced by past events and personal circumstances that left indelible marks on their cookery? While there are many promising commentaries by men regarding seventeenth- and eighteenth-century gentry women in Virginia, these records do not include the women's own perspectives. Fortunately, some women among the gentry, including Anonymous (1700) and Jane (Bolling) Randolph, had begun to write informatively about their roles and activities. Their cookbooks were their private mediums for personal expression. Examination of these two cookbooks and *The Virginia Housewife* by Mary Randolph yields some of this dynastic trilogy's opinions.

As the wife of Richard Randolph, Jane (Bolling) Randolph would have succeeded Mary (Isham) Randolph as the second socially prominent matriarch at Curles Plantation. Being a role model, she would be expected to instruct her daughters on cooking skills along with other domestic virtues. Her "receit" book included recipes from her mother-in-law Mary (Isham) Randolph and kinswomen "Ms. Pr." and "Ms. Chiswell," who were Mary and Elizabeth, daughters of Col. William Randolph and Elizabeth Beverley.[8]

Anonymous (1700) largely adhered to Gervase Markham's prescription. Her recipes, for the most part, were traditional (i.e., not innovative) and reveal that she was personally conservative. In keeping with her social station and Markham's prescription, she felt she would be judged by her table and sought to provide only the best. To her, that meant haute cuisine, a style of cooking that reflected the status of her husband and family. She made sure she was correct in all domestic matters, including the preparation and presentation of foods commensurate with the social status of her guests. Although she conveyed her sense of importance through cooking and hospitality, she accepted the tight confines of her domestic domain. The implication is that she did not often venture out of her domestic arena. Through her faithful imitation of Edward Kidder's recipes, among others, Anonymous (1700) revealed that she was well aware of being her husband's representative. His status was considered first.

In contrast to Anonymous (1700), Jane (Bolling) Randolph began to move beyond the limited scope of her society by becoming active in other areas. She functioned as an accountant not only for her family during her husband's absence but also for her kin and acquaintances. Richard Randolph obviously trusted his wife's ability in this particular regard.

At the same time, as shown in her expense accounts, Jane (Bolling) Randolph entered the public sector in dealing with the local labor force. In this respect she transformed her home base into a quasi-public one. It was not fully a public life, since her social circle encompassed only local acquaintances and relatives. She was a transitional figure in the sense that she was both exploring new possibilities and stretching her boundaries as well as upholding old traditions as she supported her spouse's status in the eyes of the community through her cookery and hospitality. While she provided the plentiful and traditional array of meats and sugared sweets in her menus, she also incorporated new recipes with the old. She thought she could appropriately include some Native American elements with her persimmon beer and use of Kipscacuanna as a purging agent.

Jane (Bolling) Randolph obviously took pride in her work and had a strong sense of her domestic role. She shared some of her recipes with The Compiler (1744). Her confidence is reflected not only by her neatly written name and date on the title page of her cookery book, but also by the fact that she drew up a will of her own. Furthermore her portrait is rather telling. Instead of posing prettily in satin, laces, and flowers as her peers did, she stood confidently in a simple yet elegant gown and held a thick tome. Her accomplishments and sense of self-worth set an example that her descendant Mary Randolph would subsequently expand upon. It is also interesting to note that Jane (Bolling) Randolph's belief in herself as an individual must have irritated the ever socially conscious and overly critical William Byrd, because she was the only nearby Randolph wife who was never mentioned in his famous secret diaries. Obviously Byrd found the other Randolph wives more amiable.

Anonymous (1700), Jane (Bolling) Randolph, and probably Randolph's daughter Jane conducted themselves in accordance with Markham's prescription, interpreted in the light of changing times and individual circumstances. Since meat was a status symbol, these women agreed that the greater the number of meat creations in a menu, the better.[9] The table might have included roast beef and mutton, veal cutlets, bacon, chicken fricassee, roast turkey, sugar-cured ham, "bisk" (bisque) of pigeons, boiled fowl, pickled pork, potted tongue, smoked joints, savory balls, and "ragoos" (ragouts) with sweetbreads. Not to be excluded were meat pasties and pies. Gervase Markham would have approved.

Mary Randolph's culinary background and skills permitted the expansion of her domestic activities into a public sphere, i.e., the men's domain. Her cooking skills had provided her an acceptable outlet through public entertaining. Through this channel she went on to other achievements including inventing the hot water bathtub and the refrigerator. The wheeled bathtub included a spigot and heated brazier. The refrigerator, a tubular frame filled with ice, was set upon a tub and placed inside a box with an inner lining of charcoal, and this box was set within a larger box.[10] The icebox fascinated her 1815 guest Harriot Pinckney Horry, who sketched this wonder. Mrs. Horry noted that Mrs. Randolph paid fifty cents daily for five pecks of ice to put inside it. Mrs. Randolph's "excellent fare" such as "pans of butters, meats, and other foods" could be kept chilled for twenty-four hours. "The use of ice for the preservation of food was just beginning to reveal its revolutionary potential."[11]

Although a recipe for metheglin is attributed to a "Mary Randolph" and written in a younger hand, it is more likely that this recipe was copied at a later time. (Two different hands attributing the recipe to "Mrs. Mary Randolph" differ from the hand that wrote the text.) The language and quasi-superstitious overtones of this recipe unmistakably date it from the late seventeenth or early eighteenth century and thus would fit a recipe from Mary (Isham) Randolph's time. Mary Randolph's version of this recipe would not only be more modern in terms of language but also would have omitted the added stipulation that the metheglin just "had to be made" before the first of October. That particular world no longer existed. Furthermore, this would not accurately reflect Mary Randolph's personality or her more enlightened mind. Her empirical recipes reflect her more logical approach with careful measurements and labor-saving preparation. She was living in a world at the threshold of modern thinking.

When Mary Randolph published *The Virginia Housewife* in 1824, it became an instant cookery classic. Her publication helped shape a new era in Virginian cooking, since her cookery was much more democratic in ingredients and approach than earlier cooking methods. Many vernacular dishes were introduced, and large-scale use of vegetables was encouraged. Fewer, simplified, and yet still elegant dishes also meant more time out of the kitchen. She remembered only too well the past experiences of her youth and made it a priority to keep such work to a minimum. She wanted to prevent "the horrible drudgery of keeping house all day, when one hour devoted to it in the morning would release her from trouble until the next day."[12]

She was almost certainly familiar with her great-grandmother's recipes. Like Jane (Bolling) Randolph and Anonymous (1700), she had recipes for "Beef à la Mode," "Red Beet Roots," "Oyster Loaves," "Jumbals," "Caveech Fish," and "Hash Calf's Head," among others. Even the largely forgotten tansy and pipkin reappeared in one of her recipes.[13] Her recipes for pickled walnuts, wafers, and sturgeon were similar to those found in Jane (Bolling) Randolph's manuscript. "Hash Calf's Head" and "Caveech Fish," although more modern, are easily recognizable as descendants of the recipes in Anonymous (1700)'s work. Mary Randolph's upbringing would have further honed her culinary knowledge.

It is significant that Mary Randolph's abode was not in the usual plantation setting but rather in an urban environment, the city of Richmond. Her discreet though public and successful culinary career helped support the family's financial position. Mary Randolph was not an isolated hostess who associated only with guests of high standing. While she entertained genteel families who patronized her famous dinners, she also served travelers and others who stayed at her boardinghouse. In her domestic sphere turned public she reached a wider range of American citizenry than her predecessors, and the recipes in her cookbook reflect this fact. It was probably during her tenure as a famed hostess that she shared her recipes for calf's foot jelly and peach preserves with her kinswoman Mary Burton Augusta (Bolling) Banister, who in turn penned it into her cookbook between 1818 and 1821.[14] This was sometime before Mary Randolph polished them for her forthcoming book, *The Virginia Housewife.*

Starting in the kitchen, women such as Anonymous (1700), Jane (Bolling) Randolph, and Mary Randolph would use cooking to welcome guests, display hospitality, and present the latest fashions in foods. Due to their domestic upbringing, society's prescriptions, and roles as hostesses, they knew that their culinary skills would intangibly but powerfully affect their husbands' social, business, and political interactions with their guests. Individually and collectively these Virginian women made unacknowledged but major contributions to the progress and well-being of their families, their communities, and the Colony of Virginia.

Cookbooks in themselves are ahistorical, since "cooking is a tradition with social associations . . . recipes are abstracted from meteorological, political, technical and social environments, past and present."[15] Recipes are not static; they change and evolve. Over a period of time and at different locations, "certain procedures and ingredients have been preferred to others . . . collections whose pieces change from period to period."[16] The three cookbooks belonging to Anonymous (1700), Jane (Bolling) Randolph, and Mary Randolph were no exception. Each document deals with foodways along with the perceptions and life experiences of the author at a given stage in the Chesapeake region's history.

# Virginia's Cultural Boom

The two butts . . . of Sherry, from Coles, and mine was put into a hogshead and the vessell filled up with four gallons of Malago wine; . . . but it is the first great Quantity of wine that I ever bought.

—Samuel Pepys

I out and bought some things; among others, a dozen of Silver Salts. . . . They eyed mightily my great Cupboard of plate.

—Samuel Pepys

To Sir W. Penn to drink a glass of bad Syder in his new, fair, low dining-room, which is very noble. But to see how Sir W. Penn imitates me in everything, even in his having of his chimney piece in his dining-room the same with that in my wife's closet—and in everything else I perceive, wherein he can.

—Samuel Pepys

Mr. Povy's . . . where . . . he made a most excellent and large dinner of their variety, even to admiration; he bidding us in a frolique to call for what we had in mind and he would undertake to give it as—and we did—for prawns-Swan-venison after I had thought the dinner was quite done, and he did immediately produce it, which I thought great plenty.

—Samuel Pepys

That Capt. James Crews deceased did receive of Edwd Hatcher then liveing at Varina a parcel of Deer Skins & Som Furrs wch I understood to be in part of paymt for some Plate wch he had bought of ye same Capt. Crews.

—Henrico County Record Book No. 1

1 Tea Table . . . 12 plain, 2 Elbow Chairs Walnut . . . 2 Square Walnut Tables . . . 1 Corner & 2 Oval Tables . . . 1 Mahoghany Writing Table . . . 8 pictures . . . 1 Bacgamon Table . . . 1 bird Cage . . . 1 Plate Warmer . . . 1 Desk & Book Case . . . 1 Spinet . . . 5 pictures . . . 22 Blue & white China Dishes . . . 11 Red & white Gilt Do. Dishes . . . 14 Chocolate Cups & Saucers . . . 7 Decanters . . . 8 froot Glasses . . . 39 finger glasses & 10 Stands . . . 4 Glass Salts, 6 Cruits, & 2 Mustard potts . . . 18 Glass Tart Moulds . . .

24 Cider Glasses . . . 9 Strong Beer Glasses . . . 58 wine Glasses . . . 1 Sett of Glass Salvers . . . 99 Jelly Glasses . . . 11 Stone Sweet Meat Potts . . . 6 Lead Chocolate Moulds . . . 9 Tea Spoons & Case . . . 1 Tea Chest & Cannisters . . . 2 doz Ivory knives & forks . . . 5 Brass Chafing Dishes . . . 2 Japan Waters . . . 4 pipkins . . . 3 doz thin pewter plates . . . 4 doz pewter plats (used) . . . 25 pewter Dishes . . . 53 lb old pewter . . . 1 Brass Coffie pott . . . 1 Tea Chest . . . Medicens, Morters, Glasses &c . . . Sugar Chests . . . 3 pr Stilliards . . . Carving knife & fork . . . 1 preserving pan & 2 Stew pans . . . 1 Copper fish kettle . . . 2 Stew pans . . . 3 Copper Kettles . . . 2 Grid Irons, 3 Trivets.

—"Appraisement of the Estate of Philip Ludwell Esqr. Dec'd"

The blossoming of Virginia's gentry between 1670 and 1730 and its relationship with women's roles, cuisine, and entertainment can be better understood if examined against a backdrop of what constituted "cultural refinement." Its origins began with the fusion of the rising class, social prescriptions, and adoption of Georgian thought.

It is not surprising that the initial cultural awakening of colonial Virginians around 1725[1] was limited to those who formed "polite society." Gentility at this point was "worldly, not godly" and "was hierarchical, not egalitarian and it favored leisure and consumption over work and thrift"; theoretically, members of polite society had never worked nor were taught to save.[2] While this was largely true for the English aristocracy and upper classes, the conditions of colonial Virginia forced modifications of this rule. Powerful figures such as Richard Randolph in Virginia may not have performed manual labor per se, but they spent a majority of their time in supervisory capacity and in civil-political service. Genteel women such as Anonymous (1700) and Jane (Bolling) Randolph ensured the smooth running of domestic operations at home with their servants and slaves. Over time the "high toned aura"[3] of European gentility was weakened by demographics and historical circumstances, and became more egalitarian. These genteel families of Virginia differed from the gentry in England.

While hard labor dominated the lives of the lower and middling classes, the upper crust of society purchased luxury items as expressions of personal power and social elevation. More conscious of how they were judged by others, they recognized that their genteel lives rested upon properly erected facades and status-laden goods for the public to read. The old way of life filled with brass kettles, frying pans, skillets, pot hooks and racks, spits, powdering tubs, worn pewter, and other hearth hardware was no longer suitable. Simpler furnishings such as old tables and wooden bowls were replaced by coveted mahogany pieces and silverware. Refinement meant quality.

Chinese porcelain, tea sets, and silver spoons now graced the tables. Family portraits, correct attire, proper education, and impeccable conduct reflected society's ideals. All of these elements were required for special occasions as well as entertainment. The activities themselves did not change for the next two hundred years but were conducted on a more elevated level. It was a time of pronounced social division between the gentry and the rest of society.

Although this movement toward more polished civility and awareness were adopted somewhat more slowly by the middling class before 1750, they caught on rapidly after that date. Men including the clergy, professionals, officials, prosperous yeomen, and traders were expected to learn and adhere to the same standard of social refinement. Their less ostentatious but still handsome houses soon dotted the riverways and countryside. Many a citizen soon followed this new outlook as shown by their inventories, which listed signs of gentility: a looking glass, a book, or a dancing lesson. After the Revolutionary War refinement became more widespread and gave the middling classes a greater visibility in terms of social acceptance. Only then did the divisive social lines between the gentry and the middling class become somewhat blurred, since genteel manners were no longer the exclusive property of gentry. However, this did not mean that the fine dividing line between the gentry and the more prosperous citizenry became nonexistent; it only meant that the lower classes were able to cross that line. In contrast to Europe, where people aspired to aristocratic bearing, the colonial citizenry saw their ascension as part of their "emerging egalitarian society."[4]

Those exempt from such social codes were the indigent or lower classes living in the backwaters of Virginia. From their perspective, the refinement of the upper classes not only prevented social interaction on an equal footing but also served as a symbol of exclusivity. They realized that such exclusiveness strengthened and made clear the established social order. It was not until the early nineteenth century, when conditions improved and opportunities became available, that they began to catch up socially. Through the introduction of a massive market demand for high-status goods among the gentry and middle classes, the less respectable soon were adopting the same social requirements. They realized that such refinement meant, at the very least, "a hope of elevation from ordinary existence into an exalted society of superior beings."[5]

Richard Bushman, especially interested in the interrelationship of the personal ideal and the material world, believed that the houses of the gentry and aspiring middle class went beyond mere possession and pride. These more spacious houses also served as symbols of a cultural transition which stemmed from role models back in Europe. Accompanying the stately houses were newly defined social expectations concerning speech, clothing, conduct, and manners. These new rules helped distinguish the "proper style" of the gentry and the ascendant middle class alike from the lower classes. It endowed them with a power to impress, guide, and influence others. This formed the foundation of trust, an essential quality for familial respect and civic advancement, and that was their key to success.[6]

Not only were the lower classes under a social obligation to these figures, but so were the children and wives of the gentry. The formal and carefully penned letters filled with respectful greetings, self-conscious affectations, and subservience were written by children and peers of important gentry figures in the eighteenth century.[7] Jane (Bolling) Randolph showed such care and respect when she wrote a neat letter to her son John Randolph while he was in Philadelphia. She signed her note "Your loving Mother, Jane Randolph."[8] When Richard Randolph invented a specific type of horse bridle, he wrote to Thomas Jefferson in the hopes that his invention would be found worthwhile, signing it "your most Obedt. Servt. Richard Randolph."[9]

While these letters would seem artificial today, such formality was not a mere convention of the times; it was part of their genteel training, which included the proper use of

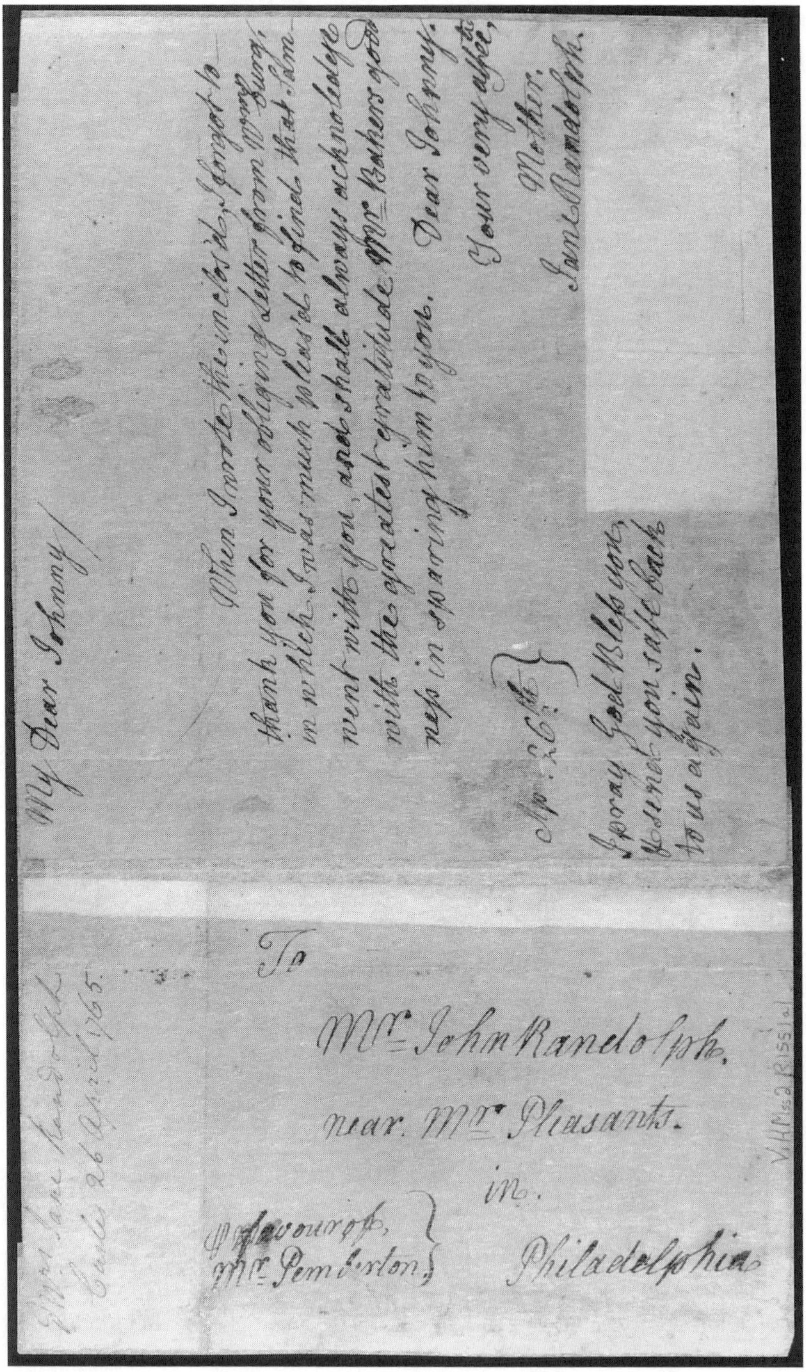
My Dear Johnny

When I wrote the inclosed, I forgot to thank you for your obliging Letter from Wmsburg, in which I was much pleas'd to find that Adam went with you, and shall always acknowledge with the greatest gratitude Mr Bakers goodness in sparing him to you.

Dear Johnny

Your very affec.te

Mother.

Jane Randolph.

Apr 26th

I pray God Bless you & send you safe back to us again.

To

Mr John Randolph.

near. Mr Pleasants.

in.

Philadelphia

favour of Mr Pemberton

Mrs Jane Randolph Cassle 26 April 1765.

Letter of Jane (Bolling) Randolph to her son John Randolph. Courtesy of the Virginia Historical Society, Richmond, Virginia.

language, the religious and moral foundation, a sense of responsibility, and careful penmanship. As Richard Bushman observed, letters were not just literary performances like dancing and other skills; letters also "resembled entering a room or engaging a polite company in conversation."[10] They were acts that had to be "carried off with aplomb and style" to prove to others that they had received proper educations, and above all, the letters revealed that they were subjects to a higher power.[11] More natural and charming letters do survive, however. In a 1797 letter addressed to Sally Pleasants at Curles, Jane Turner hinted that Sally should not "delay" setting her cap for Doctor Adams, who was "a clever fellow" and "worth catching"—although in her girlish postscript Jane directed that Sally "let no one see this."[12]

Within the framework of this elevated culture, citizens were all too aware that they were expected to "perform for themselves" both within and without their homes, and this in turn led not only to self-criticism and criticism toward others but also to public criticism.[13] The writings of William Byrd and Landon Carter show their acute awareness of these attitudes as well as their obsession with any public censure. Exactly what constituted refined manners and correct conduct that would label an individual as well bred? After all, a prosperous citizen could build a fashionable house and yet not be considered refined. In fact, gentility was an intangible sum of indoctrinated religious, moral, educational, behavioral, and civic-oriented elements. A person could learn the basics of such social customs and yet appear to be unpolished and unacceptable to the upper echelon. This could be due to lack of mastery of one or two particular aspects, such as quality of clothing or using inappropriate terms, for example *desk* instead of *escritoire*. Only when all desirable traits of gentility were thoroughly mastered could a person's character be acknowledged by others as truly genteel.

Since domesticity and religion formed the foundations for gentility, seventeenth- and eighteenth-century manuals instructed both men and women in endless detail how they should speak, dress, and comport themselves. Many a mother followed these instructions and taught them to their children, believing that correct conversation, deportment, manners, and deference were related to Christian morality. Fathers paid attention to the education of their sons. Sons and daughters learned from their parents that endeavors required capital and capital meant a foundation of work, however indirect. They also learned about the relationship between gentility, husbanding of resources for investment, and successful production, and that refinement and capitalism were interrelated. In contrast to the English members of genteel society, Virginians learned that thrift and industry were virtues.[14]

These indoctrinated and Americanized habits are reflected in the cookery books of Anonymous (1700) and Jane (Bolling) Randolph. Nothing was to be wasted, and every ingredient was to be of prime quality whenever possible. Proper dishes were to be served during religious observances. In addition, women saw to it that every family member was well instructed in the art of social behavior and table manners. In order to accomplish all these laudable goals, a stage was necessary. This came in the form of a refined architectural setting, and within that compound was the central dining room.

# The Architectural Setting

It is a good seat—with a fair grove of trees by it, and the remains of a good garden. But so let to run to ruine, both house and everything in and about it—so ill furnished and miserably looked after, I never did see in all my life. Not so much as a latch to his dining room door—which saved him nothing, for the wind blowing into the room for want thereof, flung down a great Bowpott that stood upon the side-table, and that fell upon some Venice-glasses and did him a crown's worth of hurt.

—Samuel Pepys

The Doctor, who is a man of learning, was pleased with the library.

I settled my cases in the library till about 11 o'clock when Major Chamberlayne came to see me, who is one of the biggest men in Virginia.

In the afternoon we went into the library to see some prints.

—William Byrd

The house and ground was made clean to receive the Governor. . . . In the afternoon I caused all the rut to be cut away that lay at the woodpile and the pasture to be made clean. I caused a hogshead of punch to be made for the people when they should come to muster.

We rummaged the cellar to know our stock of wine.

—William Byrd

I sent John to kill some blue wing and he had good luck. I ate some boiled beef for dinner. In the afternoon all things were put into the best order because Captain Burbydge sent word that the Governor would be here at 4 o'clock but he did not come till 5. Captain Burbydge sent his boat for him and fired as he came up the river. I received at the landing with Mr. C-s and gave him three guns. . . . After he had drunk some wine he walked in the garden and into the library till it was dark. Then we went to supper and ate some blue wing.

About 8 o'clock the Governor came down. I offered some of my [fine water]. Then we had milk tea and bread and butter for breakfast. The Governor was pleased with everything and very complaisant.

—William Byrd

In order for well-to-do Virginian planters and genteel hostesses to display their knowledge of hospitality and entertainment, there had to be a suitable setting in which they could enact their roles. Such a setting could be in their homes, placed in a tamed field, or situated on landscaped grounds. Owing to the changes in function and design within the house over time, the dining room would emerge as one of the most important aspects of the house.

Until the latter part of the seventeenth century the majority of settlers viewed their stay in Virginia as temporary while they attempted to reap great profits from tobacco, lands, or trade. Home meant "ye olde England," to which they would someday return once they had achieved financial independence. Houses were built along simple lines with no sense of permanence. The evolution of such impermanent or vernacular architecture can be studied in such classic publications as Fraser D. Neiman's *Domestic Architecture at the Clifts Plantation: The Social Context of Early Virginia Buildings* or Henry Glassie's *Folk Housing in Middle Virginia.*

Until the cultural boom only a few planters such as Adam Thoroughgood of Lynnhaven (1640), Arthur Allen at Bacon's Castle, and Governor Berkeley at his Greenspring mansion could afford to build brick dwellings. The majority of the houses built by the gentry were much more simple in construction and plan, and were not all that different from dwellings of the lower classes. Studies have shown that at least a third, if not one half, of the population occupied simple log or framed structures measuring eighteen by twenty feet. The other half of the inhabitants lived in one-and-one-half- or two-story houses two-over-two-rooms deep. Chimneys were initially part of the interior features but later were often built outside, both as a preventive gesture against fires and as a new architectural statement. Because of the floor plans of these homes, cooking and dining took place in multipurpose rooms on a daily basis. For more formal occasions, however, entertaining and dining took place in the parlor if there was one.

Such multipurpose one- or two-cell houses were found perfectly acceptable even by the gentry and would dominate the Virginia countryside throughout the eighteenth century. Later, kitchens were usually housed separately.[1] Various reasons are given for keeping the kitchen separate from the house, such as the heat of cooking and the prevention of fires, but this is open to debate. Some scholars feel that the separation of the kitchens may reflect some kind of social change, such as the separation of hired hands or slaves from the family's personal space.[2]

According to Dr. L. Daniel Mouer of Virginia Commonwealth University, there is an obscure reference to patriarch William Randolph inhabiting "a 40' x 20' frame house with a huge fireplace" at Turkey Island, and this was a "good description of a fairly successful man's house of the late seventeenth–early eighteenth century . . . [that] takes into consideration that William Randolph was a building contractor."[3] After the land at what is now Curles Plantation was purchased by William Randolph in 1699, he had a single-story house built of brick, measuring 54 feet by 22 feet. Completed before his death in 1711, the house featured two rooms with a central chimney from which projected a small firebox in each room. A garret lay beneath its wooden roof. This was to become the first home of Richard and Jane (Bolling) Randolph.[4] For their time in the Virginia wilderness they were considered truly refined. However, when compared to the English manors back in Britain, the grand houses of the wealthiest settlers often fell far short of the English standard.[5]

The simple structure built by William Randolph was not the first domestic seat built at Curles Plantation, however. It was constructed over the foundations of a circa 1635 house built by Thomas Harris and adjacent to another domicile, dated 1674, that belonged to Nathaniel Bacon the Rebel.[6] These were substantial houses for their era. What remained of the Harris house by 1699 vanished from view when it was buried under the newly constructed and parallel building that would become Richard and Jane (Bolling) Randolph's first home and then kitchen. A short distance to the west was, possibly, a brick-lined well.[7]

During the 1988 archaeological excavations (see the frontispiece), the remains of Bacon's house were discovered. Destroyed by fire, it measured only twenty feet by twenty feet and was located immediately south and parallel to the new house underneath Jane (Bolling) Randolph's mid-eighteenth-century kitchen garden beds. Partial remnants of 1676 trenches recalling tumultuous times have been found along one side of Bacon's house, while the rest of the trenches are believed to surround it. Toward the north and west, near the future site of the Randolph mansion and the banks of the James River, stood at least one unidentified seventeenth-century structure and another seventeenth-century quarter.[8]

After the restoration of King Charles II in 1660, peace returned to the British Isles. The aristocracy soon adopted Renaissance thought concerning architectural design and quickly built elegant and fashionable manors with accompanying gardens. Parlors gave way to rooms designed specifically for talking and entertaining. Stairways became roomy, airy, and graceful. In effect, mansions were now built "around a different idea"—i.e., formal entertainment. In southeastern England a style known as "a hip roofed, central-passage brick house" became the prototype that would transform other regional architecture. The middling classes and gentry, wishing to copy the habits of the wealthy, followed suit.[9]

This cultural transformation eventually reached across the Atlantic to Virginia. With Virginia's new cultural awakening in 1670–1730, dramatically heightened perceptions of what constituted proper housing became manifest among the wealthy colonists. Due to the influence of Georgian thought, the two- and four-room houses of seventeenth-century upper-class Chesapeake society gave way to more elaborate central-hall Georgian styles such as Westover, Stratford, and Nomini Hall. This architectural design was well suited to the hot climate. The Georgian central hallway allowed air to flow through the house, keeping it cool in the Virginia heat.[10] By the 1730s many of these now-famous homes lined the James River.[11] Given the backdrop of established social expectations, these airy, fashionable, and spacious houses would serve as icons of society's overall hierarchical structure.[12] Robert Hunter especially admired Robert Beverley's mansion but found Mr. Waring's perfectly respectable house less ostentatious.[13]

This movement went far beyond mere prosperity and pride. It was a symbol of a cultural transition because the building of a new house served as "a social act."[14] No longer were visitors allowed a direct access to the family house. While the new central hall isolated the visitors from other family activities located in the rear and upstairs of the house, it gave them a reference point in terms of a more defined social interaction. This very hall led to an awareness of the host's social standing. Even the rooms and layout had changed. The multifunctional rooms or parlors now gave way to rooms designed for formal entertainment such as teas, serving wine, playing cards, dances, and refined discourse.[15] Other rooms were converted for other specific functions, particularly the more elegant dining room. Since dining was a specialized form of entertainment in itself, this particular aspect will be discussed in the chapter "The Dining Room Stage."

In combination with education, manners, and rank, the grand new houses created the latest definition of "polite society."[16] Polite society included dinners and balls, which in turn focused on cookery behind the scenes. Many letters and diaries, such as that of Philip Vickers Fithian, show society's fascination with entertainment, identity of all the guests, and all the delicacies served at the table.[17]

Adopting the prevailing Georgian thought, Richard Randolph and his wife Jane were well aware of this symbolism, for they were planning to move into a new house around 1730 and greet their guests in a similar fashion. Their simple one-room structure with a loft was no longer found spacious enough for their elevated status in life. The Randolphs left their simpler home when their new framed mansion, measuring ninety-five feet by twenty-six feet, was completed. Their first home was now to be used for another purpose: as Jane's kitchen.

No Virginia mansion would be complete without a formal garden. John Bartram observed during a visit that William Byrd at Westover had established "new Gates, gravel Walks, hedges, and cedars finely twined and a little green house with two or three orange trees."[18] Another characteristic of formal gardens included terraces and parterres with gravel paths aligned in straight lines. Sometimes fences enclosed the whole plantation.[19] Richard and Jane (Bolling) Randolph's Curles Plantation had formal gardens, terraces, parterres, and a colonnade that connected the mansion and kitchen. As well-dressed and well-bred host and hostess blended harmoniously with their more gracious architectural setting, they wished their guests to perceive and admire the social message carried by their fine house and gardens.

Within the spacious confines of their refined home was the dining room, the vital stage where the hostess would offer hospitality and display her social and culinary knowledge. She knew that many a business transaction or successful social contact was often ventured at gatherings and concluded over a meal. As the culinary manuscripts belonging to Anonymous (1700) and Jane (Bolling) Randolph show, they were well aware of their crucial roles. What prepared them to perform flawlessly not only in the kitchen but also in the dining room lies in the way they perceived themselves—through a combination of England's "prescriptions," the lens of demographic accidents, and their personal experiences with other influential events in Virginia's history.

# The Kitchen

Then . . . settled my accounts with my wife for housekeeping, and do see that my kitchen, besides wine, fire, candle, soap, and many other things, come to about 30s a week or a little over.

And so home—where I find all clean and the harth and range, as it is now enlarged, set up; which pleases me very much.

—Samuel Pepys

A new mayd . . . who dresses our meat mighty well, and we mightily pleased with her.

A very pretty dinner of my Bridget and Nell's dressing, very handsome.

—Samuel Pepys

In the Kitchen
1 fish Ketle & Cover, 5 Old Coppers Sorted, ——— New Copper about 40 galls., ——— [S]tewpan and Cover, ——— pan, [Brass?] Kettle, ———[S]auspan, ——— Covers, 2 Ir[on] [Ket]tles, 8 old Iron potts, 6 ordinary Ditto, 1 frying Pan, 3 Pr. pott racks, 4 Pr. pott hooks, 1 Pr. Tongs & Shovell, 1 Dripping Pan, 3 Spitts, 2 grid Irons, 1 Iron Bread Toaster, A Pr. large hand Irons, 2 tin pyepans, 1 Brass Skillett, 1 Bell Mettle Ditto, 9 old pewter Basons, 1 old Ditto Cullendar, 1 Ditto Mazereen Dish, 12 very old pewter Dishes, 19 pewter Dishes Sorted, 3 good Soop dishes & one old one, 2 doz soop plates, 3 doz pewter plates, 1 doz and 10 old pewter plates, 10 Earthen Jarrs, 1 Old Broken pestle & Mortar . . .

In the Pantry
1 dozen Casks with Pains in them, 4RC/xx No. 2 A Jarr of Linseed Oyl, One Do. . . . of Do. about half full, 4 Tobo. hhds full of Allom Salt, 4 Casks of Ditto, 1 Ditto half full of white Salt.

—Inventory of Robert Carter

I made an indifferent dinner this day because Moll had not boiled the bacon half enough, for which I gave her some stripes . . .

I ate some green peas for dinner and was out of humor because the butter was melted oil and scolded at Moll for it.

—William Byrd

While regular menus were being prepared in the kitchen, more elite foods for honored guests were also created there according to the recipes culled from Jane (Bolling) Randolph's cherished manuscript. Through archaeological excavations and the reading of Jane (Bolling) Randolph's manuscript, some information has been learned about the eating habits of those who lived at Curles.

During the summer of 1988 when the house of Nathaniel Bacon the Rebel was discovered and excavated, the stark white brick ribs of Jane (Bolling) Randolph's kitchen foundation provided a contrast to Bacon's adjacent red brick tile floor (see the frontispiece). Under the archaeological trowel the dust began to yield more historical secrets. The deeper foundation was laid in English bond, two and a half bricks deep and buried nearly "three feet into the packed clay of the artificially constructed terrace." The ground-level foundation on a "broad spread footing" was patterned in Flemish bond. Owing to the presence of hundreds of bricks with glazed headers, the walls may have possessed the familiar checkerboard look, while the end walls provided a contrast with repetitive pattern formed by diaper work, a decorative technique popular in the early eighteenth century.[1]

When Richard and Jane (Bolling) Randolph moved into their new house, they apparently had plans to renovate their former home into a separate kitchen suitable for preparing large quantities of food for the family, hired hands, slaves, and guests. Another room was added to the structure to increase the useable space. The central wall was replaced with a larger cooking hearth and bread oven, which faced the center room. The back of this same hearth contained a brand new firebox on the other side of the cross-wall. It would keep the eastern room warm during the winters. Even the flooring was modified as part of the renovation, being lined with cobblestones in the western space. A bare rectangular spot on this floor provided evidence that a boxed-in stairway once rose to the garret. In contrast, the eastern room contained a root cellar in front of the hearth. According to Dr. L. Daniel Mouer of Virginia Commonwealth University, one of the delightful finds unearthed in this root cellar included a stoneware receptacle for either beer, vinegar, or pickled meats.[2]

The partially robbed foundation trenches, adjacent middens, and the midden by the kitchen's eastern door were filled with domestic refuse such as food remains, ceramics, stillyard (balance scale) fragments, and a "chain and dogs from a spit jack."[3] Analysis of the food remains in the archaeological laboratory not only yielded the expected "bones of beef and hogs, sheep, deer and rabbit" along with "chickens . . . quail, and ducks, geese, and passenger pigeons," but also identified "tortoise and turtle, frogs, raccoons, catfish, sturgeon and gar." Among the more unusual food scraps included a "bald eagle" and "the leg of a bear."[4] In addition, scales of a sturgeon were found hidden under a square brick floor tile in Nathaniel Bacon the Rebel's house.

Sometime before the late eighteenth century more kitchen refuse was deposited into a kitchen well and what was either an underground cooler or a meat house. Drains from a barrel cistern at the southeast corner of the kitchen,, the laundry house, and the brew house all flowed into a "stew pond" that irrigated and made fertile the kitchen garden beds below the southern terrace. These square- or rectangular-shaped flower beds were aerated for drainage purposes with thousands of pottery and wine bottle fragments.[5] A brick wall leading from the south side of the kitchen ran across the middle garden terrace toward the river, while a colonnade on the other side of the kitchen was directed toward the east end of the mansion through a bulkhead entrance to the cellar.

In the basement were a warming kitchen and storage rooms whose floors were lined with clay. Archaeological work has shown that this clay floor had been carefully pushed down over a layer of glass shards to prevent "vermin from getting to the food supply and wine cellar." The brick wall cutting across the garden beds and the colonnade effectively spelled out a private domain, or a "woman's place." The designation of this area as a private sphere is further emphasized by the fact that a small frame building within the brick wall stood at the foot of the terrace. This structure is believed to have functioned as the house for slaves who labored in the kitchen, tended the gardens, and worked elsewhere in the manorial complex. In addition, the garret in Jane's kitchen served as living quarters for the chief cook and her family.[6]

It is not likely that Jane (Bolling) Randolph and successive mistresses would have done the daily cooking, since "African and African-American women did nearly all of the gardening and food preparation," which helps explain the extensive influence of "African foodways on Southern cuisine to this day."[7] Jane probably read the recipes aloud or gave oral instructions to the trained slave cook, but she would have learned how to cook as part of her childhood upbringing. Like Sally Cary Fairfax's mother, who made an array of dishes for a special Christmas party, Jane could and did pitch in occasionally for special events. Because of her knowledge of cooking, she knew what should be the expected outcome of enslaved cooks' labors and also was able to instruct her daughters in the culinary arts.

Free or enslaved, Jane (Bolling) Randolph, her female successors, female workers, and female slaves were restricted to the southeastern quarter of the plantation, where they would be excluded from the public (male) activities such as official church and courthouse duties, and the interchange of commercial goods at the local wharf. This was unmistakably their most visible yet private domain, or sphere. However, this is not to say that this particular space was primarily their property. It was not. Since both the male and female spheres were deeply interrelated, one half could not function successfully without the other—even though this fact was not publicly acknowledged.

Men's spheres were just as carefully dictated by society's prescriptions at Curles. An east-west line, parallel to the mansion, ran in both directions. Its northern arm crossed the colonnade and passed the laundry before reaching an eighteenth-century barn. It continued along a road and fence line to various field quarters beyond. The southern arm of the same line moved along three terraces facing the James River. Quarters for the enslaved laborers and craftsmen dotted these terraces. The northern face of the mansion overlooked a parterre, the family cemetery, overseers' compounds, guest quarters, and the Quaker Road leading to Curles Church, which was built by Richard Randolph. This arrangement did not remain static, however. More additions were made later on in the century when a stable, icehouse, and storehouse were added to the northern end of the parterre, joining a string of other shops and quarters.[8]

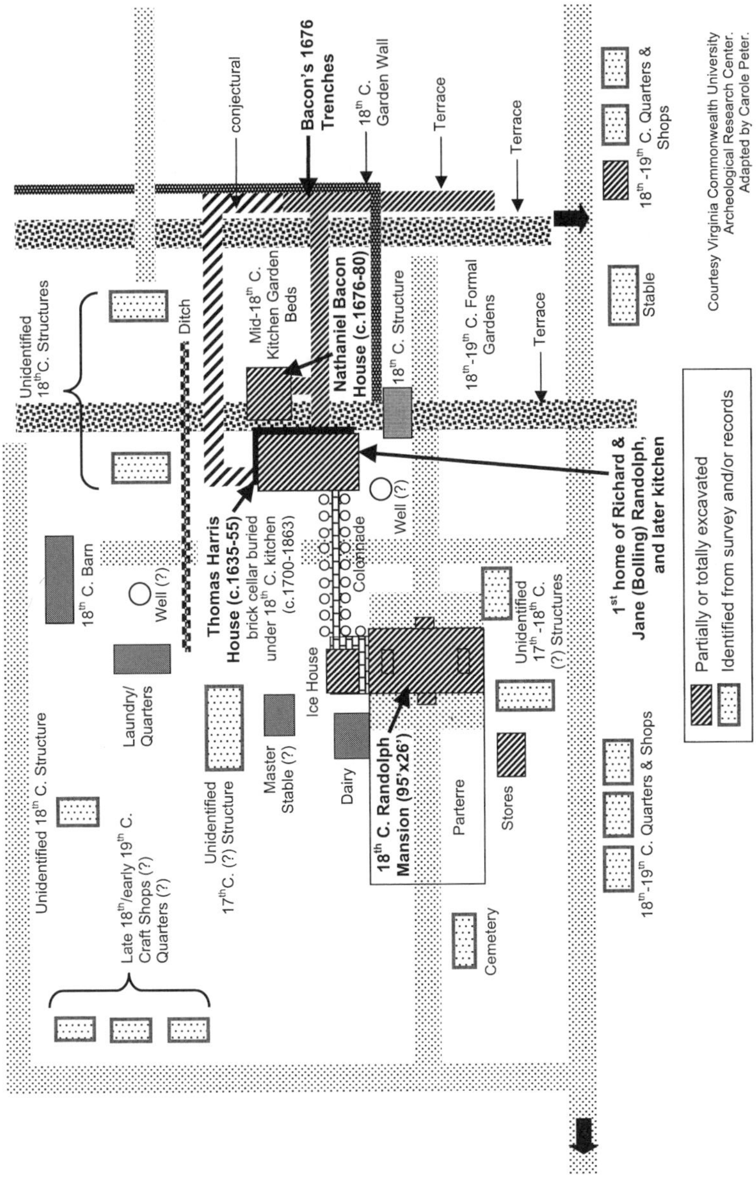


Curles Plantation site, Henrico County, Virginia. Courtesy of Virginia Commonwealth University Archeological Research Center.

Since social consciousness was established by society's prescriptions, it is no accident that specific brick walls and walks divided the Curles mansion complex into two distinct and yet entwined men's (public) and women's (private) spheres. They were simply carrying out their ages-old prescriptive duties. Richard Randolph's work was separate, facing toward the public world located in the fields, the James River quay, and the community, while his wife Jane's sphere was restricted and confined to an inner space within walls and paths. These linear boundaries clearly enclosed the kitchen and other structures in the eastern half of the compound and yet simultaneously precluded any direct contact with the public (male) sphere. The divisions of male and female spheres extended to the Randolph mansion itself. Dr. L. Daniel Mouer said, "The western rooms of the mansion, I believe, served as the dining room and parlor," adding, "East of the passage, were, I suspect, offices for the master and mistress to manage their respective domains."[9]

The very arrangement of the men's and women's spheres followed society's prescriptions perfectly. The "outward face" of the plantation served as a public meeting place between master and inhabitants from the neighborhood, the church, the community as a whole, and lastly, the sea captains who berthed their cargo-laden ships at Curles landing. In contrast, the interactions between the host and hostess and the hired hands, servants, and slaves were restricted to the interior or eastern portion of the plantation, where all domestic-related activities involving the kitchen, laundry, barns, and gardens took place. This was Curles, where the Randolph family would live in this fashion for the next three generations.

Away from the gardens and the heat of their kitchens, wives such as Mrs. Elizabeth (Randolph) Chiswell of Scotchtown, her sister Mrs. Mary (Randolph) Price of Coolwater, and The Compiler (1744) of Hanover County all interacted either with Anonymous (1700) or Mrs. Jane (Bolling) Randolph. Their networks were not just social interactions but exchanges of the latest ideas on how to serve the best victuals on the dinner table. Knowing all too well the importance of making excellent impressions on their honored guests, such wives pulled it all together in a supremely important stage called the dining room. There they would display the best of their culinary skills with seed and ratafia cakes, calf's foot jellies, sugar-glazed orange "slips" (peels), fried creams, macaroons, chocolate almonds, jumbles, and syllabubs along with peach brandy and metheglin.

# The Dining Room Stage

My wife ( . . . buying of a tablecloth and a dozen of napkins of Diaper, the first that ever I bought in my life.)

My dining room, now graced with pictures.

Bought a silver salt for my ordinary table to use.

Paid . . . the silversmiths 22*l* 18*s* 00*d* for spoons, forks, and sugar box.

In Pasternoster-row; and there bespoke something, a silver chafing dish for warming plates.

One thing I reckon remarkable in own condition is that I am come to abound in good plate, . . . having two dozen and a half.

But my love of pleasure is such that my very soul is angry with itself for my vanity in so doing.

—Samuel Pepys

At my father's about gilded leather for my dining room.

This morning my Dining room was finished with greene Serge hanging and gilt leather, which is very handsome.

And so I rose in good temper, finding a good chimney-piece made in my upper dining-room chamber and the dining room wainscote in a good forwardness, at which I am glad.

Thence to Woodstreete and there bought a fine table for my dining rome, cost me 50*s*.

—Samuel Pepys

Find Balty and Mr. How, who dined with me; and there my wife and I fell out a little about the foulness of the linen of the table.

So home to dinner, where finding the cloth laid, and much crumpled but clean, I grew angry and flung the trenchers about the room, and in a mighty heat I was; so a clean cloth was laid, and my poor wife very patient; and so to dinner.

—Samuel Pepys

> We had an elegant dinner; Beef & Greens; roast-Pig; fine boil'd Rock-Fish, Pudding, Cheese &c.-Drink: good Porter-Beer, Cyder, Rum, & Brandy Toddy. The Virginians are so kind.
>
> Philip Vickers Fithian

> At three were shown unto the dining [room], where a most elegant dinner was prepared. Mr. and Mrs. Lewis did the honor of their table in a genteel, easy manner. After tea we amused ourselves with music again. At eight we supped in as elegant a manner as we dined, and conversed upon general topics. The Colonel is a sensible, polite, accomplished gentleman and very elegant in his manners and address. . . . Mrs. L. sings delightfully.
>
> Robert Hunter

Since medieval times there had existed a strong relationship between a family's social status and the food presented at its dinner table. Among the numerous symbols of status, none has been more central than the selection, preparation, and presentation of food. For more than three hundred years, "power was embedded in meal-taking . . . menus, table settings, guest lists, and polite behavior."[1] His wife's success in offering hospitality to their guests was not only a reflection of her excellent training within the domestic circle, but also of her fine personal qualities, his status, and the family's standing in the community.

Like their English peers, the financially comfortable colonists gave food particular emphasis as a status symbol. As representatives "of a culture that says display is good, and more is better,"[2] they "flaunted their wealth" at the dinner table.[3] By their ability to offer elegant fare from their tables, men demonstrated their "political power and economic supremacy,"[4] i.e., their achievements in the public sphere. William Byrd and others of his time probably entertained thoughts similar to those of their overseas contemporary Samuel Pepys: "They full of admiration at my plate, perticularly my flagons (which endeed are noble) . . . with great mirth and satisfaction to them as I thought, and to myself to see all I have it do so much out-do, for neatness and plenty, anything done by any of them. They gone and I to bed much pleased."[5]

Seventeenth-century documentary material is limited when it concerns consumption patterns, detailed meals, or descriptions of the furnishings of rooms where people dined. The best information usually is derived from diaries, letters, receipts, and inventories, which are far from perfect. Samuel Pepys's diary gives excellent descriptions of what constituted the ideal in England and is useful for comparison, but he was not a Virginian. Letters and receipts seldom list such minutiae, while inventories often suffer from inherent bias of the appraisers. The gentry, however, did make efforts during this era to possess fine dining tables complete with diapers or linen tablecloths, fine plates or dinnerwares, silverware if possible, and other status-coded accoutrements.[6] William FitzHugh's order, dated 1 June 1688, included a dozen sturdy knives, forks, and spoons; a pair of candlesticks; a basin; a salver plate; porringers; plates; dishes—the plates to be marked with his initials and coat of arms if finances permitted. In addition, he also stressed that he wanted two of the large silver dishes suitable for "a good joint of meat."[7] These items, however restrained and tasteful, simultaneously reflected the status of the family and guests. These cultural aspirations were not limited to the upper classes. Benjamin Franklin recalled how he found a silver spoon and a china bowl on his breakfast table one morning. His wife thought he deserved such items as much as his neighbors did.[8]

Studies of forks conducted after about 1720 by Lois Call, Lorena Walsh, and Carole Stammas showed that while only 3–8 percent of the poor between 1700 and 1709 possessed forks, by the period 1768–78, 21 percent of the poor and 52 percent of the middling classes had forks listed in their inventories.[9] The figures must have been higher for the gentry, although Richard Bushman did not state what the figures might be. Besides these documentary materials, seventeenth-century cookbooks and courtesy guides provide considerable, if indirect, insight. We do know that entertainment and correct behavior were de rigueur in the seventeenth century and beyond.

Behind the scenes of hospitality and wealth, the Virginian host and hostess were in many ways different from their British peers in terms of their physical environment and their personal sense of accomplishment. Samuel Pepys lived in London, a totally urban world where he could easily purchase prepared foods at various eateries if the need arose: "And chose a small banquett and some other things against our entertainment on Thursday next. Thence to Tom Pepys and bought a dozen of trenchers, and so home."[10] Such accommodations were not possible on the isolated plantations in the rural Virginia wilderness. Taverns, or ordinaries, being few and far between, did not necessarily serve fine foods or have meals ready to serve. Many a traveler was just as well off lodging where a kindly citizen offered to share his abode and victuals. Although Samuel Pepys possessed pride in his fine possessions to a fault, his sense of accomplishment was tempered to some extent by having a mercantile career and easier access to produced goods. Pepys never had to struggle to carve out his career with limited financial resources and back-breaking labor under life-threatening conditions, or wait for months for goods to arrive from England. Settlers' sense of accomplishment was forged by sheer necessity, courage, intensive labor, forethought, and planning in the raw wilderness. They made use of local foods and created useful items out of local raw resources. The feeling of accomplishment also extended to seventeenth-century women in Virginia who adopted, adapted, or experimented with local foods such as corn and pumpkin along with their family recipes.

Although the rarity of an item on the English dinner table was now replaced by the sheer amount of food as a status symbol on the American table, the common everyday fare of the upper classes did not differ all that greatly from the lower classes in terms of everyday consumption.[11] What distinguished the two worlds lay not only in the amount of meat served on the table, but also in the very manner dishes were prepared and presented to please the eye and the taste buds. In *The Virginia Housewife,* Mary Randolph admonished her audience to be "careful not to let a particle of dry flour be seen on the meat—it has a very ill appearance."[12] As the ultimate status symbol, the amount and variety of meats formed the dividing line between the gentry and the lower classes.[13] This social distinction was the most obvious during assemblies, balls, feasts, parties, and private formal entertainments within their plantations.

Planters not only vied with one another under the guise of southern hospitality, they enjoyed each other's company. William Byrd noted, "Mrs. Randolph received us very kindly and entertained us with the best she had"; this included roast mutton.[14] Robert Hunter was impressed with Mr. Edmundson's "elegant breakfast" and his mother-in-law, "who did the honors of the table."[15] These families also exchanged food during these visits with each other as tokens of respect. William Byrd gave William Randolph some sweetmeats for his lady in 1709.[16] Genteel Virginians expected to receive, and generally were accorded, treatment appropriate to their status.

Although the abundance of local food determined many aspects of Virginian cuisine, hostesses followed the rules in the most current cookbooks only to the extent of their ability, finances, and circumstances. Some, such as Anonymous (1700), took careful note of what was en vogue and used this as her guide. Other women selected and modified specific trends commensurate with their needs. They consulted guides to "all manner of cookery, both in the English and French Mode, with the preparing of all kind of Sallets and Sauces proper thereto."[17] They took note that the French were considered the best cooks who would provide "several sauces of haut goust, with dainty ragouts, and sweet meats, as yet hardly known in this Land."[18] That Chesapeake women were concerned with adopting French cookery is attested to by many a surviving culinary work containing recipes such as "Beef à la Mode" or "Cutlets À la maintenoy." Not only was French cookery expensive, it was the current rage. Willingness to accept this expense served to inform the community of the family's affluence. Furthermore, cookbooks warned against being out of touch with current trends: "There are Rules in all Arts . . . should the Table of a great Man be serv'd in the Table that prevail'd twenty Years ago, it would not please the Guests how strictly soever he might conform to the Rules laid down at that Time."[19] No hostess would wish to risk the family's standing by being seen as lagging behind with respect to the latest fashion. To do so would have been tantamount to an admission that the family had fallen on hard times or was unsophisticated. If such an event occurred, the status of the husband, not to mention the family, would suffer.

Although Samuel Pepys saw the tables furnished with a "Bill of fare" at Guildhall "under every salt" and "persons proper for that table,"[20] it is not likely that many Virginian hostesses placed such menu cards on the table. They more likely used printed courses as a guide, as did Anonymous (1700), who painstakingly copied the long list of various courses from Edward Kidder's publication. Of the three cookbook authors discussed, Anonymous (1700) was the most sensitive in her response to society's views that menus were part of proper entertainment. The following example twice stresses the word *entertainment* and emphasizes the high social status of the host:

Entertainment for the Month of April

The First Course

Potages

Two sorts of Potages, viz A Bisk of Pidgeons, and a Potage de Sante, with a young fat Hen.

The Side-dishes

A Quarter of a Mutton forced

A large fat Pullet in a Ragoo
A Breast of Veal farced
Pidgeons with sweet Basil in their Bodies, together with a small Farce; and a large Piece of Beef in the middle.
The Second Course
For the Roast
A great Dish of Roast-meat, consisting of several fowls according to their Season, and two Sallets
The Intermesses
A Dish or Pain au Jambon
Boil'd Cream
A Ragoo of Sweet-breads of Veal and Capons-livers
A Dish of Asparagus with Sauce of Jus lie, or thick Gravy
And so there may be seven Dishes for each Course
The Marquiss d'Arci, formerly the French Kings Ambassador . . . gave such an Entertainment at his House on the 10th Day of April 1690.[21]

Anonymous (1700), Jane (Bolling) Randolph, and Mary Randolph filled their tables with numerous elegant meat dishes, fish platters, soups, pickled or fresh vegetables, warm breads, puddings, fruit preserves, garnishes, condiments, "conceits," and imported wines or elite home brews such as metheglin. The Compiler (1744) presented similar selections. With her copy of various courses serving as a model for her board, Anonymous (1700) made an extra effort to ensure that no fault would be found with her table offerings.

The sheer importance of displayed material goods, dishes, fashionable table manners, eminence of the guests, and the heavy responsibilities of the host and hostess could not be worded more clearly than the following dictum stressed by a contemporary entry of Samuel Pepys:

> Up, and again to look after the setting things right against dinner, which I did to very good content; . . . and after greeting them, and some time spent in talk, dinner was brought up, one dish after another, but a dish at a time; but all so good, but above all things, the variety of wines, and excellent of their kind, I had for them, and all in so good order, that they were mightily pleased, and myself full of content at it; and endeed it was, of a dinner of about six or eight dishes, as noble as any man need to have I think—at least, all was done in the noblest manner that ever I had any, and I have rarely seen in my life better anywhere else—even at the Court. After dinner, my Lords to cards, all the rest of us sitting about them and talking, and looking on my books and pictures and my wife's drawings which they commend mightily and might merry all day long, with exceeding good content and so till 7 at night. Thus was this entertainment over, the best of its kind, and the fullest of honour and content to me the ever I had in my life and shall not easily have so good again. The truth is, I have some fear that I am run behind—hard in the world for these last two years.[22]

Having lived in London for a time, William Byrd was familiar with current social mores and made tremendous effort to ensure that his family observed them. As hosts, these planters and merchants were pleased when things went well, because such responses were positive reflections upon their status. Taking pride from well-presented dinners at his house, William Byrd wrote that there was a "handsome dinner" and "a fine desert which the company admired."[23] Obviously, Byrd and his contemporaries cared deeply about how they were perceived by their peers and guests. Who came to dinner and who refused his invitation to dine were carefully noted in his diaries, since he connected their responses directly to his social status and respect. At the same time, like many men, he took critical notice of other wives' social skills, his relatives' responses, and his peers' and guests' conduct: "I ate some roast goose for dinner, and we were served very well, but Colonel Ludwell's boy broke a glass. In the afternoon we played again at billiards."[24]

It was surely because of these particularly high and rigid expectations that wives did not feel free to act in less than an impeccable fashion toward their guests, even when those guests were irritating. Hostesses such as Alicia Middleton were well aware of their supportive roles in public, which had to be above reproach. In private, however, Alicia was able to pen her true feelings about one guest as her outlet of expression: "He is really a bore he comes here just as if it were a tavern Friday afternoon without any invitation & stays until Monday it is too tiresome—Izard says Ma can't You tell him to go—."[25]

Since guests as well as spouses noticed everything from appearances to manners, it must have made things difficult for the mistresses. Nevertheless, many women were able to perform impeccably regardless of pressure and circumstances. Martha (Jefferson) Randolph's overseer remarked that he had never seen her disconcerted by the demands of her role: "I have never see her at all disturbed by any amount of care or trouble."[26] She lived up to society's expectations of women's roles and Christian virtues by following society's prescriptions. Anonymous (1700) and Jane (Bolling) Randolph had been determined to do the same.

Not limited to the seventeenth and eighteenth centuries, these social expectations were also true for the nineteenth century, when Dolley Madison continued the role of a successful hostess. An excellent foil to her husband James Madison's more reserved personality, she achieved great influence through her entertaining. Her fine foods, faultless service, carefully selected guests, and skillful small talk made her levees famous: "With the help of her steward, French John she set a fine table. Waterfowl, deer, game birds, and oysters were plentiful in the vicinity. Ham, fish, and game appeared four times a day, accompanied by potatoes, beets, puddings, and pies and, later, by such 'fancy' vegetables as celery, spinach, salsify, and cauliflower. Dolley had a household staff of thirty, which she often supplemented with extra slaves from neighboring plantations at thirty-five cents each for the evening, providing one waiter for each guest."[27]

Dolley Madison's guests included diplomats, congressmen, members of the cabinet, and American and European travelers. In spite of living in a "period of bitter partisanship" between her husband's party and its political opponents, she kept relations smooth. Jonathan Roberts of Pennsylvania observed that "by her deportment in her own house, you cannot discover who is [*sic*] her husband's friends or foes."[28] Dolley knew well the importance of gracious hospitality and impressive menus. She would have secretly agreed with an observation made by Voltaire: "The fate of a nation has often depended upon the good or bad digestion of a prime minister."[29] She may have expressed her satisfaction when she commented, "I derived pleasure from my indulgence."[30]

Mary Randolph was much like Dolley Madison as a hostess on a local scale in her house. She differed from her predecessors Anonymous (1700) and Jane (Bolling) Randolph in terms of physical (urban) space and thus crossed the line from her private sphere into the men's public space. However, she met no resistance. Men did not feel that her entertainment broke the unspoken cultural code, because her entertainment was a suitable activity for a woman. She was the queen of cuisine who knew how to present a spectacularly inviting groaning board. She entertained distinguished guests and planters alike with her cosmopolitan wit and social skill. She knew full well, as did Dolley Madison, that her food and entertainment made up the secret foundation of her family's income and power.

# Dining Room Decorum

A host is like a general: mishaps often reveal his genius.

—Attributed to Horace

I had for them, after oysters, at first course, a hash of rabbits and lamb; and a rare chine of beef—next a great dish of roasted fowl, cost me about 30*s*, and a tart; and then fruit and cheese. . . . I find my new table very proper, and will hold nine or ten people well, but eight with great room. . . . At night to supper; had a good sack-posset and cold meat and sent my guests away about 10 a'clock at night—both them and myself highly pleased with our management of this day. And endeed, their company was very fine and Mrs. Clerke a very witty, fine lady, though a little conceited and proud. So weary to bed. I believe this day's feast will cost me near 5*l*.

—Samuel Pepys

At noon had Sir W. Penn (who I hate with all my heart for his base treacherous tricks, but yet I think it not policy to declare it yet) and his son Wm to my house to dinner, where was also Mr. Creede and my Cozen Harry Alcocke; I having some venison given me a day or two ago, and so I had a shoulder roasted, another baked, and the umbles baked in a pie, and all very well done. We were merry as I could be in that company—and the more because I would not seem otherwise to Sir W. Penn.

—Samuel Pepys

So we went to Major Merriweather's. . . . The Major was a little surprised and was not prepared much for such guests; however he did well as he could and for fear of the worst I had brought two bottles of wine with me. . . . I ate some boiled beef for dinner. The Major sat at the upper end of the table and helped himself first. His wife did not appear.

—William Byrd

We were very courteously entertained. I ate bacon and fowl for dinner.

About 3 o'clock we dined with the Governor where everything was very polite and well served.

In the afternoon came Mr. Blair and his wife and Mrs. Hyde, who is a woman of abundance of life.

—William Byrd

Colonel Cary being an old bruiser, and swearing by God I should dine with him today . . . and doubling his fist at the same time, I did not care to contradict him for fear of a blow. He is . . . of patrician order . . . and hospitable.

—George Washington Greene

In the evening Captain Keeling came to see us to account with me for the quitrents of New Kent. I ate some supper with him, contrary to custom.

—William Byrd

—At Supper I had an agreeable conversation with Mr. & Mrs. Carter on the Times manners, &c.

. . . shelves, filled with cakes, oranges, apples, wines of all sorts, ice creams, etc., and highly lighted up.

—Philip Vickers Fithian

As French author Abbé d'Ancourt observed, "Wherever you are, imagine that you are observed, and that your behavior is attentively scanned by the rest of the Company all the while, and this will oblige you to observe yourself, and to be constantly on your guard."[1] Such decorum at table included table manners, one of the "most highly charged and deeply felt of intra-social differences, so that 'rustic' behavior is not merely quaint but barbarous. It is obviously not only interclass but interethnic."[2] As the hostess, a woman had to exhibit manners and training that would bring honor to the family name and to her guests. She had to carefully select foods that would reflect not only her husband's status but also that of her guests.[3] In addition, she had to take care that the seating arrangements were worked out in accordance with the social standing of each guest.[4] Even the placement of victuals and the manner of serving were crucial. The best possible furnishings, silverware, and plates were used. If possible, a mistress would use the most "elegant dishes . . . made of sterling silver" as a symbol of her family's standing.[5] Samuel Pepys went so far as to copy the French mode of folded, pleated, or twisted napkins as an extra touch to his table;[6] this not only honored his guests but was also a form of entertainment.

While not a great deal is known about how foods were served on the seventeenth-century table, according to Jane Carson the eighteenth-century dinner table was largely modeled after the French mode, whereby the hostess carved the "top dish" while the host took responsibility for the "bottom dish," and guests had their plates passed around the table to be served by persons sitting near the desired dishes.[7] Servants could be present to ease the proceedings with their silver waiters, which were also used to replace first-course dishes with foods for the second course.[8] The dessert course included silver spoons and other items associated with sweets.[9] While it is not certain how Anonymous (1700)'s table was served, there are indications that Jane (Bolling) Randolph may have used this French mode of presentation, since she had silver waiters among other silver items (see appendix).

The emphasis on correct presentation of foods commensurate with the status of hosts and guests continued well into the nineteenth century. Barbara Carson mentions that in 1819 Mrs. Forman of Washington, D.C., took pride in presenting her rose-decorated ice cream in one large silver goblet.[10] Guests still expected to find numerous dishes artistically arranged on the bountiful table and the interstices filled with condiments. The first and second courses still consisted largely of meat dishes, some vegetables, and an array of pickles, while dessert made up the third course.[11]

It was not until Mary Randolph's time that this custom began to change: "A dinner looks very enticing, when the steam rises from each dish on removing the covers, and if it be judiciously ordered, will have a double relish." According to Randolph, "Profusion is not elegance—a dinner justly calculated for the company, and consisting for the greater part of small articles, correctly prepared, and neatly served up, will make a much more pleasing appearance to the sight, and give a far greater gratification to the appetite, than a table loaded with food, and from the multiplicity of dishes, unavoidably neglected in the preparation, and served up cold." Fewer and simpler dishes also meant more time out of the kitchen.[12]

On the subject of table manners, hosts and hostesses made sure they behaved impeccably as guests in other people's houses as well as in their own. Many a cookbook and even one wag stated admonitions warning them not to eat in the country manner: no staring, greed, show of displeasure, or eating too fast was permitted.[13] A person was instructed "not to gnaw no bones with your Teeth, nor suck them to come at the Marrow" or fill one's cheeks like "a pair of Scotch bag pipes."[14]

The host and hostess as well as guests had to be well composed at all times, even under disagreeable circumstances. As host, Samuel Pepys refrained from showing his revulsion with a peculiar guest who, he learned, only enjoyed meat raw enough to have blood run down the sides of his mouth.[15] Pepys pretended to enjoy all his guests and ordered "a barrel of oysters and a breast of veal roasted" in their honor, and although he acted "very merry," he secretly could not abide their "dull company and impertinent" behavior.[16] As a guest, he also endured situations that were less than ideal. About the performance on the virginals by a short, ugly, red-haired woman, Pepys wrote that "she sings but after such a country manner, I was weary of it but could not but commend it. . . . Anon we sat down again to a Collacion of cheescakes, tarts, custards, and such-like, very handsome."[17] He made himself sociable on another occasion at Sir R. Ford's, where "dined, in an earthen platter a fried breast of mutton, a great many of us. But very merry; and endeed as good a meal, though as ugly a one, as ever I had in my life."[18] He clearly felt that the wares were not commensurate with his respect and status.

William Byrd felt the same way while he was a guest at the home of his brother-in-law John Custis: "Everyday at dinner we had a bottle of good wine first and then a bottle of bad."[19] Landon Carter was not so lucky a host at his own table, for the offenders were his own family members:

> I never knew the like of my family for finding fault.
> . . . Every [*sic*] speaks well of my table but they who
> constantly live at it.

If the meat is very fine, It is not done say one altho
Perhaps nobody eat hartier of it
If the bread is white and li[ght] ——— musty; but yet
many ———.
If the Sallad is fine, the melted butter it is mix'd with
is rank altho every mouthful of salad is devoured.
The pickles are quite brassy tho crisp and green, and
so the good folks go on disparing and devouring
The beer too bitter altho my brewg are the same
My coffee too weak altho no body spends so much in their
houses.[20]

As guests, hosts, and hostesses the Virginia colonists were determined to be gracious and well mannered. They did not want to be viewed by their European peers as country bumpkins, and they succeeded. In Virginia, Robert Hunter was impressed by the elegant ladies who would "have made a conspicuous figure in any company in Europe"; he added that the continued and equally elegant menus also did honor to Mr. Beverley, who "has everything within himself—no market to go to here."[21]

Proposing toasts, after the French manner, became popular in England and Virginia. Samuel Pepys may have captured his peers' admiration with his pewter flagons and interlocked pies as part of his entertainment, but their mouths surely must have been agape at Mrs. Shipman's version of a proper toast to "Sir Wm and my Lady." She consumed a pint and a half of white wine all at once—"the great draught that ever I did see a woman drink in my life."[22] In Virginia toasts were also proposed at the dinner table, according to Landon Carter and Philip Vickers Fithian.[23]

With all the classic furnishings, attractively presented high cuisine, and eminent guests, the next important requirement for host and hostess concerned the carving of meat at the table. A hostess not only had to be gracious in manner but had to use correct procedures for carving, serving, and other activities befitting the occasion. The serving of food at dinner generally began with the ladling of soup from a tureen for each guest. After the soup came platters of meat[24] and other dishes.

Graciousness required the use of refined language in referring to food and culinary procedures. The simple "cow, calf, deer, sheep, and pig" became "beef, veal, venison, mutton, and pork."[25] A hostess of standing knew the proper terminology for carving: "unbrace the mallard," "chine that salmon," or "barb the lobster."[26] She could not mention terms used in butchering. Carving had to be carried out in a particular fashion, and specific portions of meat or fowl were allotted to the guests in accordance with their status; the more prominent a guest, the more desirable were his or her servings. Many a cookbook stressed the importance of being able to "distribute the best pieces first, and it will appear very comely and decent to use a fork"[27] and to "dispose the best Delicacies to the most eminent Persons."[28] Carving was sometimes a difficult task, and as warnings, horror stories abounded about uncivilized carving.[29] Heaven forbid that anything should go seriously amiss as it did at a dinner given by William Byrd: "My wife endeavored to cut a bone of pork but Mr. Dunn took the dish and cut it for himself, which put my wife into great disorder."[30] Mr. Dunn's poor table manners were an offense to his host and hostess. The careful attention given to carving continued in the nineteenth century when Mary Randolph instructed her readers to "be sure to joint every thing that is to be separated at table, or it will be impossible to carve neatly."[31]

Last, it was desirable that the host or hostess have the finesse to deal with unexpected disasters. In spite of the fact that preparations for a dinner were conducted with the utmost care, inevitably there were times when something went wrong. When faced with such unforeseen events, the host and hostess were expected to remain poised and gracious. At one dinner Martha Washington rose to the occasion in a manner that prompted admiration: "A trifle was served at the close of a recent state dinner which, as everybody soon discovered, had been made with rancid cream. All the ladies began to watch Mrs. Washington to see what she would do—and, as was related all over town the next day, she was seen to taste and swallow her portion in self-martyrdom."[32] Her poise subsequently became the epitome of social conduct for any hostess to follow.

Anonymous (1700), Jane (Bolling) Randolph, and countless other genteel Virginia wives were prepared to bring elegance and refinement to the dinner table in the midst of the Virginia frontier. They made these possible with their correct deportment, refined manners, and correct cuisine.

# All Things French

No for I hate everything that Old England brings forth, except it be the temper of an English Husband, and the Liberty of an English Wife; I love the French Bread, French Wines, French sauces, and a French Cook; in short, I have all about me French or foreign and from my Waiting Woman to my Parot, only my Steward.

—*The English Lady's Catechism*

My wife . . . and I, to a French house to dinner . . . the table covered, and clean glasses, and all in the French manner, and a mess of potage first and then a couple of pigeons a l'esteuvé, and then a piece of boeuf-a-la-mode, all exceedingly well seasoned and to our great liking; . . . to see the pleasant and ready attendance that we had, and all things so desirous to please . . . did take me mightily . . . our dinner cost us 6*s*.

—Samuel Pepys

A good dinner we had of boeuf a la mode, but not dressed so well as my wife used to do it.

Thence to dinner, where my wife got me a pleasant French Fricasse of veale for dinner.

—Samuel Pepys

Here Mr. Moore showed us the French manner when a health is drunk, to bow to him that drunk to you, and then to the person that you drink to; which I never knew before, but it seems is now the fashion.

—Samuel Pepys

We drank a bottle of French wine.

Proceeded to Manakin Town . . . we had some French cookery for supper.

When we came home we drank a bottle of French wine and then went to bed.

—William Byrd

Then we went to dinner at C—t where the President treated us. I ate calf's head for dinner. In the afternoon we retired to the President's to drink the Queen's health, where I drank some French wine that did not agree with me but gave me the gripes.

—William Byrd

Outside cultural influences came into play and became integral parts of table decorum. In the years following the reign of Oliver Cromwell, the rising literate middle class in England preferred simple fares, hearty and substantial. Soups, broths, stews, pasties, and pies were popular along with the usual proliferation of meat dishes. Anything foreign was suspect and disapproved of, as indicated by John Evelyn's comment that a Portuguese dinner was "not at all fit for an English stomac which is for solid meats."[1]

During the latter part of the seventeenth century, the great political and cultural influences of the French court spread over Europe,[2] and French cuisine and table customs became an international culinary language. Contests were held among the French nobility to create elegant dishes or to locate special finds. At one point peas caused great excitement as a sweetmeat; they were first eaten as bon-bons. Even King Louis XIII participated in picking peas.[3] French women made themselves ill on this vegetable: "after having supped with the king, and supped well, find peas at home to eat before going to bed, at the risk of indigestion. It is a fashion, a furor."[4] It was a time of "excessive protocol and etiquette" and "exquisite manners."[5]

A famous cook, François Pierre de La Varenne, initiated the adoption of French fare in England by the publication of *The French Cook* in 1653. Sauces became based on meat juices or eggs, not on flour, although the famous roux was composed of flour, butter, onion, bouillon, and vinegar. Other flavoring agents contained pureed ingredients such as mushrooms, truffles, anchovies, vinegar, and bread crumbs.[6] The popularity of French cuisine reached its peak when Prince Charles II returned from his exile in Paris.[7] English brawn and simple roast beef had to share the spotlight with "Mutton à la Daube" and "Cutlets à la Maintenon"; and ragouts, fricassees, haricots, and sauces were incorporated into menus. Throughout Europe the elite embraced French foods and methods as status symbols, and the English were no exception. Culturally sensitive Samuel Pepys commented in his diary that he had sampled "a fine French dinner."[8]

This trend extended well into the years leading up to the Napoleonic Wars and found its way to America, as the recipes in Anonymous (1700)'s cookbook show. It should be noted, however, that many an Englishman took offense, and some refused to have anything to do with things French and felt that such dishes "have bewitcht some of the Gallants of our Nation with Epigram dishes . . . called a la mode."[9] Another poked fun at this craze: "If a lump of soot falls in the soup, to stir well in to give the soup a high *French* taste."[10] Even Prince Charles II preferred simple roast beef over fancy French foods. This disgusted a French noblewoman, who as a consequence refused to consider him as a possible suitor: "He ate no ortolans and threw himself upon a piece of beef and shoulder of mutton as if there were absolutely nothing else to eat."[11]

For most of the seventeenth century in Virginia the prescriptions for a fine table were beyond the reach of the majority, however aware contemporary publications may have made them about what constituted a proper table. Since a greater diversity of foods began to appear after 1650 with emerging gentry, resources became available for the purchase of, for example, sugar and saffron. Trade also brought food items from other countries, such as peppers from the Caribbean. Against this historical backdrop, all of these ingredients could be utilized by the colonial mistress to provide elegant dishes and beverages for the table. Hostesses thus began to present increasingly sophisticated menus to enhance their families' standing. Herein lies the importance of the earliest surviving recipes as presented in Anonymous (1700)'s manuscript, some of which date from this latter quarter, if not the second half, of the seventeenth century.

The classic French accoutrements in shapes of truffles, morels, mushrooms, pallats (palates), cocks' combs, and asparagus tops[12] appeared on English menus and remained popular up to the time of Edward Kidder's publications. Many of the recipes copied by Anonymous (1700) from Kidder's works incorporated the same classic French ingredients: cocks' combs, sweetbreads, oysters, anchovies, mushrooms, truffles, morels, capers, and tart liquids.[13] Much more than Jane (Bolling) Randolph's manuscript did, hers made sure her dishes on the Virginia frontier were just as elegant as those served back in England. By serving such fashionable foods currently in vogue, a hostess not only flattered her visitors but also demonstrated the correct decorum for the dining table.

Meat remained de rigueur and the high point of every meal. The manuscripts of Anonymous (1700) and Jane (Bolling) Randolph show that "Beef À la Mode," "Beef À la Daube," "Pullets À la Cream," "Cutlets À la Maintenoy," and "À Touert de moy," graced their tables among other delicacies. The Compiler (1744) had her own "Tort de Moyle" and possessed a wide range of French recipes.[14] It was Mary Randolph, however, who helped preserve the family's culinary tradition with her own versions of beef à la mode and other dishes. At the same time she made sure her newest dishes such as gazpacho and lemon ice met the highest—and fashionable—standards.

# Religious Aspects of Foods

[Shrove Tuesday] . . . very merry, with a special good dinner—a leg of veal and bacon, two capons and sausages and fritters, with abundance of wine.

—Samuel Pepys

Very merry at dinner . . . because Mrs. Turner and her company eate no flesh at all this Lent and I had a great deal of good flesh, which made their mouths water.

Then home to the only Lenten supper I have had of wiggs and ale.

—Samuel Pepys

To Redriffe, calling at the Half-way house; . . . where there was infinite of new cakes placed, that are made against Whitsuntide.

—Samuel Pepys

To Kate Joyces christening—where much company—good service of sweetmeats.

. . . so we had gloves and wine and wafers.

—Samuel Pepys

So home to dinner, and had an excellent Good Friday dinner of pease porridge—and apple pie.

Our dinner, it being Good Friday, was only sugar soppe and fish; the only time that we have had a Lenten dinner all this Lent.

Thence to my lady Sandwiches, where my wife all this day, having kept Good Friday very strict with fasting.

—Samuel Pepys

And there wine was offered and they drunk, I only drinking some Hypocras, which doth not breake my vowe, it being, to the best of my judgment, only a mixed compound drink, and not any wine—if I am mistaken, God forgive me.

—Samuel Pepys

To the funeral of Captain Llewellyn. . . . We had wine and biscuits according to custom.

We gave them burnt claret and cake.

—William Byrd

To 10 lbs. Butter . . . 50; To 2 Galls. Brandy . . . 70; To 1/2 Pepper, 1/2 of Ginger . . . 9; To 5 Gals. Wine . . . 150; To 8 lbs. Sugar . . . 32; To 1 Steer of 7 years . . . 600; To 3 large Weathers [sheep] . . . 450; [Total] 1361.

—Henrico County Record Book No. 1

Along with the currently fashionable French cookery, centuries-old religious practices were observed and practiced at the dinner table. This particular aspect was considered to be part of a hostess's proper training and decorum.

Seventeenth- and eighteenth-century inhabitants in Great Britain and Virginia celebrated fasts or feasts, depending on the nature of the religious holiday. Some were saints' days, while others were church days:

| | |
|---|---|
| January 1 | Circumcision |
| January 13 | Saint Hilary (Hilary Term) |
| January 25 | Conversion of Saint Paul |
| February 2 | Purification of the Virgin (Candlemas Day) |
| February 24 | Saint Mathias the Apostle |
| March 25 | Annunciation of the Virgin (Lady Day) |
| April 23 | Saint George |
| April 25 | Saint Mark the Evangelist |
| June 24 | Nativity of Saint John the Baptist (Midsummer Day) |
| June 29 | Saints Peter and Paul |
| July 2 | Visitation of the Virgin |
| July 15 | Saint Swithin |
| July 25 | Saint Christopher (Lammastide) |
| August 15 | Assumption of the Virgin |
| September 29 | Saint Michael and All Angels (Michaelmas) |
| November 1 | All Saints Day |
| November 11 | Saint Martin (Martinmas) |
| December 25 | Christmas.[1] |

Besides Lent there was Ash Wednesday, which occurred forty-six days before Easter. Easter, another major holiday, was followed by Whitsunday (Pentecost) seven weeks later. Trinity Sunday was observed only a week after Whitsunday.[2] The population measured the passing of the year through these holidays. Mrs. Mary (Isham) Randolph directed that her metheglin be made on 1 October, around Michaelmas. Early colonial deeds stipulated that rents or tithes be paid with ears of corn during the Feast of Saint Michael, and not surprisingly, this religious aspect was carried over to foods. Elizabeth Pepys saw to it that appropriate foods as dictated by church dogma as well as prescription, however unpopular, were served during Lent: "Dined at home on a poor Lenten dinner of Coleworts and bacon."[3] It is regrettable that William Byrd did not make mention of any religious observances other than occasional fasts, which were based on a decree by the governor or the council. The closest indication of William Byrd's religious expression is his intercession with God over his family's health, acceptance of God's will, and thinking of good thoughts before conducting his nightly prayers. He made no mention of Lent, other religious holidays, or even religion-influenced meals. He preferred to memorialize meat or fish at every meal.

Fortunately, it is known that Anonymous (1700), Jane (Bolling) Randolph, and The Compiler (1744) practiced at least Lent. Anonymous (1700) and The Compiler (1744) both copied a pease soup designed specifically for Lent, while Jane (Bolling) Randolph's manuscript contained a recipe for pease soup that was equally acceptable to guests and the church. Anonymous (1700) penned a good many fish recipes, presumably for family consumption, fish days, and perhaps to sell as profitable commodities. In contrast, Jane (Bolling) Randolph's repertoire of fish recipes is a mere handful, concentrating on sturgeon, eels, herring, and carp. (The possible explanation for these differences is given in the chapter titled "Seafood".)

Fritters, "wiggs," wafers, and probably pancakes were other edibles that met the Anglican Church's approval for consumption during fasts[4] and other solemn events. Anonymous (1700) had apple fritters, which were acceptable substitutes for meat. According to Frances Phipps, fritters were "fragments or cut pieces of food fried in batter."[5] Jane (Bolling) Randolph served wiggs, triangular pieces of baked dough, as part of her family's religious observance. (It was an important recipe, given her very neat penmanship.) According to Wilson, wiggs were doughnut-like cakes cut into wedges.[6] Circular wafers were thin and crisp.

The most intriguing recipes are found in Anonymous (1700)'s culinary collection in the form of "Jews Almond Cake" and "Jews Bread."[7] Although other recipes entitled "Almond Cakes" and other breads with religious titles have been carefully searched, none closely resembling these recipes has been found to date. While "Jews Bread" has been compared to challah and found somewhat different, it is believed that the titles of these recipes may be strictly biblical allusions to the absence of leavening.

Besides these religious holidays, there were other religion-based events: weddings and funerals. According to Philip Alexander Bruce, the most important events in an English settler's life included church attendance, weddings, and funerals.[8] While it is a shame that Hunter did not describe the Beverley-Randolph wedding feast, it is known that such wedding festivities lasted more than a day.

In spite of the fact that funerals were to be conducted in a decorous manner, many a funeral possessed a festive air. Neighbors and relatives would come from distant as well as nearby locales to pay their respects to the deceased and surviving family members. The surviving spouse, if any, and family members would provide beverages and foods as part of their "entertainment."[9] The funeral expenses for Elizabeth Sindrey of South Carolina in 1705 listed "66 lb. Sugar to burn the Wine."[10] Samuel Pepys mentioned that "six biscuits" were served apiece along with cakes and burnt claret at his brother's funeral.[11] Besides burnt claret and other wines, cider, beer, brandy, rum, and other spirits[12] were also served with various meats, cakes, biscuits, and other tasty accoutrements. William Byrd commented that "funeral biscuits" was served at one funeral while wine and cake were liberally provided at another funeral.[13] Twenty-five pounds of "white biscuit" and "pares" were provided at the service for Elizabeth Sindrey.[14]

Some of these funerals were so rowdy, unruly, and financially ruinous that many a testator expressed his wishes concerning funeral expenses and the provision of beverages. In 1683 Ralph Langley of York County stipulated that his executors were not to provide more than six gallons by way of beverages, apparently all he felt his estate could afford.[15] Rev. Edmund Watts directed that his funeral be conducted in a becoming manner: "Imprimis, haveing observed in the daies of my pilgramage the debauched drinking at burials tending much to the dishonor of God and his true Religion, my will is that noe strong drinke be provided or spent at my burial."[16]

# The Dinner Table

With great content, having a mess of brave plum-porridge and a roasted Pullett for dinner; and I sent for a mince-pie abroad.

. . . a good shoulder of veal, well dressed by Jane, and handsomely served to table —which pleased us much.

—Samuel Pepys

The first dinner I have made since I came hither. This cost me above 5*l* and merry we were—only, my chimney smokes.

—Samuel Pepys

My dinner was great and most neatly dressed by our own only mayde. We had a Fricasse of rabbets and chickens—a leg of mutton boiled—three carps in a dish—a great dish of a side of lamb—a dish of roasted pigeons—a dish of four lobsters—three tarts —a Lamprey pie, a most rare pie—a dish of anchovies—good wine of several sorts; and all things mighty noble and to my great content.

—Samuel Pepys

I ate some mutton hash as good as ever I ate in my life.

Colonel Randolph dined with me and I ate chicken for dinner, and our chief business was concerning a ship for his son Isham.

—William Byrd

About 3 o'clock we returned to the house and as many of the officers as could sit at the table stayed to dine with the Governor, and the rest went to take part of the hogshead in the churchyard. We had a good dinner, well served, with which the Governor seemed to be well pleased.

—William Byrd

This is a fine Sheeps-Head, Mr. Stadly shall I help you?—Or would you prefer a Bass or a Perch?—Or perhaps you will rather help yourself to some picked Crab—It is all extremely fine, Sir, I'll help myself—Well says the Colonel when we had almost finished our Dinner with a Glass of sparkling Porter on the Table before him, we have but fasted

to Day; here stands a fine Ham, & a Shoulder of excellent Mutton yet untouched—
At least, says the merry, good-hearted Man, we have kept Lent—

—Philip Vickers Fithian

I pray that instead of milk and honey the good Lord will give me some of Sister Dew's Sunday dinner.

—A deacon of Upper King and Queen Church

Amid the social pressure on them, Anonymous (1700), Jane (Bolling) Randolph, Mary Randolph, and other Chesapeake women had to be truly flawless and not fall into a "disorder" as did Byrd's wife. The meal was a crucial point of entertaining. Everything was now coming together: proper accoutrements of the room, elegant items on the table, appropriate utensils such as knives and forks, correct seating of guests, forms of entertainment, proper decorum, and exactly the right amount and choices of foods. There was also French cuisine and the colorful crowning glories: desserts, or "conceits." Fruits and tarts were timeless favorites as desserts because they were "fit to set before the most discriminating guest."[1]

Simultaneously hostesses' Christian virtues, domestic skills, and faultless personal deportment had to be visible at all times. Each also had to make sure that a midnight collation and beverages were available if a party was of long duration. If the host and hostess's children were old enough to attend, mothers would have to keep careful watch to ensure that their deportment met everyone's expectations. Like Martha Washington, they must be ready to cope with any emergency that might arise during their guests' stay. Aware that their roles were crucial, they would be careful to give an impression of calm and command toward their guests at all times.

Not only did a hostess need to be aware of the latest styles in cooking, she also had to be familiar with other requirements for the table beyond the purchase of plates and seating of guests. She had to be socially agile when orchestrating the setting of her table, since every item on the table had to be carefully balanced and arranged like "a Handel sonata."[2] The critical importance of correct placement was underscored by the inclusion of diagrams in many cookbooks:[3] "The direction of a table is no inconsiderable branch of a lady's concern."[4] There were detailed instructions to be followed, such as having tarts, custards, cakes, and certain sweetmeats, laid out with a point of a knife, handsomely presented.[5] The table included layered dish stands containing showy confections and sugared, shaped sweets; disguised meats; perfumed dishes; pewter flagons; and gleaming silver bowls. Certain family observances were followed; servants were well trained; and toasts were proposed in the latest fashion.

A hostess did have options. Certain dishes were sometimes offered in artistic forms since artifice was all the rage in the eighteenth century.[6] Many an item was transformed: "It is candied, it is reshaped, it is disguised."[7] Pies might be served in the shape of what they contained, such as carp pies in the form of fish.[8] In observance of his eighteenth marriage anniversary, Sir William Penn served not only a chine of beef and "other good cheer" but also "eighteen mince pies in a dish."[9] Chopped meats might be mixed with other ingredients and molded into a "hedgehog" by covering the meat with sliced almonds for "quills."[10] The Compiler (1744) made sure she possessed a recipe for "Hedgehogg." Anonymous (1700) may have practiced similar artifices, since she had two recipes that indicated disguise: "How to Pickle Codlins Like Mango" and "Pidgeon Pairs," a carefully shaped meat covered with scalded chopped spinach and strips of bacon.[11] These colorful and aromatic dishes were entertainment indeed.

Another popular form of disguise carried over from the seventeenth century into the eighteenth century concerned the camouflaging of a meat's flavor and serving it as another. One cook served a venison pasty that actually was a pasty of salted pork. Such recipes showed not only the cook's thrift but also her skill. However, this approach sometimes backfired with the consumer. Samuel Pepys dined on a "damned venison pasty that stunk like the devil; however, I did not know it till dinner was done."[12]

In contrast to most of their British peers, who heavily utilized perfumes in their foods, Anonymous (1700) and Jane (Bolling) Randolph (and her namesakes) did not resort often to using ambergris or musk to scent their foods. This implies that their entertaining was much more simple and straightforward in this regard. They emphasized instead impeccable manners toward each other and served attractive foods. William Byrd noted in his diary that "I complimented the Governor [Alexander Spotswood] who seemed to be a very good man and was very courteous to me and told me I had been recommended to him by several of my friends in England . . . I ate boiled ——— for dinner."[13]

All foods had to be presented in the best condition possible, free from discoloration and spoilage. Meats had to be cooked to perfection, vegetables crisp, breads hot, and syllabubs curdled just so. Oranges had to be spotless, jellies clear, and preserved fruits coated with expensive sugar. A list of other weighty accoutrements gracing the table would include pasties, puddings, tarts, and sugar-laden desserts known as conceits.

Expensive imported wines and homemade cordials were essential to any bountiful table. Drinking was a form of ritual; it served as a marker of one's personal identity and set the mood at dinners and other social functions. It generally was not associated with drunkenness.[14] Chocolate as well as tea, coffee, refined beer, and fine wines completed a meal.

Meat was prepared in every way imaginable: boiled, baked, roasted, stewed, pickled, salted, fried, fricasseed, and à la mode. These meats would provide a wide selection for guests at a dinner table. No Virginia hostess would embarrass her spouse by having only sheep's trotters to offer to a guest, as Elizabeth Pepys did; nor would she serve "deadly foul" meals, as did host and hostess Penn.[15]

Hot vinegar mixtures ensured the fresh-looking green color of various vegetables.[16] Salads, however limited, added colorful garnishes to platters. This was clearly the purpose of the few vegetables or salads in the three courses listed by Kidder. Colonial women made sure that their vegetables looked appetizing and fresh. Careful instructions in recipes such as "French Beans" in Jane (Bolling) Randolph's manuscript stipulated that boiling vinegar be poured on the beans from time to time until they were truly green. Spices and alum not only helped preserve the color but added crunch to the vegetables.

In addition to meats, Anonymous (1700) and Jane (Bolling) Randolph made sure that pickled oysters/eels, manchets (white breads), oyster rolls, sallets (salads), pea soup,

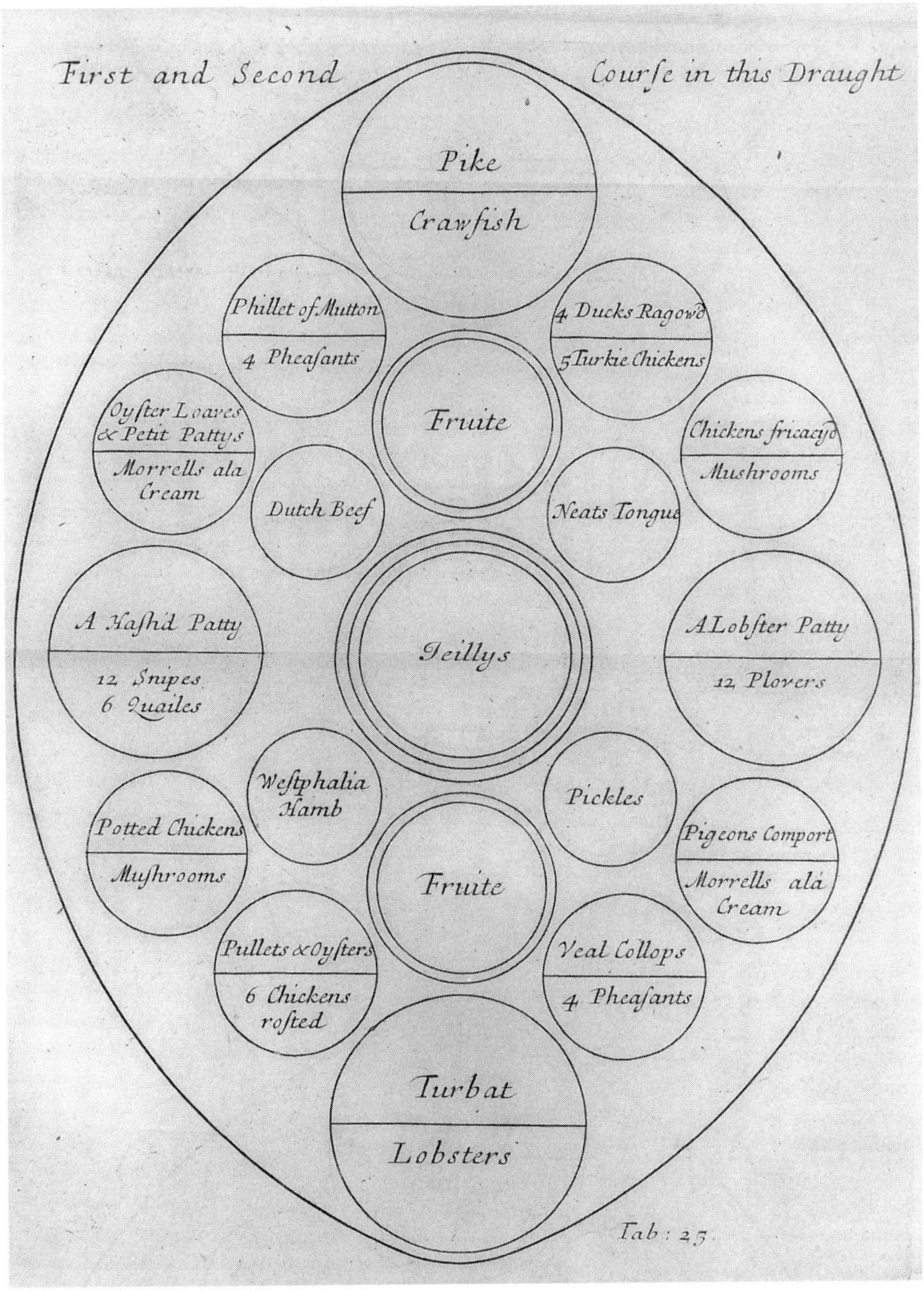


ABOVE AND OVERLEAF: First and second courses as presented by Patrick Lamb in 1710. Courtesy of the Library of Virginia, Richmond, Virginia.

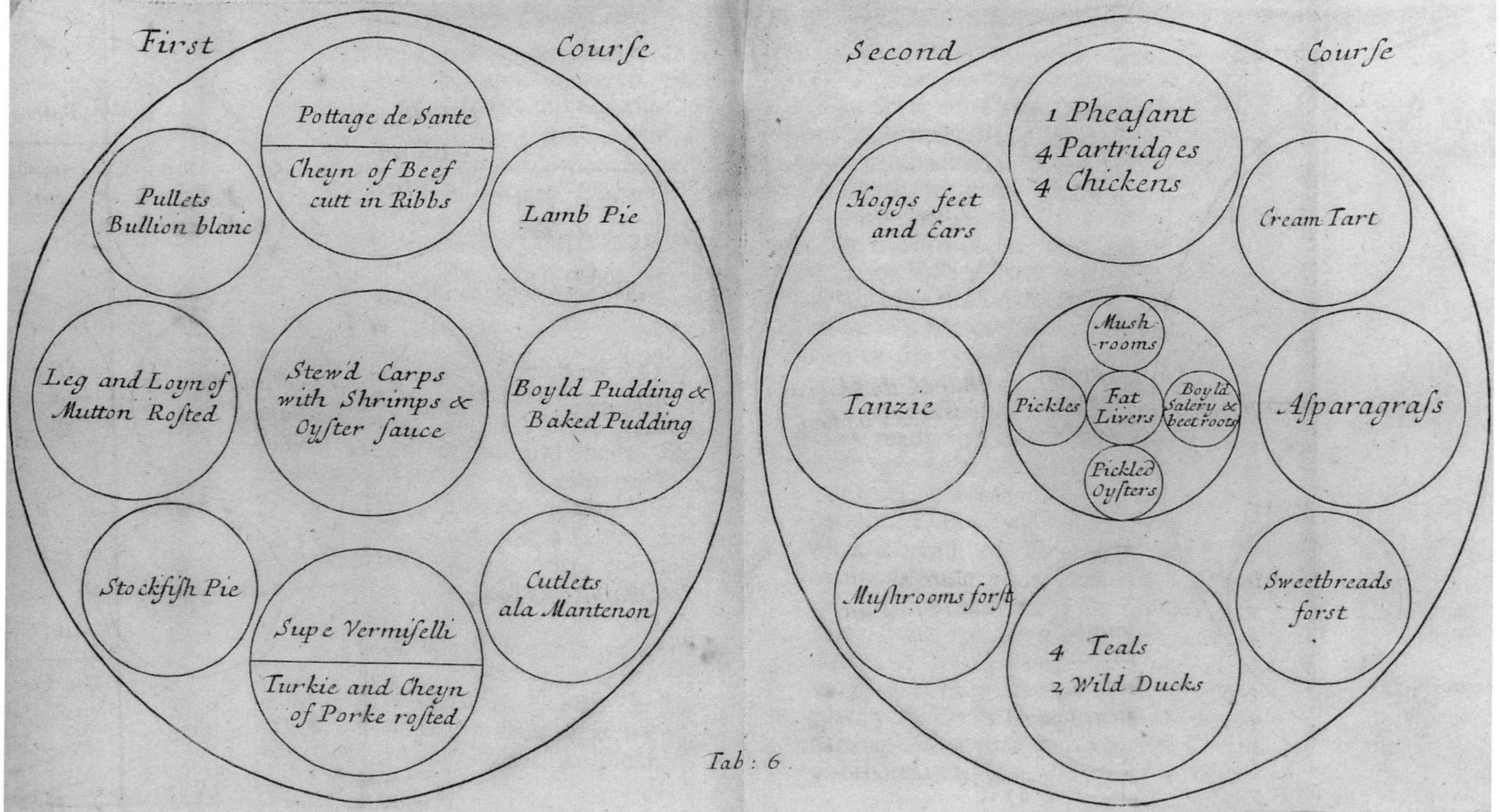
First Course
Pottage de Sante
Cheyn of Beef cutt in Ribbs
Pullets Bullion blanc
Lamb Pie
Leg and Loyn of Mutton Rosted
Stew'd Carps with Shrimps & Oyster sauce
Boyld Pudding & Baked Pudding
Stockfish Pie
Supe Vermiselli
Turkie and Cheyn of Porke rosted
Cutlets ala Mantenon
Second Course
1 Pheasant 4 Partridges 4 Chickens
Hoggs feet and Ears
Cream Tart
Tanzie
Mush-rooms
Pickles
Fat Livers
Boyld Salery & beetroots
Pickled Oysters
Asparagrass
Mushrooms forst
4 Teals 2 Wild Ducks
Sweetbreads forst

Tab: 6

"florendines" (tarts), and regalia of cucumbers, flummeries, marmalades, preserved quinces, and pickled barberries were placed on their serving tables. Jane prized her preserved peaches and quinces as well as her quince maramlade. The Compiler (1744), too, supplied an ample table with her selections. Anonymous (1700) had orange, almond, and pistachia (pistachio) butters, while Jane (Bolling) Randolph liked to offer potato pie. Jumbals, various creams and fools, puddings, assorted cakes, sugared fruits, and conceits such as candied angelica and fried cream joined other recipes in these manuscripts.

Desserts were almost as important as meat dishes because they served as a grand finale. Sugar-glazed cakes should never crumble under a knife, nor should carraway comfits fall off its sides. Characteristics such as color, shape, texture, and transparency were taken seriously. Tinted cakes should look as enticing as the beautifully clear, colored calves' feet jellies that sparkled like green, yellow, and red jewels.[17] "Guided by taste and experience, she [the hostess] practiced an art—not a science."[18]

For more than three hundred years "power was embedded in meal-taking . . . menus, table settings, guest lists, and polite behavior."[19] A husband was fully aware of his wife's duties and expected her not to fail. Although as a rule this was not normally acknowledged, Bishop James Madison in 1811 voiced his awareness by offering fatherly advice to his daughter Susan Randolph Madison, who was soon to be married: "What ever be your repast, how ever scanty it may be . . . receive [your husband and his unexpected guests] with a pleasing countenance . . . a hearty welcome; it will more than compensate for every other deficiency; it will more evince love for your husband, good sense in yourself, and that politeness of manners which acts as the most powerful charm, it will give to the plainest fare a zest superior to all that luxury can boast. . . . In the next place, as your husband's success in his profession will depend upon his popularity, and as the manner of a wife have no little influences in extending or lessening the respect and esteem of others for her husband, you should take care to be affable and polite to the poorest as well as the richest."[20]

It may be noted that by the very process of elevating her husband's (as well as her family's) status in a public setting, a hostess was no longer acting within her domicile but in the public sphere. Although a few women had the opportunity to serve as first lady, many performed with comparable skill and success at the local and regional levels. Some, such as Mary Randolph, achieved prominence in the public realm. Others were influential while maintaining a lower profile.

Like Mary Randolph at a later time, Anonymous (1700) and Jane (Bolling) Randolph were not typical women. They functioned to the best of their ability and on their own terms made the best use of the opportunities that came their way. Through their cookbooks (foodways), Anonymous (1700) and Jane (Bolling) Randolph provided glimpses into the social, ideational, and food behavioral systems that were already in full force in the late seventeenth and early eighteenth centuries. Although many of their recipes retained a medieval or English flavor, their dinners were stamped with their own indelible marks. The fact that Anonymous (1700) wished to serve elegant foods at such an early date is truly significant not only in historical terms but also for cultural or foodway implications. Her recipes provide aspects of documented food behavior at an early date in Virginia.

The next section of the book will examine the various categories of foods found in Anonymous (1700)'s and Jane (Bolling) Randolph's manuscripts, since they passed the torch of cookery to their successor Mary Randolph. It was indeed a colonial Virginia culinary dynasty in the best sense of the word.

# PART TWO

# Meats ~ One

Supped upon a Westphalia ham.

Dined alone upon some marrow bones, and had a fine piece of roast beef but being alone I eat none.

The best powdered goose that ever I eat.

A very good dinner . . . of a powdered leg of pork and a loin of lamb roasted.

A couple of large Chickens, were dressed and a good mess of Creame—which anon we had with good content.

He [Sir William Hicks] did give us the meanest dinner-of beef-shoulder and umbles of venison . . . and a few pigeons; and all in the meanest manner that ever I did see—to the basest degree.

—Samuel Pepys

Wee were never more merrie, nor fedde on more plentie of good oysters, fish, flesh, wild foule, and good bread; nor never had better fires in England then in the drie warme smokie houses of Kecoughtan.

—Captain John Smith

That he saw John Woodson Jr. go to the Curle Swamp in the main creek with his dog and gun . . . and that he shot ducks there out of his canoe.

—Henrico County Deeds, Wills, Etc., 1688–97

Did we but know your wants before the fall, we could secure any quantity that can be needed: because that is the proper time for killing and packing of pork.

—William Byrd

After selling Joseph two Beeves and some Pork—rode to Capt. Henry Downe's.

Clear, frosty Weather, our people busie butchering the Swine.

—Robert Rose

I caused a beef to be killed this day because the weather was cool.

I caused Moll to be beaten for not making the shoats [fat].

I ate roast shoat for dinner.

—William Byrd

Owing to the continuous warfare in Europe and the fact that it was not yet possible to have fodder for livestock last through the winter, meat became scarce after 1550. Enough fodder did not become a reality until the eighteenth century.[1] This subsequent scarcity of fresh meats led to an upsurge in salting, smoking, and pickling, which both preserved and tenderized the tough meat fibers. Salted beef became the norm in the winters for those unable to afford fresh meat.[2] The following two poems beautifully exemplify English society's primary focus on numerous meats, with roast beef being a national favorite:

They both provide, against Christmas do come
to wellcome good neighbor good cheer to have some
Good bread and good drink, a good fire in the hall,
brawn, pudding, and souse, and good mustard withal:
Beef, Mutton, and Pork, shread-pies of the best, of meat
pig, veal, goose, and capon, and turkey well drest,
Cheese, apple, and nuts, jolly carols to hear,
as then in the countrey is counted good cheer.[3]

When mighty roast beef was the Englishman's food,
It ennobled our hearts and enriched our blood,
Our soldiers were brave and our courtiers were good,
Oh! the roast beef of old England.[4]

Luxury as defined by privileged families of the seventeenth through nineteenth centuries was not confined to rare or status-laden items but also applied to the meals themselves, especially expensive meats. Samuel Pepys of London and William Byrd II of Virginia were all too aware of such social symbolism, since they commemorated meat at practically every meal. Poultry, once considered a poor man's food, became prohibitively expensive. Inhabitants, such as Samuel Pepys, who purchased poultry proved that they had "risen in the world":[5] "At night my wife and I had a good supper by ourselfs, of a pullet=hashed; which pleased me much to see my condition come to allow ourselfs a dish like that."[6]

Since meat was the "central element of the traditional British diet" and carried a "high cultural value," a family's standard of living was largely judged not only "by the amount of meat eaten" but also against the prominence and variety of meat dishes on the ideal dinner table.[7] Beef was the first choice of the British. Venison, "a prerogative of the crown," was also held in special esteem, even in pies made of umbles.[8] Meat was considered too valuable to waste. Samuel Pepys and his peers ate the remainder of their king's royal menu with the royal servants at the backstairs, and he found the meat to be superb.[9]

This social value of meat was part of the culinary heritage that the immigrants brought with them to Virginia in the seventeenth century. Therefore, it is not surprising that beef and other prime cuts occupy such a large portion of the manuscripts belonging to Anonymous (1700), Jane (Bolling) Randolph, The Compiler (1744), and Mary Randolph. They were selected for their obvious status and also because they were consistently eaten throughout the three centuries by all classes of people. There were recipes for boiled, salted, potted, roasted, collared, forced, and hashed beef along with other specialties such as beef à la mode and Portugal beef.

Along with this culinary heritage and basic foodstuffs such as oats and wheat, the earliest settlers also brought their nearly fatal perceptions with them to Jamestown. Their ideas concerning the cultivation and gathering of food resources were based on the circumstances they had known on an island of well-tended gardens and domesticated livestock. Virginia, however, turned out to be quite alien: excessive heat and humidity, disease-bearing swamps, unfamiliar vegetation, wild species, and Native American guerrilla warfare.

In order to survive, the settlers quickly adopted Native American methods of procuring and preparing foods. These methods have since become part of America's classic cuisine: barbecues and clambakes, clam and corn chowders, steamed seafood, and pemmican.[10] Variations of the famed Brunswick stews were also favored by colonists, who used this term for the "game soup" created by women of the Powhatan, Cherokee, and Chickahominy tribes.[11] These Native Americans also introduced into the settlers' diet ground acorns from the live oak trees, which could thicken venison soup or be used in conjunction with hominy or rice.[12] The Choctaw tribe taught them how to grind sassafras leaves into filé powder to enhance and thicken stews, and this became the basic characteristic of Creole cooking for gumbos.[13]

One of the new things the inhabitants learned involved the preparation of meats. According to L. Daniel Mouer, the technique of using hickory ash instead of saltpeter in the first rubbing of meats was derived from the Native Americans.[14] Mary Randolph used hickory ashes on her ham to prevent spoilage.[15] By sharing their culinary knowledge, the Native Americans left a "permanent mark on American cooking habits."[16]

The majority of meat in the settlers' diet was provided by swine, sheep, cattle, and other livestock. Wild game such as deer, squirrel, rabbit, polecat, beaver, and anything else available was also eaten.[17] The cookbooks of Anonymous (1700), Jane (Bolling) Randolph, The Compiler (1744), and Mary Randolph did not include these wild meats or quail, raccoon, or bear, which their predecessors definitely used. Anonymous (1700) and The Compiler (1744) had rabbit dishes, either boiled or fricasseed, while Jane (Bolling) Randolph's manuscript listed a sauce for a hare dish.[18] In contrast, Mary Randolph preferred curried, roasted, boiled, and sauce-covered rabbit.[19]

Meats such as beef continued to be status food, and a plentiful supply was highly valued. In 1656 John Hammond wrote: "Cattle and Hogs are everywhere, which yeeld beef, veal, milk, butter, cheese and other made dishes, porke, bacon and pigs, and that are as sweet and savoury meat as the world affords."[20] Given the extraordinary hardships the settlers endured for most of the seventeenth century, meat probably grew even more important as a central role in their diets. Pigs adapted especially well in the wild and offered a unique flavor for which future Virginia hams would be justly famous.[21] A Frenchman commented that the

Virginians had a "special way of curing" meat through salting and smoking in their smoke-houses and that this meat was found to be superior to that of the French in terms of flavor and quality.[22]

Shoats were highly prized not only because meats ensured the settlers' chance of survival by providing valuable protein, but also as legal tender, bartering items, and as legacies to offspring. In 1631 Andrew Whowell bequeathed sows to his children.[23] Capt. Stephen Gill's 1653 inventory revealed 600 pounds of "Neate Pork," and Thomas Deacon's estate showed that a bill of 995 pounds of pork needed to be paid in 1647.[24] According to Lyman Carrier, slaughtered hogs yielded 75 percent edible meat, in contrast to slaughtered cattle, which resulted in 50–60 percent edible meat.[25] Prices in 1648 were reasonable—beef could be sold at two pence, half-penny a pound, while pork was sold at three pence a pound.[26]

Besides being consumed, pork also figured in cases of punitive damages and criminal activities. Because of his age, William Hatcher escaped hanging by Governor Berkeley for his "mutinous words" during Bacon's Rebellion. Instead, he was fined eight thousand pounds of "drest porke," which was to be delivered with "all expedition" unto "his majesties commander of his forces in Henrico County for the supply of the soldiers." In February 1684 Benjamin Hatcher testified that he heard Lewis Watkins claim that Thomas Holmes was a "hog-stealer" since he stole several of his prized porkers. After Hatcher responded that "it is a hard thing to say," Watkins replied that "he would prove it." Emotions continued to run high over swine. In 1692 Edward Oliver was accused by Henry Turner of stealing his hogs and keeping a "powdering tubb in the cornfield."[27]

During the time of Bacon's Rebellion and its destructive aftermath, inhabitants of all classes suffered serious losses, including sources of meat. The following testimonies of the settlers reflect the sheer necessity of feeding starving soldiers and the desperation of hungry and otherwise honest neighbors driven to stealing food. In 1679 Samuel Knibbe mentioned that Edward Good had broken into his father's loft and stolen some meat "for his belly."[28] Margaret Thomas gave her own compelling testimony that some three years earlier a sheep, mutton, cow, calf, and hogs were taken and killed by Trent and Sherman families and their servants from other estates; it seems the families survived by either converting the meat for their own use or selling it to the starving soldiers.[29]

In contrast to beef and pork, mutton and lamb never gained the popularity they enjoyed in England. Until about 1700 sheep were viewed as primarily sources of wool and thus were limited in number: "Mutton is somewhat scarce."[30] Only later did mutton and lamb begin appearing more often on dinner tables as herds became larger. One possible factor for their limited use in cuisine may be that these greasier meats were difficult to preserve well in the hot Virginia climate and thus had to be consumed immediately or salted to prevent spoilage. A contemporary account noted that fresh meat would not keep during the summer and thus often was lent "from one to another" and "repaied again."[31] In contrast hogs, a major staple, were not slaughtered during the summer and thus seldom were eaten fresh.

However, the historical record may be biased, both by omission and by selection. Sheep may have been fewer in number, but they were still valued as sources of meat. Thirty-year-old Joane Jones made a deposition about an illegal sheep killing on 1 April 1680, claiming that Henry Sherman and his maid had "sett the dogg upon one sheep" and that the sheep was "brought dead into the garden," where "he drest & carryed it into his house and converted it to his owne use."[32] Even William Byrd's dietary record contradicts this supposed unpopularity of mutton, since he mentions mutton many times as a regular feature of his diet. Perhaps mutton was considered an everyday meat and thus not worth recording unless it was prepared in an elaborate manner. This was the case for Anonymous (1700), The Compiler (1744), and Mary Randolph. Besides boiled or roasted mutton, their recipes include "Mutton à la Royale," "Mutton à la Daube," and mutton cutlets. It is not possible to determine whether Jane (Bolling) Randolph's manuscript also had mutton recipes, since a number of the meat recipes are missing; the surviving portion of the index does not mention mutton, however.

Writers stated that Virginians also ate a great deal of venison, which was available in abundance in the colony's early years. Durand wrote in 1686–87 that "there are such great number of . . . deer that you cannot enter a house without being served venison. It is very good in pies, boiled or baked."[33] This is a studied contrast to Samuel Pepys's comment about a particular type of venison dish: "where we had some rare pot venison and Ale to abundance."[34] Although the number of deer declined by the turn of the eighteenth century, deer were not yet difficult to find. It is interesting to see that Jane (Bolling) Randolph's collection included a recipe for umble pie called Black Pudding similar to those contemporary British sources; it was not viewed as a vernacular dish.[35] Apparently these settlers shared the view that their beef, veal, mutton, and pork were "as good as Europe."[36]

Not to be overlooked as sources of meat were wild fowl and domesticated poultry such as chickens, ducks, and geese. Instead of being viewed as a poor man's food, as they were in England for a time, poultry and native fowl incited admiration. John Hammond noted that "wilde Turkeys are frequent, and so large that I have seen some weigh neer threescore pounds; other beasts that are whose flesh is whole and savourie, such are unknowne to us."[37]

Pigeons were considered fine meat, according to the upper classes in Britain. Samuel Pepys treated Mr. Hawley with "six of my pigeons which my wife is resolved to kill here."[38] European visitors in America noted that "pigeons are raised by people of quality, the common people scorning such small animals"[39] and that their "flesh" was the "most palatable of any bird's flesh I have ever tasted."[40] Pigeons were elegant enough for Anonymous (1700), Jane (Bolling) Randolph, The Compiler (1744), and Mary Randolph to include in their culinary manuscripts. Anonymous (1700) made sure her pigeons were elegantly served at table by molding them into the shape of "Pidgeon Pairs." If the prescriptive culinary publications are any indication, they probably served pigeon with other meat dishes upon festive tables.

It is said that "hog and hominy" fare along with johnny cakes and pone became colonial mainstays among all social classes.[41] Care must be taken concerning inherent bias in the written record since people usually presented ideal images on paper. In spite of problems dealing with measurements and sampling bias, the archaeological record has been proven more reliable than documentary sources. A bear leg was excavated at Curles, a fine example of the disparity found between the written record and archaeological evidence. In addition Miller's and Bowen's studies prove that by 1640 beef was dominant over pork and other meats.[42] This emphasis on meat extended well into the late nineteenth century. It is no accident that the most important or expensive meat dishes (including beef, seafood, and poultry) are missing from Jane (Bolling) Randolph's cookbook. These missing recipes show that meat was the most important feature of a meal, and every hostess wanted to make sure she possessed excellent meat recipes for her table.

William Byrd did not see anything amiss with squirrel or blue wing. Given the nature of his daily entries, Byrd is probably one of the most reliable contemporary sources we have concerning everyday cuisine. However, he seldom described these dishes in great detail. Even when discussing parties, foodstuffs were given the same brevity. He appeared not to have been interested in describing the way food was presented. However, Byrd enjoyed a wide variety of meats prepared in every conceivable manner, be it baked, boiled, fried, fricasseed, hashed, stewed, roasted, or served cold. The meals in themselves were not necessarily fancy, as Byrd clearly attested to from time to time when mentioning goose giblets and tripe, but meat took precedence over fish.

The omission of regular meats in the manuscripts of Anonymous (1700) and Jane (Bolling) Randolph indicate that their recipes were strictly for entertaining. Cookbooks such as these, according to Sandy Oliver, were part of "prescriptive" literature,[43] since their manuscripts were meant to serve as guides for a more elevated form of entertaining.

A Virginia hostess's dinner table, like that of her English predecessors, provided a status-laden "riot of meat,"[44] accompanied by fish. This could range from a large side of basted beef for a barbecue to thirty dishes of meat served on the table for twenty guests.[45] Anonymous (1700) and Jane (Bolling) Randolph's manuscripts s listed roast beef and mutton, veal cutlets, bacon, chicken fricassee, roast turkey, sugar-cured ham, "bisk" (bisque) of pigeons, boiled fowl, pickled pork, potted tongue, smoked joints, savory balls, and "ragoos" (ragouts) with sweetbreads. Not to be excluded were meat pasties and pies. The Compiler (1744) was similarly elegant in her updated choices. She joined Anonymous (1700), Jane (Bolling) Randolph, and Mary Randolph, who sought to present only the best dishes for their families and friends. The majority of their meat recipes reflected high cuisine and their places in society. Gervase Markham would have approved and given them high marks.

# Meats ~ Two

> About 2 o'clock we went to dinner and I ate some of the beef that was preserved after the new manner and found it very juicy and not very salt. It is the best way of saving meat and will preserve it for several years free from taint and was found out by chance by a poor carpenter who keeps the secret to himself and gets abundance of money.
>
> —William Byrd

> My Dear Grand Papa [Thomas Jefferson]: . . . there was a great Barbacue at Charlottsville to day at which Mr. Jones delivered an oration.
>
> —Ann Cary Randolph

The three authors had their own preferred cooking methods and distinctive touches: Anonymous (1700) was "traditional," Jane (Bolling) Randolph "transitional," and Mary Randolph "modern." "Traditional" refers to an Old World outlook, influenced by Markham's prescriptions. No additional or new ingredients, improvements, or innovations were included. "Transitional" refers to a time marked by the adoption of new ingredients or innovations, as shown by Jane (Bolling) Randolph's use of Native American persimmons, and "kipscacuanna" (ipecac), and inclusion of an old tobacco ointment. Her manuscript recipes were transitional since she sometimes continued old family standbys, such as the bran–sour drink mixture to preserve meats, and yet was also innovative: instead of boiling her hams in a saline solution, she used the curing method with sugar and salt and used blood for coloring instead of cochineal. "Modern" refers to streamlined spices and greater use of vegetables such as parsley and asparagus with meat instead of fruits. Mary Randolph explored new recipes such as olla, escalloped tomatoes, and lemon ice. Tomatoes, vegetables, and everyday meats and fish for fine meals were simply but effectively presented on her table. Her recipes were less elitist than were those of the other two authors. Measurements were more precise, a reflection of better scientific understanding and a burgeoning republican culture. Mary Randolph epitomized this progressive outlook.

The medieval practice of mixing meats with fruits and other flavorings persisted, as illustrated by the "vestigal mince pie."[1] The cookbooks of Anonymous (1700) and Jane (Bolling) Randolph had mince pies filled with neat's tongue, mutton or veal, candied fruits, currants, raisins, and the peel of oranges or lemons. Mrs. Street's version consisted exclusively of apples, currants, candied peel, the juices of lemons and oranges, and suet; there was no trace of meat in sight. In contrast, The Compiler (1744)'s mince pie recipe contains meat and fruits limited to currants and candied peels.[2]

Anonymous (1700) gave meat dishes heavy emphasis, and the index of such dishes in her manuscript is long compared to those found in Jane (Bolling) Randolph's and The Compiler (1744)'s manuscripts. Anonymous (1700)'s special interest in elaborate meat dishes is evident from the fact that she copied many recipes from Edward Kidder's book. She also included a newly fashionable dish called "Bisk of Pigeons," even though it was frowned upon by her English peers because of its French origins.[3] Other recipes included "Scotch Collops," "Mutton à la Daube," "Mutton à la Royale," "Cutlets Alamaintenoy," "Pigeons in Surtout," "Pidgeon Pairs," and "Pullets à la Cream." The Compiler (1744), though of slightly later date, had similar recipes in more modern form. She possessed recipes for collaring a pig, chicken fricassee, and beef à la mode, which were traditional standbys. However, she had other meat dishes not found in Anonymous (1700)'s, Jane (Bolling) Randolph's, or Mary Randolph's collections, such as hashed calf's head, "Beef Royal," "To harsh Mutton," "Geese à la Soabe," and a hedgehog dish.[4] It would be interesting to discover whether her recipe for hashed calf's head resembles the one listed in the index but missing in Jane (Bolling) Randolph's manuscript. It is clear, though, that Anonymous (1700)'s recipes reflected the latest fads available from England.

Anonymous (1700)'s recipes for brawn of a hog's head and calf's chaldron are truly arresting because these dishes were popular on dinner tables in the first half of the seventeenth century. Prepared heads and other parts of animals reflected a time when no scrap of meat was wasted. Brawn, according to Lorna Sass, was the flesh (muscle) of a boar, either collared and boiled or set aside for pickling and potting.[5] However, the term could and probably did include other fleshy and edible meats as well, as suggested by Karen Hess, who states that brawn consisted of "the fleshy part, the muscle, of the leg."[6] *The Oxford English Dictionary* states that brawn could be the flesh of boar or swine.[7] Brawn was considered a great delicacy. John Murrell made mention of "brawne" in his 1621 edition.[8] However, none of the other cookbooks examined by the author yielded a recipe for a brawn of a hog's head. In spite of this, it may be significant that the archaeological excavation of the site called The Maine (c. 1618–25) by Alain Outlaw near Jamestown in Virginia yielded a number of hogs heads. Presumably this cheaper cut of meat was relegated to the settlers while other, more choice cuts were sent to the governor in the form of tithes.[9] The settlers' hogs' heads certainly were not as elaborately dressed as the one prepared by Anonymous (1700). More likely their hogs heads were either simply boiled or roasted and quickly consumed.

Anonymous (1700)'s "Brawn of a Hogs Head" is undeniably old in terms of language, ingredients, method of preparation, and resulting overall flavor, and the dish by then was passé. Anonymous (1700)'s method of cooking brawn was by simple boiling. A published recipe entitled "To make tender and delicate brawne" called for collared brawn to be put into water-filled kettles that were then covered and put into ovens for a certain length of time; this new method of preparation was touted as being far superior to the "olde manner of boyling brawne in great and huge kettles."[10]

Most sixteenth-century feasts included brawn as an entree served with mustard, usually around December, Michaelmas, and the Lenten holidays.[11] Referring to December, one eighteenth-century cookbook noted that "this Month, Brawn is in season, and must always be serv'd either in the Collar or Slice, before the Dinner comes on the Table to be eat with

Mustard."[12] Samuel Pepys mentioned in his diary that he gave a "collar of brawn" for breakfast.[13] When French cookery became all the rage by 1690, brawn declined in popularity. After 1690 it would reappear occasionally since it regained its common use in rural communities. According to Roger Goodburn of Oxford, England, brawn was still being consumed in Lincolnshire among the elder citizenry in rural areas of England in 1993.[14] It can still be found today in some meat markets, and mixed with tongue into a form of headcheese, it can be found at London's Smithfield Market.[15] Perhaps Anonymous (1700)'s recipe was handed down for generations.

Calf's chaldron, a dish consisting of a highly seasoned sauce containing dressed entrails of a beast, also declined in popularity. Used in dishes as early as 1604, if not earlier, chaldron became popular by 1655.[16] Anonymous (1700)'s carefully penned recipe "To make a Fricassy of a Calfs Chaldron C——" was widely used at the time, but like brawn, it gradually faded from genteel tables by the end of the seventeenth century:

> To make a Fricassy of a Calfs Chaldron C——
>
> [Take] [a] Calfs Chaldron, after it is little more than half [boyled] and when it is Cold, Cut it into little bits as big [as] [Wal]nuts, Season ye whole with beaten Cloves, Salt, [Nutm]eg, Mace, a little pepper, an Onion, Parsley, & a Tarragon all Shred very Small, then put it into a [fry]ing pan with a Ladle full of Strong broth, & a little [?]t Butter, when it is fryed enough, have a little [lea]r made with ye Mutton-gravy, ye juce of a Lemon [&] [Ora]nge, ye yolkes of three or four Eggs & a little grated [Nut]meg, put all to your Chaldron in ye pan, toss your [Fri]cassy two or three times, then Dish it, & so Serve it up.[17]

According to Mrs. Ernest Goodburn of Winterton, England, a professional cook now retired, this dish was still being served on English tables in Yorkshire about sixty years ago. She provided a modern version of the recipe, which is hardly changed from Anonymous (1700)'s recipe:

> Fricassy of a Calf's Chaldron
>
> Stew until half cooked, strain. When it is cold, cut into pieces as big as a walnut. Season with beaten cloves, salt, nutmeg, mace, a little pepper, an onion, parsley and tarragon. Put into a warm pan with a ladle full of strong broth with a little Lemon & orange juice, the broth made from mutton gravy. Cook until tender. Add 3 or 4 yolks of eggs, stirred in, and add chopped parsley & nutmeg and serve.[18]

Anonymous (1700)'s brawn and chaldron recipes exemplify her traditional outlook. By the time of Jane (Bolling) Randolph's and Mary Randolph's manuscripts, brawn and chaldron had disappeared from the American table.

Jane (Bolling) Randolph's collection presented more elegant meat courses for the table, including potted meat dishes to tide the family over the winter. Some of Mary Randolph's recipes resemble recipes listed in Jane (Bolling) Randolph's and Anonymous (1700)'s cookbooks. In spite of the different titles, Anonymous (1700)'s "Cutlets Alamaintenoy" and Mary Randolph's "Scotch Collops of Veal" are quite similar. These contrast with The Compiler (1744)'s recipe for "Neck/Loyn of Mutton in Cutlets," which calls for broiling egg-coated mutton with herbs such as "savory spice," then serving it in a sauce called ragout and completing the dish by adding bits of fruit.[19] These three items are classic characteristics of fashionable and French-influenced seventeenth-century cooking, and in this sense Anonymous (1700) was purely traditional. In contrast, Mary Randolph chose to fry and then stew her cutlets until tender and flavor them with a tart sauce containing vinegar, wine, and garlic. Only one spice, mace, was used, and greens (parsley) replaced the fruit. Although Mary Randolph's taste was modern, these cooks shared an interest in serving this dish in the most visually attractive manner possible.

Mary Randolph did not restrict herself to high-status meats to the degree that Anonymous (1700) and Jane (Bolling) Randolph did. She published recipes for vernacular meat dishes enjoyed by all classes. These dishes could be presented by a middle-class housewife with easily affordable local ingredients. Mary Randolph's "A Nice Little Dish of Beef," "To Roast Large Fowls," and "To Stuff a Ham" served as models for her audience to emulate.[20]

A striking feature in these culinary collections is that venison is barely acknowledged. A traditional English venison pasty appeared in the c. 1700 manuscript, while a single recipe using venison, now unfortunately missing, was included in Jane (Bolling) Randolph's collection. For unknown reasons Mary Randolph and The Compiler (1744) did not include venison in their repertoires of vernacular foods. Perhaps venison was no longer as plentiful as it had been or was considered an everyday meat. Surprisingly, turkey was also seldom used. The culinary pages of Anonymous (1700) and Jane (Bolling) Randolph each listed only one turkey dish. The former dressed up her turkey in a pie, but the latter turkey recipe is unknown since it is among the recipes lost from her manuscript. Mary Randolph provided three elegant recipes for turkey and included sauce and jelly as suitable accompaniments.[21] Perhaps turkey also was considered too common unless prepared in a fashionable mode.

The meat recipes compiled by Anonymous (1700) are of interest in that they are older in content and utilized parts of meat that were little used by the late eighteenth century or early nineteenth century. Beef was the prime choice, followed by veal, mutton, lamb, ham, and fowl. This supports the archaeological evidence presented by Bowen and Miller.[22] This pattern of preference continued to the nineteenth century.

The skinless aspect of Anonymous (1700)'s beef sausages may or may not be significant. Beef sausages with skins became popular on English breakfast tables shortly after the 1630s. Since sausage meats often were potted before they were rolled and fried, they saved time and were especially favored by farmers and country laborers. The gentry preferred meat in the form of rolled balls or forcemeats for garnish.[23] In the published editions either beef is presented with skins or pork without skins is used for fillings. Since the author has not found any recipe for beef sausage without skins in any of the published works to date, this skinless beef sausage may be a cherished family recipe and a vernacular dish brought over to Virginia. Beef sausages are not found among Jane (Bolling) Randolph's and Mary Randolph's recipes. Like her British predecessors, Mary Randolph used pork with skins,[24] which may have been a short-term preservation method.[25] Her choice may also have been personal preference.

Beef à la mode was penned in Anonymous (1700), Jane (Bolling) Randolph, and Mary Randolph's cookbook creations. Although sharing the same name, these dishes differed not only in method of preparation but also in terms of ingredients. Anonymous (1700)'s recipe featured beef cooked in a pan with savory spices and sealed with pastry—in short, a larger and heavier version of the beloved dishes of England. Again Anonymous (1700) was traditional and conservative in her mental outlook. In contrast, the recipe in Jane's manuscript specifies that the meat be pickled with salts and then baked slowly in an oven with traditional spices. This recipe was transitional, partly traditional and partly new, and more closely resembled Anonymous (1700)'s recipe for beef than for beef à la mode.

Mary Randolph's "Beef À la Mode" is striking in that it preserves several seventeenth-century elements that were declining in use: marrow, forcemeat balls, and walnut and mushroom catsups. The marrow served the function of the lard, butter, and suet of the other two recipes, and also served as a moistening and flavoring agent. Wine helped flavor and tenderize the meat and is much more reminiscent of our wine-flavored roasts today. Her baking technique was similar to those in the Anonymous (1700) and Jane (Bolling) Randolph versions when it came to slow cooking. Mary Randolph used a metal lid instead of the pastry lid used by Anonymous (1700), while the recipe in Jane's collection used a pot in the final baking phase. In this particular example Mary Randolph was more traditional than usual, but the use of the wine and precise directions pointed toward a more modern approach. The three authors' techniques had common roots but differed in accordance with the authors' preferences and the changing times. This was also true of The Compiler (1744), who preferred her own slightly more modernized beef à la mode versions in "To Stew Beef Allamode" and to "pott Beef" as good as venison.

Since hogs were valued in colonial Virginia, both the Anonymous (1700) and Jane (Bolling) Randolph manuscripts offered recipes for "Collar Pig." So did The Compiler (1744), who titled her recipe "To Collier a Pig." Anonymous (1700)'s recipe, again, was already ancient by the time she penned it in her cookbook. One is struck not only by the age-old methods of preparation in her recipe but also the more old-fashioned language and seventeenth-century ingredients compared to those used in Jane (Bolling) Randolph's collection. Anonymous (1700)'s personal conservatism remained consistent. Jane (Bolling) Randolph offered two recipes for pork. The first was quite traditional, right down to the pickling and collaring. Her sack-coated pork was boiled in mint water and bran after soaking overnight in plain water. Besides the familiar spices, she used sage, lemon peel, and sweet herbs instead of cloves. Even sack was used to enhance flavor. In her second recipe she reduced the range of spices employed and used a boiled vinegar solution to pickle her simply boiled pork, and she experimented with bay leaves.[26]

Both cooks specified that, once cooked, pork was to be tightly rebound—presumably using fresh, woven material. The recipes reflect Anonymous (1700)'s traditional perceptions about her domestic role through cooking and show that Jane (Bolling) Randolph was interested in combining customary methods with new approaches. One recipe was traditional, the other more innovative. The recipe in Jane's cookbook was unmistakably old in technique and, yet, was innovative. These subtle changes indicate that Jane—and probably her daughter—was exploring all possibilities of preservation and that she was willing to make her own contributions.

For reasons not understood, Mary Randolph did not include a recipe for collaring pigs in her cookbook. Instead she possessed recipes for "a shote's head," "To make shoat cutlets,"

"To roast a pig," and "To Barbecue Shote."[27] These recipes were just as messy and time-consuming but reflected her more modern choices.

The recipes involving hams offer further illustration of the similarities and differences between Anonymous (1700) and Jane (Bolling) Randolph's collections. In these recipes they are traditional in their methods and use of salts and sugars. Sugar had long been associated with hams, as in the much-admired Westphalian hams in Germany. Sugar was eventually "purged" from meat recipes, including hams.[28] Not only was saltpeter an essential ingredient to prevent spoilage, but other types of salts also had important functions. The coarse-grained bay salt penetrated the tissues inwardly, in contrast with the more refined table salts, which moved outward from the surface of the meat. Saltpeter was not the only ingredient that colored the meat red; so did cochineal.[29]

Although proof is lacking due to a number of missing meat recipes, it is believed that the pickled pork recipe is Jane's. The use of cochineal reflects her willingness to innovate. This author has not seen this in other recipes, published or otherwise: "with a Dram of Cochineal & lett it Stand till it be cold & then putt in your Pork."[30] Cochineal, derived mainly from a female insect in Mexico, was one of the most expensive coloring agents that could be purchased during the colonial times. It was later replaced by saunders, known as red sandalwood. Mary Randolph mentioned this ingredient in connection with blancmange rather than meat.[31]

Mary Randolph's confident personality, inquiring mind, and bent for innovation enabled her to realize her true worth as Richmond's leading hostess. Her emphasis on precise measurements and instructions that were "direct, down-to-earth and authoritative"[32] reflects her more modern perspective concerning her role in the domestic field. Not only did she eliminate the pickle and sugar combination in her hams, but she made use of hickory ashes as a preservative. Her discussion on the subject of hogs is absolutely thorough, ranging from the age of the corn-fed hog, to the careful preparation of the meat in the salt tub, to hanging the pieces correctly in the smokehouse.[33]

For unknown reasons chickens were not high on the list for these cooks and were not prepared intact. Generally, the recipes found in the culinary works of Jane (Bolling) Randolph and Anonymous (1700) included either boiled or shredded chicken for pies, fricassees, and "Battalia Pye." Anonymous (1700)'s recipes reflect the flavors of the seventeenth century, while Jane (Bolling) Randolph's listed versions have a more modernized flavor. Heavy spices such as anchovies and sweet herbs were skipped, and lemon juice instead of the usual claret or verjuice was used. Chicken was stewed rather than fried. These more subtle flavorings reflected a shift away from richly spiced dishes, but her recipes retain other older elements—they are clearly transitional in nature.

Mary Randolph used a fricassee recipe similar to Jane (Bolling) Randolph's but also used roasted, boiled, and fried chicken—preparations familiar to all of us today.[34] She apparently set her sights not only on high society patrons but also on the masses.

Pigeons were considered a delicacy by the upper classes and were elaborately prepared by all three cooks. Anonymous (1700) offered four recipes for pigeon dressed in the French fashion,[35] while Jane (Bolling) Randolph's pages held a recipe for pigeon pie.[36] The Compiler (1744) possessed a pigeon recipe that none of these three cooks had: "Ragoo of

Pidgeons."[37] Pigeon recipes were high cuisine because of their elaborate nature, expensive ingredients, and showy presentation. These recipes contrast greatly with Mary Randolph's simple methods—boiled or roasted. However, she presented pigeons with either broccoli or asparagus and a parsley-butter sauce.[38] All of these women shared the view that pigeons were suitable for entertaining.

Changes in the selection of meats through time reflected changes in attitudes toward specific foods and family status. The three cookbooks by Anonymous (1700), Jane (Bolling) Randolph, and Mary Randolph contain, in a sense, dynastic and time-tested recipes.

# Seafood

In Fish-Street my wife and I bought a bit of salmon of 8*d.* Mr. Walgrave and I dined below in the buttery by ourselfs upon a good dish of buttered salmon.

So came to Hungerford where very good trouts eels and cray fish dinner, a bad mean town.

I bought two eeles upon the Thames, cost me 6*s.*

—Samuel Pepys

So he and I to eat herrings at the Dog Tavern.

So we had a dish of Mackerel and pease.

—Samuel Pepys

I had a pretty dinner for them—viz: a brace of stewed Carps, six roasted chicken, and a Jowle of salmon hot, for the first cours—a tanzy and two neats' tongues and chees the second.

—Samuel Pepys

At Southampton we went to the Mayors and there dined, and had Sturgeon of their own catching the last week, which doth not happen in 20 year, and it was well ordered.

—Samuel Pepys

We had a lobster to supper, which, with a crabb Peg Pen sent my wife this afternoon; the reason of which we cannot think, but something there is of plot or design in it—for we have a little while carried ourselfs pretty strange to them.

—Samuel Pepys

We ate some [anchovies] and drank some wine and strong beer.

I ate sallet and shad for dinner.

—William Byrd

I ate some fish for dinner sent us by my neighbor Parish.

I ate salt fish.

Mr. Randolph sent us a sturgeon.

—William Byrd

Each Wednesday & Saturday we dine on Fish all the Summer, always plenty of Rock, Perch, & Crabs, & often Sheeps-Head and Trout!

—Philip Vickers Fithian

In England fish and other seafood were not only considered important supplements on the table,[1] but were required by the rulings of the Church of England. Considering that there were 166 fast days, including Lent, during the course of the year,[2] seafood was prepared and preserved in every conceivable manner. Noting that it was recently Shrove Tuesday, Samuel Pepys wrote that he had just received a "barrel of pickled oysters" from a sea captain, which was "a very great favour"; he also had an "all fish-dinner, it being Goodfriday."[3] Certain seafoods, however, were not easily available even to the wealthy and therefore carried a great social cachet. Sturgeon fit this particular category since the British monarch had, and still retains, the right to all sturgeon caught in English rivers.[4] Pepys was honored with a barrel of sturgeon, and he made a similar gesture when he sent "two Keggs of Sturgeon" to his cousin Roger Pepys at Cambridge.[5]

Long-term preservation of seafood was a problem to be contended with, as illustrated by one of Samuel Pepys's notations. His stomach, he declared, was "turned" when a dish of sturgeon crawling with worms was served at his table; he refused to eat it and attributed the cause not to the age of the fish but to the "staleness of the pickle."[6] Naturally, relatively fresh seafood was preferred over pickled fish, oysters, and scallops in barrels whenever possible. Dried herring fared especially well, being heavily salted and preserved in brine or carefully smoked in a drying process.

Fish, already prepared, was more easily (and safely) obtained in some kind of eatery, aboard a ship, in a pie, or pickled in a fresh solution. Since Samuel Pepys ate out often, it is not surprising that a respectable number of his meals consisted of already prepared seafood. He and his friends had "two brave dishes of meat, one of fish, a carp and some other fishes, as well done as ever I eat any."[7] Aboard one ship he "spoiled" his dinner through Mr. Dunn's inadvertent mistake of giving him a bottle of oil instead of vinegar.[8] This entry reveals one accompaniment that was acceptable with seafood and one that was not.

Samuel Pepys's entries highlight the ease of obtaining reasonably fresh or preserved seafood even though he lived in the crowded streets of London. This is a vivid contrast to the Virginia settlers who supplemented their meat dishes with seafood from nearby waterways. Their fish, shellfish, and oysters were relatively cheap, more plentiful, and unmistakably fresher than those found in Pepys's London. "There were excellent thirty sorts of fish."[9] It was reported that "the rivers afford innumerable sortes of choyce fish (if they will take the paines to make wyers or hier the Natives, who for a small matter will undertake it)."[10] Of fresh and saltwater shellfish, "no Country can boast of more Variety, greater Plenty . . . their several Kinds among them s[t]urgeon, trout, conger-eels and lampreys, crabs."[11]

Landon Carter mentioned that he and his family were "blessed" by the local river with "fish crabs every day all the Summer," "the finest Prawn I ever saw," and "very good oysters for Sauces of all kinds"; he added that oysters were done in "every shape, raw, stewed, caked in fritters and pickled," and that he had six bushels of pickled oysters and two bushels of oyster dressing.[12] Regular folk, such as Parson Robert Rose, obtained their seafood through their own hunting activities, but their seafood was just as fresh. Unfortunately, the limited entries of the lower classes usually do not describe how their fish was prepared or preserved. This was reflected in Byrd's and Rose's diary entries: "I ate fish for dinner which we catch in great quantity" and "went a fishing and Catched above 5 Doz. of Carp."[13]

Seafood was utilized not only as legal tender or for bartering but also as a potential source of revenue. Abraham Womeck declared during a 1691 court session that he would pay John Burton forty shillings and "one barrel of Mackerell."[14] Proclamations given by the governor in the 1620s regulated prices of fish shipped in barrels for export or local sales. "Canada dry" fish by the hundred cost twenty-four pounds of tobacco, while "Canada wet" fish fetched a price of thirty pounds of tobacco. Other fish "by the hundred" were sold for ten pounds of tobacco.[15]

The seafood recipes found in the cookbooks belonging to Anonymous (1700) and Jane (Bolling) Randolph are striking in terms of studied contrasts. Anonymous (1700) took advantage of opportunities to salt, pickle, or preserve fish as well as prepare fresh seafood delicacies for her dinner table. She made sure she had a recipe for fish smelts, "caveech fish," collared eels, and pickled oysters. Caveech fish, browned in a skillet, were stored in a vinegar-and-spice-filled vessel and then covered with olive oil; the vessel was to be tied "up Close" to prevent spoilage.[16] Seafood approved for serving honored guests meant crawfish soup, buttered lobster, fish pies, collared eels, and rolls filled with dressed oysters. Pike was roasted, while eels, carp, trout, oysters, and lampreys ended up in pies. A cod's-head dish was prepared in the French mode, which included barberries, liver, and lemons. These ingredients not only provided vivid colors to attract the eye but also added sharp flavors to an otherwise bland-tasting dish.

Although her fish menus appear to be more elaborate than those served at William Byrd's Westover plantation, since he and Samuel Pepys made no mention of similar dishes such as crawfish soup, this may not be the case, given Byrd's brief description of menus. It should also be noted that, given her variety of seafoods and proximity to waterways, it is surprising that Anonymous (1700) made no mention of sturgeon or other types of available fish. Apparently her selection of fish to be included in her cookbook was based on elitism as well as personal preference.

In contrast, Jane (Bolling) Randolph's cookbook mentions only one recipe for boiling fresh carp, which is unfortunately missing from her manuscript. Her other recipes focus solely on preservation, be it sturgeon, eels, herring, or sprats. Her eels were rolled up and pickled in a collared manner like Anonymous (1700) used. Her recipe for pickled sprats was by then an old one, using such terms as "lare" (layer). Out of the three recipes for sturgeon, Jane penned one that emphasized careful cleaning and boiling of the fish before its preservation in a vinegar and spice solution.

Jane (Bolling) Randolph's interest in sturgeon is not surprising. As in England, in Virginia sturgeon was one of the most highly prized seafoods in terms of social status, but with a different twist. Unlike in England, it was not restricted by law or class in terms of usage in Virginia. Sturgeon was much more commonplace in the colonial diet since most settlers lived near the waterways or the Chesapeake Bay. One visitor was especially impressed when, during his boat ride to Jamestown, "an eight-foot sturgeon" leaped into his sloop.[17] William Byrd received a present of sturgeon from Mr. Randolph.[18] Jane (Bolling) Randolph obviously held sturgeon in high esteem and found it to be appropriate for her guests. With her particular attention to preserving sturgeon, no worm-infested sturgeon would ever be found on her table.

The limited choices of seafood in Jane (Bolling) Randolph's cookbook are not reflected in the archaeological record. According to Dr. L. Daniel Mouer, plentiful fish swam in the nearby James River, including "white bass, striped bass, yellow perch, pickerels, shad, alewives, porgeys, or any of the other dozens of food fish species which are common to this stretch of the James River."[19] Anonymous (1700) had a recipe for trout and pike, but neither she nor Jane (Bolling) Randolph made mention of scallops in their hoard of recipes. An eighteenth-century slave quarter at Curles yielded a variety of fish remains, and the late-eighteenth-century trash deposits by the kitchen contained skeletal remains of sturgeon, catfish, and gar. Mouer speculates that Jane (Bolling) Randolph's family viewed these fish as somewhat less desirable, suitable only for slaves or as profitable commodities.[20] However, it is possible that the Randolph family may simply have disliked fish. Or, given the indications in her medical recipes that some members of her family may have suffered from allergies, they may have been allergic to shellfish. Jane (Bolling) Randolph's repertoire did not include lobsters, crabs, mussels, or other shellfish even though they must have been available. The only exception was oysters, mentioned in only one recipe for crisped oyster rolls. Jane (Bolling) Randolph stressed, "You must stew the oysters very nice."[21]

The manuscript belonging to The Compiler (1744) yields a limited number of seafood recipes, all fit for her guests. Besides the dependable salmon and carp pies, stewed carps and eels, cod's head, oyster loaves, and pickled sturgeon, she made sure she had buttered crabs, pike, and sowles (sole).[22] These were not listed in Anonymous (1700)'s or Jane (Bolling) Randolph's manuscripts.

Mary Randolph's fish recipes contrast sharply with fish recipes belonging to Anonymous (1700) and Jane (Bolling) Randolph. All of Mary Randolph's recipes for sturgeon were designed to have that fish freshly prepared on the table, not pickled or preserved. She provided baked and stuffed sturgeon with mushroom catsup and red wine. There are also recipes for sturgeon cutlets, sturgeon steaks, and boiled sturgeon, all freshly prepared and seasoned with gravies, catsups, wines, butter, and fried parsley. Shad was either baked, boiled, roasted, or broiled. Rockfish was boiled, while perch was fried.[23]

Her dressed cod's head and shoulders recipe is a modernized descendant of Anonymous (1700)'s recipe for cod's head. Anonymous (1700) simply boiled her cod's head.

Mary Randolph went a step further in her preparations. After crisping the boiled cod's head and shoulders brown with flour, butter, and bread crumbs before the fire, Mary Randolph added the familiar lemon slices, barberries, roe, and liver. Then a "little of the lobster out of the sauce in lumps" was poured over it. The only differences in the ingredients were the presence of scraped horseradish and the use of a few small fried fish or oysters instead of anchovies. If shellfish was not available, then two small anchovies and a clove-studded onion could be mixed with a spoonful of walnut liquor and then strained into a sauceboat. This is more like Anonymous (1700)'s version.[24]

Another obvious descendant found in *The Virginia Housewife* was "Caveech Fish." Anonymous (1700)'s version is definitely older, speaking from another time. She used nutmeg, cloves, mace, salt, and English pepper as seasonings for her round fish slices, which were then fried in "Sweet Oyl"; then boiled vinegar with garlic cloves and whole pepper was poured over her fish pieces in the pot before more sweet oil was added to it.[25] Mary Randolph used flour instead of spices to coat her round fish pieces before frying and added onions to her vinegar solution, but she used mace and whole pepper along with oil for her potted fish, as did Anonymous (1700).[26] Again, Mary Randolph's recipe is more streamlined.

Mary Randolph also possessed a recipe called "To Stew Carp" that is similar to a recipe of Anonymous (1700), but changes in tastes and preparation methods are obvious. Anonymous (1700)'s elaborate recipe was modeled after Edward Kidder and highly spiced and garnished with blood-flavored gravy, spawn, milt, liver, and toasts.[27] Mary Randolph's version used water, red wine, and lemon pickle instead of Anonymous (1700)'s claret, white wine, and vinegar; and Mary used walnut catsup, mushroom powder, cayenne, and horseradish to flavor her dish and then served it with pickled mushrooms and more horseradish.[28]

Mary Randolph not only differed from Anonymous (1700) and Jane (Bolling) Randolph by her use of fish that any housewife could obtain, but she also provided many new versions of seafood dishes. She had salted cod and dressed cod dishes, boiled and broiled eels, fried and scalloped oysters in the shell, and chowder, which were not derived from Anonymous (1700) or Jane (Bolling) Randolph.[29] However, her recipe for oyster rolls is similar in concept, even though much more simplified. Stewed and buttered oysters were simply mixed with some bread crumbs and cream before they were spooned into the oyster rolls. They were also placed in the oven to crisp. Her oyster rolls were more modern in their simplicity, but the principles were the same as those found among Anonymous (1700)'s and Jane (Bolling) Randolph's recipes.

Since the relationships among these recipe versions of Mary Randolph, Anonymous (1700), and Jane (Bolling) Randolph's recipes are apparent, it may be that Mary Randolph was familiar with or had seen the others' recipes, if not their culinary manuscripts. Family recipes often were shared and handed down for generations. Since she was well educated, it is possible that Mary Randolph had inherited or used the family's book by Several Hands published in 1714.[30]

In Virginia the dinner table loaded with meat and seafood became a symbol of a family's wealth and status. The cornucopia of plenty was the American status symbol, in contrast to Britain's emphasis on the rarity of an item. Anonymous (1700), Jane (Bolling) Randolph, and Mary Randolph took advantage of locally available seafood that they deemed appropriate for their guests and took great care that a lot of flavor and colors were added to stimulate the taste buds and appeal to the eye. They also made sure that there were other plentiful edibles on their tables to provide visual and tasteful contrasts to the main dishes.

# Condiments

Down into the Hold of the India Shipp, and there . . . —pepper scatter[ed] through every chink, you trod upon it; and in cloves and nutmegs, I walked above the knees —whole room full—.

—Samuel Pepys

And we went to a blind alehouse . . . to a couple of wretched, dirty seamen, who . . . had got together about 37 *lb* of Cloves and 10 *lb* of Nuttmeggs. And we bought . . . the first at 5*s*-6*d* per *lb*., and the latter at 4*s*—and paid them in gold; But it would never have been allowed by my conscience to have wrought the poor wretches, who told how dangerously they had got some and dearly paid for the rest of these goods.

—Samuel Pepys

A good cake there was, but no marks found; but I privately found the clove, the mark of the knave, and privately put it into Captain Cocke's piece, which made some mirth because of his lately being known by his buying of clove and mace of the East Indian prizes.

—Samuel Pepys

As I walked before the cellar window I heard something running, at which I went and called the boy and it was a vinegar barrel which had not been well stopped.

—William Byrd

Nich. Osborne did give me a barrell of Samphire.

—Samuel Pepys

That colony has found out the way of propagating the fly, of which they make cocheneal in perfection, and I am informed Lord Lay is concerned in the project.

—William Byrd

Another characteristic of English cookery before Jamestown was the extensive use of spices and salt, a holdover from medieval times. Though traditionally spices were heavily used as food preservatives or to hide the flavor of tainted meat, they were subsequently widely used in dishes regardless of need.[1]

Recent studies of 4,578 recipes from 96 cookbooks in 36 countries, conducted by Cornell University's behavioral scientist Paul Sherman and his student Jennifer Billing, raise the possibility that spices were not used so much as flavorsome preservatives as they were "savory antiseptics." Spices, they concluded, were used to "kill disease-causing bacteria and fungi in food." Onions, garlic, allspice, and oregano were found to be 100 percent effective in terms of bacterial inhibition and were followed, in decreasing percentages in terms of effectiveness, by the rest of the spices known to man.[2]

Spices, other than everyday salt, were costly and hard to come by except by those fortunate enough to have the financial means to purchase them. One of the ubiquitous spices was nutmeg, which no housewife would be found without. In contrast, saffron was an exotic spice used only among the moneyed classes.[3] Jane (Bolling) Randolph had a recipe containing saffron.[4]

Once sugar became accessible to the public and found to be another natural preservative, the use of spices and flavorings declined, and as a result, "food became simplified."[5] There were varieties of white salt, such as common salt from salt licks, bay salt, saltpeter, and other grades of salt obtained from other exotic locales.

No course was complete without some condiments such as walnuts and mushrooms, either pickled or fresh, or highly flavored dressings such as barberry sauce. It is interesting that Anonymous (1700), Jane (Bolling) Randolph, and Mary Randolph all had recipes for pickled walnuts that still retained a medieval character. Landon Carter also prized these pickled walnuts: "I had a jugg of Vinegar yesterday from Dr. Mortimer, so that my Walnuts may be immediately pickled."[6] Another favored pickle was the gherkin, and Anonymous (1700) made sure she had a recipe for it. Samuel Pepys mentioned that Captain Cock gave his wife a glass of "Girkins," which "are rare things."[7]

Hostesses and cooks were well aware that sauces not only added flavor to meat, poultry, and seafood dishes but also provided splashes of attractive colors. Furthermore, sauces provided flavorsome alternatives to the ubiquitous but sometimes tiresome spices. One Spanish sauce, much admired by Samuel Pepys during a visit with the Duke of York, consisted of a mixture of parsley, toast, vinegar, salt, and pepper ground up in a mortar and served as a condiment.[8]

Poorly prepared or spoiled sauces by cooks instantly invited displeasure from the masters. This was a serious sign of waste and incompetence, not to mention that it ruined a meal. Furthermore, the woman responsible for the bad sauce was considered to have failed her "prescriptive" duty. Both Samuel Pepys and William Byrd did not hesitate to show their ire at such carelessness: "My wife and I all alone to a leg of Mutton, the sawce of wich being made sweet, I was angry at it and eat none, but only dined upon the Marrowbone that we [had] beside"; and "out of humor with Moll because she had not made good sauce."[9] Anonymous (1700) stressed the use of "lears," an old term for sauces, while Mary Randolph made the most of all kinds of sauces and gravies.

Vinegar, claret, capers, anchovies, oysters, forced meat balls, sweetmeats, marrow, and sippets were classic choices. Vinegar, claret, and capers added a touch of tartness and flavor to the menu, and forced meat balls and sweetmeats provided additional protein to the main meat dish. Anchovies served as a less expensive substitute for salt. Anonymous (1700) and Jane (Bolling) Randolph used these ingredients in their recipes. Around the mid-eighteenth century these favorites started fading from the scene when social tastes and trends changed. Such changes are reflected in the wide array of sauces listed in Mary Randolph's manuscript: barbecue, caper, celery, claret, gravy, lobster, shrimp, mushroom, mint, parsley, and orange, among others.[10]

One seventeenth-century fad was adding perfumes such as musk and ambergris to salads, omelettes, scrambled eggs, fritters, meats, puddings, tarts, and conceits. Pepys mentioned receiving "perfumed comfits" ultimately derived from a Portuguese merchant.[11] Since perfumes were tokens of luxury, only well-to-do families could purchase them. As a result of changing tastes, their use as flavorings diminished by the mid-eighteenth century, when they were replaced in England by rose water.[12] In contrast, perfumes were not often cultivated in Virginia. Anonymous (1700) and Jane (Bolling) Randolph used musk and ambergris as flavoring agents along with sugar, but only sparingly and only for a few recipes. Rose water, orange water, and later vanilla were preferred by Anonymous, Jane (Bolling) Randolph, and other women cooks and became popular.

# Corn and Other Grains

And those who came were resolved to be Englishmen,
Gone to the world's end, but English every one,
And they ate the white corn kernels, parched in the sun,
And they knew it not, but they'd not be English again.

—Attributed to Stephen Vincent Benét

The bosun of the ship did bring us out of the Kettle a piece of hot salt beef and some brown bread and brandy; and there we did make a little meal, but so good as I never would desire to eat better meat while I live—only, I would have cleaner dishes.

—Samuel Pepys

With fish, oysters, bread, and deere, they kindly traded with me and my men, being no lesse in doubt of my intent, then I of theirs; . . . With sixteene bushells of Corne, I returned towards our Forte.

—Captain John Smith

While wee are tending corn to feed our wives & children, the Indians (if wee have no guard over us) would butcher us in our fields, they being so frequent about us, that wee dare not stir from our plantations.

—from "Some Grievances of Rappahannock"

Rich'd Ripley came down in ye Evening with his Canoe carrying with three Men, one barril of Corn, as much barley. . . .

—Robert Rose

My people made an end of shelling the corn.

We began to cut our wheat and found it good and in good order.

I ate whole hominy for dinner.

—William Byrd

I drank some tea and ate some bread and butter.

Ate water gruel for breakfast.

I ate boiled pork and rice for dinner.

—William Byrd

The famous trio of corn, squash, and beans mentioned by Capt. John Smith along with hominy were quickly adopted by the settlers, who depended on them for survival.[1] The early inventories of Andrew Whowell, Thomas Deacon, Capt. Stephen Gill, and Hugh Mackinyell show hominy sifters, corn, and Indian beans.[2] Aware of its value, William Byrd and other observers stressed the importance of corn in the early years of Virginia's history and in their everyday diets. If it had not been for the "fruitfulness" of corn, "it would have proved very difficult to have settled some of the Plantations in America."[3] Being the "most useful grain in the whole world," it not only yielded "five hundred for one [acre]" but also made good bread, frumenty, malts, and beer, and it would keep well for seven years.[4] According to Byrd, most of the "inhabitants of America live solely on tis corn because it is very healthful and nourishing. For this reason they use it for baking and cooking, indeed for all things."[5]

The Virginia settlers quickly adopted the Native American method of using fresh wood ashes not only as a salt substitute but also as an agent for converting corn into hominy[6]: "They take the corn and parch it in hot ashes, til it becomes brown, then clean it, pound it in a mortar and sift it, this powder is mixed with sugar. About 1 quarter of a pint, diluted in a pint of water, is a hearty traveling dinner."[7] The ashes also served as a cover when baking corn cakes on the hearth. Parson Robert Rose mentioned a hoecake, which was so called because baked on a hoe before the fire.[8]

While the use of coarse and refined white breads was confined to specific social classes in England,[9] these were readily available during times of plenty. Coarse bread meant rough rye or wheat loaves, which were consumed by both the lower-middle and poorer classes. More-refined white breads, such as manchets, made of fine white flour, were either made by the housewife of the manor or purchased in London shops.[10] Although white bread was popular with the upper classes in Virginia, it had to share the spotlight with cornmeal products. Even gentlemen preferred pone for bread (from *appone*, an Algonquian Indian word) over wheat bread.[11]

Given the importance of corn, along with beans and squash, in the Virginia settler's diet, it is intriguing that such items do not appear in Anonymous (1700)'s, Jane (Bolling) Randolph's, and The Compiler (1744)'s manuscripts. These omissions further support the speculation that their cookbook collections were viewed mainly for entertaining purposes or festive events, not for everyday eating. It is only much later into the eighteenth century that more mundane items such as "to eat bread with butter" or Mrs. Munford's muffins, begin to appear in cookbook manuscripts, but even these were made with fine flour, not cornmeal.

Mary Randolph is quite a study in contrast to Anonymous (1700) and Jane (Bolling) Randolph. She mentioned not only elegant meals but also everyday foods that any housewife could make in a short time. She possessed recipes for cornmeal-based polenta and batter bread, along with boiled cornmeal mush, cornmeal bread, boiled Indian meal, and batter cakes (cornmeal and hominy). She even included johnnycakes and puddings made of hominy.[12] Her cornmeal mush recipe is the simple and basic one that people had been preparing and consuming for more than two hundred years.

Another important grain, rice, was quickly recognized as a potentially profitable crop as well as another suitable staple for the dinner table. In 1647 Gov. William Berkeley was among those who took advantage of the opportunity to cultivate rice, and he got 156 excellent bushels of rice to show for his pains. It is no accident that his rice was planted and tended by slaves who were familiar with it in their native Africa.[13]

According to *The Carolina Rice Kitchen* by Karen Hess, the early history of rice in South Carolina kitchens was "inextricably bound up with slavery; it was the black hands of African slaves which cultivated the rice and cooked it." This is not surprising since rice was cultivated in India and Africa. Furthermore, it was these enslaved cooks who were "responsible for the near-mythic reputation of southern cookery." Hess adds that the "historical roles of these cooks in shaping the palate of the South" cannot be sufficiently praised or acknowledged.[14]

Rice was not originally a staple found on the plantation tables of European planters. However, the use of rice eventually spread. In South Carolina, rice, especially "Carolina Gold," was so valued that it was "revered and . . . eaten at virtually every meal . . . in soups, main dishes, side dishes, desserts, and breads." Hess mentions that William Salmon made reference to this South Carolina rice as the best in his 1710 publication *Botanologica.*[15]

Hess believes that rice was introduced to South Carolina by one of two possible routes. One source could have been the Jews fleeing from Persia, who took their knowledge of rice with them to Provence, France. Later centuries saw a huge exodus of persecuted Huguenots to other parts of Europe and America, including the state of South Carolina. An alternative route was through the Middle East and Africa. Rice was brought by the Arabs from Baghdad to their settlements along the western coast of Africa, where it was adopted by the natives as an important staple. It was there that the knowledge of rice cultivation was perfected, and this centuries-old knowledge of rice cultivation was carried by the slaves when they were shipped to South Carolina.[16]

It is believed that the type of rice cultivated by Governor Berkeley and other planters in Virginia was like the dry type of rice that could be grown as a crop with other grains. Daniel Littlefield believed that the cultivation of rice came to an end because of Virginia's primary focus on tobacco crops.[17] According to Hess, however, the combined competition of the superior South Carolina rice and more profitable Virginia wheat were also important factors that caused the decline of rice cultivation.[18]

According to Karen Hess, the earliest known rice recipe printed in the English language was "Boiled Rice dry" in Sir Kenelm Digby's 1669 publication *The Closet of the Eminently Learned Sir Kenelm Digbei Kt. Opened.* No other known recipe followed until 1747, when Hannah Glasse published "A Currey the Indian Way" in her book *The Art of Cookery Made Plain and Easy.*[19] Mentioned in the Virginia manuscripts before 1747, rice was apparently consumed for some years before publication in cookbooks.

It is of great interest that there are rice recipes in Anonymous (1700)'s, Jane (Bolling) Randolph's, and The Compiler (1744)'s cookbooks. One recipe for rice pudding in Anonymous (1700)'s manuscript is characteristic of the seventeenth century since it is unmistakably older in language, content, and preparation methods. She also possessed a recipe for a rice florendine, an archetypically English dish of medieval origins in Britain. Her rice florendine was somewhat similar to her rice pudding recipe except the former mixture was poured into a pastry-lined dish and baked.

The index of "Jane Randolph Her Cookery Book" lists a "Rice Pudding to Make" on page 3. What remains of that page no longer contains this recipe, and therefore it cannot be compared to the one mentioned in Anonymous (1700)'s cookbook. It may have been somewhat similar to a rice pudding found in The Compiler (1744)'s collection, but proof is lacking. This recipe does prove that Jane Randolph's family members were familiar with and used rice. The recipe for "Yallow Rice Cream" stands out among the dessert recipes in The Compiler (1744)'s manuscript.[20] Is the yellow color a reference to the "Carolina Gold" rice mentioned by Karen Hess?

Mary Randolph published "Rice Pudding" in her book *The Virginia Housewife*. It is a modernized version of Anonymous (1700)'s rice florendine. By having the rice mashed and the mixture poured into a paste-lined dish, Mary Randolph may have felt it was no longer necessary to add grated biscuits as a thickening agent. She also printed recipes for rice milk, rice waffles, rice bread, and rice journey or johnnycakes. Both her rice milk and rice journey or johnnycakes were old recipes known to practically every settler. These two recipes were by far more homely and democratic than her novel recipe for boiled rice served with a spicy curry sauce.[21] This particular recipe is among Mary Randolph's adaptions that show East Indian influence.

Only the finest wheat flour was considered acceptable for use when creating cakes, pastry, breads, rusks, muffins, biscuits, cookies, wigs, wafers, and French rolls. Jane (Bolling) Randolph must have used the best flour for her carefully penned recipe for wafers, a recipe that would be recopied. Whole wheat flour was not favored among the Virginia gentry, according to Karen Hess.[22] No coarse flour or bread such as rough brown bread is found in any recipes of Anonymous (1700), Jane (Bolling) Randolph, or The Compiler (1744). Nor is there any mention of rye, cornmeal, millet, or coarsely cracked wheat flour in any of their recipe collections. Large loaves were "associated with the peasants and the poor."[23]

Manchets, small rolls or loaves of bread made up of the finest white flour, were popular among the British gentry from the fourteenth century to the seventeenth century.[24] The 1653 recipe for "Lady of Arundel's Manchet" was one of many popular recipes in Lady Arundel's publication and in other works, such as *A True Gentlewoman's Delight* by the Countess of Kent in the same year.[25] According to Elizabeth David, only the wealthy could have manchets for their breakfast or dinner, and these became the "common ancestor" of "the eighteenth-century fine breads known as French rolls and French bread."[26] Manchets were baked in a "cooler oven" than normally found for breads, while French rolls were baked in a "quick oven" and the crust was then grated off.[27] Queen Elizabeth I's manchets were made from Heston wheat cultivated near Hounslow, London, considered the most superior wheat flour of all.[28] By the end of the eighteenth century in Europe manchets had pretty much disappeared from various cookbooks since they had been replaced by French rolls. It is surprising that Anonymous (1700) did not possess a recipe for manchet, since her manuscript covers this particular time period. That she and Jane (Bolling) Randolph included elegant French rolls in their collections indicates that these rolls replaced manchets and also reflected a current social trend. The Compiler (1744) had her own three versions of French bread.[29]

It cannot be overlooked that the first group of missing pages from Anonymous (1700)'s manuscript may once have contained a recipe for manchet. Mary Randolph's recipe entitled "To Make a Bread" was not all that different from the manchet prototype, as it called for the best white flour.[30] Anonymous (1700)'s recipe for Savoy biscuits also used only the finest flour. Anonymous (1700) and Jane (Bolling) Randolph, however, did utilize oats for their archetypical flummery dishes, which were steeped in British culinary tradition.

Unlike her predecessors, Mary Randolph made use of "cornmeal, oats, buckwheat, homony, rice, sago, arrowroot and cassava" flours. She held recipes for buckwheat cakes, rice bread, sago cream, and arrowroot pudding; and she had a barley cream recipe, as did The Compiler (1744). These called for everyday ingredients any housewife could purchase. Although Mary Randolph possessed refined recipes such as French rolls, her use of various grains reveals that Mary Randolph was far more democratic than were Anonymous (1700) and Jane (Bolling) Randolph. Although she did not focus on exclusiveness in her book, she did share the belief with Anonymous (1700) and Jane (Bolling) Randolph that breads, cakes, biscuits, and other dishes should be prepared with discrimination and served in the best manner.[31]

# Dairy Products

Good huswife in dairie, that needes not be tolde,
deserveth hir fee to be paid hir in golde.

—Thomas Tusser

"It was the best butter," the March Hare meekly replied.

—Lewis Carroll

Was very angry at my people's eating a fine pudding (made me by Slater the Cooke last Thursday) without my wife's leave.

—Samuel Pepys

So home to eat something, such as we have, bread and butter and milk; and so to bed.

—Samuel Pepys

Where Hawley brought a piece of his Cheshire cheese, and we were merry with it.

Called for a biscuit and a piece of cheese and gill of sack.

Such plenty of milke-meats (she keeping a great dairy) and so good as I never met with.

—Samuel Pepys

To the Red Lyon, where we . . . drink and eat some of the best cheese-cakes that ever I eat in my life; . . . W Hewers took us into his lodging, which is very handsome, and there did treat us very highly with cheesecakes, cream, tarts, and other good things.

—Samuel Pepys

Through Epsum towne to our Inne, in the way stopping a poor woman with her milk-pail and in one of my gilt Tumblers did drink our bellyfuls of milk, better than any Creame; and so to our Inne and there had a dish of creame, but it was sour and so had no pleasure in it.

—Samuel Pepys

Wrote to borrow 3 bushels of salt from Col. Tayloe for Butter making.

—Landon Carter

I ate nothing but pudding and stewed apples for dinner.

Here I ate custard and was merry.

—William Byrd

Dairy products formed another important part of the settler's diet similar to his peers in Britain. Often referred to as "white meats," cheeses and other protein-rich dairy foods were available to all social classes.[1] This is evident in the inventories of Thomas Deacon, Capt. Stephen Gill, and Hugh Mackinyell, which listed the usual butter, milk trays, and cheese presses.[2]

Surprisingly, butter in Europe was in the exclusive domain of the truly wealthy, even in Holland. Perhaps owing to the fact that extensive labor was required, butter did not come into common use until the latter part of the eighteenth century.[3] Samuel Pepys made a note of it when he and his wife received "a ferkin of butter . . . which is very welcome" from Captain Cuttance.[4] This may have been different in Virginia. Each colonist possessed a cow or two and time and/or indentured servants to do the intensive labor. Parson Robert Rose made an agreement with Andrew Reid "for all His butter next year."[5]

Although butter and cream combinations characterized Tudor cooking, they never replaced the preferred beef suet and marrow puddings.[6] Many recipes of Anonymous (1700) and Jane (Bolling) Randolph contained beef suet and marrow instead of butter and cream, a holdover from the seventeenth century. However, Anonymous (1700) did take the trouble to copy elegant butter recipes as part of her high cuisine: orange, almond, and pistachia (pistachio). It is also interesting that orange and almond butter were also found among the pages of The Compiler (1744)'s manuscript.[7]

As indicated by a 1684 letter probably addressed to Nehemiah Grew in England, Cheshire cheese was considered a rarity in Virginia. John Clayton desired that his contact find people skilled in the making of Cheshire cheese and send him some "at James City, Virginy."[8] Anonymous (1700) made sure she had a recipe for this coveted Cheshire cheese. Neither Jane (Bolling) Randolph, Mary Randolph, nor The Compiler (1744) had a recipe for Cheshire cheese among their collections, but the latter possessed one cheese called "Anseoff's[?],"[9] which was not found in any of the other three authors' culinary works.

Compared to Jane (Bolling) Randolph and Mary Randolph, Anonymous (1700) continued to stand out through her dairy-based dishes such as cheesecakes, cheesecake meat, almond cheesecakes, and almond cream to jelly. Her concoction called "Fry'd Cream" was elegant indeed. After this creamy mixture was boiled to a certain thickness, it was spread evenly on either a cheese plate or mazareen (mazarine), cut into diamond squares, and then deep-fried in sweet suet. There were also recipes for custard, gooseberry fool, milk-based pudding, posset, and whipped syllabub. Jane (Bolling) Randolph's manuscript also contained a recipe touted to be the best way of making cheesecakes, which paralleled those found in Anonymous (1700)'s manuscript.

The most elaborate and outstanding labor-intensive dairy-based dish was Anonymous (1700)'s recipe for junket, once made with cream cheese or cream and now prepared with curds sweetened and flavored. Scalded cream topped this mixture. Junket therefore was considered the absolute height of refined dining. Popularly associated with Devonshire, it was known in other districts as "curds and cream."[10] To prepare a rennet bag for rennin was time-consuming and tedious activity. Rennin was a requisite enzyme that would convert milk into cheese or a rich junket. The Compiler (1744) and Elizabeth (Tucker) Coalter possessed recipes for rennet and a rennet bag, respectively, a reflection of their prominent social status.[11] Elizabeth (Tucker) Coalter's manuscript had Mary Randolph's recipe for rennet before it was published in 1824.[12] It is possible that Mary Randolph had seen the recipe by Anonymous (1700), since her version was similar to Anonymous (1700)'s but more modernized.

Jane (Bolling) Randolph and Mary Randolph shared other dishes in common with Anonymous (1700): custards, creams, and milk-based puddings. Anonymous (1700)'s chocolate cream consisted of scraped chocolate added to the mixture of boiled cream and eggs. The Compiler (1744)'s chocolate cream closely resembled Anonymous (1700)'s version, in which the chocolate shavings were mixed into her boiled cream and eggs.[13] Jane (Bolling) Randolph did not have custard or chocolate cream listed among her recipes, but she did have hot chocolate, which required a lot of labor. She wrote that the chocolate nuts (cocoa beans) first had to be carefully washed and roasted to remove the hulls and then rolled "on the stone" until they became a paste; the recipe suggested that bits of the hull should be added to make the chocolate "froth."[14]

Mary Randolph's custard was thoroughly her own in a more streamlined form. It was baked in cups in a Dutch oven. She added eggs or cream to her lemon cream,[15] whereas Anonymous (1700) had never used eggs or cream in her lemon cream recipe. Anonymous (1700) used only egg whites with her mixture. Mary Randolph's chocolate cream, however, roughly paralleled the chocolate cream recipe found in recipes of Anonymous (1700) and The Compiler (1744). Her chocolate was also scraped and boiled, but she thickened and flavored it with eggs, milk, and a vanilla bean.[16] The addition of the vanilla bean clearly set Mary Randolph apart from the others and placed her in a more modern time.

All three of the authors penned their versions of what constituted a proper almond pudding. Anonymous (1700)'s elegantly flavored mixture was poured into a deep dish lined with a puff paste. The preparations for the recipe point to its late-seventeenth-century origins. In contrast, the version found in Jane (Bolling) Randolph's cookbook was short and sweet and more simplified in ingredients. Butter now had replaced the marrow, but its descent from the older recipe is apparent. Mary Randolph's recipe[17] is a curious mixture of both old and new trends. It was just as richly flavored as Anonymous (1700)'s recipe, but rice flour or crackers were added to the mixture before it was poured into a paste-lined dish and baked. These three recipes are fine examples of evolutionary and personal changes that took place over time.

The Compiler (1744) outdid them all with her large collection of puddings and creams. There were four recipes for orange puddings alone as well as hasty, lemon, marrow, Italian, carrot, calves' feet puddings and almond, tower, "Yallow Rice," posset, "Codlin," and grape creams.[18]

All these recipes clearly demonstrate the important role dairy products played in the diet of the settlers. Dairy products were not only nutritious and sweet tasting, they served as a filler, a meat substitute, and an impromptu dish elegant enough to fit nicely on the table. Being such versatile items, these dairy byproducts were highly valued by Virginia hostesses.

# Vegetables

A salet and two or three bones of mutton were provided for a matter of ten of us, which was very strange.

I had a good Quarter of Lamb and a salat.

—Samuel Pepys

I to Sir W. Penn's . . . I supped with them, that is, eat some butter and radishes, which is my excuse for not eating of any other of their victuals, which I hate because of their sluttery.

—Samuel Pepys

To the King's head, and . . . eat a tansy and so parted . . .

Mr. Sheply, Hawley and Moore dine with me on a piece of beef and cabbage, and a collar of brawn.

—Samuel Pepys

To my father's to dinner, where nothing but a small dish of powdered beef and a dish of carrots, they being all busy to get things ready for my Brother John to go tomorrow.

—Samuel Pepys

I ordered Tom to plant some [l-c-s] seed.

I ate mutton and sallet for dinner . . . I walked in the garden.

I ate some beans and bacon.

I . . . was angry with Moll for neglecting to boil some artichokes for dinner.

—William Byrd

The wealthy are attentive to the raising of vegetables, but very little so to fruits. The poorer people attend to neither, living principally on milk and animal diet. This is the more inexcusable, as the climate requires indispensably a free use of vegetable food, for health as well as comfort, and is very friendly to the raising of fruits.

—Thomas Jefferson

> I . . . ate milk and rhubarb for breakfast.
>
> I ate some pea soup for dinner.
>
> —William Byrd

> If you would be so kind as to send me over a barrel of potatoes carefully put up, it would be a most engaging present.
>
> —William Byrd

As a subject, vegetables remains a topic of debate among culinary circles. Study of the subject proves to be unreliable because of the prevailing argument over whether vegetables were eaten commonly or infrequently.[1] Some food historians insist that vegetables were not mentioned in seventeenth- and eighteenth-century English or American culinary books because they did not require fancy preparation methods; they were either cooked simply or eaten raw. Other sources argue that vegetables were accepted gradually since they were perceived by various classes as "unfashionable" and fit only for the poor.[2] In addition, the "medieval suspicion of raw vegetables and fruit" as "toxic agents" took its time disappearing from public consciousness.[3] Samuel Pepys wrote in his diary that "Sir W. Batten tells me that Mr. Newburne . . . is dead of eating Cowcumbers, of which the other day I heard another, I think Sir Nich. Crisps Son."[4] Anonymous (1700) showed no such hesitation about cucumbers, since she possessed a recipe for a "Regalia of Cowcumbers."

In seveteenth-century Britain vegetables were served in limited amounts because they were suspected of causing social embarrassments such as flatulence and melancholy.[5] This suspicion also prevailed in America, though to a lesser degree. John Randolph commented that Jerusalem artichokes tended to create "commotions in the belly."[6] On the one hand they seem to have been used primarily as garnishes or in soups in seventeenth- and eighteenth-century recipes;[7] and Anonymous (1700)'s entreés reflected a prevailing perception of vegetables as hors d'oeuvres.[8] The written records of Jane (Bolling) Randolph, William Byrd, and Landon Carter also revealed limited use of vegetables.

On the other hand, vegetables such as artichokes, asparagus, cauliflower, and peppers found in Anonymous (1700)'s and Jane (Bolling) Randolph's manuscripts were strictly luxurious items for the tables of the wealthy, since they were considered "rare and Extock [exotic]" plants.[9] Vegetables such as parsley, carrots, peas, and asparagus were well liked by most people. Jane (Bolling) Randolph or her daughter Jane had a recipe for "French Beans" appropriate for guests, yet she made no mention of locally available vegetables such as "beans . . . squash, or pumpkins, or black-eyed peas."[10] A scrap of paper found among the pages of Anonymous (1700)'s manuscript mentioned "affrecan skarlit beans." These were actually scarlet runner beans that came from Central America, but their origin was wrongly attributed to Africa. However, it is interesting to note that the word "affrecan" was significant to the writer, who may have received these beans from an African slave.

Asparagus was a favored vegetable. "We came to Gilford and there passed our time in the garden cutting of Sparagus for supper, the best that ever I eat in my life but in that house last year," wrote Samuel Pepys.[11] He even went so far as to buy at Farechurch-street "a hundred of sparrowgrass, cost 18*d*."[12] Peas also found favor in his eyes: "to Wilkinsons, where we had bespoke a dish of pease, where we eate them very merrily."[13] And he sampled pea soup: "to the Cock . . . they dined with myself . . . and mighty merry, this house being famous for good meat, and perticularly pease-porridge."[14]

A 1648 English advertisement, conveniently overlooking early difficulties, focused on how vegetables thrived in Virginia: "That they have roots of several kinds, potatoes, asparagus, carrots, turnips, parsnips, onions and artichokes"; and "That they have store of Indian peas, better than ours, beans, lupines, and the like."[15] The writings of William Byrd have preserved for posterity other native American vegetables used during his lifetime: "shumake," "chapacow," "puccoons," "musquaspen," "tockawaigh," and "burmillions"—"all these are Indian vegetables or pot herbs . . . therefore . . . not at all or imperfectly known . . . others too long to mention."[16] Broccoli and asparagus, among other vegetables, continued to be cultivated in the early eighteenth century.[17] Philip Vickers Fithian commented that he "had th honour of taking a walk with Mrs. Carter through the Garden— . . . I think uncommon to see this Season peas all up two & three Inches— . . . Mrs. Carter shewed me her Apricot-grafts; Asparagus Beds &c."[18]

The lower classes also possessed vegetable gardens. Parson Robert Rose wrote: "Fine warm weather, some rain, busie about gardening"; "planted peese"; and "got ground ready for Turnips."[19] They seem to have entertained a more practical, if not always fond, attitude toward vegetables. According to Rose, he "preached at the Upper Church, was forced to go with Mr. Corbin to eat green peas."[20] Perhaps only vegetables of a certain class were considered delicacies worth mentioning in cookbooks for entertaining and the rest were everyday vegetables too commonplace to be worth listing.

Vegetables also served as much-needed cash crops that were exported back to Britain.[21] These included assorted squash and beans, pumpkins, gourds, dwarf beans (Indian beans), cymlings, potatoes, peas, French beans, red cabbage, carrots, turnips, and spinach.[22] The shipping of these vegetables yielded profits that were used by the planters to achieve and compete with their neighbors through the purchase of precious commodities or other high-status items. Landon Carter wrote that "pease . . . are of some use in buying necessary Molasses, Sugar and Chocolate."[23]

Only a few individuals, including John Randolph of Williamsburg and Thomas Jefferson, realized the true worth of vegetables. John Randolph wrote and published the earliest American book on kitchen gardening, *Treatise on gardening.* Even though an avid agriculturist, Thomas Jefferson valued his copy of John Randolph's publication, which was also held in high esteem by Edmund Ruffin, another agriculturist.[24] John Adams added his own commentary on vegetables: "Nowhere in the world do people have such a variety of good garden things to grow and eat as in these colonies. Still our daily fare can be monotonous. How beneficial it would be if more of our countrymen thought as freely as does Mr. Thomas Jefferson about fruits and vegetables."[25]

Although Thomas Jefferson is well known to have cultivated a wide variety of vegetables in his own garden after his trip to France, it was Amelia Simmons who published recipes using "pumpkins" and "squash" along with red- and yellow-skinned potatoes.[26] Mary Randolph was yet to publish her work.

Vegetables gained greater acceptance in the nineteenth century, although documentary sources do not explain this new trend. Mary Randolph listed at least forty vegetables, both native and foreign, in her classic, *The Virginia Housewife*. Her vegetables are familiar to us today, including the tomato and okra. She also stressed close watch over vegetables so that they would be cooked to perfection and not overcooked.[27]

Only further study can determine the actual perception of vegetables in seventeenth- and eighteenth-century Britain and Virginia. It is not clear whether vegetables were considered beneath recording by certain social classes, whether there were lingering cultural suspicions, or whether they were so simply prepared that no one felt the need to describe them in great detail.

# Fruits

So to supper and some apples and ale, and to bed with great pleasure-blessed be God.
—Samuel Pepys

So to my Lady Battens and sat with her a while, Sir W. Batten being gone out of towne; . . . did it out of design to get some oranges for my feast tomorrow of her—which I did.

In Mr. Petts garden I eat some (and the first cherries I have eat this year) off the tree where the King himself had been gathering some this morning.

. . . to Blackburys . . . where I eat some peaches and apricotes; a very pretty place.
—Samuel Pepys

Marmalet of quinces as per his note 1 ct weight is 11:04: . . . Conserves of sloes 9 potts 02:16: . . . Conserves of Barberryes 7 potts net 30 li is 03.
—"Accompts of the Tristam and Jane"

Mr. Mumford sent us some peaches.

Colonel Hill sent his man with a basket of apricots, of which my wife ate twelve immediately and I ate eight.

—William Byrd

Then I read some Italian and ate some cherries.

I ate abundance of peaches and figs before dinner.

I ate some stewed quince and drank some cider and ate apples till about 5 o'clock.

I ate some milk and quince.

I gave [Harry] four great pomegranates for the Governor which grew at Westover.
—William Byrd

Mrs. Randolph sent my wife some apples as fine as ever I saw.

I ate two apples and some watermelon.

—William Byrd

> Sup'd on Crabs & an elegant dish of Strawberries & cream—How natural, how agreeable, how majestic this place seems! . . . we have fine Fish, & every Day good Fruit for Dinner, caulded Apples, Hurtle-Berries with milk &c.
>
> —Philip Vickers Fithian

The concept of fruits in the garden or orchard was carried over from Britain to Virginia. Virginians took great pride in their fruits. Anonymous (1700) and The Compiler (1744) utilized most of these available fruits. Robert Beverley observed: "I don't know any English Plant, Grain or Fruit, that miscarries in Virginia . . . apples, nectarines, apricots, peaches, European grapevines, almonds, pomegranates, figs, wheat, barley."[1] Philip Vickers Fithian enjoyed his panoramic view: "The Apricots are in their fullest Bloom; Peaches, also, & Plumbs, & several sorts of Cheries are blossoming; as I look from my Window & see Groves of Peach Trees on the Banks of Nomoni."[2]

Fruits, however, were hard to come by for the lower classes during the difficult years of the seventeenth century. Since fruits were found desirable for their valuable nutrition and added variation to a monotonous diet, local court records contain numerous references to thefts of fruits. Stealing a neighbor's fruit was a serious offense, since having enough food could spell the difference between survival and starvation. When John Puckett, twenty-nine years old, made a deposition in court in 1679 that he witnessed Thomas Burton Sr. "takeing up apple trees belonging to George Freeman," Burton's defense was that the apples would be wasted by the cattle and thus be useless for George Freeman and that, besides, it would "doe his children good."[3]

Native American fruits were cultivated along with the familiar European fruits. William Byrd made mention of "different types of pears and cherries, grapes, strawberries and mulberries."[4] Not to be overlooked were "persimmons, cranberries, huckleberries, raspberries and chinkquapins" along with native melons such as "muskmelons and macocks."[5]

According to some published sources, there was lingering suspicion in the seventeenth century that fruits other than apples, oranges, lemons, and grapes were as potentially harmful as vegetables were, both in Britain and Virginia.[6] Letters and diaries both support and refute this assertion. The people took advantage of fruit in the orchards whenever possible, but any new or unfamiliar fruits were looked upon with mistrust. Samuel Pepys hesitated at drinking a new and brightly colored beverage called orange juice. Although he found it a "very fine drink" mixed with sugar, he feared that "it being new, I was doubtful whether it might not do me hurt."[7] They also assumed that fruit was harmful only if consumed in excess or at inappropriate times. William Byrd of Virginia complained in his diary that eating five apricots put his "belly out of order" and he had consumed "so many pears that I was a little griped in the evening."[8] At the same time some fruits were perceived as sources of possible physical relief. Byrd wrote that he "was exceedingly griped in my belly. I ate as many cherries as I could get for it, but they did no good."[9]

Other factors that could explain the scarcity of fruits at some tables were the seasons; the expense of certain fruits—for example, grapes and Seville oranges; and the current events. Anonymous (1700)'s copy of the proper courses from Edward Kidder reveals that almost no fruits were listed as entrées. They were primarily added as colorful garnishes.

Grapes were highly prized in both England and Virginia. Samuel Pepys wrote: "Captain Country . . . come with some Grapes. . . . And my wife and I eat some. . . . But the grapes are rare things. . . . My wife had put up some of the grapes in a basket . . . to be sent to the King";[10] and "Mrs. John Stith sent my wife some grapes."[11] A recipe Anonymous (1700) had for sugared grapes, as part of her elegant cuisine, involved a great deal of labor, including making a cut in each grape with a needle to remove the seeds and then boiling and drying them in liquefied sugar.[12] The Compiler (1744)'s version is similar.[13]

When oranges became rare and exorbitant in England due to the current war with the Dutch, Samuel Pepys inveigled to get coveted oranges from Mrs. Batten and also griped that he had to pay for "oranges, 3*d*."[14] He wrote that "[China] oranges" were "now a great rarity since the wars; none to be had."[15] For Virginians, such as William Byrd I, who could afford them, Seville oranges had to be ordered from Spain through an agent.

Besides the usual fruits, there were raisins, prunes, dates, currants, dried figs, and almonds.[16] These were used extensively for fruit-studded cakes, puddings, desserts, beverages, and as medical simples. Many a "seed" cake incorporated these fruits, while fermented raisins could also be used as a base for Malaga or artificial wines and as flavoring for medical drinks.[17] Anonymous (1700) and Jane (Bolling) Randolph had recipes for such seed cakes; one from a Mrs. Cary was considered fine. Recipes for Malaga and artificial wines were also found in Jane (Bolling) Randolph's collection, the latter incomplete as if the writer had been interrupted.

Fruits were also used in jellies, preserves, marmalades, cordials, ratafias, and in various candied forms such as orange comfits and suckets. Some of Anonymous (1700)'s desserts were literally lifted out of England as the best tokens of British cooking tradition: orange marmalade, gooseberry preserves, gooseberry fool, marmalade of quinces and raspberries, barberry and damson preserves, and dried cherries. Anonymous (1700)'s recipe for orange marmalade is unmistakably old, both in labor-intensive technique and language. Jane (Bolling) Randolph, The Compiler (1744), and Mary Randolph could afford copious amounts of sugar for their sugar-based preserves and other desserts.

Anonymous (1700) had one old recipe for gooseberry preserves in which, again, needles were used to pick out the seeds. Her recipe for gooseberry fool called for boiled and strained gooseberries added to a bowl of boiled, thickened, and flavored cream. Mary Randolph's gooseberry recipes were both similar and dissimilar to those. The gooseberries were simply boiled in a sugar syrup, and the cream was then added to the mixture.[18] While Mary Randolph's "Gooseberry Fool" is more streamlined, it is an obvious descendant of Anonymous (1700)'s recipe.

Cherries were a status symbol during this time. Anonymous (1700) had two recipes for preserving cherries, with or without the pits. Again, both were labor-intensive. Jane (Bolling) Randolph's version belonged to a relatively progressive time. She had one recipe for sugared and dried cherries from Mr. Sylvanus Bevin of Plow Court, London, and another from Mrs. Lanthorn for bottled cherries. In contrast, Mary Randolph's recipe, "Cherries," was similar to Anonymous (1700)'s recipe for preserving cherries with the stones. Her cherries, intact with stems, were carefully boiled in sugar to the point of becoming transparent.

The Compiler (1744) also possessed somewhat similar recipes for preserved gooseberries, gooseberry fool, and three ways of keeping cherries. She had a greater selection of updated recipes to choose from publications.[19]

One fruit-based recipe stands out in Anonymous (1700)'s collection in terms of age and elegance: "Taffity Tarts." This recipe, not commonly seen in published cookbooks, was not found among Jane (Bolling) Randolph's, Mary Randolph's, and The Compiler (1744)'s collections. Being a variation of the word *taffeta,* it referred to the silky or taffeta-like texture of fruit-filled tarts.[20] Anonymous (1700) made her apple paste from her recipe "Apple Pape for Taffity Tarts," which consisted of stewed and strained apples. It was sprinkled with sugar and cinnamon before being put into the tarts. Taffety Tarts served as a nice dessert on the dinner table.

# Sugar

My wife . . . making of Marmalett of Quince, which she now doth very well herself. I left her at it.

I took leave of her in the garden, plucking appricotes for preserving, and went away.

—Samuel Pepys

As yet they made but bare muscavadoes, so moist and full of molasses, so ill-cured that they were barely worth the bringing home to England.

—Richard Ligon

Edward Grinden, gent., 14 Jan. 1627: That Wm. Mills stole 3 lbs of sugar and 6 lbs of currents from the store.

—"Minutes of the Council and General Court 1622–1629"

For Eight barrells of Candy oyl at 3 li per barrell is 24 li . . . 448 li Powder sugar 4 ct as per Contra sould to divers Merchants and Planters at 5 li per ct is in tobacco 002240; Loafe Sugar at 5 li and 6 li per ct 3 barrells sould for 001312.

—"Accompts of the Tristam and Jane"

Abt. 2c Loafe Sugar, 1 chest Oranges, 6 Chocolate, 40 Musc'o sugr ye rest Rum
To mr. Jonathan Walke-Barbadoes.

—William Byrd

I desire these following Goods may bee sent on my particular account, vizt.
. . . About 1200 Gallons of Rum.
3000 lbs. Muscovado Sugar.
1 Barrell of White S. about 2 cwt.
3 tun of Molasses.
1 Caske Limejuice and 2 cwt. Ginger.

—William Byrd

> You . . . to return in Comoditys . . . Muscovado Sugr (if cheap & good) is now wanted. . . . Send yor goods by, to deliver up James River as high as Westover, w:h is abt two miles above where the Great Ships ride—
>
> —William Byrd

Until the arrival of Caribbean sugars, the best sugar came from Madeira in relatively small loaves weighing about three or four pounds apiece. Other sugars could be obtained from Italian and Baltic refineries that utilized sugar exported from India, Persia, and North Africa.[1] These sugars were expensive. After its discovery by Christopher Columbus in 1493, sugar cane flourished as a valuable cash crop in the lower central Caribbean.[2] By 1643 large amounts of refined sugar were being produced in Barbados, and the American colonies were among the major purchasers. Prices varied, depending on the type, size, and grade of sugar purchased. Processed or white double-refined sugars were the most expensive and could weigh from five pounds to thirty-five or forty pounds. The larger ones could be fourteen inches in diameter and three feet high. The preferred sizes found in households, however, weighed fourteen pounds.[3]

When Princess Catharine of Braganza arrived in England for her marriage to King Charles II, part of her dowry was "in Sugars and other Comoditys."[4] Samuel Pepys, ever sensitive about correct social mores, gave Mrs. Hunt a box of sugar and a sugar loaf for Mr. Shelton, and in return he received a "feacho" of "fine sugar" as a reward for his previous year's service.[5]

In an article entitled "Time, Sugar and Sweetness," Sidney W. Mintz discussed the expense of sugar and strong demand for it among the wealthy. Since sugar is a created need, he carefully analyzed the pertinent factors that contributed to Europe's great consumption of sugar. The critical factors turned out to be "political and economic forces behind the availability of sugar" as well as "slavery, indentured labour and the production of primary commodities in the Third World." There was a direct relationship between human behavior and economy with "the growth of industrialization and slavery." This led to change in dietary habits, and sugar served as a quick and cheap energy substitute for factory workers.[6]

By the 1660s there were fifty sugar refineries alone in London that could convert raw sugar from the Caribbean. This was a revolutionary change from only two sugar refineries in England in the mid-sixteenth century. As a consequence, many family fortunes were made through the establishment of sugar refineries.[7] However, only the wealthier classes could afford to purchase these expensive single- and double-refined sugars along with Lisbon sugar. Other, less expensive sugars were muscovado sugar, molasses, blackstrap, and treacle, each representing a step down in extent of refinement.[8] These cheaper grades of sugar were found perfectly suitable for specific purposes. Anonymous (1700) and Jane (Bolling) Randolph used treacle for their gingerbread recipes.

According to Elizabeth David, muscovado sugar derived its name from a Portuguese word, *mazcavado,* which meant "impure" or "unrefined." She added, however, that the word could also be derived from a Spanish word, *masacabado,* which meant a more finished state before it was mixed with molasses. Barbados, Trinidad, and Jamaica were the main sources for muscovado sugar. It was found useful by the British citizenry in their wine-making and brewing businesses.[9]

In contrast to these various sugars, Lisbon sugar consisted of tricolored loaves. The base was made of white sugar while the middle portion consisted of yellow sugar, and the top portion was brown sugar. The partially refined loaves originated from the Azores, Madeira, and Brazil. According to Elizabeth David, Lisbon sugar was prized even though it was partially refined.[10] Jane (Bolling) Randolph's recipe for oatmeal flummery may indicate the use of Lisbon sugar: "one spoonful of L Sugar."[11]

By 1676 the price of sugar dropped, enabling the middle class in England and the American colonies to have access to this sweetening agent.[12] But it was still expensive and highly valued in the colonies. A "keg of brown sugar was worth a set of chairs, and four loaves of white sugar had the same value as a walnut chest."[13] Even well-to-do Elizabeth (Cary) Fairfax carefully hoarded her conical loaf of sugar, which was to be used only for special occasions such as one teatime during January 1772. She allowed her daughter Sally Cary Fairfax to experience a momentous event, which was noted in Sally's diary in her girlish hand: "I craked a loaf of sugar."[14] Jane (Bolling) Randolph's manuscript contained a notation: "5734 lbs Sugar @ 10*d*[?] P Lb."

The only way the settlers could obtain sugar was to purchase muscovy sugar, molasses, or treacle if they could afford it. Honey was a natural alternative. Parson Rose mentioned that he "saw Mary, Duncans wife, making sugar" after girdling the trees in midwinter.[15] Since honey was an important ingredient for metheglin, apparently honey must have been available to the Randolph family whenever they wished to make Mrs. Mary (Isham) Randolph's metheglin.

In contrast to Elizabeth (Cary) Fairfax, who hoarded her conical loaf of sugar, Anonymous (1700) and Jane (Bolling) Randolph used copious amounts of various sugars in their recipes, especially for preserving fruits, making marmalades and jellies, and candying angelica, grapes, and orange "slips." The Compiler (1744) must have had plenty on hand as well, given her special interest in sugar-laden recipes. They all preferred the most expensive double-refined sugar but did use single-refined sugar as well. They knew that the amount of sugar had to be close to the weight of the fruit, give or take a small amount, depending on the type and sourness of the fruit.[16] Cherries did not require as much sugar as apricots and peaches. Quinces and barbaries, however, required a lot of sugar. The women also had to know the appropriate temperature of boiling sugar for each type of preparation. Sugar was either to be skimmed from time to time in the preserving pan or boiled to candy height for candying. The process took much experience and skill.

As part of their preparation to present attractive and mouthwatering dishes, not only did sugar need to be clipped off the sugar loaf with sugar snippers, it had to be broken up into lumps and made smooth. The recipes belonging to Anonymous (1700) and Jane (Bolling) Randolph's manuscripts often mentioned that sugar had to be first "searced" through a hair bag, a fine sieve, or similar material. This involved a lot of labor.

Both Anonymous (1700) and Jane (Bolling) Randolph or her namesake had cake recipes with strict directions concerning icing. These cake recipes stressed the importance of not spreading the glaze on prematurely. If the glaze was applied to a warm cake, the cake could crumble to pieces. If the glazed cake was placed in a still-overheated oven, then the glaze would not only harden but turn yellow. The heat had to be exactly right to harden the glaze and yet keep it pristine white, the ideal color prescribed in the seventeenth century by Sir Kenelm Digby, who said that such glazes should be like "silver between polished and matte or like a looking glass."[17] A high standard indeed.

Although Anonymous (1700) and Jane (Bolling) Randolph utilized expensive white sugars in their recipes, neither of them used muscovado sugar for preserving their fruits because its use would have produced different results in terms of taste and color.[18] They knew that only white sugar would do for orange marmalade or Taffety Tarts.

A better idea of how much sugar Anonymous (1700) and Jane (Bolling) Randolph used is best reflected in their endless array of sweet desserts, preserves, marmalades, jellies, candied fruits, seed and sugar cakes, tarts, syllabubs, almond cream, macaroons, and sugar-cured hams on their tables. Such a display of sugar-laden foods not only emphasized their social status but also stressed their determination to serve only the best to their guests, frontier conditions notwithstanding. Their legacy was carried over to the eighteenth century by Mary Randolph, who believed in the same exacting standards.

# The Crowning Glory

Anon we sat down again to a Collacion of cheesecakes, tarts, custards and such-like, very handsome.

We liked very well their Codlin tarts.

Then my wife and I . . . went to Mrs. Jem, in expectation to eat a sack posset.

—Samuel Pepys

My wife to the making of Christmas-pies all day.

My wife . . . having sat up up till 4 this morning seeing her maids make mince-pies.

—Samuel Pepys

She gave me some ginger-bread made in cakes like chocolatte, very good.

By and by to my house to a very good supper, and mighty merry and good music playing; and after supper to dancing and singing till about 12 at night; and then we had a good sack-posset for them and an excellent Cake, cost me near 20s, of our Jane's making, which was cut into twenty pieces, there being by this time so many of our company . . . and so to dancing again and singing with extraordinary great pleasure.

—Samuel Pepys

I desire you to send mee two or three bottles of Orange flower water, Some of your best Suckets and another barrell of refined Sugar.

—William Byrd

We had a very handsome dinner, and particularly a fine desert which the company admired.

I ate some apple pie for supper.

I ate some apple pudding for dinner.

I ate some cake and drank some milk and water.

—William Byrd

At night ventured to the ball at the capitol where I stayed till 10 and ate three jellies.

—William Byrd

Mama made 6 mince pies & 7 custards, 12 tarts, 1 chicking pye, and 4 puddings for the ball.

—Sally Cary Fairfax

The timeless custom of including sweets on the dinner table for guests gave the hostess an opportunity to show off her specialized skills, and she knew that her confections would serve as an important finale to the entire meal. Accompanied by fine wines, cordials, syllabubs, and shrubs, sweets were the high point of the menu that would ultimately determine the outcome of postdinner conversation. Since hostesses inherited or learned their culinary knowledge from their mothers, their peers, their cultural heritage, and from cookbooks, it is not surprising that their desserts remained traditionally British.

The big factor behind each hostess's choice of desserts was what was locally available and each's supply of imported foodstuffs. Secondly, they preferred to choose and select recipes that they felt were the best to serve their guests. Virginia hostesses did not share these secrets with their free or enslaved cooks on their plantations, since desserts were true forms of art that presented hostesses with opportunities to show off their skills.

Published cookbooks dating from the sixteenth to the eighteenth centuries stressed the high status of various recipes: the "excellent Marmelade" that was a New Year's gift to Queen Mary;[1] the preserved quinces prepared for "King Edward";[2] a posset made in the "Earl of Arundel's Way";[3] along with "Prince Bisket,"[4] "Countesse Cakes,"[5] and "The Lady Arran's Daughter's Wedding Supper."[6] While members of the British gentry may have been able to emulate some of these recipes, the gentry in Virginia would not have been able to do so—but not for want of trying. Various cookbook authors offered their versions of what should be served each month. Patrick Lamb made a neat listing of what should be served in the first and second courses for each month, such as brawn for the first course with other edibles in the month of January.[7] Anonymous (1700) took great pains to copy the ideal courses as printed in Edward Kidder's book, since she could use them as a guideline on what constituted the current fashion in entertaining.

Anonymous (1700) and Jane (Bolling) Randolph possessed the usual custards, puddings, hart's horn or oatmeal flummeries, mince pies, and gooseberry fools, and other sweets were faithful and traditional British standbys that any hostess could rely upon. Anonymous (1700)'s old recipe for codlin (apple) cakes included a postscript on how to color them: red—"with a dram of scuganell, a dram of almond, a bit of sugar and a little water."[8] In contrast, Anonymous (1700) copied recipes for chocolate almonds, chocolate cream, almond cream to jelly, candied fruit, creams and biscuits, fried cream, and "Touet Demoy." The Compiler (1744) had her own "Tarte de Moyle," "Almonds Allamode," almonds in chocolate, chocolate puffs, and trifle.[9] Her choices were different but just as pleasing and stylish.

Not to be overlooked were sparkling, clear jellies made of calves' feet or neats' feet, an old-time favorite. Anonymous (1700) and Jane (Bolling) Randolph possessed these classics. There were other jellies, marmalades, jams, and preserves. Jane (Bolling) Randolph once possessed a jam recipe for her cake, while Anonymous (1700) offered colored or ribboned jellies. Anonymous's recipe directed that separate muslin bags containing saffron, spinage (spinach) juice, and scutcheneale (cochineal) be added to the jelly-filled pipkins. As the colors rose, they were to be strained with egg whites and made clear. This is similar to Randle Holme's 1688 list of courses, which included "jelly of five or six colors."[10]

Other fine, dainty confections for the table were candied oranges, orange slips, sugared angelica, biscuits, macaroons, flavored jumbles, and cakes. The word *cake,* as used during that period, referred not only to cakes as we know them but to what we would call miniature cakes, cookies, or hardened-syrup confections today. Anonymous (1700), Jane (Bolling) Randolph, and The Compiler (1744) had recipes for Shrewsbury cakes, sugar cakes, little plum cakes, and candylike sweets. Anonymous (1700) directed that her Portugal cakes, studded with currants, be baked in hart (heart-shaped?) pans. Anonymous (1700)'s manuscript continued to yield more surprises. There were cake recipes shared by Madame Orlis or Orless, Mrs. Price, Mrs. Cary, and T. M., among others. There were light, plain, rich, seed, and fine cakes. Many of these recipes cautioned the reader to keep stirring the batter until it was put in the oven; otherwise it would fall. Caraway comfits could be added to the frosting if desired. It was imperative that the appearance, texture, and flavor of these cakes be crowd pleasers without fail.

Elizabeth David believed that seed cakes may have been symbolic, reflecting the sowing of wheat in the spring. Furthermore, many a seed cake was affiliated with Lent. Caraway, anise, cumin, and coriander seeds would be coated with sugar and added to the cake batter or glaze. Rich wigs, mentioned in a previous chapter, could also be served as spice cakes studded with caraway instead of currants. Ginger was another beloved spice in British culinary lore.[11]

It is immediately apparent from reading various recipes for regular-sized cakes belonging to Anonymous (1700) and Jane (Bolling) Randolph that these women had money to spend not only on sugar but also on spices and dried fruits. Both continued the cultural favorite gingerbread with their own recipes. They could afford to purchase the expensive currants, raisins of the sun, and candied citron for their cakes. Malaga raisins were among the most expensive items, and yet both Anonymous (1700) and Jane (Bolling) Randolph made sure to have them on hand for their cakes as well as vinegar and Malaga-wine making. These dried fruits, which involved tremendous amounts of labor because they had to be carefully stoned, picked over, and cleaned by hand, had been shipped through the Mediterranean trade routes from Malaga, Spain, and the Greek islands.[12] Rose and orange waters were used as flavorings. (The vanilla bean was not available in America until Thomas Jefferson brought it from France in 1784.[13])

Cakes flavored with saffron were also popular during this time,[14] since Saffron Waldon in England provided a plentiful supply. It is interesting that saffron cakes do not appear in either Anonymous (1700)'s or Jane (Bolling) Randolph's repertoire. Anonymous (1700) preferred to use saffron to color her jellies, while Jane (Bolling) Randolph's cookbook contained saffron syrup.

Jumble recipes added an extra sparkle to the manuscripts of Anonymous (1700) and Jane (Bolling) Randolph. Almond paste, an old British favorite, could be flavored and shaped as the cook pleased. Anonymous (1700) flavored her almond paste with sugar, eggs, cream, butter, caraway, coriander, and rosewater before she shaped it into knots. The recipe for French "jumblets" in Jane (Bolling) Randolph's manuscript was already an old one, consisting of beaten almonds, water, and lemon peel. Each long roll was dipped in egg whites and then coated with sugar before baking. The other "jumblet" recipe, donated by Mrs. Byrd of Westover, was similar. They were made of beaten almonds and cold water, with an egg white added to make the batter froth. Because of its soft consistency, Mrs. Byrd stipulated that this mixture be squeezed through a "squirt." The mention of this term as part of the cooking repertoire is unusual in any British cookery manuscript or published edition, but it is rare in American manuscripts.[15] To date, only one other recipe printed before 1744 that mentions using a squirt has been located by the author.[16]

A congealing agent known as gum dragon was mentioned by the well-to-do in the mid-seventeenth century before it gave way to shaved hart's horn or isinglass. Gum dragon and isinglass were time-consuming to make since these items had to be soaked overnight to soften before they could be added to other ingredients. John Murrell and Thomas Dawson mentioned "gum dragon" and "gum dragant," respectively, in their 1617 and 1653/54 publications.[17] It was utilized in Anonymous (1700)'s and Jane (Bolling) Randolph's manuscripts when recipes needed something to hold its shape.[18] However, isinglass was not used since it was expensive and did not come into a more common use until later in the eighteenth century. Mary Randolph did use isinglass, however, for her blancmange.[19]

It was Mary Randolph who introduced many new dishes that would become part of our cuisine today: new creams such as sago or raspberry, lemon ice, trifle, floating island, burnt custard, and ice cream.[20] While these dishes were mostly unheard of in Anonymous (1700) and Jane (Bolling) Randolph's time, The Compiler (1744) did possess a recipe for trifle. Mary Randolph's recipes appeared during a time of great technical as well as social change. Her approach and outlook were much more precise and exacting, and her recipes reflect this. Furthermore, the sheer force of her personality enabled her to make innovative dishes that she took pride in and would eventually publish in book form.

However different their approaches toward desserts and confections, Anonymous (1700), Jane (Bolling) Randolph, and Mary Randolph were all well aware of their important roles in entertaining their guests. They recognized that in the eyes of society their menus and their status were related. Therefore they took great pains that every course was presented in the most attractive and colorful manner possible. They gave careful attention to their choices of desserts and delicacies and made them memorable enough to spark admiration. Their accomplishments along with the successes of other aspiring hostesses would make southern hospitality famous.

# Beverages

Mr. Peter Barr sent me a Terce of Clarret, which is very welcome.

And so to his [Commissioner's] house, and had syllabub.

—Samuel Pepys

When we have a very fine dinner, good Musique and a great deal of Wine . . . my head troubled with wine; and I, very merry, went to bed,—my head akeing all night.

—Samuel Pepys

I did give him a morning draught of Muscadine.

He hath also sent each of us some anchovies, Olives and Muscatt; but I know not yet what that is, and am ashamed to ask.

—Samuel Pepys

I had some broth made me to drink, which I love.

So to his house, where I drank a cup of Syder.

Here my Cosen Norton gave me a brave cup of Metheglin, the first I ever drank.

And after a dish of Coffee, home.

—Samuel Pepys

When I returned drank some syllabub.

At night we drank some punch and were merry.

—William Byrd

About Noon a great Number of people at prayers, disturbed by a Retailer of Whiskey, one Wm. Miller.

I have drunk more whiskey than ever I did before, and find when a Man is heartily fatiqued, anything will do instead of claret

—Robert Rose

I ate pickled oysters and chocolate.

And ate chocolate for breakfast with Mr. Isham Randolph, who went away immediately after.

—William Byrd

Mrs. Carter made a dish of Tea. At Coffee, she sent me a dish—& the Coloniel both ignorant—He smelt, siped—At last with great gravity he asks what's this?—Do you ask Sir—Poh!—And out he throws it splash a sacrifice to Vulcan

—Philip Vickers Fithian

To Day I drank her Health from my Heart in generous Medaira—Yes, best of Women, when you are the Toast I drink wine with Pleasure

—Philips Vickers Fithian

In the Evening the Coloniel began with a small Still to distill some Brandy from a Liquor made of Pisimmonds.

—Philips Vickers Fithian

Owing to society's poor standards of sanitation and other sources of contamination, water was seldom used as a thirst-quenching drink or in cookery. "Not very well occasioned by my fatigue and drinking too much River water" was the explanation offered by Parson Robert Rose for his poor condition.[1] Recipes in cookbooks reveal the careful search for and use of safer waters, such as rainwater or water collected from a spring. This water could be safely added to everyday beers such as small beer, cider, and ale, which were acceptable for all social classes.

The true benefits of milk beyond infancy or for medical value were not yet realized in the seventeenth century. In Britain whey was believed to be a more healthful beverage than milk, which was perceived useful only for infants and the infirm. Samuel Pepys made mention of drinking whey from time to time for his health; he perceived milk as useful for medical purposes, such as stopping heartburn.[2]

Attitudes toward milk appear to have been similar though somewhat different in the Virginia wilderness, where perhaps due to painful experience, every scrap of food and drop of beverage was valued. Many early inventories show that milk and other milk products were stored in sheds, coolers, or cellars where they were less apt to spoil in the humid climate.[3] William Byrd made numerous references to drinking plain or boiled milk for breakfast or shortly before bedtime.[4] Milk was also perceived to be of medicinal value, since William Byrd noted that his daughter Evie had a bad fever and "to increase [it] they had given her milk."[5] However, in contrast to William Byrd, neither Anonymous (1700) nor Jane (Bolling) Randolph mentioned milk or whey in their cookbooks, again supporting the fact that their recipes were for entertaining occasions and not for everyday consumption.

Beverages differed among the social classes in Britain, since only the wealthy could afford such luxuries as imported wines. The Navigation Act of 1651 forbade the admission of non-English ships to England's ports as an attempt to ruin the Dutch trade, while the Wine Act of 1688 imposed heavy taxes. This had an impact upon the wealthy, who turned to relatively expensive Portuguese and Levant wines, while beer and ale consumption increased among the masses.[6] Although the preparation of home-brewed beverages was still prevalent, the practice was beginning to disappear with the advent of other commercially available drinks.[7] Samuel Pepys, however, sometimes preferred homemade brews over commercial beverages because he at times found the latter disappointing, commenting that "their drink doth not please me, till I did send to Goody Stankes for some of hers, which is very small and fresh, with a little taste of wormewood, which ever after did please me very well."[8] Other ordinary beverages such as spring beer or small beer were also consumed.[9]

Later in the seventeenth century the wine restrictions were eased to meet the public demand for Canary, Sack, Madeira, and Rhenish wines. Sack from the Canary Islands became so highly favored that it became immortalized in Shakespeare's "Sir John Sack and Sugar" in *Henry IV.* In an urban setting Samuel Pepys was able to sample various beverages such as Rhenish wine, raspberry sack, and sack.[10]

Once these more expensive drinks became affordable for the upper class, many set up wine cellars where they could purchase and store local or foreign wines. Samuel Pepys noted that "he bid me go down to his wine-cellar, where upon several shelves there stood bottles of all sorts of wine . . . with labells pasted upon each bottle."[11] Pepys was aware that a well-stocked cellar was a prime commentary about a host's social status and was determined to have one of his own as soon as his finances permitted it. He eventually got his set of wine bottles with his "crest upon them . . . about five or six dozen."[12] He ended up with "two terices of claret—two quarter-cask of canary, and a smaller vessel of sack—a vessel of tent, another of Malaga, and another of white wine . . . —which I believe none of my friends [of my name] now alive ever had of his own at one tyme."[13]

It was also during this time that tea, chocolate, and coffee first made their appearances on the British scene. Samuel Pepys pointedly made no comment about a strange brew called tea: "Did send for a Cupp of Tee (a China drink) of which I never had drank before and went away."[14] In spite of Pepys's lack of enthusiasm, these imported Chinese teas would soon conquer England and become its national beverage. According to Pepys, chocolate was an improvement over tea: "We three to Creeds chamber and there sat a good while and drank Chocolate."[15] Perhaps the coffeehouse where Samuel Pepys went to "drink Jocolatte" was a place at Queen's Head Alley that provided an "excellent West Indian drink called Chocolate."[16] Coffee also served as society's status-laden fad since a Turkish merchant established the first coffee shop in London in 1652.[17] Coffeehouses were favored stopping places since drinks were served there in settings suitable for business or social purposes. According to Driver and Berriedale-Johnson, as well as Drummond and Wilbraham, only the wealthy could afford these three new beverages until the mid-eighteenth century, when prices fell because of a flooded market.[18] Only then could the middling classes afford to purchase these beverages.

In Virginia the locals held the same cultural values. An account of items sold in Virginia in 1637 included "10 butts of sacke which is 40 quarter caske at 250 li per Caske in Tobacco . . . 010000."[19] Hugh Jones commented that they "likewise used a great deal of chocolate, tea and coffee . . . commodities brought from the West Indies, and the Continent, which cannot be brought to England without spoiling."[20] William Byrd and other planters made numerous references to chocolate, coffee, and tea in their diaries, showing that they were conducting their lives as would any proper Englishman living in Virginia. As in Britain, these drinks were prohibitively expensive and served as status symbols, as did imported wines of the previous century. Tea sets were visible extensions of this social-class consciousness.[21] Not until the mid-eighteenth century did coffee, tea, and chocolate became popular beverages of the day for the middling classes.[22] William Byrd found coffee at both the governor's[23] and tea at the coffeehouses.[24] As late as 13 January 1772 young Sally Cary Fairfax penned in her diary that "mama made tea for a wonder indeed."[25] It is interesting that Anonymous (1700) and Jane (Bolling) Randolph made no mention of coffee or tea in their recipes except for medicinal teas. Yet Jane (Bolling) Randolph's will revealed that she possessed a chased-silver milk or tea pot, perhaps used for her teas.

Since local water resources were less than ideal, carrying malaria and other diseases, beverages other than tea, coffee, and chocolate were either imported or home-brewed.[26] On 30 May 1625 a John Twke [*sic*] made a deposition in court saying that "he doth know yt Thomas Edwardes did Deliuer a pipe of Seack to Mr. Robert Bennet in ye *Abigall* and this Examnt thinketh the price was two hundred and sixtie pound waight of Tobacco."[27]

When sack as well as Madeira, Canary, and Rhenish wines were exported to Virginia, they were usually sent to wealthy Virginia inhabitants, such as William Byrd, who could afford them: "I drew off some brandy that came from madeira that was very good"[28] and "We drank some Rhenish wine and sugar."[29] However, they had to pay the rates regulated yearly by an Act of Assembly in Virginia for alcoholic imports.[30] According to Dr. L. Daniel Mouer, the yard of the Randolph mansion at Curles was littered with hundreds, if not thousands, of shattered wine bottle fragments.[31] Richard Randolph had his wine bottles sealed with his initials and dates.[32]

The rest of Virginia's inhabitants made their own brews, either for their own use or for profit. Everyday beer, such as small beer or malt-based beverages, and cider were the dependable standbys. Beverley commented that the poorer classes drank beer made from molasses and bran, or malted Indian corn, persimmon (cakes), or potatoes.[33] The inventory of Stephen Gill in 1653 listed "Hony . . . trecle . . . Hops . . . Butter . . . 2 Bushels of Wheat . . . 3 bushels of Moalt."[34] These ingredients were useful for making beer. In 1688 William Byrd, father of William Byrd the diarist, placed an order for such malts: "I fear I shall want also some of it w'ch you or I forgott."[35] During a beer-brewing session Thomas Jefferson requested Richard Randolph to "send me two gross of your beer jugs; the one gross be quart jugs, and the other pottle (half-gallon) do."[36] Landon Carter, on the other hand, had his malt recipe in Virginia; it contained molasses donated to him years before by a brewer in Weymouth, England.[37]

Historic inventories in Virginia provide evidence that cider was a commonplace beverage for all classes. By 1648 Richard Bennett's orchard yielded twenty butts of excellent cider.[38] One day in August 1681 Thomas Cocke near Curles served cider to his hired hands, both blacks and whites.[39] Even William Byrd made his own cider[40] and drank the same with the governor.[41] It may not be surprising that Anonymous (1700) and Jane (Bolling) Randolph did not include any recipe for cider in their manuscripts since it was accepted by all classes. Even Mary Randolph mentioned cider only once—as an ingredient for a mince meat pie.[42]

Besides the usual beer and cider, the settlers concocted their own wines, such as perry from pears, peach or French brandy, and fruit-based wines from available fruits in their cultivated orchards and gardens. William Byrd tasted perry, which turned out to be "very good."[43] Philip Vickers Fithian wrote that peach brandy was distilled at the Carter plantation.[44] It was not until the latter part of the seventeenth century that imported wines became more accessible to the middling classes.[45] Even Parson Robert Rose could occasionally purchase a foreign wine or liquor such as rum: "Went with Mr. Cruden to Mrs. Brooke's, brought Home Wine, Rum and other Necessarys."[46]

Housewives such as Anonymous (1700) and Jane (Bolling) Randolph were steeped in the ways of distilling wines and beers as part of their domestic training. Besides the ubiquitous beer and cider, drinks of the day included simple fruit juices, flavored waters, homemade and imported wines, and elegant shrubs.[47] Anonymous (1700) possessed spring beer. In addition to her neatly penned recipes for spring beer and bitter wine, Jane (Bolling) Randolph's manuscript also had a recipe for small beer. Anonymous (1700) also favored beverages such as gooseberry, raspberry, cherry, and cowslip wines as well as shrub, syllabub, and peach brandy. Jane (Bolling) Randolph's manuscript included some of these beverages as well as ratafia.

Other home-brewed wines made from cherries, blackberries, elderberries, mulberries, and currants are found in Anonymous (1700)'s and The Compiler (1744)'s manuscripts. Jane (Bolling) Randolph also had some of these wines, but one of her handwritten beer recipes stands out in her collection: persimmon beer. A Native American drink, it was made from the extract of persimmons and distilled. It is not clear whether she adopted this increasingly popular beverage from her fellow settlers[48] or wrote down a cultural piece of knowledge, given the fact that she was a descendant of Pocahontas. Apparently persimmon beer and small beers were acceptable in Jane (Bolling) Randolph's viewpoint, since she included them in her cookbook.

Metheglin, a fine beverage dating back to medieval times, was valued by the upper classes in Britain. As a guest in the king's dining quarters, Samuel Pepys made much of it: "I, drinking no wine, had Metheglin for the King's own drinking, which did please me mightily."[49] In spite of its high status, even members of the middling classes in Virginia were making metheglin for profit, including George Felton, an ancient planter of twenty-five years standing, whose metheglin yielded a profit of thirty pounds a year.[50]

Jane (Bolling) Randolph included Mary (Isham) Randolph's recipe for metheglin in her manuscript. Although written in a latter hand, the language and the stipulation that it had to be brewed before the first of October (nearly Michaelmas) points to an earlier Mary Randolph and an earlier recipe from a different era. This is likely Mary (Isham) Randolph, not Jane's descendant Mary Randolph, author of *The Virginia Housewife*.

In the midst of the Virginia wilderness Anonymous (1700), Jane (Bolling) Randolph, and Mary Randolph, as hostesses, endeavored to have only the finest beverages—tea, coffee, chocolate, imported wines, and refined home brews—on their tables to honor their guests. Somehow they succeeded.

# Tobacco

Thomas Charles, aged 23, on 1 August 1679: That he heard Mrs. Katherine Isham say that Edward Good had stolen her tobo upon which one of her servts. replyed that they believed Edward Good had it not, whereupon she replyed that the said Edward Good & Edward Lester had it betwixt them, &c.

—Henrico County Record Book No. 1

John Edwards, aged 27, 1 9bris 1679: Mrs. Isham sayed that she believed Edward Good had stole her tobo (that Rogue).

—Henrico County Record Book No. 1

Thomas Davis, aged 27, on 2 Feb. 1679: Stated in court that his "master Coll Wm Farrar" had paid Coll Fra Epes 1 hogshead of tobacco—"500 & odd pounds neat."

—Henrico County Record Book No. 1

Since 1624 a Virginia law had been in effect that no planter could sell his tobacco until he had paid his years' tithes (or church support) to the parish in which he resided.

—Robert Rose

Tobacco Creditors Vizt . . . Shipt aboard the shippe called the *Tristram and Jane* of London at several times and from severall places as Kickhowtan, backe river, Ould Pocoson, New Pocoson, Accamach, etc. in Virginia 99 hogshead of Tobacco . . . 0031800.

—"Accompts of the Tristam and Jane"

Began to water our Tobo plants. . . . Rain this Morning, planted about 7,000 or 8,000 Tobo plants

—Robert Rose

I received a letter from poor Captain C—l—v who gave me to understand that he had been run down by another ship and that all the tobacco was lost. My part of this misfortune was 36 hogsheads. . . . Captain Wilcox was so kind as to offer his pinnace to go down to see if anything was saved of the Captain C—l—v lading.

—William Byrd

> In the afternoon while the Captain smoked his pipe I settled my books again.
>
> Then I went to the store and opened some thing's there. I sent 15 hogsheads more of tobacco on board Captain Burbydge. . . . In the afternoon my sloop returned and was loaded again with 15 hogsheads to send to Captain Bradby.
>
> —William Byrd

Tobacco, as an import, was highly favored in Britain not only as a profitable commodity but also for its medical virtues. The fumes of tobacco were especially valued during the times of plague, since it was said that not a single tobacconist died during a plague. After seeing plague-stricken houses marked with red crosses upon the doors, Samuel Pepys became ill at ease about himself and hurriedly purchased a "roll=tobacco to smell to and chew—which took away the apprehension."[1] He was but one of many who valued the preventive properties of tobacco.

The importance of tobacco in Virginia reached nearly mythic proportions when the settlers quickly learned that it was a "highly profitable enterprise for England."[2] The value of tobacco for the settlers started off with a bang. For the years 1615–19, 1621–22, and 1626–28 a pound of tobacco fetched prices from three shillings to three shillings and six pence. The intervening years showed only a moderate dip, down to two shillings. It was not until the 1630s that the demand for tobacco collided with a glutted market, and prices then fluctuated wildly from one pence to nine pence. In 1640 the price recovered somewhat, shooting back up to twelve pence, but the market did not regain the prices in shillings until 1713, when a pound of tobacco meant a payment of three shillings. This also immediately disappeared until 1766, when four shillings was the paying price. During the intervals prices continued to rise and fall, depending on demand and the market. This uneven pattern of practically ruinous prices did not deter the inhabitants, since the volume of tobacco shipped to England kept growing steadily. That a humble twenty thousand pounds of tobacco exported in 1617 increased to an average of some 55 million pounds by the mid-eighteenth century[3] showed that the colonists felt that tobacco was still a profitable venture. This fact was part of the basis for Virginia's cultural boom between the 1660s and 1730. The English also profited from this tobacco crop. The labor of one Virginian planter meant not only considerable revenue from tobacco surplus but also employment for English sailors, processors, and tradesmen.[4] Furthermore, a medium of exchange was truly needed in Virginia. Since the "balance of trade was heavily in favor of the Mother Country" and English coin was scarce on the frontier, tobacco was quickly adopted as the new legal tender and fixed in terms of pounds and salaries.[5]

Great care and attention were given to the packing of tobacco for shipment overseas because that affected the prices it would fetch on the market. In a 1656 deed with Nicholas Trott, John Claxon agreed to sell a piece of land on Back Creek in York County, complete with servants, stocks, and tobacco crops. These crops of sweet-scented tobacco were to be packed with care, the "Topp Leaves" and the "ground Leaves" by themselves, and also to be "well Cured strooke dry and sorted . . . wth:out fraud or deceipt."[6] As author Melvin Herndon put it, tobacco became "the life and soul of the colony."[7] An early Virginian settler described the influence of tobacco even better: in 1655 William Grimes gave Ann Harden a heifer called "Hogshead."[8]

Tobacco therefore was not only the king of all crops in terms of Virginia's colonial economy, it was also said to possess "phenomenal curative properties."[9] During the reign of King James I, tobacco was perceived to serve as a purge for phlegm and certain humors, an antidote for poisons, and a healer of wounds. Tobacco was also claimed to heal the gout and ague and "counteract drunkenness."[10] While a number of tobacco ointment recipes have been located in seventeenth- and eighteenth-century publications, none of them matches the unmistakably reverential tone of Jane (Bolling) Randolph's most intriguing recipe called "The Oyntment of Tobacco."[11] It was a guaranteed panacea for all kinds of bodily imperfections ranging from "blotches and scabs," to "appostumes," to "venemous beasts" and "gout," to "passions." This sticky morass also created wonders with gunshot wounds and "poysoned arrows." Was the creator of this recipe speaking from personal experience with frontier warfare? Were gunshot wounds suffered from local muskets and guns, and were these poisoned arrows a reference to Native American guerrilla warfare? This almost sacred fervor and questions were raised by Dr. L. Daniel Mouer in his article "Jane Randolph Her Cookbook" in his *Digging Sites and Telling Stories: Essays in Interpretive Historical Archaeology.*[12] Jane (Bolling) Randolph's recipe clearly reflected the almost religious importance of tobacco in Virginia's consciousness and its pivotal economic role in Virginia society.

Besides caring for their own families, colonial women like Anonymous (1700), Jane (Bolling) Randolph, and Margaret Good often nursed friends and indigents beyond the boundaries of their plantations.[13] By moving beyond the physical boundaries of their own plantations to offer their privately learned skills to those in need, they provided public service. In that respect, each of these women transformed her sphere into a semi-public one.

# Medicines

Sir W. Batten did advise me to take Juniper water. . . . This evening Mr. Hollyard sends me an electuary to take, a wallnutt quantity of it, going to bed, which I did.

Then I drank a glass or two of Hypocras. . . . And so home and to bed—and by the help of Mithrydate slept very well.

So to bed, drinking butter-ale.

—Samuel Pepys

To Mrs. Martha Stratton for trouble & means when ye dec'd was lame Sick & unable to help himself is allowed 300 lbs tobo.

—Henrico County Order Book & Wills, 1678–93

This Evening my son Hugh was taken with a violent cough, a wheezing Rattling in his throat, and a very great agitation of his lungs which made me apprehensive of the present reigning disorder, sore throat, and on the early, gave him 8 gr. of Jalop, 2 of mer.

Left Col. Fry's where his son was ill of a Distemper that answerd to the Description of St. Vitus' Dance.

—Robert Rose

Then came Colonel Randolph who was just recovered of a dangerous sickness.

Mr Finney and Tom Randolph, who dined with us. They told me Colonel Randolph has the gout very much.

About 11 o'clock came Mr. Bland, just from Colonel Randolph's, who he said was very sick.

John Randolph . . . told me his father was very sick and desired a bottle of sack, which I sent him.

The Doctor returned from his journey and told me . . . that Colonel Randolph was extremely sick and in great danger.

Colonel Randolph died this evening about 5 o'clock.

—William Byrd

I should not have minded if Dick Randolp [*sic*] had been there but must confess I was much disappointed, as I understood he was attending his poor father, who is at the point of death.

—Robert Hunter

Coll. R. R. (Richard Randolph) of Curles after a tedious Gouty and Bilous disorder yielded to the fate that awaits us all sooner or later (last month).

—James Currie

The medical remedies in Anonymous (1700)'s and Jane (Bolling) Randolph's receipt collections reflect centuries-old humoral theories of Galen and Hippocrates. This ancient humoral theory stipulated that life consisted of "the four elements, the four qualities, and the four humors. The elements were fire, air, earth, and water; the four qualities were hot, cold, moist, and dry; and the four humors were phlegm, black bile, yellow bile, and blood."[1] As these theories were understood, throughout the ages disease and pain were the results of humors that had either broken down[2] or were out of their proper alignment. The goal was to restore these bodily humors into a harmonious balance. One colonist wrote: "Call'd for a half a gill of bitters to qualify my humours; & a dish of tea to cheer me."[3]

Although great leaps in scientific discovery were gaining ground in the seventeenth and eighteenth centuries, remnants of a medieval and superstitious era still lingered. Even the term "receipt" is medical in origin, since Samuel Johnson's dictionary defines it as a medical formula.[4] This is especially evident in the medical cures found in the manuscripts belonging to Anonymous (1700), Jane (Bolling) Randolph, and to a lesser extent, The Compiler (1744). During the latter part of the eighteenth century medical theory evolved into its more recognizable and present form. Although Mary Randolph did not publish medical cures, her other recipes clearly reflected her era's new way of thinking. Her recipes were scientific, precise, and methodical in approach. There were no remaining medieval flavors reflected in terms such as "with God's Blessing" or utilizing every available herb and plant to expel the disease from the body.

Curative recipes touted by illustrious persons and famed physicians were the most sought after. Lady Elizabeth (Talbot) Gray's prestigious rank as Countess of Kent certainly was one of the factors behind her posthumous 1654 best-seller entitled *Choice Manuall, or Rare and Select Secrets in Physick and Chyrurgery . . . Conserving, Candying, &c.* Remedies by physicians of high repute were also much in demand by the public, especially "Dr. Stephen's Water" as found in John Partridge's 1573 volume, William Vaughan's work, Sir Hugh Platt's 1611 edition, and John Murrell's 1617 publication, among others.[5] They also had the option of trying out recipes such as "King Charles II's Surfeit Water" and "To dissolve the Stone, which is one of the Physicians greatest secrets."[6] Anonymous (1700) and The Compiler (1744) made sure they had "Dr. Stephen's Water" as well as "Lady Allen's Water."

However, one of Jane (Bolling) Randolph's medical recipes stands out among these collections: a cure for "broken cancer." It was purchased from "old Lady Arundel in Germany for the princely sum of £300."[7] Jane was well aware of her family's financial ability to purchase such a status-laden recipe.

Regardless of class, the ages-old humoral principle in all its varied manifestations was universally practiced. To deal with these disordered humors, these printed materials recommended treatment in the form of purgation, phlebotomy (bloodletting) and emetics. In 1657 in York County, Virginia, Dr. Mode's bill to George Light included "a phlebothany to Jno Simmonds and a phlebothany to your mayd."[8] It is interesting that neither Anonymous (1700) nor Jane mentioned any use of bloodletting. They may have felt that bloodletting was such a common medical technique that it was not necessary to include any reference to it. In contrast, William Byrd was a firm believer in the practice: "Our cook Moll was taken sick. I caused her to be bled."[9]

In addition to these ancient practices, other popular treatments were "physick" drinks, which served as sweating or cleansing agents, laxatives, or neutralizing formulas for ills such as fevers and colic. William Byrd got into a fight with his wife Lucy, who did not follow the doctor's instructions to give their ill child the "oil of bitters" three times a day.[10]

Since fruits, vegetables, and fibers found in coarse breads were not commonly seen on the genteel table, many inhabitants consumed excessive amounts of heavy pasties, bread, and meats. Constipation was a common complaint, as revealed by diaries and letters. "Physick" drinks were designed to solve this problem, as evidenced in an entry by Samuel Pepys: "Early in the morning my last night's physick worked. . . . Then up my maid rose and made me a posset."[11] William Byrd wrote that he "met Dick Cocke's servant who in the absence of the Doctor sent him to me for two or three purgatives"; however, while Byrd gave him "some blackroot sufficient for three doeses," he refused "to send him any laudanum because I think it is bad for the gripes."[12] Anonymous (1700) and Jane (Bolling) Randolph made much use of these popular purgatives with their surfeit waters and other medical simples.

Medical knowledge did not remain static in either Europe or Virginia. During this time of great social change, venerated medical tenets were beginning to be questioned in terms of their effectiveness and accuracy. During the era of scientific discoveries, the ancient humoral theory would eventually give way to a new understanding of the human body as either a machine or a vessel containing chemical relationships.[13] Although remnants of medieval "magic, folk-lore, and superstition"[14] lingered for a long time, they would finally give way to logic and reason toward the end of the eighteenth century. King Charles II still practiced the ages-old prerogative of the "Royal Touch" on patients suffering from scrofula ("King's Evil"), even though William Harvey had demonstrated the design and efficiency of blood circulation in the body.[15] Samuel Pepys did not know whether his good health resulted from "my Hare's-foot which is my preservative against wind . . . or my keeping my back cool . . . or whether it be my taking of a pill of Turpentine every morning."[16] Even William Byrd, an educated man, wondered if his griping of the belly was due to "cherry wine, or else pulling my coat off about noon."[17] This odd juxtaposition of differing medical lore was the cultural heritage of Anonymous (1700) and Jane (Bolling) Randolph.

Although the colonists in America continued these medical practices, the alien surroundings in Virginia forced them to seek new cures for unfamiliar diseases such as "ague" (malaria),[18] sleeping sickness,[19] and other swamp-related fevers. Some learned through explorations, while others took note of the Native Americans' use of certain ingredients for specific ills. The Native Americans, as one settler observed, ground their sassafras leaves into powder before applying it to wounds.[20]

Even though the Native Americans had generously shared their foodstuffs with the settlers, the revered leaders of various tribes did not share their medical knowledge. Their intimate knowledge of herbs, plants, and roots was considered sacred and therefore not to be shared with outsiders. Nevertheless, some cultural transmission took place, because it is known that the settlers quickly adopted some of these native ingredients such as sassafras, various barks, and ipecac. Sassafras quickly became valuable since it was believed to be an effective drug for dysentery and skin diseases as well as an astringent or stimulant. Jane (Bolling) Randolph extracted an oil from sassafras roots for anointing rheumatic joints while the patient drank distilled sassafras liquid. She also expressed great interest in matters pertaining to gout, or the stone, while Anonymous (1700) focused on possible plagues. The Compiler (1744) preferred medicinal waters and syrups. Mary Randolph did not list any medical recipes in her voluminous work, but it is possible that she had them written in a separate manuscript.

Although the medical recipes of Anonymous (1700) and Jane (Bolling) Randolph varied in scope and subject matter, it is clear that the majority of their recipes were based on English cures. In contrast to seventeenth-century European physicians, who viewed and rejected cinchona bark as an "additive" rather than a purgative agent,[21] these settlers made much use of it as a valuable source of quinine for the treatment of malaria: "My son Pat's fever returned with such violence that his Mother was frightened, sate up with him all Night— . . . The child's fever went off, gave him the Bark."[22] During one of his sick bouts, William Byrd gave one of his rare praises: "I ate nothing all the rest of the day but bark. My wife gave it me and looked after me with a great deal of tenderness."[23] Anonymous (1700) and Jane (Bolling) Randolph made use of various barks, such as Peruvian bark to reduce fevers and to purge the body.

Another major factor of medical care in Virginia concerned the limited number of learned physicians who could travel widely throughout their isolated settlements. These physicians, however skilled, were often looked upon with fear, suspicion, and skepticism by a population that preferred its do-it-yourself simples as did their counterparts in England. Physicians were often resorted to only during times of desperation or when the skills of the local practitioner failed to effect a cure. Dr. Will Irby provided sweating medicine for hapless Elizabeth (Gilliam) Maybury and her daughter, who were known to suffer from some distemper. Since they felt "rather worse" instead of better, he agreed not to receive any payment in tobacco if his cure proved ultimately ineffective.[24] Landon Carter, being among the skeptical, got into an argument with Dr. Mortimer by requesting him to divulge the contents of the prescriptions for his ailing sons. Dr. Mortimer gave him a "blast" for his trouble.[25]

Since these skilled practitioners were few and far between and too many other claimants were more or less quacks, housewives such as Margaret Good were expected to possess some medical knowledge. This was in order for her to care for her family members, as well as neighbors, hired hands, indigents, and slaves. This particular subject was considered a vital part of her proper domestic training.[26]

Since such Christian virtues were part of a woman's prescriptive upbringing, housewives such as Margaret Good and Jane (Bolling) Randolph developed their knowledge by inheriting oral instructions from their mothers or other women. They were viewed by all as immediate, local, and familial caregivers to the family and community. They may or may not have had medical volumes within their abodes, but they were well versed in the medicinal use of popular herbs, plants, and roots as part of their domestic training. William Byrd, well aware of the requirement for good deeds, noted that he was angry with his wife Lucy when he perceived her to be negligent in this regard: "In the evening I quarreled with my wife for not taking care of the sick women, which she took very ill of me and was out of humor over it."[27] When he became ill with a fever and sore throat, he griped that "my wife took no notice of my complaint . . . Mrs. Cocke had the goodness to come and sit above an hour with me. Mrs. Dunn gave me the bark in the night."[28]

By the time Anonymous (1700) penned her receipts, dangers of typhoid, dysentery, malaria, and other diseases had lessened somewhat, now that settlers were living in healthier territory. However, other disorders such as smallpox and similar pestilential diseases brought in through ships from abroad were still serious concerns. Anonymous (1700) and Jane (Bolling) Randolph wanted to be prepared for any illness by either memorizing oral family knowledge of medical simples or writing down the best remedies in their cookery manuscripts.

On closer inspection of Anonymous (1700)'s medical lore, it is surprising that her cookery manuscript contained only a small number of medical cures, given the normally high interest in the subject. Although the majority of her medical recipes were medical beverages, she did possess salves and medicinal waters. Perhaps the majority of her medical formulas were penned in a separate manuscript, as Landon Carter had done. It is also possible that she copied only what prescriptive literature and oral knowledge guaranteed desirable results.

Recipes for "plague water" were so coveted that every household possessed at least one. During the great plague outbreak in London in 1665, Samuel Pepys received a bottle of plague water from Lady Carteret.[29] Anonymous (1700)'s extraordinarily long recipe for plague water from P. Hart revealed the more superstitious aspects of seventeenth-century thought, since it specified forty herbs and flowering plants to be gathered and mixed according to explicit directions. The recipe, which calls for a number of plants not indigenous to the United States, such as pellitory-of-the-wall and tormentil, is obviously British.

In contrast to Anonymous (1700)'s, Jane (Bolling) Randolph's medical collection was a veritable pharmacy modeled after those touted in Britain. Like Anonymous (1700), Jane (Bolling) Randolph followed prescriptive social standards by believing that the more expensive or elitist the cure, the more worthy it was to add to her collection. Jane was careful to mention that certain and costly deadly poisons should be used with great care. She noted that the dosage was determined by whether the invalid was a child or an adult. One of her recipes may have come from England since it utilized red cicers (chickpeas) and "coob" seeds, which could be obtained from any "Druggist."[30] This would be possible for people living in the city but not in the remote frontier more than three thousand miles away unless such a skilled person lived among them. Likely these had to be ordered from overseas or the formula came from a British publication.

Jane (Bolling) Randolph also included Mrs. Barrett's "approv'd Oyntment" for a dreaded disease known as "Irreptilis or St. Anthony's fire."[31] This ailment was known as the fatal "sacred fire" as early as 1089, and many a victim of erysipelas sought the curative powers from Saint Anthony to restore their inflamed bodies from its rosy color, and thus back to life.[32] In 1668 Samuel Pepys penned in his diary that "my lord Crew, who is very sick, to great danger, by an Irisipulus."[33] Today the ailment is known as a streptococcal infection of the skin that turns it vivid red, especially around the face and scalp.[34]

One of Jane (Bolling) Randolph's most intriguing recipes was her prescription for kipscacuanna, a purging agent. According to Dr. Helen Rountree, this novel spelling appears to be a variation of the Native American term *Ipecacuanna.*[35] Known as "Indian Physick" or "Ipecoacanna," it was used by Landon Carter as part of his medical regimen when treating ill slaves.[36] William Byrd treated himself with it.[37]

Jane (Bolling) Randolph searched for relief for her family by focusing primarily on treatments for gout. Her great interest in gout is one of the most revealing aspects in her entire manuscript. Given the fact that her husband Richard, possibly one of his brothers, her father-in-law William, her son Richard, and kinsman John Randolph of Roanoke all suffered from a hereditary disorder known as gout and/or the stone, it is not surprising that she collected a good number of extolled cures for gout in her manuscript. William Byrd's diary entries referred to his attempts to alleviate the pain from gout: "Then went to visit Colonel Randolph who had the gout in his hand. In about an hour we returned again to Will Randolph's for supper"; and "Tom Randolph came and brought me word that Colonel Randolph had the gout in his stomach, for which I sent him some [b-v-r mineral]."[38]

Gout was a disease usually restricted to the wealthier classes since they could afford rich food on a regular basis. Gout reflected one's inability to metabolize nucleoprotein and afflicted many, who suffered the intense pain of uric acid crystals collecting in the joints (especially the big toe). Samuel Pepys had a "cere-cloth" placed on his sensitive foot to draw out the pain.[39] Since people were unaware that no alcoholic beverage should be consumed by those afflicted with gout, the recipes were found to be variable in effectiveness. Jane (Bolling) Randolph's manuscript included a recipe for the stone and drunkenness reflected such doubtful results. It will work, the manuscript notes, if given with "God's Blessing." Obviously all promising remedies had to be considered for something as agonizing as gout.

While Anonymous (1700) kept pretty much to her cultural heritage with her plague water and other medical beverages, Jane (Bolling) Randolph went a step further. While her medical collection could not be properly cited as an early example of creolization of foodways, it could not be characterized as wholly British. She was widening her boundaries by her willingness to use Native American ingredients such as sassafras, tobacco ointment, kipscacuanna, and persimmons.

Anonymous (1700) and Jane (Bolling) Randolph were evidently raised to be skilled in medical diagnosis, selection of appropriate cures, and creation of concoctions for all kinds of illnesses. Although they were physically in a "private space," they in reality had crossed that invisible line by caring for their families, indigents, hired hands, slaves, and kinsmen. They now functioned in the public world by providing a public service.

# Conclusions

#285. Archeabald Cary Esqr. pr Mr. Wayles
Glasses Cookery.

—*Virginia Gazette Day Book*

Gentlemen and Ladies appear'd at the Capitol, where a Ball was open'd, and after dancing some Time, withdrew to Supper, there being a very handsome Collation spread on three Tables, in three different Rooms, consisting of near 100 Dishes, after the most delicate Taste. There was also provided a great Variety of the choicest and best Liquors. . . . The whole affair was conducted with Great Decency and good Order, and an unaffected Chearfulness appeared in the Countenances of the Company.

—*Virginia Gazette*

The enduring prescriptions that the early settlers brought with them to Virginia regarding the role of women in the domestic and public spheres are consistent with the prescriptions given in Gervase Markham's classic cookbook, *The English Hus-Wife,* published in 1615. His book reiterated that men served in the public sphere (e.g., held public office) and provided status-bearing goods. Women were to keep themselves busy as household managers, supervising everything from planting gardens to keeping rooms clean. A woman's role was in the domestic niche, and her home was the arena in which she was expected to distinguish herself.[1]

Although activities carried out within the domestic sector were not given as high status as those in the public sphere, there were nevertheless gradations of value and standing. A woman's status was multidimensional. Although anthropologists recognize that women of all cultures fulfill multifaceted roles in the course of their lives,[2] their sphere was limited to a narrow area of their domestic activities, namely the home plantation, relatives, and the church. In contrast, the men's sphere was more fluid in nature, encompassing a wide range of activities including political involvement and civic duties. It also permitted change. Men's sphere contained the essential ingredient of being away from, being separate from, and lying outside the domestic sphere assigned to women.

Aware of prescriptions given in publications such as Gervase Markham's *The English Hus-Wife,* men enforced them, carefully spelling out to the women their duties and what was expected of them. However, Colonial Virginia presented an entirely different set of circumstances that eventually broke the rules given by Markham. Due to a combination of demographic accidents and Revolutionary War opportunities, Chesapeake women were much more active in the public sphere than historians and anthropologists formerly believed. They took up deliberate strategies to manipulate the "reality" around them.

The men's economic base (plantation, crops, tobacco, wealth, furnishings, etc.) provided a springboard from which women were to conduct their supportive roles (elevation of status through cuisine) as hostesses. A family's dining room played a central role in the extension of hospitality, and the hostess's achievements in the selection, preparation, and presentation of foods and the entertainment of her guests around the table were noted carefully by all concerned. Success as a hostess could do much to maintain and enhance a family's standing and strengthen her husband's position in the public sphere.

In spite of Markham's powerful prescriptions, recognition of the importance of their roles, and deriving status as a consequence, women still desired to go beyond their traditional boundaries. Many of them disliked their confinement or certain responsibilities and felt that they deserved better; Susanna Clay, for instance, wrote: "recall that hateful season to all housekeepers (the putting up of Pork)."[3]

Education was a crucial factor, since it was more than likely that many more women would have been active in the public sphere had they been well educated. This would have far-reaching consequences for the course of Virginia history. Though many could read, most of them could not write, and therefore many of their private thoughts have been lost to us. In addition to this problem, there were indications that women were trained not to write their true feelings on paper. Recall that Sally Cary Fairfax felt she could not express her true thoughts on paper in case of prying eyes.[4] Instead they had a more elegant and subtle way of achieving their goals through exemplary behavior and used cooking and hospitality to widen their spheres. They extended cooking into an expression of their unsolicited views (recall the patriotic desserts) and "a sense of identity."[5]

The three cookbooks created by Anonymous (1700), Jane (Bolling) Randolph, and Mary Randolph provide insights into the lives of Virginia women as Chesapeake society evolved. Cookbooks in themselves are ahistorical since "cooking is a tradition with social associations, something organic which can grow or wither, improve or decline. . . . recipes are abstracted from meteorological, political, technical, and social environments, past and present."[6] Furthermore, recipes do change. Over a period of time and in different locations, "certain procedures and ingredients have been preferred to others . . . collections whose pieces change from period to period."[7] The three cookbooks under study were no exception. Nevertheless, all of these receipt books not only dealt with foodways but also reflected the perceptions and life experiences of their authors at given stages in the region's history.

Anonymous (1700) adhered closely to Markham's prescriptions and French fashion, and faithfully copied a number of recipes and menus published by Edward Kidder. Although obviously well educated, she was not creative in the sense that she did not experiment with Native American foods or make an attempt to stretch beyond her boundaries. She concentrated on presenting numerous meat dishes, plentiful sugared fruits, and expensive items such as chocolate almonds. No indications of her private thoughts concerning her role is given other than her conservatism. In fact, she identified more closely with the outlook of English society than with the new possibilities inherent in late-seventeenth-century Virginia. She was determined to be as "civilized" as her London peers in the midst of the

Chesapeake frontier and within her domestic circle. In keeping with her station and Markham's prescription, she felt she would be judged by her table and sought to provide only the best. To her, that meant haute cuisine, which reflected the standing of her husband and family.

Jane (Bolling) Randolph was also well educated for her day. Her manuscript reflects a later period and her position as a transitional figure, partly traditional and partly experimental. Although she still preserved and followed many traditional dictates of behavior and the domestic arts, she was prepared to innovate and experiment with many recipes and new ingredients. She incorporated new recipes with the old, thus showing a further evolution in Virginia cookery. Besides the plentiful and traditional array of meats and sugared sweets, she provided persimmon beer and potato custard. She experimented with the use of blood and cochineal to color her meats and with kipscacuanna as a potentially useful medical remedy. Unlike Anonymous (1700), she was willing to break new ground and thought the "best" cuisine could appropriately include some Native American foods and beverages.

Jane (Bolling) Randolph was also willing to build on her success in the culinary arts and, as a hostess, to stretch the boundaries of her domestic role, a sphere to which, according to tradition, she should limit herself. In addition to writing her cookbook, she took up accounting and in later life drew up her own will, which listed a number of silver articles. It may be significant that she waited until after her husband's death to write her own will. She obviously took pride in her work and had a strong sense of her role in her domestic niche. Her accomplishments and sense of self-worth set an example upon which her descendant Mary Randolph would subsequently expand.

In contrast to Jane (Bolling) Randolph and Anonymous (1700), who lived on plantations, Mary Randolph, the third of the authors, ran a boardinghouse in the city of Richmond. As Dr. L. Daniel Mouer states in his article "Reading 'Jane Randolph Her Book'," Mary and David M. Randolph had inhabited the "Early Republic world," which was "cleanly on the other side of Revolution and Enlightenment."[8] An outstanding hostess, she introduced many vernacular dishes and encouraged the large-scale use of regional vegetables. She also confidently simplified meals and the management of their preparation, actions that helped to shape a new era in Virginia cooking. Her cooking was much more democratic in feeling and approach than the other two women's cooking, which partially accounted for the great success and influence of her 1824 publication, *The Virginia Housewife.* She saw herself as an upholder of her husband's status and also as important in her own right. She had her own worthy contributions to make, and her creative mind and practical bent led her to invent the refrigerator and the bathtub. She felt at ease writing a cookbook and earning a living running a boardinghouse, which was a financial success. Mary Randolph's contributions signaled the beginning of a new chapter for Virginia women.

Each of the three authors conducted herself in accordance with Markham's prescription, interpreted in the light of changing times and individual circumstances. Hesitantly at first, but with growing confidence, boundaries were tested, stretched, and at times surmounted.

The nature of The Compiler (1744)'s nonaccretive manuscript served both as a supportive model for and contrasting foil to these three culinary works. She simultaneously preferred the latest culinary trends and made sure there was more than one variety of a recipe. Had she lived a longer life, it would have been interesting to see whether she matured or not over time in terms of culinary skills and personal growth. This will never be known. However, she shared the same belief that her table was to be found faultless by the presentation of the best foods available.

While much would still need to be accomplished in years to come, the women of Virginia did not wait passively for their role to change. They made use of the opportunities available to them to help point the way. Individually and collectively these women made major contributions to the well-being and progress of their families, their communities, and the colony of Virginia.

Lastly, Anonymous (1700) and Jane (Bolling) Randolph's culinary creations served as an influential background and foundation for Mary Randolph, and consequently, her published classic, *The Virginia Housewife,* in 1824. All three authors participated in a colonial cooking dynasty in the best Virginia tradition.

# PART THREE

John Pleasants and Isham Randolph came to see me and dined with us. I ate no meat for dinner.

—William Byrd

There was also Mrs. Chiswell. I went with them to Doctor B—r—t [Barret?] and ate beef for dinner.

—William Byrd

Rode to Will Randolph's where I saw his wife [Mary Isham] and gave her joy. She seems to be a good-humored woman and is handsome. Here I dined and ate boiled beef for dinner.

—William Byrd

Beverley Randolph went with me. We got there by 2 and dined, when I ate boiled chine. After dinner we talked and drank till 9.

—William Byrd

Col. Dick [Randolph] breakfasted with us . . . and Capt. Bolling, and were also persuaded to stay to dinner when I ate boiled pigeon and bacon.

—William Byrd

Captain Talman . . . dined with us and I ate roasted pigeon.

—William Byrd

About 12 came Beverley Randolph's wife, Annie Bolling, Betty Randolph, Molly Randolph, Fanny Davenport, and Will Randolph to dinner and I ate roast turkey.

—William Byrd

Breakfasted with Mr. A. Cary, or rather, with his Mother-in-law—left Warwick about 11, & came to Richmond.

Rode with Mr. Quin to Warwick to visit Mrs. Cary & returned—

—Robert Rose

With Mr. Chizwell & Harvie, set out about 5, breakfasted at Mr. Charles Barrets.

—Robert Rose

It rained very hard and I was wet to the skin, but when I came to Colonel Randolph's they gave me clothes. . . . About 12 o'clock we went to dinner and I ate some chicken fricassee.

—William Byrd

Unless some pops in unexpectedly—Mrs. Washington and myself will do what I believe has not been done within the last twenty years by us—that is to set down to dinner by ourselves.

—George Washington

Advertisement for Edward Kidder's cooking school. The Library of Congress, Rare Book and Special Collections, Washington, D.C.

"Unidentified cookbook, c. 1700"
Anonymous

*"Unidentified cookbook, c. 1700"—Anonymous*

**[Missing Title]**

——— [s]ome strong broath and a bundle of Sweet hearbs and Thy[me] one whole Spice, & Anchovis A peice of Lemon peal wth halfe ——— & white wine forced meat Balls, & some Oysters putt in a Dish ——— fresh Butter & the Yoakes of 2 Eggs to Thicken it, haveing ye o[ne] side Broyled with Salt Strowed over it & put it On the Harsh in [ye] Midle of the dish ye Oynions & the hearbs, taken out you may put [i]n Capers & thin Slices of Bacon & putt abt: ye Dish some on y[e] harsh.

*Comments*

~ **Harsh** is a variation for **Hash.** John Evelyn used this term through his recipes #118, "To make a cold harsh," and #119, "To make a harsh of fresh salmon" (Evelyn, The Manuscript, #118–19). Also known as hach or hacee, it is a "Dish-meat made of any kind of flesh minced or in Gobbets stewed in strong broth with Spices, and served up in a dish with Sippets: to Hash is to stew any meat that is cold" (Holme, *Academy,* Bk. 3, Chap. 3, 82). The recipe at left is a meat dish of some kind, perhaps for a hashed calf's head.

**To Coller a Pigg**

First take yor: Pigg Besh him Cutt Down ye back & Belly but take no—— [o]f the head If you will have him Coller wth: his head on if not þn Cutt his head of & take all the bones out: then lay him in white wine Vineg[ar] or Vergese & watter: lett him Lye in this Pickle 12 hours you must putt in 2 handfulls of salt & when he hath Lane So Longe take it out & tak[e] some Cloves Mace Nutmegs Salt and peper Beat these Small & Strow on the sides of ye Pigg A good Large One will take a Qr. of an Ounce of white Peper one penny worth of Cloves & Mace one Nutmegg & a Little Salt þn take few Sweet hearbs Shread:t About half a Spoonfull When they be Shread Very well then Strow them in ye inside of [ye] Pigg & So Roll it Up: Close to ye head: Roll ye insides of ye Flitches Inward: Butt If you take of the head then Role the One flank Upon the Other Except ye Pigg be Very Learge so th[at] it will make a Collar then Lap a Strong Cloath abt: it & bind it [wth] Tape as hard as ye Can then boyle ye Same Pickle it Lay a Season in & put in half an Ounce of white peper & So Let Boyle un[til] it be tender wch will be in 2 hours or their about when it is boy[led] ——— it as before the Coller is Cold, & bind it againe a Strait.

~ A **collar** is the neck piece of brawn [obsolete], tied up in a roll or coil (*Oxford English Dictionary,* 1933 ed. [*OED*] 2:615). **Vergese** is an old term for verjuice, which is the "acid juice of unripe grapes, crabapples, or other sour fruit" (*OED,* 12:131). **Strow**, a dialect, is equivalent to strew (*OED,* 10:1164). A **flitch** is the "side of an animal" or "a side of bacon." It usually refers to "a hog, salted and cured" (*OED,* 4:332).

*Contemporary Recipe #1*

**To Hash a Calve's Head**

Let your Calve's head be half boyled & cut it in small peces, toung & all; put it into a stupan; put to it a prettie deel of sallt and anchove pepper, Cloves, & a Oinon, a bundell of sweethearbes, and as much sider or white Wine & water as will cover it. Stu this till ye licker be half wasted, then put in 7 yolks of egges beaten with a spoonful of Viniger; put it in & stir it on ye fire till it is thick & sarve it up with ye brans fried & forsed Meat balls & slised Lemon. (Blencowe, *Receipt Book,* 19)

*Contemporary Recipe #2*

**To hash a Calves Head**

Take your Calves head and cleave it in two and wash it out in certain waters, that it may boyl white; then put it a boyling and scum it when it is almost boyled, take it up, and let it cool; Hash it in slices as thin as you can, then put it into your Stew-pan, with a ladleful or two of Strong Broth, and as much White Wine, three or four Onions whole, and a little Timeminced, with two or three Anchovies, a little Salt, with a little Oyster liquor, if you have it; put all these a stewing together, when they are enough, toss it up with the yolks of two eggs, and a little drawn butter; you may have a Pipkin with about half a pinte of Oysters stewed up in a little gravie, with as many Mushrooms, being thickened with a little drawn Butter, and seasoned with Nutmeg; take off your Pipkin, lay the bones of your Calves Head in the bottom of your dish with sippets, then pour out your Hash with your Lear into the dish, and spread it abroad, and put your Oysters and Mushrooms, and that Lear all over your Calves head; then having your thin sliced Bacon, before boyled, and part thereof fryed in eggs, lay it around on the dishes side; the one fryed, and the other boyled; you may add Sassages also about it, so garnish it with Lemmon; only grate a Nutmeg, strow it on the top, and let it go up Smoaking. (Rabisha, *Whole Body* [1661], 74–75)

**How to Souse a Pig and collar it like a Brawn.**

After you have stuck the Pig let him bleed well, then with scalding water and Rozin finely beaten take off the Hair, let him lye in cold water a little space, shifted two or three times, that he may look white, then cut off the Feet, slit him open and take out his inwards, and cut off his head, take the two sides asunder, lay them in cold water, steep it there a day and a night, shifting the water thrice, then take out the bones, roll up each side several, tying them as hard as possible, in the fashion of a Collar of Brawn, then tye it up in a Cloth hard, and put the head whole in another, then boyle it in water and Salt, Cloves, Mace, and Nutmeg, and a handful of *Rosemary,* and some Sweet herbs while it is very tender, take it up and let it cool; then put it into the liquor that boyled it, adding thereto two quarts of Small Beer, set the two Collars in a Dish, garnished with Salt, (with the head entire in the middle) and stick in two Sprigs of Rosemary flowred and serve it with Sawcer of Mustard. (Cromwell, *Court & Kitchen,* 50–51)

**Brawn made of a Sucking-Pig, otherwise called souced Pig.**

Chuse not a spotted Pig for handsomeness-sake, but one that is white; scald him, and cut off his head, parting him down the back, draw and bone him, the sides being throughly cleansed from the blood, and soaked in several clean waters, dry the sides thereof, season them with Nutmeg, Ginger and Salt, rowl them, and put them up in clean Clothes; then take as much water as will cover it in the boiling-pan two inches over and above, and add two quarts of White-wine thereunto. When the liquor boils, put in your Collars, with Salt, Mace, sliced Ginger, Parsley-roots, and Fennel-roots scraped and picked; being half boil'd, put in a quart of White-wine more, being quite boil'd, put in slices of Lemon to it with the whole peel. Having souc'd it two or three days, dish it out on plates with Vinegar; or serve it in Collars with Mustard and Sugar. (Woolley, *Compleat Cook's Guide,* 124–25)

*"Unidentified cookbook, c. 1700"—Anonymous* | *Comments*

**Yeast Cake**

One fourth of a Cake to a Qrt of flour, if you make your bread at 9 at night it will rise for 8 o clock breakfast do send the receipt for Toilet soap-Bettie.

~ This refers to a cake of yeast.

**To make a Fricassy of a Calfs Chaldron C——**

[Take] [a] Calfs Chaldron, after it is little more than half [boyled] and when it is Cold, Cut it into little bits as big [as] [Wal]nuts, Season ye whole with beaten Cloves, Salt, [Nutm]eg, Mace, a little pepper, an Onion, Parsley, & a Tarragon all Shred very Small, then put it into a [fry]ing pan with a Ladle full of Strong broth, & a little [?]t Butter, when it is fryed enough, have a little [lea]r made with ye Mutton-gravy, ye juce of a Lemon [&] [Ora]nge, ye yolkes of three or four Eggs & a little grated [Nut]meg, put all to your Chaldron in ye pan, toss your [Fri]cassy two or three times, then Dish it, & so Serve it up,

~ See page 81 for more about **chaldron**. **Lear** was "a thickening for sauces, soup, etc., a thickened sauce" (*OED*, 6:156). Normally "lear" would be used between the words "little" and "made," but on the original page when it was first examined, the author used the word "butter" instead of lear. The edges of this fragile page have since crumbled away to the extent that only the letter "r" remains. Anonymous (1700) repeated her error until she realized it in another recipe. She then crossed out the word "butter" and replaced it with the correct word, "lear."

**To make beef Sausages without Skins**

Unto Eight pound of Lean beef put 6 lbs beef Suett Shread ye beef & Mixt it together: Season it with peper & Salt wth: a Lettle Rosemar[y] [mix] them in a Morter till they be like paste then rowl them up L[ike] Sausages as you use them: but do not fry them too much.

~ No sausage recipe has been located to date containing beef without skins.

**To make Harts horne Gelly**

Take 2 oz of harts horne: 1 qt. of watter: 1 Spreg of Rosemary 1 blade of M[ace] [&?] boyle it together till it be enought, wch: the you mayst know by Setting a Li[quid] to Cule & if it will gelly then Strain it & put in some Rose watter ye ju[ice] of one Lemon: then Sweeten it wth: Sugar or Syrup of Oranges or Lemon[s]

~ **Hart's horn** is the horn or antler of a hart. The substance is extracted by the process of "rasping, slicing, or calcining the horns of harts" and now from bones of calves. It serves as "a nutritive jelly" (*OED*, 5:107).

**To Collar Beeff**

[Take] [a] [Fl]ank of Beeff: Take of ye Inside Skin Lay it in Spring wa[tter] ——— Lettle Bay Salt & 3 or 4 pennyworth of Salt Peter 3 days then [take] it out of ye pickle & dry it well wth: a Cloth then Strew over [ye] [s]ide with 1/2 oz Cloves as much Mace & Notmeggs & 1/2 oz of white peper so rowl it up as you do Brawn þn Bake it with ye Weaven Batch þn hang it up as you do a Neats Tongue

~ **Pennyworth** is the "amount of anything" that can be purchased "for a penny" (*OED*, 8:650). **Bay Salt** is domestic sea-salt or marine salt consisting of crystals obtained by slow evaporation by the sun's heat. It is now mostly brine pumped up from rock-salt strata (*OED*, 10:59). **Salt Peter** is saltpetre, or potassium nitrate, used for pickling meats, gunpowder and medicinal uses (*OED*, 9:65). **Weaven Batch**—this appears to be an error involving the letter "w."

*Contemporary Recipe #1*

*Contemporary Recipe #2*

———

———

**To fricate Calves Chadrons**

Take a calves Chaldron, after it is little more then half boiled, and when it is cold, cut it into little bits as big as Walnuts; season it with beaten cloves, Salt, Nutmeg, Mace, and a little Pepper, an Onion, Parsley, and a little Tarragon, all shred very small, then put it into a frying-pan, with a Ladle-ful of strong broth and a little piece of sweet butter, so fry it, when it is fryed enough, have a little lear made with a the gravy of Mutton, the juyce of a Lemon and Orange, the yolks of three or four Eggs, an a little Nutmeg grated therein; put all this to your Chaldrons in the Pan, toss your Fricat two or three times, then dish it, and so serve it up. (W. M., *Compleat Cook,* 8)

———

**To make most rare Sausages without Skins.**

Take a Leg of young Pork, cut off all the Lean, and mince it very small, but leave none of the strings or skins amongst it; then take two Pound of Beef-suet shred small, two Handfuls of Red-sage, a little Pepper, Salt and Nutmeg, with a small piece of an Onion: Mince them together with the Flesh and Suet, and being fine minced, put the Yolks of two or three Eggs, and mixing all together, make it into a Paste; and when you use it rowl out as many pieces as your please, in the form of an ordinary Sausage, and fry them. This Paste will keep a Fortnight upon Occasion. (Howard, *England's Newest Way* [1710], 144)

———

**To make a Jelly of Harts-horn.**

Take a quart of running water, and three ounces of Harts-horn scraped very fine, then put it into a stone Jug, and set the Jug in a Kettle of water over the fire, and let it boyle two or three houres untill it jelly, then put into it three or four spoonfuls of Rose-water, or white Wine, then strain it: you may put into it Musk, or Ambergreece, and season it as you please. (Kent, *Choice Manual,* 14)

———

**To Coller Beef**

Take a piece of Beef of the flanck, and peel off the inner skin, then rub it over with saltpeetr beaten fine, then lay in strong brine 48 hours; then roll it up with pepper, cloves, and mace, and a little sweett herbs shred very small. When it is fast taped up, put it in a pot, and put in so much smooth strong ale as will cover it. When it is well baked, and so cold as you may well handle it, take off the tape and shape it as

**To Collar Beef the best Way.**

Take a piece of the thin Flank of Beef, let it be cut broder by two Inches at the thin end than at the thick end; take off the inward and the outward Skins; and if it be a large piece of Beef, then take six Ounces of Salt-Peter, and beat it fine, and a Quart of Peter's Salt, and a Quart of Bay Salt, and beat it very fine, and rub on the Salt-Peter first, and then the Peter-Salt, and then the Bay-salt, and let it lie in Salt a Night and two Days,

*"Unidentified cookbook, c. 1700"—Anonymous*

*Comments*

It should be Leaven Batch, a baker's term. Leaven was a dough left unbaked until it turned sour, when it was baked in a batch (Holme, *Academy,* Bk. 3, Chap. 3, 85).

The letter þ, or thorn, represents a "th" sound. In handwritten documents, the letter often resembles an elaborate "y". Anonymous (1700) and Jane (Bolling) Randolph employ it frequently in these manuscripts, most often in the words "þn" (then) and "þm" (them).

**To Make a Lame pasty**

Take a hind quarter of Lame bone it & lay it in press þn beat your Suite wth: a Roleing pin Sprinkleing watter on it Season it wth: peper Salt Cloves Nutmegg then Lay it under your Meat lett it Stand 2 hou[rs] and 1/2 in the Oven the Same Seasoning for Venson Only butter

———

**To Make Mince Pyes**

Of Mutton or Veal take a Legg of Either & Shread it Small to ——— of Meat ad 8 lb. of Suitt Shread it together then Season it wth: peper Salt Cloves Mace Nutmegg put in 6: lbs. of Currants 2 lbs of Reasons Stond [a] pint of Cannary & Rose watter & Some Sweetmeets Sugar to your tast you may putt in a few apples: if you gett Marrow insted [o]f Suitt theyle be the petter

~ **Canary** was a light and sweet wine imported from the Canary Islands (*OED,* 2:60). **Marrow,** an extracted "soft vascular substance" from the bone cavities of animals, was "regarded as a dainty" (*OED,* 6:182).

The "p" is confused with "b" in the word "petter." This is but one example of such errors found in her culinary collection.

*Contemporary Recipe #1*

you please; then sow it up in a thin cloath very fast and keep it in an upper roome. It will keep in winter a quarter of a year very well. (Blencowe, *Receipt Book,* 5)

*Contemporary Recipe #2*

then take half an Ounce of Nutmegs, half an Ounce of Mace, one Ounce of Pepper and a few Cloves, and beat them all, but not too fine, then wash the Beef in a Pale of Pump-water very clean, and dry it in a course Cloath, then season it with your Spice all over, and roll it up hard, and bind it up close with broad Tape, and put it in a deep Earthen-pot, and put to it a quart of Claret, and a pound of Butter and tie it over with double Paper, or cover it over with course Paste, and bake it with Household Bread; and when it is bak'd, take it out of the Pot, and roul it up in a Course Towel, and tie it at both ends and hang it up to drain till it is cold; then wrap it up in white Pepper, and keep it in a dry place, but not near the Fire, to keep it for use. (Hall, *Queen's Royal Cookery,* 6–7)

**Lamb Pasty:**

Bone your Lamb, cut it four square, season it with Salt, beaten Pepper, Cloves, Mace, Nutmeg, and minc'd Thyme, lay in some Beef-suet and your Lamb thereupon, making a high border about it; then turning over your Sheet, close and bake your Pasty; when it is enough liquor it with Claret, Sugar, Vinegar, and the Yolks of Eggs beaten up together if you would have your Sauce only savoury, and not sweet, let it be Gravy only, or the Baking of Bones in Claret-Wine. (Salmon, *Family Dictionary,* 169)

**To make a Lamb-Pasty.**

Bone your Lamb, skin it, and cut it four square in the manner of a Pasty, season it with Salt, Pepper beaten small, Cloves, Mace, Nutmeg, and minced Thyme: Let your Paste be rich cold buttered Paste: Lay your Lamb upon minced Beef-suet, and put on an high border about it, then turn over your Sheet, close, finish and bake your Pasty; when it is baked and drawn, put in a lear of White-wine, Sugar, Vinegar beaten up with the Yolks of two or three Eggs; if you would have it savoury and not sweet, add the more Spice in the seasoning, and let your Lear be only Gravey, or the baking of Bones and some Meat in Claret-wine as before: This you may observe in all other baked Meats betwixt the Lears of sweet and savoury. (Hall, *Queen's Royal Cookery,* 42–43)

**A minc't pie**

Take a Legge of Mutton, and cut the best of the flesh from the bone, and parboyle it well: then put to it three pound of the best Mutton suet, and shred it, very small: then spread it abroad, and season it with *Pepper* and *Salt, Cloues* and *Mace;* then put in good store of *Currants,* great *Raisins* and *Prunes* cleane washt and pickt, a few *Dates* slic't, and some *Orenge* pills slic't: then being all well mixt together, put it into a coffin, or into diuers coffins, and so bake them: and when they are serued vp open the liddes, and strow store of *Sugar* on the top of the meate, and vpon the lid. And in this sort you may also bake Beefe or Veale; onley the Beefe would not bee parboyld, and the Veale will aske a double quantity of Suet. (Markham, *English House-Wife,* 114)

———

*"Unidentified cookbook, c. 1700"—Anonymous*

*Comments*

**To Make Brawn of a hogs head**

[Ta]ke the head & pull out all the Bones & Lay it in watter for a day or tw[o] [shi]fting ye watter till ye Blood is Clean out then take the think End of one [Flan]ck to ye thick end of ye other & Rowl it up as hard as you can then [boi]l it till it is tender then take it up & Sett it on end then weigh ——— till it is quit[e] Cold then [putt] it in[to] ———.

~ See pages 80–81 for more about **brawn**. **Shift** or **shifting** meant changing the water in which something was steeped or changing water for another (*OED*, 9:693).

Various sixteenth- and seventeenth-century cookbooks contained recipes for brawn, but none available to the author utilized only the head of a hog.

Mary Randolph did possess a recipe that gave elaborate instructions for collaring a calf's head, but not that of a hog. After cooking it, her collared meat was pressed (presumably by weights) and then kept in a mixture of vinegar and water (Randolph, *Virginia Housewife*, 52). Anonymous (1700)'s version hinted that her collar of brawn was also weighted down as it cooled.

**To make a Fricassy of Mushrooms**

Make ready your Mushrooms as you do for Stewing, & whe[n] you have poured away ye black liquar that Comes from them put them into a Frying-pan with a piece of Sweet Butter little parsly, Thyme, Sweet-Marjoram; a piece of Onion Shr[ed] very Small, a little Salt, & fine beaten Pepper, fry them till they are enough, then having ye above-mentioned Lear ready, put it to ye Mushrooms while they are in ye pan toss them two or three times, turn them forth & Serve the[m].

———

**To Make a Giblet-Pye.**

Let ye Goose-Giblets be Scalded & well picked then Set them over ye fire with just Water enought to Cover them, Seasoning them pretty high with Salt, Pepper, an Onion, & a bunch of Sweet-herbs when thay are Stewed very tender take them out of ye Liquor & Set them by to Cool afterwards thay are to be put into a Standing Pye or into a pan with good Puff-paste round it, a Conveniant quantity of Butter, & ye yolks of hard Eggs, Balls of forced Meat may also be laid over them, leaving a hole on ye top of ye lid to pour in half ye Liquor ye Giblets were Stewed in, just befo[re] your Pye is Set in ye Oyen.

~ **Force-meat** is "meat chopped fine, spiced, and highly seasoned" and was "chiefly used for stuffing or as a garnish" (*OED*, 4:422).

Oyen (oven) is but one of several such errors found in these manuscripts.

**Dowlet-Pye**

Let Veal roasted or parboil'd be Chopt Small with Beef Su[et] and Sweet-harbs Seasoning them with Sugar, Nutmeg and Cinnamon then beat as many Eggs as will moisten the whole Mass & make it up into Balls Shaptd like Eggs, Sticking a Date in ye middle of Each. these are to be lade in a Pye with some Plums over them, either ripe or dry Dry, according to ye Season of ye Year. a little before [y]ou Draw it pour in White

~ **Dowlet** is not found in the *OED* or other available dictionaries.

*Contemporary Recipe #1*

**To boil Brawn.**

Take your brawn four and twentie houres, and wash and scrape it four or five times, then take it out of the water, and lay it on a fair table, then throw a handfull of Salt on every coller, then bind them up as fast as you can, with Hemp, Bass, or Incle, then put them into your kettle when the water boyleth, and when it boileth, scum it clean, let it boil untill it be so tender that you may thrust a straw through it, then let it cool untill the next morning, by the souced meats you may know who to souce it. (Kent, *Gentlewoman's Delight,* 75–76)

*Contemporary Recipe #2*

———

*Contemporary Recipe #1*

**Mushrooms Fricassed:**

Having stewed them, put away the Liquor, and put them into a Frying-pan with a piece of Butter, some stript Thyme, sweet Majoram, and an Onion shred very small, also a little Salt, and beaten Pepper; and when they are fryed, make a Leer, or Sauce, with three or four Eggs dissolved with some Claret-Wine, and the Juice of two or three Oranges, grated Nutmeg, and the Gravy of a Leg of Mutton; shake them well, and give them three or four tosses in the Pan: dish them, and garnish the Dish with Orange and Lemon, and rub it with a Shallot, or Onion, and so serve 'em up. (Salmon, *Family Dictionary,* 213–14)

*Contemporary Recipe #2*

———

*Contemporary Recipe #1*

**39. Jiblet Pye.**

Take your Jiblets and scald them, put them on the Fire and stew them very tender; season them with Salt and Pepper pretty high, with a Bunch of sweet Herbs, an Onion, and just Water enough to cover them; then take them out of the Liquor and let them stand to be cold; then put them in your Patty-pan with good Puff-paste-round it, and put in what quantity of Butter you think fitting, with the Yolks of hard Eggs, and lay over it Force-meat-balls; and when you have lidded your Pye leave a hole a top, and just as it goes into the Oven, put in half the Liquor that the Jiblet was stewed in; bake it not too much; send it up. (Howard, *England's Newest Way* [1710], 19)

*Contemporary Recipe #2*

**A Giblet Pie**

Your Goose Giblets being scalded and well picked, set them over the Fire with just Water enough to cover them, seasoning them pretty high with Salt, Pepper, an Onion, and a Bunch of sweet Herbs. When they are stewed very tender, take them out of the Liquor, and set them by to cool: Afterwards they are to be put into a standing Pie, or into a Pan with good Puff-paste round it, a convenient Quantity of Butter, and the Yolks of hard Eggs: Balls of Forced-Meat may also be laid over them, leaving a Hole on the Top of the Lid, to pour in half the Liquor the Giblets were stewed in, just before your Pie is set in the Oven. (*Lady's Companion,* 2:120)

*Contemporary Recipe #1*

**33. Dowlet Pye**

Take Veal perboil'd or roasted, and cut it small, with sweet Herbs and Beef-suet; then put some into seasoned with Sugar, Nutmeg and Cinnamon if you like it; then beat as many Eggs as will wet it; then make it like Eggs, and stick a Date in the middle of each of them, and lay them in a Pye, and put some dried Plumbs over them, and if in time of year put in ripe Plumbs; then take White-wine, Sugar and Butter,

*Contemporary Recipe #2*

**A Dowlet Pye.**

Let a Leg of Veal be either roasted or parboil'd; then mince it small with Beef-Suet, and sweet Herbs. Then put some into the Pye, season'd with Nutmeg and Cinnamon; then beat as many Eggs as will wet it; and make it up like Eggs, and stick a Date in the middle of each of them, and lay them in a Pye, and lay some dry'd Plums over them; then put it in the Oven; before you draw it, take White-wine, Sugar and Butter; and

*"Unidentified cookbook, c. 1700"—Anonymous*

Wine, Butter & Sugar Scalding-hot and give it a shake or two—in order to be Sent to table.

**Egg-Pye**

Having boil'd twenty Eggs, mince ye yolks Small & put to them three or four Spoonfuls of ye best Canary-Wine; with the same quantity of Orange-flower Water Season ye whole with fine Sugar, Nutmeg, Cloves & Mace, & lay a Layer of [w]et & dry Sweet-Meats then beat up a pound & a quarter of fresh Butter with half a Pint of Cream, and mingle all ye ingredients together in order to be put into your Pye. When it is drawn pour in a little heated White-Wine beaten with ye yolks of an Egg greated Nutmeg and Sugar.

**To make a Calfs-Chaldron-Pye**

**To Stew Pigeons**

Take six Pigeons with their Giblets Cut the Pigeons in quart[ers] put þm. in ye. Stew-pan wth. two blades of mace, a little pepper & salt, & just water enough to stew þm. without burning, when they are tender thick ye liquor wth. ye yolk of two egg, three Spoonfulls of thick Sweet cream, a bit of butter & a little shred thyme & parsly, shake þm. all together and garnish it with lemon.

**To make Stove Veal**

Take a fillet of Veal of a Cow-Calf cut away an jnch of ye. middle bone on each side, that ye meat may lie flat in ye Stew-pan. Cut of ye Udder, and Slice it in long pieces, and roll it in Seasoning of pepper. Salt. Nutmeg, & Sweet-herbs finely shred make holes through ye. fillet & stick in these Seasond pieces of fat Udder as thick as you Can till ye whole is Stuffd in, then lay

*Comments*

~ **Sweet meats,** in this context, are found in the shape of "preserved or candied fruits, sugared nuts, etc." (*OED,* 10:314).

~ This recipe was left unfinished.

———

~ **Capers** are the flower buds of a shrub, *Capparis spinosa,* and are used for pickling (*OED,* 2:91).

Iurning is clearly written as such. The word "turning" is intended.

*Contemporary Recipe #1*

and pour it in a little before you draw it, scald the Wine, and give it a shake or two together; send it. (Howard, *England's Newest Way* [1710], 16)

**Egg-Pye**

Boil eighteen Eggs, cut the Yolks small, and put to them three or four Spoonfuls of Orange-flower Water, and as much Sack; season it with Cloves, Mace, Nutmeg, fine Sugar, and lay a layer of wet and dry Sweetmeats; then melt a Pound and a quarter of sweet Butter; beat it with half a Pint of Cream; mix all these Ingredients together, and put it in your Pye, and bake it; when it is drawn, scald a little White wine, and thicken it with the Yolk of an Egg; put in Sugar and grated Nutmeg; pour it on your Pye; give it a Shake or two, and serve it. (Middleton, *Five Hundred New Receipts,* 1:203)

**To make a Calf's Chaldron Pie**

Take a Calves Chaldron, half boil it & cool it; when it is cold, mince it as small as grated bread, with half a pound of Marrow; season it with salt, beaten Cloves; Mace Nutmeg, a little Onion, and some of the outmost rind of a Lemon minced very small, and wring in the juyce of a half a lemon, and them mix all to-gether, then make a piece of of puff paste, and lay a Leaf thereof in a silver dish. of the bigness to contain the meat, then put in your meat, and cover it with another Leaf of the same paste, and bake it; and when it is baked take it out and open it, and put in the juyce of two or three oranges, stir it well together then cover it agian and serve it. Be sure none of your orange kernels be among your Pye-meat. (W. M., *Compleat Cook,* 10–11)

**To Stew Pidgeons**

Take six Pigeons with their Giblets cut the Pigeons in Quarters, and put them in the stew-pan wth two blades of Mace, a little Pepper, and salt, and just Water enough to to Stew them without burning, when they are tender, Thick the Liquor wth the yolk of one Egg, three Spoonfuls of of thick Sweet Cream, a bit of Butter, and a little shred Thyme and Parsly; shake þm all up together, and garnish it with Lemon. (Several Hands, *Collection* [1714], 10–11)

**To make Stove Veal**

Take a Fillet of Veal of a Cow Calf, cut away an Inch of the middle Bone on each side, that the Meat may lie flat in the Stew-pan; cut off the Udder, and slice it in long Pieces, and roll it in Seasoning of Pepper, Salt, Nutmeg, and Sweet-herbs finely shred; make Holes through the Fillet, and stick in these season'd Pieces of fat Udder as thick as you can, 'till the whole is stuff'd

*Contemporary Recipe #2*

pour into it; let it scald a little, give it a shake or two, and serve it up. (Nott, *Cook's and Confectioner's Dictionary,* #16)

———

**To make a Chadron Pie**

Take a Calf's Chadron, and parboil it, then when it is cold, shred it very small; then shred a pound of Suet very fine, then season it with half an ounce of Cinnamon, and two Nutmegs, and a little beaten Cloves and Mace, a little shred Limon and Orange peel, four good Pippins shred small, a little Rose-water, and a half a pint of Sack if it be a large Chardon, if not, a quarter of a pint will be enough, and a pound of and a half of Currans; mix all these together with a quarter of a pound of Sugar and a little Sack; then fill your Pies or Florendine with this Meat. This Florendine mustbak'd in puff Paste, or cold Paste. (Hall, *Queen's Royal Cookery,* 30–31)

———

———

*"Unidentified cookbook, c. 1700"—Anonymous*

*Comments*

butter in ye pan, & put in the meat, Set it on a gentle fire, lurning and Shaking it as you have occasion then scum off the fat, and put in one onion stuck with Cloves a lemon pared. and Cut in half, & Squeezed in Continue to shake it, if your fire be as Slow as as it ought to be, twill take five hours to make it ready, one hour before it is so, put in a large pint of Strong broth, when ye meat is just enough Set on a pint of Oysters, & a pint of mushrooms, with a little of ye. broth, & two Spoon-fulls of Capers. let ye meat be again Clean Scum'd from the fat, before you use ye liquor, thicken with flower & pour it into ye. dish to ye meat.

**A very good Pease-Soup**

Put three or four pound of lean Coarse beef, with three pints of peass, into two gallons of water, let it boil till ye meat is all to rags, and half an hour before you strain it out, put in two or three Anchovis, then strain it from ye husks and meat, and put in ye sauce-pan as much as much as you want for that meal with an onion stuck with Cloves, a race of ginger bruised, a little pepper let it boil thus near half an hour, Stir in a piece of butter, and fry some force-meat balls, bacon, and french-bread Cut in dice, with Spinnage boiled green to put to it in the dish.

~ **Race of ginger** referred both to a measure and the roots of ginger (*OED*, 8:87–88).

**Pease-Soup for Lent or any Fasting day.**

Put a quart of good breaking pease to three quarts of water, and boil them till they are tender then take out some of the Clear liquar, and strain the pease as Clean as you can from the husks. take some butter and boil it, and when it breaks in the middle put to it an onion and some mint Cut very small Spinnage and sorril and a little Sallery Cut large. stir it often, and let it boyl about a quarter of an hour then shake in some flower with one hand, and some of your thin liquor with the other. then put in the thick strained liquar some pepper, mace, and salt and boil it an hour longer. then put into as much as will make a large dish one pint of sweet thick Cream put a french-roll Crispt. and dipt in milk in the middle of the dish.

**Green Pea Soup.**

Make it exactly as you do the dried pea soup, only in place of the celery-seed, put a handful of mint chopped small, and a pint of young peas which must be boiled in the soup till tender; thicken it with a quarter of a pound of butter, and two spoonsful of flour. (Randolph, *Virginia Housewife*, 34)

~ Mary's simplified recipe reflected the evolutionary changes in recipes over time and the changing tastes of society.

**To Pot Cheshire Cheese**

Take three pound of Cheshire Cheese & put it in a morter wth. half a pound of ye best fresh butter you can get pound þm. together, & in ye beating add a glass or or two of rich Canary. & half an ounce of mace finely beat & sifted that it may not be discern'd: when all is extremely well mix'd. press it hard down into a

*Contemporary Recipe #1*

*Contemporary Recipe #2*

in; then lay Butter in the Pan, and put in the Meat; set it on a gentle Fire, turning and shaking it as you have occasion; then scum off the Fat, and put in one Onion stuck with Cloves, a Lemon pared, and cut in half, and squeez'd in: Continue to shake it. If your Fire be as slow as it ought to be, 'twill take Five Hours to make it ready: One Hour before it is so put in a large pint of strong Broth. When the Meat is just enough, set on a pint of Oysters, and a pint of Mushrooms, with a little of the Broth, and two spoonfulls of Capers. Let the Meat be again clean scum'd from the Fat, before you use the Liquor; thicken this with Flower, and pour it into the Dish to the Meat. 'Tis a grateful, savoury Dish. (Several Hands, *Collection* [1714], 28)

**A very good Pease-Soup**

Put three or four pound of lean coarse Beef, with three pints of Pease, into two gallons of Water; let it boil 'till the Meat is all to rags; and half an hour before you strain it out, put in two or three Anchovies; then strain it from the Husks and Meat, and put into the Sauce-pan as much as you want for that Meal, with an Onion stuck with Cloves, a race of Ginger bruised, a little faggot of Thyme, Savory, and Parsley, and a little Pepper: Let it boil thus near half an hour; stir in a piece of Butter, and fry some Forc'd-meat-Balls, Bacon, and French-bread cut in Dice, with Spinnage boiled green, to put to it in the Dish. (Several Hands, *Collection* [1714], 3)

———

**Pease-Soop for Lent, or any Fasting-Day**

Put a quart of good breaking Pease to three quarts of Water, and boil them 'till they are tender; then take out some of the Clear Liquor, and strain the Pease as clean as you can from the Husks: Take some Butter and boil it, and when it breaks in the middle, put to it an Onion an some Mint cut very small, Spinnage and Sorrell, and a little Sallery cut large; stir it often, and let it boil about a quarter of an hour; then shake in some flower with one Hand, and some of your thin Liquor with the other; then put in the thick strained Liquor, some Pepper, Mace, and Salt, and boil it an hour longer; then put into as much as will make a large Dish, one pint of sweet thick Cream; put a French-Roul crispt and dipt in Milk, in the middle of the Dish. (Several Hands, *Collection* [1714], 5–6)

———

**To Pot Cheshire Cheese**

Take three Pounds of Cheshire Cheese, and put it in a Mortar, wth half a Pound of the best fresh Butter, pound them together and in the beating add two Glasses of rich canary, [Sack] and half an Ounce of Mace, so finely beat and sifted that it may not be discern'd; when all is extremely well mix'd, press it down

———

*"Unidentified cookbook, c. 1700"—Anonymous*

gallypo[t] cover it with melted butter. & keep it cool a slice of this exceeds all ye cream cheeses that can be made.

**To make Mince Pyes. Mrs. Street**

Take one pound of Suet, One pound Currants, One pound of apples being right golden runnets, one pound of sugar, one ounce of Cloves Mace & Nutmegs each beaten together the juice of two Lemons & one Sevil Orange with the rinds finedly greated, a gill of sack, Candyed Orang and Lemon Peel & Citron,

**To Caveech Fish.**

When ye fish is gutted and wash'd, Cut it in round peices, and Split the head, when so done, wipe them very dry, then take Nutmeg, Cloves, and Mace, and English pepper, beat them very fine, and mix salt with them, and Season the fish there with, then fry them in Sweet Oyl, till it is brown and dry, turning every peice on all sides. then set them a Cooling, and take as much Vinegar as will Cover the fish, boyling in the Vinegar 2 or 3 Cloves of garlick, and some whole pepper, when boyld together take it off of the fire, and Set them a Cooling, and when all is Cold, put the fish into a pot, then pour the pickle to it, when so done pour half a pint of Sweet Oyl [c]over, tye it up Close and keep it for use. the above receipt is Calculated for about 8 lbs of fish. the firmest fish is the best to be done, and if done well, will keep twelve Months

**To Pickle Green Peppers**

Cut out ye Seeds Leaveing the Stock on: put þm in Coold watter make astrong Brine that will bare an Egg, then wash them out and put them in ye Pickle and keep them Over a hott Emberse coverd clous. till they turn Yellow then shift them unto fair watter Evere day till they Green: Then put them into Veneger t[o] Use.

**To Pickle Codlins like mangoe.**

Make a brine of Salt and water; Strong enough to bear an egg, into which put half a hundred of the fairest and largest Codlins you Can get, they must be full grown but not full ripe, let them lie in this brine nine & ten days, Shifting ye pickle every other day, then dry them and very Carefully Scoop out ye Core, take out ye. Stalk so whole, as that it may fit in again and you may leave ye eye in. if you dont put your Scoop quite through fill it in ye room of ye Core, with ginger sliced thi[n] and Cut short, a Clove of garlick, and whole mustard-seed, as much as it will hold, put in ye piece,

*Comments*

~ **Gill** is a specific measurement for liquids, being one fourth of a standard pint (*OED,* 4:163).

**To Caveach Fish**

Cut the fish in pieces the thickness of your hand, wash it and dry it in a cloth, sprinkle on some pepper and salt, dredge it with flour, and fry it a nice brown; when it gets cold, put in a pot with a little chopped onion between the layers, take as much vinegar as will cover it, mix with it some oil, pounded mace, and whole black pepper, pour it on and stop the pot closely. This is a very convenient article, as it makes an excellent and ready addition to a dinner or supper. When served up, it should be garnished with green fennel or parsley. (Randolph, *Virginia Housewife,* 103–4)

~ One can see the similarities between Anonymous (1700)'s version and Mary Randolph's rendition.

**Caveech** refers to a certain way mackerel is pickled, "according to a West Indian method" (*OED,* 2:203). The **sweet oil** referred to any oil of pleasant or mild taste, especially olive oil (*OED,* 10:310).

~ This type of recipe is seldom found in seventeenth- or eighteenth-century publications.

~ **Codlins** (or codlings) in this instance refers to a variety of apple. With its "elongated" shape and "rather tapering towards the eye," it was known as "Kentish Codling, etc." (*OED,* 2:584). **Mango** is the fruit of *Mangifera indica,* found in India and other tropical regions. The green fruit was used for "pickles and conserves" (*OED,* 6:118).

*Contemporary Recipe #1*

*Contemporary Recipe #2*

hard into a Gallipot, cover it with melted Butter and keep it cool; a slice of this exceed any of the Cream Cheeses that can possibly be made and is generally more acceptable. (Several Hands, *Collection,* [1724], 1:20)

———

———

**To Pickle Mackerel, call'd Caveach**

Cut your Mackarel into round Pieces, and divide one into five or six Pieces: To six large Mackarel you may take one ounce of beaten Pepper, three large Nutmegs, a little Mace, and a handful of Salt; mix your Salt and beaten Spice together, and make two or three holes in each Piece, and thrust the Seasoning into these holes with your finger; rub the Pieces all over with the Seasoning; fry them brown in Oil, and let them stand 'till they are cold; then put them into Vinegar, and cover them with Oil. They will keep, well cover'd, a great while, and are delicious. (Several Hands, *Collection,* [1714], 43)

———

———

———

**To Pickle Codlins, like Mangoe**

Make a Brine of Salt and Water strong enough to bear an Egg, into which put half a Hundred of the fairest and largest Codlins you can get; they must be full grown, but not full ripe; let them lie in this Brine nine or ten Days, shifting the Pickle every other Day; then dry them, and very carefully scoop out the Core: Take out the Stalk so whole, as that it may fit in again; and you may leave the Eye in, if you don't put your Scoop quite through: Fill it, in the room of the Core, with Ginger sliced thin, and cut short, a Clove or Garlick, and whole Mustard-seed, as much as it will hold: Put

———

*"Unidentified cookbook, c. 1700"—Anonymous* | *Comments*

and tie it up tight, make your pickle of as much white-wine Vinegar as will Cover them with sliced ginger, Cloves of garlick, & whole mustard-seed, pore this pickle boiling hot upon them every other day, for a fortnight or three weeks Stone jars are best for all Sorts of Pickles And this is as good a way any for a midling large Cucomber, only dont let them to put ye. garlick and mustard-seed in, for they keep much longer and eat much Crisper, if you let them be whole.

**To Pickle Elder Buds**

Take ye largest & youngest shoots of elder, which puts out ye middle of May ye middle stalks is best peel off ye outward peel or skin & lay þm. in a strong brine of salt & water for one night, & then dry þm. in a cloth, piece by piece, in ye mean time make your pickle of half whit-wine & half beer-vinegar to each quart of pickle you must put an ounce of white or red pepper, an ounce of ginger sliced, a little mace, & a few corns of jamica pepper, when ye spice has boil'd in ye pickle pour it hot upon ye shoots, stop þm. close, & set ye jar two hours before ye fire, turning it often.

~ Recipes for pickling elder buds were not often published in the seventeenth- or eighteenth-century cookbooks, but the following recipes help give a general time frame.

The scientific name for **elder buds** is *Sambucus nigra,* a low elder tree or shrub (*OED,* 3:72). **Jamaica pepper**, an aromatic spice made from dried berries (*Eugenia Pimenta*), came from the Allspice tree of the West Indies (*OED,* 1:241; 5:548).

**To order a Runnit Bag for a Junket**

Take a Calves bag clean it well with warm water & dry it well with a Cloath Then take a good handfull of Cloves half a handfull of Salt lay these thick on the bagg inside and out besever let the inside of the bagg be turnd out to dry the butter, put it to dry in an Oven or the Sun & when dry'd hang it up in a paper bagg for use and it will keep good 12 Month as often as it gives dry it again

**To Prepare the Stomach of the Calf for Rennet.**

As soon as it is taken out cut it open length-way, empty it of its contents and wash it in several changes of warm water, rub it with salt and let it remain two or three days, then wash it, stretch it on slender sticks and dry it in the shade; when as dry as parchment, which it will resemble, put it in paper bags and keep it in a dry place; it will remain good two years. (Randolph, *Virginia Housewife,* 55)

~ Mary Randolph's version above is shorter and more streamlined, while another Randolph descendant, E. Tucker-Coalter, had her own version at the far right.

Both **Runnet** and **rennet** are archaic (*OED,* 8:913). Defined as a "mass of curdled milk found in the stomach of an unweaned calf or other animal," it is "used for curdling milk in the making of cheese, etc." and is also the "fourth stomach of a ruminant" and thus connected with a "rennet bag" (*OED,* 8:448).

*Contemporary Recipe #1*

in the Piece, and tie it up tight. Make your Pickle of as much White-wine-Vinegar as will cover them, with sliced Ginger, Cloves of Garlick, and whole Mustard-seed: Pour this Pickle boiling hot upon them every other Day, for a Fortnight or Three Weeks. Stone-Jars are best for all sorts of Pickles.

And this is as good a Way as any for a midling large *Cucumber:* only don't cut them to put the Garlick and Mustard-seed in; for they keep much longer, and eat much crisper, if you let them be whole. But neither *Cucumbers, Peaches,* nor *Melons* are comparable to Codlins, for imitating the right *Mangoe.* (Several Hands, *Collection* [1714], 46–47)

**To pickle Elder-buds in *March*, before the tree leaves.**

Having gathered what quantity you please before they are blown, and put them into wine-vinegar, they are a good sallet. If in case they are full blown, as in *June,* they serve to make strong Elder-vinegar, and themselves no sallet: This Vinegar is good to make sauce for divers sorts of meat. (Rabisha, *Whole Body* [1673], 2)

**To make a Rennet Bag.**

Let the Calf such as much as he will, just before his is killed: then take the Bag out of the Calf, and let it lie twelve hours, covered over in stinging Nettles till 'tis very red; then take out your Curd, and wash your Bag clean, and salt it within-side and without, and let it lie sprinkled with Salt twenty-four hours, and wash your Curd in warm new Milk, and pick it, and put away all that is yellow and hollow, and keep what is white and close, and wash it well, and sprinkle it with Salt, and when the Bag has lain twenty-four hours, put it into the Bag again, and put to it three spoonfulls of the Stroakings of a Cow, beat up with the yolk of an Egg or two, twelve Cloves, and two blades of Mace and put a Skewer through and hand it in a Pot; then make the Rennet-water thus:

Take half a pint of fair Water, a little Salt, six tops of the reddish of black Thorn, and as many Sprigs of Burnet, and two of Sweet-marjoram., boil these in the Water, and strain it out, when 'tis cold, put one half in the Bag, and the Bag lye in the other half, and take it out as you use it, and when you want, make more Rennet, which you may do six or seven times; three spoonfuls of this Rennet will make a large *Cheshire* or *Chedder* Cheese, and half as much to a common Cheese. (E. Smith, *The Compleat Housewife* [1729], 55–56)

*Contemporary Recipe #2*

**To pickle Elder, or many other buds of trees in the Spring, that useth to serve for Spring-sallets.**

Give them one or two walms with Vinegar, Salt, whole Pepper, long Mace, and a Lemmon-Pill cut in pieces, then drain them, and let the Buds and the Liquor cool severally; afterwards put them in a Pot, and cover them with your Pickle. (Rabisha, *Whole Body* [1673], 8)

**Rennet bag to prepare for use-**

Let the Veal suck a short time before it is killed- Open the Rennet bag and take out, on a clean dish the Curd you find therein- Pick it clean of Motes and hairs- wash it quickly in strong salt and Water Press it dry, and sprinkle it well with salt- wash the Rennet bag in several waters and steep it in strong salt and Water an hour or two- pick it quite white and Rub the inside well with salt put in the Curd and tie it close- Have a small stone pot lay salt at the bottom and put in yr. Rennet bag surrounding it closely with salt- The night before you wish to use it take out the Rennet bag wash it clean of the salt (but do not untie it) in cold water- put it in a pint of Cold to steep all night, and in the morning put back the Rennet bag into the Pot of Salt as before-Bottle the Water it was steeped in- it will keep in a cool place some days- If you wish to make Curd put a spoonful of this Water to each quart of milk in the Morning, while warm from the Cow- It will turn in a short time[.]~ (Tucker Coalter, *Cookbook,* 15–16)

*"Unidentified cookbook, c. 1700"—Anonymous*

*Comments*

**To make a Junket**

Take a bitt of the Same bagg the bigness of half a Crown Steep it in 4 Spoonfulls of Rose water but for want of it use warm water which Liquor will do for 3 pints of milk to mix it in blood warm if you like the milk Sweet Sweettend it before the runnet is in Observe it may be fit for ye Table in an hours time

~ **Junket** was the height of elegant dining in the seventeenth century because of its rich ingredients. Only a few cookbooks at the time included this recipe. Defined by *OED* as a dish consisting of sweetened and flavored curds, it was topped with a layer of scalded cream. Especially associated with Devonshire, it was also known as curds and cream in other districts (*OED,* 5:632).

**A Whipt Sillibub Extraordinary**

Take a quart of Cream: and boil it let it Stand till tis Cold then take a pint of white wine; pare a Lemon thin, and Steep the peel in the wine two howers before you use it, to this add the juice of a Lemon and as much Sugar as will make it very Sweet: put all this together into a bason & whisk it all one way till tis pritty thick: Fill your Glasses and keep it a day before you use it, twill keep good three or four days. Let your Cream be full Measure and your wine rather less, if you like it perfum'd put a grain or two or Amber-greese

~ **Sillabub,** or syllabub, a popular "drink or dish made of milk or cream, is curdled by an admixture of wine, cider or other acid, and often sweetened and flavored" (*OED,* 9:50). **Amber-greese** refers to ambergris, a waxy and marbled substance usually found floating at sea. Created by the secretions in the intestines of the sperm whale, it is used in perfumery (*OED,* 1:269).

**Eggs Minc'd Pyes**

Take Six Eggs, boyle them very hard and Shred them Small. Shred the double quantity of good Suet very fine, put Currants neatly wash'd and pick'd, one pound or more if your Eggs ware large; the peel of one Lemon very fine Shred, half the juice and five or Six Spoonfuls of Sack, Mace Nutmeg Sugar and a little Salt, Candy'd Citron or Orange-peel if you would have them rich.

~ **Sack** was a "dry wine," usually from a "class of white wines formerly imported from Spain and the Canaries" (*OED,* 9:10).

**To make Fry'd Cream**

Take a quart of good new Cream, the yolks of Seven eggs, a bit of Lemon-peel, a greated Nutmeg, two Spoonfuls of Sack, as much Orange-flower water, butter your Sauce-pan, and put it over the fire, Stir it all the while one way with a little white whisk, and as you Stir, strew in flower very lightly, till tis thick and Smooth, then tis boil'd enough, and may be pour'd out upon a Cheese-plate or Mazareen, Spread it with a knife exactly even, about halfe an jnch thick, then Cut it in diamond-Squares, and fry it in a pan-full of boiling Sweet Suet

~ A **cheese plate** was described as "a small plate, 5 or 6 inches in diameter, used for cheese or the end of dinner" (*OED,* 2:316). Known as a **mazareen** or **mazarine** dish or plate, it is normally made of metal (*OED,* 6:262).

**A very rich Almond-Cream, to Jelly.**

Make a very Strong jelly of hart's horn, and that it may be So, put half a pound of good harts-horn to a quart and a half a pint of water, let it boil away near half, Strain it off through a jelly-bag, then have ready beaten to a very fine paste Six ounces of Almonds, which must be Carefully beat with one Spoonful of good Orange-flower-water, with Six or eight Spoonfuls

~ This was an elegant dessert indeed.

*Contemporary Recipe #1*

*Contemporary Recipe #2*

**To make a Junket.**
Take Ewes or Goats Milk, if you have neither of these then take Cowes Milk, and put it over the fire to warm, then put in a little Runnet to it, then pour it out into a dish and let it cool, then strew on Cinnamon and Sugar, then take some of your aforesaid Cream and lay on it, scrape on Sugar, and serve it. (Kent, *Gentlewoman's Delight,* 105)

**To make excellent Junquet.**
Take new warm Milk from the Cow, put to it a sufficient Quantity of Runit, and when your curd is come take it from the Whey, and strew on it Sugar and cinnamon, over which pour Cream, strewing Rose-water and Sugar upon the Cream. (Middleton, *Five Hundred New Receipts,* 1:161)

**A Whipt Silibub, Extraordinary.**
Take a quart of Cream, and boil it, let it stand 'till 'tis cold; then take a Pint of White-wine; pare a Lemon thin, and steep the Peel in the Wine two Hours before you use it; to this add the Juice of a Lemon, and as much Sugar as will make it very sweet: Put all this together into a Bason, and whisk it all one way 'till 'tis pretty thick: Fill your Glasses and keep it a Day before you use it; 'twill keep good three or four Days. Let your Cream be full Measure, and your Wine rather less. If you like it Perfum'd, put a grain or two of Ambergreese. (Several Hands, *Collection* [1714], 76)

———

**Egg Minc'd-Pyes.**
Take six Eggs, boil them very hard, and shred them small; shred the double quantity of good Suet very fine; put Currants neatly wash'd and pick'd, one pound or more if your Eggs ware large; the Peel of one Lemon very fine shred, half the Juice, and five or six spoonfuls of Sack, Mace, Nutmeg, Sugar, and a little Salt; Candy'd Citron, or Orange-peel, if you have them rich. (Several Hands, *Collection* [1714], 92–93)

———

**To make Fry'd Cream**
Take a quart of good new Cream, the Yolks of seven Eggs, a bit of Lemon-peel, a grated Nutmeg, two spoonfuls of Sack, as much Orange flower Water: Butter your Sauce-pan, and put it over the Fire; stir it all the while one way with a little white Whisk, and as you stir, strew in Flower very lightly, 'till 'tis thick and smooth; then 'tis boil'd enough, and may be pour'd out upon a Cheese-plate or Mazareen; spread it with a Knife exactly even, about half an Inch thick, then cut it in Diamond-squares, and fry it in a Pan-full of boiling sweet Suet. (Several Hands, *Collection* [1714], 71–72)

———

**A very Rich Almond Cream, to Jelly.**
Make a very strong Jelly of Hart's horn; and that it may be so, put half a pound of good Harts-horn to a quart and half a pint of Water; let it boil away near half; strain it off through a Jelly-bag; then have ready beaten to a very fine Paste six ounces of Almonds, which must be carefully beat with one spoonful of good Orange-flower-Water, with six or eight spoonfuls

———

*"Unidentified cookbook, c. 1700"—Anonymous* | *Comments*

of Cream, then take a near as much Cream as you have jelly & put both in a Skillet, & Strain in your almonds, Sweeten it to your taste, Set it over ye fire, & Stir it wth. Care Constantly till it is ready to boil So take it off & keep it Stirring till is near Cold, then pour it into narrow-bottomd-glasses, when you would turn it out put your glasses into warm water a minute.

**To make a Pretty Sort of Flummery.**

Put three large handfuls of Oat-meal ground Small, into two quarts of fair water, let it Steep a day and Night, then pour off the Clear water, and put the Same quantity of fresh water to it Strain it through a fine hair-Sieve, and boil it till as thick as hasty-pudding, Stir it all the while, that it may be extremely Smooth, and when you first Strain it out, before you Set it on the fire, put in one Spoonful of Sugar, and two of Orange-flow[er] water; when tis boil'd enough, pour it into shallow dishes, for use.

———

**To make Harts horn Flummery**

Put a pound of harts-horn Shavings to three quarts of Spring-water, boil it very gently over a Soft fire till tis Consumed to one quart, then Strain it through a fine Sieve into your bason, and let it Stand till Cold, then just melt it over the fire, and put to it half a pint of white wine, a pint of new thick Cream, and four Spoonfuls of Orange-flower water Scald your Cream and let it be Cold before you mix it with wine and jelly, put in duble-refind-Sugar to your taste, and then beat it all one way for an hour and an half at least, for if you are not thus Carefull in beating, twill neither mix nor look to please you. let the Cups you pour it into be dipp'd in water, befor you pour it in, keep it ye Cups a day before you use it, then you must turn it out, Eat it wth. Cream or wine.

**To Make heartshorne flummary**

Take a pound of Heartshorn shaveing, put to it three quarts of Spring Water boil it very gently over a Slow fire, till it is Consum'd to a quart. then Strain it through a fine Sive into your Bason and let it stand till Cold, then Just melt it over the fire, and put to it half a point of White Wine apoint of new Thick Cream and let it be cold before your mix it with the Wine and Jelly ----- Sweeten it with double Refine Sugar to your Tast and then beat all one way for an Hour and a half at least, for it you are not thus ----- Careful in beating it will never mix nor look to please you let the Cups you pore it into be dipt in Cold Water it will not Turn out well Keep it in the Cups a Day before you use it When its sent to Table You must Turn it Out and Stick it all over with blanch'd Almonds ----- Cut in Slips -----. (The Compiler [1744], Manuscript cookbook, 94)

~ This is a good example of a recipe used for decades with little change over time.

**To make Orange-Posset.**

Squeeze the juice of two Sevil-Oranges, and one Lemon, into a China-bason that holds about a quart: Sweeten this juice like a Surrup with Double-refind Surgar put to it two Spoonsfuls of Orange-flower-water, and Strain it through a fine Sieve. boil a large pint of

~ See page 278 for more on **possets**. **Seville oranges** are bitter oranges (*Citrus Bigardia*), usually used for making marmalades (*OED*, 9:574). **Double-refined sugar** is the purest grade of sugar. The manufacture of sugar included double refined, refined, refused, sifted, stamped, and strained sugars (*OED*,

*Contemporary Recipe #1* | *Contemporary Recipe #2*

of very thick sweet Cream: then take a near as much Cream as your have Jelly, and put both into a Skellet, and strain in your Almonds, sweeten it to your Taste with Double-refin'd Sugar; set it over the Fire, and stir it with Care constantly 'till 'tis ready to boil; so take them off, and keep it stirring 'till it is near cold; then pour it into narrow-bottom'd Drinking-glasses, in which let it stand a whole Day. When you would turn it out, put your Glasses into warm Water for a Minute, and 'twill turn out like a Sugar-loaf. This is call'd *Steeple Cream*. (Several Hands, *Collection* [1714], 69–70)

**To make a pretty Sort of Flummery.**

Put three large handfuls of Oat-meal ground small, into two quarts of Fair-Water, let it steep a Day and Night; then pour off the clear Water, and put the same quantity of fresh Water to it; strain it through a fine Hair-Sieve, and boil it 'till tis as thick as Hasty-pudding; stir it all the while, that it may be extremely smooth; (and when you first strain it out, before you set it on the Fire, put in one spoonful of Sugar, and two of good Orange-flow(er)-Water,) When 'tis boil'd enough, pour it into shallow Dishes, for your Use. (Several Hands, *Collection* [1714], 74)

———

**To make Hart's-horn Flummery.**

Put a pound of Harts-horn-Shavings to three quarts of Spring-Water, boil it very gently over a soft Fire 'till 'tis consumed to one quart; then strain it through a fine Sieve into your Bason, and let it stand 'till cold; then just melt it over the Fire, and put to it half a pint of White-wine, a pint of new thick Cream, and four spoonfuls of Orange-flower-Water; scald your Cream, and let it be cold before your mix it with the Wine and Jelly; put in double-refin'd Sugar to your Taste, and then beat it all one way for an Hour and a half at least; For if you are not thus carefull in beating, 'twill neither mix nor look to please you. Let the Cups your pour it into be dip'd in clean Water for if they are dry, it will not turn out well: Keep it in the Cups a Day before you use it. When 'tis sent to Table, you must turn it out, and stick it all over, the top the blanch'd Almonds cut in Slips. Eat it in Cream, or Wine, which you like best. (Several Hands, *Collection* [1714], 75)

———

**To make Orange-Posset.**

Squeeze the Juice of two *Sevil*-Oranges, and one Lemon, into a *China*-Bason that holds about a quart; sweeten this Juice like a Syrop with Double-refin'd Sugar, put to it two spoonfuls of Orange-flower-Water, and strain it through a fine Sieve; boil a large pint of

———

*"Unidentified cookbook, c. 1700"—Anonymous*

thick Cream, with some of the Orange-peel in it Cut thin when tis pretty Cool: pour it into the bason of juice through a funil, which must be held as high as you Can from the bason. it must Stand a day before you use it when it goes to table, Stick Slips of Candy'd Orange, Lemon, and Citron-peel on the top.

**To make a very good Barley-Gruil.**

Of three Ounces of Pearl-barley make a quart of barley-water, Shift it once or twice, put to it four ounces of Currants Clean pick'd and washed, when they are plumpt, pour the gruel out to Cool a little, and beat up the yolks of three eggs and put into it, with half a pint of White-wine, and half a pint of new thick Cream, the Peel of a Lemon, and as much Sugar as you like, Stur it gently over the fire till tis as thick as Cream. Tis a pretty wholsome Spoon-meat for Suppers.

**C--- Hargrave Pudding**

Take one pound of Currants, one pound of Suit, Six Eggs three Spoonfuls of flower, Nutmeg and Salt, Cut the Suet Small and boyle it four hours,

**An Excellent plumb pudding,**

Take one pound of Suet Shred very Small and Sifted, one pound of Reasons Ston'd, four Spoonfuls of flower, and four Spoonfuls of Sugar five Eggs but three whites, beat the Eggs with a little Salt, tie it up Close, and boil it four Hours at least.

**Panada for a Sick or weak Stomack,**

Put the Crumb of a penny white loaf grated into a quart of Cold water, Set both on the fire together, with a blade of Mace: When tis boiled Smooth take it off the fire, and put in a bit of Lemon peel the juice of a Lemon, A Glass of Sack and Sugar to your taste: this is very Nourishing, and never offends the Stomack, Some Season with butter sugar adding Currants which on Some Occasions are proper: but the first is the most grateful and Innocent,

**A Pancake Pudding,**

Take a quart of Milk, four Eggs, two large Spoonfuls of flower, a little Salt and a very little grated Ginger, butter your Dish, and bake it, pour melted butter over it when it Comes out of the Oven: tis a Cheap and very Acceptable pudding, being less offensive to ye Stomack then fry'd pancakes

*Comments*

10:114). **Slips** presumably refer to the peels. The word is defined as dialectic for "to strip, peel, skin" or an "excised piece of the form" (*OED,* 9:216, 221). It is believed that Anonymous (1700) meant something similar, such as strips of peel.

———

~ Col. William Byrd commented that he "ate cold lamb" with a person whose abbreviated name has been tentatively translated as "Mrs. Hargrave" (Byrd, *Another Secret Diary,* 78).

———

~ **Panada** is a dish of bread boiled in water into a pulp and flavored with sugar, currants, nutmeg, or other ingredients according to taste (*OED,* 7:414).

———

*Contemporary Recipe #1* | *Contemporary Recipe #2*

thick Cream, with some of the Orange-peel in it cut thin: When 'tis pretty cool, pour it into the Bason of Juice through a Funnel which must be held as high as you can from the Bason: It must stand a Day before you use it. When it goes to Table, stick Slips of Candy'd Orange, Lemon, and Citron-peel on the top. (Several Hands, *Collection* [1714], 70–71)

**To make a very good Barley-Gruel.**
Of three ounces of Pearl-barley make a quart of Barley-Water; shift it once or twice, if it is not white; put to it four ounces of Currants clean pick'd and wash'd; when they are plumpt, pour the Gruel out to cool a little, and beat up the Yolks of three Eggs and put into it, with a half a pint of White-wine, and half a pint of new thick Cream, the Peel of a Lemon, and as much Sugar as you like; stir it gently over the Fire 'till 'tis as thick as Cream. 'Tis a pretty wholsome Spoon-meat for Suppers. (Several Hands, *Collection* [1714], 72–73)

———

———

———

**An excellent Plumb-Pudding.**
Take one pound of Suet, shred very small and sifted, one pound of Raisons ston'd, four spoonsfulls of Flower, and four spoonfuls of Sugar, five Eggs, but three Whites; beat the Eggs with a little Salt: Tie it up close, and boil it four Hours at least. (Several Hands, *Collection* [1714], 89)

———

**Panada, for a Sick or Weak Stomach.**
Put the Crum of a Peny White Loaf grated into a quart of cold Water, set both on the Fire together, with a blade of Mace: When 'tis boiled smooth, take it off the Fire, and put in a bit of Lemon-peel, the Juice of a Lemon, a Glass of Sack, and Sugar to your Taste. This is very Nourishing, and never offends the Stomach. Some season with Butter and Sugar, adding Currants, which on some Occasions are proper; but the first is the most grateful and Innocent. (Several Hands, *Collection* [1714], 76–77)

———

**A Pancake Pudding**
Take a Quart of Milk, four Eggs, two large Spoonfuls of Flower, a little Salt, and a very little grated Ginger; butter your Dish, and bake it; pour melted Butter over it when it comes out of the Oven: 'Tis a cheap and very acceptable Pudding, being less offensive to the Stomach than fry'd Pancakes. (Several Hands, *Collection* [1724], 2:24)

———

*"Unidentified cookbook, c. 1700"—Anonymous*

*Comments*

**T Make Cheescake Meat**

To 1 quart of milk take 6 Eggs break them & beat them well mixt þm with your milk put it over the fier keep it Stiring till it comes to firm and then strain it from the whaye=take 2 Ounces of Butter & work it in well with your hand: when it is hott putt a lettle Salt in then lett it Coole [?] then take 12 Cloves 2 or 3 blades of Mace one Quarter of an Nutmeg beat them & putt þm into ye Curd put in ye Sugar to your tast a Lettle Wine & Rose=watter beat ye yolks of 2 Eggs & Mix with the Curd & put in Currants to your minde

~ While there are several variations on this theme, a close match has not been located to date. The "T" was penned without an "o."

**A Nother**

Take 6 q of milk & 1 Spoonfull of Running So make it into a tender Curd þn take 6 Eggs 1/2 p of milk 1/2 lb of Sugar 1/2 lb Currants 1 lb of Butter melted & 1 Nutmeg greated So mix it up and fill ye Coffins with it

~ Although **running** has not been seen in examined publications so far, this term is an obsolete and dialectic form of "rennet" (*OED,* 8:914).

**To Make a Custare**

Take 3 pts: Cream: & 12 Eggs beatthem & put þm into ye Cream then put in 3/4 lb. Sugar & as much Salt as will ley on a 3 pence: Put in 1/4 pt rose watter then Strain it & blow of ye froth yt will be upon it after it is Strainnd then harden ye Crust & put it in & bake it a lettle above 1/4 an hour

———

**To Make a Maids Dish**

Take ye Curd of 1 qtt of milk tured wth 6 Eggs & 1/4 lb of Almonds past: Break it into ye Curd & put in 1/4 ptt of Cream & 5 or 6 Eggs & 2 Nutmegs: & as much fine Sugar as will Sweeten it & 2 Greans of musk & Ambergrease dissoled into 6 Spoonfuls of Rose=watter: & beak it in a Dish, you may make Cheascaks with the Same ingredients only ad 1/4 lb. of Currance & 2 or 3 oz of Butter

~ Perhaps Anonymous (1700) meant "made dish"? According to Karen Hess, a **made dish** usually meant a special culinary creation conceived and executed by the cook. They were never major dishes and often included eggs (Hess, *Martha Washington's Booke,* 100). In Holme's view, however, a "Made Dish" was a dish "compounded or made of several sorts of Meat minced, or cut in pieces." Then the meat was either stewed or baked in paste, "being liquor'd with Wine, Butter and Sugar" (Holme, *Academy,* Bk. 3, Chap. 3, 83).

**To Make Jumballs**

Take One pound & halfe of flower Dryed One pound of fine Sug:r put it into Six yoalkes of Eggs & three whites Butter ye Bigness of an Egg A quarter of a

~ "A kind of fine sweet cake or biscuit," a **jumbal,** or jumble, was "often made up in the form of rings or rolls" (*OED,* 5:626).

| *Contemporary Recipe #1* | *Contemporary Recipe #2* |
| --- | --- |
| **To make a Cheese-cake the best way**<br>Take two gallons of new milk, put into it two spoonfuls and a half of runnet, heat the milk little less then blood-warm, cover it close with a cloth, until you see the cheese be gathered, then with a scumming dish gently take out the whay, so when you have drained the curd as clean as you can, put the curd into a sieve, and let it drain very well there, then to two quarts of curd take a quart of thick cream, a pound of sweet butter, twelve eggs, a pound and a half of currants, a penny worth of cloves, nutmeg and mace beaten, half a pound of good sugar, a quarter of a pint of rose-water, so mingle it well together, and put it in puff-paste. (Cromwell, *Court & Kitchen,* 136–37) | ——— |
| **A Good Cheese-cake, with Curd.**<br>To a Pound and half of Cheese-curd, put ten Ounces of Butter, beat both in a Mortar, till all looks like Butter; then ad a quarter of a Pound of Almonds, beat with Orange-flower-Water; a Pound of sugar, eight Eggs, half the Whites, a little beaten Mace, and a little Cream, beat all together: A quarter of an Hour bakes them in Puff-crust, and in a quick Oven. (Several Hands, *Collection* [1734], 50–51) | ——— |
| **A Custard.**<br>Boil a Quart of Cream, with a Stick of Cinnamon, a quarter'd Nutmeg and large Mace; when near cold, mix it with eight Yolks of Eggs, and four Whites well beat, sweeten'd with refin'd Sugar; add to it Sack and Orange-flower-Water; set it on the Fire, and stir it till a white Froth ariseth; scum it off; then fill up your Crust, being dry'd in the Oven. (R. Smith, *Court Cookery* [1724], 1:124) | **A Custard**<br>Boyle a quart of creame with a stick of—cinnamon a quartered nuttmeg and large mace when halfe cold mix it with 8 yolks of Eggs and 4 Whites well beat Sugar Sack orange flower water sett it on the fier and Stirr it till a white froth ariseth Scum it of then fill your Custards being dryed in the oven. (Anonymous [c. 1720], handwritten notes in *E. Kidder's Receipts,* 22) |
| **To Make a baked Dish.**<br>Take a quarter of a pound of Almonds, and beat them very fine with Rose-water, a pint of Cream, and the Yelks of 8 Eggs, so season it with Sugar and Nutmegs, and you may, if you will put in the Juice of Herbs to make it look green, so put it into a Dish with a Puff-past, or you may boil it either. (*Pastry-Cook's Vade-Mecum,* 37) | **Almond Cheese-Cakes.**<br>Take two Quarts of Milk warm from the Cow, set it with a little Runnet, and when it is turn'd gather your Curds; then take a Pound of Almonds, blanch and beat them in a Marble Morter very fine with a Glass of Sack and some Rose-water; season them with Cloves, Mace and a little Cinnamon beat fine, half a Pound of Sugar, half a Pint of Sack, and half a Pound of butter melted thick; beat in six Eggs leaving out half the Whites, and a Pound of Currants; mix all these Ingredients together, and fill your Cheese-Cakes; bake them in a gentle Oven. (Middleton, *Five Hundred New Receipts,* 1:80–81) |
| **To make good Jumbals**<br>Take a pound and a half of fine Flower, a pound of fine Sugar, both settled and dried in an Oven, six Yelkes, and three Whites of Eggs, six Spoonfuls of sweet | ——— |

*"Unidentified cookbook, c. 1700"—Anonymous*

*Comments*

pound of Corriander & Carraway Seeds & Six Spoonfulls of Cream as much Rose watter: make it up make Light paste & role it & make it up in Knots

**To Make Mackaroons**

Blanch apd: of Almonds in warm watter þn wash them in Cold & dry them in a Clooth then pound þm in astone or wooden Morter Very well: Ad some Rose watter to keep þm from Oyleing þn put the whits of 3 Eggs in the pounding: have ready one 1 lb of Loaf Sugar sifted mix it wth the Almonds when you are almost ready whip up ye whits of 3: or :4 Eggs to Snow so mixt together & Drap them on wafars and Lay them on Tinn Plates or Capp paper in the Oven before they goe in Durst them with Loaf Sugar

~ A **macaroon** is "a small sweet cake or biscuit consisting chiefly of ground almonds, white of egg, and sugar" (*OED,* 6:3). **Capp paper** refers to "a kind of wrapping paper" (*OED,* 2:97).

**A Carrat Pudding**

Take a pint of Cream halfe a pint of Milk three Large Carroats grated halfe a penny lofe Grated Seven Eggs halfe the whites Mixt all these together well, then put in Bits of Canded Lemon and Sittron peal when its going into the Oven, you must melt A quarter of a pound of Butter & Stur it in When you put it in the Dish put in Some bitts of Marrow & bake it in an hour

———

**To make Rice Pudding**

Take 1/4 lb. of Rice beaten & Searched 1 qtt of Milk or Cream Set ye milk over ye fier to boyle then Stir in ye rice and let it boyle ab:tt 1/4 an hour then fill it out & Stir in 1/2 lb of Butter ye yolks of 6 Eggs and 1 white Sume Sugar 3 or 4 Spoonfulls of Rose watter & a lettle Cinnamond & Nuttmeg Nutmeg Stir in 1/4 lb Currants ye last thing ye: fill it out into a Dish & bake it.

———

**To Make a Marrow Pudding**

Take ye Marrow of 2 Bones & 1/2 lb Bisket Shread thin 1/2 oz Candyed Orang Peel & as much Lemon Season it wth: Mace Nutmeg Cinnomond & Salt beat 12 Eggs with 1/4 of pint Sack: a Lettle Rose watter 3 pints of Cream mixt it altogether with 1/2 lb Sugar & lay round with puft past

~ A **bisket**, or biscuit, could be made in a number of forms and was composed of only flour and water (or milk), without leaven. Usually it was a "kind of crisp dry bread more or less hard, prepared generally in thin flat cakes," but "confectionary and fancy biscuits were [also] variously composed" (*OED,* 1:877).

*Contemporary Recipe #1*

Cream, as much Rose-water, the quantity of an Egg of sweet butter, mingle all these together make a Paste stiff, work it better than a quarter of an hour, then break it abroad, and put in some Anniseeds, or Coriander-seeds, or Carraway-seeds, as much as you please, you may put in Musk and Ambergrease; roll them in rolls, and make them into what form you please, lay them upon Plates thin-butter'd, prick them all over, then bake them as you do diet Bread, If this will be too thin, add more Flower and sugar according to Discretion. (*Pastry-Cook's Vade-Mecum,* 11–12)

**To make Macroones**

Take one pound of fine white Sugar beat and searced very fine, and one pound of blanched Almonds beat very fine: you are to note, when you beat Almonds, you must wet them either with Rosewater or other water to prevent oyling; then mix the Sugar and almonds well together, put them into a dish ad dry them over a gentle fire; then take the whites of five Eggs well beaten with Rosewater, and wet the almonds with it, so wet that you may make them up with your knife into Cakes, and lay them on a paper that is buttered very thin, and bake them in an Oven where Bread hath beene bak'd, a quarter of an houre. (Cooper, *Art of Cookery,* 152)

**A Carrott Pudding**

Boyle 2 large Carrotts when cold pound them in a mortar Streine them through a seive mix them with 2 grated bisketts halfe a pound of butter Sack and orange flower water sugar and a little Salt a pints of cream mixed with 7 yolks of Eggs and 2 Whites beat them together and putt them in a dish coverd with Puff Past—and garnish the brim. (Anonymous [c. 1720], handwritten notes in *E. Kidder's Receipts,* 21)

**A Rice Pudding.**

Take six Ounces of the Flour of Rice, put it in a Quart of Milk, and let it boil till it is pretty thick, stirring it all the While; then pour it in a Pan, and stir in it half a Pound of Butter, and six Ounces of Sugar. When it is cold, grate in a Nutmeg, and beat and stir all this together; put a little fine Paste at the Bottom of your Dish, and bake it. (Harrison, *House-Keeper's Pocket-Book,* 117)

**Marrow Pudding**

Take a quart of cream boyled & cold, and 12 eggs well beat, leave out 4 whites: slis 4 biskits and 4 Oranges pile & lay them in a dish fit to bak it on & a few Currants: the marrow out of 2 bones: sweeten it as you please: half an houer will bake it. (Blencowe, *Receipt Book,* 12)

*Contemporary Recipe #2*

**To make Macaroons.**

Take a Pound of blanch'd Almonds, one Pound of Sugar, and a little Rose-water, beat them in a Mortar, adding a little Flour; put it in a Dish over a Chafing-Dish of Coals, stirring them 'till they come clear from the Dish, and put in a grain of Musk; then lay them on butter'd Papers, very longish; ice 'em with Loaf-Sugar sifted over them, and bake them in a gentle Oven. (Middleton, *Five Hundred New Receipts,* 1:52)

———

**Rice-Pudden**

TAKE a pint of thick cream, set it on the fire, and put into it three spoonfuls of the flour of Rice; stir it; when it is thick, pour it into a pan, and put to it a pound of fresh butter; stir it till it is almost cold; then add a grated nutmeg, a little salt, sugar, and sack, the yolks of six eggs; stir it well together, put puffe-paste at the bottom of the dish; pour it in, and bake it about an hour. (Atkyns, *Family Magazine,* 1:55)

**7. Marrow Pudding**

Take a Quart of Cream, and boil it with a Blade of Mace, set it to be cold a little: then beat ten Eggs, leaving out half the Whites, and put to your Cream; then cut a penny Loaf into Slices, and lay a Layer of Bread, and a Layer of Marrow With a few Raisins of the Sun; and so do till you have laid out your penny Loaf, and three quarters of a pound of Marrow: Then sweeten

*"Unidentified cookbook, c. 1700"—Anonymous*

*Comments*

**To Make Almond Pudding**

Take 2 oz: Almonds blanch em & beat em in a morter wth: 2 Spoonfulls Rose watter to keep-em from Oyling: Then boyle a pint of thick Cream with a lettle whole Mace & Nutmeg: Let it Cool: beat 6 Eggs: 1/2 ye whits Cast by when the Cream is as Cold as milk from ye Cowe put it to the Eggs keep it Sturring all the while: Then put in the Almonds & 2 oz Napes Biskett greated 2 oz powdered Sugar a little Salt: 1 oz Lemon & Cittron peel candied a Glace Sack 4 oz Marrow in large peices put it into a Deep dish wth puff paste rownd it Lett some of ye marrow & Cittron be put on the top Just as it is -going into ye Oven

~ **Napes Biskett** is Naples Biscuit.

**To Make a Tansey**

Take 20 Eggs beat þm well and a Double handfull of Spinage Stamp it and Strain it beat a Lettle Tansey with ye Spinage & put it a mong ye Eggs with a pint of Cream & Rowles Greated with Salt and Sugar then put it in a Skillet well Buttered with a Lump of Butter in it & keep Sturing till it is as Thick as puding then Butter a Dish put in & Lay it over Coles for above an hour & then turn it out & Serve it with Rose watter Butter & Sugar and Eat it

~ **Spinage** is an old term for spinach (*OED,* 10:603). **Tansey,** or tansy (*Tanacetum vulgare*), is "an erect herbacious plant," about "two feet high," that grows "yellow rayless button-like flowers." With its bitter taste and strong aromatic scent, it was utilized in medicine as a "stomachic." The curly type of tansy was used similarly to parsley for garnishing dishes (*OED,* 11:78). It was associated "with bitter herbs of Passover" (Hess, *Martha Washington's Booke,* 125).

**To make Goosberry Fool ye beast way**

Take a Quart of Goosberrys and Scold them Tender & Draine them well from the watter throught a Cullindar and wth ye back of a Spoon forse ye best parts of them throught a Cullindar & þn take a Quart or 3 pints of Cream Cutt a Large Nutmeg into Large peices into it and some Rose watter & Sugar Sweeten it According to your Taste sett all on a Gentle fier and Stire it till you See it off a good thickness then take it off and Coole it a Lettle then putt it into a basens and Stur in ye Goosberys & Serve it to the Table when it is Cold

———

**To make Flomary**

Take a handfull of Oatmeal & put it to a Quart of watter & boyle it very well till you have boyled it allnost a half a way þn Straine it throught a hair Sive & keep it

~ Although Anonymous (1700) did not use the same title, there is no question about her ultimate source. Jane (Bolling) Randolph also had a recipe for oatmeal flummery.

*Contemporary Recipe #1*

*Contemporary Recipe #2*

your Cream and Eggs, and put in two Spoonfuls of Orange-flower-water: Pour it over your Bread with a thin Puff-paste in the bottom, and round the sides of your Dish; send it. (Howard, *England's Newest Way* [1710], 4)

**To make Almond Puddings.**

Take a pound of Almonds blanched, and beat them very small, with a little Rosewater, boyl good milk with a flake of Mace, and a litle sliced Nutmeg, when it is boyled take it clean from the spice, then take the quantity of a penny loaf grate it, and searce it through a Collender, and then put it into the milk, and let it stand till it be prettie cool, then put in the almonds, and five or six yolks of Eggs, and a little salt and Sugar, what you thinke fit, and good store of Beef suet, and Marrow very finely shred. (Kent, *Gentlewoman's Delight,* 21–22)

**Almond puddings.**

Grate a 2 penny loaf. Take ye equal weight of beef suit minc'd & some marrow, half a pound of almonds pounded very fine with rose water, almost a spoonful of mace cutt very small, 6 eggs & leave of it 2 whites well beat. Mix it with milk or cream boyling hot, sweeten it as you please, & put in a little sack & sweetmeats cutin large pieces. You may sprinkle your puddings with Rose or Oringe water.

Now bread is so small we use a 2 penny loaf & half, to ye same quantity of almonds. (Blencowe, *Receipt Book,* 9)

**A Tansey**

Boyl a quart of cream or milk wth. a Stick of cinnamon, quarter'd nutmeg, and large mace; when half cold mix it with 20 yolks of eggs and 10 whites strain it, then put to it 4 grated biskets, 1/2 a pound of butter; a pint of Spinnage juice, and a little Tansey Sack and orange flower water; Sugar & a little Salt: then gather it to a body over the fire and pour it into your dish being well butter'd when it is bak'd turn it on a pye plate; Squeese on it an orange grate on Sugar and garnish it with Slic'd orange and a little tansey made in a plate cut as you please[.] (Kidder, *E. Kidder's Receipts* [1720], D3)

———

**To make a Gooseberry Fool the best Way.**

Take a quart of Gooseberries and scald them tender, and drain them from the Water through a Cullender, and with the back of a Spoon, force all the best part of them through the Cullender, and then take a quart of three pints of new Cream and six Eggs, Yolks and Whites, beat them well and put them to the Cream, cut a large Nutmeg in large pieces into it, and some Rosewater and Sugar, sweeten it according to your Pallet, set all on a gentle Fire and stir it till you see it of a good thickness; then take it off and cool it a little, then put it into white earthen Cream-bowls, and when it is cold, serve it to the Table. (Hall, *Queen's Royal Cookery,* 55–56)

———

**To make Flummery that will thicken Sause excellently, instead of Flour or grated Bread.**

Take a good handful of beaten Oatmeal, and put it into a quart of Water, and boil it very well, till you have

———

*"Unidentified cookbook, c. 1700"—Anonymous* | *Comments*

by you for use // it will thicken Sause as well as Greated bread or flower for some things better then Eggs

**To preserve Corrans**

Take Corrans the ripest and largest than can Be gott prick them with a nedle then wheigh Them and to a pound of Corrans take a pound And quarter of loaf Suger and threequarters of A pint Juce of Currans as thou prick them Strow Some of the Sugar upon them then Sett the Juce And Sugar over the fire only Save out some of The Sugar to Strow in Sometimes as it boyleth let It boyle over a quick fire and Skim it cleane and Then putt in the Currans and lett it boyle Gently Till the Currans be tender and then putt them Into potts and lett the Syrup boyle allmost to a Jelly and putt it into the potts to the Corrans And the next day paper them up close

———

**To make Jelly of Currans mb**

Take Currans when they are full ripe and Sprip Them of the Stalks then bruse them with a Spon and Strane them throw a peace of Canves butt Not lett the Seeds goe throw: then Measure them And to a pinte of Juce take a pound of Sugar Beaten Sett it on a Charcoall fire Save Sum of the Sugar out to Strew in now and then as it boyleth To keep its Colour and lett it boyle & Skim it ~Cleam & Strow in some Sugar now & then & lett it Titt it will Jelly then putt it into they botts

~ Here more examples of phonic errors such as "Titt," "Sprip," "Cleam," and "botts" are found among Anonymous (1700)'s collections.

**To make Currant wine**

Take 6 lb. of Currants Strip them: Putt to þm a Gallon of watter: Let them Stand together all night the next day press them throught a hare Bagg then put to them 3 lb. Sugar: Stir it till ye Sugar is dissolved: then put it into a Cask yt it wile fill lett it have a good vent till it hath done working or hissing So you may make a Greater or lesser Quantity

———

**To make Balme wine**

To 1 Gllan of watter 1 lb Sugar boyle þm an hour & scum it well þn Strain it & while it is very hott put in a good hanfull of dry'd Balm or hanfull & half of Green To ye Quantity of about 8 Gallons put in East and let it work as Bear put it up in a Cask wth ye Balme after a fortnight Bottle it & a fortnight more Drink it

~ **Balm,** "prized for its fragrance and medical properties," is an "aromatic resinous product" or a mixture of "resin and volatile oils" extracted from "various trees of the genus *Balsam odendron.*" (*OED,* 1:642).

*Contemporary Recipe #1*

boiled almost one half of it away; then strain it through a Hair-sieve, and let it stand by you, and as you need it, make use of it; it is far better than grated Bread, or Flour, or in some Cases, than Eggs. (Hall, *Queen's Royal Cookery,* 102)

**To preserve Currans.**

Part them in the tops lay a lain of Currans, and a lain of Sugar, and so boil them as fast as your doe Resberries, doe not put in the spoon, but scum them, boyle them till the Sirrup be prettie thick, then take them off, and let them stand, till they be cold, and put them in a glass. (Kent, *Gentlewoman's Delight,* 38)

**Jelly of Currants.**

Take your Currants and strip them from the Stalks into a Gally-pot, which Pot you must put into a Kettle of Water over the Fire 'till they be enough; strain them through a Flannel Jelly-bag, but don't squeeze it; add to the Liquor its weight in double refin'd Sugar, boil both up for a quarter of an Hour very gently, then put it into Glasses. (Several Hands, *Collection* [1714], 80)

**To Make Currant Wine (Mrs. Durhame)**

To a Bushal of Currants full ripe and strip'd, but pick'd clean from the leaves, put two gallons of watter. Let it infuse a day or two then strain it off, & to every gallon of Liquor put three pound & a half of suger. Then Tun it up, but not stop it close till it has done fermenting. Bottle it when 'tis fine, which may be in three months. (Blencowe, *Receipt Book,* 32)

**To make Balme-water.**

Take fiue ounces of dried Balme, Time, Pennie-Royall, of each three ounces, of Cinamon four ounces, of Cardamon one drachme, graines halfe an ounce, sweet Fennell seedes an ounce, Nutmegs and Ginger of each a drachme, Galingall, *Calamus,* and Cypress, Cubebs, and Pepper of each two drachmes, of *Calamus* roots halfe a drachme, of *Diptimus* one drachme, bruise these things, and put them into a pottle of Sack, and steepe them twenty foure houres, and vse them like the rest. (Murrell, *Daily Exercise,* #70)

*Contemporary Recipe #2*

———

———

———

**To make Balm-Water.**

Take a peck of balm; bruise it between your two hands; and then take two quarts of the best sack; put them into cold still, and paste up the still, and let it infuse three days; then distill it, and you will find it a most excellent thing against any gripes, as also for the stomach and heart put sugar-candy to it. (Atkyns, *Family Magazine,* 2:313)

*"Unidentified cookbook, c. 1700"—Anonymous*

**To make Elder Wine**

To every Gallon watter take 4 lbs. Malago Raisons pick'd and Chopt: Put the Raisons into ye watter & lett it Stand 7 dayes Stirring it every day: þn Strain it of & to every Gall of this put 1 pint of Juce of Elderberrys þn put it into a Vessel and let it work: & when it hath don working: Stop it up: Let it Stand about 6 weeks: then Rack it of into another Vessell & lett it stand 2: 3 : or : 4 mo/n þn draw it of into Bottles for use

*Comments*

~ **Malago raisins,** also found as malaca, malligo, and mallagoe, were from a "seaport in the south of Spain," as were Malago wines, which came from Malaga, Spain (*OED,* 6:76). **Rack** (obsolete) referred to drawing off liquids such as wines and ciders from the lees (*OED,* 8:93).

**To make Metheglin**

Put to 3 Gall:s watter 1 Gall: of huney: Stir it well together & boyle it one hour & Scum it well & cule it quick & set it a working in a tub wth good Ale Yeast as they do Ale & when you have it in ye Casque intended & its don working Then put in ye bung of ye Cask in a thing bag these following Spices: To ye Quantity of a Barrl 4 lbs Ginger 1 1/2 oz Cloves & 1 1/2 oz Cinnomond let the Bag down with a string half way into ye Barral being maid in ye fall it may Stand till ye Spring then after working bottle it

~ **Metheglin,** now an archaic term, was a popular alcoholic beverage established during medieval times. Defined as "originally peculiar to Wales," it is "a spiced or medicated" mixture of "fermented honey and water" (*OED,* 6:264, 393). It is not to be confused with mead. **Ale yeast** is defined as a "yeast produced in the brewing of ale" (*OED,* 1:213).

**To Preserve Cherrys with out Stone**

Take the fairest preserving Cherries that you can Gett First wipe them cleane then put out the Stones Then wheigh them and to a pound of Cherrys take A pound and quarter of Loaf Sugar beaten and Sifted and at Least halfe a pinte of Juce of Cherreys And Strow the bottom of your Skillet with Sugar And lay the Cherryes in one by one and betwee[n] Every layer of Cherrys Strow Suger and wett it With Juce till all your Juce is in then Sett it Over a quick fire and lett it boyle and Skim it Clean and take them of Some times and Shake Them about and Skime them cleane and Sett them On again and Soe doe till the Cherrys are cleare And the Syrup Jelly and then take them of And putt into your potts and the next day paper Them up Close

———

*Contemporary Recipe #1*

**Another, very Wholesome.**

To every Gallon of pick'd Elder-berries, put a full Gallon of Water, boil them together 'till the Berries are tender, then strain it off through a fine Sieve; let what will run through, but don't press the Berries; to every Gallon of the Liquor put two full Pounds of good *Lisbon*-Sugar: This Sort for present Drinking. What you design to keep some Years, must have two Pounds and a half of Sugar; boil the Liquor and Sugar together, and scum it clean in the boiling as long as any will rise; when cool, work it with Yeast for a Night and Day; put it into the Vessel, and when it has done working, stop it close for five or six Months; Bottle it then, if fine. This ought to be the constant Drink for all Gouty People: If well boil'd and work'd, it never ferments in the Bottle or Stomach. (Several Hands, *Collection* [1724], 1:83–84)

**To make white Metheglin**

Take to three gallons of Spring-water one of Honey; first let it gently melt, then boil for an hour, continuualy skimming it; then put it into an earthen or wooden vessel, and when it is little more than bloodwarm set it with Ale-yeast, and so let it stand twelve hours: then take off the yeast, and bottle it. Put in it Limon-peel and Cloves, or what best pleaseth your taste of Herbs or Spices. Eringo-roots put into it when it is boiling, maketh it much better. So do Clove-gillyflowers; a quantity of which make the Meath look like Claret-wine. I observe that Meath requireth some strong herbs to make it quick and smart upon the Palate; as Rosemary, Bay-leaves, Sage, Thyme, Marjoram, Winter-savory, and such like, which would be too Strong and bitter in Ale or Beer. (Digby, *Closet of the Eminently Learned Sir Kenelm Digby,* 66–67)

**To do Cherries liquid, without Stones**

Take good preserving Cherries that are ripe, take away their Stalks and Stones, and boil Sugar *a Soufle,* and put your Cherries in to it, and make them boil a good pace over a good Fire, and scum them very carefully; this done, take them from the Fire, and let them stand and cool, then set them over a good Fire again, and make them boil apace; then take them off again, and scum them if it be needful, and so put them into Pots, and cover them up when they are cold. (Hall, *Queen's Royal Cookery,* 167–68)

*Contemporary Recipe #2*

**Elderberry Wine**

To every Gallon of Water put four pound of *Malagia* Raisins chop'd small, let these stand in an open Vessel for a Week or nine Days a Cloth being laid over it, stir them well every Day; then draw off what Liquor will run and press the rest out of the Raisins in a Hair Bag, and put the Liquor up in a close Cask. Boil and scum this Liquor very well, then to every Gallon of this Liquor put in a pint of the Juice of ripe Elderberries cold, and afterwards stop it close, and let it stand for six Weeks, then draw it off, as far as it is fine, into another Vessel, and put half a pound of common Sugar to every Gallon of Liquor, and when it is become pure and fine, bottle it for Use. (C. Carter, *Compleat City and Country Cook,* 214)

———

———

*"Unidentified cookbook, c. 1700"—Anonymous*

*Comments*

**To Preserve Cherrys with Stones mb**

Take ye fairest preserving Cherrys that you can gett First whipe þm And cut of halfe the Stalk and put a knife to the Stone on the side Of the Cherrys þn wheigh them and to a pound of Cherrys take a pound and quarter of Sugar beaten and Sifted and at Least halfe a pint of Juce of Cherrys and Strow the bottom of your Skillit with Sugar and Lay the Cherrys in one by one and between every Layer Strow Sugar and wett with Juce till all Juce is in but keep out some Sugar to Strow in now and then as it boyleth then sett it over a quick f[ire] and let it boyle and Skime it Cleane and as it boyleth Strow in Some of your Sugar and take them of Sometimes and Shake þm about and skim them Cleane and set them on againe and soe do till the Cherrys are so Cleare that one may se the Stones and the Syrup thick then take them of the fier and let them Stand in a basson till next day or the next day after then Set it over a quick fier and Lett them boyle & se if any Skim will rise then put it into your potts and the next day paper them up

———

**To make Cherry wine**

Squeese the Juce out of the Cherrys wth: your hands then Strain it throught a Canvass: bagg then put to 1 Gall: Liquar 3 lbs good muscovado Sugar then put it into a Cask wth out boyling: lett it Stand wth: a Vent open till it hath done working or hissing then Stop it up Close Lett it Stand 3 weeks till it is Settled: then Bottle it off

~ **Muscovado** is "raw or unrefined sugar obtained from the juice of the sugar cane by evaporation and draining off the molasses" (*OED*, 6:778).

**To Make Gooseberry wine**

Take of Spring watter 9 Gallons to wch: you must allow an 100 lbs of goosberrys and abt 26 lbs of white powder Sugar and order it as followeth Boyle ye watter over a gentle fier an hour or more then take it of and let it Stand to coole in Some wooden Vessell when it is almost cold put your Goosberrys in they being first beaten or Stampt all to mash in a Maurter as you do apples for Cyder and mixt them well with ye watter and let them Stand close covered two days & a night then Strain it throught an hair Sive and next throught a flanning bag and when So done put in ye Sugar and Stir it abute till it be well dissolved then tun it up into ye Cask and let it Stand unstopt 3 weeks and then Stop it very close and let it Stand till the 10: mon. then bottle it: you must gather the Goosberrys when full ripe and in dry weather they must be all of ye Yellow Sert the Quantity above mentioned will make 12 Gallons you must put it into a wine or Cyder Vessell & let it be full with in 2 or 3 Inches of the bung you may make a

———

*Contemporary Recipe #1*

**A way to dry Cherries.**

Take three quarters of a pound of *Sugar,* and a pound of *Cherries,* their stalks and stones taken from them, then put a spoonfull of clean water in the Skillet, and so lay a lay of *Cherries* and another of *Sugar,* till your quantity be out, then set them on the fire, and boyle them as fast as conveniently you can,now and then shaking them about the Skillet, for fear of burning, and when you think they are enough, and clear, then take them off the fire, and let them stand till they be halfe cold, then take them out as clear from the Syrupe as you can, and lay them one by one upon sheets of glasse, setting them either abroad in the sunne, or in a window where the sunne may continually be upon them. If they dry not so fast as your would have them, then in the turning scrape some loafe *Sugar* finely upon them, add no greater heat then the sunne will afford, which will be sufficient if they be well tended, and let no dew fall them by any means, but in the evening set them in some warm Cupboard. ( Jenner, *Book of Fruits & Flowers,* 40)

**To make Cherry-wine.**

The Lady *Newport* makes it near after the same manner: But she first picks the Stones as well as the Stalks from the Cherries, then breaks them very Well with Hands or Ladle, and after twelve Hours fermenting together, strains them through a Napkin, wring it very well, to press all out that can come; which, she putteth into Barrels to ferment with Sugar; and after a long time settling, draws it into bottles, it will draw well to the last, if you drink it out of the Barrel, without bottling. (Hall, *Queen's Royal Cookery,* 170)

———

*Contemporary Recipe #2*

———

———

———

*"Unidentified cookbook, c. 1700"—Anonymous*

greater or Lessor Quantity as you please allowing to every gallon of watter 11 lbs of goose-berrys and 3 lbs of white Sugar

**To preserve Goosberrys**

Take ye fairest Goose-berrys you can get & Cut of ye Tops to 1 lb Goose-berrys 1 1/2 lbs of duble refinde Sugar: breake it on pieces & dip it in watter and put it in a Skillit wth 4 Spoonfulls of watter more: Then Set it on a Charcole fier Let it boyle & Scum it very clean So let it boyle till it will draw an hair Slitt you Goose-berrys wth: a needle down the Side & put them in & wth a needle: they have boyled a lettle take þm of & Shake them rown Gentley then Set them on the Grownd: So let them Stand 1/4 of an hour then set it on ye fier againe so continue doeing the same till they be Clear then put it in your Glasses for your use

**To make Lozenges.**

Take Loaf Sugar single refind beat it serce it through a fine sive: þn take to 1 lb Sugar 40 Drops of Oyl of mint Wormwood Carraways or rosemary & a Spoonfull of Gum Dragon layd in watter þn put it together in a Stone morter & pound it till it will come to a past: þn take it out & rowl it in lumps & make it what form your please þn put it on tin plates & put þm in an Oven after you have Baked bread: till they be dry

**To Make Jelly of Oranges mb**

Take the fairest Civill Oringes the Best and Highest Colored and freest from Spotts and bruses Then weigh them and take their wheight in Double Refined Sugar then pare them very Thin or Scrape them then cutt them in half And pick outt all the meat and put in a Basson and pick out all the Seeds and Strings Very cleane then cover it very close with a Plate then lay the halves in watter 24 hours Shifting them morning and night the next Day putt them into a kettle of clean watter And cover it very close with a plate and lett Their be a very clear fire under it and keep It boyling a good pase all the while and Lett them boyl while they be Soft y/t you May thrust a Strow throw them then take Them of the fire and putt them into a wooden Plates then take Strings very cleane out of them Then cutt them as thin as your knife then Take your Sugar and break it into Small Lump And dip it into watter and putt it into a Skillet Over a Clear fire and Lett it boyle to a Candy Height then putt in the Oranges and let it boyle A good while then putt in the meat of th:e

*Comments*

~ The use of a needle to pick out the seeds was an old sixteenth–seventeenth century technique.

~ **Lozenges** in this case refer to "small cake[s] or tablet[s], originally diamond-shaped, of medicated or flavored sugar, etc., to be held and dissolved in the mouth" (*OED*, 6:481). **Serce** is an archaic word for a sieve or strainer; in this instance it is used as a verb (*OED*, 9:332).

~ **Candy Height** is equivalent to "candy-high," a certain point in the boiling of sugar when the sugar reaches the "candying or crystallizing" stage (*OED*, 2:66).

*Contemporary Recipe #1*

**To preserve Gooseberries.**
Take of the fairest Goosberies when they begin to be ripe, cutting off the blackes and the crownes, and pricke them through with a needle, then take twise so much clarified Sugar as the weight of them, put them into the hot sugar and let them boyle-vp suddenly, letting them stand in the sirrup till they they be cold, then let them boyle vppe againe the third time, put them in your pots or glasses warme. (Murrell, *Delightful Daily Exercise,* #45)

**Lozenges**
Take Blossoms of flowers, and beat them in a bowl-dish, and put them in a much clarified sugar as may come to the colour of the cover, then boil them with sitrring, till it is come to Sugar againe; then beat it fine and searse it, and so work it up to a paste with a little Gum Dragon, steep it in Rose-water, then print it with your mould, and being dry, keep it up. (W. M., *Queen's Delight,* 68)

———

*Contemporary Recipe #2*

**To preserve Goosberries.**
Take the fairest Goosberries you can get with the stalks one, prick three or four holes in every one of them, then take the weight of them in Sugar, lay the best part of the Sugar in the bottome of a Silver or peuter dish, then lay your Goosberries one by one upon it, strew some of the rest of the Sugar upon them, and put two spoonfuls of the water into half a pound, then set the Goosberries on a chafing dish of coales, and let them stand uncovered scalding upon the fire a prettie while before they boil, but not too long, for then they will grow red, and when they be boyled, let them not boyl too fast, when they be enough put them up, you must put the rest of the Sugar on them as they boil, and that will harden them, and keep them from breaking. (Kent, *Gentlewoman's Delight,* 39)

———

———

*"Unidentified cookbook, c. 1700"—Anonymous*

*Comments*

oringes And let it boyle as Long againe as it did before then putt it in potts if thou will putt in some ambergrese thou mast

**To Candy Orange Chips**

Take the Best Civell Oranges and Scrape them and Then pare them pretty thick then Sett them over The fire in a kettle of watter and lett them boyle Till they be very tender then lay them a drying on pla[tes] The next day make a Syrup when it is boyled and Scimed cleane then putt in the Chips and lett them Boyle a letle while then putt thm into a basson And Lett them Stand a day or two then take the[m] Out and whash them in Scalding watter and Soe Lay them a drying againe and the next day Take as much dooble Refined Suger as you Think will Serve and to a pound of Sugar a pint Of watter and boyle it to a Candey height and Then dip them in as fast as you can lay them A drying

~ **Chips** are thin and irregular slices of fruit (*OED*, 2:355).

**To Make Orange Watter**

Take ye out side Rinds of 100 Larges Oranges Cut þm very small put to them 1 Gall Brandy & two Gall: watter & wth: yeast or malasses put it into a Close Vessell & let it worke two or three days then put to it a Gall more of Brandy & a quart of Bay Salt & draw it of in your Limbeck

~ **Molasses** is an "uncrystallized syrup drained from raw sugar" or "syrup obtained from sugar in the process of refining" (*OED*, 6:587).

**To Make Marmalet of Oranges**

Take 25 right Sevil Oranges: high coloured free from Spots & bruises Scrape or or pare of the out side as thin as ye Edge of A Knife & cut þm in halfves and pick out all ye meat & Lay the halves in watter 24 houers & Shift them night & morning & ye next day set on ye Oranges in fresh Spring watter & make þm boyle pretty fast & when ye watter Grows bitter: tak þn out and put to þm: fresh watter & lett þm boyle till they are so tender that you can thrust a strow throw

~ **Marmalet** (obsolete) is marmalade, "a preserve or confection made by boiling fruits (originally quinces, now usually Seville oranges) with sugar, so as to form a consistent mass" (*OED*, 6:177). A **trencher** is "a flat piece of wood, square or circular, on which meat was served and cut; a plate or platter of wood, metal or earthenware" (*OED*, 11:323).

*Contemporary Recipe #1*

**To make Oring chipps, a very cordial thing against the paine or wind in the Stomacke.**

Take your fairest cleere Oringes, and pare off the outermost peele as thinne as a paper, cut your peeles in pieces halfe an inch long, then take foure times the waight of your peeles in double refined sugar, boyle them to a candie height with as much rose-water as will desolue it, and then put in your peele into the hot sugar, and let it boyle, alwayes stirring it till it begin to candie, and to growe into crumbles: then lay it in a sheete of glasse, & set it in a warme Ouen or stoue till you see it bee dry, then keepe it in a Boxe and eate of it euery morning and Euening. (Murrell, *Delightful Daily Exercise,* #56)

**To make Orange or Lemon-water.**

To one hundred Oranges or Lemons, you must have 3 gallons of Brandy and 2 quarts of Sack. Pare off the outer Rinds very thin, and steep them in the Brandy one Night; the next day distil them in a cold Still, a gallon with the proportion of Peels is enough for one Still, and of that you may draw off between 3 and 4 quarts; draw it off till you taste it being to be sowrish; sweeten it to your Taste with double-refin'd Sugar, mix first, second, and third Running together; if 'tis Lemon-water it should be perfum'd; put two grains of Ambergrease and one of Musk ground fine, tie it in a Rag and let it hang 5 or 6 days in a Bottle, and then put it in another, and so for a great many if you please, or else you may put 3 or 4 Drops of Tincture of Ambergrease in it; cork it very well; the Orange is an excellent Water for the Stomach, and the Lemon is a fine entertaining Water. (E. Smith, *Compleat Housewife* [1729], 223)

---

*Contemporary Recipe #2*

**To candy Lemons and Oranges.**

Take the peels of your Oranges and Lemons, the white cut away, then lay them in water five or six dayes, shifting them twice every day, then seeth them till they are very tender, then take them out of the water, and let them lye till they be cold, then cut them in small pieces square, the bignesse of a penny or lesse, then take to every three two ounces of Sugar, put to it a quantity of fair water, and a lesse quantity of Rosewater, and make a sirupe thereof, then skum it very clean, and put in your peels, and let them boyle for the space of an hour or longer, if you find your liquor wanting you may pput in more water at your pleasure, then boyle them a little space after with a little sharp fire, stirring it alwayes for burning, then take it off the fire three or four times, stirring them all the while, and set them on again untill they be candied. (Kent, *Gentlewoman's Delight,* 55)

**A Cordial Orange-Water.**

Take three Quarts of good Brandy, and the Rinds of a dozen and a half of Oranges, pare them very thin, that none of the White go in, let them steep in the Brandy three Days and Nights close stopt; then take five pints of Fair-Water, and a pound and a half of double-refin'd Sugar : Boil this Syrop half an Hour, and scum it as any rises ; then strain it through a Jelly-bag, and let it stand 'till cold; then mix it with the Brandy, which must be first pour'd from the Peels, and settled: Keep it for Use.

Thus you may do *Lemons,* which is a pleasanter Cordial. (Several Hands, *Collection* [1714], 117–18)

---

*"Unidentified cookbook, c. 1700"—Anonymous* | *Comments*

them þn take þm up & dry þm, in a Linnen Cloth keep þm Covered wth: a Cloth Scraping ye outsids a little before you cut þm them Cutt them very thin on a trencher one way: & then Cutt þm very thin Crose the other way then take their weight in fine Lofe Sugar: Break it in Lumps: & having a large porringer of watter iust dip the Lumps of Sugar in ye watter & throw þm into the preserving pan þn put the pan over Charcole fier to Clarifie the Sugar Skuming it well þn put in ye Cut Orange & let it boyle a good while þn pick out ye Skings & ye kirnels from meat of ye Orange into ye pan with ye other letting it boyle as long as it did before then put it into potts you may put in Some Amber Grease if you please & boyle in it

**To Candy Oranges**

Take 12 fresh Sevil Oranges Lay em in Spring watter 48 houres: Change ye watter once þn take 3 lbs Loafe Sugar & 3 pts watter let it boyle taking of the Skum þn put in ye Oranges lit em boyle abt an hour þn take em of & Let þm lye in the Syrup abt a week or two þn take of ye Oranges & lay þm on a Sive to dry when they are very dry taken 1 lb Sugar & as much watter as will wet it: boyle to Candy height So dip in the Oranges & lay þm in a Sive to dry on a Stove

———

**To Make Orange or Lemon Cakes**

When ye Oranges boyle in a Syrup take up some of þm & beat em Small & þn put in Some Orange or Lemon Juce: then take ye wtt of it in Loaf Sugar mixt it together & boyle it abt 1/4 an houer So lett it Stand till Cold: then Drop it on Tin plates & set it on a stove to dry

———

**To Preserve Damsons mb**

First wheigh them and to a pound of damsons Take a pound of lofe Sugar then put your knife To the Stones on the Side then breake your Sugar Into little lumps and dip it into fare watter Pretty well and Sett it over a quick fire and Skim it cleane and Let it boyle till it will draw A haire then putt in your damsons and Lett Them Just boyle as Slow as posable and Skim Them clean and allwaies when they begin to Boyle take them of the fire and Shake them Round the Skillet and Soe doe till the damsons Are very tender but not breat then power them Into a basson and the next day Set them over The fier and doe as bfore a little, while the Damsons are hott threw and So do againe the Next day but this time you must doe as before Till the damsons are hott threw then take the damsons up into your potts and lett

~ **Damsons** are small plums, either black or dark purple in color. Originally from Syria, they were brought to Greece and Italy in early times, where they were cultivated (*OED*, 3:22). **Breat** here may be a variation of an archaic word, "breek," a version of today's "break" (*OED*, 1:1070).

*Contemporary Recipe #1* *Contemporary Recipe #2*

**To rough-Candie Orenges with Sugar.**
Take a deepe earthen Bason, and fiue round wires, according to the bignesse of the Pan, lay your Orenge rindes on the lowest wire, and lay another wire on it, and then lade that wire also with your fruit, and lay on the third wire, and lade it also, and so with the rest, then couer all with Sugar boiled to a Candie height, and set the Pan vpon a soft mat or cushion seauen or eight houres, then poure out all the Sugar that will run from the wires, and let them drop an houre after, vntill it haue quite done, then take them out, &c. (Murrell, *Daily Exercise*, #60)

———

**Lemon-Cakes.**
Take a pound of double-refin'd Sugar, beat and sift it very fine, wet it with Juice of Lemon, boil it almost to a Candy-height, then drop it on Plates; set it in a warm place, 'till they will slip off the Plates. They are grateful, and proper to quench Thirst. You may shred the Peel very fine, and boil up with one half, if you like it; but add fresh Juice with that, or 'twill be too thick to drop neatly. (Several Hands, *Collection* [1714], 79)

———

**To preserve Damsons.**
Take a pound or something more of pure Sugar finely beaten, and then take a pound of Damsons and cut one scotch in the side of each of them, then put a row of Sugar in a silver dish or bason, and then lay in a row of Plums, and then cover it with Sugar, and so lay it in till they be all in, and then take two spoonfuls of clean water, and make a hole in the middle of them, and set it over a very soft fire, and look to it carefully, for fear the Sugar should burn, and when the Sugar is all dissolved, shake them together, and stirre them gently, and then set them down and cover them till they be cold, and when they are cold, set them upon the coales again, and then let them boyle gently till they be ready, and when they are ready take them down, and take them every one by its stem, and cover them with the skins as well as you

———

*"Unidentified cookbook, c. 1700"—Anonymous* | *Comments*

your Syrup Boyle till it is allmost to a Jelly then putt it to Your damsons and the next day paper them up Close

**To Make Malmelett of Damsons**

Take ye Damsons w/n: they are ffresh gathered and wipe them and put them in ye infuseing pott or any thing else when thou dost put them in Stope them very close and So let them infuse till they be very tender: Lett no watter come to them then take þm: out & put þm in a hair Sive & what will come through weight & put to it as much Sugar as it weighteth finely beaten & boyl it over a quick fier & Skum it clean: and when it will come clean from ye Skillet & Jelly : put it up in potts

———

**R.T. To Make Syrup of Gelly Flowers**

Take ye flowers & Cutt þm none but ye read for your use: Then pore as much Scalding watter on þm as well cover them: Then set þm over [some?] hott embers: till ye good ness is come from ye flowers then Strain þm out then renew to ye said Watter fresh flowers till you think it is a Strong Enough and to a quairt of Liquor put 3 lbs. of Loaf Sugar then put it Over a Charcole fier till ye Sugar is desolved & then Scum rise then sett it by in the Same thing: 2 or 3 days þn Scum it Clean & bottle it

~ See page 348 for more about **gillyflowers**.

**Dr: Oven:s Recpt: for making y/e: like**

To Quart of Liquor 4 lb of Loaf Sugar only Sturing ye Sugar Letting it Stand or: dayes: till the Scum is Rise then scime it of and Bottle it/n.

———

**To Make Consarve of Barbarys mb**

First Strip them of the Stalks and then put them In a Infusing pot and Set it in a kettle of watter And make the watter boyle till the Barberrys Are very tender then put them threw a Seive And then measure it and to a pinte of Juce Take a pound and three quarters of Sugar

~ **Barberries** are "long, red, sharply acid berries" that can be picked from a shrub, *Berberis vulgaris*, a native of Europe and North America (*OED*, 1:666).

*Contemporary Recipe #1*

can, and then put them all one by one in a dish, and if the sirupe be not boyled enough, set it over and let it boyle a little longer, and when the Plums be cold, put them in a gally-pot or glasse, and pour the sirupe to them while it is a little warm, you must not forget to take away the skin of the Plums as it riseth. (Kent, *Gentlewoman's Delight,* 53–54)

**To make an excellent Tart-stuffe of Damsons.**
Take a pottle of Damsons and put them into an earthen pot, stopped very close, and put it into a potte of boyling water, letting it boyle foure or fiue houres but neuer vnstop it in that time, & then straine through a cushen canuasse like conserues, then put it into the earthern pot againe, putting to euery pound of that pulfe a pound of hard Sugar, a graine of Muske, then stopp the pot againe and set it into a pot of boyling water, and let it boyle two houres close couered, then poure it into a siluer or earthen bason, set it vpon a chafeing-dish of coales and boyle it til it be thicke, alwayes stiring it still that it burne not too: then take the waight of the pulfe of double-refined sugar, boyled to the height of a candy, then put in your pulpe into the hotte sugar, boyle it, alwayes stirring it till it come from the bottom, box it in Marmelate boxes and when it is could set it in a hot ouen till it be candied on the top, and keepe it all the yeare. (Murrell, *Delightful Daily Exercise,* #27)

**Syrup of Clove July Floors**
Take half pound of floors put þm into a pott & power 3[?] Gills of Boylling water upon þm cover it & Lett it Stand 3 or 4 hours then Strain it through a Seive & put two pound of Dbl Loaf Sugr to one pint & Give a boill or two & Scum it very well-you may clear it up wth whites of Eggs[.] (Fairfax Family, *Arcana Fairfaxiana Manuscripta,* 157)

———

**To make Conserve of Barberies.**
In the heat of the day gather the fairest red Barberies, pick them cleane, and put them into a deepe pot, and set in boiling water vntill they be tender, then straine them though a cushion canuas and boile thrice their weight in double refined Sugar to a Candie height, and

*Contemporary Recipe #2*

**To make Marmalade of Damsons.**
Take a Gallon of large ripe Damsons; peel off the Skins of three Quarts of them, put the Quart unskinned in the bottom of an earthen Pan, and those that are skinned upon them; cover the Pot so close that no Water can get in; then set on a Kettle of Water; put in the Vessel of Damesons; boil them till they are tender, then take out their Stones, and both Skins and Stones of the undermost: Then take as much Sugar as they weigh, put to the Pulp, make it boil a pace, scume it well, and when it is boil'd enough, put it in a Pot for use. (Nott, *Cook's and Confectioner's Dictionary,* #5)

**6. To make Syrup of Gilly-Flowers**
Take 600 of Gilly-Flowers, cut them off to the White, then take a Quart of White-wine, put it into a Skillet; and when it boils, pour it into a Gally-pot, and put your flowers into it hot, then let it stand upon Coals to keep hot for three Days; then strain it out, and to a Pint of Liquor, put a pound and a quarter of Sugar, you will have almost two pints of Liquor; boil it to Syrup, and put it up (when cold) into a Glass Glass Bottle. You may do it in Borage-Water instead of White-wine, if you please. (Howard, *England's Newest Way* [1726], 196)

———

———

*"Unidentified cookbook, c. 1700"—Anonymous* | *Comments*

at Least, beat it Small and sifte it and put It into the Juce and lett it Stand while Next day and then Sett over a quick fire & Lett it boyl fine[?] and[?] Skim it clean and lett it Boyle till is is Jelly then putt it in yore Potts and the next day paper it up

**To Preserve Barberys**

Take ye fairest & ripest Barberys Slit them on ye side wth a needle & pick out the Stones & Strow serched Sugar on them: put them in Earthen or Silver then take to a 1 lb of Barberys 1: lb 1/4 of Loaf Sugar beaten bruse Some of ye Barberys & Strain out ye iuce mix it wth: watter & to 1 lb of Sugar 1 pint of watter: Set ye Sugar & watter over a Quick Charcole fier to Clarifie it wth: the whites of 2 Eggs beaten Scum it clean then put in the Barberys & set them over a quick fier Some times take þm: of ye fier & Shak þm round parting & putting þm down in ye Syrup wth ye back of a Spoon they must not boyl long but when they loak Clear take þm up in pots þn boyl the Syrup over a Quick feir & try it droping a Lettle on a plate brim & if when cold it be thick: then pore it on the Barberys: ye next day papr þm

———

**To Preserve Mulberrys mb**

Take the Best Mullberrys that you can gett And to a pound of Mullberrys take a pound Of loaf Sugar break it in lumps and dip it in Watter and Sett it on the fire and skim it Cleane and lett it boyle to a Candey height & then put the Mullberrys in and Lett them Boyle very Softly and when they are boyled Very tender then putt them in to a pott & Lett them Stand three dayes and then boyle them againe and then putt them into a pott The next day paper them up

~ **Mulberries** are the fruit of any tree of the genus *Morus*, especially the black mulberry; it also often applies, in English dialect, to the blackberry, *Rubus fruticosus*, otherwise called raspberry (*OED*, 6:748).

**To make malmalet of Apricocks**

Take Soand Apricocks through ripe: Paire þm & Cut them in halfes Then take out the stones & way þm: and to 1 lb of Apricocks take 1 lb of Duble refind Sugar beaten & sifted Then take y/r Apricocks & Slice þm into ye Sugar as thin as you can Put þm over a quick fier and as fast as the Scum rises take it of as Clean as you can Stiring it sofley untill it will Come Cleane from ye Skillet—Then put it into ye potts

———

**To make Chocolat almonds**

Take your Sugar & beat it & Serch it then: great youre Chocolatt: þn take to 1 lb Sugar: 5 oz. of Chocolatt mix þm well together þm put in 2 Spoonfull Gumdragon Soaked in rosewater & a grn musk & ambergreas & beat þm all well together in morter þn rowl þm out &

**Almonds in Chocolat**

Take 3 quarters of a pound of Sugar and half a pound of Chocolat and make of it a high Candey~then put in two pound of right Jordon Almonds and keep them Sturing tell they are almost Cold then lay them out to dry on Sives and coulier them thus for the couller Red

*Contemporary Recipe #1*

coole it a little, and put in your pulp, and and boile it halfe an houre, coole it againe vntill it be blood-warme, and then pot it vp. (Murrell, *Daily Exercise,* #33)

**To preserve Barberies red.**
Take a pound of the fairest Barberies & stone them on the one side with a needle, then take halfe a pound of other Barberies and stampe them and straine them, put to that sirrup two pound of clarified sugar, then put your Barberies into a Crooked lane pot such as you make a pudding in, then put your two pound of clarified Sugar in your Barberies, then couer your pot close and set it into a pot of boyling water, and let it boyle foure houers, then take vp your Barberies and put them vp in galley-pots or glasses, then boyle your sirup till it be thicke and put it warme to the Barberies, and when it is cold bind it vppe close from the ayre, and so keep it for your vse. (Murrell, *Delightful Daily Exercise,* #19)

**To preserve Mulberries.**
Take as many Mulberries as you please, and as much Sugar as they weigh: First wet the Sugar with some juyce of Mulberries, stir your Sugar together, then put in your Mulberries, then boil them apace, till you thinke they are boyled enough, then take them off, and boil the Sirupe a while, and put it into the Mulberries, let them stand till they be cold. (Kent, *Gentlewoman's,* 42–43)

**To make Marmalade of ripe Apricocks**
Pare, stone and cut your Apricocks, into thin slices; then to a Pound of Fruit, put a Pound of double - refin'd Sugar, and a quarter of a Pint of strong Codlin Liquor; boil it as fast as your can, and when the Fruit is tender, and clear from the Scum, which you are carefully to take off, then set it off the Fire, and break what pieces you think too big: then fill your Glasses, and Paper them when cold. (Several Hands, *Collection* [1724], 2:34)

**To make Chocolate Almonds**
Take a pound of Chocolate finely grated, and a pound and half of the best Sugar finely sifted; then soak Gum-dragon in Orange-flower-water, and work them into what form you please. The Paste must be stiff, dry them in a Stove. (E. Smith, *Compleat Housewife* [1729], 181)

*Contemporary Recipe #2*

**How to Preserve Barberies.**
First take the fairest *Barberies,* and of them the greatest bunches you can get, and with a needle take out the stones on the one side of them, then weigh out to every halfe pound of them one pound of *Sugar,* put them into a Preserving pan, strow the *Sugar* on them, and let them boyl a quarter of an hour softly, then taking out the *Barberies* let the Syrupe boyle a quarter of an hour more, then put in the Barberies againe, and let them boyl a pretty while with the Syrupe, then take them from the Syrupe, and let them both stand till they be cold, and so put them up. ( Jenner, *Book of Fruits & Flowers,* 8)

**Another Way of preserving Mulberries wet**
Boil your Sugar 'till it is a little pearled, allowing three Pounds of it for four Pounds of Mulberries, and give them a light covered boiling in the same Sugar, gently stirring the Pan, by means of the Handles. That done, remove it from the Fire, and set it by 'till the next Day, when you are to drain off the Syrup, in order to bring it to its pearled Quality. Afterwards slip in your Fruit, adding a little more pearled Sugar, if it be requisite, and dispose of all in Pots as soon as they are sufficiently cool'd. (*Lady's Companion,* 2:252)

**To make Marmalade of Apricocks**
Gather your Apricocks just turn'd from the green of a very pale yellow, pare them thin and weight them, three quarters of a pound of double-refind'd Sugar to a pound of Apricocks; then cut them in halves, take out the Stones and slice them thin; beat your Sugar and put it in your Preserving-pan with your slic'd Apricots, and three or four Spoonfuls of Water: boil and scum them, and when they are tender put them in Glasses.
(E. Smith, *Compleat Housewife* [1729], 189)

---

*"Unidentified cookbook, c. 1700"—Anonymous*

mark þm wth: ye molds & lay þm on tin plats to dry turn þm every day.

*Comments*

Scutcheneel~~for Yallow Termermick of Saffron for blew Stone blew for Green the Juice of Spinage and Steep your Gum in ye Juice of your Green . . . (The Compiler [1744], Manuscript cookbook, 15)

~ In spite of similar titles, all three examples show how differently each version was prepared.

**To Make Codlens Cakes mb**

Take the fairest Codlins Greene that you can gett First Putt them into boyling watter and lett them Scold a Very little while upon the fier then take them up of The fier and cover them and soe lett them Scold in The hott Lycuor till they are very tender butt nott Breek then take them up and peale them then Scrap The pullpe of the Coarest then putt your pulpe throw A very fine Seve then putt to they pulpe a little Juce Of Spinage anough to Coller it green then wheigh your pulfe and to a pound of pulfe take a pound of Loaf Sugar Then Sett your pulpe over a quick fier and lett it boyle About a quarter of an hour with out Sugar then putt in one Quarter of the Sugar that belongeth to the quantity and Lett it boyle a while till it comes clear from the Skillet Then breake the rest of your Sugar into little lumps and Just dip it into Some clear watter and Soe putt it into Your Skillit and lett it boyle with a quick fier and Skim It cleane and lett it boyle while it will draw a heire which Must be ready when the pulpe cumes clear from ye: Skillit Of pulfe and keep it Sturing butt not lett it boyle butt keep it Sturing till it is mixt together then take it up Of the fier and power it into a basson of Earthen or Silver And keep it Stirring till it is cold then putt it into your molds

the Caullirin to make Red Codlens Cakes

take to a pound & halfe of pulfe take 1/4 a dram of Scuganell 1/4 a dram of almon & a Lettle Sugar about an ounse & a lettle waiter about two Spoonefulls

~ **Scuganell** is a variation of "scutchanele" or "scutchaneal," better known today as "cochineal" (*OED*, 2:564). The carmine coloring was obtained from the dried bodies of an insect, *Coccus cacti*, in Mexico and other cacti. Besides its use for coloring, it was also used for dyes and in medicine as an "antispasmodic" (*OED*, 9:305).

Anonymous (1700) appears to have used the words "pulfe" and "pulpe" interchangeably.

**To Make Jelly of Pipens mb**

Take cleane pipens free from Spotts & bruses pare them Very thin then quarter them & pick out the kernells butt Doe not Core them, to a quarter of hundred of pipens Take three pints of runing watter and putt them in a Pipkin and lett them boyle till all the tast is out of Them then take them of and lett the Lyquar run throw A haire Seive and put to a pinte of Lyquor one pound of Sugar beatten and Sifted then put them over a quick Fire keep it Cleane Skimed and to a pinte of Lyquor Two Lemmons lett it boyle till it will Jelly it may Be tryed by Setting Some to cole thou maist cutt Same Lemmon and Oringe peale and lay in the bottom of they potts and the next day paper them

~ Anonymous (1700)'s recipe is unusual for its stipulation that the pippins not be cored. Most recipes had cored pippins. **Pippins** refer to numerous varieties of apples raised from seed (*OED*, 7:898). A **pipkin** can be described as "a small earthenware pot or pan, used chiefly in cooking" (*OED*, 7:898–99). **Quick fire** refers to a certain flame temperature, in this case a brisk or strongly burning flame (*OED*, 8:52).

*Contemporary Recipe #1*

*Contemporary Recipe #2*

**To make Pippen Cakes.**
Pare Pippins and quarter them, boil them, they are tender in fair Water, then rub them through a hair Sieve, and to one pound of Pippins, put three quarters of a pound of Sugar; boil the yelow peel of a Limon until it be tender, then mix it very small, and mix it altogether, then make it as hot on the Fire as you can hold your finger in it. Then run it on Plates, and set it into an Oven after Tarts, The next morning cut it into what Fashion you please, then dry it. If you love it sharp, you may mix Juice of Limons with it. (*Pastry-Cook's Vade-Mecum,* 50–51)

———

**To make Jelly of Pippins.**
Take Pippens and pare them, and quarter them, and coar them, lay them in water, and when you set them on the fire, shift them in another water, and put them in a skillet, put as much water as will cover them and a little more, set them over the fire, and make them boil as fast as you can, when the Apples are soft, and the liquor taste strong of the Apples, then take them off, and strain them through a piece of canvass gently; take to a pound of juyce a pound of Sugar, then set it on the fire, when it is melted, strain in into a bason, and rince you skillet again, set it on the fire, and when it is boyled up, then scum it, and make it boyl as fast as you can, and when it is almost boiled, put in the juyce of three Lemons strained through a cloth, if you will have Orange pill, pare it thin, that the white be not

**To make Pippen Jelly**
Pare and quarter 12 or 14 good Pipins, and put about a pint and half of Water, and let it boil, and when the virtue of the Pipins is out in the Water, then put it into a Hair-Sieve, and let it settle all night, and then lay a whole piece of Citron sliced into that Liquor to soak out of the Sugar, and the next day, get all ready, when you go about it, and put a pound of double refin'd Sugar to a pint of that Liquor, and when it Boils put in some slices of Pipins cut the wrong way till you come to the Kennels, boil it quick which will soon be done, and put in the Glasses with thin slices of Citron, and a little Juice of Lemons. (*Pastry-Cook's Vade-Mecum,* 23–24)

*"Unidentified cookbook, c. 1700"—Anonymous* | *Comments*

**To Make Pipens Pastt mb**

Take the fairest pipens fresh Gathered Skald them very Tender then peale them and take the pulfe cleane from The core then beat the pulfe in a morter and putt it Throw a Sieve then wheigh the pulfe and take the Wheight of it in Sugar and make a candy of it and when It will draw a heire and the pulfe boyles then putt it in The Candy and Stir it well together and then putt it in Your moalds and Set it in a Stove or oven to drey Turning it Every day till it is dry

———

**The Make an Apple pape for taffitty tarts**

Stew Your Apples in alittle watter till they are Enought then work þm Through a Seive & Season þm with Sugar Cinomon and rose watter

~ **Taffity** alluded to the "dainty" or "delicate" texture of something, such as "Taffity Tarts and Pies" (*OED,* 11:24). This particular dessert is seldom seen in publications. Holme's version called Tarts more closely resembled Anonymous (1700)'s recipe with its stewed or baked apples "laid in paste" and flavored with sugar, orangado or lemon in suckets. His other recipe, called Taffety Tarts, was more like a fruit tart. The paste was shaped round, square or long and topped with layered apples. Sugar, lemon peel, and fennel seeds were then strown over it. During baking, these tarts were iced (Holme, *Academy,* Bk. 3, Chap. 3, 85).

**To green Codlins**

Take Kentish Codlins coddle them whole & take of the skins then take fresh watter: putt into it a Bitt of Allom & a hanfull of white Sugar put in the Codlins & Stop them very Close & put them by a good fier þt they keep hot but not boyle for an hour & half: then they are fitt for use.

~ **Allom** is common alum, a "whitish transparent mineral salt" used for a number of purposes, including medical use (*OED,* 1:259).

*Contemporary Recipe #1*

seen, and then lay it in the water all night, then boil them in water till the pill be soft, then cut them in long peeces, then put it into the Sirrup, and stir it about, and fill your glasses, and let it stand till it be cold, and then it is ready to eat. (Kent, *Gentlewoman's Delight,* 35–36)

**To make an excellent greene Paste without any colouring.**

Qvoddle greene Apples reasonably tender, pill off the outward skinne, and throw all the barke of the Apples into a Posnet of seething water, and so let it boile as fast as it can vntill it turne greene, then take them vp and straine the pulp, then boile the weight of it in Sugar to a Candie height, and put your pulp into the seething Sugar, and let it boile vntill it grow stiffe, then fashion it on a pie-plate, or a sheete of glasse, and print it on mowlds, and drie it in a Stoue or a warme Ouen some tenne or twelue dayes that it be perfectly drie, and then you may keepe it all the yeere. (Murrell, *Daily Exercise,* #8)

**A pippen Tart.**

Take Pippins of the fairest, and pare them, and then diuide them iust in the halfes, and take out the chores cleane: then hauing rold out the coffin flat, and raisd vp a small verdge of an inch, or more high, lay in the Pippins with the hollow side downeward, as close one to another as may be: then lay here and there a cloue, and here and there a whole sticke of Sinamon, and a little bit of butter: then couer all cleane ouer with Sugar, and so couer the coffin, and bake it according to hte manner of Tarts; and when it is bak't, then draw it out, and hauing boyled *Butter* and *rose-water* together, anoynt all the lid ouer therewith, and then scrape or strow on it good store of *Sugar,* and so set it in the ouen againe, and after seue it vp. (Markham, *English House-Wife,* 116)

**To coddle Codlings green, to serve up with Cream.**

Take Apples from the tree fit to coddle, put them into a broad Pan (or Skillet) of water, set them over an heap of charcoal fire; so that they may be alwayes scalding hot, and never boyl, kept lose covered; only to have an eye on them that now and then they may be turned in the pan; This constant sober heat without boyling (and being kept close) Causeth their greenness; when they are tender, take off the outward skin; your cream being

*Contemporary Recipe #2*

**To make Paste of Pippins, the Geneva fashion, some with leaves, some like Plums, with stalks and stones in them.**

Take your Pippins, and pare them and cut them in quarters: then boile them in faire water till they be tender; then straine them and dry the pulp upon a chafindish of coales: then weigh it, and take as much sugar as it weigheth, and boile it to *Manus Christi,* and put them together: then fashion them upon a Pieplate and put it into an Oven being very sleightly heat: the next Morning you may turne it, and put them off the plates upon sheets of Paper upon a hurdle, and so put them into an Oven of like heat, and there let them remaine foure or five dayes, puting every day a Chafindish of coales into the Oven: and when they be thorow dry you may box them, and keepe them all the yeare. (R. H., *Closet,* 11)

**To make Tarts of the Jelly of Pippens.**

For making of your Jelly of Pippens, you must take of your fairest Apples, pared, quartered, and cored, for every pound of them, take a three quarters of a pound of fine Sugar, put them into a stew-pan, and almost cover them with clear Spring-water, put to them three or four sticks of Cinamon, cover your pan very close with a lid, set them upon Charcoals, and let them boyl up softly, until they come to a colour, see that your fire be not too fierce and stir them sometimes that they d not burn; when they are enough they will look as red as Ruby, and clear as crystall, then take them off the fire, and put them in a dish; when they are cold, you may fill them into Coffins dryed, like Hearts or Diamonds: and stick them with Orangado and Cittern, and serve them up as a dish, or garnish other rich Tarts or Baked meats with them: you may also put them on thin sheets of rich Paste, and make them with in the manner of Taffety-Tarts. (Rabisha, *Whole Body* [1673], 185–86)

**To pickle Codlins**

Gather your Codlins half grown, and without Spots, for if they are spotted, they are commonly Worm-eaten; scald them in Water till the Skin will come off easily, then put them again into old Water, and small piece of Allum to green in a Brass pan over the Fire; which they will soon do if they are kept close cover'd. (Bradley, *Complete Body of Husbandry,* 123)

*"Unidentified cookbook, c. 1700"—Anonymous*

*Comments*

**To Candy Angellico**

Take y/e Stalke of Angelico before they be too old Cut þm in long peices from the Leaves & put þm ino a pot of cold water to boyle letting þm boy[le] till ye be very tender: Then take them up & String þm: taking of ye out side þn put them into warm watter & let þm Stand till they be as grean as Grass for ye Greener ye better ye watter being very warm but not boyl all ye while Then take þm up and dry þm in a Cloth and to 1 lb Angellico take 3/4 lb loaf Sugar beaten Small: then take ye Sugar and put into a bason putting in a Spoonfull or two of watter into it Setting it on a Charcole fier & let it boyle till it is pretty thick: Then put in your Angelico & lett it boyle till it is pretty thick: Then put in your Angelico & let it boyle a lettle till it begins to Cand or yo[u] may if you please after you have dryd the Angelico lay it in a Bason & betwen every lay Strow Loaf Sugar between very Small & let them stew over a Charcol fier till they begin to Candy. But the first is counted the best way to boyle the Sugar first because the Angelico is so moist that it will be a Long while before it will thicken Then take a pye plate & strow it over wth: Some Sugar & take them up as hott as you can and twist them in what fashion you please Letting them Stand on the plates till they be through dry and turn them every day

~ **Angelica** is an aromatic plant "indigenous to Europe, . . . cultived (since 1568) in England," and "featured in a confection called 'Candied Angelica.'" It was also used in other dishes and in medicine (*OED*, 1:324).

**To Preserve Dry & Candy Grapes mb**

Take Large fair Grapes before they be througly ripe the Greenest when they Look clear when you have pricked them & With a Small cutt on the Side then take them and throw them Into as much Sifted Sugar as will cover them your Sugar Must first boyle apase then putt them in and Sudenly Take them of the fier and lett them Stand and infuse till The next day then warm them and then take them up And Sett them a drying if you mean to preserve them in Putt in a lettle fresh Sugar into the Surup and let it boyle Againe by it Self and when it is boyled Some thing thick Put in youre Grapes againe and Sett them over the fier And warm them two or three times then let them Stand till They are colde if you will dry them then when they be Drained putt them into fresh Sugar being bouyled to a Candy Height Soe take them up out of the hott Sugar and dry them In a Stove or oven turn them every day till thay be Dry and when they are throughly: dry you may put Some of them in your Candy pott

**To preserve Grapes whole**

Take Grapes when they are so clear that you can see through them when they are above half ripe before they change Couller and are not Spect stone them in their sides and as you Stone them strow Sugar over them and for every pound of Grapes a pound of Double Refin'd Sugar Clarefy your Sugar well and boyl it to Candey hight then put in your Grapes and boyl them up quick and when they look clear they are enough then set them by for a Day and ye next Day-make Jelly of Pippens or of some of the Worst Grapes and give the Grapes a boyl in the Jelly and putt them in your glasses and fill them up & [recipe ends] (The Compiler [1744], Manuscript cookbook, 8).

~ This incomplete recipe revealed that it was a more simplified version by the time The Compiler (1744) copied it, but it kept the key elements of preserving grapes.

*Contemporary Recipe #1*

boyled up, and season'd, you may put them in whole or in halves, all over your cream; being very well sprinkled with Rose water: so scrape on sugar, and send them up. (Rabisha, *Whole Body* [1673], 38)

**To preserve Angelico roots.**
Take the roots and wash them, then slice them very thin and lay them in water three or four dayes, change the water every day, then put the roots in a pot of water, and set them in the embers all night, in the morning put away the water, then take to a pound of roots four pints of water, and two pound of Sugar, let it boyle, and skum it clean, then put in the roots, they will be boyled before the sirupe, then take them up, and boyle the sirupe after, they will ask you a whole dayes work, for they must boyle very softly; at Saint *Andrewes* time is the best time to doe them in all the year. (Kent, *Gentlewoman's Delight,* 63)

**To preserve Grapes.**
Take of the fairest bunch of the whitest Grapes, gathered in the heate of the day, picke out the smallest Grapes with a penknife and make your bunches cleare, and also your stalkes cleane; then take out the stones with a needle on the one side, but make not the hole to bigge: then take the weight of halfe your grapes in Sugar clarified, with as much Rose-water as will dissolue it, then put your grapes into the hot boyling Sugar and let them boyle vp to the top of the posnet, then take it off and let it coole: when it hath boyled vp the third time, let it stand in the sirrup till the next day, then set it on the fire againe, and let it boyle, cooling it now and then, and boyle your sirrup till it be thicke, and between hot and cold, put it into pots or glasses for your vse. (Murrell, *Delightful Daily Exercies,* #51)

*Contemporary Recipe #2*

**To Candy Angelica.**
Take ye stalkes in May & boyle them in fair Water till ye rinde Will pill off. That doe & then make yr Syrop wth fair Water & Sugar & boyle them in it Untill they be tender. Lett them Lye in ye same Syrope 2 or 3 dayes. then take them out & pleit them. & boyling a fresh Syrope to a high Candy-height, putt in Yr stalkes & take them prsently off ye fyre stirring them too & fro. Then take them forth & lay them on a Pye-plate one by one. & When they are cold Drye them before ye fyre or in a Warme Ouen. (Fairfax Family, *Arcana Fairfaxiana Manuscripta,* 74)

———

*"Unidentified cookbook, c. 1700"—Anonymous* | *Comments*

**To Make Consarve of Lavinder flovers mb**

Take the flowers being new gathred as many as you Please and beat them very fine take three times their Wheight of white Sugar putt in a little at a time and Beat it till it is all in then put it in your potts Stir It some times else it will Spoyle

———

**To Make Rasberry Wine mb**

When you have gathered the Rasberrys putt in a handfull or two into a pott and then Strow Sugar and then put in Rasberreys Againe and Soe doe every day as you Gather them till you have Gott as many as you intend, to make wine of then putt them into a vesle and boyle Such a quantity of Sugar as you think The Rasberrys will bear they will not beare So much as the Cherrys when it is boyled put it boyling hott into the vesle Stir it well together when it is cold next day cover it & Lett it Stand two or three weekes a working till the Colour Is out of the Rasberrys then bottle it up and putt a Lettle Sugar into Every Bottle

———

**To Make Rasberry Cakes**

Take Rasberrys & pick em & put them in an Earthen Bason & mash them wth ye Back of a Spoone very well then make a good Charcole fier & Set them theiron & make it boyle as fast as you can: keep them Sturing all the while till it be dry then put it in a Bason & weight it & take ye weight in Sugar finely beaten & put it in ye Skillit again & Stur it very well & Sett over ye fier: againe keep it Sturing all ye while till it is hott But it must not boyle after the Sugar is in But when it is hott put it in a bason & lett it Cool a while keeping it Sturing then put it in the Moulds & put them in a Stove & put in a Little fire & lett þm Stand all night then take þm out of ye moulds & turn þm on Clean plates twice a day till they be dry

———

**To Make Jeley of Rasberrys**

Take Rasberrys & pick them & mash þm & Strain þm & to 1 pd Juice 1 lb Loaf Sugar beaten & Sett it on a Charcoal fier & Stir it till it be dissolved þn let it Stand & boyle as fast as it Can & when ye Skum rise Scumming all ye whi[le] till it will jelly then take it out & put it in the Potts

———

*Contemporary Recipe #1*

**Conserve of flowers of Lavander**

Take the flowers being new, so many as you please, and beat them with three times their weight of white Sugar, after the same manner as Rosemary flowers; they will kep one year.

*The Vertues.*

The Brain, the Stomach, Liver, Spleen, and Womb it maketh warm, and is good in the Suffocation of the Womb, hardness of the spleen and for the apoplex. (W. M., *Queen's Delight,* 236)

**36. How to make good Raspberry VVine.**

Take a gallon of Sack, in which let two gallons of Raspberries stand steeping the space of twenty four hours, then strain them and put to the liquor three pound of Raisins of the Sun stoned, let them stand together four or five dayes, being sometimes stirred together: Then pour off the clearest, and put it up in Bottles, and set it in a cold place. (M. B., *Ladies Cabinet,* 67)

*Contemporary Recipe #2*

**To make a Conserve of Lavendar Flowers**

Beat the Flowers while they are fresh, with three times their Weight in fine Sugar, in a marble Mortar with a wooden Pestle, and put them into a Gally-pot, and cover them close for use. (Nott, *Cook's and Confectioner's Dictionary,* #28)

———

**To make past of Respasses.**

Take of the clearest and ribest Rasberies, stamp them & straine them through a cushion canuas, and dry it vpon a chaffindish of coales in a silver or earthen dish alwayes stirring it, then take twise as mch double refined sugar as the pulp doth weight with a graine of Muske, and boyle it to a candy height with as much Rose-water as will dissolue it, then put it in your pulpe and let it boyle very softly, alwayes stirring it till it growe something thicke, alwayes stirring it till it come from the bottome of the posnet, then lay it vpon a sheete of glasse in what fashion you please, and set it into a warme Ouen or Stoue, and when you see it candy vpon the top, turne it and let it candy on the other side, and in ten or twelue dayes it will be dry enough, then boxe it and keepe it dry for your vse. (Murrell, *Delightful Daily Exercise,* #41)

**Jelly of Raspisses.**

First, strain your Raspisses, and to every quart of Juice, add a pound and an half of Sugar, pick out some of the fairest, and having strewed Sugar in the bottom of the Skillet, lay them in one by one; then put the Juice upon them with Some Sugar, reserving some to put in when they boil; let them boil apace and add Sugar continually, till they are enough. (Hall, *Queen's Royal Cookery,* 158)

**To make Quodiniock of Raspices, or English Currans.**

Take Raspices ripe and well coloured, and put them in a dish, & put to them four spoonfulls of Rose-water, and mix them together with the back of a spoon; then wring the liquid substance thorow a linnen cloth; season it by your mouth with sugar till it it be sweet enough; then boil it upon a Chafindish of coals in a dish, till it be ready to print; then print it in your moulds, and box it, and so keep them.

Your moulds must ly in water one night before you use them : and an hour before you print with them, take them out of the water. (R. H., *Closet,* 21)

———

*"Unidentified cookbook, c. 1700"—Anonymous*

*Comments*

### To Make Marmalett of Rasps

Take Rasps & pick Clean: þn marsh þm & put þm in aSkillet over a fier and make þm boyl apace till they be very thick but not so thick as for Cakes: [?] then put it in an Earthen bason & bake ye weight in Sugar finely beaten then put the pulp & Sugar into ye Skillit again ab:tt 1/8 of an hour and try it by cooling a Lettle in a Spoon If it cut it is anought

———

### To preserve Rasps

Take ye fairest Rasps when they are fresh gathered & weight them and take ye weight in Loaf Sugar & break it in peices & wett it wth: watter & sett it over a fier make it boyle & Scum it Clean & put in ye Rasps & let them boyle very fast but a Lettle while & Sometimes Shake þm round the Skllett & scum em Clean: So put þm in ye potts one by one þn boyl up the Syrup Scum it Clean & put it to them

~ **Rasps** are raspberries (*OED*, 8:139).

### To Preaserve Green Walnutts

Take ye: beast green Walnutts You can gett when thay are so young that one may run a nedle throught þm: Then Cast of the Stalks & noses then prick them all over full of holes wth: a nedle haveing ready a Little of watter put þm: in & make them boyle apace: a lettle while þn Shift þm in another water & let them boyle till they are tender Shifting þm:often þn: peel them & haveing ready two boyling watter: putt them in & let them have a warm or two over the fier in Each water then take them up into a Cleane Cloth & dry them þn : way them & take their weight in Sugar & to Each pound of Sugar 1 pd of watter Set it over a quick fier & scum it well Then put in y/r walnutts & Let þm: boyl 1/2 an hour or rather more þn: take þm: of ye fier & let þm stand all ye night ye next day heat it againe: Scalding hot: Then take ye Walnuts up into ye pots & lay þm eaven: þn: boyle up ye Syrup till it be Pretty thick scum it very well & pour it on þm ye next day paper þm:

~ "Stalks & noses" is an old term not often seen in publications. Presumably these referred to the sliver of the inner shell located between the "wings" of the walnut.

*Contemporary Recipe #1*

*Contemporary Recipe #2*

---

---

**To preserve Raspices.**

Take of your fairest and well coloured Raspices, and pick off their stalkes very cleane; then wash them, but in any case see that you bruise them not; then weigh them, & to every pound of Raspices, you must take six ounces of hard sugar, and six ounces of sugar-candy, and clarifie it with halfe a pinte of faire water, and foure ounces of juice of Raspices: being clarified, boil it to a weake sirup, and then put in your Raspices, stirring them up and down, and so let them boile till they bee enough, that is, using them as your Cherries, and so you may keepe them all the yeare. (R. H., *Closet,* 7)

---

**To preserue greene Walnuts before they be shelled.**

Take your Walnuts also when they may easily be pierced with a pin, pare them thinne, and lay them a weeke together in brine, then parboile them very tender in seauen or eight waters, then take them vp, and dry them with a faire cloath, and sticke in euery one two or three Cloues, and couer them in clarified Sugar, and boile them a good houre close couered, then powre them into an earthen pot, and let them stand a weeke, & then warme them againe, and power them into a Colender, to let the sirupe drop from them; then boile the sirupe by itselfe vntill it be somewhat thicke with fresh Sugar, and being but warme pot them. (Murrell, *Daily Exercise,* #24)

**Take Five Hundred New Walnuts**

This is the way to make compote. It should be begun on St. John's Day, which is the twenty-fourth of June. First, around that time, take five hundred new walnuts, being careful that the shells and the kernels are not yet formed, and that the shells are not yet too hard or too soft. Peel them all around, make holes through them in three places or in the form of a cross, put them to soak in Seine or well water, and change the water every day. Let them soak ten or twelve days (they will turn black) unti there is no bittern when you chew them. Then boil them awhile in sweet water, for as long as it takes to say a *miserere,* or until they are neither too hard nor too soft. After this, throuw out the water and put them in a sack to drain. Take honey, a *sextier* or as much as will thoroughly cover them, and melt it until it is runny and foamy. When it is cooled to lukewarm again, add the nuts. Leave them two or three days, then drain them. Take as much of your honey as will cover them, put it on the fire, bring it once to a rapid boil, skim it, and take it off the fire. In each of the holes in the nuts stick a clove one one side and a little piece of cut ginger in the other. When the honey is luke-warm, put the nuts in it and then turn them two or three times a day. After four days take them out and boil the honey again; if there is not enough, add more. Boil it, skim it, boil it, and then add the nuts. Do this every week for a month. Then leave them in an earthenware pot or a cask; and turn them once a week. (Bayard, *Medieval Home Companion,* 121–22)

*"Unidentified cookbook, c. 1700"—Anonymous*

**To make marmalett of Quinces red**

Pare your Quinces thin: Quarter & Core þm & save ye cors & Cover þm with watter in a porrenger: Then weight ye Quinces & to 1 lb Quinces 1 lb sugar & 3/4 pt: of water then brake ye sugar into ye watter & set it over a quick fier: Stir it till ye Sugar is dissolved: þn: cover it a while: þn: Scume it clean & put in ye Quinces and keep them Close covered: & let them boyle till they are tender: Sometimes Stir them doing þm: dwn with a knife or ye back of a Spoon: then take þm: up into a silver or Earthen Bason & mash þm: very well wth: a Spoon or ladle skcum ye Syrup well & put in ye Quinces againe keeping þm close Cover'd all ye while Except some times to stir them & let it boyl till it be so thick that when you stir it you may see ye Bottom of ye Skillett þn: take ye potts: Set þm before ye fier till they be warm þn wipe þm & put in ye marmalett: & Cover þm: not till nex day ye Cores that where put into a Lettle watter must be put in a lettle bag and tyed & boyled in among ye Quinces till you take þm: up to mash them & then take it out: its Cheafly to set a Glas on it and make it Cutt well

*Comments*

~ **Quinces**, "hard" and "yellowish pear-shaped fruit" of a "small tree (*Pyrus Cydonia*)" from the pear family, was used in cookery "as a preserve or to flavour dishes of other fruits" (*OED*, 8:63).

**To make white Malmalett**

Put your Quinces in a Skillit of Cold watter & set þm over a gentle fier & Scald þm til they are tender & will peel: Thay must not boyl & when very tender take þm: up into a Clean Cloth: covering them to keep þm: white: Then Scrape þm: from ye Cooers And to 1 lb Pulp 1 lb Sugar: brake ye Sugar in lumps: dip þm in watter & put it over a quick fier it must not be Coverd at all but Stired over Sometimes untill ye Sugar be melted: þn let it Stand till the scum rises & when it boyles Scum it clean: Then put it ye Quinces Stir it often making it boyle pretty fast till it be thick enought wch: well be when you can see ye Bottom of ye Skillit or presering pan as your Stir it. Then warm ye potts & if thou will make Cakes take some out before it boyles and fill it into ye moldes

———

**To Preserve Quinces**

Take ye fairest Quinces you can get & scald þm: till they be tender Then take þm: up & pare them as thin as you can & then get a Scoop & take out ye Cores & keep þm: fresh: & then weight your Quinces and take their weight 1 Loaf Sugar: & to 1 lb Sugar take 1 ptt watter & then brake ye Sugar: Then Put it over ye fier: & let it Just boyl Then Scum it & put in your Quinces & ye kirnels in a Cloth & let it boyl till thay be ready

———

*Contemporary Recipe #1*

**Quinces liquid**

Take them very yellow, and without spots, cut them into quarters, and seeth them in water, until they be well sod, and very soft; then drain them, & put your sugar in the same water, which you shall seeth a little more than sirrup; put your Quinces in again, and put in their seeds, taken out first and wrapped into a linnen cloath, for to give them a colour, and when they are enough, take them out. (LaVarenne, *French Cook,* 272)

*Contemporary Recipe #2*

**To preserve Quinces red.**

Take your Quinces and weigh them, to a pound put a pound of Sugar, and half a pint of water, put your water to your Sugar, and let it stand, your Quinces must be scalded till they be tender, take them off, pare them, and core them, but not too much, then put them in the skillet where the Sugar is, then set them on the fire, and let them boil two hours, if it be not enough, boil it a little more, pour it to the Quinces, and stop it close. (Kent, *Gentlewoman's Delight,* 45)

**To make white Quince Marmalade**

Scald your Quinces tender, take off the Skin and pulp them from the Core very fine, and to every pound of Quince have a pound and a half of double-refin'd Sugar in Lumps, and half a pint of Water; dip your Sugar in the Water, and boil and scum till 'tis a thick Syrup: then put in your Quince, boil and scum it on a quick Fire a quarter of an hour, so put it in your Pots. (E. Smith, *Compleat Housewife* [1729], 190)

**1. The best way to Preserve Quinces white**

First pare and core the Quinces, and boyl them in fair water till they be very tender, not covering them; Then taking them out of the water, take to every pound of them two pound of Sugar, and half a Pint of water, and boyle it to a sirrup, scumming it well; then put in some of the Jelly that is washed from the Quince kernels, and after that making it boyle a little, put in your Quinces, boyl them very fast, keeping the holes

**To make past of Quinces or Peaches.**

Take yellow peare quinces boyle them tender in their skins, then pare them and scrape the clearest of the pulpe from the coare, but not too neere for the coare is grauelly, then take so much refined sugar as this pulp doth weigh, and boyle it to a candy height with as much Rose-water as will dissolue it with a graine of muske, then put your pulpe in a faire cloth, and wring out the water very dry, then put it ito your hott sugar and stirre it with a spoone as it boyleth till it come cleane from the bottome of the posnet, then lay it one sheet of glasse in what fashion you please, and set it into a warme ouen or stoue, and the next day turne it, and when it is through dry with a candy all ouer, you may box it and vse it all the yeere: you may likewise make the same of Peaches, but not mingled together, for the one tast spoileth the other, neither dry the pulpe vpon the fire, for I find that it spoyleth the colour of the past. (Murrell, *Delightful Daily Exercise,* #11)

---

*"Unidentified cookbook, c. 1700"—Anonymous*

*Comments*

þn: take þm up & let them Stand 2 or 3 days & and if it do not Jely þn you must boyle þm a gaine: & then put them in your pots & Glasses

**To make Quince Cake**

Take ye fairest Quinces you can gett pare þm & quarter þm & core þm Then boyle þm over a Cleare Charcoal fier in fair watter till they be soft: keep þm Covered all ye while þn take þm up & let þm Stand Draining and þn pulp through a hair Sive & weight þm pulp and to 1 lb of pulp Take 1 1/4 lb loaf Sugar breake ye Sugar and dip it in watter & put in a Bellmettle Skillit over a Clear Charcoal fier Let it boyle and cume it very clean & let it boyle to a candy height & then put in ye pulp and keep it Stiring of the fier till it is all dissolved Then put it over the fier: & let it Just boyle: Then take it up & if you will Colour it then put in your Colouring and let it Just boyl and then take it up in Earthen Bason & put it in your molds upon tin plats and put them in a stove Turing them every daye till they be dry

———

**To keep Codlings Green all the Year**

Take right Codlings, Coddle them soft not to break them then take of the thin skin put them in the same licker with a hand full of apple leavs over them then set them over a slow fire to green when they are green set them to Cool then take the Codlings and mash them Core and all when they are all Cold lay a laying of pulp and a laying of Codlings till the pot is full & when quite Cold melt some Motten suet and pour over them and stop them Cloce.

~ This recipe, different from most similar recipes, used apple leaves to make codlins green.

**To make Quince Caks**

Take Quinces boyl them very tender then strane the pap and to a pound of pap take a pound and two ounces of double refined suga[r] wett it and melt it over a soft fire then boyle it to a Candy hight then put in your pap and boyle it till you Can see the bottom of the preserving pan then drop it upon tin plates of what shape you pleas

~ **Pap, papp, pape,** and **pappe** are obsolete terms for the "pulp of an apple, especially when roasted" (*OED*, 7:434). This presumably applied to quinces, since they are part of the apple family. A **preserving pan** was specifically for "making and keeping preserves" (*OED*, 8:1310).

**To Make Almon Cakes mb**

Take the best Jordan almons that you can gett & Lay þm In watther all night and the next blance them into fair Watther and then beat them while they are as fine as flower And to a pound of almons put in two Sponefulls of rose Watter as thou beatst them but put in but 5 or 6 draps At a time to keep it from oyling & when y/e are beaten Wheight them & to Six ounce of almons take two pounds Of flower mixt y/e flouer & the almons litely together While it is as flower againe then

~ **Jordan** was a particularly "fine variety of almond, chiefly from Malaga" (*OED*, 5:603).

*Contemporary Recipe #1*

upwards, (as neer as you can) for fear of breaking; and when they are so tender that you may thrust a rush thorow them, take them off, and put them up in your glasses, having first saved some sirrup till it be cold, to fill up your glasses. (M. B., *Ladies Cabinet,* 1–2)

**To make thin quince cakes**

To make thinne Quince cakes: take your Quince when it is boiled soft as before said, and drie it vpon a Pewter plate with a soft heat and be euer stirring of it with a slice till it be hard; then take searsed suger quantity for quantity and strow it into the quince, as you beat it in a wood-den or stone morter; and so roule them thinne and print them. (Markham, *English Hus-Wife,* 69)

**To Preserve Pepins Green.**

Take green Pipins and Codle them, shifting the Water thrice till they be green, and when they are tender as to eat them, take them up and feel them, and put them into as much clarified Sugar as will cover them, and let them boil leisurely half an hour, then take them up and boil the syrup by it self a little more, then put in your Pipins when it is cold, and keep them all the Year, the Water must be hot before you put in your Pipins to Codle. (*Pastry-Cook's Vade-Mecum,* 28–29)

**To make Cakes of Almonds.**

Take one pound and a half of fine Flower, of Sugar twelve ounces beaten very fine, mingle them well together, then take half a pound of Almonds, blanch them, and grind them fine in a Morter, then strain them with as much Sack as will mingle the Flower, Sugar, and Almonds together, make a paste, bake them in an oven not too hot. (Kent, *Gentlewoman's Delight,* 56)

*Contemporary Recipe #2*

**To make Mackaroons or Almond Cakes.**

Take half a pound of sweet Almonds, and steep them all night in fair Water, then blanch and dry them, and beat them very small in a Mortar, put in about three Spoonfuls of Rose-water to keep them from Oiling, then take half a pound of Sugar finely beaten, and put it to the Almonds and stir them together, and set it upon a Chaffing dish of Coals, and let it heat, stirring them, not boiling; then take three Whites of Eggs and beat them with a Rod to make them froth, then take

*"Unidentified cookbook, c. 1700"—Anonymous*

*Comments*

put in one pound of Sugar & mixt it as before & one pound of Butter Slice ye Butter very then into Watter and then dry it in a Cloth and mix it as before and then put in y/e yolks Of Eight Eggs being well beaten mix it all lightly Together & then make it out into cakes & bake them Vpon tin plates Save out Sum butter to butter the Plats & bake them when y/e Scorching of ye oven is over.

**To Make a Rice or Almond Florendine mb**

Boyle 8 oz of Rice very Thicke & tender in Milk þn mix in 10 oz of fresh butter a Lettle Beaten Mace & Cinamond & Salt, a pint of Cream wth: Cold a Glass of Sack 6 yolks of Eggs 8 oz of Candid Lemon & Cittron Sliced a Spoonfull of Oringe or Rose watter 8 oz of Currants, Sweetten it with fine Sugar putt A thin paste over ye Bottom of ye Dish þn: put it in & Couer it with pufe paste Bake it dust on fine Sugar and ~~Eat~~[?] it.

~ **Florendine** (or **florentine**) was a "kind of pie or tart, especially meat baked in a dish with a cover of paste" (*OED*, 4:343). Meat was not always required in such dishes, however, as proven by the following examples.

**To Make Cheese Cake**

Take 6 qtt. milk & 1 Spoonful of Runnet so make it into a tender Curd þn take 6 Eggs 1/2 qtt: milk 1/2 Sugar 1/2 Currants 1 lb Butter melted & 1 nutmeg greated So mix it up & fill your Coffins with it

**To make Savoy Bisketts**

First take the Yolkes of 12 Eggs and break them into a bowle and 5 Whites putting thereto 4 Spoonfulls of Rose water haveing ready a pound of double refind Sugar that is finely Searched then beat up your Eggs with a white rod, with some of your Sugar, you must beat them soe long untill thay be thick & white like a Creame and then weigh a pound and 2 Ounces of the finest flower, and mix that in very well and lay them out upon Wafers and bake them.

~ A **Savoy Biskett** resembles a spongy, fingerlike paste dusted with sugar and joined during baking, and it is also known as a sponge cake baked in a mold (*OED*, 9:144). According to Karen Hess, there were wafers made the "French Way," with batter poured onto a buttered iron, pressed, and then baked (Hess, *Martha Washington's Booke*, 154). This may be how Anonymous (1700) prepared her "Savoy Bisketts." **Wafer irons** are circular-shaped irons often decorated with elaborate designs (*OED*, 12:5).

**To Make a Good Cake mb**

Take halfe a peck of fine flower a pound & halfe of Sweet butter Three quarters of a pint of Creame a quarter of a pinte of Sack as Much rose watter 2 nuttmegs a penyworth of Cloves & Mace three Ounces of candid Oranges & Leamon peale & Sitren ye greatest part Sittron half a pound of fine Sugar four Eggs but clean out two white 1 pound of Courrans a quart of ye best ale yest & as much Salt As will ly upon a Sixpence one or two Graines of amber greese bake it in an oven an houer þn beat ye whits of three Eggs, Six ounces of Double refind Sugar þn: wash ye cake all over & Sett it in ye oven a while againe

~ A **peck** is an equivalent of one fourth of a bushel or two gallons (*OED*, 7:598).

*Contemporary Recipe #1*

*Contemporary Recipe #2*

the froth and put it to yur Stuff when cold, and stir it together, then heat your Oven as hot as for a Tart; then take white Paper and slick it very well, and put your Stuff upon it, a Spoonful in a place, and scrape some hard Sugar upon them, when you set them into the Oven one Fagot will heat the Oven. (*Pastry-Cook's Vade-Mecum,* 33–34)

**To make a Rice Florentine**

Boyle the Rice with Milke or water, and season it with Nutmeg, Cynamon, Salt, Sugar and Carrawayes, Rose-water, sliced Dates, lumps of Marow, two or three yolks of Eggs, a little Cream, if it be too thin put in a little grated Bread, and put it into Puff-paste in a dish, and bake it: you may make a Puddling thus in Guts, shredding the Dates and Marrow finer. (Cooper, *Art of Cookery,* 156–57)

———

———

———

**Savoy Biskets**

Beat up a Dozen of Eggs, and but half the Whites, (take great Care they be new), in three or four Spoonfuls of Orange-Flower Water, and strew in a pound of double-refin'd Sugar, finely beaten and sifted: When your Eggs and Sugar is of the Substance and Colour of Cream, dry a pound of the finest Flower, and mix therein: Make them in what size you will, and bake them on Tin plates, first flower'd, in a very slack Oven[.] (R. Smith, *Court Cookery* [1723], 2:44–45)

———

**4. How to make very good Cakes.**

Take half a Peck of fine Flour, five pound of Currans, one pound of Carraway-Comfits, half a pound of Marmalade of Oranges, a dozen Eggs, leave out half the Whites, one pound of Butter, half a pint of Sack, a little Rose-water, Cloves, Mace and Nutmeg; mould them together with a litle new Ale-yeast, and as much Creame as will make them up into Cakes; then Ice them with Sugar and Whites of Eggs, and bake them in a gentle Oven. (Howard, *England's Newest Way* [1710], 108)

———

*"Unidentified cookbook, c. 1700"—Anonymous*

*Comments*

**To Make Chease Cakes mb**

Take a gallon of new milk=turn it with Runnet & when it is come you must putt in your Skiming dish & gather it togather & put it into your Straining Cloth & hang it up & lett it draine till all ye way is out of it þn put it into your morte[r] & beate it wth: halfe a pound of fresh butter, þn mix it wth: Currants & rose watter & Sugar & a Little greatted bread a Little nutmeg & Salt & soe put it into your past a quarter of an hour will bake þm your oven must be pretty quick or Else y/e will be heavey you must put in four Eggs beaten

———

**To Make Flitters mb**

Take of Brandy & Sherry halfe a pinte of Each 1/2 oz of fine Sugar 1/2 an oz of Cinamon Mace & Ginger 4 Eggs will beatten wth a little Salt 8 oz of Naple biskatt or white bread gratted a pinte of Cream mix this tgther & make it thicker þn batter for pancakes wth: fine flower þn fry þm: wth: Clarified hoggs Leard y/e pan must be allmost full wth: it boy[le] Strike þm in formes of a trencher wth: a knife in Lettle bitts w/n: frided up þn fine Sugar & sarve þm you may putt all bread or little or no flower.

∼ "Flitters" appear to be fritters in this context.

**To Make A Cake mb**

Dry 7 lbs of flower þn: rub into it 2 lb of butter þn: mix into it 6 oz of Cloves 1 mace & Cinamond 2 lbs of Suger 1: lb of Candid Lemon & Cittron slliced 4 oz of dates Sliced 12 Eggs whipp three whites to Snow a quart of ale yest a pint of Sacke 1/4 of pint of rose watter þn: melt one pound of butter 1 quart of Cream make it Blood Warm & putt it all into ye flower & mix it well together þn mix into it 6: lbs of Currants & put it into a buttered hoop & Backe it 3 houres & 1/4 make ye icing Ready to Leay on Just as ye Caks Comes out of the Oven and harden it Enove

———

**To Make Rusk mb**

To a peck of flower take twenty Eggs & beat them very well and þn: take a quart of Ale yeast & Strain it in ye Eggs þn take A pound of Sugar & a pound of fresh butter & mix ye Butter in in a quart of Milk but you must not make it hott & a bout a handfull of Carraway Seeds & then Mixt it all together you must not Ned it but put it in little bitts Severall times Over & then Lett them Stand a Risen a while þn make þm up & putt two one upon another & Sett þm in ye Oven as fast as you can & when they are baked anufe take them out & Splite them in two & set them in againe A Lettle When the Oven is allmost Cold

∼ A **rusk** is a piece of bread that has been "re-fired" to render it hard. Rusks were sometimes sweetened (*OED*, 8:923).

*Contemporary Recipe #1*

**49. To season Cheese-cakes.**

Take a Gallon of new Milk warm from the Cow, set it with a spoonful of Runnet; as son as it comes, strain the Runnet from the Curds; rub 'em through a little Range with the back of a Spoon; season 'em with half a quarter of an Ounce of Cloves, Mace and Cinnamon beat fine, a little Salt, half a pound of Sugar, a little Rose-water, half a Pint of Sack, half a pound of butter melted thick; beat in six Eggs, leave out half the Whites, put in a pound of Currans, and it is fit for use.

The same Ingredients for Rice-cakes, only you must boil the Rice tender before; the same way for Almond-cakes, only beat them in a Stone-mortar, with a Glass of Sack, and a little Rose-water. (Howard, *England's Newest Way* [1710], 24)

*Contemporary Recipe #2*

**To season Cheese-cakes**

Take a Gallon of New Milk warm from the Cow, set it with a Spoonful of Rennet; and as soon as it comes, strain the Rennet from the Curds; rub them through a Range with the back of a Spoon; season them with a half a quarter of an Ounce of Cloves, Mace, and Cinnamon beat fine, a little Salt, half a Pound of Sugar, a little Rosewater, half a Pint of Sack, half a Pound of Butter melted thick; beat in half a dozen Eggs, leaving out three of the Whites; put in a Pound of Currants, and it is fit for use (Nott, *Cook's and Confectioner's Dictionary,* #79)

**To make Fritter-stuffe.**

Take fine flower, and three or four Eggs, and put into the flower, and a piece of Butter, and let them boyle all together in a dish or chaffer, and put in *sugar, cinamon, ginger,* and *rose water,* and in the boyling put in a little grated Bread, to make it big, then put into a dish, and beat it well together, and so put it into your mould, and fry it with clarified butter, but your Butter may not be too hot, nor too cold. (Jenner, *Book of Fruits & Flowers,* 49)

**To make Good Fritters.**

Mix half a pint of good Cream, very thick with Flower, beat six Eggs, leaving out four Whites, and to the Eggs put six spoonfuls of Sack, and strain them in the Batter; put in a little grated Nutmeg, Ginger and Cinamon, all very fine, also a little Salt; then put in another half pint of Cream, and beat the Batter near an Hour: pare and slice your Apples thin, dip every Piece in the Batter, and throw them in a Pan-full of boiling Lard. (Several Hands, *Collection* [1714], 98)

---

**To make the hard Bisket.**

TAKE half a peck of fine Flour, one ounce of Carraway-seeds, the whites of two Eggs, a quarter of a pint of Ale-yeast, and as much warm Water as will make it into a stiff Paste; then make it in long rolls. Bake it an hour; the next day pare it round; then slice it in Slices about half an inch thick; dry it in the Oven; then draw it and turn it, and dry the other side; they will keep the whole Year. (E. Smith, *Compleat Housewife* [1729], 135)

*"Unidentified cookbook, c. 1700"—Anonymous*

*Comments*

**To Make the Icing for a Cake mb**

Beat & Sift 1 lb of dauble refind Sugar through a Sive þn: whipp ye whits of 6 3ggs to Snow very thick þn put in ye Sugar by degres in beat it together 1/2 of an hour tell ~~thick~~ it will but iust runn put in a little Rose watter Just as ye Cake cumes out of ye oven whett it all over wth: rose watter þn lay on the Icing all over ye topp and Sides Lett it Stand tell it be Cold

It is interesting that Anonymous (1700) used "3" for the letter "E," given her attention to the neatness of her penmanship.

**To Make little Cakes**

Take 1 1/2 lb flower & 1/2 lb white Sugar 1 lb Currants mix them well together Then take Six Eggs 1 lb of Butter 2 Spoonfulls of Rose watter: a little Cloves and mace beaten Work them together till it is like a Custard: then put to them ye flower & Sugar Currants & work them together little balls & lay them upon tin plats & bake them in a Gentle Oven

———

**R:M: A Receipt for a Cake**

Take 1/2 peck fine flower well dryed: 1 lb Currants 3 lbs Butter Sliced thin and rubed in the flower till it be fine 2 lb sugar: 1 oz of Cloves mace & Nuttmegs beatten together 1 lb of almonds blanched & beaten fine put in 1 or 2 Spoonfuls Rose watter as you beat them to keep þm from oyling as much Cittron-Candid-orange & lemon peal as you please mix these all well together take 1 qtt of milk boyled & let it be almost cold: 1 qtt good ale yest 1/4 pint Rose watter 2 or 3 Spoonfulls of Brandy 12 Eggs half ye whits left out beat them well together & before ye Oven be quite hott mix your Cake: When mix Cover it & lay it 1/2 hour befre ye fire to Rise Then paper ye hoop & Butter ye paper well both sides & Bottom lett it be asoaking Oven & Bake it 3 hours & while it is Baking take for 1 Cake 2 lbs the finest loaf Sugar: beaten & Sifted and well beat together with ye whites of 3 Eggs a little Rose-watter & when you draw it out of ye oven & it hath stood a little Ice it top and sides Spread it as Smoth as you can wth a knife & then Strew it thick wth: Carraway Comfits & it well baked it well keep a month it must not be set in the Oven after it be Iced

Cakes containing dried fruits and/or seeds were interchangeable with recipes for seed, caraway, and plum cakes.

**Comfits** are sweetmeats made of "some fruit, root, etc. and preserved with sugar," and now each is "usually a small round mass of sugar enclosing a caraway seed, almond or sugar plum, etc." (*OED,* 3:661).

**T - M Receipt to make a Cake**

Take forty Eggs 4 lbs Sugar 4 lbs flower 4 lbs butter 2 nutmegs Cinnomon Cloves & Carraway Seeds Beat the Eggs one houer and Eggs & Sugar turn over another hour Mix the butter & flower well together And then put them into the Eggs & Sugar and then Beat it up wth one's hand If you Like Currants put in some Else it is

———

*Contemporary Recipe #1*

*Contemporary Recipe #2*

**To make little Cakes**

Take a pound and quarter of Flower, dry it, and cool it; then work into it half a pound of Butter, which has lain all night in Damask Rose-water before you use it, put in half a pound of Loaf-Sugar beaten very fine, and a pound and half of Currants washed, and temper all these with four Yelkes, and two Whites of Eggs beaten very well, with as much thick Cream as will make them into a Paste. This quantity will make 16 or 17 Cakes, the Oven must be as hot for small Manchet; half an hour, or little more will bake them; prick them when you bake them [.] (*Pastry-Cook's Vade-Mecum,* 48–49)

**A Seed Cake**

Take 3 pound of Smooth carraway comfitts 6 pound of flower halfe a pound of Sugar an ounce of Spice rubbed in very fine with 2 pound of butter make a hole in the flower and putt in 3 pints of Ale yest halfe a-pint of Sack a little orange flower-water a pint of warm milk mixed together strew a little flower thereon and Lett it lie to rise put it in a hoop and bake it Strow over it double refind Sugar and rough carraway comfitts. (Anonymous [c. 1720], handwritten notes in *E. Kidder's Receipts,* 26)

*"Unidentified cookbook, c. 1700"—Anonymous*

*Comments*

well enought with out Butter ye pan well & so Bake it in a Tin pudding pan It must be kept beating wth ones hand till it goes into the Oven Else it will fall

**Dutch Bread or Rusk**

Take 4 lbs flower: 1/2 lb Butter 2 Spoonfulls of Sugar sifted a pint & 1/4 of Milk the butter must be mielted in the Milk lett it be almost Cold before you put it into ye flower & ad 1/4 a pind of good yeast & 5 Eggs work all into paste & make it up into Little loafes of ye bigness of halfe penney bread then let it Stand before the fier till it is well Risen when is Baked Cutt þm into halfes & Set them into ye Oven to Crispe

**Plane Wigs**

Dry 3 lbs fflower mix 2 lbs & 1/2 with a pint of East & almost as much warm milk þn lay it by ye fier half an hour & while it is warme work in 3/4 lb Butter & 1/2 lb Suger & as much Carraway Seed as you please ye 1/2 lb of flower goes in the working it up wth the Butter & Spice So make them up & bake them in a Quick Oven

~ **Wiggs** (**wigs**) were wedge-shaped cakes or buns made of fine flour and often used during Lent (*OED*, 12:118). A **quartern**, now obsolete, is a dialect for a "quarter of anything" (*OED*, 8:33).

**To Make Genger Bread**

Take 1 peck of flower 4 oz Carraway seeds 6: oz Ginger 1 Suger 1 1/2 lb Butter Slice ye Butter thin & rub it in the flower: then mix them well then: take 1 Gallon Treacle 1 ptt: milk mix the treacle & milk together: then make up your bread & work it till it will Cut fast þn make it into Cakes or what you please It much not be baked to much & when baked dip each Cake into boyling water as they come hott out of ye Oven & let þm dry.

**To make Ginger Bread**

Take 4 pound of Flower 3 pound of the thickest Treakle as much Ginger as you think fitt and as much Cloves Mace & Nutmeg and Cinamon as will lay on a half Crown to your Flower & Treakle make it up very stif then make your Cakes as you please 2 inches thick will take an hours baking then have redy a Kettle of boyling Water & Just dip it in to make it have aGloss Loaves of this butter'd hot is good[.] (The Compiler [1744], Manuscript cookbook, 57).

**To Make Naples Biskets**

Take 1 1/2 lbs flower well dryed in an Oven & 2 lbs Sugar dryed & finely beaten and search'd throught a Sive then take in 12 Eggs & beat them well mix these well together wth a few Carraway & Coriander Seeds: well beaten & 3 or 4 Spoonfulls rose watter, then beat it all togeth very well ab: 1/2 hour and not let it Stand then Butter the molds & fill them but not to full & bake them, But ye Oven must not be so hott as to Collour a paper in a Considerable time

~ **Naples Bisket** (obsolete) was a once popular biscuit "affiliated with Naples in Southern Italy" (*OED*, 7:20). According to Hess, it is rare to find a recipe for this biscuit in culinary manuscripts from the seventeenth century, and she believes that they were imported (Hess, *Martha Washington's Booke*, 155). The Compiler (1744) also had a recipe for "Naples Biskett," but it was quite different in content.

*Contemporary Recipe #1*

*Contemporary Recipe #2*

———

———

**To make Wigs.**

Take three pounds and a half of Flour, and three quarters of a pound of Butter, and rub it into the Flour till none of it be seen, then take a pint or more of new Milk, and make it very warm, and half a pint of new Ale-yeast, then make it into a light Paste. Put in Carraway-seeds, and what Spice you please; then make it up, and lay it before the Fire to rise; then work in three quarters of a pound of Sugar, and then roll them into what Form you please, pretty thin, and put them on Tin-plates, and hold them before the Oven to rise again. Before you set them in, your Oven must be pretty quick. (E. Smith, *Compleat Housewife* [1729], 129)

———

**Gingerbread Cakes**

Take 3 pound of flower one pound of Sugar one pound of butter rubbed in very fine 2 ounces of Ginger and a grated Nuttmeg mix it with a pound of Treacle and a quarter of a pint of creame warmed together then make up your bread stiff and roule them out cutt them with little Cakes and Bake them in a Slack oven[.] (Kidder, *E. Kidder's Receipts* [1720], 27)

**Another way**

Take a quarter of a Peck of flower 2 pound and 3 quarters of Treacle a quarter of a pound of Ginger halfe an ounce of Carraway and-coriander seeds bruised make it into large Cakes putt it what sweetmeats you please into either of them when they are baked dip them in boyling water to glaze them. (Anonymous [c. 1720], handwritten notes in *E. Kidder's Receipts,* 28)

**Naples Bisket:**

To make these so much in use: Take a pound of fine Flour, and the like weight of Sugar, eight Eggs, and two spoonfuls of Rose-water, an ounce of Carraway-seeds beaten small: mix them well together, and put them, when made, into a fit thiness with fair Water, into Tin Coffins, and bake them moderately in a gentle Oven, glazing them over with Water, in which Sugar has been dissolved. (Salmon, *Family Dictionary,* 218)

**To make Naples Biskets**

Take a Pound and half of fine Flour, and as much double-refin'd Sugar, twelve Eggs, three Spoonfuls of Rose-water, and an Ounce and half of Carraway-seeds finely powned, mix them all well together with Water; then put them into Tin-plates, and bake in a moderate Oven, dissolve some Sugar in Water and glaze them over. (Nott, *Cook's and Confectioner's Dictionary,* #1)

*"Unidentified cookbook, c. 1700"—Anonymous*

### To Make Shrewsberry Cakes

Take 3 lbs flower 1 lb Sugar dry them both in an Oven then take ye Sugar & beat it very fine & Search it very fine then take 1 lb fresh Butter & Cutt it into ye flower & mix them together: and 3 Spoonfull Sack as much rose water: & 3 Egs beaten: & mix thes well together: and knead it very well: then Rowl it very thin & Cutt it round by a trencher or sum other Round thing then Butter tin plates & put them on þn prick them then bake þm: but the Oven must not be so hott as for ye Biskets

*Comments*

———

### To Make Seed Cake

Take 6 lbs flower well dryed 3 lbs Butter broken & rub'd in Cold, ten Eggs half the whites Cast by, 10 Spoonfulls Rose watter, 1/4 ptt Sack 1/2 ptt Cream, 1 ptt of Ale yeast Let ye Eggs & liquor be Straind into ye flower & Butter & lett it Stand by ye fier 1/2 an hour to rise þn take 2 1/2 lbs Carraway Cumfits & 1/2 orange Peal: Lemon peal & Citron peel, Sliced work ye Carraway & Citron into it lay it on double papers and Round it with Cap paper, two hours time in a good Oven may bake it

~ As old favorites, **seed cakes** were usually flavored with "caraway seeds" and "sweetened" (*OED*, 9:385).

### To Make Portugal Cakes

Take 1 lb flower, 1 lb Butter 1 lb Sugar 1 lb Currants 12 Eggs taking out half the whites Setting ye flower & Sugar before ye fier to dry & beat ye Eggs & Butter together one way tile it comes to be like Cream: then take ye flower & Sugar & Curants & mix them well together

———

### To Make Plumb Cake

Take 4 lbs flower well dryed: 3 lbs Currants well clean'd & dryd 1 lb Raysins stond 10 Eggs 1/2 the whits Cast by 1/4 pt Sack 1 ptt Barme: 1 pt Cream warm enought to dissolve 1/2 lb butter: 4 Spoonfull of Rose watter 1/4 Sugar 1/2 oz Nutmegs 1/2 lb Lemon & Citron peel 1/4 lb Dates: sliced thin a Little Salt and Ginger: all ye dry & hard things mix together wth: a Stirrer not with hands for that will make it heavey þn Strane in all ye liqued things mix it all together wth: the Stirer þn turn it out into a hoop buttered þn put it in the Oven to bake it abt 2 1/2 hours Look to it Some times that it Catch not make ye Ice as before mentioned

~ **Barme** is the "froth" that appears on the "top of the fermenting malt liquors" and is utilized as leaven for breads and in the fermentation of liquors (*OED*, 1:675).

*Contemporary Recipe #1*

**To make *Shrewsbury* Cakes.**
Take four pound of Flower, two Pound of Butter, one Pound and a halfe a fine Sugar sifted, four Eggs, a little beaten Cinnamon, a little Rose or Orange-flower-Water, and make a Hole in the Flower, and put them in, when they are beaten, melt the Butter, and mix it well with the Sugar, Rose-water, Cinnamon, The Eggs and Flower into a Paste, and roll it thin, and cut them by the bottom of a Glass; but if you would have them the size of *Shrewsbury* Cakes, cut them by a small round Trencher; bake them in an Oven, hot enough for small Tarts, on Tin Plates, or butter'd Paper. (R. Smith, *Court Cookery* [1724], 209)

*Contemporary Recipe #2*

**To make Shrewsbury-Cakes.**
Take to one pound of Sugar, three pounds of the finest Flour, a Nutmeg grated, some beaten Cinnamon; the Sugar and Spice must be sifted into the Flour, and wet it with three Eggs, and as much melted Butter as will make it of good thickness to roll into a Paste; mould it well and roll it, and cut it into what shape you please. Perfume them, and prick them before they go into the Oven. (E. Smith, *Compleat Housewife* [1729], 129–30)

**3. How to make a good Seed-cake.**
Take a quarter of a Peck of Flour, two pound of Butter beaten to a Cream, a pound and three quarters of fine Sugar, one Ounce of Carraway-seeds, three Ounces of candied Orange-peel and Citron, ten Eggs, leave out half the Whites, a little Rose-water, a Glass of Sack, a little Cloves, Mace and Nutmeg, a little new Barm, and half a pint of Cream; mix it up and lay it by the Fire to rise; then bake it in a Hoop, and butter your Paper: When it is baked, Ice it over with Whites of Eggs, and Sugar, and set it in again to harden. (Howard, *England's Newest Way* [1710], 108)

———

**A good Sort of Portugal Cakes.**
Take a pound of new Butter, and six Eggs, leaving out two Whites; then work it together with your Hand, 'till the Eggs are perfectly mixt in the Butter; to this put one pound of Loaf-Sugar sifted, a pound of fine Flower dry'd, half a pound of Currants, a little beaten Mace, mix all together; Butter the Pans; fill and bake them in an Oven that won't colour a White Paper. (Several Hands, *Collection* [1714], 87–88)

**To make Portugal Cakes**
Take two pound of new Butter, twelve Eggs, leaving out four Whites, work them together with your Hand, 'till the Eggs are througly mixt with the Butter; add to this two pound of sifted loaf Sugar, two pound of fine Flour dry'd, a pound of Currants and some beaten Mace; mix all together, butter your Pans, fill them and bake them in an Oven so moderately hot, that it will not colour a white Sheet of Paper. (Nott, *Cook's and Confectioner's Dictionary,* #12)

———

**Another Plum-Cake.**
Take four pounds of flour, four pounds of Currants, and twelve Eggs, half the whites taken out, near a pint of Yeast, a pound and half of Butter, a good half pint of Cream; three quarters of a pound of Loaf-sugar, beaten Mace, Nutmegs and Cinnamon, half an ounce beaten fine; mingle the Spices and Sugar with the Flour; beat the Eggs well and to them a quarter of a pint of Rose-water, that had a little Musk and Amber-grease dissolved in it; put Butter and Cream into a Jug, and put it in a Pot of boiling Water to melt; when you have mixed the Cake strew a little Flour over it; Cover it with a very hot Napkin, and set it before the Fire to rise; butter and flour your Hoop, and just as your Oven is ready, put your Currants into boiling Water to plump; Dry them in a hot Cloth, and mix them in your

*"Unidentified cookbook, c. 1700"—Anonymous*

*Comments*

**To make Caraway Cakes/**

Take 1 1/4 lbs Jordan Almonds being blanched Slice them as thin as you can then take 9 lbs flower & 5 lbs Butter sliced ye Butter into ye flower rub it wt : your hand together untill it is like all flower then beat 6 Eggs very well & boyl 3/4 pint Cream þn take a qt & 1/2 pint of good ale Barme & 3/4 pint of Canary put ye Eggs to ye Sack & Stur it well: þn take 1 lb Candied Citron and Slice it very thin in Bro:[?] pieces 4 lbs of Carraway Cumfits 4 grs. of musk put ye musk into ye flower & ye Barm & Eggs together and when ye Cream is hott put Some of it into ye Egs keep it Sturing so put it all in: and when ye Oven is ready þn mixt ye Cake & put it ye Citron Carraways ye last things Bake it on wafer paper wth: other paper under it Put it in the Oven as Fast as you Can

———

**To Make the Jews Almond Cakes**

Take 1 lb Almonds: blanch them & beat þm with 3 Spoonfulls Orange flower: watter then take 1/2 lb of Duble refin'd Sugar & ye youlks of 4 Eggs & beat þm altogether in a morter very well: Then put in 2 Grs: of musk or amber Grease, To make ye past you must take 1/4 lb of double refind sugar 1/2 lb of flower dry'd: & 2 Eggs but one white & wth: a little watter make a Stiff past and So make it into what form you please

~ This title and "To Make Jews Bread" do not appear in any of the published cookbooks examined to date by the author. Perhaps these were two cherished recipes handed down through the family. The title at the left is believed to be a biblical allusion because of the absence of any leavening agent.

**To Make Jews Bread**

Take 11 yolks of Eggs & beat þm very well wth: a little amber watter abt: a spoonfull: then put to it 1 lb of Duble-refined Sugar & 1 lb flower Then put it into ye: pans & put them into a moderate Oven

~ **Amber water** might refer to water flavored with a grain or two of ambergris, which is sometimes called amber as an abbreviation. It could also be spermaceti, known as "white amber," but it is not to be confused with the fossilized yellowish resin also known as amber (*OED*, 1:268).

**To make Little Cakes**

Take 1 1/2 lbs flower 1 lb white Sugar 1 lb Currants mix them well together Then take Six Eggs 1 lb Butter either fresh or Salt washed 3 Spoonfulls Rose watter a little Cloves & mace beaten: Work them together till it is like a Custard: Then put to them ye flower Sugar & Currants & work þm together into little balls: & lay them upon tin plates & bake them in a Gentle Oven

~ In spite of its different title, the following recipe contains the same basic outlines.

*Contemporary Recipe #1* *Contemporary Recipe #2*

Cake. You may put in half a pound of candied Orange, and Lemon, and Citron; let not your Oven be too hot, two hours will bake it, three if 'tis double the quantity. Mix it with a broad Pudding-stick, not with your Hands; when your Cake is just drawn, pour all over it a gill of Brandy or Sack; then ice it. (E. Smith, *Compleat Housewife* [1729], 136–37)

**My Lady H——'s way to make a Carraway Cake.** Take three pound and a half of the finest Flour, and dry it in an Oven one pound and a half of sweet Butter, and rub it in the Flour until it be crumbled very small, that none of it be seen; then take three quarters of a pint of new Ale-yeast, and half a pint of Sack, and half a pint of new Milk, six spoonfuls of Rose-water, four Yolks and two Whites of Eggs; then let it lie before the Fire half an hour or more; and when you go to make it up, put in three quarters of a pound of Carraway Comfits, and a pound and a half of Biskets; put it in the Oven, and let it stand an hour and half. (Hall, *Queen's Royal Cookery,* 42–43)

———

**To make Almond Cakes.**

Take a pound of Almonds, blanch and beat them exceeding fine with a little Rose or Orange-flower-water; then beat three Eggs, but two Whites, and put to them a pound of Sugar sifted, and then put in your Almonds, and all beat together very well; butter sheets of white Paper, and lay the Cakes in what form you please, and bake them.

You may perfume them, if you like it; bake them in a cool Oven. (E. Smith, *Compleat Housewife* [1729], 130)

———

———

———

**To make little Plum-cakes.**

TAKE two pounds of Flour dried in the Oven and half a pound of Sugar finely powdered four yolks of Eggs, two whites, half a pound of Butter washed with Rose-water, six spoonfuls of Cream warmed, a pound and half of Currants unwashed, but picked and rubbed very clean in a Cloth; mix all together and make them up in Cakes, and bake them in an Oven almost as hot as for Manchet. Let them stand half an hour till they be coloured on both sides; then take down the

———

*"Unidentified cookbook, c. 1700"—Anonymous*

*Comments*

**To make Scutchaneale**

Take 1/4 oz Scutchaneal & pound it to power & then take 1/4 lb of duble refined Sugar & 1 oz of Boach allom & 1/4 pint watter, & put it into a Skillet over a Clear charcole fier : & let it boyl about a 1/4 hour þn take it of & when it is cold put it in a Bottle for use

~ **Boach allom** is an unidentified type of salt. Only wealthy or well-to-do families could afford scutchaneale.

**C-H Puding**

Take one pound of Currants, one pound of Suit, Six Eggs three Spaens fulls of flower, Nutmeg and Salt, Cut your Suet small and boyule it 4 howers

———

**For a Cold**

Take an oz of Lickerish 1/4 oz of Sweet fenel seeds and three pints of water boyld and pour it upon them bruse the Lickerish and Seeds let it stand by the fire two or three hours to infuse Drink 1/4 of pint in a morning fastin and two or three hours after Diner and when you go to Bed

~ There are many recipes concerning treatments for colds, but none of the recipes examined by the author mentions the combination of fennel seeds and licorice.

**To make Minced Pyes, Mrs. Street**

One Ounce of Mace & Nutmegs & Clovs, beaten together one Pound of Currants, One pound of apples, one Pound of Suet, one pund of Sugar, ye juice of two Lemons and one Sevil Orange with ye rinds finely grated, a Gill of Sack Candy'd Oranged & Lemon Peel & Citron,

———

**A Receipt for to make Stoutens Bitter**

Take one Doz: of the Rindes of Civell Oranges, one ounce of Gentian Roots Sliced Steep the Orange Rinds and the Gentian Roots three Weeks then Strain it out and add one Dram of Scotchaneal and one Dram of Saffron put the Saffron 9 pence and Scocthaneal 9 pence half an ounce in a fine Linin or muslin bagg and let it Stand three Weeks Longer, the Quantaty is for one Quart

~ **Gentian** is a "plant belonging to the genus *Gentiana* (esp. *Gentiana lutea*)," which yields the "gentian root of the pharmacopoeia" (*OED,* 4:115). **Saffron** was a real luxury since it was very expensive. It was procured as dried stigmas of "*Crocus sativus.*" Saffron was used for coloring confectionaries, liquors, etc., and in medicine as "a cordial or sudorific" (*OED,* 9:30).

**An Artificial Wine to keep ye Body soluble**

Take a Gallon of boiling Water, and pour it upon three pounds of Raysons of ye Son Ston'd and well bruse'd by Squeezing and pressing get out the juce as thorowly as you can from the Skins, and haveing Strain'd, put to it a pound of brown sugar Candy,

———

*Contemporary Recipe #1*

Oven-lid, and let them stand a little to soak. (E. Smith, *Compleat Housewife* [1729], 117)

**8. Excellent Pudding.**
Take a Quart of Cream, boil it with two Manchets, and grate in one Nutmeg, six Yolks and four Whites of Eggs well beaten, with your Bread and Cream at least half an Hour together; then put into it a pound of Beef-suet finely minced, half a pound of Sugar, a little Salt, bake it three quarters of an Hour in a quick Oven, the same way boiled without Suet as long is as good. (Howard, *England's Newest Way* [1710], 4–5)

**To Make *Stoughton's* Bitter, Doctor *Ratcliff's* way.**
Take one quart of the best French brandy, one drachm of cochineal, two ounces of gentian; six Seville orange-peels; let these ingredients stand a week in a bottle or jug and pour off the liquor thro' a strainer. (Atkyns, *Family Magazine*, 2:307)

*Contemporary Recipe #2*

**A Boil'd Pudding.**
Take a Pound of Beef-suet shred very fine, then stone three quarters of a Pound of Raisins, then take some grated Nutmegs, a large Spoonful of Sugar, a little Salt, some Sack, four Eggs, three Spoonfuls of Cream and five Spoonfuls of Flour; mix these together, tie it up in a Cloth, and let it boil three Hours. Melt Butter, and pour over it. (Harrison, *House-Keeper's Pocket-Book*, 117)

*"Unidentified cookbook, c. 1700"—Anonymous*

**To Make a Water against the Plague**

Any Surfeit Ague or the gripes or most approved and Experienced p P. Hart Take of Sage one handfull as much

| | | |
|---|---|---|
| Time | Mint | Egrimony |
| Angelico | Cardius | Bame |
| Bitton | Wormwood | Drgones |
| Burneyet | Redd Roses | Carduf |
| Scordium | Buriage | Lavender |
| Tormintle | Scabius | Isoope |
| Rew | Varvaine | Pelitory of ye wall |
| Popies | Margerum | Rosa Solis |
| Rosemary | Mary Gold flowers | Buigles flowers |
| Camemile | Cowslips | Celandine |
| of Cloves | Pempernell | ffennell |
| Mugwort | Sinnomon | Aneseeds |
| Nutmegs | Coriander | |

Each a quarter of a ounce with Some figs & Rasons and a bout half a pound of Lyquorish Sliced ye figs and raisons to be Stoned-

You may take all the harbs and Speices and add or deminish as you have ocasion or need Cut y/e harbs a lettle And Steep them in brandy or leay of Sack twenty four hours then draw it of Either in a Limbeck or cold Still but the Latter is best you may Eether Sweeten it with Sugar alltogether or put as your use it for many Like it Not to drink Sweetned at all~you may take four five or Six Spoonfulls att a time for the plauge take tenn Spoonfulls and Sweenten it with it for the Ague take for or five Spoonfulls an hour before you Expect the colde and Lay to Sweet if you feill any Chilliness or other Simtoms of its aproach take presently two or three Spoonfulls more And if you fieall it coming take two or three Spoonfulls more but none after the cold fitt comes upon you if you can get into a Swett wth: it before y/e cold fitt takes you & Lay in y/e sweet turn over two hours or an houre at Least: after the time the could fitt Should come, it then cures your ague this is a new receit of the cordiall watter it be mad this way Shread the harbs pretty Small put them in a pot & cover þm over wth: watter Stir þm & push them down in ye watter once a day & when they begin to firment Sett it of quickly ye watter will blader so þn Still it of Set it by & Still it over againe at Leasure & then put up 12 bottls of this watter wth: a few fresh harbs into y/e: Still againe & power over 6 bottles of Brandy on the top & Stop it up close & Still it of you may draw of it 12 bottles of very good watter & Stronge making it thus Whearas Steeping ye harbs: in brandy you can draw of but Soe many quarts as you have brandy but this may makes it very Stronge of ye harbs over ye other dos & halfe the quantity of Brandy Serves

*Comments*

**Bitton** (**bettony** or **bittony** [obsolete]), is a plant of the genus *Stachys betnica* whose spiked purple flowers and ovate crenate leaves were attributed with magical and medicinal virtues (*OED,* 1:831, 834). **Burneyet** is **burnet,** a "popular name of plants" of the "genera *Sanguisorba,*" which are commonly found in meadows and chalky ground and which were known respectively as the "Great" or "Common Burnet" and the "Lesser" or "Salad Burnet" (*OED,* 1:1192). **Scordium** is a name for "Water-Germander," a plant once used in medicine "as a sudorific, an antidote for poisons, etc." (*OED,* 9:239). **Tormintle,** also known as tormentil or septfoil, is "a low growing herb, *Potentilla Tormentilla* . . . of trailing habit" that is commonly "found in heaths and dry pastures" and whose "astringent roots" were used "from early times in medicine, and in tanning" (*OED,* 11:161). **Rew (rue)** is recognized as a "perennial evergreen shrub of the genus *Ruta,* especially *Ruta gravedens,*" and has "bitter" and "strong-scented leaves . . . used for medicinal purposes" (*OED,* 8:869). **Mugwort** (or **motherwort**), "a plant known as "*Artemisia vulgaris*" and other species such as wormwood (*A. Absinthium*), was "famous for an uterine & antispasmodic" (*OED,* 6:747). **Cardius (cardus, carduus)**, a Latin name for thistle, in England was more familiarly called *Carduus benedictus* or Blessed thistle (*OED,* 2:115). **Wormwood,** a plant identified as *Artemesia Absinthium,* is "proverbial for its bitter taste"; its "leaves and tops" were used as medicinal "tonics and vermifuge," and when used in brewing and protecting clothes and bedding from moths, it yielded a "dark green oil" (*OED,* 12:312). **Scabius** can be any of the "herbaceous plants of the genus *Scabiosa*" and was once believed effective as a "cure of certain skin diseases" (*OED,* 9:157). **Varvaine,** or vervain, is "a common European and British herbaceous plant known in scientific circles as *Verbena officinalis*" and prized for its "reputed medicinal properties" (*OED,* 12:151). **Margerum** is marjoram, an "aromatic herb used in cookery" (*OED,* 6:166). **Egrimony** is agrimony, which covers a genus of plants (*N.O. Rosaceae*) and includes liverwort; it was valued for its ability to "open liver & spleen" (*OED,* 1:191). **Bame** (archaic) is balm (*OED,* 1:645). **Drgone (dragon)** refers to either the name of plants shaped like a dragon's claw or to a dragon plant found in the species of *Draecana* (*OED,* 3:636). **Isoope** is an obsolete term for hyssop (*OED,* 5:509). **Pellitory of ye wall** is a "low bushy plant with small oviate leave and greenish flowers" that grows "upon or at the foot of walls"; its "pungent flavor" was used in medicines as a "salivant" and as remedies for "local irritant" and toothache (*OED,* 7:626). An archaic term, **Rosa Solis** was the herbal plant **sundew,** which "grows on mossy grounds" and was used in wines and at one time flavored cordials (*OED,* 8:798). **Celandine**

*Contemporary Recipe #1*

**To make the Plague or Surfeit water**

| | |
|---|---|
| Dragons | Wood Sorill |
| mugwort | feverfue |
| Agrimony | Scabious |
| Bettony | Carrdus |
| Baum | Sage |
| wormwood | hearts Ease |
| Pimpernell | |
| fumatary | Tormentill |
| | Angelico |
| Rue | Wild Time |
| Calendine | Scordium |
| Burnett | Mary Gold floors |
| | Rid popy floors |
| Spearmint | Clove July floors |

of Each of these one pound
Rosemary
Cowslip floors
Tormentill Root
Each of these half pound
Elicamplane Root
Butterbur Root

Sett all thes above 3 or 4 days upon a table before you Use þm & Shred þm very Small then putt þm into any Convenient thing as a Large cream pott or Kettle ading to them ad followeth

| | |
|---|---|
| Each | Sweet fennell Seeds |
| an Ou | Carroway Seeds |
| nce | Cardium well bruis'd |
| | Cloves |
| | Nutmeg Cinemon |
| | Venice Treackle |
| | Diascordium |
| | of Each Ounce |

To all these add 3 Gallons of good brandy and lett them Stand to Infuse 4 dayes - Stirring þm once a day & keeping ye pott coverd then Still þm in a Close Still keeping it col[?] wth wett cloths when the Surfeit water begins to Grow Sower taking more you may boill some of ye Smallest water in fine Sugr. & Little Amber Grease to a Syrup to Sweeten ye Rest. (Fairfax Family, *Arcana Fairfaxiana Manuscripta,* 156)

*Contemporary Recipe #2*

———

*"Unidentified cookbook, c. 1700"—Anonymous*

*Comments*

can refer to either of two separate plants with yellow flowers, and the "old herbalists" probably correctly identified it as a species of the same plant as the "greater & lesser Chelidonia" of ancient times; it could pertain to the Common or Greater Celandine (*Chelidonium majus*), which is known by still another name, Lyte swallow-wort, whose "thick yellow juice" was considered a "powerful remedy" for poor eyesight (*OED*, 2:209). **Ague** is an old word for an acute, violent, or malarial fever (*OED*, 1:192).

**To Make Surfitt Watter**

Take two Gallons of Brandy half a pound of Licorish one pound of figs one pound of Reasons two ounces of Sadra root beaten to powder two pecks of popy flowers cut out ye black & Six peny worth of Raisons a quarter of an ounce of Safron infused amongst it take two ounces of annis seed one ounce of Cordanum Seeds one ounce of Sweet fenell Seeds a quarter of an ounce of Scutchaneell bruse it & disolve it in halfe a pint of Sack bruse the Seeds Slice ye licorish & figs Stone ye reasons & put þm all into a glase & let þm Stand two or three weeks ye take ye Lyquorish from ye ingredience þn put into the Lyquorish two quarts of Sack & one pound of good Sugar þn put in the Scutchanall and Straine it againe this is is good watter to breath out any distemper of Surfit or cold take a quarter of a pinte and goe to bed it will causs the party to sweet.

~ **Surfeit waters** ("surfeit" applied to any "excessive amount or supply") were created to deal not only with excessive eating or drinking, but also with any sickness, such as intemperance and fevers (*OED*, 10:233). **Sadra root** is unidentified. **Distemper** referred to an illness, disease, or "disturbed humour" (*OED*, 3:520).

**To Make Doca. Stevens Watter**

Take Angelico dragon and cardus of Each one pound of rosemary brown Sage brown fennell maiden Hop Sparemint cordium balm Salendine dittander wormwood Sabius burnit rew phillipendilo prosper egrymony ormentall bittone Gentury Sasafrax wood pillobory vervine mugwort Roses solis of each of these take half a pound genium roots of each four ounces heare is the full quantity of yeabs four ounces Seedary roots

and roots for Seven Gallons of Sack these Herbs are to be picked and weighed exactly as above mentioned and then washed and put to run and then Shread indiferent Small and so Slice the roots and doe the like to them as to the harbs and so put the wine to them Stop it close four dayes then Still it in a limbick with a delibarate fire and be sure set it cole and the watter is good a gainst the plague

**Doctor Stephens's Water**

Take a Gallon of Gasking Wine the take Ginger and Gallingale Cinamon Camamile Nutmeg Graines Cloves Anny seeds & Fennil Seeds Carraway Seeds of Each a Dram then take Sage Mint Read Rose Time Pellitorne of the wall Rosemary Wild Marigom Argnea every of them one handfull then pound the Spice & wring the herbes & putt alltogether into half white Wine & half Brandy & let it stand twelve hours sturing it Divers times & still them in a Limbrick & Sweeten it to your Teast with loaf Suger then bottle it up[.] (The Compiler [1744], Manuscript cookbook, 44).

~ **Maidenhop** is not located in *OED*, but perhaps it is a female hop? **Sparemint (spearmint)** is a common garden mint used in cookery (*OED*, 10:541). **Dittander**, now **dittany**, is a "labiate plant" named pepper wort or dittany of Crete that was once famous for its "alleged medicinal virtues" (*OED*, 3:543–44). **Phillipendilo** (also known as **filipendula** or **philypendula**) is a drop wort that has "tuberous root-fibers" (*OED*, 7:214). It can be found in common, field, and mountain drop worts (*OED*, 3:682). **Prosper** and **wood pillobory** are not identified. **Gentury** could

*Contemporary Recipe #1*

**Surfeit Water.**

Two Gallons of Anniseed Water, half a bushell of Poppeys, & steep them in ye Anniseed Water for a fortnight. Cover them & stir them every Day. Then strain of ye Poppeys & take 2 oz. of Anniseeds & 2 oz. of Cardimum seeds, two Oz. of Coriander seeds, 2 Oz. of Liquorish sliced. Bruise ye seeds, figgs, & Raisons, of each a pound. Ye Raisons being ston'd, put all these into ye Anniseed Water. After it have lain 3 or 4 Days strain it & bottle it off. (Blencowe, *Receipt Book,* 49)

**The Copy of Doctor Stephens Water.**

First take a gallon of the best Gascoyn Wine; then take Ginger, Gallingale, Cinamon, Nutmegs, Grains, Cloves, Anniseeds, Fennell-seeds, Carroway-seeds, of each of them a dram weight: then take wild Time, Hysop, Lavender, Sage, Mints, red Roses, Garden Time, Pellitory of the wall, and Rosemary, of each of them one good handfull, and bray the Herbs very small, and stamp the Spices all together very small: put all together into the Wine, and close it fast twelve hours, and stir it divers times: then still it in a Limbeck, and keep the first water, for it is the best; and then keep the second, for it is good, but no so good as the first. E. C. (R. H., *Closet,* 44)

*Contemporary Recipe #2*

**King Charles II's Surfeit Water.**

TAKE a gallon of the best Aqua-vitae, a quart of brandy, a quart of Aniseed-water, a pint of Poppy-water, and a pint of Damask Rose-water: put these in a large glass Jar, and put to it a pound of fine powder'd Sugar a pound and a half of Raisins stoned, a quarter of a pound of Dates stoned and sliced, 1 ounce of Cinnamon bruised, Cloves 1 ounce, 4 nutmegs bruised, 1 stick of Liquorice scrap'd and slic'd; let all these stand nine days close cover'd, stirring it 3 or four times a day; then add to it three pounds of fresh Poppies, or three handfuls of dry'd Poppies, a Sprig of Angelica, 2 or 3 of balm; so let it stand a Week longer, then strain it out and bottle it. (E. Smith, *Compleat Housewife* [1729], 223–24)

———

*"Unidentified cookbook, c. 1700"—Anonymous*

*Comments*

mean **centaury,** and if so, this plant with medical properties is more familiar as mor and yellow centaury or common and lesser centaury and is an herb somewhat like marjoram or Saint-John's-wort (*OED,* 2:220). **Sasafrax** is **sassafras,** a native tree in North America whose dried bark was used in medicines (*OED,* 9:115). **Seedary** is believed to be **zedoary,** an "aromatic tuberous root of the species of Curcuma" found in the East Indies and neighboring countries; sold in long or round shapes, it was "used as a drug" (*OED,* 12:88). **Limbick** is an **alembic,** "an appratus formerly used in distilling" that had a beak or nose that "conveyed the vaporous products to a receiver, in which they were condensed" (*OED,* 6:294). **Dr. Stephens** may be the Irish physician Dr. Richard Steevens (1653–1710) whose famed medical knowledge was printed posthumously (*Dictionary of National Biography,* 18:1035–36).

**To make a Cordial watter**

Take 1 qtt of Spring watter a handfull of Bame & mint & marygold flowers & leaves & put þm in a pipkin & infuse þm over a Soft fier untill it be 1/2 dissolved: A lettle before you take it of ye fier add to it 1/4 ptt: Juce of Oranges þn Strain it Then add to 16 lb Sugar: make it into a thin Syrup then let it stand till it be Cold add to it 1 lb worth saffron tyed up in a thin rag: put this into two Quarts Brandy infuse in the Brandy 1/2 qt peel of 1 orange keep it for your use

~ A **cordial** could be a medicine, food, or beverage, depending on its use. As a medicine it stimulated the heart and circulation and thus served as a "comforting or exhilarating drink"; or it could be an "aromatized and sweetened spirit, used as a beverage" (*OED,* 2:987).

**To make the best Surfeit Watter**

Take 3 Gall: Brandy: & 1 peck poppys: 1/2 peck: Cloves Gilyflowers 2 Bunches mint 2 Bunches bame 1 handfull of Angelico: 1/2 peck Marygold flowers: 1 qtt Burage flower watter 1 qt Buglass watter 1 oz Groundsell Seed 1 oz of fennel Seed 1 oz Cardimums: 1 oz Saffron: 2 oz long pepper: 1 oz Cloves: 1 oz nutmegs 1 1/2 oz Cinamon: 1 lb figgs: 1/2 lb dates 1 lb of Resons of ye Son Stond 1 oz Carraway seeds brused þm all & let it Stand twelf dayes and strain þm out and put 1 qt Poppy watter & Sweeten it wth 2 lbs white Sugar maid in a thin Syrop: this is Excellent for any distemper a wine Glase full to be taken at a time in a feaver or ague or Griping or Collick or Stone:

~ The use of poppy seeds in these recipes helped yield a powerful and soporific effect due to its underlying opium qualities. **Burage** is **borage,** part of the "common British species (*Borago officinalis*)" which "has bright blue flowers and prickly hair-covered leaves and stems"; highly "esteemed" in the past as a "cordial," it is still used today for making "cool tankard, claret, etc." (*OED,* 1:999). **Buglass (bugloss),** known to "old herbalists" as "*Helminthia echroides,*" or prickly ox-tongue, covers "several boraginaceous plants," especially small, corn, or field bugloss (*OED,* 1:1161). **Groundsell (groundsel),** which covers a number of plants under the genus *Seneco,* especially the "common groundsel," is a European weed that was largely used for medicinal purposes (*OED,* 4:457). **Long pepper** is prepared from the "immature fruit-spikes of the allied plants *Piper (Charica) officinarium* and *P. Longum (C. Roxburghii)*" and was also "formerly supposed to be the flowers or unripe fruits of *P. nigrum*" (*OED,* 7:663).

*Contemporary Recipe #1*

*Contemporary Recipe #2*

**To make Surffet Water.**

Take a quart of Aqua Vitae, two Handfulls of Popeys, ye blacks being taken away, two handfull of ye flowers of Gilleflowers, & two handfull of ye flower of Marigolds, half a pint of red rosewater, two Nutmegs sliced, ye like quantity of mace, & more of cinamon, ye like qnty of Ginger, half a quarter of a pound of raisins of ye sun stoned. Putt all these into a wide mouth'd glass, & sett it in ye sun 9 days. Then strain it & put to it half a pound of sugar; so keep it for your use. (Blencowe, *Receipt Book,* 41)

*"Unidentified cookbook, c. 1700"—Anonymous*

**A Receipt to make Sweet watter**

Take 1 gallon of runing watter, of Lavender tops 2 handfull of pinks 2 handfulls of red huney suckles-flowers or Ttrefoile 2 handfulls, of Lemon thyme 2 handfulls, of Sweet brier 2 handfulls, of Damask roses 1 handfulls of cloves brused 2 ounces, Infuse all these 4 dayes Sturring them once a day then Still þm: of wth: a gentle fier, Bottle it tye a paper wth holes prick on it

**For a Cordiale Spirit**

Take a few of ye tops & flower of Rosemary, Balm, Angelico, Swett Marjorum, Wormwod: Centrey Angelico Seeds Carraway a few Anniseeds Cubib Cardamum Calamus, Virginia Snake root, a few of Barbadoes bayberries, Angelico Roots a Lettle Liquorish a lettle bark of Sassfrax, a lettle Jention Roots

**An Approved Salve**

Take 1/2 lb Pure Rosin of Frankincence, Virginy-wax, Hart-Suett, Venice Turpentine of each: 4 oz ye best Mastick: 1 oz: Camphire 2 drms Beat your gum into a fine powder: Then take part of your wax & suett & anoyn[t] your Skillet all over: Then put in your Gums & melt þm over a Soft fier. Then take ye other part of your Suett & wax & anonynt a nother Skillit into wch: Strain your gums throught a strong Canvass: But if you beat & Sarch your Gums you need not Strain þm, at all, But put it into two quarts of white wine with out fistication, & put in ye Campheir & boyle it till all ye wine be Consumed wch: may be known by setting some of it in a Spoon & if no moister issue from it it is enought: It must be stirred all ye time that it boyls and after till is blood warm & þn make it up in Rouls for your use

Vertue viz

It is good for all manner of Maladies wounds old or Green in wha[t] place soever or festers ingendred in ye fleash it healeth more in 9 day[s] then other Salves in a month: It suffers not dead flesh to grow or bide where it cometh. It is good for ye head ack being applyed to ye Temples. It is good for sinews Shrunk or stif wth labour: It is good to draw out Iron-Thorns or shroubs out of ye fleash: It is good to healp ye biting or Stinging of Venemaus Beasts: It help[eth?] botches or felons its good for aches of ye Spleen Kidnys or Reins of ye Back: It breaketh Impasthumes & all manner of Swellings either in man or woman. It is good for ye Swellings of ye Dropsie: It is a Soveraign medicine for all aching

*Comments*

~ **Trefoile**, or **trefoil**, with its triple leaves, is a clover, but the term also applies to other plants with trifoliate leaves, such as wood sorrel (*OED,* 11:316).

Clover was a natural room freshener.

~ **Cubib** (or **cubeb**), a berry found on the "climbing shrub *Piper Cubela* or *Cubebe officinalis* and native of Java and adjacent islands," resembles a grain of pepper, has a "pungent spicy flavor," and is used in "medicine and cookery"; there was also a cubib of an "allied African species" known as *Piper clusii* (*OED,* 2:1233). Valued for its antidotal properties to "snake-poison," **Virginia snake root** is the "root of *Polygala senega* or *Aristolochia serpentaria*" (*OED,* 9:301).

~ **Frankincence** (or **frankincense**) is an "aromatic gum resin" derived from the genus *Boswellia* or a resin from firs or pines; the former is used for burning as incense (*OED,* 4:512). **Virginy wax** is **virgin's wax,** a "fresh, new, or unused bees-wax, sometimes that produced by the first swarm of bees"; during later times it meant purified or high quality wax for more general use (*OED,* 12:234). **Mastic,** a "gum or resin which exudes from the bark of *Pistacia Lentiscus* and some other trees," was once commonly used in medicine (*OED,* 6:219). **Gum** might refer to **sweet gum,** used for its stiffening properties "in the arts" or for use in drugs and perfumes (*OED,* 10:506). **Fistication** could not be found in *OED* but may be connected with the verb "fisticate" or "fistucate," an obsolete word meaning "ram down" (*OED,* 4:261). **Iron-Thorns,** though not identified in *OED,* may simply be thorns, since a shrub is also mentioned. These **botches** allude to bumps, swelliings, tumors, and even goiters (*OED,* 1:1011). A **felon** either was a "small abcess," a "boil," or "an inflamed sore" (*OED,* 4:148). **Reins** concerned the "region of the kidney" (*OED,* 8:389). **Impasthumes** (**impostumes**) is an obsolete term for a "purulent swelling or cyst in any part of the body" or an abscess (*OED,* 5:104). **Pilles** (**piles**) is an old term for hemorrhoids (*OED,* 7:856) or **Hemrods,** as it is spelled here (*OED,* 5:17).

*Contemporary Recipe #1*

**A speciall sweet water to perfume clothes in the folding being washed.**
Take a quart of Damask Rose water and put it into a glasse, put unto it a handfull of Lavender flowers, two ounces of Orris, a dramme of Musk, the weight of four-pence of Amber-greece, as much Civet, four drops of oyle of Cloves; stop this close, and set it in the Sun a fortnight: put one spoonfull of this water into a bason of common water, and put it into a glasse, and so sprinkle your cloths therewith in your folding the dregs left in the bottom (when the water is spent) will make as much more, if you keep them and put fresh Rose-water to it. (R. H., *Closet,* 16)

---

**To make an Ointment, called *Flos Unguentorum.***
Take rosin, *Perrosin,* and half a pound of Virgin Wax, Frankincese a quarter of a pound, of Mastick half an ounce, of Sheeps Tallow a quarter of a pound, of Camphire two drachms, melt that that is to melt, and powder that that is to powder, and boyl it over the fire, and strain it through a cloth into a pottle of white Wine, and boil it altogether, and then let it cool a little, and then put thereto a quartern of Turpentine, and stire it well together, till it be cold, and keep it well: This Ointment is good for Sores old and new; it suffereth no corruption in the Wound, nor no evil flesh to be gendered in it, and it is good for headach, and for all manner of Imposthumes in the body, and for boyling eares and cheeks, and for sauce-flegm in the face, and for Sinews that be knit, or stiffe, or sprung with travall; it doth draw out a Thorn, or Iron, in what place soever it be, and it is good for biting or stinging of venomous Beasts; it rotteh [sic] and healeth all manner of Botches without, and it is go for a Fester, and Canker, and *Noli me Tangere,* and it draweth out all manner of aking of the Liver, and of the spleen, and of the Mensis, and it is good for aking and swelling of many members, and for all members, and it ceaseth the Flux of Menstrua, and of Emeroids, and it is a special thing to make a sumed? cloth to heal all manner of Sores, and it searcheth farthest inward of any Ointment (Kent, *Choice Manual,* 55–57)

*Contemporary Recipe #2*

**To make Sweet Water.**
Take Rose leafs, Bay leafs, Lavender, Sweet Marjoram, Eglantine, Pinks, of each two handfuls, Cloves, Cinamon, *ana* one ounce: bruise all these, and pour upon them two quarts of strong Ale, (that is neer the grounds) let them infuse twenty four hours, then distil it, and draw it till the Ingredients remain almost dry. (Digby, *Choice and Experimental Receipts* [1668], 296)

---

---

*"Unidentified cookbook, c. 1700"—Anonymous*

of Sinews for Scabs or Shakeing Palsie or Gout and it healps watter bettwen ye Skins & ye fleash: It is good for ye [P]illes & hemrods if inward It good to prevent miscarrying if a plaister to lower back.

**A Receipt most Excellent to Cure Sore niples & Sore breasts as also approved for feling[?] out feir of burns or scalds: its also excelent for bruizes to take inward or outward**

Take 2 qtt of Cream of 1 nights Gathering in May thenc take these hearbs Sanicle, Buglass; Strawberry leaves, Violet leaves, Columbine leaves, brown Shage, Woodbine leaves, & adders tongue, take all these haveing been never wett of each 1 handfull & rub þm in a Cloth & chop them but not very small & put þm in ye cream & set it over ye fier & keeping it Sturing & as ye oyle riseth take it of: Thous must take care it do not burn: & when ye oyl is clean of then pour it into a glass or pott & let it stand till it be cold: Then turn it forth: & take ye settling of ye Bottom Clean away: Then put it into a pewter dish over a Chafing dish of Charcoal & when it is melted slice in 1/4 oz white Virgins wax & 6 Spoonfulls Red rose watter: & let þm boyle till there riseth no froth or Scum & let it boyle leisurely a lettle while, & then take it up in potts & keep it for they use: This must be made in May ye 3 m/n.

*Comments*

~ **Sanicle** is a plant found under the genus *Sanicula,* such as black snakeroot, or other genera, such as saxifrage (great sanicle and lady's mantle) (*OED,* IX:96). **Woodbine,** which includes various plants of "a climbing habit," is now obsolete, but it once covered convolulus and ivy and now primarily refers to the U.S. Virginia creeper and the West Indian plant known as Spanish woodbine (*OED,* 12:265–66). **Adders tongue** represents a genus of ferns, *Ophioglossum Linn,* whose "simple spike springing from the base of the barren frond, which clasps it when young . . . suggests the mouth and tongue of a serpent" (*OED,* 1:103).

## MR. KIDDER'S RECEIPTS

*Forced Meat Balls*

**Sweet Balls**

Take part of a Leg of Lamb or veal and mince it with ye same quantity of beef suet, put thereto a good Quantity of Currants, Season it with sweet Spice a little lemon Piele 3 or 4 Yolks of Eggs and a few sweet herbs mix it well togather and make it into Balls.

~ Not all the recipes attributed to Kidder were actually published by him. At least one was from another source. Only the first five of Kidder's recipes in the 1740 edition will be repeated here to show that they are almost exactly the same as the 1720 edition. After this point the right column will be left blank with the understanding that the recipes were the same unless otherwise noted. The differences usually are found in the page numbers.

**Savory Balls**

Take part of a leg of Lamb or veal and mince it wth ye same Quantity of beef Suet, a little lean Bacon, Sweet herbs, a Shallot and an anchovey, beat it in a morter till it's as Smooth as wax, Season it wth Savory Spice and make it into little Balls.

———

**Another Way**

Take ye flesh of a foul, beef Suet & marrow ye same Quantity 6 or 8 Oysters, lean bacon, Sweet herbs & Savory Spice Pound it and make it-into little balls.

———

*Contemporary Recipe #1*

**A poultus for sore breasts in weomen**

To helpe weomens sore breasts, when they are sweld or els inflamed: Take violet leaues and cut them smal, and seeth them in milke or running water with wheat bran, or wheat bread crummes: they lay it to the sore as hort as the part can endure it. (Markham, *English Hus-Wife,* 26)

MR. KIDDER'S RECEIPTS

*Forced Meat Balls*

**Sweet Balls.**

Take part of a Leg of Lamb or Veal & Scrape it fine & shred the same quantity of Beef Suet; put thereto a good quantity of Currants, Season it with Sweet Spice, a little Lemon Peel, 3 or 4 Yolks of eggs, & a few Sweet-herbs; mix it well together & make it into little balls[.] (Kidder, *E. Kidder's Receipts* [1720], A1, 2)

**Savoury Balls.**

Take part of a Leg of Lamb or Veal & Scrape it fine with the Same quantity minced of beef Suet, a little lean bacon, Sweet-herbs, a Shallot & an Anchovie - beat it in a Mortar till it is as Smooth as wax, Season it with Savoury Spice & make it into little balls. (Kidder, *E. Kidder's Receipts* [1720], A1, 2)

**Another Way**

Take the flesh of Fowl, Beef Suet & Marrow the same quantity 6 or 8 Oysters, lean bacon, Sweet-herbs, & Savoury Spice, pound it & make it into little balls. (Kidder, *E. Kidder's Receipts* [1720], A1, 2)

*Contemporary Recipe #2*

———

MR. KIDDER'S RECEIPTS

*Forced Meat Balls*

**Sweet Balls.**

Take part of a Leg of Lamb or Veal & Scrap it fine & shred the same quantity of Beef Suet; put thereto a good quantity of Currants, Season it with Sweet Spice, a little Lemon Peel, 3 or 4 Yolks of eggs, & a few Sweet-herbs; mix it well together & make it into little balls[.] (Kidder, *E. Kidder's Receipts* [1740], 2)

**Savoury Balls.**

Take part of a Leg of Lamb or Veal & Scrape it fine with the Same quantity minced of beef Suet, a little lean bacon, Sweet-herbs, a Shallot & an Anchovie - beat it in a Mortar till it is as Smooth as wax, Season it with Savoury Spice & make it into little balls. (Kidder, *E. Kidder's Receipts* [1740], 2)

**Another Way**

Take the flesh of a Fowl, Beef Suet & Marrow ye same quantity 6 or 8 Oysters, lean bacon, Sweet-herbs, & Savoury Spice, pound it & make it into little balls. (Kidder, *E. Kidder's Receipts* [1740], 2)

*"Unidentified cookbook, c. 1700"—Anonymous*

*Comments*

**A Caudle for Sweet Pyes**

Take Sack and white wine a like in Quantity a little verjuce and Sugar boyle it and brew it wth 2 or 3 Eggs as Butterd Ale when the Pyes are baked pour it in a ye funnell and Shake it togather.

~ **Caudle** is a "warm drink consisting of a thin gruel, mixed with wine or ale, sweetened and spiced" that was given to "sick" patients, especially women "in childbed" and their visitors (*OED,* 2:192). **Buttered ale,** once a popular beverage, was "composed of sugar, cinnamon, butter, and beer brewed without hops" (*OED,* 1:213).

**A Lear for Savory Pyes**

Take Clarret, Gravey, Oyester Liquor, 2 or 3 Anchoveys, a ffaggot of Sweet herbs, and an onyion boyle it up and thicken it wth Brown Butter then pour it into your Savory Pyes when Called for

~ A **ffaggot (faggot)** alludes to a bundle or bunch of something, such as herbs (*OED,* 4:19).

**A Lear for Fish Pyes**

Take Clarret White wine and vinegar oyster Liquor, Anchoveys and Drawn Butter when yr Pyes are baked pour it in at the funnell

~ **Claret** wine ranged from yellowish to light red in color but is different from the red and white wines ; in c. 1600 it was "then used for red wines generally . . . now Bordeaux," and in 1616 it was a reference to French wines, colored whites, deep yellows, or reds (*OED,* 2:461).

**A Lear for Pasties**

Season ye bones of that meat you make your Pasty of Cover þn wth water and bake then with ye Pasty when they are baked strain ye Liquor out into ye Pasty.

———

**A Ragooe for made Dishes**

Take Clarret, Gravey Sweet herbs and Savory Spice Toss up in it Lambstones Cocks Combs boyled blanched & Sliced wth sliced Sweet breads Oyesters Mushrooms Truffells Murrells thiken these wth Brown Butter and use it when Called for.

~ **Ragooe (ragout)** consisted of small pieces of meat stewed with vegetables and highly flavored (*OED,* 8:110). **Lambstones** are lamb testicles (*OED,* 6:34). A **truffle** can be any of the various underground fungi of the family *Tuberaceae,* esp. the edible fungus of the genus *Tuber,* a native of central and southern Europe; English and French truffles are esteemed delicacies (*OED,* 11:419). A **murrell** (or **morel**) is an edible fungus of the genus *Morchella,* esp. *Morchella esculenta* (*OED,* 6:662).

**A Regalia of Coocumbers**

Take 12 Coocumbers and Slice them as for Eating put them in a Corse Cloath beat and Squeese þm very dry flower and fry them brown then put to þm clarret Gravey Savory Spice and a bitt of butter rould up in flower Toss þm: up thick they are Sauce for Mutton or Lamb.

———

Sweet Spice is Cloves Mace Nutmeg Cinnamon Sugar & Salt

Savory Spice is pepper salt Cloves mace & nutmeg-

———

*Contemporary Recipe #1*

**A Caudle for Sweet Pyes**
Take Sack & white-wine alike in quantity a little Verjuice & Sugar; boyl it & brew it, with 2 or 3 Eggs as butterd Ale, when the Pyes are bak'd, pour it in at the Funnel & Shake it togather. (Kidder, *E. Kidder's Receipts* [1720], A1, 2)

**A Lear for Savoury Pyes.**
Take Claret gravy Oyster liquor, 2 or 3 Anchovies, a faggot of Sweet-herbs & an Onion boyl it up & thicken it with brown butter; then pour it into your Savoury Pyes when call'd for. (Kidder, *E. Kidder's Receipts* [1720], A.2, 3)

**A Lear for Fish Pyes.**
Take Claret white Wine, Vineager, Oyster Liquor, Anchovies & drawn butter; when ye Pyes are bak'd, pour it in with the Funnel (Kidder, *E. Kidder's Receipts* [1720], A.2, 3)

**A Lear for Pasties.**
Season the bones of that meat you make your Pasty off, cover them with water & bake them with the Pasty when bak'd, Strain the liquor out into the Pasty. (Kidder, *E. Kidder's Receipts* [1720], A.2, 3)

**A Ragoo for Made Dishes.**
Take Claret gravy, Sweet-herbs and Savoury Spice Toss up in it Lamb-Stones, Cox-Combes, boil'd, blanch'd & Slic'd wth Slic'd Sweet-breads, Oysters, Mushrooms, Truffells & Murrells, thicken it these with brown butter, use it when call'd for. (Kidder, *E. Kidder's Receipts* [1720], A.2, 3)

**A Regalia of Cowcumbers.**
Take Twelve Cowcumbers and Slice them as for eating, beat and Squeeze them very dry; flower and fry them brown, then put to them Claret gravy, Savoury Spice and a bit of butter rouled up in flower; toss them up thick, they are Sauce for Mutton or Lamb. (Kidder, *E. Kidder's Receipts* [1720], A.2, 3)

---

*Contemporary Recipe #2*

**A Caudle for Sweet Pyes**
Take Sack & white-wine alike in quantity a little Verjuice & Sugar; boyl it & brew it, with 2 or 3 Eggs as butterd Ale, when the Pyes are bak'd, pour it in at ye Funnell & Shake it togather (Kidder, *E. Kidder's Receipts* [1740], 2)

**A Lear for Savoury Pyes.**
Take Claret gravey Oyster liquor, 2 or 3 Anchovies, a faggot of Sweet-herbs & an Onjon boyl it up & thicken it with Brown butter; then pour it into your Savoury Pyes when call'd for. (Kidder, *E. Kidder's Receipts* [1740], 3)

**A Lear for Fish Pyes.**
Same

**A Lear for Pasties.**
Same

**A Ragoo for Made Dishes.**
Same

**A Regalia of Cowcumbers.**
Same

---

*"Unidentified cookbook, c. 1700"—Anonymous* | *Comments*

*All Sorts of Paste*

**Puff Past**

Lay down a pd of flower break into it 2 ounces of butter & 2 eggs þm make it into past wth. cold water þn work ye other part of ye

~ This recipe was never finished.

**Past for a Pastry**

Lay down a peck of flower work it up wth. 6 pd. of butter 4 eggs wth Cold water

———

**Paste for a high Pye**

Lay down a peck of flower work it up wth. 3 pd. of butter melted in a sauce pan of boyling liquar make it into a stiff past

———

**Past Royall for Patty Pans.**

Lay down a pd. of flower work it up wth 1/2 a pd. of butter 2 ounces of fine Sugar & 4 eggs

———

**Past for A Custard**

Lay down flower & make it into a stiff past past with boyling water sprinkle it wth a little cold water to keep it from cracking

———

*Sweet Pyes*

**A Lamb Pye.**

Cut an hind quarter of lamb into thin slices season it wth. sweet spice lay it in ye pye mixt wth 1/2 a pd. of raisons of ye sun stond 1/2 a pd of currants 2 or 3 spannish potatoes boyld blanchd & sliced or an artichoke bottome or 2 with prunnelas damsons goosberries & graps cittron lemons chips & oringoe roots lay on butter & close ye pye wn. tis bakd make for it a caudle

~ **Spanish potatoes** are Carolina or sweet potatoes (*OED*, 10:1185). **Prunnelas** (obsolete) are a "variety of plum or prune, either fresh or dried," that were considered the finest (*OED*, 8:1536). **Oringoe roots** are **eryngo** or **eringo roots** (obsolete), candied roots of the sea holly (*Erygium maritimum*) that were considered sweetmeats and aphrodisiacs (*OED*, 3:280–81).

**A Chicken Pye**

Take 6 small Chickens roul up a piece of butter in sweet spice & put into þm. þn. season & lay þm. in ye wth. ye marrow of 2 bones rould up in ye batter of eggs wth. preserves & fruite as ye Lamb pye & a caudle

———

*Contemporary Recipe #1*

*All Sorts of Paste*

**Puff Paste**

Lay down a pound of flower, break into it 2 ounces of butter & 2 eggs: then make it into Paste with cold water; then work the other part of the pound of butter to the Stiffness of your paste; then roul out yor. paste into a Square Sheet: Stick it all over with bitts of butter, flower it, and roul it up like a collar, double it up at both ends that they meet in ye middle, roul it out again as aforesaid, till all the pound of butter is in. (Kidder, *E. Kidder's Receipts* [1720], A, 1)

**Past for a Pastry**

Lay down a Peck of flower, work it up with six pound of butter and four eggs with cold water. (Kidder, *E. Kidder's Receipts* [1720], A, 1)

**Past for a high Pye**

Lay down a peck of flower and work it up with 3 pound of butter melted in a Sauce-pan of boyling liquor and make it into a Stiff paste[.] (Kidder, *E. Kidder's Receipts* [1720], A, 1)

**Past Royall: for Patty Pans.**

Lay down a pound of flower and work it up with 1/2 a pound of butter, 2 ounces of fine sugar & 4 eggs. (Kidder, *E. Kidder's Receipts* [1720], A, 1)

**Past for A Custard**

Lay down flower & make it into a Stiff Paste with boyling water, Sprinkle it with cold water, to keep it from cracking. (Kidder, *E. Kidder's Receipts* [1720], A, 1)

*Sweet Pyes*

**A Lamb Pye**

Cut an hind quarter of Lamb into thin Slices, season it with Sweet Spice & lay it in the Pye mixt with half a pound of raisons of the Sun Ston'd, 1/2 a pound of Currants, 2 or 3 Spainish Pottatoes, boil'd, blanch'd & Slic'd or an Artichoke bottom or two, with Prunellas Damsons Gooseberries, Grapes, Citron & Lemon Chips, lay on butter & close the Pye; when 'tis bak'd make for it a Caudle~(Kidder, *E. Kidder's Receipts* [1720], B, 4)

**A Chicken Pye**

Take 6 Small Chickens roul up a piece of butter in Sweet Spice & put it into them then season them & lay them in the Pye wth ye mar-row of 2 bones with fruit & preserves as the Lamb Pye with a Caudle. (Kidder, *E. Kidder's Receipts* [1720], B, 4)

*Contemporary Recipe #2*

*All Sorts of Paste*

**Puff Paste**

Same

**Past for a Pastry**

Same

**Past for a high Pye**

Same

**Past Royall for Patty Pans.**

Same

**Past for A Custard**

Same

*Sweet Pyes*

**A Lamb Pye**

Same

**A Chicken Pye**

Same

*"Unidentified cookbook, c. 1700"—Anonymous*

**Mincd Pyes**

Shred a pd. of neats tongue perboyled wth. 2 pd of beef suet 5 pipens a green lemon picle season it wth an ounce of Sweet spice a pd. of sugar 2 pt. of Currants 1/2 a pt. of Sack a little orange flower water ye juice of 3 lemons a quarter of a pd. of lemon cittron & orange piele mix these together & fill yor: pyes.

**Egg Pyes**

Shred ye yolks of 20 hard eggs wth. ye same weight of marraw & beef suet season it wth sweet spice wth cittron & lemon picle & close ye pyes.

**Another way**

Shred ye yolks of 20 eggs wth cittron & lemon piele season it wth sweet spice þn mix it wth. a qt of Custard stuff ready made gather it to a body on ye fier yor. pyes being dry'd in ye. oven fill þm wth. this batter as custards wn. thay are baked stick þm. wth. sliced Citrron & strew þm with Collard biskets.

**A Lumber Pye**

Take a pd. an half of a fillet of Veal, mince it wth. ye same quantity of beef suet season it wth. sweet spice 5 pippens an handfull of spinnage & hard lettuce tyme & parsley mix it with a penney loaf grated ye. yolks of 2 or 3 eggs sack & orange flower water a pd. & an halfe of Currants wth. preserves ye lamb pye & a Caudle: An humble pye is thus made

**An Artichoke Pye**

Take ye. bottoms of 6 or 8 artichokes being boyld & sliced season þm wth sweet spice mix þm wth. ye marraw of 3 bones with fruite & preserves as ye. lamb pye: A skarrot or a potatoe pye is made ye same way

*Comments*

~ **Pipens (pippens)** is the name given to "numerous varieties of apple raised from seed" (*OED*, 7:899).

———

———

———

~ **Skarrot** might mean skerret, a perennial plant of the water parsnip species, which was often used in medicine (*OED*, 9:152).

*Contemporary Recipe #1*

**Minc'd Pyes.**

Shred a pound of neats tongue parboil'd wth two pound of beef Suet 5 Pippins and a green Lemon Peel: Season it with an Ounce of Sweet Spice, a pound of Sugar; 2 pound of Currants, 1/2 a pint of Sack, a little Orange flower water, the juyce of 3 Lemons, a quarter of a pound of Citron Lemon and Orange peel: mix these togather & fill your pyes

Sweet Spice is Cloves, Mace, Nutmeg, Cincinamon, Sugar & Salt. (Kidder, *E. Kidder's Receipts* [1720], B, 4)

**Another way.**

Shred the yolks of 20 eggs with the Same weight of marrow and beef Suet, Season it with sweet Spice with Citron and Lemon, fill and close the pyes. (Kidder, *E. Kidder's Receipts* [1720], B, 1)

**Egg Pyes.**

Shred the Yolks of 20 hard eggs wth. Citron and Lemon peel, Season it with Sweet Spice, then mix them with a quart of custard Stuff ready made, gather it to a body over the fire, your pies being dry'd in the Oven, fill them with this batter as Custards, when bak'd Stick them with Slic'd citron, and Strew them with coloured biskets (Kidder, *E. Kidder's Receipts* [1720], B, 1)

**A Lumber Pye.**

Take a pound of a half of a fillet of Veal & mince it with the Same quantity of beef Suet, Season it with Sweet Spice, 5 pippins an handfull of Spinnage and an hard lettice, thyme and parsley, mix it with a penny grated white loaf; the yolks of 2 or 3 eggs, Sack and Orange flower water; a pound & an 1/2 of Currants & preserves as the lamb pye & a caudle. An Humble Pye is made the Same way. (Kidder, *E. Kidder's Receipts* [1720], B, 1)

**An Artichoke Pye.**

Take the bottoms of 6 or 8 artichokes being boil'd & sliced, Season them with Sweet Spice, and mix them with the marrow of 3 bones, with fruit & preserves as ye lamb pye and a caudle. A Skerret or Pottatoe Pye's made the Same way. (Kidder, *E. Kidder's Receipts* [1720], B, 1)

*Contemporary Recipe #2*

**Minc'd Pyes.**

Same

**Another way.**

Same

**Egg Pyes.**

Same

**A Lumber Pye.**

Same

**An Artichoke Pye.**

Same

*"Unidentified cookbook, c. 1700"—Anonymous*

*Comments*

*Savory Pyes.*

**A Lamb Pye.**

Cut an hind quarter of Lamb into thin slices season in wth. savory spice lay þm in ye. pye wth an hard lettuce & artichoke bottoms ye. tops of an hundred of asparragus lay on butter & Close ye. pye wn. tis bakd, pour it a Lear

**Another way**

Season yor. lamb steaks wth. savory spice lay þm. in ye pye wth. sliced lambstons sweatbreads savory balls & oysters lay on butter and Close ye pye. when its baked pour in a Lear

**A Mutton Pye.**

Season yor mutten steaks wth. savory spice fill ye pye lay on butter & close it. when tis bakd toss up an handfull of chopt Capers Cowcumbers & oysters in gravy and anchovy and drawn butter

**A Kid Pye.**

Cut yor. kid in pieces. lard it wth. bacon & season it with savory spice lay on butter & close it. when tis bakd take a qt. of large oysters dry þm. in a Cloth & fry þm. brown toss þm. up in 1/2 pt of white wine oysters liquor gravy & barberries thicken it with eggs & drawn butter Cut up ye lid & pour it into ye pye

**A Hare Pye.**

Cut it in pieces break ye. bones & season it wth. savory spice & lay it in ye. pye wth. balls sliced lemon butter & close the pye

**A Hen Pye.**

Cut it in pices season & lay it in ye pye lay in balls yolks of hard eggs butter & close ye. pye wn. tis bakd pour in a lear thickend wth. eggs.

**A Pigeon Pye.**

Truss and season your pidgeos wth. savory spice lard þm. wth. bacon & stuff þm. wth. forced meat lay on lamstons & Sweet breads butter & Close ye. pye put in a Lear

A Chicken or a Capon pye is made ye. same way

~ A **capon** refers to "a castrated cock" (*OED*, 2:96).

*Contemporary Recipe #1*

*Savory Pyes*

**A Lamb Pye.**
Cut an hind quarter of Lamb into thin Slices, Season it with Savoury Spice and lay them in the Pye with an hard Lettice & Artichoke bottoms, the top of an hundred of Asparragus, lay on butter and close ye Pye; when it is bak'd pour into it a Lear[.] (Kidder, *E. Kidder's Receipts* [1720], C, 5)

**Another way**
Season your Lamb with savory seasoning Lay them in the Coffin with sliced Lambstones hard Lettice Artichoke bottom the tops of 100 Asparragus Lay on butter and close the Pye. A Lear. (Anonymous [c. 1720], handwritten notes in *E. Kidder's Receipts,* 9)

**A Mutton Pye**
Season your mutton Stakes with Savoury Spice, fill the Pye, lay on butter and close the Pye; when it is bak'd, toss up an handfull of chopt capers, Cowcumbers & Oysters in gravy, an anchovy & drawn butter. (Kidder, *E. Kidder's Receipts* [1720], C, 5)

**A Kid Pye**
Cutt your Kidd in peices Lard it with bacon season it with savory seasoning Lay on butter and close your Pye when tis bakd take a quart of large oysters dry them in a Cloth and fry them brown toss them up in half a pint of white wine oyster liquor gravy barberies and thicken it with eggs and drawn butter cutt up the Lid and poure in Into your Pye. (Anonymous [c. 1720], handwritten notes in *E. Kidder's Receipts,* 10)

**A Hare Pye**
Cut it in pieces, Season & lay it in the pye with balls, Slic'd lemon butter and close the pye[.] (Kidder, *E. Kidder's Receipts* [1720], C, 5)

**A Hen Pye**
Cut it in pieces, Season it and lay it in the Pye with balls, yolks of hard eggs, Slic'd lemon butter & close the pye: when it is bak'd, pour in a Lear thicken'd with eggs. (Kidder, *E. Kidder's Receipts* [1720], C, 5)

**A Pidgeon Pye.**
Truss and Season your Pidgeons wth. Savoury Spice, lard them with bacon & stuff þm. wth. forc'd meat & lay þm. in ye pye wth. ingredients for Savoury pyes wth. butter & close ye pye a Lear. *A Chicken* or *Capon* pye's made ye same way. (Kidder, *E. Kidder's Receipts* [1720], C, 5)

*Contemporary Recipe #2*

*Savory Pyes*

**A Lamb Pye.**
Same

———

**A Mutton Pye**
Same

———

**A Hare Pye**
Same

**A Hen Pye**
Same

**A Pidgeon Pye.**
Same

*"Unidentified cookbook, c. 1700"—Anonymous*

*Comments*

**A Calves head Pye.**
Almost boyle ye. Calves head take out ye. bones season it wth. savory spice, mix it wth. sliced sweet-breads shiverd pallats cocks-comes oysters mushrooms & balls lay on butter & close ye. pye. & put in a Lear wth. it is bakt.

~ **Sweetbreads** are organ meats of animals, such as the pancreas, thumus, heart, stomach, gullet, and neck (*OED,* X:480). The **pallat** (obsolete) alludes to the palate of the animal (*OED,* 7:389, 398).

**A Neats Tongue Pye.**
Halfe boyle ye. tongues blanch & slice þm. season þm. wth. savory spice wth. balls scliced lemon butter & close ye. pye wn. tis bakd take a pt. of gravy sweet-breads pallats & cock combs tosed up & pourd into ye pye

~ **Neat's tongue** is ox tongue, used as an article of food (*OED,* 7:58).

**A Venison Pye.**
Raise an high round pye þn. shred a pd. of beef suet & put it in ye. bottome þn. cut yor. venson in pieces & season it wth. pepper & salt lay it on ye. suet þn. lay on butter & close ye. pye & bake it 6 hours

———

**A Lambstone & Sweetbread pye**
Boyle blanch & slice þm season & lay þm. in ye. pye wth. sliced artichoke bottoms lay on butter & close ye. pye. A Lear.

~ Although attributed by Anonymous (1700) to E. Kidder, this recipe was not found in any of his published works except for a handwritten version, which follows.

**A Battalia Pye.**
Take 4 small Chickens 4 squab pidgeons 4 sucking rabbits cut þm in pieces & seasons þm. wth. savory spice lay þm. in ye. pye wth. 4 sweetbreads sliced & as many sheeps tongues 2 shiverd Pallats 2 pare of lamstons 20 or 30 cocks-combs wth. savory balls & oysters lay on butter & close ye. pye wn. bakd pour in a Lear

~ **Squabs** are young pigeons (*OED,* 10:719).

*Cold Pyes*

**A Veale Pye.**
Raise an hightround pye þn. cut a fillit of veal into 3 or 4 fillets seasons it wth. savory spice mincd sage and sweetherbs lay it in ye. pye wth. slices of bacon at the bottome & betwixt each piece lay on butter & close ye. pye wn. tis bakd & half cold fill it up wth. clarrifid butter

———

**A Turkey Pye.**
Bone yor. turkey season it wth. savory spice & lay in in ye. pye wth. 2 Capons or 2 wild ducks Cut in pieces to fill up ye. Corners wn. tis baked & half Cold fill it up wth: Clarrifide butter

A Goose pye is made this way wth 2 rabbits

~ Anonymous (1700) did not include the last notation about cold pies in her recipe. **Clarified butter** is a description for melted, purified, and potted butter for culinary use (*OED,* 1:1217; *OED,* 2:462).

*Contemporary Recipe #1*

**A Calves head Pye.**
Almost boyl the Calves head, take out all the bones and cut it into thin Slices and lay it in the Pye with the Ingredients for Savoury Pyes. *A Lear*. (Kidder, *E. Kidder's Receipts* [1720], C.1)

**A Neats Tongue Pye.**
Half boyl the Tongues. blanch & Slice them Season them with Savoury Spice with balls, slic'd Lemon and butter, and close the Pye: when it is bak'd pour into it a Ragooe (Kidder, *E. Kidder's Receipts* [1720], C.1)

**A Venison Pye.**
Raise a round high pye, then shred a pound of beef Suet and put it in ye bottom, cut your Venison in pieces and Season it with pepper and Salt and lay it on the Suet, lay on butter and close ye pye and bake it Six hours. (Kidder, *E. Kidder's Receipts* [1720], C.1)

**A Lambstone & Sweetbread Pye.**
Boyle blanch and Slice them with savory seasoning & Lay them in the-coffin with Sliced Artichoke bottoms-butter and close the Pye. A Lear. (Anonymous [c. 1720], handwritten notes in *E. Kidder's Receipts,* 12)

**A Battalia Pye**
Take 4 small Chickens, 4 squob Pidgeons, 4 Sucking Rabbits, cut them in pieces, Season it with Savoury Spice and lay them in the pye with 4 Sweetbreads Sliced and as many Sheeps tongues, 2 Shiver'd Pallats 2 pare of Lamb Stones, 20 or 30 cocks combs with Savoury balls & Oysters, lay on butter & close the pye A Lear. (Kidder, *E. Kidder's Receipts* [1720], C.1)

*Cold Pyes*

**A Veal Pye**
Raise an high pye, then cut a Fillet of Veal into 3 or 4 Fillets; Season it with Savoury Spice, a little minc'd Sage and Sweetherbs, lay it in ye Pye with Slices of bacon at the bottom & betwixt each piece, lay on butter and close the pye[.] (Kidder, *E. Kidder's Receipts* [1720], C. 2)

**A Turkey Pye.**
Bone the Turkey, Season it wth Savoury Spice and lay it in the pye wth 2 Capons or 2 wild ducks cut in pieces to fill up the corners, lay on butter and close the pye

A Goose pye is made the same way wth 2 Rabbits

All cold Pyes when they are bak'd and half cold must be filled up with Clarify'd butter. (Kidder, *E. Kidder's Receipts* [1720], C.1)

*Contemporary Recipe #2*

**A Calves head Pye.**
Same

**A Neats Tongue Pye.**
Same

**A Venison Pye.**
Same

———

**A Battalia Pye**
Same

*Cold Pyes*

**A Veal Pye**
Same

**A Turkey Pye.**
Same

*"Unidentified cookbook, c. 1700"—Anonymous* | *Comments*

*Fish Pyes.*

**A Carp. Pye.**

Bleed yor. Carp at ye. taile open ye. belley draw & wash out ye. blood wth. a little Clarret vinegar & salt þn season yor. Carp wth. savory spice & shred sweet herbs lay it in yor. pye wth a pt. of large oysters & butter & Close ye pye wn. tis bakd pour into ye lear ye. blood & Claret & pour it into ye. pye

———

**A Trout Pye.**

Cut wash & scale þm, lard þm with pieces of a silver Eele rowl'd up in spice, & sweet herbs & bay leaves powder'd lay on & between þm slic'd Artichoke bottoms mushrooms oysters caper dried lemon & butter & close ye pye.

———

**An Eele Pye**

Cut wash & season þm with sweet Spice an handfull of butter & close ye Pye.

———

**A Lamprey Pye**

Cut wash & season þm with sweet Spice lay þm in ye pye with dried lemon cittron butter & close ye Pye.

~ **Lampreys** resemble eels in shape but have no scales, and they have suckerlike mouths and fistulas (openings) on the tops of their heads (*OED*, 6:43).

**An Oyster Pye**

Parboyle a quantity of large Oysters in their own liquor mince þm small & pound þm in a mortar with pistasia Nuts marrow & sweet Herbs an onion & savory Spice & a little grated bread or season þm as aforsaid whole lay on butter & close ye Pye.

———

*Pasties*

**A Venison Pastie**

Bone a side or haunch of Venison cut it square & season it with pepper & salt make it up in your aforsaid pastie past a peck of flower for a buck pasty & 3 quarters for a doe 2 pound of beef suet at ye bottom of your Buck pasty & a pound & half for a doe

A Lamb pasty is made as ye Doe.

~ **Buck** is "the male of the fallow deer" (*OED*, 2:1148).

**A Beef Pasty**

Is cut out & season'd over night with pepper salt a little red wine & cutchenele þn made up as ye buck pasty To Each of these Pasties pour in a Lear.

~ **Cutchenele** is a variation of *scutcheneal* or *cochineal*.

*Contemporary Recipe #1*

*Fish Pyes*

**A Carp Pye.**
Bleed your carp at the tail, open the belly draw & wash out the blood wth a little clarret, vineagar & Salt, then season your carp with savoury Spice & shread sweet herbs lay it in the pye with a pint of large oysters butter & close the pye when it is bak'd put into the lear, ye blood & clarret and pour it into ye pye. (Kidder, *E. Kidder's Receipts* [1720], C.3)

**A Trout Pye.**
Cut wash and Scale them lard them with pieces of a Silver eele roul'd up in Spice, and sweetherbs and bay leaves powder'd lay on and between them Slic'd Artichoke bottoms, mushrooms, oysters, capers, diced lemon; lay on butter and close the pye. [Kidder, *E. Kidder's Receipts* [1720], C.3)

**An Eele Pye**
Cut and season them with Spice, an handfull of currants, butter & close the pye. (Kidder, *E. Kidder's Receipts* [1720], C.3, 7)

**A Lamprey Pye**
A Lamprey Pye is made the Same way with dic'd Lemon and citron. (Kidder, *E. Kidder's Receipts* [1720], C.3).

**An Oyster Pye**
Parboyl a quart of large Oysters in their own liquor, mince them Small and pound them in a mortar with pistacho=nuts, marrow and Sweet-herbs, an onion and Savoury Spice and a little grated bread or Season them as aforsaid whole, lay on butter and close the pye. (Kidder, *E. Kidder's Receipts* [1720], C.3)

*Pasties*

**A Venison Pasty.**
Bone a side of haunch of venison, cut it square & Season it with pepper & Salt make it up in yor. aforsaid pasty past: a peck of flower for a buk pasty & 3 quartrs. for a doe. 2 pound of butter at ye bottom of yor. buck pasty & a pd. & 1/2 for a doe.

A Lamb Pasty is made as the Doe. (Kidder, *E. Kidder's Receipts* [1720], I, 13)

**A Beef Pasty**
so cut out & seaso'd over night with pepper, Salt, a little red wine & Cochineel: Then made up as the Buck Pasty.

To each of these Pasties pour in a Lear. (Kidder, *E. Kidder's Receipts* [1720], I, 13)

*Contemporary Recipe #2*

*Fish Pyes*

**A Carp Pye.**
Same

**A Trout Pye**
Same

**An Eele Pye**
Same

**A Lamprey Pye**
Same

**An Oyster Pye**
Same

*Pasties*

**A Venison Pasty**
Same

**A Beef Pastie**
Is cutt out and Seasoned over night with—Pepper, Salt, a little red wine and cutcheneale then made up as the Buck Pastie. For any of these poure in a Lear. (Anonymous [c. 1720], handwritten notes in *E. Kidder's Receipts,* 16)

*"Unidentified cookbook, c. 1700"—Anonymous*

*Comments*

*Florendines and Puddings*

**A Florendine of a Kidney of Veal**

Shred ye kidney fat & all with a little spinnage parsley & lettuce 3 pippins & orange peele season it with sweet spice & sugar a good handfull of Currants 2 or 3 grated biskets sack & orange flower water 2 or 3 Eggs mix it into a body & put it in a dish cover'd with puffe past lay on a cut lid of ye same & garnish ye brim of ye dish.

———

**A Rice Florendine**

Boyl 1/2 a pd of rice tender in fair water þn put to it a quart of milk boyl it thick & season it with sweet spice & sugar mix it with 8 Eggs well beat 1/2 a pd of currants 1/2 a pd of butter 3 grated biskets sack & orange flower water put it in a dish being cover'd & garnish'd with puffe paste as aforsd.

———

**A Florendine of Oranges & Apples**

Cut 6 Sevil Oranges in halfes save ye Juice pull out ye pulpe & lay þm in water 24 hours shifting þm 3 or 4 times then boyl þm in 3 or 4 waters in ye 4th water put to þm a pd of fine sugar & their juice boyl þm to a syrrup & keep þm in this sirrup in an Earthen pot when you use them in thin slices. Two of these oranges will make a florendine mixt with ten Pippins par'd quarter'd & boyl'd up in water & sugar lay þm in a dish being cover'd with puff paste lay on a cut lid & garnish ye brim.

A Florendine of currants & apples is thus made.

———

**A Touet Demoy**

Beat 1/2 a pd of blanch'd Almonds in a mortar with a quarter of a pd of citron ye white of capon 4 grated biskets sweet spice & sugar sack and orange flower water mix it with a pint of Cream & ye Eggs being well beat þm bring all these Ingredients to a body over ye fire & having a dish cover'd with puff past put part of it into ye bottom squeese on it a lemon & put in the marrow of 2 bones in peices þn lay on ye other part of ye Ingredients & cover it with a cut lid.

**A Tart de Moyle**

Take Puff past and lay round your Dish then lay a layer of biskett and a layer of Marrow or butter and then a layer of all Sorts of wet Sweet Meats or as many as you have and so do tell the Dish is full then boyl a point of Cream and thicken it with four Eggs and a Spoonfull of~Orainge flower Water Sweeten it with good Suger to your Tast and half an hour will~~~bake it. . . .

A Side Dish[.] (The Compiler [1744], Manuscript cookbook, 76)

~ This recipe is a good example of how recipes with the same or similar titles can become quite different in terms of ingredients within a short time.

*Contemporary Recipe #1*

*Florendines and Puddings*

**A Florendine of a Kidney of Veal.**
Shread the kidney fat & all with a little Spinnage, parsley and lettice, 3 pippins and orange peel; Season it with Sweet Spice and Sugar and a good handfull of currants; 2 or 3 grated biskets, Sack & Orange flower water; 2 or 3 eggs; mix it into a body and put in a dish being covered wth. puff past lay on a cut - lid and garnish the brim. (Kidder, *E. Kidder's Receipts* [1720], D, 8)

**A Rice Florendine**
Boyl 1/2 a pound of rice tender in fair water, þn. put to it a quart of milk or cream boyl it thick & season it with Sweet spice & Sugar mix it wth. 8 eggs well beat 1/2 a pound of currants 1/2 a pound of butter & ye marrow of two bones, 3 grated biskets. sack and orange flower water, put it in a dish being covered & garnish'd as aforesaid. (Kidder, *E. Kidder's Receipts* [1720], D, 8)

**A Florendine of oranges & apples**
Cut 6 Sevil oranges in halves, save the juice pull out the pulp and lay them in water 24 hours shifting them 3 or 4 times then boyl them in 3 or 4 waters; in the 4th. water put to them a pound of fine Sugar and their juyce; boyl them to a Syrrup, & keep them in this Syrrup in an earthen pot; when you use þm cut them in thin Slices Two of these Oranges will make a Florendine, mixt with 10 pippins pared, quartered & boyl'd up in water and Sugar; lay them in a dish being cover'd & garnish'd as before (Kidder, *E. Kidder's Receipts* [1720], D, 8)

**A Tort de moy**
Blanch 1/2 a pound of jordan almonds & beat them in a mortar with a quarter of a pnd. of citron, ye white of a capon; 4 grated Biskets sweet Spice and sugar, Sack and orange flower water: then mix it with a pint of cream and 7 eggs being well beat and the marrow of 2 bones in pieces; then bring all these ingredients to a body over ye fire & put it in a dish being cover'd and garnished with puff paste. (Kidder, *E. Kidder's Receipts* [1720], D.1)

*Contemporary Recipe #2*

*Florendines and Puddings*

**A Florendine of a Kidney of Veal.**
Same

**A Rice Florendine**
Same

**A Florendine of oranges & apples**
Same

**A Tort de moy**
Same

*"Unidentified cookbook, c. 1700"—Anonymous* | *Comments*

### A Custard

Boyl a quart of Cream or milk with a stick of Cinnamon a quarter'd nutmeg & large mace wn half cold mix it with 8 Eggs leave but four whites well beat sugar sack & orange flower water set it on ye fire & stir it till a white froth ariseth scum it of then fill your custards being dry'd in ye oven

~ This recipe is not identical to an earlier recipe with the same title.

### An Almond Custard

Blanch & beat them in a mortar very fine in ye beating add thereto a little milk press it thro a Seive & make it as aforsd.

———

### A marrow Pudding.

Boyl a quart of Cream or milk with a stick of cinnamon a quarterd nutmeg & large mace þn mixt it with 8 Eggs well beat a little salt sugar sack & orange flower water strain it þn put to it 3 grated biskets an hand full of currants as many raisons of ye sun ye marrow of 2 bones all to 4 large peices gather it to a boyl over the fire & put it in a dish having ye brim thereof garnishd with puffe paste & rais'd in ye oven lay on ye 4 peices of marrow colourd pasts & knots slic'd citron & lemon peele halfe an hour will bake it.

~ "Colourd **pasts** & **knots**" might refer to some kind of confection. Pastes were known to be "various confections of doughy consistence" (*OED*, 7:539). It is believed that **knots** are similar to knops, which are flower buds (Hess, *Martha Washington's Booke,* 438).

### An ALmond Pudding

Take 1/2 a pd of Jordan Almonds blanch & pound þm in a mortar with a quarter of a pd of Pistachia Nuts 4 grated biskets 3 quarter of pd of butter sack & orange flower water then mix it with a quart of cream being boyld & mixed with 8 Eggs sweet spice & sugar put it in a dish being cover'd & garnished with puff paste

~ Note that Anonymous used a combination of capital and small letters in this recipe and in "Orange Pudding."

### A Carrot Pudding

Boyle two large Carrots wn cold pound þm in a mortar strain þm thro a seive mix þm with 2 grated biskets 1/2 pd of butter sack & orange flower water sugar & a little salt a pt. of cream mixd with 7 yolks of Eggs & 2 whites beat these together & put þm in a dish cover'd with puffe past & garnish ye brim

———

### An Orange PUDDing

Take ye Peels of 2 sevil oranges boyld up as for a florendine of oranges & apples pound & season þm as ye carrots.

———

| *Contemporary Recipe #1* | *Contemporary Recipe #2* |
|---|---|
| **A Custard**<br>Boyl a quart of cream or milk, with a Stick of Cinnamon, quarter'd Nutmeg and large Mace when half cold, mix it with eight yolks of eggs & four whites well beat Sugar Sack and Orange flower water. Set it on the fire and Stirr it untill a white froth ariseth, Schum it off then fill your custard being dry'd in the Oven. (Kidder, *E. Kidder's Receipts* [1720], D.3) | **A Custard**<br>Same |
| **An Almond Custard.**<br>Blanch and pound them in a mortar very fine: in the beating add thereto a little milk press it through a Sive, and make it as your aforesaid custard (Kidder, *E. Kidder's Receipts* [1720], D.3) | **An Almond Custard.**<br>Same |
| **A Marrow Pudding.**<br>Boyl a quart of cream or milk with a stick of cinnam on a quarter'd nutmeg and large mace, then mix it with 8 eggs well beat; a little Salt, Sugar Sack and orange flower water, strain it, then put to it, 3 grated biskets, an handfull of currants, as many raysons of the Sun, the marrow of 2 bones all to 4 large pieces : then gather it to a body over ye fire & put it in a dish having the brim thereof garnished with puff past and rais'd in the oven : then lay on the 4 pieces of marrow, colour'd knots & pasts, slic'd citron and lemon peel. (Kidder, *E. Kidder's Receipts* [1720], D.1) | **A Marrow Pudding.**<br>Same |
| **An Almond Pudding.**<br>Take 1/2 a pound of jordan almonds, blanch & pound þm. in a mortar wth. 4 grated biskets and three quarters of a pound of butter, Sack and orang flower water, then mix it wth. a quart of cream being boyl'd & mixt wth. 8 eggs sweet spice & Sugar, pour it into yor. dish being cover'd & garnish'd with. puff paste. (Kidder, *E. Kidder's Receipts* [1720], D.1) | **An Almond Pudding.**<br>Same |
| **A Carrot Pudding.**<br>Boyl 2 large carrots, when cold pound them, in a mortar, strain them thro a sive, mix them wth two grated biskets, 1/2 a pound of butter; sack and Orange flower water, Sugar and a little Salt, a pint of cream mixt with 7 yolks of eggs and two whites, beat these together and put them in a dish covered and garnished. (Kidder, *E. Kidder's Receipts* [1720], D.2) | **A Carrot Pudding.**<br>Same |
| **An Orange Pudding.**<br>Take ye peels of 2 Sevil Oranges boyld up as for a florendine of oranges and apples. pound & season þm. as ye Carrots. (Kidder, *E. Kidder's Receipts* [1720], D.2) | **An Orange Pudding.**<br>Same |

*"Unidentified cookbook, c. 1700"—Anonymous*

*Comments*

**A Tansie**

Boyl a qt of Cream or milk with a stick of cinnamon, a quarter'd nutmeg & large Mace wn halfe cold mix with it 20 yolks of Eggs & 10 Whites strain it then put to it 4 grated biskets 1/2 a pd of butter a pt of spinnage juice & a little tansie sack & orange flower water sugar & a little salt gather it to a body over ye fire & pour it into your dish being well butter'd wn tis bak'd turn it on a pye plate squeese on it an orange grate on sugar garnish it with slic'd orange & a little tanise made in a plate cut as you please.

———

**A Calves foot Pudding**

Take 2 calves feet shred þm very fine mix þm with a penny white loaf grated being scalded with a pint of cream put to it 1/2 pd of shred beef suet & 8 Eggs an handfull of plumpt currants season it with sweet spice & sugar a little sack & orange flower water sugar & little salt ye marrow of 2 bones put it in a veal caul being wash'd over with ye batter of Eggs þn wet a cloth & put it therein tye it up close when ye pot boyls put it in boyl it about 2 hours then turn it in a dish stick on it slic'd almonds & cittron then pour on it sack verjuice & drawn butter scrape on sugar.

~ **Caul** can be "any investing membrane or structure" and in this particular case meant the "amnion or inner membrane inclosing the foetus before birth" (*OED*, 2:192).

**A Quaking Pudding**

Take a qt of cream & beat 3 or 4 spoonfulls with 2 or 3 spoonfulls of flower of rice a penny grated white loaf & 7 Eggs put to it orange flower water sugar & sweet spice butter ye cloth & tye it up but not too close wn ye pot boyls put it in boyl it an hour þn turn it in a dish stick it with slic'd citron þn let ye sauce be sack & orange flower water with ye Juice of Lemons sugar & drawn butter.

~ **Drawn butter,** melted butter whipped up into a sauce, sometimes with a little water, was in popular use in the seventeenth century (Hess, *Martha Washington's Booke,* 181).

*Cakes*

**A Butter Cake.**

Take 6 pd of currants 5 pd of flower an ounce of cloves & mace a little cinnamon 1/2 an ounce of cloves & nutmegs 1/2 a pd. of pounded & blanchd almons 1/2 a pd. of Sugar 3 quarters of a pd. of cittron lemon & orange piele 1/2 a pt. of sack a little hony water a qt. of good ale yest a pt. of cream & a pd. & 1/2 of butter melted therein mix it together in a kettle over ye fier sturing it wth your hand till tis very smooth let it be as hott as you can bear it þn. put it in an hoop wth. a paper flowerd at ye bottom

~ Although the title of the recipe to the right is different from the one on the left, the contents match.

*Contemporary Recipe #1*

**A Tansey**

Boyl a quart of cream or milk wth. a stick of cinnamon, quarter'd nutmeg, and large mace; when half cold mix it with 20 yolks of eggs and 10 whites strain it, then put to it 4 grated biskets, 1/2 a pound of butter; a pint of Spinnage juice, and a little Tansey Sack and orange flower water; Sugar & a little Salt: then gather it to a body over the fire and pour it into your dish being well butter'd when it is bak'd turn it on a pye plate; Squeese on it an orange grate on Sugar and garnish it with Slic'd orange and a little tansey made in a plate cut as you please[.] (Kidder, *E. Kidder's Receipts* [1720], D.3)

**A Calves foot Pudding**

Take 2 Calves feet shred them very fine mix them with a penny loaf grated & Scalded with a pint of cream put to it 1/2 pnd. of shred beef suet 8 eggs & a hand full of plumpt currants, season it wth sweet spice & sugar a little sack & orange flower water; ye mar-row of 2 bones þn put it in a veal caul being wash'd over with ye batter of eggs then wet a cloth & put it therein, tye it close up wn. ye pot boyls put it in, boyl it about 2 hours, þn. turn it in a dish, Stick on it slic'd almonds and citron, let the sauce be, Sack & orange flower water wth. lemon juyce sugar & drawn butter. (Kidder, *E. Kidder's Receipts* [1720], D.2).

**A quaking Pudding.**

Take a qrt. of cream & beat 3 or 4 spoonfuls wth. 3 or 4 spoonfulls of flower of rice, a penny loaf grated & 7 eggs orange flower water sugar & sweet spice, butter the cloth & tye it up but not too close, boyl it about an hour stick on it slic'd citron, let ye Sauce be Sack & orange flower water lemon juyce Sugar & drawn butter. (Kidder, *E. Kidder's Receipts* [1720], D.2)

*Cakes*

**A Plumb Cake**

Take 6 pound of Currants, 5 Pound of Flower an ounce of Cloves & Mace, a little Cinnamon 1/2 an Ounce of Nutmegs, 1/2 a Pnd. of pounded & blanchd Almonds, 1/2 a Pd. of Sugar, 3 quarters of a pound of Slic'd Citron, Lemon & Orange Peel; 1/2 a pint of Sack a little honey water & a quart of ale yest, a quart of Cream, & 2 Pound and 1/2 of butter melted & pour'd into the middle thereof; then Strew a little flower thereon & let it lye to rise, then lay it before ye fire to rise: þn. work it up till it is very smooth, then put it in an hoop with a paper flower'd at the bottom. (Kidder, *E. Kidder's Receipts* [1720], E, 9)

*Contemporary Recipe #2*

**A Tansey**

Same

**A Calves foot Pudding.**

Same

**A quaking Pudding.**

Same

*Cakes*

**A Plumb Cake**

Same

| *"Unidentified cookbook, c. 1700"—Anonymous* | *Comments* |
| --- | --- |

**The Iceing**

Beat & sift a pd. of dubble refind sugar & put to it 4 eggs put in but one at a time beat þm. in a basson wth. a silver spoon till tis very leight & white

—

**A Seed Cake.**

Take a pd. of smooth carraways 6 pd. of flower 1/2 a pd. of sugar an ounce of spice & 2 pd of butter rub'd in very fine þn make an hole in ye flower & put in a qt of yest & 4 eggs well beat 1/2 a pt. of sack a little orange flower water & a pt. of warmed milk mixt together þn. strew a little flower thereon let it lye to rise þn. put it in an hoop & strew over it doubble refind sugar & rough carraways

—

**A Leight Seed Cake.**

Take 1/2 a quarter of flower a little ginger nutmeg 3 spoonfulls of ale yest & 3 eggs well beat 3 quarters of a pt. of milk 1/2 a pd. of butter warmed together 6 ounces of smooth carraways work it warm together wth. yor. hands

—

**Chees Cakes.**

Boyle a quart of cream or milk wth. 8 eggs well beat stir it till tis a curd þn. strain it and mix it wth. ye. curd of 3 quarts of milk 3 quarters of a pd. of fresh butter 2 greated biskets 2 ounces of blanchd almonds pounded wth. a little sack & orange flower water 1/2 a pd. of currants & 7 eggs spice & salt beat it up wth. a little cream till tis very leight þn fill your chesscakes

You may make cheescakes ye same way wth. ye curd of a gallon of milk with out ye eggs curd

—

**Portugall Cakes.**

Put a pd. of fine sugar a pd. of fresh butter 5 eggs & a little beaten mace into a flatt pan beat it up wth. yor. hands till very leight and Looks curdling þn. put thereto a pd. of flower 1/2 a pd. of curratnts very clean pickt & dry'd beat þm together fill yor. hart pans & bake þm in a slack oven

You may make seed Cakes ye same way only put Carraways seeds insteed of Currants.

—

**Ginger bread Cakes**

Take 3 pd. of flower a pd. of sugar & a pd. of butter rubb'd in very fine an ounce of ginger & a greated nutmeg mix it wth. a pd. of treacle þn & a quarter of a pt. of cream warm'd together þn make up yor. bread stiff roul þn. out þm. in little cakes & bake them in a slack oven

~ **Treacle** is an "uncrystallized syrup produced in the process of refined sugar (molasses)" (*OED*, 11:306).

| *Contemporary Recipe #1* | *Contemporary Recipe #2* |
|---|---|
| **The Iceing.**<br>Beat & Sift a pound and a half of double refin'd Sugar & put to it the whites of 6 eggs, put in but one at a time & beat them in a bason wth. a silver spoon till it be very light and white. (Kidder, *E. Kidder's Receipts* [1720], E, 9). | **The Iceing.**<br>Same |
| **A Seed Cake**<br>Take 2 pound of Smooth Carraways 6 pound of flower, 1/2 a pound of Sugar, an ounce of Sweet Spice with Citron, Lemon peele, then make an hole in ye flower & put in 1/2 a pint of yest & 8 eggs well beat, 1/2 a pint of Sack, a lttle Orange flower water; a pint of Cream & 2 pound of butter warm'd together; then strew a lttle flower thereon, let it lye to rise then put in an hoop and strew over it double refin'd Sugar and rough Carraways. (Kidder, *E. Kidder's Receipts* [1720], E, 9) | **A Seed Cake**<br>Same |
| **A Light Seed Cake**<br>Take 1/2 a quartern of flower a little ginger, Nutmeg, 3 Spoonfulls of ale yest & 3 eggs well beat, 3 quarters of a pint of milk, 1/2 a pound of butter and 6 ounces of Smooth carraways, work it warm together wth your hand. (Kidder, *E. Kidder's Receipts* [1720], E, 1) | **A Light Seed Cake**<br>Same |
| **Cheese Cakes.**<br>Take the curd of a gallon of milk, 3 quarters of a pound of fresh butter, 2 grated biskets, 2 Ounces of blanch'd Almonds pounded with a little Sack and Orange flower water, 1/2 a pound of Currants and 7 Eggs Spice and Sugar; beat it up with a little Cream till it is very light; then fill your Cheese-cakes[.] (Kidder, *E. Kidder's Receipts* [1720], E, 2) | **Cheese Cakes.**<br>Same |
| **Portugal Cakes.**<br>Put a pound of fine Sugar, a pound of fresh butter, 5 eggs & a little beaten mace into a flat pan beat it up with your hands till it is very light, þn put thereto a pound of flower, 1/2 a pound of currants very clean pickt & dry'd; beat them together, fill~your heart pans and bake them in a Slack Oven<br>You may make Seed Cakes the Same way: only put Carraway Seeds instead of currants. (Kidder, *E. Kidder's Receipts* [1720], E, 1) | **Portugal Cakes.**<br>Same |
| **Ginger-bread Cakes.**<br>Take 3 pound of flower, a pound of Sugar and a pound of butter rubb'd very fine, an Ounce of ginger and a grated nutmeg; mix it with a pound and a quarter of treacle: then make up stiff, roul it out and cut them in little Cakes and bake them in a Slack Oven[.] (Kidder, *E. Kidder's Receipts* [1720], E.1) | **Ginger-bread Cakes.**<br>Same |

*"Unidentified cookbook, c. 1700"—Anonymous* | *Comments*

**Another way**

Take a quartern of flower 2 pd. & 3 quarters of treacle an ounce of ginger 1/2 an ounce of Carraway & Coriander seeds bruis'd make it into large Cakes put it into either of þm. what sweet meats you please wn. they are bak'd dip þm. in boyling water to glease þm.

———

**Shrewsbury Cakes**

Take a pd. of fresh butter a pd. of dubble refind sugar sifted fine a little beaten mace & 4 eggs beat þm all together wth your hands till tis very leight & looks curdling þn. put to þm. a pd. & 1/2 of flower roul þm out into little cakes.

———

**Wiggs**

Take a quartern of flower 1/2 a pd. of Sugar an handfull of Car -Carraway seeds þn. put into þn. midle of ye flower 1/2 a pt of yest with a pd. & 1/2 of butter milted in a pt. of milk & pourd to ye yest stirring it wth. yor: hands strew flower let it lye to rise þn. make þm up.

———

*Broths*

**Strong Broths**

Take 3 or 4 gallons of water & put therein a leg & shin of beef Cut into 5 or 6 pieces boyle it 12 hours now & then stirr it with a stick & cover it Close wn. tis boyl'd strain & Coole it let it stand till it will jelley þn. take ye fatt from ye top & ye dross from ye bottome

———

**Gravey**

Cut a piece of beef into thin slices & fry it brown in a stewpan wth 2 or 3 onions 2 or 3 lean slices of beacon þn. pour to it a ladle or 2 of strong broth rubbing ye brown of from ye pan very Clean ad to it more strong broth Clarret wine & white wine anchovys a faggot of sweet herbs season it & let it stew very well and þn. strain it of

———

**Plum Porrage**

Take 2 gallons of strong broth put to it 2 pd. of Currants 2 pd. raisons of ye sun 1/2 an ounce of sweet spice a pd. of sugar a pt. of Clarret a pt. of sack ye juice of 3 oranges & 3 lemons thicken it with grated biskets with a pd. of pruants

~ The following two recipes are identical in spite of the differences in titles. **Pruants** (archaic) are prunes (*OED*, 7:1533).

*Contemporary Recipe #1*

**Another way.**
Take a quartern of flower, 2 pound and 3 quarters of treacle and 1/2 a pound of butter warm'd together, an Ounce of Ginger, 1/2 an Ounce of Carraway and Coriander Seeds bruis'd make it into large Cakes put it into either of them what Sweet meats you please when they are bak'd dip them into boiling water to glaze them[.] (Kidder, *E. Kidder's Receipts* [1720], E.2).

**Shrewsbury Cakes.**
Take a pound of fresh butter, a pound of double refin'd Sugar sifted, a little beaten mace and 4 eggs, beat them all together with your hands till it is very light: then put thereto a pound and 1/2 of flower and roul them out into little Cakes. (Kidder, *E. Kidder's Receipts* [1720], E.1)

**Wiggs**
Take a quartern of flower, 1/2 a pd. of Sugar a handfull of Carraway seed: then put into ye middle of the flower, 1/2 a pnt. of yest wth a pnd. & 1/2 of butter melted in a pt. of milk & pour'd to ye yest stirring it wth. yor: hands strew flower let them lye to rise, then make up yor. wiggs. (Anonymous [c. 1720], handwritten notes in *E. Kidder's Receipts,* 29)

*Broths*

**Strong-broth**
Take 3 or 4 gallons of water and put therein a leg and Shinn of beef, and a crag of mutton cut into pieces boyle it 12 hours, now and then stir it with a stick and cover it close: when it is boyl'd strain and cool it, let it stand till 'twill jelly, then take the fatt from the top & the dross from the bottom[.] (Kidder, *E. Kidder's Receipts* [1720], F, 10)

**Gravey**
Cut a piece of beef into thinn Slices and fry it brown in a stew-pan with 2 or 3 onions, 2 o r 3 lean slices of bacon then pour to it a ladle or 2 of Strong broth, rubbing the brown off from the pan very clean add to it more Strong broth, clarret, white wine anchovies, a faggot of Sweetherbs, Season it and let it Stew very well, then strain it off. (Kidder, *E. Kidder's Receipts* [1720], F, 10)

**Plum-Pottage**
Take two gallons of Strong broth; put to it~two pound of currants, two pound of raisons of the Sun, half an ounce of sweet Spice, a pound of Sugar a quart of clarret, a pint of Sack, the juice of three oranges and three lemons; thicken it with grated biskets, or rice flower with a pound of pruants. (Kidder, *E. Kidder's Receipts* [1720], F, 1)

*Contemporary Recipe #2*

**Another way.**
Same

**Shrewsbury Cakes.**
Same

———

*Broths*

**Strong-broth**
Same

**Gravey**
Same

**Plum Pottage**
Same

*"Unidentified cookbook, c. 1700"—Anonymous*

**Brown Pottage Royall.**

Set a gallon of strong broth on ye fier wth 2 shiverd pallats Cocks Comes lambstones slic'd wth. savory balls a pt. of gravy 2 handfulls of spinage & young lettuce minc'd boyle these together wth. a duck ye. leg & wing bones being brock & pull'd out & ye breast slashed & brownd in a pan of fatt þn put to it 2 french rouls sliced & dry'd hard & brown put ye pottage in a dish & ye duck in ye midle lay about it a little vermachelly boyled up in a little strong broth savory balls & sweetbreads garnish it wth. scalded parsly turnip beet roots & barberies

*Comments*

**Pottage (potage)** has two meanings. In this context it is a "dish made of vegetables alone," or mixed with meat, and "boiled to softness" with seasonings; it is also known as soup (*OED*, 7:1193). **Vermachelly**, or **vermicelli**, of Italian origin, is a paste made of wheat flour, cheese, egg yolks, sugar, and saffron that was molded into long, slender, hard threads (*OED*, 12:132). Mary Randolph published a recipe on how to make this vermicelli (Randolph, *Virginia Housewife*, 100–101).

**Pease Suop.**

Boyle a quart of good seed pease tender & thick strane & wash it throu wth. a pt. of milk þn. put thereto a pt. of strong broth boyld wth. balls a little sparemint & a dryd french roul season it wth. pepper & salt Cut a turnip in dice fry it and put it in

———

**Green Pease Soop.**

Wipe your pescode sheal & scald ye shells strain & pound þm. in a morter wth. scalded parsly young onons & a little mint þn. sokk a french roul boyle these together in clear mutten broath a faggot of sweet herbs seasond wth. pepper salt & nutmeg þn. strane it thro a Culender put ye pottage in a dish put in ye midle your larded veal a forcd foul Chicken or rabbit garnish it wth. scalded parsly Cabbatch lettuce and some of ye peas

You may make Asparragas Soop ye same way as Pease

Although the following two recipes are identical in contents, their titles differ. **Pescode** actually is **peascod,** a pea pod (*OED*, 7:595).

**A Crawfish Soop**

Cleanse yor. Crawfish boyle þm in water salt and spice pull of thare feet & tails & fry þm. break ye rest of þm. in a stone morter season it wth. savory spice & an onion hard eggs greated bread & sweet hearbs boyld in strong broth strain it þn. put to it scalded Chopt parsley and french rouls þn. put þm therein wth. a few slicd lemon ye feet and tails of ye Crawfish

A **crawfish** is a **crayfish,** "a general name for large crustacea other than crab," which resembles "a small lobster, and is found in rivers and brooks" (*OED*, 2:1164).

*Contemporary Recipe #1*

**Brown Pottage Royall**

Set a gallon of strong broth on the fire wth 2 shiver'd pallats, coxcombs, lambstones slic'd with Savory-balls, a pint of gravy, 2 handfulls of Spinnage & young lettice minc'd boyl these together with a duck the leg & wing bones being broke and pull'd out and the breast Slash'd & brown'd in a pan of fatt þn put to it 2 french rowls Slic'd and dry'd hard and brown. Then put the Pottage in a dish and duck in the middle, lay a bout it a little vermachelly boyl'd up in a little Strong broth Savory balls & Sweetbreads garnish it with Scalded parsley turnips, beat root, and barberries[.] (Kidder, *E. Kidder's Receipts* [1720], F, 10)

**Peas Soop**

Boyle a quart of good Seed peas tender & thick, Strain and wash it thro with a pint of milk: then put thereto a quart of Strong broth boyld with balls, a little Spire mint & a dry'd French rowl and Season it with pepper & Salt[.] (Kidder, *E. Kidder's Receipts* [1720], F, 1)

**Green Pease Pottage**

Wipe your Peascods then sheal and scald the shells, strein and pound them in a mortar, with scalded Parsly, young onions, & a little mint than soak a white french Roule boyle these together in clear mutton broth a faggot of sweetherbs, seasond with pepper salt and Nuttmeg than streine it through a cullender Putt the Pottage in a Dish

Garnish it with scalded Parsly Cabbage Lettice and some of the Pease Putt in the middle of your dish your Larded Veale a forc'd foule Chickens or Rabbits. (Anonymous [c. 1720], handwritten notes in *E. Kidder's Receipts,* 32)

**A Crawfish Soop**

Cleanse your crawfish and boyl them in watr. Salt and Spice; pull off their feet and tails and fry þm break the rest of them in a Stone mortar; Season them with Savory Spice and an onion, hard eggs, grated bread, and Sweetherbs boyl'd in Strong broth; strain it; then put to it Scalded chopt parsley & french rowls, then put them therein with a few dry'd mushrooms, garnish the dish with slic'd lemon and the feet and tails of the crawfish. A Lobster Soop is done the same way. (Kidder, *E. Kidder's Receipts* [1720], F.1)

*Contemporary Recipe #2*

**Brown Pottage Royall**

Same

**Peas Soop**

Same

**Green Pease Soop**

Wipe your Peascods, then shell, and scald the Shells, strain and pound them in a Mortar, with scalded Parsley, young Onion, and a little Mint; boil these together in clear Mutton-Broth, with a Faggot of sweet Herbs, season'd with Pepper, Salt, and Nutmeg; then strain it through a Culinder; put the Pottage in a Dish and put it in the middle larded Veal, a forc'd Fowl, Chicken, or Rabbet; garnish it with scalded Parsley, and Cabbage-Lettuce[.] (R. Smith, *Court Cookery* [1724], 1:9)

**A Crawfish Soop**

Same

*"Unidentified cookbook, c. 1700"—Anonymous*

*Comments*

**A Bisk of Pidgeons.**
Your pidgeons being clean washd & perboyled put þm. into strong broth & stew þm. þn. make for þm. a ragooe wth. gravy artichoke bottoms potatoes & onons savory spice lemon juice & dicd lemon & bacon Cut as for larding wth. mushrooms truffells & murrells pour ye. broth into ye dish haveing dryd Carved Cippets þn. place yor. pidgeons & pour on ye. ragooe wth. 1/2 a pt .of hott Cream garnish it wth scalded parley beet roots & lemon

~ A **bisk**, or **bisque**, is "a rich soup made by boiling down birds, etc." (*OED*, 1:879). **Artichoke bottom** refers to the "fleshy base" of a thistlelike flower, originally from "Barbary and the south of Europe," that was "widely cultivated in kitchen-gardens" (*OED*, 1:470). **Cippets** are **sippets**, small pieces of "toasted or fried bread, usually served in soups or broth, or with meat" and also used to sop up gravy, etc. (*OED*, 9:99).

**To Boyle a Leg of Mutton.**
Boyle yor. mutton in water & salt as usuall for ye. sauce toss up a little strong broth gravy pickled Cowcumbers and samphire shred barberries a dicd lemon white wine salt and nutmeg grated bread thicken it wth. 2 eggs & a little butter rould up in flower

———

**A Nother way.**
Lard yor mutton wth. lemon piele & beet roots boyle it as usuall let ye sauce be strong broth white wine gravy oysters anchovys onons a faggot of sweet herbs savory spice & a piece of butter rould up in flower

———

**To Boyle Rabbits.**
Truss þm. for boyling & lard þm. wth. bacon þn. boyle þm. quick and white for ye. sauce take ye. boyld liver shred it wth. fatt bacon toss these up together in strong broth white wine & vineger mace salt & nutmeg set parsly minced barberries & drawn butter lay yor. rabbits in a dish pour ye. lear all over þm. garnish þm. wth. slicd lemon & barberries

———

**To Boyle Pidgeons.**
Stuff yor. pidgeons wth sweet herbs Chopt bacon a little grated bread butter & spice ye yolk of an egg þn. boyle þm. as aforesaid & garnish þm. wth. sliced lemon & barbarries

———

*Contemporary Recipe #1*

**A Bisk of Pidgeons**

Your Pidgeons being clean washd & perboyled putt them into strong broth and stew them make for them a Ragooe with Gravy Artichoke bottoms slicd Potatoes and onions season them with savory seasoning and Lemon juice and lemon cut like dice and bacon cutt as for Larding also mushrooms truffells & murrells pour the broth into the dish haveing seasoned and dryed carved cippets then place your Pidgeons and poure on a Ragooe with 1/2 a pint of hott creame garnish it with Scalded Parsly Beet root and Lemon. (Anonymous [c. 1720], handwritten notes in *E. Kidder's Receipts,* 33)

**To Boyle a Legg of Mutton**

Boyle your Mutton in water and salt as usuall for the sauce Toss up a little strong broth white wine Gravy Pickled-Cucumbers and Samphire and barberries shred a dicd Lemon White wine salt and Nutmeg grated bread thicken it with 2 Eggs and a piece of butter rould in flower[.] (Anonymous [c. 1720], handwritten notes in *E. Kidder's Receipts,* 35)

**Another way**

Lard your Mutton with Lemon piele and beet root boyle it as usuall Lett thesauce be strong broth White wine Gravy oysters with their liquor Anchoves onions a faggot of sweetherbs savory seasoning and a piece of butter rould up in flower[.] Anonymous [c. 1720], handwritten notes in E. Kidder's Receipts, 35)

**To Boyl Rabbits.**

Truss them for boyling and lard them wth. bacon, then boyl them quick and white: for ye sauce take ye boyl'd liver Shread it with fat bacon, toss these up together in strong broth, whitewine & vineager, mace, Salt and nutmeg minc'd, Sett parsley Barberries & drawn butter then lay your Rabbits in a dish, pour ye lear all over them and garnish it with Slic'd lemon & barberries[.] (Kidder, *E. Kidder's Receipts* [1720], F.2)

**To Boyle Pidgeons**

Stuff your Pidgeons with Sweetherbs, chopt, bacon, a little grated bread, butter and Spice, the yolk of an egg: tye them at both ends and boyl them as aforesaid, and garnish them with slic'd lemon & barberries. (Kidder, *E. Kidder's Receipts* [1720], F.2)

*Contemporary Recipe #2*

**A Bisque of Pidgeons, or Soop with a Ragoo**

Same

**To Boil a Leg of Mutton**

Lard your Mutton with Lemon-peel and Beet-Root, and boil it as usual: For Sauce, take strong Broth and White-wine, Gravy, Oysters, Anchovies, an Onion, a Faggot of Herbs, Pepper, Salt, and Mace, and a Piece of Butter roll'd up in Flower. (R. Smith, *Court Cookery* [1724], 1:59)

———

**To Boyl Rabbits.**

Same

**To Boyle Pidgeons**

Same

*"Unidentified cookbook, c. 1700"—Anonymous*

**To Boyle Pullets & oysters**

Boyle þm. in water & salt wth a good piece of bacon for sauce draw up a pd. of butter wth a little strong broth white wine & a qt. of large oysters þn. put yor. 3 pullets in a dish Cut yor. bacon & lay about þm. wth a pd. & 1/2 of fryd sausages garnish it wth. slicd lemon.

**To Boyle Fouls.**

Boyle þm. as usuall for sauce toss up sweet breads artichoke artichoke bottoms lambstons Cocks Combs hard eggs all slicd in strong broth & white wine wth. pistastia nuts asparragus tops & spice thicken it wth. a bitt of butter rould up in flower & garnish it wth. slicd lemon

*Made Dishes*

**Scotcht Collops**

Take ye skin from a fillet of veal & Cut it in to thin Collops hack & scotch þm. wth. ye. back of a knife lard half of þm. with. bacon fry þm. wth. a little brown butter þn take þm. out & put þm. into another tossing pan þn set ye pan they were fryd in over ye fier again wash it out wth. a little strong broth þn. pour it to ye. Collops doe this to every panfull till all is fryde þn. stew & toss þm. wth. a pt. of oysters 2 anchovys 2 Shiverd pallats Cocks Combs lambstons and savory balls sliced sweet breads onions a faggot of sweetherbs thicken it wth brown butter & garnish it wth. sliced lemon & orange

**Ollives of Veal**

Take 8 or 10 scotcht Collops wash þm. over wth. ye batter of eggs þn. season & lay over þm. a little forced meat roul þm. up and roast þm. þn make for þm. a ragoue as ye. Collops & garnish þm. wth sliced orange

*Comments*

A **pullet** is a "young (domestic) fowl between the ages of chicken and mature fowl or a young hen" (*OED,* 8:1581).

———

This category in this manuscript and in Kidder's editions is entitled "Made Dishes." **Scotch collops** alludes to "a savory dish made of diced veal, bacon, forced meat and several other ingredients"; to **scotch** meant "to score or hatch," or "to make incisions" (obsolete), and **collops,** per se, is a dialect for slices of meat either fried or broiled (*OED,* 2:624; 9:249).

Mary Randolph's version shows that she kept the same basic outline but adapted it to her own taste and chose catsup to flavor it.

**Scotch Collops of Veal.**

They may be made of the nice part of the rack, or cut from the fillet, rub a little salt and pepper on them and fry them a light brown, have a rich gravy seasoned with wine and any kind of catsup you chuse, with a few cloves of garlic and some pounded mace, thicken it, put the collops in and stew them a short time, take them out strain the gravy over and garnish with bunches of parsley fried crisp, and thin slices of middling of bacon curles around a skewer and boiled. (Randolph, *Virginia Housewife,* 47–48)

**Veal Olives.**

Take the bone out of the fillet and cut then slices the size of the leg, beat them flat, rub them with the yelk of an egg beaten, lay on each piece a thin slice of boiled ham, sprinkle salt, pepper, grated nutmeg, chopped parsley and bread crumbs over all, roll them up tight and secure them with skewers, rub them with egg and roll them in bread crumbs, lay them on a tin dripping pan and set them in an oven, when brown on one side turn them, and when sufficiently done, lay them in a rich highly seasoned gravy made of proper thickness, stew them till tender, garnish with forcemeat

*Contemporary Recipe #1*

**To boyl Pullets & Oysters.**
Boyle them in water and Salt, with a good piece of bacon: for Sauce draw up a pound of butter with a little white-wine, Strong broth and a quart of oysters: then put your 3 pullets in a dish cut your bacon and lay it about them, wth. a pound and 1/2 of fry'd Sauceages and garnish it with Sliced lemon. Or you may boyl your pullets in bladders and Send them up in a ragooe. (Kidder, *E. Kidder's Receipts* [1720], F.2)

**To Boyle Foules**
Boyle them as aforesaid for the sauce toss up Veale sweetbreads Atichoke bottom Cocks combs hard Eggs all Slicd in strong broth Pistasher nutts white wine asparragus tops and spice thicken it wth a bitt of butter rould up in flower and garnished with slicd Lemons. (Anonymous [c. 1720], handwritten notes in *E. Kidder's Receipts,* 37)

*Made Dishes*

**Scotcht Collops**
Take the skin from a Fillet of Veal, & cut it into thin Collops, hack and scotch them wth ye back of a knife, lard half of them with bacon fry them, wth a little brown butter, then take them out & put them into another tossing pan, then set the pan they were fry'd in over the fire again, wash it out wth. a little strong broth rubbing it with your ladle, then pour it to the Collops do this to every panfull till all are fry'd: then Stew & toss them up with a pint of Oysters, 2 Anchovies, 2 Shiver'd pallats, cocks combs, lamb-stones, & Sweet breads blanch'd & Sliced, savory balls, onions, a faggot of sweetherbs; thicken it with brown butter & garnish it with Slic'd Orange[.] (Kidder, *E. Kidder's Receipts* [1720], F.3)

**Ollives of Veal**
Take 8 or 10 Scotcht Collops wash them over wth the batter of eggs, then Season & lay over them a little forc'd meat, roul them up & roast them, then make for them a ragooe, & garnish it with Slic'd Orange. (Kidder, *E. Kidder's Receipts* [1720], F.3)

*Contemporary Recipe #2*

**To boyle Pullets & Oysters.**
Same

**An admirable Way to boil Fowls**
Boil them as aforesaid; to the Sauce, toss up Sweet-breads, Artichoke-bottoms, Lamb stones, Cocks Combs, and hard Eggs, all sliced in strong-Broth, and White-wine, with Asparagus-Tops, and Spice; thicken it with a bit of butter kneaded in Flower; garnish the Dish with sliced Lemon. (R. Smith, *Court Cookery* [1724], 1:23)

*Made Dishes*

**Scotcht Collops**
Same

**Ollives of Veal**
Same

*"Unidentified cookbook, c. 1700"—Anonymous*

*Comments*

balls and green pickles sliced. (Randolph, *Virginia Housewife,* 48)

~ This is a good example of how the basic steps of a recipe are preserved over time and yet are more modernized with new additions or flavors.

**Pidgeon Pairs.**

Bone your pidgeons all but one leg & put that thro ye. side out at ye. vent Cut of ye. toes & fill þm. wth. forcd meat made of ye. hart & liver & Cover þm. wth. a tender forced meat being washd over wth. ye. batter of eggs & shape þm. like pares þn. wash þm. over & roul þm. in scalded Chopt spinnage Cover þm. wth. thin slices of bacon & put þm. in bladers boyle þm an hour & half þn. take þm. out of ye. bladers lay þm. before ye fier 1/2 an hour þn. make for them a ragooe & garnish þm. wth slicd lemon

———

**A Calves Head hashd**

Your Calves head being slitt & Cleans'd half boyld & cold Cut one side into thin slices fry it in a pan of brown butter þn having a toss pan on ye. stow wth. a pt. of gravy as much strong broth a quarter of a pt. of Clarret as much white wine & a handful of savory balls 2 or 3 shiverd pallats a pt of oysters Cocks combs lambstons & sweet breads blanchd & slicd wth. mushrooms truffels & murrells 2 or 3 anchovys as many shallots a faggot of sweetherbs toss'd up & stewd together season it wth. savory spice þn. scotch ye. other side Cross & Cross flower bast & broyle it

The hash being thickened wth. brown butter put it in ye. dish lay over & about it fryd balls & ye tongue slicd & larded wth bacon lemon piele & beet root þn. fry in ye. batter of eggs sliced sweet breads Carved Cippits & oysters lay in ye. head & place these on & about ye dish & garnish it wth. slicd orange and lemon

———

**A Ragooe of a Breast of Veal.**

Bone a breast of veal Cut an handsome square piece þn cut ye. other part into small pieces brown it in butter þn. stew & toss it up in a pt. of gravy a little Clarrat whit wine strong broth & an onion 2 or 3 anchovys Cocks Combs lambstons & sweetbreads blanchd & slicd wth. savory balls oysters truffels murrels mushrooms savory spice & Lemon juce þn. toss it up thicken it wth. brown butter put ye regooe in ye dish Lay on ye square piece dicd lemon sweetbreads Cippets & bacon fryd in ye. batter of eggs & garnish it wth. slicd orangs

———

*Contemporary Recipe #1*

**Pidgeon Pears**

Bone your pidgeons all but one leg, and put yt. thrô ye side out at ye vent; cut of ye toes & fill them wth forcd meat, made of ye heart & liver, & cover them with a tender forc'd meat being wash'd wth ye batter of eggs; & shape them like pears; þn wash þm over & roul þm in scalded chopt spinnage, cover þm wth thin Slices of bacon, & put þm in bladders, boyl þm an hour & 1/2 then take them out of the bladders, and lay þm before the fire to crisp them, then make for þm a raggooe. (Kidder, *E. Kidder's Receipts* [1720], F.6)

**A Calves head hash'd**

Your Calves head being Slitt & cleans'd half boyld & cold cut One side into thin Slices fry it then having a tossing pan on the Stow with a Ragooe for made dishes, toss it up and Stow it together: then Scotch the other Side cross and cross, flower, bast and broyle it. The hash being thicken'd wth brown butter, put it in the dish, lay ovr. & about it fry'd balls & the tongue Slicd and larded wth bacon, lemon peel and beet root; then fry in the batter of eggs, Slic'd Sweetbreads, carv'd Sippets and Oysters, lay in the head, and place these on & about the dish & garnish it wth Slic'd Orange and Lemon. (Kidder, *E. Kidder's Receipts* [1720], F.5)

**A Ragooe of a breast of veal.**

Bone a breast of veal cut an handsom Square piece then Cut the other part into Small pieces, brown it in butter then stew & toss it up in your ragooe for made dishes, thicken it with brown butter; then put the ragooe in ye dish lay on ye Square piece, dic'd lemon, Sweetbreads, Sippets, and bacon fry'd in the batter of eggs, & garnish it with Slic'd Orange. (Kidder, *E. Kidder's Receipts* [1720], F.5)

*Contemporary Recipe #2*

**Pidgeon Pears.**

Same

**A Calves head hash'd.**

Same

**A Ragooe of a breast of Veal**

Same

*"Unidentified cookbook, c. 1700"—Anonymous* | *Comments*

**A Ragooe of Sweet Breads**

Set lard & force ye sweetbreads wth. mushrooms ye tender ends of pallats Cocks Combs boyld tender beat it in a morter mixt wth. fine herbs & spice a little grat'd bread & an egg or 2 þn. fry þm. thus forsd toss þm up in gravy Clarrot white wine wth Cocks Combs & mushrooms spice & oysters a dicd lemon thicken it wth brown butter & garnish it wth. slicd lemon

———

**Chickens Forcd wth. Oysters**

Lard & truss þm. make a forcing of oysters sweet-breads parsly truffels mushrooms & onions Chop these together and season it mix it wth. a piece of butter ye yolks of 1 or 2 eggs tye þm. at both ends & roast þm. þn. make for þm. a fine ragooe & garnish it wth slicd lemon

———

**Bombarded.**

Take a fillit of veal Cut out of it 5 lean pieces as thick as yor. hand round þm up a little þn lard very thick on ye. round side lard 5 sheeps tongues being boyld & blanch'd þn make a well season'd forc'd meat wth. veal red beacon beef suet & an anchovy þn roul it up into a ball being well beat þn make another tender forcd meat wth. veal fat bacon beef suet mushrooms spinage parsly tyme sweet marjoram winter-savory & green onions season & beat it þn but yor forc'd ball into part of this forcd meat put it in a veal Caul & bake it in a little pott þn roul up that which is left in another veal Caul wett wth ye batter of eggs roul it up like apolonia sausage tye it at both ends & slightly round & boyle it

Your forced ball being bak'd put in the midle of yor. dish yor. larded veal being stewd in strong broth & fryd in ye. batter of eggs lay round it & ye. tongues fryd brown between each þn pour on a ragooe lay about it ye. other forcd meat Cut as thin as an half Crown & fryd in ye. batter of eggs þn squese on it an orange & garnish it wth. slicd orange & lemon.

~ **Bombard,** as used in cookery, means "to stuff"—especially a fillet of veal (*OED,* 1:9978).

**A Brown Fricasse of Chickens & Rabbits.**

Cut þm in pieces & fry þm. in brown butter þn. having ready hott a pt. of gravy, a little Clarret white wine & strong broth anchovy 2 shiver'd pallats a faggot of sweet harbs, savory balls & spice thicken it wth. brown butter and squese on a lemon

———

*Contemporary Recipe #1*

**A Ragooe of Sweet Breads**

Set Lard & Force ye Sweet-breads wth. mushrooms, ye tender ends of pallats cocks combs boyld tender, beat it in a mortar mixt wth. fine herbs; & Spice a little grated bread & an egge, or two then fry them thus forsed, toss þm up in a ragooe, thicken it with brown butter, & squeese on it a lemon, garnish it with Slic'd lemon & barberries. (Kidder, *E. Kidder's Receipts* [1720], F.5)

**Chickens forc'd wth Oysters**

Lard & Truss þm make a forcing of oysters, Sweetherbs, Parsley, Truffels, Mushrooms, & Onions; chop these together and Season it, mix it with a piece of butter the yolk of an egg then tye them at both ends and roast them; then make for a Ragooe & garnish them with Slic'd Lemon. (Kidder, *E. Kidder's Receipts* [1720], F.3)

**Bombarded Veal.**

Take a fillet of veal cut out of it 5 lean pieces, as thick as yor hand, roun them up a little then lard very thick on the round side, lard 5 sheeps tongues being boyl'd blanch'd & larded wth. lemon peel & beet root; þn. make a well seasoned forc'd meat wth Veal, lean Bacon beef Suet & an anchovy, roul it up into a ball being well beat þn. make a another tender forcd meat wth veal fat bacon, beef suet, mushrooms, Spinnage, parsley, thyme, Sweet majoram, winter Savory and green onions Season and beat it. Then put your forc'd ball into part of this forc'd meat, put it in a veal caul & bake it in a little pot; then roul up that which is left~in another veal caul, wet with the batter of eggs, roul it up like polonia Sauceage, tye it at both ends & Slightly round and boyl it~Your forc'd ball being bak'd, put it the middle of the dish, yor. Larded Veal being stew'd in strong broth lay around it & ye tongues fry'd brown between each, then pour on them a ragooe, lay about it the other forcd meat cut as thin as a half Crown & fry'd in the batter of eggs; then squeese on it an Orange and garnish it with slic'd Lemon. (Kidder, *E. Kidder's Receipts* [1720], F.4)

**A brown Fricasse of Chickens or Rabbits**

Cut them in pieces & fry them in butter then~having ready hot a pint of gravy, a little Clarret whitewine & Strong broth, 2 anchovys, 2 Shiver'd pallats, a faggot of sweet-herbs, Savory Balls and Spice, thicken it with brown butter and Squeese on a lemon. (Kidder, *E. Kidder's Receipts* [1720], G.1)

*Contemporary Recipe #2*

**A Ragooe of Sweet Breads**

Same

**Chickens forc'd wth. Oysters**

Same

**Bombarded Veal**

Same

**A brown Fricasse of Chickens or Rabbits**

Same

| *"Unidentified cookbook, c. 1700"—Anonymous* | *Comments* |
| --- | --- |
| **A White Frigasee of ye Same.**<br>Cut þm in pieces wash þm from ye. blood & fry þm on a a soft fier & put þm in a tossing pan wth. a little strong broth season þm. and toss þm. up when allmost anought put to them a pt. of Cream thicken it with a bitt of butter rould up in flower | ——— |
| **A Frigasee of Lamb.**<br>Cut an hind quarter of lamb into thin slices season it wth. savory spice sweet herbs & a shallot þn fry þm & toss þm up in strong broth whit wine oysters balls & pallats a little brown butter or an egg or 2 to thicken it or a bitt of butter rould up in flower garnsh. it wth. slicd Lemon | ——— |
| **Pidgeons in Surtout.**<br>Cleanse yor. pidgeons þn. make forcing for þm. tye a large scotcht collop on ye breast of each spitt & cover þm. wth. paper & rost þm. þn. make for þm. a fine ragooe & garnish þm. with slicd Lemon | ~ **Surtout** refers to "various fancy dishes" in the form of "an outer covering or integument" in cookery (*OED*, 10:248). |
| **Cutlets Alamaintenoy**<br>Season yor. cutlets of mutton wth. savory spice & shred sweet herbs þn dip 2 scotcht Collops in ye. batter of eggs & Clap on each side of each Cutlet & þn a rasher of bacon on each side broyle þm or bring þm off in ye oven wn. they are drest take of ye bacon & send up yor. Collops and Cutlets wrapt in Clean white paper as letters or you may leave þm out ——— s[end?] þm up in a ragooe & garsh. þm wth. slicd orange or Lemon | ——— |
| **To Roast a hare.**<br>Set & lard it wth. bacon make for it a pudding of grated bread ye. hart & liver being perboyld & Chopt small wth. beef suet & sweet herbs mixt wth. marrow C(ream) spice eggs þn. sou up ye belley & roast him, wn. tis roast let yor. butter be drawn up wth. Cream gravy or Clarrot | ——— |
| **Pullets Ala Cream.**<br>Lard & force yor. pullets of there own flest boyld ham mushrooms sweet breads oysters anchovys grated bread ye yolk of an egg a little Cream spice & herbs roast þm. þn. pour on þm. a fine ragooe of mushrooms oysters sweet breads Cocks Combs truffels murrells & Cream thickend wth. eggs. | ——— |

*Contemporary Recipe #1*

**A White Fricase of ye Same**
Cut them in pieces & wash them from the blood, fry them on a a soft fire, & then put them in a tossing pan with a little strong broth: season them and toss them up with mushrooms & oysters; wn almost enough put to them a pint of cream & thicken it with a bit of butter rould up in flower. (Kidder, *E. Kidder's Receipts* [1720], G.1)

**A Frigasee of Lamb**
Cut an hind quarter of lamb into thin Slices, Season it with Savoury Spice, Sweet herbs & a shallot then fry them & toss þm up in strong broth, white wine, oysters, balls & pallats, a little brown butter to thicken it or a bit of butter roul'd up in flower garnish. (Kidder, *E. Kidder's Receipts* [1720], G.1)

**Pidgeons in Surtout**
Cleanse your pidgeons, then make a forcing for a þm tye a large Scotcht Collop and a Rasher of bacon on ye breast of each: Spit and cover them with paper & roast them then make for them a ragooe, and garnish them wth. Slic'd Lemon[.] (Kidder, *E. Kidder's Receipts* [1720], G. 2)

**Cutlets, A la Maintenoy**
Season your cutlets of mutton wth Savoury Spice & Shread sweet herbs: then dip 2 Scotcht collops in ye better of eggs & clap on each Side of each cutlet, & then a rasher of bacon on each side, broyl them upon paper, or bring them off in the oven, when they are drest take off the bacon and send them up in a ragooe; and garnish them wth. Slic'd orange & lemon. (Kidder, *E. Kidder's Receipts* [1720], G.2)

**To Roast a Hare**
Sett & lard it with bacon make for it a pudding of grated bread the heart and liver being parboiled & chopt small with beef Suet & sweetherbs mix with marrow cream spice eggs then sew up the belly and roast him, when 'tis roasted let yor. butter be drawn up with cream gravy or clarret. (Kidder, *E. Kidder's Receipts* [1720], G)

**Pullets a la Cream**
Lard & force your Pullets of their own flesh boyl'd ham, mushrooms, sweet breads, oysters, anchovys, grated bread, ye yolk of an egg, a little cream, spice & herbs þn roast þm & pour on them a fine white ragooe of mushrooms, oysters sweetbreads cocks combs, truffles, murrells & cream thickend with eggs. (Kidder, *E. Kidder's Receipts* [1720], G1)

*Contemporary Recipe #2*

**A White Fricase of ye Same.**
Same

**A Frigasee of Lamb**
Same

**Pidgeons in Surtout**
Same

**Cutlets, A la Maintenoy**
Same

**To Roast a hare**
Same

**Pullets a la Cream**
Same

| *"Unidentified cookbook, c. 1700"—Anonymous* | *Comments* |
|---|---|
| **Portugall Beef.**<br>Brown ye. thin of a rump of beef in a pan of brown butter & force ye. lean of it wth. suet bacon boyld Chessnuts anchovys savory spice & an onion stew it in a pan of strong broth till tis very tender þn. make for it a ragooe wth. gravy pickled gerkins boyld Cheesnuts thicken it with brown butter & garnish it wth. slicd Lemon | ——— |
| **A Leg of Mutton Ala Daube.**<br>Lard yor. meat wth. beacon half roast it draw if off ye. spitt and put it in as small a pott as will boyle it put to it a qt of white wine strong broth a pt. of vinegar whole spice bay leaves swete marjoram winter savory & green onions wn. ye. meat is ready make seace wth. some of ye. liquor mushrooms dicd Lemon 2 or 3 anchovys thicken it wth. brown butter & garnish it wth. slicd Lemon | ——— |
| **A Leg of Mutton Ala Royall**<br>Lard yor. mutton & slices of veal wth. bacon roald up in spice and sweet herbs þn. bring þm. to a brown in milted lard boyled ye. leg in strong broth all sorts of sweet herbs an onion stick wth. Cloves wn. tis ready lay in ye. dish lay round it ye. Collops þn. poar On a ragooe & garnish it wth. slicd orange & Lemon | ——— |
| **A Leg of Mutton Forcd.**<br>Take ye. meat out of ye. leg Close to ye. skin & bone mince it wth. a pd. of beef suet & a good quantity of tyme parsly & onions beat it morter season it wth. savory spice & 2 anchovys þn. wash wash ye. inside of ye. skin with ye. batter of eggs & fill it bast flower & bake it ye. sauce may be seasond greavy & put to it a regalia of Cowcumber Coliflowers & french beans | ~ The contemporary recipes have identical contents but again, different titles. |
| **Oysters Loves.**<br>Cut a round hole in ye. tops of 5 french rouls take out ye. Crumb & smear þm. over ye. sides wth. a tender forcd meat made of set oysters part of an Eele pistastia nuts mushrooms herbs anchovys marrow spice ye. yolks of 2 hard eggs beat these well in a morter wth. one raw egg þn. fry þm. crisp in lard & fill þm. wth. a qt. of oysters ye. rest of ye. Eele Cut like [blank] mushrooms anchovys tossed up in there liquor 1/2 a pt. of white wine thicken it wth eggs & a bitt of butter rould up in flower | ——— |

*Contemporary Recipe #1*

**Portugal Beef**

Brown the skin of a Rump of beef in a Pan of brown butter then force the Lean of it with Suitt bacon boyld Cheesnutts Anchovey savory seasoning an onion stew it in a Pan of Strong broth till it is very tender then make for it a Ragooe with Pickled Jerkins - boyled Cheesnutts thicken it with brown butter and putt it in the dish poure the Ragooe it garnish it with sliced Lemons. (Anonymous [c. 1720], handwritten notes in *E. Kidder's Receipts,* 46)

**A Goose Turkey or Leg of Mutton a la Daube.**

Lard it with bacon half roast it, draw it of ye spitt and put it in as small a pott as will boyle it put to it a quart of white wine strong broth a pt of vinegar, whole spice, bay leaves, sweet marjoram winter savoury & green onions: when tis ready lay in ye dish; make sauce wth some of ye liquor; mushrooms dicd lemon: 2 or 3 anchovies: thicken it wth brown butter & garnish it wth Slicd lemon. (Kidder, *E. Kidder's Receipts* [1720], F.7)

**A Leg of Mutton a la Royal**

Lard your mutton and Slices of veal wth. bacon rouled up in Spice and Sweet-herbs then bringing them to a brown in melted lard, boyl the leg of mutton in Strong broth, all Sorts of Sweet-herbs, an onion Stuck wth. cloves when it is ready lay it in the dish lay round it the Collops þn pour on it a Ragooe and garnish it wth. lemon & oranges. (Kidder, *E. Kidder's Receipts* [1720], G)

**A Leg of Lamb Forc'd**

Take the meat out of ye leg close to the Skin & bone mince it with a pd of beef Suet, thyme, parsley & onions, beat it in a mortar with Savoury spice and 2 anchovies: then wash the inside of the Skin with ye batter of eggs & fill it, bast flower & bake it the Sauce may be season'd gravy, OR put to it a regalia of cow-cumbers colliflowers & french beans. (Kidder, *E. Kidder's Receipts* [1720], G.2)

**Oyster Loaves**

cut a round hole in ye tops of 5 french rouls and take out all ye crumb & smear þm over ye sides wth a tender forcd meat made of sett oysters part of an Eele þn fry þm crisp in lard & fill þm wth a quart of oysters: ye rest of ye eel cut like lard spice mushrooms, anchovys tossed up in yr. liqr. 1/2 a pint of white wine; thicken it with a bit of butter roul'd up in flower[.] (Kidder, *E. Kidder's Receipts* [1720], F.7)

*Contemporary Recipe #2*

**Portugal Beef**

Brown a thin Rump of Beef in a Pan of brown Butter, and force the Lean of it with Suet, Bacon, boil'd Chesnuts, an Onion, and season it; stew it in a Pan of strong Broth, and make for it a Ragoo with Gravy, pickl'd Gerkins, and boil'd Chesnuts; thicken it with brown Butter, and garnish it with slic'd Lemon. (R. Smith, *Court Cookery* [1724], 1:63)

**A Goose Turkey or Leg of Mutton a la Daube.**

Same

**A Leg of Mutton a la Royal**

Same

**A Leg of Lamb Forc'd**

Same

**Oyster Loaves**

Same

*"Unidentified cookbook, c. 1700"—Anonymous* | *Comments*

**To Roul a Breast of Mutton.**
Bone ye. mutton make a savory forcd meat for it wash it over wth. ye. batter of eggs þn. spred ye. forcd meat on it roul it in a Collar bine it wth. pack thread & roast it put under a regalia of Cowcumbers

———

**Beef Almode.**
Take a good Buttock of Beef interlarded wth. great lard rould up in savory spice minced sage parsly & green onions put it in a green sauce Sauce pan & cover it close wth. course past wn tis halfe don turn it let it stand over ye. fire or a stow 12 hours or in an oven this is fitt to eat cold or if to be eaten hott you may slice it out thin wn. tis cold & toss it up in a fine ragooe

———

**Veal Alamode**
Take a good fillet of Veal mince it small with the same quantity of Beef Suet beat it with an Egge or 2 to bind it season it with Savory Spice & make it into ye form of a thick round pyes, fill it thus lay in thin slices of Bacon squab pidgeons slic'd sweetbreads tops of Asparagus yolks of hard Eggs ye tender Ends of shiver'd pallats & cocks combs boyl'd blanch'd & sliced.

~ One of these two recipes has a different title from the preceding recipe.

**Sausages:**
Take pork more lean þn fat & shred it þn take of ye fleak of pork & mince it season Each a part with minc'd sage & pretty high with Savory spice clear your small guts & fill þm mixing some bits of fat between ye minc'd meats sprinkle it with a little red wine & twill fill ye better þn tye them in Links.

———

**Polonia Sausages.**
Take a peice of red gammon of Bacon & half boyl it mince with as much bacon lard put to it minc'd sage thyme & Savory spice ye yolks of Eggs & as much red wine as will bring it to a pretty thick body mix þm wth yor hands & fill þm mixing some bit of fat between ye mincd meat sprinkle a little wine & twill fill ye better þn tye þm in links.

~ **Gammon** alludes to "the ham or haunch of swine" (*OED*, 4:41).

*To Dress fish*

**To Boyle a Codds Head:**
Set a Kettle on ye fire with water vinegar & salt a faggot of sweet herbs & an onion or [2?] when ye liquor boyls put put in ye head on a fish plat[e] in ye boyling put in cold water & vinegar when tis boyld

~ **Spawn** is an outdated term for "the milt of a fish" (*OED*, 9:531). **Milt** is the "roe or spawn of the male fish," or "the 'soft roe' of fishes" (*OED*, 6:452).

*Contemporary Recipe #1*

**To Roul a Breast of Veal or Mutton.**
Bone your meat and make a savoury forcd meat for it, wash it over wth the batter of eggs; þn spread the forc'd meat on it, roul it in a collar and bind it with pack thread & roast it: put under it a regalia of cowcumber. (Kidder, *E. Kidder's Receipts* [1720], G.2)

**Beeff Alamode.**
Take a good buttock of beef interlarded wth. great lard rould up in savoury Spice and Sweet-herbs; put it in a great Sauce pan & cover it close & Sett it ye oven all night, this is fit to eat cold. (Kidder, *E. Kidder's Receipts* [1720], F.6)

**Veal Alamode A la Daube.**
Take a good fillet of veal interlarded as ye beef, and to ye stewing of it a little white wine; then make for it a ragooe & garnish it with slic'd lemon. (Kidder, *E. Kidder's Receipts* [1720], F.6)

**Sausages:**
Take pork more lean than fat & shred it, then take of ye flake of pork & mince it; season each a part wth minc'd sage, & pretty high wth savoury spice: then clear yor. small gutts & fill þm mixing some bitts of fat & a little wine wth. it; then tye them in links. (Kidder, *E. Kidder's Receipts* [1720], F.7)

**Polonia Sausages.**
Take a peice of red gammon of bacon and half boyl it mince it wth as much bacon lard, put to it minc'd sage, thyme, & savory Spice ye yolks of Eggs & as much red wine as will bring it to a pretty thick body; mix þm wth. your hands & fill þm in large skins & dry them as hamm in links. (Kidder, *E. Kidder's Receipts* [1720], F.7)

*To Dress Fish*

**To Boyle a Codds-head**
Set a Kettle on the fire with water: vineagar & Salt; a faggot of Sweetherbs & an Onion or two when the liquor boyl's put in the head on a fish bottom, and in the boyling put in cold water & vineagar, when it is

*Contemporary Recipe #2*

**To Roul a Breast of Veal or Mutton.**
Same

**Beeff Alamode.**
Same

**Veale Alamode**
Take a good fillett of Veale interLarded as the beef add to the stowing of it a little Whitewine When this is cold you may slice it out thin and toss it up in a fine Ragooe of mushrooms. (Anonymous [c. 1720], handwritten notes in *E. Kidder's Receipts,* 50)

**Saucidges**
Take Pork more Lean then fatt and shred it - then take of the flitch of Pork and mince it - season each a part with minced Sage and pretty high with savory seasoning clear your Small Gutts and fill them mixing some bitts of fleak between the minced meat Sprinkle a little wine with it it will fill the better tye them in Links (Anonymous [c. 1720], handwritten notes in *E. Kidder's Receipts,* 51)

**Polonia Sausages.**
Take a peice of Red Gammon of bacon and halfe boyle it with as much bacon Lard, then putt to it minc'd sage thyme & savory season: the yolks of 12 Eggs and as much Red wine as will bring it to a Pritty thick body mix them with your hands and fill them in Skins as big as 4 ordinary saucidges hang them in a Chimney a while and eat them with oyle and vinegar. (Anonymous [c. 1720], handwritten notes in *E. Kidder's Receipts,* 51)

*To Dress Fish*

**To Boyle a Codds head**
Same

*"Unidentified cookbook, c. 1700"—Anonymous* | *Comments*

drain & spounge it for the sauce take gravy & claret boyld up with a faggot of sweet hearbs & an onion 2 or 3 anchovies drawn up with 2 pound of drawn butter 1/2 a pint of shrimps & ye meat of a Lobster shred fine put ye head in a dish pour ye Sauce thereon stick small toasts on ye head lay on & about it ye Spawn milt & liver garnish it with fry'd parsley slice'd lemon & barberries.

**To Butter Lobsters.**

Take out ye meat & put in a Sauce pan with a little Season'd gravey a nutmeg a little vinegar & drawn butter fill ye Shells & set ye rest in plates.

———

**To Stew Carps**

Take a brace of living carps knock þm on ye head open ye bellies wash out ye blood with vinegar & salt þn cut þm close to ye tale to ye bone & wash þm clean put þm in a broad Saucepan & put thereto a quart of claret 1/2 a pint of white wine 1/2 a pint of vinegar a pint of water a faggot of Herbs a nutmeg slic'd large mace 4 or 5 cloves 2 or 3 racers of Ginger whole pepper & an Anchovy cover þm close & stew þm a quarter of an hour þn put to it ye blood of ye Carp & a ladle of drawn butter lay about ye Spawn milt & liver stick on þm toasts & eat ye lear as broth or thicken it with brown butter.

~ **Brace** at this time meant "two things taken together; a pair; a couple" (*OED*, 1:1042).

**A Carpe Larded With Eele in a Ragooe.**

Take a live carpe slice & scale him from head to tail in 4 or 5 slices on ye one side to ye bone then take a good silver Eele & cut it as for lard as long and as thick as yr little finger rould in Sweet herbs powder'd bay leaves & Savory Spice than lard it thick on ye slosh'd side fry it in a good pan of lard then make for it a ragooe with gravey white wine vinegar claret ye Spawn mushrooms capers grated nutmeg mace a little pepper & salt thicken it with brown butter & garnish it with slic'd lemon.

———

**To Roast A Pike**

Scale & slash a pike from head to tail & lard it with Eels flesh rould in sweet herbs & spice bast & bread it roast it at length or turn ye tail into ye mouth & bring it of in ye oven let ye Sauce be drawn butter ye row & liver with mushrooms, capers & oysters.

———

*Contemporary Recipe #1*

*Contemporary Recipe #2*

boyl'd take it up & put it in a dish that fits your fish bottom; for the Sauce take gravy & clarret boyl'd up with a faggot of Sweet - hearbs & an Onion; 2 or 3 anchovys drawn up with 2 pound of butter a pint of Shrimps oystrs. ye. meat of a Lobster shred fine þn. put the Sauce in Silver or China Basons, stick Small toast on the head, lay on and about it the Spaune milt & liver, garnish it with fry'd Parsley, Slice'd Lemon, Barberries & horse - radish. and fryed fish[.] (Kidder, *E. Kidder's Receipts* [1720], H, 12)

**To Butter Lobsters**

Take out the meat & put it in a sauce -pan with a little Season'd gravy and put to it a nutmeg a little vinegar and drawn butter, fill the Shells & set the rest in plates. (Kidder, *E. Kidder's Receipts* [1720], H.1)

———

**To Stew a Carp.**

Take a Brace of Carp knock them on the head open the bellies & wash out the blood with vineagar & Salt, then cut them close to the tail to the bone & wash them clean, put them in a broad Sauce pan & put thereto a quart of Clarret, half a pint of vineager a pint of a pint of water, a faggot of Sweet herbs, a Nutmeg Sliced large Mace, 4 or 5 Cloves, 2 or 3 racers of Ginger whole pepper & and an Anchovy, cover them close & Stew them a quarter of an hour then put to it the blood and Vineager, and a bit of butter rold up in flower lay about it the Spaune, milt & liver, Stick on them toasts thicken it it with brown butter. (Kidder, *E. Kidder's Receipts* [1720], H, 12)

**To Stew a Carp**

Same

**A Carp Larded wth Eele in a Ragooe.**

Take a live carp knock him on the head, Scale and Slice him from head to tail in 4 or 5 Slices on the one side to the bone: then take a good Silver eel and cut it as for larding as long and as thick as your little finger roul'd in Spice and Sweetherbs and bay leaves powder'd than lard it thick on ye Slash'd side fry it in a good pan of lard: then make for it a ragooe with gravy, white wine vineagar, clarret, the Spaune, mushrooms balls, capers, grated nutmeg, mace, a little pepper & Salt thicken it with brown butter and garnish it with Slic'd lemon. (Kidder, *E. Kidder's Receipts* [1720], H.1)

———

**To Roast A Pike.**

Scale and slash a pike from head to tail and lard it with eels flesh roul'd in Sweet herbs & Spice and fill it with fish, forc'd meat roast it at length bast and bread it : or you may turn his tail into his mouth and bring it off in the oven, let ye sauce be drawn butter, Anchovies, the row and liver with~balls mushrooms, capers & Oysters and garnish it with Slic'd lemon[.] (Kidder, *E. Kidder's Receipts* [1720], H.1)

———

*"Unidentified cookbook, c. 1700"—Anonymous*

*Comments*

**To Pott Beef.**

Take a good buttock of beef or leg of mutton piece cut it in peices & season it with Savory Spice an ounce of salt peter 1/2 a pint of Claret then having 3 or 4 pound of Beef suet lay it between every laying of Beef tye a paper over it & let it lay all night þn bake it with houshold bread þn take it out & dry it in a cloth cut it across ye grain very close & rub it in yr hands like flower if it is not season'd Enough þn season it more þn pour to it ye fat clear from ye gravey & mix it together þn put it close in potts set ye oven to settle when tis cold cover it with clarified butter.

———

**To Pott Pidgeons.**

Your pidgeons being trus'd & season'd with Savory spice put þm in a pott cover þm with butter & bake þm þn take þm out & drain þm when they are cold cover þm with clarified butter you may pot fish ye same way only bone þm when they are bak'd.

———

*Collaring*

**To Collar Beef.**

Lay your flank of Beef in ham brine 8 or 10 days þn take it out & dry it in a cloth lay it in a board take out all ye leather & skin scotch it cross & season it with savory spice 2 or 3 Anchovies an handfull or 2 or thyme parley sweet majoram winter Savory onions & fennel strew it on ye meat & rowl it in a hard collar in a cloth sow it close tye it at both Ends & put it in a collar pott with a pint of claret & cutchenell 2 qts of pump water set it in ye oven all night when tis cold take it out of ye cloth & keep it dry.

———

**To Collar Veal.**

Bone a breast of veal wash & soak it in 3 or 4 waters dry it in a cloth season it with Savory Spice shred & rashers of Bacon dipt in ye batter of Eggs & roul it up in a collar in a cloth & boyle it with water & salt with 1/2 a pint of vinegar & whole spice scum it clean when it is boyl'd take it up & when cold keep it in this pickle.

~ A **rasher** is a "thin slice of bacon or ham cooked . . . by broiling or frying" (*OED*, 8:158).

**To Collar Pigg.**

Slit yr Pigg down ye back take out all ye bones wash out all ye blood in 3 or 4 waters wipe it dry & season it with Savory Spice thyme partley & Salt rowl it in an hard collar in a cloth tye it at both Ends boyl it with ye bones in 3 pts of water an handfull of Salt a qt of

~ **Isieing glass** is **isinglass,** "a firm whitish semi-transparent substance (being a comparatively pure form of gelatin) obtained from the sounds or air-bladders of some fresh water fishes, esp. the sturgeon; used in cookery for making jellies, etc." (*OED*, 5:502).

| *Contemporary Recipe #1* | *Contemporary Recipe #2* |
| --- | --- |
| **To Pott Beef.** Take a good buttock of beef or leg of mutton piece, cut it in pieces and season it with Savoury Spice an ounce of Salt peter 1/2 a pint of Clarret then let it lye all night: then put it in a pan and lay over it 3 or 4 pound of butter, tye a paper over it and bake it with household bread: then take it out and dry it in a cloth and beat it in a mortar very fine; then pour to it the butter clear from the gravy and mix it together then put it close in potts, Sett it in the oven to Settle: when it is cold cover it with clarrified butter. (Kidder, *E. Kidder's Receipts* [1720], I, 13) | **To Pott Beef** Same |
| **To Pott Pidgeons.** Your pidgeons being trust & Season'd with Savoury Spice, put them in a pot, cover them with butter & bake them; then take them out & drain them, when cold cover them wth. clarryfide butter. You may pot fish the same way: but let them be bone'd when they are bak'd. (Kidder, *E. Kidder's Receipts* [1720], I, 13) | **To Pott Pidgeons** Same |
| *Collaring* | *Collaring* |
| **To Collar Beef** Lay your Flank of Beef in Ham brine 8 or 10 days, then dry it in a cloth and take out all the leather and Skin Scotch it cross & Season it with Savoury Spice, 2 or 3 anchovys an handfull or two of thyme Sweet marjoram winter Savoury and Onions, Strew it on the meat & roul it in a hard collar in a cloth, Sew it close & tye it at both ends and put it in a collar pot with a pint of Clarret and Cochineal and two quarts~of pump water and bake it all night: then take it out hot and tye it close at both ends then set it up on one end and put a weight upon it and let it stand till it is cold: then take it out of the cloth and keep it dry[.] (Kidder, *E. Kidder's Receipts* [1720], I.1, 14) | **To Collar Beef** Same |
| **To Collar Veal** Bone a breast of Veal wash and Soake it in 3 or 4 waters, dry it in a cloth and Season it with Savoury Spice Shread Sweet - herbs and rashers of Bacon, dipt in the batter of eggs and roul them up in a collar in a cloth and boyl it in water and Salt with 1/2 a pint of vineagar and whole Spice Scum it clean when it is boyl'd take it up and when cold keep it in this Pickle[.] (Kidder, *E. Kidder's Receipts* [1720], I.2) | **To Collar Veal** Same |
| **To Collar Pig** Slit the Pig down the back take out all the bones wash out all the blood in 3 or 4 waters, wipe it dry, and Season it with Savoury Spice, thyme parsley & Salt and roul it in a hard collar, tye it close in a dry cloth and boyl it with the bones in 3 pints of water, an handfull | **To Collar Pig** Same |

*"Unidentified cookbook, c. 1700"—Anonymous*

*Comments*

vineger a faggot of sweet herbs whole Spice a penny worth of Iseing glass when tis tender take it of when tis cold take it out of ye cloth & keep it in this pickle.

**To Collar Eels**

Scour yr large silver Eeles with Salt slitt þm down ye back take out all ye bones wash & dry them Season þm with Savory Spice minc'd parsley Thyme Sage & an Onion þn rowl Each in collars in a little cloth tye þm close & boyl þm in water & Salt with ye heads & bones & 1/2 a pint of vinegar a penny worth of Iseing glass when they are tender take þm up tye þm close again strain ye pickle & keep ye Eeles in it.

———

**To Collar Pork**

Bone a breast of pork season it with Savory spice & a good quantity of Thyme sage & parsley roal it in an hard collar in a cloth tye þm at both Ends & boyl it when tis cold keep it in Sowsing drink.

~ **Sowsing drink,** an old dialectic term for *sowre* or *sour drink,* was part of the "action or process of pickling" and consisted of a tart, vinegary, fermented liquor in which bran had been allowed to become sour and in which meat or fish was then steeped to prepare and preserve it (*OED,* 10:475, 479–80).

*Pickles*

**To Pickle Mellons or large Cucumbers.**

Take a sliver out of ye Sides of Each & take out ye pulp clean & pour on þm a brine boyling hot & let þm stand 2 or 3 days then fill þm with scrap'd horse reddish sliced garlick ginger nutmeg whole pepper & large mace put ye sliver in again & tye þm with a thread then take for ye pickle. The best white wine vinegar an handfull of salt a quarter'd nutmeg whole pepper cloves & mace 2 or 3 racers of ginger boyld together & pour it to ye melons boyling hot stow þm down close 2 days when your intend to green þm set þm over ye fire in a bell metal pott in these pickles till they are scalding hot & green þn pour þm into Earthen potts slow þm down close when they are cold cover þm with a wet bladder & leather.

Thus cover all other pickles.

———

**To Pickle Gerkins**

Wipe þm clean & put þm in a brine strong enough to bear an Egge 2 or 3 days þn drain þm from ye brine & pour on þm ye same pickle as ye Melons boyling hot: having some dill seeds in yr Pots Stow þm down close 2 or 3 days green þm in a bell metal pot & cover þm as before

~ The following recipe also has a different title but identical contents.

*Contemporary Recipe #1*

of Salt, a quart of vineager, a faggot of Sweet - herbs, whole Spice a pennyworth of Iceing glass when it is boyl'd tender take it off and when cold take it out of the cloth & keep it in this pickle. (Kidder, *E. Kidder's Receipts* [1720], I.2)

**To Collar Eeles.**

Seower yor. large Silver eeles with Salt, Slit þm. down the back, take out the bones wash & dry them & Season þm. with Savory Spice, minc'd parsley, thyme, Sage and an onion then roul each in collars, in a little cloth, tye them close and boyl them in water & Salt wth. ye heads & bones & 1/2 a pint of vinegar a faggot of herbs ginger a penny - worth of iceinglass when they are tender take þm. up tye them close again Strain ye pickle & keep the Eeles in it. (Kidder, *E. Kidder's Receipts* [1720], I.1, 14)

**To Collar Pork.**

Bone a breast of pork Season it with Savoury Spice & a good quantity of Sage, & parsley & thyme roul it in an hard collar in a cloth tye it close and boyl it when its cold keep it in Sousing drink. (Kidder, *E. Kidder's Receipts* [1720], I.2)

*Pickles*

**To Pickle Mellons or large Cucumbers.**

Scoop them at one end and take out the pulp clean, and fill them with Scrap'd horse - raddish, Slic'd garlick, ginger; nutmeg, whole pepper and large mace; then for the pickle: The best white - wine vineagar, an handfull of Salt, a quarter'd nutmeg, whole pepper, cloves and mace and 2 or 3 racers of ginger boyl'd all together. And pour it to the Mellons boyling hot & Stow them down close 2 days; when your intend to green them, Set them over the fire in a bell - mettle pot in their pickle till they are Scalding hot and green~ then pour them into your pots, Stow them down close: when cold cover them with a wet bladder and leather.

Thus cover all other pickles. (Kidder, *E. Kidder's Receipts* [1720], K, 15)

**To Pickle Gerkin Cowcumbers.**

Put them in a brine 2 or 3 days Strong enough to bear an egg; then drain them from the brine and pour on them the Same pickle as the Mellons boyling hot and green them and cover them as before[.] (Kidder, *E. Kidder's Receipts* [1720], K, 15)

*Contemporary Recipe #2*

**To Collar Eeles.**

Same

**To Collar Pork**

Same

*Pickles*

**To Pickle Mellons or large Cucumbers**

Same

**Cowcumbers.**

Same

*"Unidentified cookbook, c. 1700"—Anonymous*

*Comments*

**To Pickle french Beans.**

Put þm a month in Brine strong Enough to bear an Egge þn drain þm from ye Brine & pour on þm ye same pickle as ye mellons boyling hot & green þm ye same way

———

**To Pickle Walnuts.**

Scald þm & put þm in water & salt for 9 or 10 days changing it every day þn take þm out & rub þm in a course cloth þn pour on þm ye same pickle as ye mellons boyling hot adding thereto some mustard seed.

———

**To Pickle Mushrooms**

Take yr small hard buttons cut ye dirt from ye bottom of ye stalks wash þm with salt water & milk & rub þm with flannel þn put þm into another pan of salt water & milk & rub þm till they are clean þn boyl salt water & milk when it boyls throw in yr mushrooms & when they are boyld quick & white straine þm & throw þm into water & salt salt for 2 or 3 days changing it twice a day þn. let ye pickel be halfe white wine & half vineger wth. slicd nutmeg ginger whole peper cloves & mace þn. slop þm in glasses

Calliflowers is don ye same way

**To Pickle Mushroms**

Take the button Mushrooms wipe them with a piece of Flannell throw them into~Milk & Water & then set on a pan of Milk & Water equall alike & take out yor Mushrooms and put them in when it boyls let them boyl up quick for half a quarter of an hour~then pore them into a Sive let them dreen tell they are Cold then make yor Pickle of the best White Veniger and put in Cloves Mace long Pepper & a Race of~Ginger boyld in it & when it is boyld a quarter of an hour & a quarter an Nutmeg~and put in let it stand tell it is cold put them into a pott Tye them down Close with Leather and pore a little of the best Oyle over them to keep them. (The Compiler [1744], Manuscript cookbook, 86).

~ The last part of the Anonymous recipe was written by another hand. It is similar to the one copied above by The Compiler (1744).

**To Pickle beet Root & Turnips.**

Boyle yor. beet roots in water & salt a pt.of vinegar a little Cutchenele when they are half boyld put in ye. turnips being pared wn. they are boyled take þm. off ye fier & keep þm. in this pickle.

———

**To Pickle Red Cabbatch.**

Slice ye. Cabbatch thin & put to it a Cold pickle of vinegar & spice

———

*Contemporary Recipe #1*

**To Pickle French Beans.**
Put them a month in brine strong enough to bear an egg; then drain them from the brine and pour on them ye same pickle as the Mellons boyling hot & green them the Same way[.] (Kidder, *E. Kidder's Receipts* [1720], K, 15)

**To Pickle Walnuts.**
Scal'd them and put them into water & salt for 9 or 10 days, changing it every day, then take them out & rub them with a course cloth & pour on them ye same pickle as the mellons, adding thereto a little mustard Seed. (Kidder, *E. Kidder's Receipts* [1720], K.1)

**To Pickle Mushrooms.**
Take your Small hard buttons, cut ye dirt from ye bottom of ye Stalks, wash them with water & rub them very clean with flannell, then boyl water & Salt; when it boyls throw in your mushrooms & when they are boyld quick & white, Strain them thro a cloth, then throw them into cold water & Salt for 2 or 3 days, changing it twice a day, then let the pickle be white wine vineager with Slic'd nutmeg, ginger, pepper, cloves & mace then stop þm. up in glasses. Calliflowers may be done ye Same way[.] (Kidder, *E. Kidder's Receipts* [1720], K.1)

**To Pickle Beat Roots & Turnips.**
Boyle your Beat Root in water & Salt, a pint of vinegar, a little Cochineal, when they are half boyl'd put in ye Turnips being pare'd, when they are boil'd take them off the fire & keep them in this pickle. (Kidder, *E. Kidder's Receipts* [1720], K.1]

**To Pickle Red Cabbage**
Slice the Cabbage thinn & put to it a pickle of vineagar & Spice cold. [Kidder, *E. Kidder's Receipts* [1720], K.1)

*Contemporary Recipe #2*

**To Pickle French Beans**
Same

**To Pickle Walnuts**
Same

**To Pickle Mushrooms.**
Same

**To Pickle beet Root & Turnips**
Same

**To Pickle Red Cabbage**
Same

*"Unidentified cookbook, c. 1700"—Anonymous*

**To Pickle Arstation Flowers**

Pickle þm in half white wine & 1/2 vineger & sugar.

*Comments:* ~ **Aristation Flowers** are not listed in *OED*, but are believed to be nasturtiums. Mary Randolph had a recipe called "To Pickle Nasturtiums" on page 207.

**To Pickle Onions**

Boyle yor. small white onions in water & salt strain & Coole þm in a Cloth þn. put to þm. a pickle of vinegar & spice boyling hott

*Comments:* ———

**To Pickle Barberries.**

Pickle þm : being pickt in bunches only in water & salt strong enough to bear an egg

*Comments:* ———

**To Pickle Smelts**

Lay þm in a pan in rows lay on þm .slicd lemon ginger nutmeg mace peper and pay leaves powderd & sald let ye. pickle be red wine vinegar bruis[d] Cutchenele & peter salt

You may eat þm as anchovys

*Comments:* ~ **Smelts** refer to "a small fish, *Osmerus eperlanus*, allied to the salmon, and emitting a peculiar odour" (*OED*, 9:271). **Peter salt** or **petre-salt** is saltpetre (*OED*, 7: 751).

**To Pickle Oysters.**

Take a quart of large oysters in ye. full of ye. moon perboyld in there one liquar for ye. pickle take ye liquar a pt of white wine & vineger mace pepper & salt boyle & scum it wth. tis Cold keep ye. oysters in this pickle

*Comments:* ———

**To Pickle Pidgeons.**

Boyle þm. with whole spice in 3 pts. of water a pt. of white wine & a pt. of vineger wn. boyled take þm. up & wn. cold keep þm in this pickle.

*Comments:* ———

**To Pickle Tongues.**

Blanch þm. being boyld in water & salt & put þm in a pott or barrell and make ye pickle of as much white wine vineger as will fill it boyld up wth. savory spice ginger a faggot of sweet herbs wn. Cold put in ye. tongues wth. slicd lemon & cover it close wn. you eat þm. beat up some of ye pickle wth. very good oil & garnish it wth. sliced lemon

*Comments:* ~ This is another recipe attributed to E. Kidder by Anonymous (1700) that has a different title from the following recipe.

| *Contemporary Recipe #1* | *Contemporary Recipe #2* |
|---|---|
| **To Pickle Aristacon Flowers or Clove Gilly Flowers** Pickle them in half white-wine & half Vineger & Sugar when boyl'd & cold (Kidder, *E. Kidder's Receipts* [1720], K.2) | **To Pickle Aristacon Flowers or Clove Gilly Flowers** Same |
| **To Pickle Onions** Boyle your small white onions in water & Salt, Strain and cool them in a cloth, then let the Pickle be Vineager and Spice cold as the Mushrooms. (Kidder, *E. Kidder's Receipts* [1720], K.1) | **To Pickle Onions** Same |
| **[To Pickle Barberries]** Barberries are pickled it only in strong Brine of water & Salt. (Kidder, *E. Kidder's Receipts* [1720], K.2) | **To Pickle Barberries** Same |
| **To Pickle Smelts** Lay þm. in a pot in rows, lay on þm. slic'd Lemon, ginger, nutmeg, mace, pepper & bay leaves powder'd, salt. let ye. pickle be red wine vineager, bruis'd Cochinele, peter salt, let ye pickle be boyl'd & cold & pour'd on þm & Cover þm close. You may eat þm as anchovys[.] (Kidder, *E. Kidder's Receipts* [1720], K.2) | **To Pickle Smelts** Same |
| **To Pickle Oysters** Take a qrt. of large Oysters in ye full of ye moon, parboyl'd in yr. own liqr. for ye pickle, take ye liqr. a pnt. of white wine, & vineager, mace, pepper & salt, boyl & Scum it wn cold keep ye Oysters in this pickle. (Kidder, *E. Kidder's Receipts* [1720], K.2) | **To Pickle Oysters** Same |
| **To Pickle Pidgeons** Boyl them wth whole Spice, in 3 pts of water, a pt. of white wine, & a pt. of vineager; when boyl'd take them up & when cold keep them in this pickle. (Kidder, *E. Kidder's Receipts* [1720], K.2) | **To Pickle Pidgeons** Same |
| **To Machinate Tongues** Blanch them being boyld in water and salt and putt them in a Pott or barrell and make the Pickle of as much White wine vineger as will fill it boyld up with savory seasoning Ginger a faggott of herbs When they are cold putt in the Tongues with Slicd Lemon and cover it When you eat them beat up some of the Pickle with very good oyle garnish'd with Sliced Lemons. (Anonymous [c. 1720], handwritten notes in *E. Kidder's Receipts,* 64) | |

*"Unidentified cookbook, c. 1700"—Anonymous*

*Comments*

**To Salt Hams & Tongues.**

Take 3 or 4 gallons of water & put to it 4 pd. of white sald 4 pd. of bay salt a pd. of peter salt a quarter of a pd. of salt peter & 2 ounces of prunela salt & a pd. of brown sugar let it boyle a quarter of an hour wn. tis cold sever it from ye. bottom into ye. vessel you keep it in

Let hams ley in this pickle 4 or 5 weeks
A Clood of dutch beef as long.
Tongues a fortnight
Collard beef 8 or 10 days
Dry þm. in a stow or wood Chimney

~ **Prunella salt** (*Sal prunella*), a "fused nitre cast into the shape of cakes or balls" or "a salt burnt on charcoal in contrast to salt peter," was used in medicine (*OED,* 9:58). **A clod of beefe** pertains to the "coarse part of the neck of a steer" (Hess, *Martha Washington's Booke,* 83).

*Jellies*

**Harts horn Jelley**

Put 1/2 a pound of hartes horn into an Earthen pan wth. 2 qts of spring water cover it close & set in ye oven all night þn. strain it into a clean pipkin wth. 1/2 a pd. of double refind sugar & 1/2 a pt. of rhennish wine ye. juice of 3 or 4 lemons 3 or 4 blads of mace & ye whits of 4 or 5 eggs well beat let it simer over ye. fier & mix it that it curdle not þn. stirr it well together on ye. fier run it thro a napkin & turn it up again till tis all clear

~ **Rhenish wine** is "produced in the Rhine region" (*OED,* 8:625).

**Calves foot Jelley.**

Boyle a pair of calves feet in water wth. ye meat cut off from ye bons season it as ye. harts horn jelley wn. tis could take ye. fatt from ye top & ye dross from ye bottome

———

**To Run Colours.**

Have in yor. severall small pipkins strong jelley ready seasond have also severall muslain raggs tyde up close one wth. bruisd cutchenele another wth. saffron & another wth. spinage juice put yor. baggs into yor. several pipkins & as you would ye colours rise fine þm. wth. ye. white of eggs and run þm thro' severall baggs

~ This is an interesting glimpse of what was used for food coloring since it reflected the cook's desire to make food appear appetizing.

**Blamangoes.**

Put 1/2 a pd. of harts horn into an earthern pipkin wth. 2 qts of spring water þn. run ye. jelley thro' a napkin put to it 1/2 a pd. of jordan almonds well beat mix wth. it orange flower water a pt. of milk or cream ye. juice of 2 or 3 lemons & double refind sugar let it simer over ye. fier & take care least it burn to run it thro' a sive 2 or 3 tymes put it in glasses & colour it if you please

~ **Blamangoes** was not located in *OED,* but archaic **blamange** was listed. Known as **blancmange,** it was originally a dish "composed usually of fowl, but also of other meat, minced with cream, rice, almonds, sugar, egges, etc.," and today it is "a sweetmeat made of dissolved isinglass or gelatine boiled with milk, etc." and formed into a white jelly; corn flour also could be incorporated into the mix if desired (*OED,* 1:898, 900).

*Contemporary Recipe #1*

**To Salt Hams & Tongues**

Take 3 or 4 gallons of water, put to it 4 pound of bay salt 4 pound of white Salt, a pound of petre Salt a quarter of a pound of Salt petre, 2 ounces of pranella Salt & a pound of brown Sugar: let it boil a quarter of an hour, Scum it well, when it is cold Sever it from the bottom into the vessel you keep it in

Let Hams lye in this pickle 4 or 5 weeks
A Clod of Dutch Beef as long
Tongues a fortnight
Collard Beeff 8 or 10 days
Dry them in a Stove, or wth. wood in a Chimney.

(Kidder, *E. Kidder's Receipts* [1720], L.3)

*Jellies*

**Harts-horn Jelley.**

Put 1/2 pound of harts -horn into an earthen=pan with 2 quarts of Spring water, cover it close & set it in the oven all night, then Strain it into a clean pipkin wth 1/2 a pint of rhennish wine and 1/2 a pound of double refin'd Sugar, the juice of 3 or 4 blades of mace & the whites of 4 or 5 eggs well beat and mix it that it curdle not Set it on the fire and Stir it well together then let it Stand over the fire till it ariseth with a thick Skum; run it thrô a napkin and turn it up again till it is all clear. (Kidder, *E. Kidder's Receipts* [1720], L.16)

**Riban Jelley.**

If made wth ye colour'd jelleys hereafter mention'd First run one of those colours in a glass, wn. it is cold, run another as cold as you can & þn another & so all ye rest. (Kidder, *E. Kidder's Receipts* [1720], L.16)

**To Run Colours.**

Have in yor. Severall small pipkins strong jellies ready season'd have also several muslin rags ty'd up close one wth bruisd cochineal, another wth Saffron & another wth Spinnage juice put yor bags into yor Several pipkins & as you would ye colours rise fine þm with the whites of eggs, and run them thrô Severall bags. (Kidder, *E. Kidder's Receipts* [1720], L.16)

**Blamangoes.**

Make your jelly of 1/2 of harts horn and 2 qts of Spring water, run it thrô a napkin, put to it 1/2 a pound of jordan almonds well beat, mix with it orange flower water, a pint of milk or cream the juice of 2 or 3 lemons and double refind Sugar; let it simmer over the fire and take care least it burn too run it thrô a Sive 2 or 3 times colour it if you please and put it in glasses. (Kidder, *E. Kidder's Receipts* [1720], L.1)

*Contemporary Recipe #2*

**To Salt Hams & Tongues**

Same

*Jellies*

**Harts-horn Jelley.**

Same

**Riban Jelley.**

Same

**To Run Colours.**

Same

**Blamangoes.**

Same

*"Unidentified cookbook, c. 1700"—Anonymous*

*Comments*

**A Whipt Sillabub**

Take a pt. of creame wth. a little orange flower water 2 or 3 ounces of fine sugar ye. juice of a lemon ye white of 3 eggs wisk these up leight together in a broad earthern:pan & having in yor. glasses rhennish wine & sugar & clarret & sugar lay on ye. froth wth. a spoon heapt up as leight as you can

———

**A Sack Posset.**

Take 14 eggs leave out ye. whits beat þm. wth. a quarter of a pd. of fine sugar oringoe roots sliced very thin wth. a quarter of a pt. of sack mix it well together set it on ye. fier & keep it stirring all one way wn. tis scalding hott let another whilst you stir it pour into it a qt. of cream boyling hott wth. a greatd nutmeg boyld in it þn. take it off ye. fier clap ahott pye plate on it & let it stand a quarter of an hour

~ A **posset**, a drink made of "hot milk curdled with ale, wine or other liquor" and often flavored with "sugar, spices & other ingredients," was considered a delicacy as well as a cure for the common cold and other afflictions (*OED*, 7:1158). Anonymous (1700)'s version utilized cream instead of milk, but it served the same principle.

**Chocolate Cream**

Take a pt. of cream wth. a spoonfull of chrapt chocolate boyle þm. well together mix wth. it ye yolks of 2 eggs & thicken & mill it on ye fire þn. pour it into yor. chocolate cups

———

**Lemon Cream.**

Take ye juice of 3 or 4 lemons & boyle some of ye. picle in spring water þn. take ye same quantity of that water as lemon juice put to it orange flower water 1/2 a pd. of doubble refind sugar þn beat ye. whits of 12 eggs & strain þm. þn. mix þm. together & keep it stirring over a charcole fier till tis pritty thick þn. put it in glasses

Orange creame is made ye. same way only thickened with yolks of eggs instead of whits

———

**Orange Butter.**

Take ye. yolks of 5 hard eggs put to it orange flower water & a little fine sugar & a pd. of butter work it thro' a sive

Almond & pistastia butter is thus made but let þm be blanchd & pounded

———

**To Codle Codlings.**

Put yor. fair Codlings in a brass pan wth. water over a charcole fier till tis scalding hott keep þm. close cover'd wn. they will skin þn. skin þm. & put þm. in again wth. a little vineger & let þm. ley till they are green

———

*Contemporary Recipe #1*

**A Whipt Sillabub**

Take a pint of Cream with a little orange flowor water, 2 or 3 ounces of fine Sugar the juice of a lemon, the white of 3 eggs: whisk these up light together and having in your glasses rhennish wine and Sugar and clarret & Sugar, lay on the froth wth. a Spoon heaped up as high as you can. (Kidder, *E. Kidder's Receipts* [1720], L.1)

**A Sack Posset.**

Take 14 eggs, leave out the whites & beat them with a quarter of a pound of white Sugar oringoe roots slic'd very thin with a quarter of a pint of Sack, mix it well together, Set it on the fire and keep Stirring it all one way: when it is scalding hott let another whilst you stirr it, pour into it a qrt of cream boyling hot with a grated nutmeg boil'd in it: Then take it off the fire, clap a hot pye plate on it and let it Stand a quarter of an hour. (Kidder, *E. Kidder's Receipts* [1720], L.1)

**Chocolate Cream.**

Take a pint of Cream wth a spoonfull of scrapt Chocolate boyl it well together mix wth it ye yolks of 2 eggs & thicken & mill it on the fire þn put it in glasses. (Kidder, *E. Kidder's Receipts* [1720], L.2)

**Lemon Cream.**

Take the juice of 3 or 4 Lemons & boyle some of the peel in spring water then take double the quantity of that water as Lemon juice then put to it orange flower water & 1/2 a pound of double refin'd sugar þn beat the whites of 12 eggs & strain them þn mix them together & keep it stirring over a charcoal fire till tis pritty thick þn put it in glasses. Orange Cream it made the same way only thickened with yolks of eggs instead of whites. (Kidder, *E. Kidder's Receipts* [1720], L.2)

**Orange Butter**

Take ye yolks of 5 hard eggs, a pound of butter, a little fine Sugar & a spoonfull of orange flower water & work it thrô a Sive Almond & Pistatia butter is made ye same way only blanch & pound them. (Kidder, *E. Kidder's Receipts* [1720], L.1)

**To Coddle Codlings.**

Put your fair Codlings in a brass pan wth water over a charcole fire till tis Scalding hott~keep them close cover'd, when they will Skin then~Skin them and put them in again with a little vineager and let them lye till they are green[.] (Kidder, *E. Kidder's Receipts* [1720], L.3)

*Contemporary Recipe #2*

**A Whipt Sillabub**

Same

**A Sack Posset.**

Same

**Chocolate Cream.**

Same

**Lemon Cream**

Same

**Orange Butter**

Same

**To Codle Codlings**

Same

*"Unidentified cookbook, c. 1700"—Anonymous*

*Comments*

**To Bottle Goosberries.**

When they are full grown before they turn fill þm. into wide mouth bottles cork þm. close & set set þm in a slack oven till they are tender & some crack þn. take þm. out & pitch ye. corks

Damsons Bullas pare plums or Currants are don ye same way as goosberries only doe these wn. they are ripe

~ **Bullas** is her spelling for **bullace,** a wild plum colored dark blue, black, or white (*OED,* 1:167). **Pare plums** are shaped like pears (*OED,* 7:590).

**[Missing Title]**

Put 1/2 pound of harts-horn into an Earthen pan wth 2 Quarts of Water cover it close & set it in ye oven all night þn. strain it into a clean pipkin wth. 1/2 a pound of Sugar & 1/2 a pint of wine ye juice of 3 or 4 Lemons 3 or 4 blads of Mace & ye whits of 4 or 5 eggs well beat let it simer over ye fier & mix it that it curdle not.

~ Two copies of a recipe, possible flummery, were written on two scraps of paper at a later date. The first scrap of paper had a name inscribed on the reverse side:

Peterfield Trent Peter
Petl? Th H H H

Peterfield Trent was a son of Alexander and Frances Trent of Henrico County, Virginia (Trent Genealogical Chart, #27057). He married Angelica Wilkinson there on 5 March 1771 (*Virginia Gazette,* 21 March 1771, 3).

**[Untitled]**

french huneasuckkles
Luppins Crown imperal
Rockets Dasiss Ememessey[?]
Dabble
Vukelisis Rackelises Rankespurs
Wallflowers Stock Gilleflowers
Curnashons hollehokes Gunkquils
Harts=East french Maragoles affrecan
Skarlit=Beens Salaxtes Crocuses
Bellflower

~ This list of badly spelled flowers and plants also included errors in the use of correct letters of the alphabet. Found on the reverse side of this second scrap of paper was a recipe for fish sauce.

**Huneasuckkles** are **honeysuckles,** while **luppins** mean **lupins. Ememessey** is unidentified, while there is doubt about **dabble. Vukelisis** may be a corruption for **bugles** or **bugloss** in the plural sense. One can only guess at **Rackelises. Rankespurs** refer to **larkspurs.**

**Curnashons** allude to **carnations,** and **hollehokes** are **hollyhocks. Gunkquils** probably are **jonquils,** while **Harts=East** is surely **heartsease. Affrecan skarlit-beens,** while erroneously attributed, are scarlet runner beans. **Salaxtes** is somewhat obscure.

**Mrs. Pr- fish Sass**

Take Back Beef & Cut it small & put it in your pan with a little water & let it Stue over ye fier till it is Broun then stir it till ye brown Cumes of of ye pan then pore it of & put more water till you have as much as you want then put your meet in a saspan with a little water & wine Onyon Ancho-vis pepper & Salt & when you think all ye grease is out of ye meet then put it to ye other gravey & when ye want to use it put half a pound ——— to a pint of Grave[y]——— ——— ———.

~ **Mrs. Pr.** is believed to be Mary (Randolph) Price.

*Contemporary Recipe #1*

**To Bottle Goosberries etc**

When they are full grown before they turn fill them into wide mouth'd bottles cork them close & set them in a slack oven till they are tender & crackt, then take them out & pitch ye corks

Thus you may keep
Damsons Bullace
Pears Plums or
Currants etc.

Only do these when they are ripe. (Kidder, *E. Kidder's Receipts* [1720], L.3)

*Contemporary Recipe #2*

**To Bottle Goosberries**

Same

The order

**First Dishes**
Pottages of all sorts
a dish of fish
beans & beacon
a ham & chickens
pullets & oysters
boyled tongues & udders
a ledg of veal bacon & herbs
a calves head bacon & herbs
a calves head hashed
a goose or turkey ala daube
a legg of veal or mutton ala daube
a bisk of pidgeons
a forcd leg of veal boyld
a powderd haunch of venison
a powderd leg of pork
a leg of mutton & turnips
a piece of salt beef carrots
pullets bacon & cabbatch
boyld foulds & marraw bons
a turbit & small fish

**Bottome Dishes**
A chine of veal or mutton
a jaggot of mutton
a neck of veal
pidgeons in surtout
pudings of sorts
roast beef mincd pyes
cold ham: slicd tongus
potted meats & fouls
a venison pasty
cold lobsters salmon
or sturgen
a haunch of venison roast
a leg of mutton roast wth. oysters
lamb in joynts
a chine & turkey
roast tongues & udders
chickens & asparragus
hens wth. eggs
a roast pike
a calves head roast

**Side Dishes**
Bombarded veal
Scotcht Collops
A forced leg of Lamb
Cutlets forcd
Frigasees white or brown
A ragooe of any sort
Puddings of any sort
Atourt or tansie
Pease beans or french beans
Scollopt oysters
Ollives of veal
Carp in a ragooe
Pidgeons & asparragus
Lambstons & Sweetbreads
Stewed or forcd Carp
Chickens ala Cream
A pompetone

~

**For ye. midle of the table**
A Grand sallad
Pickles of all sorts
A sallad & butter
A hott or Cold pye
Tarts Chees Cakes puffs
A Custards
jellies & Creams
Blamangoes
A dish of fruite
A sweet meat tart
A patty of Lobsters
Cold Lobsters

**Second Course**
A dish of wild foul
Green geese or ducklings
Roast Chickens or pidgeons
Lamb in joynts
Fryd fish
Turkey pouts or Leverits
Partriges Cocks or Snips
Teasants quails or Larks
Wild ducks or teail
Buttard Lobsters or Crabs
Artichokes boyld
Asparragus & eggs
Scollopt oysters
Pitty Patties
A tourt or tansie
Tarts Cheascaks puffs & Custards
a dish of Pease
A ragooe of mushrooms
Lobsters ragoode or rousted

**Plates**
A ponpetone
Oyster, Loves
Tourts of marrow or Cream
Artichokes in Cream
Eggs la swith
Portugall eggs
Cutlets, ollives of veal
Patties of oysters
Crawfish prawns shrimps
Fritters of a peecocks or oysters
Vnion tansie
Polonia sausages
Slicd tongues
Salmongandy
Potting Collaring or Pickles of any sort: Marraw or Spinnage toast
Veal puffs
Sweetbreads larded & roasted

The Order for Bills of Fair

FIRST DISHES
1
*Pottages of all Sorts.*
A Dish of Fish.
*Beans and Bacon.*
A Ham and Chickens.
*Pullets and Oysters.*
Boyl'd tongues & Udders.
*A Leg of Veal, Bacon & herbs.*
A Calves head Bacon & herbs.
*A Neck of Veal Bacon herbs.*
A Calves head hash'd.
*A Goose or Turkey* a la Daub.
A Leg of Veal or Mutton a la Daub.
*A Bisk of Pidgeons.*
A forc'd Leg of Veal boyl'd.
*A Powder'd haunch of Venision.*
A Powder'd Leg of Pork.
*A Leg of Mutton and Turnips.*
A piece of salt Beef *and* Carrots.
*Pullets Bacon & Cabbage.*
Boyl'd Fowls & marrow Bones.
*A Turbut & Small fish.*
A Ham or red tongues wth.
*Chickens or Pidgeons wth.*
Herbs forc'd or plain.
*A Boyl'd Turkey & Oysters.*
Stew'd Giblets.
*A Leg of Lamb & Spin-nage or gooseberries.*
Boyl'd Rabbits.

MIDDLE DISHES
2
A grand Sallad of Pickles.
*A hot or cold Pye.*
Tarts Cheescakes.
*Puffs & custards.*
Jellies, Creams & Blamangoes.
*A Dish of Fruit.*
A Sweet-meat Tart.
*A Patty of Lobsters.*
*Cold Lobsters.*
*Puddings.*

BOTTOM DISHES
3
A Chine of Veal or Mutton.
*A Gigot of mutton.*
A neck of Veal. Pidgeons
*in* Surtout. Puddings of
any sort. Roast Beef.
*minc'd Pyes.* Cold Ham.
*Slic'd tongue.* A Venison
Pasty. *Potted meats or*
*Fowls.* Cold Lobster.
*Salmon or Sturgeon.*
A haunch of Venison *roast*
a Leg of mutton roast wth.
Oysters. Lamb in Joynts.
*A Chine & Turkey.* Chick-
*ens or Pidgeons roast with.*
Asparagus, Pullets *or Turkey*
*wth. eggs.* A roast Pike.
*a Calves head roasted Pid-*
*geons pears.* Bombarded-
Veal. *Roast Turkey or*
*Fowls wth.* Sausages.

SIDE DISHES
4
Bombarded Veal.
*Scotch'd Collops.*
a forc'd leg of Lamb.
*Cutlets a la Maintenoy.*
Cutlets forc'd.
*Fricassies white or brown.*
A Ragooe of any sort.
a Tourt or Tansie. *Peas,*
Beans or French-beans.
Scollop'd Oysters.
*Ollives of Veal.*
Carp in a Ragooe.
*Chickens & Asparagus.*
Lamb-stones & Sweetbreads.
*Stew'd or forc'd Carp.*
Chickens a la Creame.
*A Pompetone.*

SECOND COURSE
5
A dish of wild or tame
Fowl of any sort. Rabbits,
*Ducklings,* Green Geese or
*Pidgeons,* Turkey Pouts,
*Leverets,* Partridges.
*Woodcocks or* Snips.
*Pheasants,* Quails *Larks*
Wheat-ears, *Ducks Widge-*
*ons,* Plovers.
*A Comport of Pidgeons.*
Pidgeons broild or *Stew'd*
*Butter'd Lobsters or Crabs.*
Artichokes boyld.
*Asparagus & eggs.*
Schollop'd Oystiers.
*Pitty Patties.*
A Tourt or Tansy.
*Tarts, Cheese-cakes,*
Puffs & Custards.
*A Dish of Peas.*
A Ragooe of Mushrooms.
*A Ragooe of any sort.*
Lobsters Ragoo'd or Roast.
*A Pompetone.*
Oyster Loaves.
*Tourts of Marrow or Cream.*
Veal Cutletts.
*Ollives of Veal.*
Patties of Oysters.
*Craw-fish Prawns, Shrimps.*
Fitters of Abricocks *or*
Oysters.
*Polonia Sausages.*
Slic'd Tongue.
*Solomon gundy.*
Potting collaring or Pick
les *of any Sort.*

(Kidder, *E. Kidder Receipts* [1720], last page)

# "Jane Randolph her Cookery Book, 1743"

# Account Book, 1739

These accounts, dated from 1739 to 1742, were found among the first few pages in Jane (Bolling) Randolph's culinary manuscript. The accounts have been edited separately for the ease of the reader.

| | | | | | | | | |
|---|---|---|---|---|---|---|---|---|
| **1739** | | Dr. | Cur. | | | | | |
| 19 Oct | Mrs. Margery | | *s* | *d* | | | | |
| | To 1 Flanll. Petticoate | @ | 3 | 9 | | | 3 | 9 |
| | To 1 pr. Stockings | @ | 3 | 9 | | | 3 | 9 |
| | To 2 Yds. Flanll. | @ | 2 | | | | 4 | |
| | To George's acct. | | 1 | | | | 1 | |
| | To 1 pr. Stockings | | | | | | | |
| | To 1 pr. Gloves | | 3 | | | | 3 | |
| | To 1½ Yd. Check | | 1 | | | | 1 | 6 |
| | To 1¼ Yd. Linsey Woolsey | | 1 | 8 | | | 2 | 1 |
| | To 2½ Yds. Rushia | @ | | 4½ | | | | 11½ |
| | | | | | Cur. £ | 1 | | |

[*facing page*]
P. Contra Cr.

| | | | | | | | |
|---|---|---|---|---|---|---|---|
| **1739** | | Dr. | Cur. | | | | |
| 21 Oct | Cate | | *s* | *d* | | | |
| | To 2 Yds. Stripe Cotton | @ | 2 | 6 | | 5 | |
| | To 2 Yds. Dutch Do. | @ | 2 | 2 | | 4 | 4 |
| 22 | To 1 Check Apron & Beads | @ | 3 | | | 3 | |
| | To 1 paper of pins | @ | | 7½*d* | | | 7½ |
| | To 1 piece none so pretty | @ | | Do. | | | 7½ |
| | | | | | Cur. £. | 13 | 7 |
| | | | | | | 1 | 3 |
| | Remains Due by Ballance | | | | | 12 | 4 |

[*facing page*]

| | | | |
|---|---|---|---|
| 1739 | P Contra Cr. | | |
| 21 Oct. | By Cash reced one Shill : & 3 pence | 1 | 3 |

| | | | | | | | |
|---|---|---|---|---|---|---|---|
| **1739** | | Dr. | Cur. | | | | |
| 21 Oct | Joan | | *s* | *d* | | | |
| | To 3½ Yds. Cotton | @ | 2 | 2 | | 7 | 7 |

[*facing page*]

| | | | | |
|---|---|---|---|---|
| | P Contra | Cr. | | |
| 9br7 | by Cash | | 3 | |
| | by Do. | | 1 | 7 |

| | | | | | | | |
|---|---|---|---|---|---|---|---|
| **1739** | | Dr. | | | Ster. | | |
| 22 Oct | Sam | | *s* | *d* | | | |
| | To 1 pr. stockings | @ | 3 | | | 3 | |
| | To 1 Worsted Cap | @ | 1 | | | 1 | |
| | | | | | Ster. | 4 | |
| | | | | | Cur. | 5 | |
| | | | | | | 2 | 11½ |
| | Remain/Due by Ballance | | | | Cur. £. | 2 | ½ |

[*facing page*]

| | | | | |
|---|---|---|---|---|
| 1739 | P Contra | Cr. | 2 | 11½ |
| 22 Oct | By Cash reced | | | |

| | | | | | | | |
|---|---|---|---|---|---|---|---|
| **1739** | | Dr. | | | | | |
| 19 Oct | mr. Peter Randolph | | s | d | | | |
| | | | | Ster. | | | |
| | To 19 Yds. Linen | @ | | *7d* per yd | | 11 | 1 |
| | To 14½ Yds. Do. | @ | | 8½ | | 10 | 3¾[?] |
| | To 1 pr. of Worsted hose | | | 18 | | 1 | 6 |
| | To 9½ yds. Linen | @ | | 11 | | 8 | 8½ |
| | To 2 pr. Children hose | | | | | 2 | |
| | To ¾ Yds Ribband | @ | | *8d* | | | 6 |
| | To Do. | | | | | | 6 |
| | To Do. | | | | | | 6 |
| | To 1 pr. Red Hose | | | | | 3 | |
| | To 2 pr. Womens hose | @ | 3*s* | | | 6 | |
| | To 16½ Yds. White kowl | @ | | *7d* | | 9 | 8 |
| | To Pins | | | | | 2 | 7 |
| | To 100 sowing Needles | @ | 6*s* pr 1000 | | | | 7 |
| | To ½ ll. Thread | @ | 10*s* | | | 5 | |
| | To 2 pr. Stockings | @ | 3 | 6 | | 7 | |
| | To 1 Hair Cap | @ | | *6d* | | | 6 |
| | To 1 Bible | @ | 18*s* | | | 18 | |
| | | | | Ster. £. | 4 | 7 | 5¼ |
| | | | | Cur. | 5 | 9 | 3½ |

[*facing page*]
P Contra
By Charged by R R in Private
acct L folo. 109

| | | | | | | | |
|---|---|---|---|---|---|---|---|
| **1739** | | Dr. | | | | | |
| 20 Oct | Major John Bolling | | s | d | | | |
| | | | | Ster. | | | |
| | To 1 prs. Dutch Cotton | | | | | 19 | 7 |
| | To 21¼ Yds. Rushia Linen | @ | | 4½*d* | | 8 | |
| | To 24 Yds. Do. | @ | | 10½ | 1 | 1 | |
| | To 3 pr. Boys hose 3s Twist | | | *3d.* | | 3 | 3 |
| | To 11 Worsted Caps | @ | | *9d* | | 8 | 3 |
| | | | | Ster. £. | 3 | 0 | 1 |
| | | | | Cur. | 3 | 15 | |

[*facing page*]
P Contra Cr.

| | | | | | | | |
|---|---|---|---|---|---|---|---|
| **1739** | | Dr. | | | | | |
| 20 Oct | Madm Carey | | s | d | | | |
| | | | | Ster. | | | |
| | To 7 prs. Stockings | @ | | 12*d* | | 7 | |
| | To 1 pr. Do. | @ | | 24 | | 2 | |
| | To 19 Yds. Rushia Cloth | @ | | 4½ | | 7 | 1½ |
| | To 20 hanks Worsted | @ | | 1 | | 1 | 8 |
| | To 1 busk | @ | | 4 | | | 4 |
| | To 2 borders 10 Petticoats | @ | | 14 | | 2 | 4 |
| | To 4½ Yds. Ribband | @ | | 8 | | 3 | |

| | | | | | | |
|---|---|---|---|---|---|---|
| | To 10½ yds. Ell Wide Check | @ | 15 | | 13 | 1½ |
| Ster. | To 4 prs. Gloves | @ | 14 | | 4 | 8 |
| £4:9:10 | To 3 pr. Stockings | @ | 42 | | 10 | 6 |
| | To pr. Norwich Gloves | @ | 42 | | 7 | |
| | To 18 oz: Thread | @ | 6 | | 9 | |
| Curs | To 1 pr. Coarse Do. | @ | 28 | | 2 | 4 |
| £5:12:3½ | To 6 Worsted Caps | @ | 9 | | 4 | 6 |
| | To 3 Yds. Diapr. | @ | 21 | | 5 | 3 |
| | To 1 pr. scales & wafer | | | | [?] | [?] |

[*facing page*]

P Contra Cr.

**1739** Dr.

| | | | | | | | | |
|---|---|---|---|---|---|---|---|---|
| 13 Oct | Coll : Richd. Randolph | | *s* | *d* | | | | |
| | To 600 Pins at 2s P 1000 | | | | Ster. | | | |
| | and sowing Needles to ye | | 2 | | | | | |
| | Irish men yt. Brot ye Butter | | 5 | | | | 1 | |
| 19 | To ½ Yd. Lawn | @ | 9s | | | | 4 | 6 |
| | To 2½ Yds. Do. | @ | 2 | 10 | | | 7 | 1 |
| 21 | To 2 pr. Drawn Pocketts | @ | 1 | | | | 2 | |
| | To 6 prs. Mittins | @ | 1 | 6 | | | 9 | |
| | To 2 pr. Gloves | @ | 10 | | | | 1 | 8 |
| | To 3 Yds. canvass for Sampler | @ | 1 | 6 | | | 4 | 6 |
| 23 | To 35 Yds. Check | @ | 1 | 6 | | 2 | 12 | 6 |
| | To 3 pr. Childrens Stockings | @ | | 4½ | | | 1 | 1½ |
| | To 1 Flanll. Petticoate | @ | 3 | | | | 3 | |
| | To 7¼ Yds. Stripe Flanll. | @ | 1: | 8 | | | 12 | 1 |
| 26 | To mr. Pleasants acct. | | | | | 2 | 2 | 3 |
| 29 | To 1 Piece Cotton | @ | 12 | | | | 12 | |
| 30 | To 24 Yds. Rushia Cloth | @ | | 10½ | | 1 | 1 | |
| | To 23½ Yds. Do. | @ | | 4½ | | | 8 | 9¾ |
| | To 3 Yds. Do. | @ | | Do. | | | 1 | 1½ |
| | To Ned's acct. | | | | | | 8 | |
| 31 | To ye Gardner's acct. | | | | | | 7 | 9 |
| | | | | | Ster. £. | 9 | 19 | 4¾ |
| | | | | | Cur. | 12 | 9 | 3 |

[*facing page*]

| | | | | |
|---|---|---|---|---|
| | P Contra Cr. | | | |
| | 1742 By Cash Reciev'd of Jean | | 7 | 7 |
| June 2d : | | | | |
| April 2 | To Margery | 1 | | |

**1739** Dr.

| | | | | | | | |
|---|---|---|---|---|---|---|---|
| 21 Oct | mr. Joseph Hobson | | *s* | *d* | | | |
| | To 2 pr. Stockings | | | Cur. | | 3 | 9 |
| | To 23 Ells Rushia | @ | | 9d | | 17 | |
| | | | | Cur. £. | 1 | | 9 |
| | | | | | | 9 | 2 |
| | Remains/Due p Ballance | | | | | 11 | 7 |

[*facing page*]

| | | | | | | | | |
|---|---|---|---|---|---|---|---|---|
| 1739 | P Contra Cr. | | | | | | | |
| 21 Oct | By Cash reced nine Shillings & 2 pence | | | | | | 9 | 2 |

| | | | | | | | | |
|---|---|---|---|---|---|---|---|---|
| **1739** | | Dr. | | | | | | |
| 20 Oct | Beverly Randolph Esqr. | | s | *d* | | | | |
| | To 1 pr. Stockings | @ | 4s | | | | 4 | |
| | To 1 pr. Do. | @ | 1 | 9*d* | | | 1 | 9 |
| 21 | To 2 pr. Do. | @ | 4 | 3 | | | 8 | 6 |
| | | | | | Ster. £ | | 14 | 3 |
| | To two fans | | | | Cur. | | 17 | 10 |
| | To four yrds. Riband | | | | | | 3 | |
| | | | | | | 1 | | 10 |

[*facing page*]
P Contra Cr.

| | | | | | | | | |
|---|---|---|---|---|---|---|---|---|
| **1739** | | Dr. | | | | | | |
| 23 Oct | mrs. Baugh | | s | *d* | Ster. | | | |
| | To 2 pr. Stockings | @ | | 8*d* | | | 1 | 4 |
| | | | | | Cur. | | 1 | 8 |

[*facing page*]
P Contra Cr.

| | | | | | | | | |
|---|---|---|---|---|---|---|---|---|
| **1739** | | Dr. | | | | | | |
| 17 Oct | mr. Sackvill Brewer | | s | *d* | Ster. | | | |
| | To 2 pr. Stockings | @ | 4s | | Ster. | | 8 | |
| | | | | | Cur. | | 10 | |

[*facing page*]
P Contra Cr.

*"Jane Randolph her Cookery Book, 1743"*

***Jane Randolph***
***her***
***Cook Book***
M E
T? J?[faint] Miss

Jane Randolph her
Cookery Book
January 18th 1743
1 Spoonful
nutmeg
Jane Randolph
Sugar to make
Her Book
Robarty[? ] March 29th 1796
1796
1796
[left page]: Jane Randolph
her
Cook Book

*Comments*

The title page on the right half of the folio page is in the handwriting of Jane (Bolling) Randolph. Her manuscript may have been completed as a gift to her daughter Jane Randolph-Walke, who may have possessed it for only a short time, since a different "Jane Randolph Her Book" was penned more unevenly on the left half of the folio page.

Scribbled among the words and below Jane (Bolling) Randolph's name and date is a possible death date in someone's handwriting to commemorate a Jane Randolph. While the word does look like "Robarty," it is believed that the word "Departed" is intended. It is known that Jane's granddaughter Jane Randolph-Bolling did die on 29 March 1796.

The lines starting with "1 Spoonful" and "nutmeg"" were penned upside down at the bottom of the page. It is presented right side up for the ease of the reader.

**Calves Head to hash**

[Missing]

**To Hash a Calf's Head.**

Boil the head till the meat is almost enough for eating; then cut it in thin slices, take three quarters of a pint of good gravy, and add half a pint of white wine, half a nutmeg, two anchovies, a small onion stuck with cloves, and a little mace; boil these up in the liquor for a quarter of an hour, then strain it and boil it up again; put in the meat, with salt to your taste, let it stew a little, and if you choose it, you may add some sweet breads, and make some forced meat balls with veal; mix the brains with the yelks of eggs, and fry them to lay for a garnish. When the head is ready to be sent in, stir in a bit of butter. (Randolph, *Virginia Housewife,* 90)

According to Jane's index, this recipe was on this page, but it is now missing. Perhaps this version was a slightly modernized edition of Jane's recipe.

**Marmalade**

To 2: lb. Quinces, put 3/4 lb: Sugar, & a pt: spring water, put them over the fire, & boil them till they are tender; then take them up & bruise them; put then into the liquor & boil them 3/4 of an hour.

**Quinces Baked**

[Missing]

**Tansey**

[Missing]

According to the index compiled by Jane (Bolling) Randolph, there was a recipe for "tansey" on page 2.

*Contemporary Recipe #1*

*Contemporary Recipe #2*

*"Jane Randolph her Cookery Book, 1743"*

*Comments*

**Pickle Cucumbers**
[Missing]

———

**Mrs. Dudlys Cake**
4 lb: flour, mix in it two races of Ginger, 2 blades mace 1 stick cimmamon, 6 cloves 1 nutmeg, 3 lb: currants 2 lb: white sugar 18 eggs 1 pt: yest, a qt: cream mix all well together, & beat it a good white before it ———.

~ The rest of the recipe is missing because the lower portion of the page was torn off. The recipe below was found a few pages later and may be a recopy of the first one.

**Mrs. Dudlys Cake**
4 lb: flour, some spice, & ginger. 3 lb. currants, 2 lb. white sugar 18 eggs, 1 pint yest, a quart m: cream. mix these things, & beat them well before go into the oven. Half a pound Butter, & little Sack added will make it better.

**Fricassee chickens or rabbits**
[Missing]

~ Atkyns's recipe at right is almost identical to the one given in Kidder's works.

**Florendine**
[Missing]

~ It cannot be determined at this point whether Jane (Bolling) Randolph had in mind a plain, rice, or orange and apple florendine.

**To Roast a Calf's Head.**
[Missing]

**To Roast A Calf's Head.**
Wash and pick the head very nicely, having taken out the brains and tongue, prepare a good quantity of forced meat, with veal and suet well seasoned, fill the hole of the head with this forced meat, skewer and tie it together upon the spit, and roast it for an hour and a half. Beat up the brains with a little sage and parsley shread fine, a little salt, and the yelks of two or three eggs; boil the tongue, peel and cut it into large dice, and fry that and the brains, and also some of the forced meat made up into balls, with slices of bacon. Let the sauce be strong gravy, with oysters, mushrooms, capers, and a little white wine thickened. (Randolph, *Virginia Housewife,* 89–90)

~ This recipe was listed on page 6 according to Jane's index, but it is missing from the manuscript.

**Ragoo of breast of veal**
[Missing]

**Ragout of a Breast of Veal.**
Separate the joints of the brisket, and saw off the sharp ends of the ribs, trim it neatly and half roast it; put it in a stew pan with a quart of good gravy seasoned with wine, walnuts, and mushroom catsup, a teaspoonful of curry powder and a few cloves of garlic, stew it till tender, thicken the gravy and garnish with

*Contemporary Recipe #1* | *Contemporary Recipe #2*

———

———

**A brown Fricassy of Chickens or Rabbets.**
CUT them in pieces, and fry them in butter; then having ready hot a pint of gravy, a little claret, white-wine and strong broth, two anchovies, two shiver'd palates, a faggot of sweet herbs, savoury balls and spice, thicken it with brown butter, and squeeze a lemon on it. (Atkyns, *Family Magazine,* 1:33)

———

**To Roast a Calf's Head.**
After the Head is nicely wash'd and pick'd, take out the Brains and Tongue; make a large Quantity of Forc'd -meat, with a Veal and Suet well season'd, fill the Hole of the Head; skewer it, and tie it together upon the Spit: One Hour and a half roasts it: Beat up the Brains with a little Sage and Parsley finely shred, a little Salt, and the Yolks of two or three Eggs; Boil and blanch the Tongue, cut it in large Dice, and fry that and the Brains, as also some of the Forc'd -meat in Balls, and some Slices of Bacon. The Sauce is strong Broth, with Oysters, Mushrooms, Capers, and a little White-wine thicken'd. (Several Hands, *Collection* [1714], 20)

**A Ragooe of a breast of Veal**
Bone a breast of veal, cut an handsom Square piece; then cut the other part into Small pieces, brown it in butter, then stew & toss it up in your ragooe for made dishes, thicken it with brown butter; then put the ragooe in ye dish, lay on the Square piece, dic'd Lemon, Sweetbreads, Sippets, and bacon fry'd in the

*"Jane Randolph her Cookery Book, 1743"* | *Comments*

sweet breads nicely broiled. (Randolph, *Virginia Housewife*, 49)

~ Perhaps Jane's version resembled the above or the recipe at right.

**Beef to Collar**
[Missing]

**To Collar Beef**

Take a large Flank of Beef beat it with your Rowling pin to make it lye Even & cut it~Smouth take out all the Grisells & Vains then take an Ounce of Salt peter as much of salt prewnelas-beaten then take a quarter of a pound of brown Suger mix them together & Rub it with your hand-then lay it in a Tray & Sprinkle it with Pump Water let it lye 2 or 3 daies & turn it & Sprinkle it once A day then Season it with Salt peper & Nutmeg & all sorts of sweet herbs with a good deal of Sage one Sprig of Rosemary Cut them & Strow on the Collor the rowl them up hard like a Coller of brawn and put it into Water Enough to Cover it with a bunch of Sweet herbes alittle whole Mace Salt & abay leaf or 2 & an Onion & when it is baked take it out & tye it up in a Cloth tell it is cold then rowl it up hard in a Cloth & let it lye tell next day or you may keep it in the Pickle it was bake in only when it is cold take of the fat & boyl it with more Water & if it is not Season'd Enough Season it more Set it to be cold then put in your beef in along Pott & Cover it with the Pickle and boyle up the Pickle as you find Occasion once a week or 10 days. (The Compiler [1744], Manuscript cookbook, 82–83)

~ Perhaps Jane (Bolling) Randolph used one of these versions.

**Venison Pasty**
[Missing]

~ Jane (Bolling) Randolph's index placed "Venison" on page 9. However, like many of her other meat recipes, it is missing from her manuscript—a significant fact because of the high status attached to serving meats. For the 1664 cookbook published by Elizabeth Cromwell, her husband Oliver stole this venison pasty recipe, known as the "King of dainties" (Cromwell, *Court & Kitchen,* 125). Perhaps the recipe at right was one she had used.

*Contemporary Recipe #1*

*Contemporary Recipe #2*

batter of eggs, and garish it with Slic'dOrange. (Kidder, *E. Kidder's Receipts* [1720], F.5)

**To Collar a Flank of Beef**

Get a nice flank of beef, rub it well with a large portion of salt petre and common salt, let it remain ten days, then wash it clean, take off the outer and inner skin with the gristle, spread it on a board and cover the inside with the following mixture: parsley, sage, thyme, chopped fine, pepper, salt, and pounded cloves, roll it up, sew a cloth over it and bandage that with tape, boil it gently five or six hours, when cold lay it on a board without undoing it, put another board on the top with a heavy weight on it, let it remain twenty-four hours, take off the bandages, cut a thin slice from each end, serve it up garnished with green pickle and sprigs of parsley. (Randolph, *Virginia Housewife,* 42)

———

**40. Venison Pasty.**

Take three quarters of a Peck of fine Flour, and put six pound of Butter in the Flour; then beat in twelve Eggs, and make your Pasty with warm Water; bone the Venison, beat and break the bones, season it with Salt and Pepper to fill up the Pasty when it comes out of the Oven; then season your Venison with an Ounce and half of black Pepper just bruised, and Salt; then take about a pound of Beef - suet, cut it into long slices, beat it with your Rowling - pin, and strew over it Salt and Pepper; then lay the Venison on the top, season it very high with Pudding - crust rund the Pan, and put in a large Porringer of Water, and lay a Layer of good fresh butter and cover it; shake your Pasty, and when it comes out of the Oven pour in the Liquor that you made of the bones, and shake it well together; serve it to the Table. (Howard, *England's Newest Way* [1710], 19–20)

———

*"Jane Randolph her Cookery Book, 1743"*

*Comments*

**A Receipt for the Cholick**

Take 2 oz: Lignumvita
2 oz: Liquerish
2 oz: Seina
2 oz: Coriander Seed
2 oz: Elicumpane
1 oz: Rhubarb
1/2 oz: ston'd Raisons.

Put these Ingredinets into two qts. french Brand[y] & two pts: water, let them steep together ten days shaking it once a day: then strain it off. The dose is a small dram Glass full when you first feal the pain. It it does not give ease in Eight hours, take another dose p Capt: Talman.

~ **Lignumvita (lignumvitae)** is either guaiacum, a tree, or a resin from this tree (*OED*, 6:282). **Seina** refers to **senna,** "a shrub of genus *Cassia,* a native of tropical regions" (*OED*, 9:455). **Elicumpane (elicampane)** is familiar as horse-heal with its "very large yellow radiate flowers and bitter aromatic leaves and root"; it was used at one time as a "tonic and stimulant" (*OED*, 3:74). **Rhubarb** is the "medicinal rootstock (purgative and subsequently astringent) of one or more species of *Rheum*"; the common garden "English or French rhubarb" is often used as a substitute for fruit but was also used for pharmaceutical purposes as well (*OED*, 8:633).

Capt. Henry Talman sailed between England and Virginia for a number of years.

**Turkey Pie**
[Missing]

~ This meat dish is among many meat dishes absent from Jane (Bolling) Randolph's cookbook.

**Walkers Receipt to mend China**

Mix Spanish whitin with Lintseed Oil pretty soft then mend your China & put it into the Oven after Bread had been drawn that it may dry.

~ **Spanish whitin** probably alludes to **Spanish white,** "a finely powdered chalk used as a pigment or for its cleansing properties" (*OED*, 9:508). **Lintseed oil (linseed oil)** is obtained from the seed of flax (*OED*, 6:321).

**Norfolk Dumplins**

Make a good thick Batter, as for Pancakes, drop the batter into boiling water, two, or three minutes will do them. drain them in a sieve, & stir a little good butter among them.
1796

~ This particular recipe is among those added later to Jane (Bolling) Randolph's manuscript that year, perhaps by granddaughter Jane Randolph.

**Quinces Bak'd**

To 1 lb: Quince put a pint water, & 3/4 lb: Sugar, put the parings on the top. & so bake them.

———

**Muffins.**

Take a quart of flour well dri'd, & make it up with a spoonful of yest, & as much warm water as will make it. thin enoug to pour into a Jug, or any thing of that

———

*Contemporary Recipe #1*

---

**A Turkey Pye**

Bone the Turkey, Season it with savoury Spice and lay it in the pye wth 2 Capons or 2 wild ducks cut in pieces to fill up the Corners, lay on butter and close the pye.

A Goose pye is made the same way with 2 Rabbits[.] (Kidder, *E. Kidder's Receipts* [1720], C.2, 6)

---

---

**To bake Quinces, cap. xi.**

Pare them, take out ye Core, perboyle thm in water tll they be tender let the water run frō thē til they be drie: then put into every Coffin one Quince, fil a good quatity of marow. Also take sugre, Cinamon, & a litle Ginger, & fil the Coffin therewith, close it, let it bake an howre, and so serve it. (Partridge, *Treasurie*, chap. 11)

---

*Contemporary Recipe #2*

---

---

---

**Norfolk Dumplings**

Mix a good thick Batter, as for Pancakes, take half a Pint of Milk, two Eggs, a little salt, and make it into a Batter with Flour. Have ready a clean Sauce-pan of Water boiling, into which drop this Batter. Be sure the Water boils fast, and two or three Minutes will boil them; then throw them into a Sieve to drain the Water away, then turn them into a Dish, and stir a Lump of fresh Butter into them, and eat them hot, they are very good. (Glasse, *Art of Cookery*, 112)

---

---

*"Jane Randolph her Cookery Book, 1743"*

*Comments*

kind. when tis light pour it into moulds, & bake them. then cut them round, & tare them open, & butter them hot for breake fast.—Mrs. Munford.—

**Light wigs.**

Take 2 lb: flour, 1 pint milk made warm, mix these well together, & let them stand by the fire an hour to rise, then mix into it half a pound of Butter, & as much Sugar then make it into Wigs with as little Flour, as possible.

———

**[Boiled Pudding]**

[Missing]

**A Nice Boiled Pudding.**

Make up a pint of flour at sun-rise, exactly as you do for bread; see that it rises well; have a large pot of water boiling, and half an hour before the puddings are to go to table, make the dough in balls, the size of a goose-egg; throw them in the water and boil them quickly, keeping the pot covered: they must be torn asunder, as cutting will make them heavy; eat them with powdered sugar, butter, and grated nutmeg. (Randolph, *Virginia Housewife,* 152–53)

~ It is too bad this is one of many missing recipes in Jane's manuscript.

**Shaking Pudding**

[Missing]

~ It is not known from which source Jane (Bolling) Randolph may have copied her "Shaking Pudding" recipe.

**Rice Pudding**

[Missing]

**Rice Pudding.**

Boil half a pound of rice in milk, until it is quite tender; beat it well with a wooden spoon to mash the grains; add three quarters of a pound of sugar, and the same of melted butter; half a nutmeg, six eggs, a gill of wine, and some grated lemon-peel; put a paste in the dish and bake it. For change, it may be boiled, and eaten with butter, sugar, and wine. (Randolph, *Virginia Housewife,* 147)

~ This recipe is not all that different from Anonymous (1700)'s version or Howard's edition on the right. Jane's recipe may have been along the same lines.

*Contemporary Recipe #1*

*Contemporary Recipe #2*

**To make the Light Wigs**

Take a pound and half of Flour, and half a pint of Milk made warm; mix these together and cover it up, and let it lie by the Fire half an hour; then take half a pound of Sugar, and half a pound of Butter; then work these in the Paste, and make it into Wigs, with as little Flour as possible. Let the Oven be pretty quick, and they will rise very much. (E. Smith, *Compleat Housewife* [1729], 117)

———

**3. To make a rare Pudding to bake or boil.**

Beat a Pound of Almonds as small as possibly; put to them some Rose-water and Cream as oft as your beat them; then take one Pound of Beef-suet finely minced, with five Yolks of Eggs, and but two Whites; make it as thin as Batter for Fritters, mixing it with sweet thick Cream; season it with beaten Mace, Sugar and Salt; then set it into the Oven in a Pewter-dish, and when you draw it forth strew some Sugar on the Top; garnish your Dish with Sugar, and serve it always first up to the Table. (Howard, *England's Newest Way* [1710], 177)

———

**17. Shaking Pudding of Almonds.**

Take a Pint of Cream, boil it with a blade of Mace, strow it over with some beaten Almonds, a little Orange-flower or Rose-water; then take four Eggs, leave out two Whites, strain the Cream, Eggs and Almonds together; then take some Sugar and sweeten it, and thicken it with grated Bread or Bisket; then take a Cloth and rub it with Flour, and tye it up and dip it into Rose-water; then boil it, and when it is boiled eat with Butter, Sugar and White-wine, stick it with blanched Almonds; send it. (Howard, *England's Newest Way* [1710], 8)

**To make a shaking Pudding.**

Boil some large Mace, slic'd Nutmeg, and Ginger in a Quart of sweet Cream; then put in Almonds beaten with Rose-water, then beat eight Eggs, leaving out four of their Whites; strain all these together; mingle with them some slic'd Ginger, Salt, Sugar, and grated Bread; the butter a Cloth, and flour it; put in your Pudding, tye it hard, put it into boiling Water, then dish it up with Butter, Verjuice and Sugar. (Nott, *Cook's and Confectioner's Dictionary*, #247)

**A fine Rice Pudding.**

TAKE of the Flour of Rice six ounces, put it in a quart of Milk, and let it boil till 'tis pretty thick, stirring it all the while; then pour it in a Pan, and stir in it half a pound of fresh Butter, and a quarter of a pound of Sugar, or sweeten it to your Taste; when 'tis cold, grate in a Nutmeg, and beat six Eggs with a spoonful or two of Sack, and beat and stir all well together; put a little fine Paste at the bottom of your Dish, and bake it. (E. Smith, *Compleat Housewife* [1729], 99)

———

| *"Jane Randolph her Cookery Book, 1743"* | *Comments* |
| --- | --- |
| **For Fits**<br>For a child, of a Year old in a fit, give it four grains Salt of amber and in case they continue, give this dose once in two hours.<br>You may mix ten grains Salt of amber, & ten grains caster in a cup with a little water & stir it every time tis ud, which may be when a child is convuls'd the Salt of amber must be rub'd in a morter with a little sugar when tis mix'd | ~ **Fits** covered a wide range of illnesses caused by high fever or some other unidentified cause (*OED,* 4:262). **Caster** is **castor** oil. |
| **Little Plumb Cacks.**<br>Tk 2 lb: flour, 2 lb Sugar; 4 yolks of Eggs, & 2 whites, 1/2 lb Butter, wash'd in rose water, 6 spoonfuls cream, warm'd, 1/2 lb: Currants. rub'd in cloath. make it into small Cakes. | **Little Plum Cakes.**<br>Prepare them as directed for pound cake, add raisins and currants, bake them in small tin shapes, and ice them. (Randolph, *Virginia Housewife,* 164)<br>~ Mary's recipe is obviously different from Jane's version. Her recipe incorporates a recipe for a pound cake, making it quite different from Jane's breadlike concoction at left. Mary apparently preserved some old family recipes while adopting new ones. |
| **Tincture of Sacra**<br>Take 1 oz: of Hyrapicry put it into a quart of Mout Wine & let it stand two, or three days, put a little Sand into it -Shake the Bottle some times, & then rack it off. You may put on it, a quart of Rum, which will give ease in the Chollick. | ~ **Sacra** is unidentifed to date. **Hyrapicry** is a misspelling for Hiera Picra, a purgative drug composed of aloes and canella bark, and sometimes mixed with honey and other ingredients (*OED,* 5:272). **Mout wine** is an abbreviation for mountain wine, which is "a variety of Malaga wine made from grapes grown on the mountains" (*OED,* 6:711). |
| **Tartar Emetic Powders**<br>To an Ozce of Chalk finely powderd add Eight grains of Tartar Emetic NB it must be mixd with the greatest care in a Mortar by addg a little of the Chalk at a time, till the whole is well mixd & then put it up in a Viol & keep it for use. NB ten grns of this powder is a dose for a Child & the quantity may be increased accordg to the strength of the Patient up to 30 grns once in 3 or four hours | ~ **Tartar emetic** is potassium antimonyl tartrate. Although usually used as a mordant for dyeing, it is used as a poisonous substance in medicine to induce vomiting (*OED,* 11:100). **NB** is an abbreviation for the Latin phrase *Note Bene* (take careful note). |

*Contemporary Recipe #1*

*Contemporary Recipe #2*

**To make little Plumb-cakes.**

Take two pounds of Flour dried in the Oven, and half a pound of Sugar finely powder'd, four yolks of Eggs, two whites, half a pound of Butter washed with Rose-water, six spoonsfuls of Cream warmed, a pound and a half of Currants unwashed, but pick'd and rubbed very clean in a Cloth; mix all together, make them up into Cakes, and bake them up in an Oven almost as hot as for Manchet. Let them stand half an hour till they be colored on both sides; then take down the Oven-lid, and let them stand a little to soak. (E. Smith, *Compleat Housewife* [1729], 117)

**Tinctura Sacra; or, Hiera Picra.**

Take of hiera picra, as sold at the chymists or drugsters in powder, one ounce and a half, and put it into a quart of good Madeira-wine. Shake the powder well in the liquid for three or four days; then let it settle, and when clear at top, pour off for use, and fill it up again; continuing to do so to do, 'till its purgative effiicacy decays. The quantity is from three to five spoonfuls taken at night going to rest, or in the morning fasting, using exercise; and to a person in health there needs no confinement or alteration of diet. The exellency of this fine stomachick medicine is too well known to need anything to be said in its praise. (Atkyns, *Family Magazine,* 2:213)

*"Jane Randolph her Cookery Book, 1743"*

*Comments*

**The Solution of Tartar Emetic**

To 3 grains of Tartar Emetic add sixteen Tabl Spoonfulls of fair Water & 80 drops of Spirit of Hartshorn, The does is a Table Spoonfull once in 3 hours

Elizabeth Randolph
Elezabeth Pleasants
Sally Pleasa

Put eight grains of Corrosive Sublimate into a Pint of old Spirits & after it is dissolved let the Patient take night & Morng a Table spoonful of the Solution for a week & then give a strong Purge of Salts or Jalap & remember to give the purge once a week, it will be a very good way to drink half a pint of Sassafrass Tea after every dose of the Solution, NB The same precaution are to be made use of in regard to H[?]—— & Cold as in other preparations of Mine [?]

~ The three girlish signatures, written upside down at the bottom of one page, interrupted the recipe. **Spirits** are "strong alcoholic liquor for drinking" and flavored from "various substances by distillation" (*OED*, 10:619). **Corrosive sublimate** is poisonous mercuric chloride. In the form of "crystalline soluble salt" it is used as a germicide because of its corrosive action, and it was used by surgeons in 1706 to "cleanse ulcers" and other "corrupt" flesh (*OED*, 2:1022). **Jalap** serves as a "purgative drug" that is extracted from the "tuberous roots of *Exogonium (Ipomoea) Purga*" and some other plants; the key lies in its resin found in the tubers (*OED*, 5:547).

**The Wash**

To a pint of Spirits put sixteen grns of the Corrossive Sublimate & add as much Blue Stone as will make it of a greenish coulour to wash the parts affected

~ This formula has not been seen in any of the cookbooks or medical cures so far for this time period. It probably was derived from a chemistry book. **Blue stone** is either copper sulphate or vitriol (*OED*, 2:943).

**To Pot Beef**

[Missing]

~ Jane (Bolling) Randolph's recipe was mentioned in her index. Perhaps it was similar to the one below.

**The best way to pott Beef which is as good as Venison**

Take aps. of Lean Buttock of Beef Rub it over with Salt Petre it lye one Night Then take it out, Salt it very well with White and Bay Salt, put it into a pott Just fit for it, Cover it with Water and let it lye four Days, then Whipe it—well with a Cloath, Rub it with pepper finely beaten, put it close into a pott without any liquor Cover the pott Close with past, let it bake with large loaves Six hours at least then Take it out, and when tis Cold pick it clean from the Skins and Strings, beat it in a Stone Morter very fine, Then to your Tast Season it with Nutmegg Cloves and Mace finely beated to yor Tast and pour in~~~melted Butter which you may work with it like a past. put it close down and Even in your potts and Cover it with Clarifyed Butter . . . (The Compiler [1744], Manuscript cookbook, 94)

**Boil Carps**

[Missing]

~ This fish recipe is absent from Jane (Bolling) Randolph's culinary manuscript.

*Contemporary Recipe #1*

*Contemporary Recipe #2*

---

---

**To Pott Beef**

Take a Buttock of beef, bake it in a pan with nothing to it; when it is baked, take it off from the gravey. When it is cold pare off all the outside, and the fatt, and cutt it with a knife into small bitts, and pound it in a morter. Then take a goood handfull of Sage and a little Time shred small, and a little Mace and two Nuttmegs, and a little pepper and salt; mix it and beat it all with the meat, then put in a Laying of Meat, and a Laying of Butter, till your pott is full; squease it close downe, and Bake again it for an hour. When it is cold, power butter upon it and it will keep a good while. (Blencowe, *Receipt Book,* 5)

**The best way to Pot Beef, which is as good as Venison.**

Take a piece of lean Buttock-Beef, rub it over with Salt-petre; let it lie one Night, then take it out and salt it very well with White and Bay - salt, put it into a Pot just fit for it, cover it with Water, and let it lie four Days; then wipe it well with a Cloth, and rub it with Pepper finely beaten; put it down close into a Pot without any Liquor, cover the Pot close with Paste, and let it bake with large Loaves six Hours at least; then take it out, and, when 'tis cold, pick it clean from the Skins and Strings, and beat it in a Stone-Mortar very fine; then season it with Nutmeg, Cloves, and Mace finely beaten, to your Taste, and pour in melted butter, which you may work up with it like a Paste: Put it close down and even in your Pots, and cover it with clarify'd Butter. (Several Hands, *Collection* [1714], 22–23)

**To boil a Couple of Carps**

Scale them and gut them, save the Blood in Claret, and boil them in good relish'd Liquor half an Hour, make the Sauce with good strong Gravy - liquor, the Blood and Claret, a whole Onion, three or four Anchovies, shred Shalots, a quartered Nutmeg, a Blade of Mace, a little Whole Pepper, stew these together, then melt the Butter thick therein; be sure the Fish be well dreined before you put your Sauce therein; add Juice of Limon. (Howard, *England's Newest Way* [1710], 163)

**Carps boiled**

As for your Carps, you may boil in what manner you please in Wine-Vinegar, Verjuice in your Water, with a little Sage, Hysop, but when they are boil'd enough, you should eat them with a green Sause, or else with Parsley and Vinegar. (Hall, *Queen's Royal Cookery,* 80)

*"Jane Randolph her Cookery Book, 1743"* | *Comments*

**To make an Excellent ———**

Take 4 oz of Cardomum seeds ———? Seeds & 4 of Caraway Seeds 4 ——— & two quarts of sack ——— ? & Sparemint with these? things ——— Can & Still them altogether Leisurely

~ There are several recipes that start off with similar titles, but none published before 1744 closely resembles this fragmentary recipe.

**A Drink to Sweeten ye [Blood]**

Take a pound of Barley water ———? [s]ome Liqu[orish?] ——— in a ———l[?] t[h?]e ——— & four Ounces of Ven[ice] [Tu]rpentine by Drop least it Clumper, Stiring in then make it up into Roles for you— ———

Jane Ra[ndolph]

~ **Venice turpentine** is a mixture consisting of either yellow or black rosin and oil of turpentine (*OED*, 12:99).

**Preserve walnuts green**

[Missing]

———

**To make a Salve**

[Ta]ke rosin 8 ozes. Virginis wax & franiincens each 4 ounces of Mastick one ounce Harts [horn] 4 ounces Camphire 2 Drams beat [r]osin mastick & Frankincense together [in] a mortar to a fine powder, then melt Rosin & wax together & put in ye Powder when they are well melted. Strain it thro [a] Cloth into a [p]ottle of white wine & b—— ——— ——— what[?] ——— dra[?] ——— Sweeten ——— as

For yo[ur?] ——eath.

The Virtues of this Salve

First it is good for all Wounds or Sores Secondly it Cleanseth all ffesterings, Suffers no dead Flesh to Engender, the Headach, by rubbing the Temp[les] 5ly it cures a Salt ffegme fface, ——— sinnews that are grown Stiff, strains dry for Want of Blood, it draweth out ——— is stuck in the fflesh, as rusty Iron ——— & it cures the Bite of a mad Dogg pricking of any Venenous Creatures, all ffellows or White fflaws, Cankers good for all Aches of the Liver, sple[en] Arms, Leggs &c. it cures all P—— Blotches Impostumes, or Swo[llen?] part of the body, it helpeth the Genitories, it cures Gout, Palseys, Dropseys, and Wa—— the fflesh and Skinne the Himerhoides the bloody fflux, also if the belly be ano[inted] therewith it maketh Sear cloth to hea —— the afforesaid Malladies

~ This tattered recipe has sections missing, but it was for a salve. Arabella Atkyns published the first portion of the recipe and added the list of its virtues.

**Camphire** (archaic) refers to camphor until c. 1800 (*OED*, 2:55). This was a costly item (Hess, *Martha Washington's Booke*, 441). A **dram** equals sixty grains or 1/8th of an oz (*OED*, 3:639), while **rozin** is a solid substance "obtained as residue after the distillation of oil of turpentine from crude turpentine" (*OED*, 8:801). **Fflegme** is **phlegm** (*OED*, 7:783). The term **ffellows** was not found in *OED* in this sense, but perhaps it was a misspelling for "felons"? **White fflaw** stands for **whitlow** or **whitelow**, a "suppurative inflammatory sore or swelling in a finger or thumb, usually in the terminal joint" (*OED*, 12:84). **Genitories** originally referred to a testicle or testicles but now alludes to genitals (*OED*, 4:112). **Sear cloth** (cerecloth) is an old term for a special cloth used as a plaster in surgery and for other pain-related ailments (*OED*, 2:231).

*Contemporary Recipe #1*

*Contemporary Recipe #2*

———

———

———

———

———

———

———

**Sir Edward Tertile's Salve, called the Chief of all salves**

Take Rosin, eight ounces, Virgins Wax and Frankincense, of each four ounces, Mastick, one ounce, Harts suet four ounces, Camphire two drams, beat the Rosin, Mastick, and Frankincense in a Mortar together to fine powder; then melt the Rosin and Wax together, then put in the powders; and when they are well melted, strain it through a cloth into a pottle of white Wine, and boil it together, till it be somewhat thick; then let it cool, and put in the Camphire and four ounces of Venice Turpentine drop by drop, lest it clumper, sitrring it continually, then make it up into Rolls, and do with it to the pleasure of God, and heath of man. (W. M., *Queen's Closet,* 37–38)

*The Virtues*

It is good for all wounds and sores, new or old, in any part of the head or body; cleanses all festers in the flesh, and heals more in nine days, than other salves cure in a month: suffers no dead flesh to ingender; cures the head-ach, rubbing the temples therewith, a salt phlegm in the face, and sinews grown stiff or sprung with labour, or dry for want of blood; draws out whatever is fix'd in the flesh or wound; cures the bite of a mad dog, pricking of any venomous animals; is good for all fellons or white-flaws, festerings and cankers, aches of the liver, spleen, kidneys, back sides, arms or legs; cures biles, botches, swellings, and humours in any part of the body; helps the gout, and all pains of the joints in man or woman; cures wrenches, palsey, and waters between the flesh and skin, as also the piles. Fore any of the above purposes, make a cerecloth thereof, and spread it on thin white leather. (Atkyns, *Family Magazine,* 2:305)

*"Jane Randolph her Cookery Book, 1743"*

**The Black Salve**
[Missing]

*Comments*

~ Jane (Bolling) Randolph's manuscript no longer contains this recipe for a black salve. Fortunately the following recipe with a similar title has been located and might be the one Jane included in her cookbook.

**To make a very good Dish**
[Take?] [a?] leg of Lamb & put it into Jumblets ——— it with Oysters & Capers & water & ——— Vinegar & Clarret & Anchovies ——— very smal garnish the Dish ——— Sippets & Serve it.

~ This fragmentary recipe for some kind of lamb dish was penned in the gap between the two paragraphs for the salve, above.

**For Saint Anthonys Fire**
[Tak]e a Quart of Cream, and a good handfull [of] ——seleck, a good handfull of Chicken Weed, ——— [han]dfuls of ffumitory bruise them ——— then put them into the Cream, and ——— them a quarter of an hour over the ffire, ——— a Feather doe the grieved place ——— with y either Warm or Cold.

~ This damaged recipe was very old even for Jane (Bolling) Randolph's time. **St. Anthony's Fire** was known as the "sacred fire" that "proved" to be "extremely fatal in 1089," and its sufferers "sought intercession of St. Anthony" (*OED*, 4:360). **Chicken weed**, a "small weedy plant, is known as *Stellaria media*" (*OED*, 2:337). A **ffumitory** is a plant of the genus *Fumaria* or the related *Cordyalis*, which grew in great quantities (*OED*, 4:601).

**The Mouth Water**
——— Rosemary, Sage, Hysop, Plantin, [Straw?]berry leaves, Scabious Horsetail, ———, Violet leaves, Agrimony, Woodbine, ——— Maidenhair, Ground Joy, Alehoof, ——— [Ma]rshmallows, Colts foot, Dandelyon, ——nall, Bittony, Elm bark of ——— [han]dful, put them into four ——— of Spring Water, and let them boyl ——— it, till Three parts be consumed, then ——— to it four Ounces of Common Allum [Swee]ten it with Honey

~ **Hysop** (**hyssop**) is described as "a small bushy aromatic herb of the genus *Hyssopus*" and is usually found in species of *H. officinalis;* a native of Southern Europe, it was once used in medicine, such as "decoctions" (*OED*, 5:515). **Plantin** refers to **plantain** or **plantain eye bright**, a plant from the genus *Plantego*, "a low herb . . . spread out close to the ground," the extracted juice of which was used for "distemper," while the leaves were utilized for ulcers (*OED*, 8:952). **Horsetail** is a "common name of the genus *Equisetum*," which resembles a horse's tail; another variation is the female horse-tail, an old name for *Hippuris* or mare's-tail (*OED*, 5:403). **Ground joy** is not found in *OED*. **Alehoof** is defined as an "herb ground-ivy" once called hey-hove, horse hove, and hove (*OED*, 1:214).

*Contemporary Recipe #1*

**The black Salve for an Ach or Wound**

Take a quarter of a pound of unwrought Wax, two ounces of Pitch, two ounces of Rosin, two penny worth of Olisanon, half a pint of Sallet oil, half a pint of Turpentine, melt all these together on the Fire; then take one handfull of Tulson-leaves, one handfull of Plantane, one handful of Tops of Rosemary, bruise these Herbs together in a Mortar; then put them into a Pan to the aforesaid Stuff, and let them all boil together, stirring them till they be half boiled away, then strain it through a new course Cloth, so keep it all the Year in a Box, you must take it as often off from the Fire, as it riseth in the settling, or else it will run all in the Fire, and as it falleth set it on again till it seth half away.

This is very good for an Ach, if it be laid on Plaister wise, and for a Wound the same way, or with a Tent as you shall see occasion, lay it not to a bruise where the Flesh is not cut, for it will draw away all the bruised Flesh, but in such a case only anoint the bruised Flesh with Oil of Roses twice a day, and keep it warm, and it will heat without fail. This Salve will cure a burning burnt with Fire. (*Pastry-Cook's Vade Mecum,* 77–78)

*Contemporary Recipe #2*

**The plain black Salve.**

Take a pound of good sallad-oil, and half a pound of red-lead finely powder'd; put them into a skillet, and stir it well; let it boil till it be black, and let some of it cool, if it be hard enough for plaister, take it off the fire, and put it into a little beer: when 'tis cold, roll it up, and put it into oil'd papers.

The Vertues.

Tis good for bruises, swellings, burns or scalds, or to lay on the top of tents. May take four of white-lead, and four of red, two ounces of bees-wax, and two of resin, and think the best. (Atkyns, *Family Magazine,* 2:305)

*"Jane Randolph her Cookery Book, 1743"*

**To make Syrup of Hysop for Colds**

Take one handful of Hysop of figgs, Raison[ns] of the sun stoned and Dates, of Each one Ou[nce] of Callamints half a handful of Pea[rl?] bar[ley?] one ounce, boyle all these in three pints of fair Water, till it comes to a Quart, strain it and Clarify it, with two whites of Eggs, and put to it two pounds of ffine sugar and boyle it up to A Syrup.

*Comments*

~ **Callamint** is "a genus of aromatic herbs" (*Calmintha*) that was reputed for its medical curative powers (*OED,* 2:23–24). **Pearl barley** may be what Jane (Bolling) Randolph meant.

**An Excellent Remedy for a Cough as Ever**

Take two pennyworth of the best Honey, and one pennyworth of the seeds of red Nettles, pound the red Nettle Seeds very small and mix it with the Honey, give to the party as much as a Nuttmeg at any time when troubled, but Especially at Morning and Night

~ **Red nettles** (*Urtica rubra*) is a variety of the stinging nettle (*OED,* 1:104; 8:307). It was said to be effective for lung disorders (Hess, *Martha Washington's Booke,* 271).

**An Excellent Physick Drink to be taken Spring and Fall**

Take 4 Gallons of Strong Alewort, and boyle it without Hopps till it comes to three Gallons, and Work it with good Yest, and turn it up as you do your Drink, then take 6 Ounces of Pollypodium of the Oak, 6 Ounces of bay berrys, huske them and bruise them 2 Ounces of Aniseeds bruised 3 Ozs. of the Cernills of Ash Keys bruised, 3 Ozs. of Sassafras 3 Ozs. of Salldonelli, 3 Drams of Rhubarb (or 4 if Choler does much abound, 6 Ounces of the Leaves of Senna, Slice the Rhubarb thin and bruise the Pollypodium, put all these Ingredients into a Canvas bagg with a Stone to make it Sinke, tye the bagg so that it may not touch the bottom when the Drink hath Wrought a little in the Tubb then put in ye bag of ingredients & Stop ye tub close, & when it is 3 or 4 days old you may begin to drink of it you may drink almost a pint of it in the morning fasting & take a little possett Drink or water grewel after it warme At night when you go to bed you may Drink half a pint, you take of it Spring & fall, for many days together or Leave, & take it again, if it purge more then you desire it should you may Loose Less Rubarb & Sana, if not so much then put in Some more but the Quantity Sett Down is Sufficient for it should not purge above 3 or 4 tim[es?] a Day to continue it. it is Safe Drink

Its a most Eccelent Drink for any Ailment in the head or body ye wind Gout or Dropsy Palsey Megrum, head Ach, for ye Liver & Lungs, Stomack & back it bringeth away wind & water & strengthens all ye inwards parts helps ye Scurvy & ma[y] Safely be taken by old or young it restoreth ye Complexion, & hath done great Cures

~ **Alewort** alludes to a fermenting infusion of salt (*OED,* 1:213). **Pollypodium** is a fern commonly found growing on old walls and trees, hence formerly known as **polypody of the oak** or the wall (*OED,* 7:1095). An **ash key** is "a peculiar winged seed . . . called the 'ash-key.' This two-cell seed is also named **samara** of the ash tree" (*OED,* 1:485). **Salldonelli** is unidentified. **Megrum** concerns "a form of a severe headache usually confined to one side of the head," and it could also be a "nervous or sick headache," probably a variation of migraine (*OED,* 6:310).

*Contemporary Recipe #1*

**To make Syrupe of Hysope.**
Take of Hysope one handfull, of Figs, Raysins, Dates, of each an ounce, of Calamint half a handful, of French barley one ounce boyle these in three pints of water to a quart, and then straine it, and then clarifie it with the whites of 2 egs, and two pound of sugar, and so boyle them to a Syrupe, and being boiled enough, keep them all the yeare. (Platt, *Closet,* 64–65)

*Contemporary Recipe #2*

**To Make Syrup of Hysop for Colds.**
Take a handfull of Hysop, of Figs, Raisins, Dates, of each an ounce, of Collipint half an handful, French Barley one ounce, boil therein three pints of fair water to a quart, strain it and clarifie it with two whites of Eggs, then put in two pound of fine Sugar, and boil it to a syrup. (W. M., *Queen's Delight,* 206)

*"Jane Randolph her Cookery Book, 1743"*

**To make Alamode Beef**

Take a Bullocks heart cut of ye Strings Skinns & Deaf ears & fat then Stick it with a Scewer in many Places, then take an Ounce of Salt petre, with a little Salt & rub it well in, then Cast on two handful of Salt then lett it Stand 4 Days, then Bake it in a Slow oven, then take it out of the Liquor, then put it up with ye Same weight of Butter & Sewett as the meat is, with a Nuttmeg & Little Cloves & mace & half an ounce of Pepper; then put it into a pot & put it into ye Oven for half an hour

*Comments*

**Beef A-La-Mode**

Take the bone from a round of beef, fill the space with a forcemeat made of the crumbs of a stale loaf, four ounces of marrow, two heads of garlic chopped with thyme and parsley, some nutmeg, cloves, pepper, and salt, mix it to a paste with the yelks of four eggs beaten, stuff the lean part of the round with it, and make balls of the remainder; sew a fillet of strong linen wide enough to keep it round and compact, put it in a vessel just sufficiently large to hold it, add a pint of red wine, cover it with sheets of tin or iron, set it in a brick oven properly heated, and bake it three hours; when done, skim the fat from the gravy thicken it with brown flour, add some mushroom and walnut catsup, and serve it up garnished with forcemeat balls fried. It is still better when eaten cold with sallad. (Randolph, *Virginia Housewife,* 38–39)

~ A **bullock** is a "young bull, bull calf" or "a castrated bull and ox," not to be confused with a fruit of a plant called Bullock's Heart (*OED,* 1:1171). **String** of an animal alludes to "a ligament, tendon, nerve, etc." or even "an elongated muscle or muscular fibre" (*OED,* 10:1138). **Deaf ears** concerns the auricle of the heart (*OED,* 3:64).

**To make Frost meat**

Take Veal Lean beef or pork is best take a pound of pork & Shred it very Smal then take as much Sewett as mea[t] & Shred it but not so smal, then take a Little Sprig of time & Sweet Marjoram one nuttmeg half an ounce of pepper with some Cloves & mace well beat & a handfull of salt, then Roul it up into Small Balls

**Forcemeat Balls.**

Take half a pound of veal, and half a pound of suet cut fine and beat in a marble mortar or wooden bowl; add a few sweet herbs shred fine, a little mace pounded fine, a small nutmeg grated, a little lemon peel, some pepper and salt, and the yelks of two eggs; mix them well together, and make them into balls and long pieces, then roll them in flour, and fry them brown. If they are for the use of white sauce, do not fry them, but put them in a sauce pan of hot water, and let them boil a few minutes. (Randolph, *Virginia Housewife,* 109)

~ While Mary added eggs and lemon peel, one can see that she kept the basic elements of Jane's recipe.

**To make a jelly of currants**

Take the best Currants & pick them from the Stalk then put them into a pitcher of Cold water & sett them over the fire & lett them boyle 2 hours then take them off & Strain them through a Cloth then put a pound of Sugar to the Liquor & boile it till it's a Jelly then put it into Glasses & cover þm with wett paper.

**Current Jelly**

Pick full ripe currants from the stem, and put them in a stone pot, then set it in an iron pot of water-take care that no water gets in: when the currants have yielded their juice, pour them into a jelly bag- let it run as long as it will without pressing, which must be reserved for the best jelly; you may then squeeze the bag to make inferior kind. To each pint of this juice, put one pound of loaf sugar powdered-boil it fifteen or twenty minutes-skim it clean and put it in glasses; expose them daily to the sun to prevent fermentation. (Randolph, *Virginia Housewife,* 240–41)

~ This reflects Mary's modern methods and scientific bent.

*Contemporary Recipe #1*

*Contemporary Recipe #2*

**To Stew Beef Allamode**

Take a Fleshey peice of Beef take out the fatt & shins & Cores then beat it very well & flatt it with your rowling pin or Cleaver then lard it with fatt bacon quite through as long as your~meat as deep and as big as your Finger then Season it pritty high with salt pepper Cloves~Mace & Nutmeg beat fine then put it into apott with good beef brothe where nothing but—beef has bin boyl'd in and put in a handfull of Sweet herbes and a bay leaf or two so let it boyl tell it is Tender then put in a point of Clarrit with 2 Anchovies and let them stew tell you find the meat Tender enough & that there is a great deale of liquor more then will make an end of Stewing of it then take as much of it as your think fitten before you put in the Wine and other things then put all the last Addition & let it stew tell you se the liquor begins to thicken & taste well of the Spice then take it up & take out the bay leaves sherlott and—herbes and you may Eat it Either hott or Cold. (Compiler [1744], Manuscript cookbook, 62)

———

**To make a good Forc'd Meat for any Use.**

Take a pound of Veal, and full its weight in Beef-suet, a bit of Bacon; shred all together, beat it in a Mortar very fine; then season it with Sweet-herbs, Pepper, Salt, Cloves, Mace, and Nutmegs: And when you roll it up to fry, add the Yolks of two or three Eggs, to bind it. You may add Oysters, or Marrow, on extraordinary Occasions. (Several Hands, *Collection* [1714], 44–45)

———

**Jelly of Currants**

Take your Currants and strip them from the Stalks into a Gally-pot, which Pot you must put into a Kettle of Water over the Fire 'till they be enough; strain them through a Flannel Jelly-bag, but don't squeeze it; add to the Liquor its weight in double-refin'd Sugar, boil both up for a quarter of an Hour very gently, then put it into Glasses. (Several Hands, *Collection* [1714], 80)

**To make Jelly of Currants**

Strip your Currants, put them in a Jug, and infuse in Water, strain out the Juice upon sugar, sweeten to your Taste, boil it a great while till it jellies, scumming all the while, and then put it in your Glasses. (E. Smith, *Compleat Housewife* [1729], 198)

*"Jane Randolph her Cookery Book, 1743"*

*Comments*

**To Preserve Damsons &c.**

Take a pint of Damsons to a pound of sugar take a pint of water & boyle ye sugar in it till it Draws Ropey then put in ye damsons & boyle them over a Slow fire till they Crack then lett them stand till ye next Day then take out the Damsons & boyle ye sirup till it draws Ropey then put ye Damsons out again & boil them as before then lett the Damsons stand till ye next Day as before, then Sett them on a gentle fire, lett them boyle half an hour then take your Damsons out of ye Sirrip & put them into ye pott, then boil your Sirrup till it be very ropey then put in your damsons, all sorts of Plumbs are Done thus.

———

**Receipt for ye gravel**

Take of Best Rhubarb - - - 3 Drams
Juniper berries - - - 5
Cassia Fretella [?] with ye cane - - - 4
Anniseeds - - - 1
Sliced Liquorish - - - 6
ffennel seeds - - - 1
Lapis judaicus - - - 4
Mithridate - - - 3
Agaric - - - 1
Galiga - - - 1
Ginger - - - 1
Mace - - - 1

Lett all these be beaten together & take 2 English Pints of the best Rhenish wine & one pint of the best Brandy & put altogether in a Strong glass vessell And sett in ye Sun well stopt to Stand for a month or 6 weeks in ye greatest heat of the Year the more heat it has the better it is

Of this your are to take 2 or 3 spoonfuls if you apprehend the coming of the fitt and for the Space of one month 2 Spoonfuls once a week in ye morning, & there after no more but once a week one Spoonfull unless you find new Cause

The Virtues of this water

This water is of Excellent use either for ye Stone or Gravel as also against wind in the Stomach or Gutts & Doth its Operation without any kind of Trouble

~ It is likely that Jane (Bolling) Randolph obtained her recipe from some scientific or medical book. **Cassia fretella** may be **cassia fistula,** a "genus of trees, shrubs or herbs" that grow in "warmer regions of the earth"; some are known in medicine as *Senna Leaves;* the name **cassia fistula** was already given during "the Middle Ages" to one particular species, "the Pudding Pipe tree, a native of India, but cultivated in Northern Africa, the West Indies, etc., which produces the *cassia pods*" whose pulp functions as a "laxative" (*OED,* 2:151). **Lapis judaicus,** or "Jew's Stone," a "fossil spine of a large sea-urchin," is found in Syria and was used in medicine as a diuretic as well as a "lithontriptic" in matters concerning fluxes (*OED,* 6:67). **Mithridate** is an electuary composed of "many ingredients" and was considered a "universal antidote or preservative against poison & infectious disease"; King Mithridates VI, king of Pontus, used antidotes against poisons and died of old age (*OED,* 6:546). **Agaric** is a fungus, *Polyporus officinalis,* that grows on larch and is used as a "cathartic"; another form, *Polyporus fomentarius & igniarius,* is used as a styptic (*OED,* 1:175). **Galiga** is likely to be **galingale,** an "aromatic root of certain E. Indian plants of the genera *Alpinia & Kaempferia.* These were once in great use in medicine (for dyspepsia, etc.) and cookery. The English version, *Cyperus longus,* sometimes called the English galingale, has similar properties to the true galingale" (*OED,* 4:19). **Gravel** is an "aggregation of urinary crystals" that causes pain for the bearer (*OED,* 4:376).

*Contemporary Recipe #1*

**An exceeding fine Pill used for the Gowte.**
Take of Aloes 2 ounces, mastick three drammes, Agricke half an ounce, Ginger halfe a dramme, let these be poudered very fine, then take of the extraction of Rubarbe three drams, & with white wine let them bee incorporated into a masse of pills, adding unto them a drop of oyle of cloues, & as much of Nuttmegs. (Platt, *Closet,* 60)

*Contemporary Recipe #2*

**An exceeding fine Pill used for the Gowt.**
Of Aloes take two ounces, Mastick three drams, Agrick half an ounce, Ginger half a dram: let these be powdred very fine: then take of the extraction of Rubarb three drams, and with white-Wine let them be incorporated into a masse of pills, adding unto them a drop of oyle of Cloves, and as much of Nutmegs. (R. H., *Closet,* 27)

*"Jane Randolph her Cookery Book, 1743"*

*Comments*

**Lucatellus Balsom**

Take half pound of yellow Wax & Slice it thin & put it into a Skillett over a Gentle fire then put in 3 pints of Sallet Oyle well beaten with a pint of Sack & one pound of Venice Turpentine well washt in a pint of Rosewater till this[?] boyle well with continual Stirring and then put in two ounes of red Saun[ders] beaten to fine powder lett it boyle till ye water & wine be Consumed continualy Stirring it with a wooden Stick & if at any time it rise up & offer to run over take it from ye fire till it falls Down again & when you See no more Scum arises it is enough Strain it into a Gallypot & keep it for your Use

The virtues of Lucatellus Balsom

It will help any Lameness being anointed warm & a Cloth Dipt in it being melted & laid on as hot as can be endured it helpeth any outward bruise being anointed warm, or inward being Drank as much as a wallnut melted in a Draught of warm Sack for 3 Mornings Fasting it will cure ye biting a Mad Dog or any other Venomous Creatures or least Drink it inye Like quantity & anointing the place it will heal any Cutt & Stanch the bleeding of a wound by plaister of Lint being resonable hard bound upon it, & Cloth Dipt & laid upon ye sore place it helps a Surffeit drank in warm Sack as aforesaid it cure ye headach by anointing the temples with it, it cures any burn or Scald by anointing & applying ye Sear Cloth

~ **Basme** and **baume** were used by the public until c. 1600, when **balsom** came into use (*OED*, 1:643). **Red Saunders** is "red sandalwood or ruby-wood" of an East Indian tree, *Pterocarpus santalinus*, which was once used in medicine "as an astringent and tonic" (*OED*, 8:312).

**The Caustick powder**

Take yellow Arsenick an Ounce Bole Armoniack half an ounce make þm t to fine powder & mix them well together

~ Just above this recipe was penned a notation by Jane (Bolling) Randolph: "For a broken Cancer this Receipt Cost the old Lady Arundell 300 £ in germany."

**Yellow arsenic** is "a bright yellow mineral," both in its native and manufactured states; is known as arsenic trisulphide; and is usually found as "a pigment under the name of King's Yellow" (*OED*, 12:466).

**The Glistering Caustick Powder**

Take an ounce of yellow Arsenick red Precipatate & bole Armoniack of each half an ounce & mix them well together when made into fine Powder

~ **Red precipitate** is red oxide of mercury (*OED*, 8:1249).

**The Tarte Water**

Take white Sublimate an ounce red Precipatate half an ounce, grind them together very Small, put into it 3 pints of white wine Vinegar boyl it near to a quart in a pipkin & when tis cold keep it in a Glass for use

~ The meaning of **white sublimate** is uncertain. Perhaps it refers to mercuric chloride, a violently "poisonous" white crystalline powder otherwise known as corrosive sublimate. It may also be arsenious oxide (white arsenic)—although the word *arsenic* is not correctly used here—which was very poisonous and used in medicine (*OED*, 12:29).

*Contemporary Recipe #1*

**Another Sort of Lucatellus's Balsam**

Take half a pound of bees-wax, and melt it in a kettle, then put to it three pints of oil of olives, and one of sack: let it boil together, and keep it stirring a whole quarter of an hour; then take it off, and put into it a pint of Venice-turpentine, well wash'd in red rose-water; boil it again so much longer; afterwards put into it two ounces of red saunders; then boil it all together, till the skum be all boil'd in; then strain, and put it in a pot for your use: this is good for bruises, scalds, &c. (Atkyns, *Family Magazine,* 2:273)

*Contemporary Recipe #2*

———

———

———

———

———

———

**3. Caustick**

Take Arsenick, Cristaline, *sal Armoniak,* Sublimate, of each alike; boil them, being finely ground, in as much strong vinegar as the matter weigheth, until 2 third parts be consumed, and that there remain a third; then keep it in a glass close shut for thy use, as I will shew thee in divers places when occasion shal serve. (M.B., *Ladies Cabinet,* 157)

———

*"Jane Randolph her Cookery Book, 1743"*

**The Red Water**

Take a Lime Stone or two about two pound weight boyle two gallons & half of spring water rising out of a Rock against the Sun put ye Lime stones in a Earthen Pott then pour the boyling water on them Cover all close & so lett it Stand 24 hours then pour of ye Clearest & cast away the Bottom then take bolus Verus Rock Allum, white Coperas Ciralrina & Camphire of Each two ounces, beat & Searse them very fine & mix them well together with ye said Clear water & boyle them together an hour then put it into a Pott Close Stop't till it be cold then tun it into a Glass bottle close made up & use the Cleanest

**The Green Oynment**

Take fresh hogs Grease half a pound; of Venice turpentine, three Ounces Rosin half a pound, Verdegreaze half an ozce beat the rosin & verdigreaze together then putt them all into a Skillett & boyle them to a Salve then strain it into a Gallypot for use

**The use of all these things**

Take some of the Caustick Powder & mix with ye green Oyntment, & apply it to the Just bigness of the Cancer or Noli me Tangere keep it on 8 or 10 Days till it Cast of its self then lay one another till all ye dead flesh be Spent—

The white tart water is to be applye'd to ye Cancer with cloth dipt in it if need be it's good for Cancer on ye nose ringworm or any Dead flesh

The red water is to wash ye Eyes if blood Shot Pin or web also to preserve ye Sight & for any other Sore to be used warme & with a Syrringe if need be

The Green Oyntment is to be applyed to ye Cancer after ye Causticks have done working to heale & Draw out it's good to Draw any Sore

**To make a Purge**

Take one Dram of rubarb & infuse it in half a qtr. of pint of white wine over night & next morning Strain it out & Dissolve it into 1/2 an oz. of manna an one ozce of Sirrup of Roses Strain it out again & Drink it out

**For the Cholick & Stone**

Take a pint of white wine & make thereoff a possett then take off the Curd & seith it again to Clarifye it then take of Mallow seeds an ozce Alkalangey berrys an ounce Philopendula roots, an ounce Gallingall roots Do beat & Seeth these altogether in a posset Drink then Strain it & Lett the Patient Drink it as warme as he can & Lay him Down to Sweat & within two hours the Stone will break & void & he shall be whole

*Comments*

~ **Bolus**, a "medicine of round shape adapted for swallowing," is "larger than an ordinary pill" (*OED*, 1:977). **Rock alom (roche alum)**, a "whitish transparent mineral salt crystallizing in octahedrons," is "very astringent and used in dyeing as a mordaunt, tanning skins, medicine, sizing paper and making materials fireproof" (*OED*, 12:738). **White coperas,** or zinc sulphate, can also be colored blue or green and was used in medicine as an emetic (*OED*, 2:974). **Ciralrina** and **verus** have not been located in *OED*.

~ A **Gallypot (gallipot)** is a "small earthen glazed pot, esp. one used by apothecaries for ointments and medicines" (*OED*, 4:27).

~ **Noli Me Tangere,** translated as "Touch Me Not," is a species of balsam that grows in northern England. So named from "the peculiarly forcible expulsion of its ripe seeds, which occurs when it is touched," it was valued for medicinal purposes, since it was believed effective in treating "fleame & cold humours" (*OED*, 7:181). **Pin**, or **web,** is an obsolete "name for disease of the eye" characterized by "a spot or excresence like pin's head" and "a film covering the general surface" (*OED*, 7:871).

~ **Manna** is "a sweet pale yellow or whitish concrete juice obtained from incisions in the bark of the Manna-ash, *Fraxinus ornus*," found mostly "in Calabria, Sicily"; as medicine it functioned as a gentle laxative (*OED*, 6:28).

~ The title for this recipe was missing on the manuscript page, but a title found in Jane (Bolling) Randolph's index matched the page and contents. **Cholick (colic)** is recognized by "severe paroxymal griping pains in the belly" (*OED*, 2:375). **Stone** refers to "a hard morbid concretion by the body," esp. in the kidney, bladder, or gall bladder (*OED*, 10:1009). **Mallow** is a common "wild plant with hairy stems and leaves and deeply-cleft reddish-purple flowers"

*Contemporary Recipe #1*

*Contemporary Recipe #2*

———

———

———

———

———

———

**A Purge**

TAKE half a pint of milk-water; and a quarter of a pint of Canary; two drachms of rhubarb; a stick of liquorice scraped and sliced; one ounce of Coriander-seeds; a quarter of an ounce of caraway-seeds; half a score raisins of the sun stoned: put all together in a bottle. A child of a month old may take a spoonful. (Atkyns, *Family Magazine*, 2:278)

**Another:**

Dissolve half an ounce of *manna* in a little posset-drink; then strain it, and give a child of a quarter old this quantity, three mornings successively, or every other day. (Atkyns, *Family Magazine*, 2:278)

———

———

*"Jane Randolph her Cookery Book, 1743"*

*Comments*

and is known as "Common, Field, and Wild Mallow"; it is also known for its "mucilaginous qualities" (*OED,* 6:89–90). **Alkalangey berries** likely is a misspelling of **alkakingly** or **alkakengi berries,** which are also known as winter cherries and, with their "ornamental scarlet fruit," fall into the category of red nightshade (*OED,* 1:225).

**Pomatum**

Take 1 lb of hoggs Sewett in the thickest part of the Leave, take off the Skin & beat it well with ye Rowling pin, then lay it in water covered over with Sliced pippins Change the water twice a day & ye pippins once a day doe this 9 days together, then take your Sewett & put it into a Earthen pott prick it with Cloves, Slice in the Peal of an orange, & a Lemon tye it Down close & boyle it in a Skillett of water till ye Sewett be Dissolved then Strain it out into a half pint of sweet water beating it up untill it be Cold, when it is Stiff put it up for your use

**Soft Pomatum.**

Get nice sweet lard that has no salt in it, put in any agreeable perfume, beat it to a cream, and put it in small pots. (Randolph, *Virginia Housewife,* 222)

~ Like Anonymous (1700), Jane and her family members wished to keep their houses smelling fresh. According to *OED,* **pomatum** was a scented ointment originally made with apples and used for the skin (*OED,* 7:1100).

**A Cordiall water for the Stone**

Take Bay berries, Calamas, Aromaticus Galingal Gentian Roots Zedoary Ellicampany, Ginger of each one Dram, Cloves cinnamon Angelica root of each half a dram

Lett it be bruised, grosely mixt them together & Sow them in a fine Linnen bag, put them into a glass bottle, with a wide mouth, then pour a quart of Right Nants brandy on the top, & close it & Sett it by the fire side fourty Eight hours to be kept warme, & not to boyle then pour it into a bottle for your use

The Dose is a Spoonfull fasting for the gravell, if for a Cordial a Sipp att any time

~ **Calamas** may be a variation for **calamus,** popularly known as sweet calamus or sweet-scented lemongrass from Malabar; another version of native calamus was called the sweet flag or sweet rush by English herbalists (*OED,* 2:24).

**To Pickle Spratts**

Take your Sprats & cutt their heads off, & then wipe them very Dry & then Lay a lare of them into a Earthen pot, & Strew a lare of salt upon them & some blades of mace & whole pepper, & Some Cloves then Slice a Lemon very thin & Lay some Slices of Lemon between every Lare & then another Lare of sprats & then Salt & Spice & slicd Lemon as before & so doe till you pott be full almost, with white wine Vinegar & then tye it up close & in 3 weeks time they will be fitt fr use, but when you use them, be sure to tye them up close or they will decay your vinegar must be cold & raw not boyled as for other pickles, & your Lemons must be Sliced pills & all thus you may pickle white Herrings only you must take out the Gills & Gutts

~ **Spratts** are "small sea fish *Clupa Sprattus,*" commonly found "on the Atlantic coasts of Europe" (*OED,* 10:678).

*Contemporary Recipe #1*

*Contemporary Recipe #2*

**A good Pomatum for beautifying**

Take the fat of a bacon-hog unsalted, stick it full of oats, roast it by a slow fire, that it may drip away, put to the dripping some oil of sweet almonds, and two or three drops of the chymical oil of cinamon; mix them well together, and put them up for use. (Atkyns, *Family Magazine,* 1:94)

**Sprats to Pickle like Anchovies**

Take a peck of the largest Sprats, without Heads, and Salt them a little over Night; then take a Pot or Barrel, and lay in it a lay of Bay-Salt, and then a lay of Sprats and a few Bay-leaves with a little Lemon-Peel, then Salt again, thus do till you have filled the Vessel, then cover and pitch it, that no Air get in, set it in a cool Sellar, and once in a Week turn it upside down; in three Months you may eat them. (Salmon, *Family Dictionary,* 321)

**To pickle Sprats like Anchovies**

Pull the Heads off of your Sprats, and salt them a little over Night; the next Day, take a Barrel, or earthen Pot, lay in it a Layer of refined Salt, a Layer of Sprats, a little Lemon-peel, and some Bay-Leaves; then lay another Layer of Salt, and another Layer of Sprats, &c. so do 'till you have filled the Vessel; then cover it close, and close it up with Pitch, tht no Air can get in, set it in a Cellar, and turn it upside down once a Week, they will be eatable in three Months. (*Lady's Companion,* 2:189–90)

*"Jane Randolph her Cookery Book, 1743"*

*Comments*

**To pickle Mushrooms**

Take Bufftons & wash them clean from the Dirt then Sett some water on the fire & when it boyls put them in with a little Salt, & Lett them boyle a little then take them off Drain them clean from the water then take a pint of white wine & pint of vinegar & two or 3 blades of mace, with a little whole Pepper & salt then boyle the vinegar Spice & an ounce of Sugar a little then cover it & Lett it Stand till it be cold then put in your mushrooms & quarter pint of Oyle Stop them Close Down &c. for your Use

~ **Bufftons** are buttons, or the heads of mushrooms in their "unexpanded state" (*OED,* 1:1221).

**To make a Pidgeon pye in puff paste**

Take the pidgeons & quarter them & Lay them in a deep Dish with good paste under them lay them in Rowes and as easy as may be round the Dish, Season them with Pepper, & Salt Cloves & mace & quantity of Capers according to the number of pidgeons, take a good many of the tops of winter Savoury, ye yolks of Two or three hard Eggs, & a good quantity of butter, put in the Pickle of Capers a Spoonfull in the Pye or Else a Spoonfull or two of wine then cover it with very fine paste in round things about the brim of the Dish & let it stand in an Oven a little above an hour

———

**To make a Sack Possett**

Take a pound of Almonds & beat them very Small with rose water to keep them from Oyling then take a pint of sack & put in your Sugar & sett it Over a Chaffing Dish of coals till it be ready to boyle then put in your Almonds, Stirring it very well & so serve it up

———

**To make Puff Paste**

Take Almost a quart of very fine flower & 4 or 6 Eggs yolks or whites with a little Cold water as much as will make it a Stiff Paste then role it abroad & Lay little peices of butter upon it very thick & sprinkle Little flower & fold your paste role it out again in the like Sort doe so 8 or 9 times, always putting butter between ye Folds

**To Make Puff Paste.**

Sift a quart of flouer, leave out a little for rolling the paste, make up the remainder with cold water into a stiff paste, knead it well, and roll it out several times; wash the salt from a pound of butter, divide it into four parts, put one of thelm on the paste in little bits, fold it up, and continue to roll it till the butter is well mixed; then put another portion of butter, roll it in the same manner; do this till all the butter is mingled with the paste, touch it very lightly with the hands in the making, bake it in a moderate oven, that will permit it to rise, but will not make it brown. Good paste must look white and as light as a feather. (Randolph, *Virginia Housewife,* 141–42)

~ Mary's recipe is almost virtually unchanged from Jane's rendition. She simply added her own touch.

*Contemporary Recipe #1*

**To pickle Mushrooms White.**
Gather your Mushrooms when little Buttons in the morning; wash them, and rub them in clean Water and as you rub them put them in more clean Water; then boil them in fair Water, with a little Salt for half an Hour; and then strain them through a Colander clean from the Water, and let them stand till they are cold; and for your Pickle, take Vinegar, Salt, whole white Pepper, some Blades of Mace, and about two Nutmegs sliced, and boil 'em for half an Hour, and when it is cold, then put your Mushrooms into the Pickle, and keep them close[.] (Howard, *England's Newest Way* [1710], 131)

**Pigeon=Pye:**
To order and season this, Take an ounce of finely beaten Pepper to a dozen of Pigeons; put Butter rouled up in Balls, with a little fine shred Parsley, into the Belly of your Pigeons, and two pound of Butter is sufficient for the whole Pye, where in are only a dozen of Pigeons, sprinkling them like likewise, with a little Salt, before you close up the Coffin. (Salmon, *Family Dictionary,* 253)

**A Sack Posset without Cream or Eggs.**
Take half a pound of *Jordan* Almonds lay them night in Water, blanch and beat them in a Stone Mortar very fine, with a pint of Orange-flower-Water, or fair Water, a quarter and half of Sugar, a two-penny-Loaf of Bread grated; So let it boil till 'tiss thick, continually stirring it, then warm half pint of Sack, and put to it, stir it well together, and put a little Nutmeg and Cinnamon in it. (E. Smith, *Compleat Housewife* [1729], 152)

**To make a puffe Paste.**
Break two Eggs in three pints of flower, make it with cold water, then roul it out pretty pretty thick and square, then take so much Butter as paste, and lay it in rank, and divide your butter in five pieces, that you may lay it on at five severall times, roul your paste very broad, and take one part of the same Butter in little pieces al over your paste, then throw a handful of flower slightly on, then fold up your paste and beat it with a rouling pin, so roul it out again, thus doe five times and make it up. (Kent, *Gentlewoman's Delight,* 118–19)

*Contemporary Recipe #2*

**To Pickle Mushromes.**
Gather the smallest Buttons, cut off the bottom of the Stalk, and throw them into Water and Salt; then rub them with a coarse Cloth or Flannel very clean, and throw them into another Pan of clean Water: Boil them in Milk and Water: Take them out upon a clean Cloth: When they are dry, put them into Glasses, with White-Pepper-corns, and a good quantity of Mace: Pour good Oil on the top of the Pickle; it keeps them best; and put them in as small Glasses as you can, because they soon decay when they have taken Air. (Several Hands, *Collection* [1714], 48–49)

**To make a Pigeon=pye.**
TAKE a dozen of Pigeons, and two Pound of Butter; put Butter roll'd up in Balls, with Parsley shred fine, into the Bellies of your Pigeons; season them with an Ounce of Pepper finely beaten; season the Insides before you put in the Buttter, lay them in your Crust, sprinkle Salt over them, lay them over with Butter, close up your Pye, and bake it. (Nott, *Cook's and Confectioner's Dictionary,* #128)

———

**Puff - Paste another:**
Take a quart of the finest Flour, the White of three Eggs, the Yolks of two, a little cold Water, make it into a perfect Paste, then roul it abroad thin, they lay on little bits of Butter, and fold it over again, then make it broad again, and lay on more Butter, and then fold it over, and do so ten times, make it up for your use, and put your Fruit, or meat therein, and bake it. (Salmon, *Family Dictionary,* 270)

*"Jane Randolph her Cookery Book, 1743"*

**To Pickle Pork**

Boyle half a peck of bay Salt in 3 Gallons of pump water for an hour, half a pound of salt petre with a Dram of Cochineal & lett it Stand till it be cold & then putt in your Pork

*Comments*

~ It is interesting to find that Jane (Bolling) Randolph used cochineal to make her pickled pork more attractive in color.

**Mrs. Packer's Oyntment**

Take a Dozen bunches of Soap wort & 3 Do of plentin 2 ozces of bees wax thin sliced Shred the herbs very Smal then take 3 pound of fresh butter washed from ye butter milk & clarify it & then put it into a Skillett with the herbs & wax & when it turns green then Skim the top off from all the Dross into a Clean well glazed pot, & then strain it off the Dross for present use & keep the other by its self its good for any old or new Sore or wound.

~ **Soapwort** is one of the herbs of the genus *Saponaria,* especially the common species *S. officinalis,* and there is also soapwort gentian (*OED,* 9:352).

**Mrs. Tutts oyntment**

Good for any Senew Stain Bruize or pain or old Aches Take a peck or more of groundsell, pickt from the Stalks & flowers & bruise & Cutt them Smal & then putt in 3 poundes of of may butter as it comes out from the Churn only well washed & squeezed from the butter milk & Clarifyed, & put in ye herbs with the butter into a Skillett over a gentle fire & boyle it, & when when it becomes green Skim of the Top in to a Clean gallypott to keep & then Strain ye other for present use.

~ **May butter,** which served as a medicinal unguent, was prepared by melting fresh unsalted butter in the sun; after repeated action, the butter would end up a whitish color (*OED,* 6:1297).

**The Balsom which cures all new wounds or Cutts very Speedly**

Take Sallet oyle 1[?] lb pitch 3 ozs. wax & rosin of each 2 ozces natural balsom 1 ozce then boyle them to a Balsom for use

~ **Sallet oyle (salad oil)** pertains to an olive oil of "superior quality" used in "dressing salads" (*OED,* 9:47).

---

**To make Surfeit water**

Take a peck & half red corn popies Sift them from the Seeds then take a handfull of Cloves Gilly flowers strewe ye whites half a handfull of Cowslips flowers, Steep all these in 3 quarts of brandy lett them Stand a week or more then straine it out hard then put in a half pound of Raysons of the Sun Stoned 2 ozces of figgs

*Contemporary Recipe #1*

**To Pickle Pork**

When your Pork is cut into joints, Salt it with ordinary Salt, and let it lie one night before you put it into pickle, that the Blood may run from it, and then make a strong pickle of Pump-water, Bay-salt, and Salt-peter, and some ordinary Salt, and boil it, and let it stand till is cold, and when it is cold put in your Meat be sure the pickle be always above your Meat. (*Pastry-Cook's Vade Mecum,* 45)

*Contemporary Recipe #2*

**To Pickle Pork, a good way.**

Bone it, and cut it in such pieces as will lie most convenient in your Powdering-tub, which must be large and sound to hold the Meat and preserve the Brine; the narrower and deeper your Tub is, the better 'twill keep the Meat; rub every piece well with Salt-petre, then take one part Bay-salt and two parts common Salt, and rub every piece very well and cover it with Salt as you do a flitch of Bacon; then strew Salt in the bottom of your Tub, and lay the Pieces in as close as possible, strewing Salt round the sides of the Tub: As your Salt melts on the top, strew on more. It will keep a great while, and is very good. (Several Hands, *Collection* [1714], 14)

---

**An excellent Oyntment for any Bruise or Ache.**

Take two pound of *May Butter* purified, powre it out from the dregs, and put to it of *Broome* flowers and *Elder* flowers, of each a good handfull, so clean picked that you use nothing but the leaves, mix them all together in a stone pot, and boyle them seaven or eight howres in a kettell of water, being covered with a board, and kept downe with weights, keeping the kettell alwayes full of water, with the help of another kettell of boyling water ready to fill up the firest as it wasteth, and when it waxeth somewhat coole, but not cold, straine the Oyntment from the Hearbs, into a gally pot, and keep it for your use. (Jenner, *Book of Fruits,* 31)

---

**Surfeit Water**

Get a peck of red Corn Poppies, put them in a large Dish, cover them with another, and set in an Oven several Times after Household Bread is drawn; put them into a Quart of *Aqua Vitae,* with a large Nutmeg, and a Race of Ginger sliced, a small Stick of Cinnamon, a Blade of Mace, three or four Figs, four Ounces

*"Jane Randolph her Cookery Book, 1743"* | *Comments*

Sliced & ounce & quarter of Liquorish sliced half a quarter of an ozce of Cloves, D° of nuttmeg, D° of mace, a Stick & a half of Cinnamon & a race of ginger, Sliced, half a quarter of an ounce of anniseeds, D° Carryway seeds Ditto Swett fennel seeds Ditto of Cardimum Seeds & Juniper berryes together & D° & Cordiander Seeds bruise all these Seeds & Spice & put them to Steep in your brandy lett it Stand a month or 6 weeks then Straine it off for your use

**For any Strain or bruise whatsoever**

Take ye best of Rosin one pound of mutton Sewett three quarters of a pound, byle them together to the Consistency of a Salve till it comes clean from ye bottom of the Skillet, the Virtues of this Salve are Innumerable

——

**For the Stone Chollick**

Take half a pint of white wine or Renish & Squeezed Lemon in it & put an ounce of Sirrup of Marsh Mallows & half an ounce of Oyle of Sweet Almonds Stir them all together & Drink when ye fitt comes on

——

**To Coller a Pigg**

Take a Pig & chine it Down the middle & Bone it then take pepper & Salt nuttmeg & Cloves & mace well beaten together & season it with well to your Pallett then roll it up very tite with Course Tape then boyle it well in Spring water till it is tender, then make your Pickle, take Spring water & Salt & Vinegar & Some bay Leaves & boil them well together & Lett it stand till it's Cold then put in your Pigg & Lett it Stand 7 or 8 days or till it is fitt for use

~ **Chine,** an archaic verb, refers to splitting open the backbone of the animal. In cookery it was a joint "consisting of the whole or part of the backbone of the animal with the adjoining flesh"; with mutton it is the saddle, while beef can pertain to any part of the back, depending on the animal (*OED,* 2:352).

*Contemporary Recipe #1*

of Raisins of the Sun ston'd, Anniseeds, Cardamum, and Fennel Seeds of each half a Dram beaten; of Liquorice sliced half an Ounce; lay some Poppies in the Bottom of a broad glass Body, then lay a Layer of the other Ingredients, and then another Layer of Poppies, and so continue 'till the glass is full; then pour in the *Aqua Vitae,* and cover it close, and let let it infuse 'till the Liquor is very red with the Poppies, and strong of the Spice: Of this you may take two or three Spoonfuls at a Time, and when it grows low you may pour another Quart of *Aqua Vitae* to the Ingredients. You may make double the Quantity, by doubling the Ingredients, and so any Quantity in Proportion. (*Lady's Companion,* 2:323)

*Contemporary Recipe #2*

**To Collar a Pigg.**

Take a good fat Pigg of a Month or five Weeks old, and kill him and dress him fit roast, then cut off the Head, and slit him down the Back and bone him; then take a handfull of Sage, and chop it small, and two Nutmegs, and a little Mace, and a few Cloves, and beat them very fine, and a good handful of Salt; mix all these together, and season the Pigg all over with it, and roul it up hard, and tie it about with Tape, and sow it up in a clean Linen Cloath, and boil it in Water with a little Oatmeal in it, well seasoned with Salt, till it is very tender; when it is boiled, take it and hang it up in the Cloaths that it was boiled in till it is quite cold, then take some Water and put to it some Oat-meal, as if it was to make a thin Water-grwel, season it well with Salt, and put in a pint of White-wine, and half a spoonful of whole Pepper: Boil it altogether half an hour, then set it by till it is cold, and then take off the Cloaths, and put in the Pigg, and let it be eight Days in the Sousing; then use it as you please, it must be eaten with Mustard and Sage, or with Vinegar. (Hall, *Queen's Royal Cookery,* 9–10)

**163. To collar Pig.**

Take a fat Pig, cut off his Head, and chine him down the Back, and take out all the Bones, and Gristles; take care you don't cut the Skin; then lay it in Spring-water one Night, the next Morning dry it in a Cloth, and cut each side asunder; season it with Salt, whole Pepper, Nutmeg, and a little beaten Mace, a little Sage, Rosemary, and Limon-peel; rowl them up hard in a Cloth, and the sousen Drink is Bran, Milk and Water; strain out the Bran, and skim off all the Fat, and let your Collars be cold before you put them in. (Howard, *England's Newest Way* [1710], 86)

*"Jane Randolph her Cookery Book, 1743"* — *Comments*

**To keep Quinces all the Year**

Take the fairest and the largest Quinces you can get and wipe them clean, and scald them in Water lett they be a Little tender then take the Pairings of small ones, and the Coursest and boyle them very Well then take your Quinces and lay them in a pot and put your Liquor and all the pairings and lay over them so close that no Air can come and tye a Leather over them so When you Use them keep the Rest still Close Stopt and they will keep all ye Year

———

**An Excellent Oyntment for the Ague or any Ach Pain or Swelling**

Take Cammomell Smallage Feathers few Violet Leaves Mallows Elder Leaves Rice of each a good Handfull cut them very small and boyle them in a pound and a half of pork Sewet till it look Green and the Herbs somethng dry then Straine it and keep it for Use

~ **Cammomell, cammomel,** or **camomile,** an "aromatic creeping plant known as *Anthenlis nobilis,*" is located on "dry sandy commons in England" and somewhat resembles a "double daisy"; this plant was used in medicine for its "bitter and tonic properties" (*OED,* 2:51). **Smallage** is a variety of "wild celery or water parsley" (now rare) (*OED,* 9:259). **Feathers few** was her spelling for **featherfew,** a corrupted form of **feverfew.** This plant (*Pyrethrum Parthenium*) was valued for its ability to drive away fevers (*OED,* 4:122, 180).

**An Approved Syrup for a Consumption to be taken Morning and Evening two Spoonfulls a time**

Take 2 pounds of Raisins of the Sun Stoned, one pound of Figgs cut in halfs 5 Ounces of Anniseeds Brewed half a pound of English Liquorish Scraped and Sliced, a Quarter of a pound of maidenhair liverwort hearts tongue Egrimony Bettony Coltsfoot and horehound of Each 2 Handfulls boyle all these together in 5 Gallons of Spring Water untill there ———? be but 2 Left then put the same in an Earthen Pot, and let it stand close covered untill the next day then Strain it and add thereto wormwood Water and Cardias Water of Each 1/2 a pint horehund Water and Hysop water of Each a pint a Quart of Honey a pound of brown Sugar Candy half a pint of C[?]oles[?] a pottle of Red rose Water 6 pound of Powder Sugar and so boyle them Up to Syrup for Use

~ **Raisins of the sun** alludes to sun-dried grapes (*OED,* 8:121). **Liverwort,** a lichenlike plant, is also named stone liverwort and was formerly held in esteem for its effectiveness in the treatment of liver and lung-related disorders (*OED,* 6:362). **Hearts tongue** is a common name for a particular fern, *Scobpendrium vulgare* (*OED,* 5:107). **Coltsfoot,** with its "large spreading cordate leaves . . . and yellow flowers, is a common weed growing on waste land or clayey soils. It was touted as a cure for asthma and other lung ailments (*OED,* 2:641). The herb **horehound,** usually named common or white horehound, has stems and leaves covered with a "white cottony pubescens," and its "aromatic bitter juice is much used as a remedy for coughs, etc." (*OED,* 5:383).

*Contemporary Recipe #1*

**To preserve quinces to bake all the year.**
Take the best and sweetest worte, and put to it good store of Sugar; then pare and chore the *Quinces* cleane, and puyt them therein, and boyle them till they grow tender: then take out the *Quinces* and let them coole, & let the pickle in which they were boild, stand to coole also; then straine it through a raunge or siue, then put the *Quinces* into a sweete earthen pot, then powre the pickle or sirrup vnto them, so as all the *Quinces* may be quite couered all ouer; then stop vp the pot close, and and set it in a dry place, and once in sixe or seuen weeks looke vnto it; and if you see it shrinke, or doe begin to hoare or mould, then powre out the pickle or sirrup, and renewing it, boyle it ouer againe, and as before put it to the Quinces being cold and thus you may preserue them for the vse of baking, or otherwise all the yeere. (Markham, *English House-Wife,* 115–16)

---

**An excellent Medicine for the Cough of the Lungs**
Take *Fennell* and *Angelica* of each one handfull, the leaves in Summer, roots in Winter, sliced figgs twelve, but if the body by bound, twenty at least; green Licorice if you can, two or three good sticks scraped and sliced, Anniseed cleaved and bruised, two good spoonfulls, two or three Parsley roots scraped, and the pith taken out, and twenty leaves of Foale-foot, boyle all these in three pints of *Hysop* water, to a pint and halfe, then straine it out into a glasse, putting to it as much white *Sugar*-candy as will make it sweet, drink hereof, being warmed, five spoonfulls at a time, first in the morning, and last in the evening, take heed that you eat nor drink anything two howres before nor after. (Jenner, *Book of Fruits,* 19)

*Contemporary Recipe #2*

**To keep Quinces raw all the year.**
Take some of the worst Quinces and cut them into small pieces, and Coares and Parings, boyle them in water, and put to a Gallon of water, some three spoonfulls of Salt, as much Honey; boyle these together till they are very strong, and when it is cold, put it into half a pint of Vinegar in a wooden Vessel or Earthen Pot; and take then as many of yor best Quinces as will go into your Liquor, then stop them up very close that no Aire get into them, and they will keep all the yeare. (W. M., *Compleat Cook,* 27)

---

---

*"Jane Randolph her Cookery Book, 1743"*

**For an Extream Cough though of the Lungs**
Take a ripe Ashen break them & take out the Kernells put them in a Dish & Dry them in a temporable hot Oven or before the fire so beat them to powder then mix the powder with Some English honey & Stir them well together till it be Like a Conserve take of it morning & Evening as your Stomach will Serve this Cured Divers that were Lanquishing a year and more
Probatum

**To make Egg Pies**
Take a pound of eggs boyld very hard & a pound & half of Sewett & 8 Apples Shred all these very Smal then Season them with a Little Salt, nuttmeg & Cinnamon half pound of Sugar a pound & a quarter of a Little Sack & Leamon Peal

**For make Dr Butlers Oyl**
Take 2 pound of Sheeps kidneys Seuet hot out of ye Sheep half a pound of the tops of bays Rosemary, red Sage feathefew wormwood & mugwort cut these very Smal then lett the herbs & the Sewett be beat very Smal in a Stone Mortar put it into a well glazed Pipkin close coverd & sett it into a horse Dunghill for 9 Days then put a quart of Olive oyl to it & boyle it till ye herbs be Dry then put to it 4 ounces of the French Oyle of Spike [it?] then to Boyl 4 hours before the Oyle of Spike goes in & 4 hours after, keep it Stirring for fear of burning, when its Enough Strain it out it will keep 20 Years in its full Strength & Virtue being Close Covered & Cool kept

Some Adds rue to it

The Virtues

It is good for Achs, Scabs, fellons Anguish or Swellings of wounds, Tooth Ach, Bruises Over Strained Sinews or Veins Cramps Stitches Sciatica burnings Scaldings Strains or Swellings in man or beast, it is good for Swellings in the face or throat Rub the Smal of the back with this & it Easeth the pain of the Stone, half a pease bigness Chased into ye Eares & Stopped with wool all pains thereoff Probatum Est

*Comments*

———

———

~ No recipe called "Dr. Butler's Oyle" could be found in the available cookbooks examined by the author. **French Oyle of Spike** is French lavender (*Lavandula Spica*), and **spike,** once spelled **spick,** is now obsolete (*OED,* 10:596). **Oyle of Spike** refers to plain lavender (*OED,* 10:591). The oil of lavender was valued in medicine for its "cephaic, nervous & uterine" purposes and perfumery (*OED,* 6:111). **Probatum Est** is Latin for "It has been proved," a phrase commonly found in recipes or prescriptions (*OED,* 8:1403). **Dr. Butler** is believed to be Dr. William Butler (1535–1614), a physician to the English king (*Dictionary of National Biography,* 6:542).

*Contemporary Recipe #1*

**110. For a Consumption.**

Taste Ash Keyes, so soone as they looke withered, set them into an oven (the bread being drawn) in a pewter or rather an earthen dish, and being so dried, pill off the outside, and reserving the inner part of the seed or Keies, beat them to fine powder; and either mixe it with good English Honey, and So eat of it first and last, morning and evening, a pretty deal of it at once, upon the point of a knife; or else drinke of the powder in some posset Ale or thin broth. Mares milk drunk also halfe warm morning and evening, is a soveraign medicine for it, (M.B., *Ladies Cabinet,* 94).

**Another Way**

Mince them small with a Pound of Beef-suet, add a Pound of Currans, season with Salt, beaten Cinnamon, Nutmeg and Sugar, mix all well together, put them into your Crust and bake it, and when it is done, put in some Sack and Juice of Orange. (Nott, *Cook's and Confectioner's Dictionary,* #57)

**how to make the greene oyntment**

Take of red sage & rewe of ech a pound, or a quart & of yong bay Leaves & wormwood of ech 1/2 £: picke tham well butt wash tham not, : shread tham smalle: & beat tham well in a morter: then take 3 £: of sheeps suitt hot frō the sheeps bely sread it smale & beat itt with these hearbes vntill itt be all of a culler: then put tham all in a fare Boule wth a pottle of the best oyle oLiue & worke itt all together untill itt bee ā lyke softe: & then putt itt into an earthon pott, stop itt close for eight days space: then take itt & Boyle itt in a faire pane wth a soft fyer & when itt is halfe boyled putt to itt 4 ounces of oyle of spike then boyle tham all well together untill it come to a perfect greene, & then strane it throwh a faire Linen cLoth into a galley pott or some other pott, covering it cLose, but take head that you boyle it softly vntill it come to the culour, & thus its made,

The vertue of this oyntment./

If you anoynt the stomacke wth it, it helpeth ye degestion & exspelleth all obstrucktions; rubb it on the small of the backe, & it helpeth the stone: the quantitye of half a peas well rubed in behynd the eare, being stoped with blacke woole helpeth all paines therein./ it is allsoe good against all aches & Fellons & swellings of wounds, & alsoe against toothache proseeding of cold rume, it helpeth anye bruse or strane in vaine or sinewe tis good for the cramp & sciatica & all maner of burnings & scaldings stitches stifnes? or stranes in man or Beast

it is made only in maye. (Fairfax Family, *Arcana Fairfaxiana Manuscripta,* 65–66)

*Contemporary Recipe #2*

—

—

—

*"Jane Randolph her Cookery Book, 1743"*

**Dr. Colliers reciept for the Ricketts**

R the inward bark of Tamaris 2 drams Salt of Tarter & Ens Veneris of each a Dram infused into a Quart of Ale & Lett the Child Drink it for Common Drink

**Another of the Same purpose**

R hogs Lard, Leeks Ginger, Salt Souther[n] wood of each an equal quantity & made into an Oyntment, & anoint therewith the Joints & Stomack 9 Days

**Mr Chowns receipt for fitts in children**

R Peoney roots & make beads for a Necklace for the Child to wear, then take a Hazell nutt & pick out the Kernel & fill the Shell with Argentum Virum & Stop the Hole with wax, & then take powder of Antemony, Egrimony & of a Lead stone of each a Scruple & put them into a Silk bag & wear them about the neck, 4 days After Purge

**A Receipt to hinder Pissing against one's will**

A Powder of Egrimony a Dram of H H [A?] powder a Dram mixt the powders & Lett the party have 15 grains in a spoon full of Sirrup of Cloves 3 times a day

**A Receipt to Pickle herrings**

Take & Cutt of the heads tails & Finns & take out the rowes & dry them two hours then take half Quarter of an once of Cloves & mace half a nuttmeg a Dram of white Pepper & some Salt, a Quarter of an once of beaten Ginger Two Great Onions a pint of Clarrett mix the Spices all To gether & Strow upon every Lare & mix your Onions very Smal & so you must doe by your Cloves maces & nuttmeg & Lett them Stand in ye oven over night in a Earthen Pan such as your bake Collered beef in

**To Preserve cherryes without the Stone In Gelly;**

To a pound of cherryes take a pd of Sugar Clarifye your Sugar to a Sirrup & boyle it till it rope very much & be Stiff, then put in the Cherryes & by Degrees Lett the Sugar boyle over them then have Standing by you a quarter a pint of the Juice of Currants, & when the Sugar boyls over ye Cherryes att 4 Several times put in the Juice of Currants, Take ye Scum off & Lett them

*Comments*

~ **Tamaris**, a graceful evergreen shrub or small tree of the genus *Tamarisk*, grows mostly on the seashore in the south of England (*OED*, 11:65). **Salt of Tarter** is an old name for potassium carbonate or potash derived from wood ashes (*OED*, 9:100). **Ens Veneris** (obsolete) is the essence of equal amounts of "Cyprus Vitriol" and "Sal Armoniac" (*OED*, 3:199).

~ **Southernwood**, derived from a hardy and aromatic shrub or plant known as *Artemesia Abrotanum* and "originally native to the south of Europe," was valued for its medicinal purposes but by 1718 was almost "out of use in medicine" (*OED*, 9:484).

~ **Argentum Virum** is mercury or quicksilver (*OED*, 1:441). **Lead stone** is unidentified. **Scruple** is a "unit of weight," being either 20 grains, 1/3 drachm, or 1/24 of an ounce; measurements such as this were used by apothecaries (*OED*, 9:291).

~ A **grain** is the smallest English and U.S. unit, being 1/5760 of a pound Troy weight (*OED*, 4:339).

~ **Lare** is an old spelling for "layer" (*OED*, 6:30).

———

*Contemporary Recipe #1*

**An ointment for a Child that has the Ricketts.**
Take an Ounce of Beef Marrow; as much Oil of Lillies, and Tamarisk; Bee's-wax, two ounces; Gum Amoniacum dissolv'd in Vinegar, half an ounce; Juice of Briony-roots, Smallage, and Golden-Rod, of each one ounce; let it all boil, 'till the Juice of the Herbs be consum'd: With this anoint the Belly of the Child, rubbing it in with your warm Hand by the fire, half an Hour every Night. 'Tis good, if the Belly is swell'd with Rickets, Worms, or Ague. (Several Hands, *Collection* [1714], 162)

———

———

———

**To pickle Herrings Red Trout Fashion to dissolve the Bones**
Cleanse them well, and cut off the Heads; then take an earthen Pan and lay a Row of Herrings at the Bottom; sprinkle them all over with Bay Salt and Salt Peter mix'd; then lay another Row till your Pan is full, then cover them and bake them gently; and when cold they will be as red as Anchovies, and the Bones dissolved. (Carter, *Compleat City,* 110–11)

**To Preserve Cherries**
TAKE the fairest Cherries, full ripe; for every Pound of Cherries take a Pound of Loaf-Sugar, lay some of it in the bottom of the Pan; then stone the Cherries upon it, and as you stone them, strew on them now and then a little Sugar: When you set them on the Fire, to every Pound of Cherries put in half a quarter of a Pint of the Juice of red Currants, and most of the Sugar, only

*Contemporary Recipe #2*

———

———

———

———

**To pickle Herrings or Mackerel**
Cut off the Heads and Tails of your Fish, gut them, wash them, and dry them well; then take two Ounces and a half of Salt Petre, three Quarters of an Ounce of *Jamaica* Pepper, and a Quarter and half Quarter of white Pepper, and pound them small; an Ounce of sweet Marjoram and Thyme chopp'd small; mix all together, and put some within and without the Fish; lay them in an Earthen Pan, the Roes at Top, and cover them with White - Wine Vinegar, then set them into an Oven not too hot, for two Hours. This is for fifteen; and, after this Rule, do as many as you please. (*Lady's Companion,* 2:189)

**To Preserve Cherries without Stones.**
Stone your cherries, and to a pound of cherries take a pound of sugar, clarify it to a syrup and boil it till it ropes very stiff, then put in the cherries, and by degrees let the sugar boil over them, then having standing by you a quarter of a pint of juice of currants, and when the sugar boils over the cherries at four several times put it in, (be careful to take off the scum from all

*"Jane Randolph her Cookery Book, 1743"* — *Comments*

boyle till the Sirrup is become a Jelly & when done, put them in flat Potts or Glasses wett ye paper that covers them

You need not wett the paper for any Sweet meats, but what is Done in Gelly, it only keeps the paper from Sticking to ye Gelly

**M: P$^{S}$. Extraordinary Cakes**

A pound of Sweet Almonds blanched Do of the best flower beaten with a Little Orange water 8 eggs 4 whites a Quarter of a pound of Loaf Sugar beaten well together the rine of a Lemon grated.

~ **M: P$^{S}$**. is believed to refer to Mrs. Mary (Randolph) Price.

**Water for the Wine**

Take of red Sage 1/2 a pound Cardus one pound Angelica one pound Wormwood 3 Quarters of a pound Mint 1/2 a pound Baine and Rew and of Time, of Each one Large handfull. Cut them Small & put them into a Earthen pot Lett them stand 24 hours before you put them into your Still

———

**Harts horn, or Calves feet Gelly: the Best way**

Take half a pound of goods harts horn 3 quarts of Fair water, Lett it boyle very Slow till one quart be consum'd if you cannot gett harts horn one Sett of Calfs feet will make more in quantity & taste almost as well the Cooking with Care will be ye Same, Strain the liquor & Let it Stand to Cool; The Stronger you make your Jelly the more ingredients you may use, to make it Paletable; when tis Settled as it will be the Day: take of what is clear of the harts horn, & of the calfs feet jelly you must take off the fatt from the top as well as Leave ye Dross att bottom to this 2 quarts of Strong jelly you may put a Pint of Rhenish & quarter of a pint of Canary, beat up the whites of 5 eggs to a froth stir altogether with Sugar, to make it very Sweet; mix it well & sett it over the fire & Stir it till it melts & Curdles then put in the juice of 5 Large Lemons & a bitt of the peal Lett this boyle up then pour it through your jelly bag & pass the first quart or two over & over till it is perfectly fine

**To Make Jelly From Feet.**

Boil four calf's feet, that have been nicely cleaned and the hoofs taken off; when the feet are boiled to pieces, strain the liquor through a colander, and when cold, take all the grease off and put the jelly in a skillet, leaving the dregs which will be at the bottom. There should be from four feet, about two quarts of jelly; pour into it one quart of white wine, the juice of six fresh lemons, strained from the seeds, one pound and a half of powdered loaf sugar, a little pounded cinnamon and mace, and the rind thinly pared from two of the lemons; wash eight eggs very clean, whip up the whites to a froth, crush the shells and put with them, mix it with the jelly, set it on the fire, stir it occasionally till the jelly is melted, but do not touch it afterwards. When it has boiled till it looks quite clear on one side, and the dross accumulates on the other, take off carefully the thickest part of the dross, and pour the jelly in the bag; put back what runs through, until it comes quite transparent; then set a pitcher under the bag, and put a cover all over to keep out the dust-the jelly looks much prettier when it is broken to fill the glasses. The bag should be made of cotton or linen, and be suspended in a frame made for the purpose. The feet of hogs makes the palest coloured

*Contemporary Recipe #1*

leaving out some to strew in as they boil, which they must do a good Pace; shake them round often in boiling, but do not stir them; scum them well, and when the Syrup grows thick, and they look deep, pour them out into a Bason, and shake them a good while, to gather the scum together, which you must take off very clean; and when they are cold, put them into Pots. (Nott, *Cook's and Confectioner's Dictionary,* #98)

———

———

**Hart's-horn, or Calf's-foot Jelly, the best way**

Take to half a pound of good Hart's -horn, three quarts of fair Water, let it boil very slowly, 'till above one quart be consum'd; if you cannot get Hart's-horn, one set of Calf's- feet, will make more in quantity, and taste almost as well; the look, with care, will be the same; strain this Liquor, and let it stand to cool; the stronger you make your Jelly, the more Ingredients you may use; to make it Palatable, when it is settl'd, as it will be, the next Day, take off what is clear of the Hart's-horn, and of the Calf's-foot-Jelly; you must take off the Fat from the top, as well as leave the Dross at the bottom; to this two quarts of strong Jelly, you may put a pint of Rhenish, and a quarter of a pint of Canary; beat up the Whites of five Eggs to a froth; stir all together with Sugar, to make it very sweet; mix it well & set it on the Fire, and stir it 'till it Melts and Curdles; then put in the Juice of five large Lemons, and a bit of the Peel; let this boil up, then pour it through your Jelly-bag, and pass the first quart or two, over and over again, 'till 'tis perfectly Fine (Several Hands, *Collection* [1714], 64–65)

*Contemporary Recipe #2*

things that you do) let the cherries boil till your syrup is become a jelly, which you may know by trying some in a spoon; you must take them off the fire and shake them sometimes that they may not stick to the bottom of the pan, and when they are done put them in flat pots or glasses, and cover them with the jelly, and when they are cold paper them with wetted papers and tie them over with other papers and and set them by: they will Keep a year, but do not set them in the stove. You do morello cherries the same way; only if you would have them keep, add two ounces of sugar more[.] (*Young Lady's Companion,* 27–29)

———

———

———

*"Jane Randolph her Cookery Book, 1743"* | *Comments*

jelly, those of sheep are a beautiful amber colour when prepared. (Randolph, *Virginia Housewife,* 143–44)

~ Again, Mary's careful instructions reflect her attention to all the details of preparation. Yet one can see the outlines of Jane's recipe therein.

**Mrs. Barretts approv'd Oyntment**

For the Irreptilis or St. Anthony fire or a blast or any Swelling in ye Breast or in any other part or to Anoynt a woman after hard Labour or for the Piles outward or inwardly given in a Glister useing it Instead of Oil for the Same or any other sort of Burn or Scald; Take parsley Sage Plantin Houseleek elder Leaves of each 2 handfull of mallows & marsh mallows a handfull Adders tongues 2 handfulls, Fig Leaves Do Fox Gloves one handfull, Cammomel & Butter bur of each a handfull, Lett these all be pickt & beat up with 3 pd of hogs Lard in a Stone mortar & then put it in a well Glazed pipkin & Sett it in horse Dung For Ten Days after which make into an Oyntment

~ **Irreptilis,** or **erysipelas,** "a local febrile disease accompanied by diffused inflammation of the skin, producing a deep red color," was often called St. Anthony's Fire or "the rose" (*OED,* 3:281). **Blast** is a dialectical term for erysipelas (*OED,* 1:905). **Glister** is both an archaic and dialectic word for a "bright light, brilliance, lustre" and "a glistering" (*OED,* 4:221). **Houseleek,** known as common houseleek (*Sempervivum* or *Aeonium arboreum*), is a "shrubby plant with yellow flowers." It was also familiar as *Sempervivum tectorum,* "a succulent herb with pink flowers" (*OED,* 5:423). **Butter bur** (*Petasites vularis*), a plant with "large soft leaves" that grows in wet land, is so named because its leaves were used to wrap butter (*OED,* 1:1219).

**A Receipt to make ginger bread**

Three pound & half of Flower
1 lb of Sugar
4 ozces of Ginger
4 ozces of Carraway Seeds
2 oz of orange Peal

These all mixt together in ye flower a pound & half of butter melted with a Little water & then put in pound & half of Treakle into ye butter & mix it altogether

—

**A receipt to See a Cake Madam Orlis way**

Take a pound & a half of Double refined Sugar beat & sift it well then take ye whites of three new Laid Eggs & beat them to a froth & put it to ye Sugar with a Little orange flower water & beat it an Earthen pot the Ice will hold the better if you put in as much Gum Dragon as ye quantity of a nuttmeg in ye beating of it ye Gum must be put in Steep In oringe flower water a day before you use it & Lett the Cake Stand a half hour after it comes out of the Oven before you Ice it for if you use it to hot ye Ice will run & not Dry only at Top & will be apt To break when you cut the cake therefore Lett the cake Stand till it be almost Cold before you Ice it you may Sett it before a Gentle fire to dry if to hot it will turn the Ice yellow

~ **Gum dragon** is **tragacanth,** a "gum obtained from *Astragulas* by natural exudation or incision in form of whitish strings or flakes" (*OED,* 4:636). Only "partially soluble in water," it is used in medicine (chiefly as vehicle for drugs) and in the industrial arts" (*OED,* 11:230).

*Contemporary Recipe #1*

*Contemporary Recipe #2*

**Thick Ginger-bread**

A pound and half of Flower, takes up one pound of Treacle, almost as much Sugar, an ounce of beat Ginger, two ounces of Carraway-seeds, four ounces of Citron, and Lemon- peel Candy'd, the Yolks of four Eggs; cut your Sweet-meats, mix all; and bake it in large Cakes, on Tin-plates. (Several Hands, *Collection* [1714], 86–87)

*"Jane Randolph her Cookery Book, 1743"* *Comments*

**To make a Cake Madam Orlis's way**

Take 6 pound of flower Ditto of Currants Take some Cloves mace nuttmeg & 20 eggs break 8 of the yolks & break the yelks & whites of ye 12 remaining beat them together then take 3 qrs of a pound of Sugar & pound & half of butter & a quart of new ale East & quart of Cream mix the eggs & the yeast together then melt the butter & the Cream over the fire together mix half a pound

———

**An Extraordinary receipt for the Stone**

Take of Parsley break & bruise it & Strain it & take a Spoonfull of the Juice in a glass of white wine at any time you find the fitt coming on in winter you may Dry it by the fire & rub it to a powder take as much as will Lay on a half Crown this is been known to have great good in this Distemper

———

**A Receipt for the Stone**

Take 3 Large Onions Sliced thin putt them into a Porringer cover them close put in a Little Salt & half a pint of water it must Stand 24 hours Drink the one half in morning the Other at night

———

**To Pickle Onions**

Gather the Smallest Onions when ripe peal them & putt them in water & Salt a night & a Day Shifting them in fresh water & Salt 3 or 4 times in that time, then take as much white wine Vinegar as will cover them an boil it & pour it boyling on them & stop them Down Close when cold put in a Good handful of bay Salt and a qrt of pint of brown mustard or an ounce of Mustard seed bruised & Cloves mace & pepper att Discretion with a Race or two of ginger

———

**A Receipt to make hams**

Take to 3 Hams 3 Ounces of Salt Petre and a good handfull of Salt mix'd with your Salt Petre, beat it fine and rubb your Ham all over and let them lye 24 Hours then make a Pickle with 1/2 a peck of bay Salt and 2 pound of Sixpenny Sugar, make your Pickle of Spring Water, and let it be Strong Enough to bear an Egg, then put you Hams in and let them Lye a ffortnight or Three Weeks [turning?] them every day, you must have Pickle Enough to cover them, then hang them up in A Chimney a Good Height, and let them hang about a Fortnight Whett they keep of Wood flyes, you may do Tongues in the Same Pickle if you cant get bay salt, the great White Salt will do.

———

*Contemporary Recipe #1*

*Contemporary Recipe #2*

**For the wind Colick.**

Bruise Parsly seeds, and seeth them in Sack, and drink it warm when you have your pain. (R. H., *Closet,* 35)

**To make Hams of Pork like Westphalia.**

To two large Hams, or three small ones, take three pounds of common Salt, and two pounds and a half of brown coarse Sugar; mix both together, rub it well into the Hams, let them lie seven days, turning them every day, and rub the Salt in them, when you turn them; then take four ounces of Salt-petre beat small, and mix with two handfuls of common Salt, and rub that well in your Hams, and let them lie a fortnight longer: Then hang them up high in a Chimney to smoke. (E. Smith, *Compleat Housewife* [1729], 45–46)

*"Jane Randolph her Cookery Book, 1743"*

*Comments*

**A Receipt for a Burn Burn**

4 ozces hogs Lard —2[?] ounces of bees wax 3 pennysworth of Sweet Oyle 1 ounce of Lapis Calimanaris melt them Altogether Except the Lapis over a Slow fire then put in the powder & Lett it just Simmer up then Strain it through a fine ragg

———

**To Pickle french Beans**

Take your beans & wipe them in with Cloves & mace & whole pepper & Long pepper & Jamaico pepper & ginger put your Spice between your beans then put boyling Vinegar upon them three times every 5th day put a Little Salt in your Vinegar

———

**[Missing Title]**

Take Juice of Lemons Sallett oil white wine & Syrrup of Marshmallows of each 4 Spoonfulls mixt Altogether & take 3 Spoonfulls every night going to bed

~ This is some medical remedy.

**To make Juniper Water**

Take a Gallon of ye best brandy & a pound of Juniper berries well Pickt & bruized in a Mortor putt them in your brandy and Lett them Steep To All night in a great Glass or Pott close Cover'd & ye next morning putt them into your Still, Still ye First Quart off with a Gentle fire & ye next Pretty Quick You will have 2 Quarts & a pint or Something more Still no Longer Then it Comes Something strong from the brandy will Leave a water behind it; when you have Stilled what you Can then mixt it Altogether, first & Last & to every Gallon of Spirits Putt a Pound of the best blue Reasons pickt & Stoned & Cutt in Peices & Lett them Stand four or five days till it be Sweet Enough & whilst it stands 4 or 5 Days you may putt a pint of Spring water into every Gallon but you must not Putt it Altogether

~ **Juniper berries** yielded "a volatile oil (Oil of Juniper) used in medicine as a stimulant and diuretic"; thus it is "a cordial drink made from or flavored with juniper" (*OED*, 5:631).

**To Preserve Cherryes**

Which without stones & in Jelly Take a p^d^ of Cherryes 6 p^d^ of sugar Clarifye your sugar in sirrup & Boyle it till it will rope very much & Stiff yn pull on by degrees then have Standing by you the Juice of Currants & when the Sugar boyls over ye Cherryes att 4 Several Times put that in be carefull to take the Scum off & Lett them boyle till the sirrup is become a Jelly & when done putt them in flatt pots or Glass wett ye Paper

———

*Contemporary Recipe #1* | *Contemporary Recipe #2*

**To pickle French Beans**

You must purge them in Salt and Water twenty-four Hours; then take them out and dry them with a Cloth, and make your Pickle thus: Take two Quarts of Wine Vinegar, some *Jamaica Pepper* whole, whole, Ginger, Cloves and Mace, Bay Leaves and Salt; then boil it up and skim it, and put your Beans into your Pickle boiling hot, and cover it down close; then set them before the Fire and let them cool by degrees as the Fire goes out: Do so three times together every other day. (Carter, *Compleat City,* 135–36)

**Juniper Water.**

Take the best Juniper-berries 12 ounces, proof spirit of wine three gallons, a sufficient quantity of water, and distil them. You may sweeten it with sugar. It is an excellent remedy against wind in the stomach and bowels; it powerfully provokes urine, and is therefore a good diuretick in the gravel and the jaundice. (Atkyns, *Family Magazine,* 1:74)

*"Jane Randolph her Cookery Book, 1743"* | *Comments*

**To make Vinegar**

Putt to 3 Quarts of spring water a Pound Malaga Raisons washed with the Stalk on sett it in the sun in a barrell from the beginning of the Summer till ye Latter End then Draw into bottles & Lett it Stand about a week or more.

———

**Sirrup of Saffron**

Take of saffron 1/2 an Oune Pint of Mountain wine infuse them togeth[er] in a bottle Shaking itt 3 or 4 times a Day for 6 or 7 Days then Strain it through a cloth put to itt 2 lb of Loaf Sugar melt it over a gentle fire in Earthen or Silver then strain it for use

———

**To Pickle Wallnuts**

Gather your Wallnuts about the middle of July Lett them Lye in Pump water 3 weeks Shifting them every day in fresh water then take Salt & water that will bear an Egg, boyling hott pour over them for a Fortnight Shifting them once in three days, wipeing them every time For ye pickle of an hundred wallnutts if Large will require 5 quarts of vinegar when you putt your vinegar Over the fire you must putt in 3 or 4 Shallots when they are Scalded a Little take them out the quantity of Spice for 100 Walnuts is an oz of whole black Pepper 1/2 ounce of Jamaica Do. an ounce of Ginger 1/2 oz of mace & Cloves 2 Nutmegs a Clove or two of garlick

Put the Garlick with the Spice in the Vinegar Some horse Reddish butt when all these boyle pour it Over the Wallnutts it must be 3 times once in 3 weeks Some bay Leaves in ye Pickle if you put Mustard seed itt must be half a pint put not putt in till Cold.

**To Pickle English Walnuts**

The walnuts should be gathered when the nut is so young that you can run a pin into it easily; pour boiling salt and water on and let them be covered with it nine days, changing it every third day; take them out and put them on dishes in the air for a few minutes, taking care to turn them over; this will make them black much sooner; put them in a pot, strew over some whole pepper, cloves, a little garlic, mustard seed, and horse radish scraped and dried, cover them with strong cold vinegar. (Randolph, *Virginia Housewife,* 208)

~ Mary's is a more streamlined and modernized version of Jane's recipe. **Put** in the last line is probably an error for but.

**[Missing Title]**

A Pound of ye best Flower a qtr pound of Almonds blanch'd & beaten with Orange flower water 8 Eggs butt 4 whites a Quarter of a pound of Loaf Sugar beaten well together the Rhine of Lemon Grated.

~ Although the title is missing, it is clear from the ingredients that this dish is some kind of dessert.

**[Missing Title]**

One Pound of butter Do of Sugar Do of Flower qr of pd of Almonds 12 Eggs Leaving 4 whites out a quarter of a Pint of Sack

~ This is another kind of dish suitable as a dessert.

| *Contemporary Recipe #1* | *Contemporary Recipe #2* |
|---|---|
| **To make Vinegar**<br>Take two pounds of Malago reasons, & one gallon of spring water, set them (in a pot or vessel cover'd) in ye hot sun for 6 or 8 weeks & it will become vinegar. You may boyle ye water first & put it hot to ye raisins, & 'twill be vinegar sooner & keep better. (Blencowe, *Receipt Book,* 4) | —— |
| **To make Syrup of Saffron**<br>Take a pint of the best Canary, and as much Balm-water, and half an Ounce of *English* Saffron, open and pull the Saffron very well, and put it into the Liquor to infuse; let it stand close covered (so as to be hot, but not boil) twelve hours, then strain it out as hot as you can, and add to it three pound of double refin'd Sugar, boil it till it is well incorporated, and when 'tis cold bottle it, and take one spoonful in a little Sack or small Cordial, as Occasion serves. (E. Smith, *Compleat House-wife* [1729], 191) | —— |
| **To Pickle Wall-nuts**<br>Take a Hundred of the large *French* Wall-nuts, at the beginning of *July,* before they have a hard Shell: Just scald them, that the first Skin may rub off; then throw them into Water and Salt for nine or ten Days, shifting them every other Day, and keep them close cover'd from the Air; then dry them: And make your Pickle of two quarts of White-wine- Vinegar, Long-Pepper, Black-Pepper, and Ginger, of each one ounce; Cloves, Mace, and Nutmegs, of each half an ounce; beat the Spice, and with it a large spoonful of Mustard -seed; strew this between every Layer of Wall-nutts, and pour your Liquor boiling-hot upon them three or four times, or oftner, if you see Occasion: Be sure to keep them close stopt. A spoonful of this Pickle is good in Fish, or any savoury sauce. Three or four Cloves of Garlick do well if you do not disslike the Taste. (Several Hands, *Collection* [1714], 47–48) | —— |
| —— | —— |
| —— | —— |

*"Jane Randolph her Cookery Book, 1743"*

*Comments*

**Balsom wch cures all new cuts or wounds**
[Missing]

~ This remedy is missing from Jane (Bolling) Randolph's manuscript.

**A very Good Elixer**
For ye Chollick & Gravel take of Ellicampagne Roots Sliced thin of Anniseeds Coriander Seeds Sana Geneum Joy berryes of each 2 ounces Raisons of the Sun Stoned one pound putt all these in a Stone mortar or Glass bottle wch will hold a Gallon or more adding to ye Former Ingredients 3 quarts & a pint of the Smalest Aquavita or the Like Quantity of the Strongest & Water mixt together, Stop up ye bottle Close & Lett it stand in a Cellar 4 days Stir it Twice a day & after thats its Fitt to Drink but best when It hath Stood 3 weeks then Strain it off & Keep it for ye use

The Vertues of this Elixer the quantity to be taken take 4 or 5 spoonfulls before you goe to Bed & as many the next Morning when you Awake Fast after it 2 hours it purgeth very Gentle & Perfectly cures of Chollick in ye Stomack or Bowels & also the Blood Flux & Gravell in the Kidneys it may be taken in health it's good to prevent Sickness

NB If no Berries be to begott You may take Junipers Probatum Est

~ An **elixir** is a "sovereign remedy for disease" and touted to prolong life (*OED,* 3:91). **Sana Geneum** was not located in *OED,* but it was likely senna genium. **Aquavita,** an "unrectified alcohol" or "ardent spirits," was made of ethyl alcohol (ethanol) and water (*OED,* 1:422).

**The Oyntment of Tobacco**
Take of Tobacco Leaves 6 pounds hogs Lard Clarifyed 3 pounds Lett ye Herb being bruised be infused in a pint or read wine a whole night in the morning put the Lard to the herbs & Lett it boyle Over a Slow Fire to the Consuming of the wine Then strain it of the Juice of Tobacco a pint Rosin 12 ounces sett it on the Fire again & Lett it boyle to ye consumption of the Juice then take it off & Lett it stand a whole week then Sett it on a slow fire & when it boyls Putt in a Little by Little of a lime of the Powder of round beachworck roots 6 ounces then Lett it Stand boyling for half an hour Stirring it all th Time with a wooden Stick then add it half a pound of bee's wax & when its Melted take it off & Lett it Stand to Settle then pour it off gently from ye Dregs you must Stir it first nor Losse it till its Cold

The Virtues of this Oyntment

It Cures humorous Apposthumes wounds Ulcers Gun Shots blotches & Scabs Itch Stinging wth Bees or Wasps hornetts Venemous Beasts wounds made with Poysned Arrows it helps Scalding with burning Oil or Lightning & that with out a Scar it helps nasty Rotten Putryfied Ulcers though in the Lungs In Fistulaes though the bane be Afflicted it Shall Seale it without an Instrument & bring up ye flesh from ye very bottom a

~ Although there were directions for tobacco ointments printed in the seventeenth century, none matched this recipe in terms of complexity, detail, and reverential tone. The meaning of **beachworck roots** is uncertain, but perhaps they are **beech roots** (*OED,* 1:757). A **fistula** is a "long, narrow, suppurating canal of morbid origin in some part of the body" or a "pipe-like ulcer with a narrow orifice" (*OED,* 4:261). **Passion** is an allusion to a "violent access, attack or fit of disease" (*OED,* 7:533).

*Contemporary Recipe #1*

**A most excellent Balsom for any green Wound.** Take oil of St. John's-wort and Venice-turpentine, of each a litke quantity; set them over the fire in a gentle heat, half an hour, or less, that they may incorporate: then put them up, and keep it for use, as one of the best of balsams. (Atkyns, *Family Magazine,* 2:268)

———

———

*Contemporary Recipe #2*

———

———

———

*"Jane Randolph her Cookery Book, 1743"* | *Comments*

wound Dresst with This will never Putryfie a would made with a Weapon that no tent[taint?] Can follow Oint[?] with this & you need not fear any Danger of your head Aches anoint ye Temples & you Shall have Ease the Stomach being Anointed with it no Infirmety harbours there no not Asthmas nor Consumptions of ye Lungs the belly being Anointed with it Helps the Chollick & Passion it helps the Hermoriods & piles & is the best for the Gout of all sorts

**For the Plurisye**

Take half an ounce of goats blood & half a pint of the best White wine Vinegar boyle it Till half be Consum'd Drink half Presently & ye rest 6 hours After

———

**A Receipt for ye Green Sickness to me made into Pills**

Take Powder of Steal & powder of Liquoris[h] Powder of Ellicampagne powder of Anni-Seeds powder of brimstone & beaten Ginger mix half an ounce of each in ye best honey & roule them up in the Powder of Liquorish & take 4 every morning & 4 in the Afternoon

**Green sickness,** related to iron deficiency and commonly known among young women, was an "anaemic disease which mostly affects young women about the age of puberty and gives a pale or greenish tinge to the complexion" (*OED*, 4:404).

**To make Pancakes & Extrardinary way**

Take a Quart of Cream & 8 Yelks of Eggs & 2 whites of Eggs a spoonfull of flower & a pound of butter & fry it in a Little pan without butter of Suett Two Spoonfulls will be enough for a time

———

**To make Neats feet Pudding**

Take one foot Minc't Smal & a pound of Suett & a handfull of Spineage a Little Parsley mince all these together very Smal grait a nuttmeg currants & penny white loaf 12 Eggs 3 qr of a pound of butter Melted & Little salt a half pint of Milk stir all these together then butter your Dish very well which you Design to Bake it in & a good handfull of fine flower

———

**To Make White Marmalade**

Of Quinces Cutt them in 4 qtrs & coar them & to Every pound & half of Quinces thus coared putt one pound of Double Refined Sugar putt about half the Quinces & Sugar with one spoonfull of Water to boil till the Quinces be Tender & ready to break; then putt the rest of The quinces & Sugar & about 5 or 6 spoonfull of Juice of Quinces well setled with one ounce of two of Sugar boil this together till it be all of Thickness; so put it into Glasses Do not fill it to full

———

| *Contemporary Recipe #1* | *Contemporary Recipe #2* |
| --- | --- |
| **A sovreign Medicine for the Pleurisy.**<br>Put some he-goat's blood in a silver porringer, into an oven; dry it to powder: after which take a drachm of it in a glass of sack, or any other wine, or cordial-water: keep yourself warm for twenty-four hours. It was never known to fail. (Atkyns, *Family Magazine,* 2:302) | ——— |
| **For the Green-Sickness**<br>Take an ounce of the Filings of Steel, or rusty Iron beaten to Powder, and mixt it with two ounces of the flour of Brimstone; then mix it up into an Electuary with Treacle; the Party must take the quantity of a Nutmeg in the Morning fasting, and at four in the Afternoon, and continue it till cured. (E. Smith, *Compleat Housewife* [1729], 284) | ——— |
| **Pancakes another:**<br>Take one quart of Cream, eight Yolks of Eggs, a Nutmeg grated small, and all well beaten together, then half a pound of Butter, melted with some Flour, then beat all well together again, clean your Pan, put some Butter in only the first time, and so fry them. (Salmon, *Family Dictionary,* 246) | ——— |
| **A Neat's-foot Pudding.**<br>Take to a pound of Neats-foot finely shred, three quarters of a pound of Suet shred as small, a whole Nutmeg grated, Candy'd Orange minced, some Salt, and some Currants, a little grated Bread, and seven Eggs, (leave out half the Whites;) flower the Bag, and let it boil two Hours and a half at least. The Sauce is, Sack, Sugar and Butter melted. (Several Hands, *Collection* [1714], 54) | ——— |
| **Marmalade White**<br>Take six pound of Quinces, pare and core them, and then boil 'em to a Pulp, put to it two pound of Sugar, moistened well with the Juice of Quinces; boil them gently together it first till the Liquor be swelled out of the Quinces, and the Sugar dissolved, and all come into a convenient thickness, and so put it up for your use. (Salmon, *Family Dictionary,* 199) | ——— |

*"Jane Randolph her Cookery Book, 1743"*

**To make a Hasty Pudding**

Take a Quart of Cream and as much graited bread as will make it Thick & some Currants boyle very well putt some Sugar to sweeten it and then Take 4 Yolks of Eggs beaten put the Eggs in & Lett them boyle a good while & the Batter will rise it self & when you think it is enough Take it off & Serve it

*Comments*

———

**The Lady Allens water**

Marrigolds Tops Red sage Balm Rue Burnett Angelica Dragoons Wormwood Selladine Scabius Wood Bittany Egrimony Red Pimpernell mugwort wood sorrell Cardus Rosemary Scordium Sentry, Rosa Solis 3 ounces of Each of these herbs after they are pickt Ellicampagne roots Tormentill roots 3 ounces of Each These herbs roots wash them & Slice them Redury Gentian & Liquorish of each 1/2 an ounce then shred them very Smal & steep them in four Quarters of the best white wine And Slice them very Small & Steep them & putt them into an Earthen pott þt you can stop Close that no Air come to it, and let it stand 24 Hours then put þm into your Still and Starch up the Still with Paper Nose and all, that no Air can come in and Set it a Working by 4 a Clock in the Morning that it may be drawn out by Night there will be 3 pints of very Strong the rest you may Draw as long as any Strength is left in it you may keep one Quart by it Self the other you may Mingle with the Small -

P E

The Virtue of this Aforesaid Water

This Water is good for the Small Pox ffevers and Agues, the Plague or any other Distemper given Warme with a little Sugar and it will lay them in a Sweat and Drive the Distemper or Sickness from ye Heart in ffevers or any other Distemper or sickness give it with Syrup of Clove gelleflowers or Poppys, or Violets Cold for a Cordial or in any other Syrup that your Distemper requires or wth Disacordium or with Methredate and So in Womens Travells

**The Lady Allens Water**

Take Sallendine Rue Saige Wormwood Cardus Dragon Rosa Solis Mugworte Pimpernell Scabeaus Balm Scardume Bittony Flowers & Leaves Cintuory Toops & flowers Mary gold Flowers & leaves of Each a Good handfull then take the Roots of Pinory Tormentall Angellico Elicompane Ledory liquorish all clean Scraped of each half an Ounce let the herbes be dry'd in aCloath not wash'd then Shred them altogether Slice the roots thin & Mix with ye herbes and put to them 2 quarts of Sack & 2 quarts of white Wine let them Steep together in an~Earthen Pott well Glaiz'd 2 Days & Nights cover them close & keep them Sturing once~a Day and Still them of aCold Still Sweeten it & Mix it to your Tast with loaf Suger then bottle it up for Your Use[.] (The Compiler [1744], Manuscript cookbook, 42)

~ **Redury** may be a typographical error for **zedory.** **P E** stands for Probatum Est. **Diascordium** is a Latin word for "diascord" (obsolete), which was a "medicine made of dried leaves of *Teucrium scordium,* perhaps a water-germander, and many other herbs" (*OED,* 3:321). **Clove-gillyflower,** spice clove, is a truly archaic term that was in use before 1486, and it is also a clove-scented species of pink under the name *Dianthus Carysphylus* (*OED,* 2:530). The term **travel** here refers to "torment, distress, suffer affliction, labor, toil" and "suffer pains of parturition" (*OED,* 11:292).

**To Salt Hams**

Take 2 quarts of English Salt & 2 quarts of Bay salt & six pennyworth of Salt Petre put these together in a brass Skillet & sett Them over the fire & keep it stirring till it be very hott then take it off & put a Quarter of a pound of Sugar to ye salt & rubb it into your Hams very hard & sett them in a cold Place for a fortnight turning them once a week then take them from the Brine & rub them with a Little Blood Then put some brine upon them & hang them up to Dry

~ The use of blood as a coloring agent to make meat look more attractive is unusual.

*Contemporary Recipe #1*

**20. A Hasty Pudding.**

Take a Pint of Milk and put to it a handful of Raisins of the Sun, as many Currans; then take a Manchet, grate it, and put in a little Flour and Nutmeg, and let it boile a quarter of an Hour; then put in a piece of Butter in the boiling, and dish it with pieces of Butter laid up and down upon it, then send it to the Table. (Howard, *England's Newest Way* [1710], 9–10)

*Contemporary Recipe #2*

———

**The Lady Allen's Water**

Take of Balm, Rosemary, Sage, Carduus, Wormwood, Dragons, Scordium, Mugwort, Scabious, Tormentil-roots and Leaves, Angelica-roots and Leaves, Marigold-flowers and Leaves, Betony-flowers and Leaves, Centaury-tops, Pimpernel, Wood-sorrel, or other sorrel, Rue, Agrimony, Rosa Solis, of every one of these half a pound, Liquorish 4 ounces, Elecampane-roots, 2 ounces; wash the Herbs, shake and dry them in a Cloth, then shred them and slice the Roots, and put all into 3 Gallons of the best White-wine, and let them stand close covered 2 Days and 2 Nights, stirring them Morning and Evening; then take out some of the Herbs, lightly squeezing them with your hands, and fill a Still full, let them still 12 hours in a cold Still with a reasonable quick Fire: then put the rest of the Herbs and the Wine, in an Alembick, and distil them till all the Strength is out of the Herbs and Wine: mix all the Water in both Stills together, sweeten some, but not all, for Cases of great Illness, warm some of that unsweeten'd, blood-warm, and put in it a little Syrup of Gilliflowers, and go to bed, covring warm. This is a very excellent Water. (E. Smith, *Compleat Housewife* [1729], 221)

———

**To make Westphalia Hams; absolutely the best way to do them.**

Cut your Leg of Fat large Pork, as like a right Ham as you can, (Black Hogs make the best) hang it up two days, then beat it very well on the Fleshy-side with a Rolling-pin; rub in an ounce of Salt-petre (finely beaten) in every place, so let it lie a Day and Night; then take an ounce more of beaten Salt-petre, with two large handfuls of common Salt, and a handful of Bay-salt, a pound of coarse Sugar; mix all these together, and warm them thorough- hot in a Stew-pan, but be sure not to melt it; and while 'tis hot, rub it all

**Another Way.**

CUT the leg of a quarter of pork into Westphalia shape, then take white salt; set it on the fire in a skillet till 'tis dry; put to it two ounces of salt-petre finely beaten; the salt must be laid as hot as your hand can endure it; let it lie a week in salt, and then hang it in the chimney three weeks or a month to dry: two pounces of petre is enough to a quantity of salt to one ham. (Atkyns, *Family Magazine,* 1:107)

*"Jane Randolph her Cookery Book, 1743"* | *Comments*

**Eye Water**

Plantain eye bright & Salendine of each a pint 2 quarts of spring water that is against the sun rising & ounce of white Coperas putt all these together in a new Pipkin Lett them Simmer till a pint be Consumed Cover it with a Pewter Plate & stroak of the [blank] pretty often

~ **Eye bright,** a popular remedy of repute in treating weak eyes, was derived from the plant *Euphrasia officinalis,* better known as **eurphrasy,** which was attributed with virtues concerning treatment of diseased eyes (*OED,* 3:322, 485).

**(A Receipt for the Stone/Drunkeness)**

Take half a porringer of white wine & half an ounce of oil of Sweet Almonds as much Parsley seed as will Lay upon a Shilling then Sweeten it with Sirrup of marshmallows Tis a good remedy Against the stone & being drunk going to bed & morning fasting will cure it in a short time with Gods Blessing

———

**Sirrup of Marsh Mallows**

Take green mashmallard roots sliced a Quarter of a pound; Grass roots Sparrow grass roots, Licoritie reasons of the sun of each an ounce tops of the wall Pimpernell Sasafras Plantian maiden Hair both Black & white of each 3 quarters of an ounce; Red cicers to be had att any Druggist; one ounce of the four Coob seeds To be had at any Druggist Likewise Boil all these to a Gallon of water Strain it & after its Settled put to it 4 pounds of Sugar about Six pence a pound which is better then finer boil it to a Sirrupp

~ **Sparrow grass,** which was in use before 1650 for the word **asparagus,** remained in common use until the eighteenth century (*OED,* 10:523). **Red cicers,** an outdated word for **chickpeas,** "are reckoned hot and dry," according to a 1545 publication (*OED,* 2:413). **Coob seeds,** also an archaic and dialectic term, may have referred to a cobnut, a stone of a fruit, or the seeding head of wheat, clover, etc. (*OED,* 2:560).

**[Missing Title]**

Take 28 pounds of good Malagoes rubbed Clean in a coarse clout chop them smal & a peck of Sage chopped small boyle 6 Gallons of fair water one hour then putt altogether into a Vessell & Lett it stand 12 Days Stirring it every Day then Strain it through a Coarse Clout, squezin the Pulse Dry then putt it into a vessell & when it has Done working bung it Close & Lett it stand whilst it's fine

———

**To Pickle Mushrooms**

Pick them & wash them very Clean in Cold water then put them in a Large Saucepan without water only putt some salt to them & Sett them into a Clear fire Lett them boyle in their own Liquor half a Quarter of an

———

*Contemporary Recipe #1*

*Contemporary Recipe #2*

over the Ham very well, with two large handfuls more of Salt; thus let it lie 'till it melts to Brine, then turn it every Day twice and baste it with that Brine for three Weeks together: Dry it as Bacon. (Several Hands, *Collection* [1714], 40–41)

———

———

———

———

———

———

———

**90. Syrup of Marsh mallows**

Take of roots of marsh mallows two ounces; the roots of grass Sparagus, Liquoris, Raisins of the Sun stoned, of each half an ounce; the tops of mallows, marsh mallows, pellitorie of the wall, burnet, plantane, maidenhair white and black, of each an handfull; red cicers an ounce; of the four greater and four lesser cold seeds, of each three drachms; boil them in six pound of clear water till four remain, which being strained, boile into a sirrup with four pound of white sugar. (M.B., *Ladies Cabinet,* 41).

**61. An Excellent Receipt for making Elder-wine.**

Take five Gallons of Water, and twenty Pounds of *Malago*-Raisins; pick them from the Stalks, rub them clean, and shred them small: Boil the Water an Hour, and then pour it upon the Raisins, and let it stand ten Days in a Tub, stirring it now and then; then strain it through a coarse Sieve. To five Gallons of that Liquor, put four Pints of Elder-juice, the Berries being first put into a Pot, and set in a Kettle of boiling Water. The Liquor being strained, and the Juice being cold put it together, and turn it into a Vessel, and let it work; then bung it up close, and let it stand till 'tis fine, and then bottle it off. (Howard, *England's Newest Way* [1710], 127–28)

**To Pickle Mushrooms**

Take your Mushrooms and peel them, then take them out of the Water and dry them, put them in a Sauce-pan, and put to them a good deal of Salt, some blades of Mace and Nutmeg quarter'd, let them boil

**170. Another excellent Way to pickle Mushrooms**

Put your Mushrooms into Water, and wash them with a Spunge, (put them in Water as you do them) then put Water and a little Salt, when it boils put in your Mushrooms, when they boil up skim them clean, and

*"Jane Randolph her Cookery Book, 1743"* | *Comments*

hour then lay them in a Seive to Cool & have ready boiled & quite Cold some good Vinegar with Large mace Some Cloves & whole pepper white Peper is best putt your mushrooms to the Vinegar as Soon as they are cold so tye them up for use when you find the Pickle mould or mother you must putt new Pickle to them such as ye first Butt they will keep very well this way

**To Pickle Apples**

Take hard green apples att the full growth put them into salt & water 2 or 4 Days take them out & wipe them with a Little peices out of the top that your may scoop out the Coar then fill the hole with a Clove of garlick, bruizd mustard seed a Little ginger whole pepper very Little Salt when you have Done all your Apples putt on the peices you cut out & tye them on again so putt them in a stone pot & put boyling Vinegar upon them you must boyl your Vinegar two or three times & pour it in upon them hot they will be fitt for use in a fortnight

Finis

~ This is a more modern version of the seventeenth century's way of pickling codlings.

**Orange Water**

Take a Quart of Brandy putt the peal of 6 or 8 Oranges into it paired thin Lett them steep 2 or 3 Days take a pint of water & putt as much good Sugar into it; & boyle it to a Thin sirrup then take out ye peel from the brandy & put it in hot to ye brandy & oranges & Lett it Stand Close cover'd till it's Cold

———

**Cardenom water**

Take a Gallon of Strong beer grounds & putt it into a Still then putt in a half ozce of Coriander, carraway and Anniseeds and as Cardemom 2 Drams an Nutmegs, Sinnamon Cloves, mace and Ginger bruise them and put them in, and put in a handful of Spermint balm, sage and Angelica, let it steep all Night, then Still it of, and mix it together and Sweeten it

———

**To make Cowslip Wine**

To 6 Gallons of fair water take half peck Cowslip flowers two every gallon 2 pound of sugar you must not putt in your Cowslips till it boyle working it by wt; a spoonfull of beer put in when tis Cold Lett it stand 3 Days after working & then bottle it

———

*Contemporary Recipe #1*

in their own Liquor four or five Minutes over a quick Fire, then drein them from their Liquor, and let them stand till they are cold, then take all the Spice that was used in the boiling them, and as much white Wine, and White Wine Vinegar as will cover them, a little Salt, then give them a boil or two, and put them in your Pot, and when they are cold put two Spoonfuls of Oil on the top to keep them; you must change the Liquor once in six Weeks[.] (Harrison, *House-Keeper's Pocket-Book,* 109)

*Contemporary Recipe #2*

put them into cold Water, and a little Salt, let them stand twenty four Hours, and put the Water from them, and put them into White-wine Vinegar, and let them stand a Week, then take your Pickle from them, and boil it very well, put some whole Pepper, Cloves, Mace, and a little all Spice, when your Pickle is cold, put it to the Mushrooms, and keep them close stopt, or tyed with a Bladder to keep the Air from them, or else they will be apt to mother; if they do mother you may boil your Pickle again: If you please you may make your Pickle half White-wine. (Howard, *England's Newest Way* [1710], 91)

---

**Orange Water**

Squeeze the Juice of four *Sevil* Oranges into two Quarts of Water, and put in the Pulp and Zests, let them lie several Hours to steep with a good Lump of Sugar; then pour the Liquor out of one Pot into another several times, strain it to be cooled and iced[.] (E. Smith, *Compleat Housewife* [1753], 59)

**Cardamum Water.**

Take pimento, caraway, and coriander-seeds, lemon-peels, of each four ounces; proof spirits three gallons; a sufficient quantity of water; distil and sweeten it with sugar, one pound and a half. It is a cheap and good cordial, and may be used in all cases where a stomachick cordial is necessary. (Atkyns, *Family Magazine,* 1:75).

**Cowslip=Wine:**

Take three Gallons of Water, three pound of Sugar, boil them one hour and half, scum it very well; when it is boiled, take it off the Fire, and put in six quarts of Pickt Cowslips, and let it stand all Night; strain them out, then put in New-Ale-Yest, let them work well; then turn them, and let it stand five days, then Bottle it for use. (Salmon, *Family Dictionary,* 64)

*"Jane Randolph her Cookery Book, 1743"*

**To make Gravey Soop**
Boyle a Leg of beef to mashr Strain ye strong Broth through a Cullender take the fatt of take ye Gelly of the bottom boyle a cupple of ox pallats with you Leg of beef till it be tender blanch your pallats take 4 pound of Lean beef to make Gravey to make it into gravy Cut it in Little Bitts put them in a Sauce pan or harsh pan Lett them Stew keep them coverd

**To make Shrewsbury Cakes**
Fourteen pound of flower two & thirty Yolks of eggs a pint of cream four pounds of sugar four pounds of butter & ounce of Carraway seeds a quarter of pint of rose water

**To make Peas Soop**
Boil your peas in River water put them in ye water cold boil a peice of Bacon Chine bones of pork when They are half boiled putt in a quart of water putt in a quart of water To blanch them when they are boil'd Strain them through a Cullender boyl your Soop put in mint Shred spinnage some pepper toasted white bread putt a peice of butter in

*Comments*

**To Make Gravy Soup.**
Get eight pounds of coarse lean beef-wash it clean and lay it in your pot, put in the same ingredients as for the shin soup, with the same quantity of water, and follow the process directed for that. Strain the soup through a seive and serve it up clear with nothng more than toasted bread in it, two table-spoonsful of mushroom catsup will add a fine flavour to the soup. (Randolph, *Virginia Housewife,* 29–30)

~ Her version is streamlined and flavored with mushroom catsup instead of little bits of meat.

**Shrewsbury Cakes.**
Cream one pound of butter, add a pound of powdered sugar, with a pound and a half of flour, six eggs, a grated nutmeg, and a gill of brandy; work it well, roll it thin, and cut it in shapes; put them on tin sheets, and bake without discolouring them. (Randolph, *Virginia Housewife,* 163–64)

~ Jane's recipe serves as a useful contrast with her brevity and use of caraway seeds and rosewater. The copious amounts of ingredients reflect that this was for a large number of individuals. Mary's portions reflected a smaller size for an urban housewife or a small family.

**Dried Pea Soup.**
Take one quart of split peas, or Lima beans which are better, put them in three quarts of very soft water with three onions chopped up, pepper and salt; boil them two hours; wash them well and pass them through a seive; return the liquid into the pot, thicken it with a large piece of butter and flour, put in some slices of nice salt pork, and a large tea-spoonful of celery-seed pounded; boil it till the port is done, and serve it up; have some toasted bread cut into dice and fried in butter, which must be put in the tureen before you pour in the soup. (Randolph, *Virginia Housewife,* 33–34)

~ Jane's version is a transition between those of Anonymous (1700) and Mary Randolph.

*Contemporary Recipe #1*

**To Make Gravysoop (from Serjeant's Inn Cook)**

Have a good strong broth made of a Legg of beef & seson'd with time and Cloves & mace, & when 'tis well boyld, that you think it will jelly when 'tis cold, strain it off ye broth from ye meat. Then put your broth into a pot that you design to make your soop in & have in readiness these soop hearbs, viz. some Sallery & judiss & spinidge. Clean them & chop them small, & stew them well in a stew pan over a clear fire. Then put them into your broth & let them boyl gently, & some Oxes pallets, & let them be boyl'd very tender & cut them in very small slices. Then put them into your soop, & Season it with peper & salt & Nutmeg to your pallet, & dish it up with a Roasted duck or fowl in ye middle & dry some French bread & break it into your soop.

So serve it up to Table. (Blencowe, *Receipt Book,* 24)

*Contemporary Recipe #2*

**Gravy Soup**

Take the Bones of a Rump of Beef, and a piece of the Neck, and boil it till you have all the goodness out of it, then strain it off, then take a good piece of Butter, and put it in a Stew-Pan and brown it, then put to it an Onion stuck with Cloves, some Sallary and Endive, and Spinage, then take your Gravy and put to it some Pepper, Salt, and Cloves, and let it boil all together; then put in Sippits of Bread dry'd by the Fire; you may put in a Glass of red Wine. Serve it up with a french Role toasted in the middle. (Harrison, *House-Keeper's Pocket-Book,* 66)

---

**A Green-Pease-Soup.**

Take your Pease, and in shelling them, separate the Young from the Old, then boil the Old ones soft enought to strain through a Cullender; then put the Liquor and what you strained through together: With the Young Pease whole, add some whole Pepper, three Blades of Mace, and some Cloves. When the last Pease are near enough, take some Spinach, a little Mint, and a little Green Onion, not shred too fine, a little Faggot of Thyme and Sweet-Marjoram; Put these into a little Sauce-pan with a near a Pound of Butter; and as they boil up, shake in some Flour with it to the Quantity of a Drudging box full; then put a Loaf of French Bread into the Broth to boil; mingle the Broth and Herbs together: When you have season'd it to your Taste for Salt, add some small white Toast neatly cut, and the Young Pease. (Several Hands, *Collection* [1724], 1:8–9)

*"Jane Randolph her Cookery Book, 1743"*

*Comments*

**(Conserve of Roses)**

Take 2 ounces of Conserve of roses 2 ozces of brown sugar Candy 2 ounces of Raisins of the sun Stoned 1 ounce of Mithridate Ten Drops of sulphur mix'd together

~ **Drops of sulphur** refers to sulphur in a powder form and mixed with treacle, which functioned as a "laxative, resolvent, and a sudorific" and was also used in ointments for skin disorders (*OED*, 10:132).

**Raisin Vinegar**

To a gallon of fair water putt three pounds of Malaga raisins stalks & all Chop them small & Lett your Vesselll stand in the Sun all Summer close stopp'd you may make what Quantity you please thus ordere'd.

———

**Suthern Wood, the Virtues of**

Take a quantity of it and make A strong Bath for a Sore Leg, or make an Ointment with Suthern Wood, Night shaid, and Barrows fate for Splits, & craks in ye: Hands or Feet.

~ **Night shaid** is **Nightshade**, a plant of the genus *Solanum*, esp. *S. nigrum* with its black poisonous berries. One other nightshade, of the genus *Atropa*, is familiar to us as Deadly Nightshade or Belladonna (*OED*, 7:147). **Barrows fat,** a dialectic word for barrows grease, was derived from a castrated boar or a swine (*OED*, 1:683).

**A Receipt to Pott Tongues**

Take your Tongues and parboil them, then season them while they are hot with Bay Salt peter, and Comon Salt, Nutmeg Cloves, Maces, and black peper let them ly in the Season three hours then take some of the Liquor that Boild them take as much as will Cover 'em and put them in an Earthen Pott and Bake them till till they are Tender, Then pour out the Liquor and when they are Cold fill up the pott with Clarified Butter

———

**A Nother for the same**

Take a little Salt peter, with comon salt Cloves and Mace after they are Boyld- then stuff them with the Cloves and Mace and Bake them, & Cover them with Butter

N B These Tongues are to lye in Salt Tenn Days

———

*Contemporary Recipe #1*

**To make Conserve of Roses, or other flowers.**
Take the Buddes of Red Roses somwhat before they be ready to spread: cut the red part of the leaves from the white then take the red leaves and beate and grinde them in a stone morter with a pestell of wood, and to every ounce of Roses, put three ounces of suger in the grinding (after the leves are well beaten) and grinde them together till they be perfectly incorporated, then put it in a Glas made for the nonce: and of purpose, or els unto an earthen pot: stop it close, and so keepe it

Thus ye may make conserves of all kynde of flowers used thereunto[.] (Partridge, *Treasurie,* chap. 17)

*Contemporary Recipe #2*

**Conserve of red Roses.**
TAKE of red Rose-buds one pound, bruise them with a wooden pestle in a marble mortar, adding by degrees of white lump sugar powdered and sifted, three pounds; continue beating them, till no particles of the Roses can be seen, and till the whole becomes a similar mass. (Atkyns, *Family Magazine,* 1:72)

**To make Raisin-Vinegar**
Take what quantity of Spring-Water you please, put it in Stone-Bottles, and to every Bottle put two Pound of *Malaga* Raisins; tie down the Corks very close, and set them in the Chimney corner very near the Fire for a convenient Time, or you may set them in the Sun. (Middleton, *Five Hundred New Receipts,* 1:195)

———

———

———

**To pot Neats Tongues**
Your Neats Tongues must be first pickled, then cut off the Roots, blanch them and season them well with Pepper, and Salt, Cloves, Mace, and Nutmeg, while they are warm; then put them into an Earthen-pot, and cover them over with fresh Butter; when they are baked enough, take them out of the Pot, and put them into one you intend to keep them in; take off the Butter from the Gravy, and melt as much more as will cover an Inch and a half above your Tongues[.] (Middleton, *Five Hundred New Receipts,* 1:96).

———

———

———

*"Jane Randolph her Cookery Book, 1743"* | *Comments*

### To make a Plumb Cake

———

A)

Take a quarter of a peck of Flower well Dry'd before the fire, then rub in a pound and a half of Butter, then beat four Eggs with a pint of Ale yest with apint of Warm milk beaten well together, then mixt it with the Flower, season'd with one Nuttmeg a litle Cinamon with a pound of Sugar and three pounds and a half of Currants well washed pick'd and Dry'd in a Cloth then work them into Cake with two ounces of Orange peel and as much Citron, Work it up very light, and put it into your frame and set it before the Fire for an Hour, pricking it often, then put it in a Quick Oven for an Hour

### To Make the Green Oyle

Take one quart of the Best oyle put Earthen pitcher big enough to hold two quarts and in a Clear dry Day gather of Wormwood, Young Sprouts of Bayes-Sage, Sparmint Lavender Camomel take of Each of these a Handfull and Shred them and put them into the oyle Cork it up Close, and dig a Hole in the Ground, put in Your pott and apiece of Tile or Wood, on ye mouth of it to keep out the Earth from getting into it so let it lye Buried in the ground Six Weeks at least and when you take it up put the Oyle and Herbs into a Clean Bellmetle Skillet and let it Boyl Two Hours on a gentle Fire then strain it out and keep it for Your Use, keep it close stopt this Oyl is good for any use, Bruise Sprain or Swelling whatsoever

~ There were endless variations on the theme of green oils or ointments. A **bellmetal skillet** is made of "bell metal," which is an "alloy of copper & tin" (*OED,* 1:787).

### To make Plague Water

Take Bame, Avienes, Sage, Agrimony, Saladine, Pimpernell, Burnett, Dragons, Rosemary, Marigolds, Mugwort, Angelico Rew, Featherfew, Tormintell, Cardus, Scabus, Wormwood, Mint, Scordom, Rolis Solis of Each three Handfulls pick'd very Clean, and infused in three Gallons of Brandy Twenty four Hours in a Earthen pan, Close stopt, and then draw it off and putt it into your still

~ **Avienes** may allude to **avens,** which is also known under the names of wood aven or herb bennet; its cloverlike flavor was added to ale and used in medicines (*OED,* 1:581).

*Contemporary Recipe #1*

*Contemporary Recipe #2*

**To make an excellent Plumb Cake**

Take a Quarter of a peck of Flower, and dry it, three pound of Currans wash'd and pick'd clean, set them before a Fire to dry, half a pound of Raisins of the Sun, wash'd, ston'd, and shred small, half a pound of blanch'd Almonds, beat very fine, with Rose-Water, a pound of Butter melted with a pint of Cream, but not put in hot, a Pint of Ale-Yest, a penny worth of Saffron steep'd in a Pint of Sack, ten or twelve Eggs, but half the whites of them, a quarter of an Ounce of Cloves and Mace, one large Nutmeg grated, a few Carraway-Seeds, Citron, Canded Orange, and Lemon-peel slic'd; you must make it thin, or there must be more Butter and Cream; you may perfume it with Ambergreece ty'd in a Muslin Bag, and steep'd in in the Sack all Night. If you ice it, take half a Pound of Double-refin'd Sugar, sifted; then put some of the Sugar, and beat it up with the White of an Egg, and beat it with a Whisk, and a little Orange-flower Water, but do not over-wet it; then strow in all the Sugar by Degrees; then beat it all near an Hour; the Cake will take so long a baking; then draw it, and wash it over with a Brush, and put it in again for half a quarter of an hour[.] (R. Smith, *Court Cookery* [1723], 2:13–14)

———

**A green Oil, to be made in June.**

TAKE rosemary-tops, green sage, lavender-tops, feverfue, chamomile, baum, southernwood, betony, red rose-buds, of each of these one handful; of wormwood, half a handful: let -em all be chopped small, and put into two quarts of good oil; and let it stand fourteen days, stirring it three or four times a week: then boil it softly, till the herbs be dry. It is good for bruises, taken inwardly in two or three spoonfuls of warm sack or ale: . . . Outwardly anoint the bruised part with a feather, and put a piece of flanel upon the place. (Atkyns, *Family Magazine*, 2:275)

———

**Plague Water**

Take Rosa-Solis, Agrimony, Betony, Scabious, Centaury tops, Scordium, Balm, Rue, Wormwood, Mugwort, Celandine, Rosemary, Marigold-Leaves, brown Sage, Burnet, Carduus, and Dragons, of each a large handful, Angelica-roots, Peony-roots, Tormentil-roots, Elecampane-roots and Liquorish, of each an ounce; cut the Herbs, and slice the Roots and put them all into an earthen Pot, and put to them a gallon of White wine, and a quart of Brandy, and let them steep days close cover'd; then distil it in an ordinary still with a gentle Fire: You may sweeten it, but not much. (E. Smith, *Compleat Housewife* [1729], 221–22)

**Surfeit-water.**

TAKE of sage, celandine, rue, mugwort, wormwood, pimpernel, rosemary, dragons, scabious, agrimony, balm, scordium, centaury, cardius, benedictus, betony, rosa solis of each a good handful; angelica-roots, tormentil, zedoary, liquorice, half an ounce of each: slice the roots, wash the herbs, strain them dry in a cloth and shred them; put them all together into half a gallon of white-wine, and the same quantity of sack; steep them in it two days and two nights, close covered; then put it into an ordinary still, and distil it, when you use it, let it be lukewarm, sweeten'd with a little sugar, three or four spoonfuls of the small to a

*"Jane Randolph her Cookery Book, 1743"* | *Comments*

**A Very Good Plumb Cake, Not too Rich**

Take half a peck of flower one pound of Sugar, a little Spice & Salt, a little Ginger, one pound Raisons Ston'd and Shred, 3 lb Currans, plumpt, mix all these dry things together, then melt a pound of butter soft[ened?] in a quart of cream, bet eighteen eggs keep out Six whites, a little Sack, a pint of yest - mix all the liquors together, and Strain them in the other things, and mix them very well, and set them to rise what flower you use to bring it together in the hoop, may be over and above the half peck, put what sewet you please, oring & lemon peel two hours will Bake it.

Thise Reecipt is in the Book Mr. Rees gave to Jenny Walke, and is exceeding good,

———

**Cake to ice**
[Missing]

~ The recipe is no longer attached to Jane (Bolling) Randolph's cookbook, but she may have copied it from a recipe similar to the following example.

**Barberries to Pickle**

Make a pickle of Water & Salt with some of your wort Berries; so strong as to bear an Egg, letting it boil for half an hour Scumming it; & when cold; put it into an Earthen Jar, into which put your choice Barberries & stop them close up.

**To Pickle Barbaries**

Take Barbaries and Pick out some of the worst of them and make your Pickle thus with Water & bay Salt and white Salt with the Barbaries you pickt out boyle them very well and Squeese in some to make it look Red then take it of the fire and Strain it throw a Sive into thy pott you Entend to keep them in & let your liquor stand to be cold—then put in your Barbaries with as much White Wine Venigar as you think fitten with ye quantity of a pound of brown Sugar tye them down Cloce with Leather and let the Pickle be Strong Enough to bear an Egg. (The Compiler [1744], Manuscript cookbook, 85)

*Contemporary Recipe #1*

**To make a Plum-Cake.**
Take Half a Peck of Flower, and dry it, one Pound of Sugar, one Ounce of Mace, two large Nutmegs, Half an Ounce of Cinnamon, & few Cloves; all the Spice beaten together and sifted; a Quarter of an Ounce of beaten Ginger, a little Salt, a Pound of Raisins of the Sun, ston'd and shred, six Pound of currans must be plump'd before the Fire, after they are wash'd and pick'd. Mix all these dry Things together, then take a Pound of Butter, melt it softly in a Quart of Cream, beat eighteen Eggs, keep out six Whites, put to them a little Rose-water, a little Sack, a Pint of new Ale-Yest; mix all the Liquor together, and strain them; Then mix all together, and let it stand before the Fire, cover'd with a Cloth, a Quarter of an Hour, or longer; then put it in your Hoop to bake; what Flower you use to bring it together in the Hoop, may be over and above the Halfe Peck. Put what Sewet you please, Orange and Lemon-peel a Pound. Two Hours will bake it. Candy it with the Whites of three Eggs beat to a Froth, adding a Quarter of a Pound of fine Sugar searc'd and beaten together. (Lamb, *Royal Cookery,* 82–83)

**The Ice for the Cake.**
Take the Whites of three new-laid Eggs, and three quarters of a pound of fine Sugar finely beaten, beat it well together with the Whites of Eggs, and Ice the Cake; If you please, you may add a little Musk or Ambergreese.

Let your Oven be of temperate heat, and let your Cake stand therein two hours and a half before you Ice it, and afterwards, only to harden the Ice. (Hall, *Queen's Royal Cookery,* 50–51)

**Another Way to pickle Barberries.**
Take Water, and colour it red with some of the worst of your Barberries, and put Salt to it, and make it strong enough to bear an Egg; then set it over the Fire, and let it boil half an hour; scum it, and when 'tis cold, strain it over your Barberries; lay something on them to keep them in the Liquor, and cover the Pot or Glass with Leather. (E. Smith, *Compleat Housewife* [1729], 67)

*Contemporary Recipe #2*

child, six or seven spoonfuls of te strong to an older person. This water is usually drawn a pint at the first, second, and third running. (Atkyns, *Family Magazine,* 2:313)

**To make a Plum Cake.**
Take half a peck of fine Flour dry'd in an Oven; take a pound of Butter, melt it softly in a quart of Cream, beat eighteen Eggs, keeping out six of the Whites, put to them a little Sack, a little Rose-water, a pint of new Ale, mix all the Liquors together, and strain them; take a pound of Raisins of the Sun stoned and shred, six pound of Currants, wash, pick and plump them before the Fire; then take a pound of Sugar, an Ounce of Mace, half an Ounce of Cinnamon, two Nutmegs, a few Cloves; pownd all these Spices together and sift them; add also a quarter of an Ounce of beaten Ginger, and a little Salt; then mix all these together, and cover it with a Cloth and let it stand before the Fire for a quarter of an Hour, and then put it in your Hoop to bake. You may put in a pound of Orange and Lemon-peel, and what Suet you please; when it is bak'd you may ice it. (Nott, *Cook's and Confectioner's Dictionary,* #9)

———

———

*"Jane Randolph her Cookery Book, 1743"*

*Comments*

**Barberries to Preserve**

Take fair ripe Barberries, stone them, then weigh them, & to every pound of Barberies put two pound of fine loaf Shugar, Beat them & search it, then Take a deep gally pot, put in first a Layer of Shugar; Then a Layer of Barbrries So do till you have filled your pott, then tie it close down. They will keep all the Year.

———

**Bisket Drops**

Take a pound of fine Shugar, four Yolks & two whites of Eggs, Quarter of Sack Beat them well together for an hour add the Seeds in pouder & fine flower not more: beat them well together again drop this softn past upon Buttered Paper, & Bake them in a gentle Oven; as you see them, Ice them with fine Sugar.

**To make Drop Biscuit.**

Beat eight eggs very light, add to them twelve ounces of flour, and one pound of sugar; when perfectly light, drop them on tin sheets, and bake them in a quick oven. (Randolph, *Virginia Housewife,* 157)

~ Mary's version is more streamlined and modern in comparison to the ones used by Jane, her peers, and her forebears.

**Good Ale**

Take 3 Bushels malt 1/2 high & 1/2 Pail dry'd let your water boil them put into your Mashing tubb, When the Steem is gone off, so as you may see your face; then put your malt, & after mashing it well th[en] cover it with a blanket, Let it stand 2[?] hours, then draw it of Slow, then boil it three or four hours, till the hops curdles when boiled Enough, cool a little, & work that with your yest, & so put the rest of your wort in as it cools, which must be let in small Tubs, let it work till your yest begins to curdle then turn it & stop your Barrel when it has done working; Note to Every Bushels malt a Quarter of pound of hops

P Mrs Cary

**Good Ale**

To three Bushells of Malt half high and half-pale Dry'd let your. Water boil Then put it into your Mashing Tub. when the Steem is gone off so as you m[ay] see your fface in it Then put in your Malt and after mashing cover it with - - brann let it stand four hours before you let yor wort Run of. which mu[st] Run Slow then boil it two or three Hours tell you see the Hopps Curdle—put to every Bushell of Malt 1/4 pound of Hopps which must be put int[o] your wort, when you put itt into your Copper to Boyl when boyl'd Enough Cool alittle and work that with your Yest and so put the Rest of your Wort to it as it Cooles which must be sett in panns or Small Tubs to Cool let it wor[k] tell the Yest begins to Fall in Curdles Then Tun it up stop your Barrells when it has done working This Qanity makes fourteen Gallons of—Ale very Good. . . . [The Compiler [1744], Manuscript cookbook, 97)

~ **Malt** is barley or some other grain "prepared for brewing or distilling by steeping, germinating and kiln-drying or by gelatinization, etc." (*OED*, 6:92). **Hops** are either the ripened cones of the female hop plant, used for giving a bitter flavor to malt liquors," or "a climbing perennial diecious plant . . . with rough lobed leaves shaped like those of the vine" (*OED*, 5:378).

**[Untitled]**

5734 Lbs Sugar @ w 10*d* P Lb

| | |
|---|---|
| 10 | 546 Lbs Iron[?] @ 4*d* p Lb - |
| 57840 | 18.2 |
| 2892 | 9.2 |
| 107.32 | |
| 506.1 | 745 Lb. Cotton @ 1/3[?] P Lb. |
| 253.1 | 185.4? |
| | 92.81 |
| | 46.8.9 |

~ Some of the numbers and letters were not clear.

*Contemporary Recipe #1*

**Another Way.**

After having ston'd your Barberries, to every Pound of Barberries take two Pound of fine Sugar finely powder'd and searsed, lay a Layer of this Sugar into a Gallipot, and then a Layer of Barberries; and so do till have laid all in; then stop them up close for use. (Nott, *Cook's and Confectioner's Dictionary,* #24)

*Contemporary Recipe #2*

———

**7. How to make Bisket-drops.**

Take one pound of Sugar, four Yolks of Eggs, and two Whites, a little Sack, and beat it well together one Hour; and when the Oven is ready put in a few Seeds, and one pound of Flour, and beat them well together; then butter Paper and drop it on; then put them in a gentle Oven, and as you set, Ice them with fine Sugar. (Howard, *England's Newest Way* [1710], 109)

**To Make Bisket Drops**

Beat a pound of Sugar, the Yolks of four and of two Eggs, with a little Sack; then put in a pound of Flour and a few Seeds; mix all well together; butter a paper, lay your Batter on in Spoonfuls, ice them with fine Sugar and set them in a gentle Oven. (Nott, *Cook's and Confectioner's Dictionary,* #91)

———

———

———

———

*"Jane Randolph her Cookery Book, 1743"* — *Comments*

8794 Lbs. Soap @ 57*d* P Lb
5
43970
4397
4836.7
~~1187~~
430.7
215.7

**White Puddings**

Take a pint of Cream, slice thin into it a penny loaf at Night: the next morning break it wth. a spoon; put to it 4 Yolks and 2 whites of Eggs Beaten half a pound of Marrow cut into litle pieces - half a pound of best Beef's suit: shred very small 2 L: S in powder half a pound 1 greated Nutmeg & as much Cinnamon in Powder: Two or three Spoonfulls of Canary and as much D: R: W: fill the Guts, there with and boil it on a gentle fire not pricking them in the Boiling.

**Rasberry Cakes**
[Missing]

~ The following recipe might be one she copied.

**Quince Cakes**

Take pulp of Quinces, D: L: S: of each a pound Boil over a chafing dish of quick Coals: When Enough boil'd wch. will be when laying a little of it upon a Trencher & it will come from it without cleaving to it, Then take D: L: S: searsed and strew it upon[?] the The Dresser Board upon wch. put your Quince Paste; Which when cold mould up into little Cakes and print them; after they ~~let them stand~~ are printed, let them stand in a Box upon a stool by the fire two Days or more, till they are dry, (letting the Lid of the Box be open, that the heat of the fire may the better come out and pierce the[m]

~ Food was dressed on a **dresser board** (*OED*, 3:662).

*Contemporary Recipe #1*

*Contemporary Recipe #2*

**Another Sort**

Cut a penny Loaf into thin slices, and set it to soak all night in a pint of Cream, and in the Morning break it the Bole with a Spoon, till be like Pap; then put put to it four Yelks, and two whites of Eggs, and the Marrow of one Marrow-bone cut into little pieces, and half a pound of the best Beef-suet shread extraordinary small, and season it with Nutmegs, Cinnamon and Sugar, and 2 Spoonfuls of Rose-water, and a Spoonful of Sack (and a little Musk and Ambergreese, if you please) these Puddings must be boiled on a gentle Fire, and not pricked in the boiling. (*Pastry-Cook's Vade Mecum,* 42–43)

———

**Rasberry Cakes.**

Infuse your Rasberries as your do the Currants, and let the Liquor run out; then put to the Pulp of the Rasberries as much or more of the Currant Liquor as run out of the Rasberries; put the weight in Sugar, and boil it to a Candy as exactly as you did the other.

*Note.* That the Seeds of the Rasberry are not to be mixe'd, therefore 'tis best to strain them through a thin strong Cloth, that you may get all the Pulp, and leave only the dry Seeds hard prest. Quinces and Apricock clear Cakes are made the same way, only they are scalded in fair Water, 'till tender, and not by Infusion, as this small Liquid Fruit is. (Several Hands, *Collection* [1724], 2:30)

———

**To make Printed Quidony of Quinces.**

Take two pund of *Quinces,* paired, coared, and cut in small pieces, and put them into a faire posnet, with a quart of faire water, and when they are boyled tender, put into them one pound of *Sugar* clarified, with half a pint of faire water, let them boyle till all the fruit fall to the bottom of the posnet, then let the liquid substance run through a faire linnen cloath into a clean bason, then put it into a posnet, and let it boyle till it come to a jelly, then Print it in your Moulds and turne it into your boxes. You shall know when it is ready to Print, by rouling it on the back of a Spoone. (Jenner, *Book of Fruits,* 6)

**46. To make printed Quidony of Quinces**

Take two pound of Quinces, pared, coared and cut in small pieces; put them into a clean posnet with a quart of fair water, and when they are boiled tender, put into them one pound of sugar clarified with half a pint of fair water: let them boil till all the Fruit fall to to the bottome of the Posnet, then let the liquid substance run through a fair linnen cloth into a clean Bason; then put it into a Posnet, and boil it til it come to a Jellie, then print it in your moulds, and turn it into your boxes: you shall know when it is ready to print by rowling on the back of a Spoon[.] (M. B., *Ladies Cabinet,* 20–21)

*"Jane Randolph her Cookery Book, 1743"*

*Comments*

**To make an Orange Puddings**

Take the Yolks of 12 Eggs clean them from the whites & put to them half a pound of loaf Sugar finely beaten and 2 spoonfulls of Sack and as much Rose Water, Beat it all together in a pan wth. a wooden Beater till it looks thick & white, then take half apound of Butter melted & mix it wth. the Eggs wth a little greated Nutmeg & cut it into a preserv'd Orange peal. Cut into very thin Slices & bake it in a Dish with. puffe paste in the Bottom and it will be Bak'd in half an hour

———

**Mrs Byrds' Jumbals**

Take 1 lib of Almonds Blanched in cold Water, Beat them very fine put to them 1 lib D L S & the white of one Egg Beat it to a Froth Beat them till they are mixed well together and so put them into the Squirt the Oven must be no hotter than when Bread is taken out.

~ Mrs. Byrd very likely was Maria (Taylor) Byrd (1698–1771), second wife of William Byrd II of Westover. She was a well-educated Englishwoman, who was also versed in Greek (Byrd, *Another Secret Diary,* xxxv).

While it is unusual to find **squirt** in any old cookbook, it is especially rare in American recipe books. A **squirt** was an instrument that would "force or press (a viscous or ductile material) through a small orifice; to form or fashion in this manner" (*OED,* 10:750).

**Macroons**

Take 1 pound of Almonds Blanched in cold Water Beat 'em half an hour and beat well the whites of 6 Eggs then put them to your Almonds & beat them well together put to them 3/4 of a pound of sifted Sugar beat them well together Whilst the Oven is heating Lay them on Wafer's Paper you must bake them on Wiers or tin Plates.

**Macaroone.**

Blanch a pound of sweet almonds, pound them in a mortar with rose-water; whip the whites of seven eggs to a strong froth, put in one pound of powdered sugar, beat it some time, then put in the almonds, mix them well, and drop them on sheets of paper buttered; sift sugar over and bake them quickly. Be careful not to let them get discoloured. (Randolph, *Virginia Housewife,* 146)

**To make Makerooms**

Blanch Allmonds in Cold Water one pound and beat them well for an hour or more in A Marble Morter and take the White of Eight Eggs and beat them very well tell they are white and thick then Add your Allmonds and beat them well together then put to them 3 quarters of a pound of fine Sugar finely beaten and Sifted beat them together whilst your Oven is heating then lay them on Wafer Papers in what form you please you must bake them in wiers or Tin Plates. (The Compiler [1744], Manuscript cookbook, 30).

~ Mary Randolph's version is slightly modified from Jane's recipe, but one can see the influence. The recipe given by The Compiler (1744) more closely resembles Jane's version. Did they use the same publication, or did The Compiler copy this recipe from Jane?

*Contemporary Recipe #1*

**To make an Orange-Pudding.**
Take the Peel of a large *China*-Orange, mince it exceeding small, and pound it in a Mortar; then take the Yolks of sixteen Eggs well beat with a little Rose-water, and put to it a little more than half a Pound of Sugar, and as much Butter being melted, and season it with a little Nutmeg, and put it in a dish being covered with Puff-paste, and lay Puff-paste over it, and garnish it in what form you please. (Howard, *England's Newest Way* [1710], 132)

*Contemporary Recipe #2*

**A Second Sort of Orange Pudding**
Take sixteen Yolks of Eggs, beat them fine, mix them with half a Pound of fresh Butter melted, and half a Pound of white Sugar, a little Rose-water, and a little Nutmeg. Cut the Peel of a fine large Seville Orange so thin as none of the White appears, beat it fine in a Mortar, till it is like a Paste, and by degrees mixt in the above Ingredients all together, then lay a Puff-paste all over the Dish, pour in the Ingredients, and bake it. (Glasse, *Art of Cookery*, 106)

---

**To Make Almond Jumbals (Mrs. Bethel)**
Take a pound & a half of Almonds. Beat them very fine with Orange flower & Rosewater. Then (if for white) take a pound & 1/2 of Duble refined Sugar, boyl it to a Candy, then take it off ye fire. Putt in your Almonds & break all ye Lumps & stir it over a gentle fire till it be very stiff. And when it is quite cold putt to it a pound & 1/4 more of fine sugar, & ye white of an Egg; mix it well together with Your hands, then beat it well in a morter into a past. Then with Your squart make it what forme you please; you may Color some with Chocalett or Cutchaneale. Then wett it with rosewater or juice of Limon; a very gentle oven will Bake them; it is best to sett them on something that they may not touch ye bottom of ye Oven. (Blencowe, *Receipt Book,* 7)

**To make Mackeroons.**
Blanch and beat your Almonds, with Rose or Orange-flower-Water, to every Pound of Almonds put a Pound of fine Sugar and the Whites of three large Eggs, beat to a Froth, put all to the Almonds, and beat it together very well in your Mortar; when 'tis small enough, make it scalding hot in your Preserving-pan, then drop it on Wafer paper, and bake it on Sheets of Tin; be sure the Oven be not scorching. (Several Hands, *Collection* [1724], 2:26)

**Another Way**
Take two Pound of Almonds, blanch them, and beat them in a Mortar with Orange- flower or Rose-water, add to them two Pownd of fine Sugar, and the Whites of six Eggs beat to a Froth; put these to the Almonds, and pownd them together well in a Mortar; then put them into a Preserving-pan, make them scalding hot, then drop them on Wafer Papers, or Sheets of Tin, and bake them. (Nott, *Cook's and Confectioner's Dictionary,* #2)

*"Jane Randolph her Cookery Book, 1743"*

*Comments*

**To make a Plain Cake**

3 pounds of fine flower 1 1/2 pound of Butter Beat this well together then take 5 Eggs 1/2 pint good Ale, Barme 1/4 of a pint Cream, 6 spoonfulls Rose Water. Beat all these together set it over the Coals till it is Blood Warm then strain it into your flower & Butter, mix it together as high as you can then put it in a warm Cloth before the Fire half an hour then Open it abroad 2 or 3 times till you have used 3/4 of a pound of Carriaways Cumfits then make it up as quick as you Can.

———

**A Friggasie of Chickens**

Take 2 or 3 Chickens picked dry them; cut 'em into Joints, put them into a stew pan with as much Water as will cover them, Stew them half an hour put in mace, pepper, and Salt Thyme & Parsley shred fine, Let 'em stew 1/2 an hour longer then put in 1/2 a pint of white Wine a little Lemon Juice half apound of Butter so let it stew a little more Beat 3 Eggs with a little Vinegar wth. 1/4 of a Pint of thick Cream so stir them well with the Meat.

**Fricassee of Small Chickens**

Take off the legs and wings of four chickens, separate the breasts from the backs, cut off the necks and divide the backs across, clean the gizzards nicely, put them with the livers and other parts of the chicken, after being washed clean, into a sauce pan, add pepper, salt, and a little mace, cover them with water, and stew them 'till tender, then take them out, thicken half a pint of the water with two table spoonsful of flour rubbed into four ounces of butter, add half a pint of new milk, boil all together a few minutes, then add a gill of white wine, stirring it carefully that it may not curdle, put the chickens in and continue to shake the pan until they are sufficiently hot, and serve them up. (Randolph, *Virginia Housewife*, 252)

~ Although Mary's recipe focuses more on the sauce than on how the chicken should be prepared, she preserved the basic outlines of Jane's recipe.

**French Jumblets**

Take a pound of Almonds Beat them with Cold Water & some canded Lemon peal Then put it in a pewter Dish put it on the Coals 'till it is as thick as Paste- Let it cool then roll it out into round Rings & have whites of Eggs Beaten, to dip them in roll them in Double refin'd Sugar, Sugar the Paper you lay them on & Bake them in a quick Oven.

**To make ffrench Fumballs**

Take apound of Allmonds beat them well with a little Orainge flower Water and Rose Water~together and some candid Lemon Peel amongst them in a pewter Dish on a Chafindish of Coles and stur it tell it be as thick as past then take it of the fire and let it Cool the roul them out in round~Rings and have 3 or four whites of Eggs beaten Ready and Dip them and after that roul them in double Refin'd Sugar or Single will do you must boyl it then Sugar Papers and Lay them on and bake them in a quick Oven you should have Weted them. (The Compiler [1744], Manuscript cookbook, 31)

~ Her version shows that the basic elements of making jumbles had not changed much over time.

*Contemporary Recipe #1*

**To Fricassey Chickens, or Sweet-breads.**

Take two or three Chickens (if small), wash them clean from the Blood, and cut them to pieces, not too small, set them on in as much Water as will cover them; when they boil up scum them very clean, then take them out and strain the Liquor; take part of it, to which put some Pepper whole and beaten, a blade of two of Mace, and Salt to your Taste, a little Lemon-peel, a very small Onion stuck with three or four Cloves, a quarter of a pint of White -wine warm'd and put to it; boil all these together 'till the Chickens are enough; then take three spoonfuls of Cream, a little Flower mix'd with it and put to the Chickens; shake it well over the Fire 'till it begins to thicken; then take Yolks of two Eggs well beaten, a little grated Nutmeg and Juice of Lemon beat together with the Eggs; mix these with the Liquor very carefuly, by little and little, for fear it curdle; put in half a pound of good Butter, and shake it together 'till that be melted. (Several Hands, *Collection* [1714], 18–19)

**To make Iumbolds.**

Take halfe a pound of almonds, being beaten to paste with a short cake beeing grated, & 2. egs, 2. ounces of caroway seeds, being beaten and the iuice of a Lemmon: and being brought into paste, roule it into round strings, then cast it into knots, and so bake it in an ouen, and when they are baked, yce them with Rosewater and sugar, and the white of an egge beeing beaten together, then take a feather and gild them, then put them againe into the ouen, and let them stand in, a little while, & they will be yced cleane ouer with a white yce, and so boxe them vp, and you may keep them all the yeere. (Platt, *Delights,* #16)

*Contemporary Recipe #2*

**To Fricassey Chickens**

Take three Chickens, about six Months old, flea them, and cut them in Pieces, put them into your Stew-pan, with as much Gravy and Water, as just to cover them; put in two Anchovies, well washed, some whole Pepper, Salt, and a Blade of Mace, a small Onion, and a few Cloves; set them to stew ouver a gentle clear Fire, and when they are near enough, take them from the Liquor, and fry them in Vinegar, but a very little; strain the Liquor, and take as much of it as you shall want for Sauce; put to it a little Parsley, Thyme, and Sorrel boiled green, and shred fine; half a Pint of sweet Cream, two Yolks of Eggs well beaten, some grated Nutmeg; shake them all over the Fire, till tis thick; add to it half a Pound of Butter, and shake it till it's melted, and then serve it up. (R. Smith, *Court Cookery* [1723], 1:12)

**Another Way**

Beet a Pound of blanch'd Almonds very well with Damask Rose-water, put to them two Pound of double-refin'd Sugar powdered; beat the Whites of Eggs up to a Froth, and wet the Almonds and Sugar with them; and set it a Pan over a Stove, continually stirring it, till it grows so stiff, that you may make a Paste of it. Let it be cold, and then roll it into Jumbals; strew Sugar on Pewter-plates, and lay your Jumbals upon them. (Nott, *Cook's and Confectioner's Dictionary,* 17)

*"Jane Randolph her Cookery Book, 1743"*

**To make a light Cake**

To 4 pound of dried flower put 3 ll of Currants well wash'd, pick'd, & dried 4 z. of Loaf sugar beaten fine some Nutmeg, Cinnamon & Mace, mix all together and put to it 3/4 of a pint of good ale Yeast wth a pound of Butter melted in a pint and half Cream pour it in blood Warm and add to it 9 Eggs well Beaten with a Glass of Sack, stir it all well together & let it rise by the fire while your Oven is heating. Bake it in a hoop. your Oven must be no hotter then for Manchets, and an hour or less will bake it.

**Lozanges to make**

Take a pound of double refind Sugar, pound it very fine & sift it then take a quarter of a spoonfull of Sirrup of Elicampane & half a spoonfull, the Sirrup of Colts Foot and half a quarter of a spoonfull of the Oyl of Annis seed. Drop these into the Sugar & mix it well together then take half a penny worth of Gundragon You must put it soaking in Hyssop Water over Night put as much in as will bring it into a Paste then roll it into what Form you please you may put 2 grains of Amber grease in it if you Please

**To Preserve Quinces Red**

Core & pare the Quinces them weigh them To every pound of Quinces put 3/4 of a pound of Sugar & 3/4 of a pint of Water, boil the Cores in the Sirrup Then clarifie it and strain them out & when the Sirrup has boil'd a while put in the Quinces and Boil them till they begin to be soft then set them upon Embers wch may but keep hot so let them stand sometime turning them 'till the Sirrup looks like Clarret - They must be close cover'd, then put them on a quick Fire & let them boil till they look Clear the Sirrup must be boil'd if it do not jelly.

**To Make white Marmolet**

Take 2 lb of Quinces pare them & put them into Water to keep Colour pare them as quick as you can for they will loose Colour then put them into a preserving pan Take 1/2 a pound of Sugar finely Beaten and strew on them in the pan some in the Bason and the Top, put it over a soft fire & Boil it as fast as You Can put 1/2 apound of Sugar more in the boiling when it is boiled Enough put it in Glasses.

*Comments*

~ An archaic word, **manchet** was the finest kind of small wheaten "loaf or roll"; known as "pain de maine," it was "moulded into small loaves, round & flattish, or into rolls, thicker in the middle than at the ends" (*OED*, 6:108).

———

———

———

*Contemporary Recipe #1*

———

*Contemporary Recipe #2*

———

**Excellent Lozenges for a Cough.**
Take a pound of brown Sugar-candy, and a pound of Loaf-Sugar; beat and searce them thro' a fine Sieve. Take an ounce of the Juice of Liquorish, and dissolve it in three or four spoonfuls of Hysop-water over a gentle fire; then mix your Sugar and Sugar-candy with one dram of Orrace-Powder, one dram of the Powder of Elicampane, of Gum-dragon powder'd half a dram; add one dram of the Oil of Anniseeds, and one grain of Musk. Mix all these together, and work it into a Paste; and roll them into Lozenges the bigness of a Barley-corn, or something larger. (E. Smith, *Compleat Housewife* [1729], 248–49)

———

**Quinces to Preserve Red.**
When they are pared and cored, put them into cold Water, and for every pound of Quince, take one pound of Sugar, and pint of Water, make a Syrup thereof, then put in your Quinces, and set them on a slow Fire, close covered, till you see they are of good colour, and very tender, then take them out and boil your syrup till it will Jelly. (Salmon, *Family Dictionary,* 275–76)

———

**To preserve white Quinces.**
Take a pound of Quinces, boil them with the skins on, but core them and pare them, take a quarter of a pound of Sugar, with water no more then will wet the Sugar, put the Quinces into it presently, boil them as fast as may be, and skin them, when the Sirrup is thick take it up. (Kent, *Gentlewoman's Delight,* 37)

**1. The best way to Preserve Quinces White**
First pare and core the Quinces, and boyl them in fair water till they be very tender, not covering them; Then taking them out of the water, take to every pound of them two pound of Sugar, and half a Pint of water, and boyle it to a sirrup, scumming it well; then put in some of the Jelly that is washed from the Quince kernels, and after that making it boyle a little, put in your Quinces, boyl them very fast, keeping the holes upwards, (as neer as as you can) for fear of breaking; and when they are so tender that you may thrust a rush thorow them, take them off and put them up in your glasses, having first saved some sirrup till it be cold, to fill up your glasses. (M. B., *Ladies Cabinet,* 1–2)

*"Jane Randolph her Cookery Book, 1743"*

*Comments*

**To make Ginger Bread**

Take 2 pounds of Flower rub in half a pound of Butter put to it apound of Treakel and half a pound of Sugar put 1/2 an ounce of Coriander seed & as much Caraway seed 1 1/2 oz of Ginger & if it be not tender Enough put in a little Milk make them in what shape you please & bake them on Paper's.

**Ginger Bread**

Three quarts of flour, three quarters of a pound of brown sugar, a large spoonful of pounded ginger, one teaspoonful of powdered cloves, sift it, melt half a pound of butter in a quart of rich molasses, wet the flour with it, knead it well, and bake it in a slack oven. (Randolph, *Virginia Housewife,* 159)

~ It is apparent from the first recipe that Mary kept the basic outlines of Jane's recipe except for the flavorings. In the recipe far right, she was moving away from the traditional versions with her addition of pearl ash as a leavening agent. According to Hess, this particular use of pearl ash is uniquely American (Randolph, *Virginia Housewife,* 280–81).

**Tavern Biskets**

Take 1 ll flower 1 ll Butter 2 Eggs 2 spoonfulls of Yeast make them up & roll a broad sheet out & cut them wth. the Lid of a large Canister prick them full of holes.

**Tavern Biscuit.**

To one pound of flour, add half a pound of sugar, half a pound of butter, some mace and nutmeg powdered, and a glass of brandy or wine; wet it with milk, and when well kneaded, roll it thin, cut it in shapes, and bake it quickly. (Randolph, *Virginia Housewife,* 158)

~ This is an example of a recipe that can be similar by way of title but not in terms of contents or method of preparation.

**To pickle Cucumbers**

Take 3 qts Vinegar & a qt. of Water & 4 handfulls of Salt & a little Pepper well pounded, Boil it well together pour it on your Cucumbers The Liquor must be boiled once a Fortnight and & pour'd upon the Cucumbers very hot 'till they be fit for Your Use.

**To Pickle Cucumbers.**

Gather them full grown, but quite young; take off the green rind, and slice them tolerably thick; put a layer in a deep dish, strew over it some chopped onion and salt, do this until they are all in; sprinkle salt on the top, let them stand six hours, put them in a colander, when all the liquor has run off, put them in a pot, strew a little cayenne pepper over each layer, and cover them with strong cold vinegar; when the pot is full, pour on some sweet oil and tie it up close. (Randolph, *Virginia Housewife,* 203–4)

~ Mary's recipe could not be more different from Jane's version. Besides the ingredients and method of preparation, she used cold instead of hot vinegar. A **fortnight** is measured as fourteen nights or two weeks (*OED,* 4:478).

**To make minced Pyes**

To a pound of Neets Tongue 2 pounds of Beef's suit 3 Do. of Currants, Cloves, mace & Nutmeg & a little Salt Instead of Pippins Squease the Juices of 7 or 8 sower Oranges 2 Lemons, a little Canded Orange & lemon peal shred very fine Sweeten it to yr. Taste & put what perfume you like Best

———

*Contemporary Recipe #1*

**To make another sort of Ginger-bread.**
Take a pound and half of *London* Treacle, two Eggs beaten, a pound of Butter melted, half a pound of brown Sugar, one ounce of beaten Ginger; and of Cloves, Mace, Coriander-seeds and Carraway-seeds, of each half an ounce; mix all these together with as much Flour as will knead it into a Paste; roll it out, and cut it into what Form you please. Bake it in a quick Oven on Tin-Plates; a little time will bake it[.] (E. Smith, *Compleat Housewife* [1729], 134)

*Contemporary Recipe #2*

**Plebian Ginger Bread**
Mix three large spoonsful of pounded ginger with three quarts of flour, sift it, dissolve three teaspoonsful of pearl ash in a cup of water, and pour it on the flour; melt half a pound of butter in a quart of molasses, mix it with the flour, knead it well, cut it in shapes, and bake it. (Randolph, *Virginia Housewife,* 159)

**Another sort of little Cakes.**
Take a pound of Flour, and a pound of Butter. Rub the Butter into the Flour, two spoonfuls of Yeast, and two Eggs. Make it up into a Paste, slick white Paper, roll your Paste out the thickness of a Crown, cut them out with the top of a Tin Canister; sift fine Sugar over them, and lay them on the slick'd Paper. Bake them after Tarts an hour. (E. Smith, *Compleat Housewife* [1729], 133)

**To make Biskets.**
To a quart of Flour, take a quarter of a pound of Butter, and a quarter of a pound of Sugar, one Egg, and what Carraway-seeds you please, wet the Milk as stiff as you can; then roll them out very thin; cut them with a small Glass. Bake them on Tin-Plates, your Oven must be slack. Prick them very well just as you set them in, and keep them dry when baked. (E. Smith, *Compleat Housewife* [1729], 134)

**Cowcumbers to Pickle:**
Take Cowcumbers, and wipe them clean, then put them into a Pot, strowing between every lay of Cowcumbers, bruised Pepper, Cloves, and large Mace, bruised Pepper, a little whole Ginger, a little Fennel, and a little Dill, boil them together and skim them, then take it off the Fire, and pour it on your Cowcumbers, stove them in very close: And when the Pickle is stale, take them out, and put in fresh Vinegar, Cloves, Mace, Pepper, Salt, Fenell and Dill. (Salmon, *Family Dictionary,* 64)

———

**To make Minced Pies.**
Take a large Neats tongue, shread it very well, three pound and a half of Suet very well shread, currans three pound, halfe an ounce of beaten Cloves and Mace, season it with Salt when you think't fit, halfe a preserved Orange, or instead of it Orange Pils, a quarter of a pound of Sugar, a little Lemon Pill sliced very thin, put all these together very well, put to it two spoonfuls of Verjuyce, and a quarter of a Pint of Sack, &c. (W. M., *Compleat Cook,* 74–75)

———

*"Jane Randolph her Cookery Book, 1743"*

**To make Gooseberry Cream**

Take the Yolks of 7 Eggs 2 quarts of Cream & the pulp of a qt of Gooseberries Boil the Cream then let it stand till the Steam is of and then mix it wth. the Eggs then put & on the Fire 'till tis ready to Boil Sweeten the Pulp to your Taste, & pour the Cream and Eggs together & put it in yr Dishes

**Sauce for Hare**

Take some Beef and boil it with Salt Pepper and Nutmeg some Mace & a little Anchovie & let it boil very well & then Boil it up wth. Butter you may put in some Clarret if you will.

**To Candy Angillica**

Take the tenderest stalk of Angillica Boil it & strip it then take the Weight thereof in Sugar & as much Water as will wet the Sugar set it over the Fire 'till it begins to be thick then put in the Angillica Let it simper over a soft fire till it grows thick, turn it often to keep it from Burning when you find it begin to candy Open it and lay it abroad to dry.

**To make a liquid Soap**

Take 2 oz. of hard Soap 2 oz. pot Ashes a pint of Brandy a little Cloves, Mace & Cinnamon just boil it up - let it stand to cool then pour it off & keep it you may add sweet Gum in it you must put in the spice again and stop it Close.

Pr Doctr. Tscheffiely

**To make lie of Pot Ashes**

Make a strong lime Water strong Enough to bear an Egg it must be made with boiling Water then put it on your Pot Ashes in the same Manner your other lie is made.

**A Plumb Cake pr Mrs. Cary**

Take 6 ll flower, nutmegs, Mace, Cinnamon of Each 1/2 an Oz mix them in the Flower 6 ll Currants plump them well one ll Sugar half ot if mixt in the Currts the rest in the flower 1 qt. Cream boil'd then slice 1 ll and half Butter in the Cream to melt one pint and half of Yeast 2 doz Eggs half the Whites strain your Eggs & Yest on one side of the Flower the Cream & Butter on

*Comments*

~ This recipe is different from another recipe of the same name penned on a later page of her manuscript.

———

———

**Liquid Soap**

Take two Ounces Pot ashes, a Pint of Brandy a quarter of an ounce of Mace, Cloves, Cinnamon, a little Orange Peel, two Ounces Hard Soap. you may add Sweet Gum to it if you Please Just Boil it up and it is Done

By Mrs. Jane Randolph[.] (The Compiler [1744], Manuscript cookbook, 88)

~ Dr. Tschiffeli, a Swiss "Chemist and Practitioner in Physick," also assayed metals and ores in Richmond (*Virginia Gazette,* 9 June 1738, 4).

~ No close parallels have been found to date.

———

*Contemporary Recipe #1*

*Contemporary Recipe #2*

---

**To make Sauce for Venison, or a Hare.**

Take half a Pint of Claret, and a little Oyster-liquhr, and put to it some good Gravy, and a large Onion stuck with cloves, and some whole Cinnamon and Nutmeg cut in slices; then let it boil till the Onion is boil'd tender; then take out the Onion and whole Spice, and put to it three Anchovies, and a Piece of Butter, shake it well together, and send it to the Table. (Howard, *England's Newest Way* [1710], 137)

**Sauce for a Hare**

Take half a Pint of Red-Wine, and a little Oyster-Liquor, and put to it some good Gravy, and a large Onion stuck with Cloves, and some whole Cinnamon, and Nutmeg, cut in Slices; then let it boil 'till the Onion is boil'd tender; then take out the Onion and whole Spice, and put to it three Anchovies, and a Piece of Butter, shake it up well together, and send it to the Table. (*Lady's Companion,* 1:447)

---

**To candy Angelica**

Boil the Stalks of Angelica in Water, till they are tender; then peel them, and put them into other warm Water, and cover them; let them stand over a gentle Fire till they become very green; then lay them on a Cloth to dry; take their weight in fine Sugar, with a little Rose-water, and boil it to a Candy height. Then put in your Angelica, boil them up quick; then take them out and dry them for use. (Nott, *Cook's and Confectioner's Dictionary,* #54)

---

---

**A Plum Cake.**

TAKE five pounds of fine Flour, and put to it half a pound of Sugar; and of Nutmegs, Cloves, and Mace finely beaten, of each half an ounce, and a little Salt, mix these well together, then take a quart of Cream, let it boil, and take it off, and cut into it three pounds of fresh Butter, let it stand till 'tis melted, and when 'tis blood warm mix with it a quart of Ale-yeast, and a pint of

**Plumb Cake Mrs. Cary or Pudding**

1¼ lbs Flour 1 lb Sugar 1 lb Butter 12 Eggs-cream the Butter and Flour together till quite light Beat the Yolks and whites of Eggs seperately beat the sugar into the Yolks and when light mix the whites then keep them with the Butter and Flour-and put in 1¼ lbs stoned Raisins, cut up or the same of Currans with 3 spoonfuls beaten mace and 2 Wine Glasses French Brandy—

*"Jane Randolph her Cookery Book, 1743"*

the other The Cream must be hot then mix them all together make the Cake very tender Let it stand by the fire 'till the Oven is hot make your Coffin of Paper well Butter'd, let it stand in the Oven 2 hours.

**A very good plain Cake**

Take 3 lb of Flower, 3/4 of a pound of Butter 3/4 of a pound of a pound of Sugar 3/4 of a pint of Yest & Spice to your Taste make it up with warm milk.

**A very good sauce for broil'd Chickens**

Take 1/2 a pint of Gravy a Shalott, parsley & Thyme shred Small thicken it wth. a bit of Butter

**To Clear Soap**

When you refine your soap to every lb of Do.put in 6 lb. of Lie.

**To make lie for Pot Ashes**

You must have a bottom to your Tub full of holes then cover it wth. Straw, sprinkle on it Lime then make your Ashes moist Enough to make into Balls Then put them on your Lime stir them well & fill the Tub with boiling Water & cover it Close let it stand 24 hours then draw off the first lie put it by & cover it Close & Then put up more Water to make a second lie & draw that off & cover it & so a 3d put on the 1st lie & put a rowl of Woolen Cloth 1 End in the Lie & the other over the side of the Pot so that the liquor run through the Cloths on the hearth wch. must be hot then draw a Lie from that

**Hard Soap**

[Missing]

*Comments*

———

~ Here is another meat-related dish that was listed in the index but missing from the manuscript.

———

~ Given all these soap formulas and instructions for making pot ashes, it is not surprising that Mary Randolph continued this tradition. However, she wrote her own set of long instructions and careful observations on soap making. Her version reflected her choices and the times she lived in (see Randolph, *Virginia Housewife*, 222–23).

**Hard Soap**

Take six bushells of Ashes half a bushell quick lime make your False~Bottom with a baskett. mix your ashes and lime very well before you Put it in the Tub. so that it will Roll up in Balls. then Pack it Pretty Tite in the Cask and overtop it with Boyling water this being done Cover it Close Immediately let it Stand for about twelve Hours. Put as much fatt. as you think will do. for the Pott. then beat it up till it be Well mixed, with three quarts of Cool Lye, Set it Boyling as fast as you Can as it Boyls feed it with lye, by Mrs. Jane Randolph[.] (The Compiler [1744], Manuscript cookbook, 89)

*Contemporary Recipe #1*

Sack, and twenty Eggs, ten whites well beaten; put six pounds of Currants to your Flour, and make a hole in the middle, and pour in the Milk and other things, and make up your Cake, mixing it well with your Hands; cover it warm, and set it before the fire to rise for half an hour; then put it in the Hoop; if the Oven be hot two hours will bake it; the Oven must be quick; you may perfume it with Ambergrease, or put Sweet-meats in it if you please. Ice it when cold, and paper it up. (E. Smith, *Compleat Housewife* [1729], 123–24)

*Contemporary Recipe #2*

It must be bak'd in a quick Oven and the top must be hot enough to turn it unless covered with Paper-This very nice in a Pudding but too large for amoderate company. (Tucker Coalter, *Cookbook,* 37)

*"Jane Randolph her Cookery Book, 1743"*

*Comments*

**To make Gooseberry Cream**

Take some preserv'd Gooseberries & having some good Cream season'd with Cinnamon, Nutmeg, mace, & Sugar, rose Water and Eggs, dish it up & when 'tis cold take up the Gooseberries, wth. a pin and Stick them in rounds as thick as they can lie upon the Cream.

———

**Cheese Cakes the best Way**

Take 2 Gallons new Milk put into it 2½ spoonfulls of Runnet when the Cheese is come take a scumming dish and whey it well then put in a Sifter and strain it well there then to 2 qts Curds take 1 pt. of good thick Cream 1 lb Butter 1 doz. Eggs 1½ lb Currants, Cloves, Nutmegs, mace & half a pound of Sugar a quarter of a pt. of rose Water mix all together and bake it in puff Paste.

**To make Cheese Cakes**

To two quarts of Curds put one quart of good thick Cream 1 pound Butter 12 Egg[s] 1½ lb Currants spice to your Tast half a pound Sugr. a quarter of a point Rose Water, mix alltogether and Bake it in puff past. To turn your milk put 2 spoons full of Runnet into 2 Galls. of Milk before you put any thing into ye Curds beat them very fine in a Morte[r.] (The Compiler [1744], Manuscript cookbook)

~ While not exactly identical, this version is basically similar to Jane (Bolling) Randolph's recipe and the published recipes to the right.

**Bisket Bread**

Take half a peck of Flower the whites of 6 Eggs a pint of Yest as much warm Water as will make it into a Paste so bake it in a long roll when it is 2 days old pare it and slice it then Sugar it & dry it in an Oven & keep it all the Year.

———

**Good Ale**

Take 3 Bushs. Malt ½ high 1½ pail dry'd Let Your Water boil then put into your mashing Tub when the Steem is gone off so as you may see your Face; then put your Malt & after mashing it well cover it with a Blanket Let it stand 2 hours then draw it off Slow - Then boil it 3 or 4 hours 'till the hops curdle when boiled Enough Cool a little & work that wth your Yest & so put the rest of your wort in as it Cools wch. must be set in small Tubbs Let it work till your Yest begins to curdle then turn it up & stop your Barrell when it has done Working.

N B To every bush:ll Malt ¼ of a pound of hops NB.

**Good Ale**

Take three Bushels of Malt half high and the other Pale~Dryed, let your water boyl then Pour it into the Mashing Tub, let it stand till the Steem is gone off so as you may See your face in it than Put in your Malt, wash it well and Cover it with a Blanket let it Stand two hours then draw it of Slow and boyl it two hours then work a Little of it with yeast then as it Cools Put in more till you have it all in. Put your hop in the Tub that you draw your Bear of in, lesse it should not do well.

By Mrs. Jane Randolph (The Compiler [1744], Manuscript cookbook, 88)

~ **Wort** alludes to the "infusion of malt or other grain which after fermentation becomes beer," or with spirits, "unfermented beer"; it is also a "plant, herb, or vegetable, used for food and medicine, and is

*Contemporary Recipe #1*

**To make Gooseberry Cream**

First boyle, or you may preserve your Gooseberries, then having a clear Cream, boyled up and seasoned, with old Cinamon, Nutmeg, Mace, Sugar, Rose-water and Eggs, dish it up and when it is cold, take up the Gooseberries with a pin, and stick them on in rounds as thick as they can lye upon the said Cream; garnishing your Dish with them; and strow them over with the finest Sugar, and serve them up. (Cromwell, *Court & Kitchen,* 60)

**To make a Cheese-cake the best way**

Take two gallons of new milk, put into it two spoonfuls and a half a runnet, heat the milk little less then blood-warm, cover it close with a cloth, until you see the cheese be gathered, then with a scumming dish gently take out the whay, so when you have drained the curd as clean as you can, put the curd into a Sieve, and let it drain very well there, then to two quarts of curd take a quart of thick cream, a pound of sweet butter, twelve eggs, a pound and a half of currants, a penny worth of cloves, nutmeg and mace beaten, half a pound of good sugar, a quarter of a pint of rose-water, so mingle it well together, and put it in puff-paste. (Cromwell, *Court & Kitchen,* 136–37)

**7. To make Bisket-bread**

Take half a peck of Flower fine, two Ounces of Anniseeds, two Ounces of Corriander- seed, the whites of six Eggs, a pint of Ale-Yeast, with as much warm-water, as will make it up into a Paste, so bake it in a long Roul; when it is two days old, pare it, and slice it, then Sugar it, and dry it in an Oven, and so keep it all the Year. (Woolley, *Compleat Cook's Guide,* 244)

**To brew Ale, or Beer**

Put half a Hogshead of Water into your Copper, cover it with Bran; when it is scalding hot, put a third Part of it into the mashing Tub, and let it stand till the Steam is so far spent that you can see your Face in the Liquor; then put in two Bushels of Malt; stir the Malt and Liquor well together; in the mean time let the rest of the Water boil in the Copper; then put out the Fire, that the Heat of the Liquor may be allay'd; then put the other Part of it into the mashing Tub, and stir it well again; put in also a Shovel or two of hot Coles to take off any ill Taint of the Malt, and so let it stand for two Hours. In the mean time heat half a Hogshead more of Liquor, and when you have drawn off your first Wort, put Part of it upon the Grains, and stir in a Bushel and half more of fresh Malt; then put in the rest of the Liquor, and stir it as before; then put your first Wort into the Copper again making it scalding hot, and put

*Contemporary Recipe #2*

**To make Gooseberry Cream**

First preserve your Gooseberries (as you are taught in the Book of Preserves) then having a clear Cream, boyled up, and seasoned, with old Cinamon, Nutmeg, Mace, Sugar, Rose-water and Eggs, (as you have read before) dish it up, and when it is cold, take up your Gooseberries with a pin and stick them on in rows, as thick as they can lie upon the said Cream; Garnish your dish with them; strow them over with Sugar, and send them up. (Rabisha, *Whole Body* [1673], 41)

**3. To make Cheese-Cakes, the best way**

Take two Gallons of New Milk, put into them two spoonfuls and a half of Runnet, heat the Milk little less than Blod-warm, cover it close with a Cloath, till you see the Cheese be gathered, then with a scumming-dish gently take over the whey, when you have dreyn'd the Curd as clean as you can, put it into a Siev, and let it drain very well there; then to two quart of Curds, take a quart of thick Cream, a pound of Sweet Butter, twelve Eggs, a pound and half of Currans, a penny worth of Cloves, Nutmeg and Mace beaten, half a pound of good Sugar, a quarter of a pint of Rose-water; mingle it well together, and put it into Puff-paste. (Woolley, *Compleat Cook's Guide,* 242–43)

———

———

*"Jane Randolph her Cookery Book, 1743"* | *Comments*

often called pot-herb. It fell out of use after the mid-seventeenth century" (*OED*, XII: 325).

**Small Beer**

Have your Water ready boil'd agst your Ale is run off then putt it on your Grains By Degrees till it is of the same Hight as it was before, Let it stand 2 hours then draw it off slow then boil it with the hops that came out off the Ale Boil it an hour or more then work it as before it you think these hops won't doe put in more

**Small Beer**

After this Ale you must have your Water Ready boyl'd against yor Ale is Runn off your Malt and put it by degrees on your Granes tell it is of the hight as it was before let it stand 2 hours then let it Run of slow as the other and boyl it wi[th] the hopps that comes out of the Ale but if you think them hopps not Enoug[h] put in with Discretion boyl this an hour or more, Cool it and work it [as] the Ale this will make Sixteen Gallons of Good Small Beer—[.] (The Compiler, [1744], Manuscript cookbook, 97)

~ **Small beer** is defined as a weak beer (*OED*, 9:759).

**To make Metheglein**

Make your honey and water strong Enough to bare an Egg then boil it away to abt. 6 Inches then take it off and set it to cool the Yest must be very good, - work'd very well by the fire then mix it off with your wort wch. must be a little warm than set it to work, being cover'd- with a Blankett when it has done working turn it into a clean dry Cask & take 1 Oz. Cloves Do of Mace & as much Ginger some Nutmeg groasly beaten tie them up in a rag and put them up into the Cask & stop it very well Let it stand 3 months & then bottle it 7 weeks time it will be fit to drink.

Pr mrs Mary Randolph

NB Pr Mrs Mary Randolph

You must brew this drink the first of October

~ This is a family recipe donated by Mary (Isham) Randolph, the matriarch of the Randolph family. There are myriad variations on how metheglin should be made, but all agreed that water, honey, and a bag of herbs are the essential ingredients.

**Tansie very good**

Take a pint of Milk as much Cream as much Spinage juice fifteen Eggs a little Salt leave out the 1/2 the whites strain them into the other things put in near a pint of greated Bread or Bisket a whole Nutmeg greated

*Contemporary Recipe #1*

part of it into into a second mashing Tub, and when the Steam is gone, stir in it a Bushel and half more of fresh Malt; then put in the rest of the Wort and stir it well, and let it stand two Hours; then heat another half Hogshead of Water, and when what was put into the first mashing Tub has stood two Hours, draw it off, and also that Wort in the second mashing tub, and take the Grains out of the second mashing Tub, and put them into the first; then put the Liquor in the Copper into it, and let it stand an Hour and an half; in the mean time heat another half Hogshead of Water, and put upon the Grains, and let it stand as before. Boil the first Wort with a Pound of Hops for two Hours, or till it looks curdly for Beer; boil the second Wort with six Ounces of Hops for Ale, an Hour and a half, and boil the Hops of both Worts in your other Liquor for Table Beer, an Hour and a half. (Nott, *Cook's and Confectioner's Dictionary,* #1)

*Contemporary Recipe #2*

**A very good Tansie**

Take a pint of Milk, and a pint of Cream, about a pint of Juice of spinnage, which must be well dried, after washing, before you stamp it; strain it and pour it in, beat fifteen Eggs, with a little Salt, leave out eight

**To make a Tansy to bake.**

TAKE twenty Eggs, but eight Whites, beat the Eggs very well, and strain them into a quart of thick cream, one Nutmeg, and three *Naples*-biskets grated as much juice of Spinage, with a sprig or two of Tansy, as will

*"Jane Randolph her Cookery Book, 1743"* | *Comments*

as much Sugar as will make it very sweet thicken over the fire in a Skillet as thick as a hasty Pudding then butter a Dish & bake it half an hour.

**Flummery**

Put 3 large handfulls of Oat meal ground fine into 2 qts of Water Let it steep 24 hours then pour of the clear Water & put the same Quantity ~~of Water~~ on it again then strain it through a fine hair sifter & boil it 'till 'tis as thick as hasty Pudding Stir it all the while to make it smooth When you put it on the fire put in one spoonfull of Sugar & 2 of Oatmeal water When it is boiled Enough put it into shallow Dishes.

~ The following recipe was also utilized by Anonymous (1700) in her culinary manuscript.

**A rich plumb Pudding**

Take 1 lb Suit shred fine 1 lb Rai[sins] Ston'd 4 spoonfulls of Flower & 4 Do. of Sugar 5 Eggs but 3 whites beats the Eggs wth. a little Sack & salt boil 4 hours at Least

———

**London Wiggs**

Take 1/4 of a peck of Flower put to it 1/2 a pound of Sugar as much Carraways Mix these and put them to the fire to dry & melt 1 1/2 pound Butter hot over the fire stir it often and add to it near a qt of good milk or Cream when the butter is melted in the Cream pour it into the middle of the Flower a little Sack a pint & half of good Yest Let stand before the Fire to rise Before you lay them on tin plates to bake.

———

**Plumb Cake Extraordinary**

Take 7 lb of Flower & 2 1/2 lb Butter & put the Butter into the Flower 7 lb Currants 2 Nutmegs 1/2 an Oz Mace 1/4 an Oz of Cloves 7 lb Sugar 16 Eggs leave out 4 whites put a full pt & half of good Yest warm as much Cream as you think will wet it pour Sack to Cream to make it as thick as Batter, Beat 1 lb Almonds wth. Sack or O.F. Water grosly beaten put in a pound of Candied Orange Lemon & Citron & mix all and put it into your hoop wth a paste under it to save the Bottom

**An Extraordinary plum cake.**

Take Seven Pound of fine Flower and two Pound and half of Butter, Put the butter unto the Flower Seven Pounds of Currants and two large Nuttmeggs, with half an Ounce of Mace and a Quarter of an Ounce of Cloves all Finely beat and Grated four Pound of Sugar, Sixteen Eggs leaving out four whites. Put in a full Pint and half of ale Yeast, Warm as much Cream as you think will wet it and Pour Sack to your Cream to make it as thick as butter, beat also one Pound of Allmonds with Sack and Orange Flower water, but dont let them be fine, but Grosly Beat. Put in a Pound of Candyed Orange, Lemon, and Citron Peel or more if you desire it very

*Contemporary Recipe #1*

Whites, strain them into the other things, put in near a pint of grated Bread or Bisket, grated in a whole large Nutmeg, and as much Sugar as will make it very sweet, thicken it over the Fire as thick as a Hasty-Pudding; put it into a butter'd Dish, and a Cool Oven; Half an Hour bakes it. (Several Hands, *Collection* [1714], 61)

*Contemporary Recipe #2*

make it as green as Grass; sweeten it to your taste; then butter your Dish very well, and set it into an Oven, no hotter than for Custrards; watch it, and as soon as 'tis done, take it out of the Oven, and turn it on a Pye-plate; scrape Sugar, and squeese Orange upon it. Garnish the Dish with Orange and lemon, and serve it up. (E. Smith, *Compleat Housewife* [1729], 92)

**To make a pretty Sort of Flummery**

Put three large handfuls of Oatmeal ground small, into two quarts of Fair Water, let it Steep a Day and Night; then pour off the clear Water, and put the Same quantity of fresh Water to it; strain it through a fine Hair-Sieve, and boil it 'till 'tis as thick as Hasty-pudding; stir it all the while, that it may be extremely smooth; (and when you first strain it out, before you set it on the Fire, put in one spoonful of sugar, and two of good Orange-flow(er) Water,) When 'tis boil'd enough, pour it into shallow Dishes, for your Use. (Several Hands, *Collection* [1714], 74)

———

**An excellent Plumb - Pudding**

Take one pound of Suet, shred very small and sifted, one pound of Raisons ston'd, and four spoonfuls of Flower, and four spoonfuls of Sugar, five Eggs, but three Whites; beat the Eggs with a little Salt: Tie it up close, and boil it four Hours at least. (Several Hands, *Collection* [1714], 89)

———

**The London Wiggs**

Take a quarter of a peck of Flower, put to it half a pound of Sugar, and as much Carraways, smooth or rough, as you like; mix these and set them to the Fire to dry, and then make a pound and half of Butter hot over a gentle Fire; stir it often, and add to it near a quart of good Milk or Cream; when the Butter is melted in the Cream, pour it into the middle of the Flower, and to it pour a little Sack, and full a pint and half of very good Ale- yeast; let it stand be-fore the Fire to rise, before you lay them on your Tin-plates to bake. (Several Hands, *Collection* [1714], 92)

———

**A Plumb Cake extraordinary.**

Take seven pound of fine Flower, and two pound and half of Butter, put the Butter into the Flower; seven pound of Currants, and two large Nutmegs, with half an ounce of Mace, and a quarter of an ounce of Cloves, all finely beat and grated; one pound of Sugar, sixteen Eggs, leaving out four Whites, put in a full pint and half of Ale-yeast; warm as much Cream as you think will wet it, and pour Sack to your Cream, to make it as thick as Batter; beat also one pound of Almonds, with Sack or Orange-flower-Water; but don't let them be fine, but grosly beat; put in a pound of Candy'd Orange, Lemon & Citron-peel, or more, if you desire

———

*"Jane Randolph her Cookery Book, 1743"* | *Comments*

Rich mix all and Put into your Hoop~with a Paste under it to Save the Bottom. This was Given by one of the Housewives in England and is as good as ever was made/ (The Compiler [1744], Manuscript cookbook, 88)

~ The recipe for "Plumb Cake Extraordinary" was apparently quite popular among different housewives. Mary Randolph had her own recipe for "A Rich Fruit Cake," which ran along the same basic lines but was modernized (see Randolph, *Virginia Housewife,* 162–63).

**Icing for the Cake**

The whites of 5 Eggs whipt of up to a Froth 1 lb D. L. S. whip it all the whi(le) The Cake is baking.

———

**Wild Fowl to stew**

Half roast them then set them over a Chafing Dish of Coals wth. a pint of Clarret as much Gravey season'd wth a Shallot & spice stew it 'till it is well mixt.

———

**Onions to pickle**

Take little Onions, peal them & put them in salt & Water all night then pour that away & put more Stronger than the 1st Set them on the in this Just let 'em boil & scum them take em of the Fire to cool make a pickle of white Vinegar pepper & mace & Ginger Let all stand to be cool then dry the Onions from the brine & put 'em into the pickle you may add mustard seed.

———

**French Bread**

Take a qt. of flower put to it 3 spoonfulls of Yest an equal Quantity of & Water warm the Bigness of a Walnut of Butter a little salt make it up light & drop 'em on Tinn plates, Set them Before the fire to rise Bake them in a Quick Oven you may add 3 Eggs but 1 white if you like it.

———

*Contemporary Recipe #1*

it very rich; mix all and put it into your Hoop with a Paste under it to save the bottom. This was given by one of the nicest House-wives in *England;* and is as good as ever was made[.] (Several Hands, *Collection* [1714], 93–94)

**Iceing for the Cake**

Take the Whites of five Eggs, whipt up to a froth and put a pound of Double-refin'd sugar, sifted, a grain of Ambergreese, and three spoonfuls of Orange-flower-water; whip it all the while the Cake is in the Oven; when it comes out of the Oven, Ice it; but set it no more: Leave out the Perfume if it be offensive. (Several Hands, *Collection* [1714], 94)

**To Stew Wild-Fowl**

Half roast them, and cut into Pieces, set them over a Chafing-dish of Coals, add half a Pint of Claret, and as much good Gravy, which must be first boil'd and season'd wih Shallot and Spice; let it stew in this Liquor till 'tis high Colour'd and well mix'd, and they eat better than off the Spit. (Several Hands, *Collection* [1724], 2:7)

**To Pickle Small Onions.**

Take small Onions, peel of the outward Skin, and put them in Salt and Water all Night; pour that away, and put a fresh Pickle of Salt and Water, made stronger than the first; set them on the Fire in this, and let them just boil, scum them well, and take them off the Fire, set them by to cool, and make a Pickle of White-wine Vinegar, Pepper, Mace, and a little Ginger; let all stand to be cold, then dry the Onions from the Brine, and put them into the Pickle; if you add Mustard-seed, they will keep some Time: They taste and look very pretty among green Pickles. (Several Hands, *Collection* [1724], 2:17–18)

———

*Contemporary Recipe #2*

———

———

———

———

*"Jane Randolph her Cookery Book, 1743"* | *Comments*

**Puffs**

Thicken a pint of milk with flower then pour it out to cool then do to it three Eggs, a little Salt and Shugar beat all in a morter fry them in Lard with a Quick fire they must be dropt Small, and will be Round, &[c]

———

**Herb Dumplins**

Take some grated bread Sifted through a Cullander Almost as much Suit Shred fine, put in thyme Shugar marjoram Savory & pennerial a like Quantity Let all be Shred Very fine put some Currants a spoonfull of Shugar Beat two Eggs two Spoonfuls of Sack mix all the others together a little nutmeg, & Rub yr hands with flower & Roul them up as big as Tinnis Balls boil them half an hour melt yr. Butter wit[h] a glass of Sack & Strew Shugar [ov]er them; Let your water Boil before your water boil Juce of Lemon and orange garnish with Barberies

~ **Pennerial** is **pennyroyal,** "a species of mint" that was esteemed for its "supposed medicinal virtures" (*OED,* 7:650).

**Queens Pancakes**

Take 6 Eggs, well beat a pound & half of Flower mixt together with Cream a pound Sweet Butter Melted one Nutmeg grat'd a little Salt fry them with =out any thing on a quick fire

———

**To Collar Els**

Skin them & split th[e][m down the back, & bone them Season them with nutmeg pepper, & Salt, & sweet herbs Sprinkle the seasoning on the Inside of the Els, roul them Like a Collar of braun in a Cloath boil Very tender in Vinagar Salt and water when they are cold put them into the liquor and keep them

———

| *Contemporary Recipe #1* | *Contemporary Recipe #2* |
| --- | --- |
| **Puffs to Fry instead of Fritters.** Take a pint of Milk, and mix as much Flower as will make it a Hasty Pudding; take care to mix it with a little of the Milk at first, and so more and more, that when you set it on the Fire to thicken, it may not grow lumpy; pour it out to cool, and then add to it three Eggs, a little Salt and Sugar, beat all in a Morter; fry them in good Lard over a quick Fire: They are to be drop'd small, and will be round. (Several Hands, *Collection* [1724], 2:24) | ——— |
| **Herb Dumplins.** Take the Crumb of a Two-penny Loaf grated, sift it through a Cullender, take almost as much fresh Beef suet, shred and sifted, put in Thyme, sweet Marjoram, Savory, and as much Penny-royal as all the other Herbs together; let all be shred extreamly small; put in a few Currants neatly pick'd and wash'd, a little Salt, grated Nutmeg, and a spoonful of Sugar, beat two Eggs with two spoonfuls of Sack, mingle all these; rub a little Flower on your Hands, and roll them up as big as Tennis Balls; boil them half an Hour; melt your Butter with a Glass of Sack, and strew Sugar over them; 'tis best to let your Water boil before you put them in. (Several Hands, *Collection* [1724], 2:25) | ——— |
| **Queen's Pancakes** Take six Eggs, well beat, and a Pound and half of Flower, mix'd together with Cream, and a Pound of sweet Butter melted, and one Nutmeg grated; fry them in a Pan, without any thing in it, on a quick Fire. (R. Smith, *Court Cookery* [1723], 69) | ——— |
| **Another Way** Cut two large Eels down the back, after you have skin'd them, and take out the Bone; chop a Handful of sweet Herbs, and season them with Nutmeg, Pepper, and Salt; strew the Herbs on the Inside of the Eel; roll them up like a Collar of Brawn; put them in a Cloth, and boil them very tender in vinegar and Salt; take them up, and when they are cold, put them into the Liquor for three or four Days; if too sharp, put in Water when you boil them. (R. Smith, *Court Cookery* [1723], 1:92–93) | **To collar Eels.** TAKE your Eel and cut it open, take out the Bones, and cut off the Head and Tail, and lay the Eel flat on a Dresser, and shred Sage as fine as possible, and mix it with black Pepper beat, Nutmeg grated, and Salt, and lay it all over the Eel, and roll it up hard in little Cloths, and tye it up tight at each end; then set over some Water with Pepper and Salt, five or six Cloves, three or four blades of Mace, a Bay-leaf or two; boil it and the Bones and Head and Tail well together; then take out the Head and Tail and put it away, and put in your Eels, and let them boil till they are tender; then take them out of the Liquor, and boil the Liquor longer; then take it off, and when 'tis cold, put it to your Eels, but do not take off the little Cloths till you use them. (E. Smith, *Compleat Housewife* [1729], 7) |

*"Jane Randolph her Cookery Book, 1743"*

*Comments*

**Sturgeon to keep**

Boil it very tender in Salt & water, then take it up to cool when the liquor is cold Scim it clean; then take Some of that Liquor as muc[h] Sharp Vinagar some cloves Mace nutmeg & pepper boil it up then when tis cold put in yr. Sturgin cover it clos dont make it to Salt

———

**To Pickle Beets Rots or turnips**

Boil yr. beet roots in water Salt and Spice, a pint Vinagar when they are 1/2 boiled put in yr. turnips Being pard, when they are boild; take them of & keep them in this pickle

**Red Beet Roots**

Are not so much used as they deserve to be; they are dressed in the same way as parsnips, only neither scraped nor cut till after they are boiled; they will take from an hour and a half to three hours in boiling, according to their size; to be sent to the table with salt fish, boiled beef, &c. When young, large, and juicy, it is a very good variety, an excellent garnish, and easily converted into a very cheap and pleasant pickle. (Randolph, *Virginia Housewife,* 123)

~ It is either from Anonymous (1700) or E. Kidder's recipe that Jane (Bolling) Randolph copied her recipe for beet roots. Mary Randolph's version is a good example of her streamlined recipes.

**Carrot Pudding**

Take a large Carrot Boild tender rub'd through a hare sifter half a pound- melted butter 8 Eggs 1/2 the[ir] whites 3 Spoonfulls Sack Rose water, half a pint Cream Nutmeg, greated Bread or Naples biskit little bake 1/2 an hour

———

**Apple Fritters**

Take fine dried flower, to Every Spoonfull of flower, take a Sponfull milk, or & as much Cream & an Egg 1/2 an nutmeg grated as much mace 3 spoonfuls Sack mix all these together pair the apples & Slice þm in round Slices one Each Fritter

**Apple Fritters.**

Pare some apples and cut them in thin slices, put them in a bowl, with a glass of brandy, some white wine, a quarter of a pound of pounded sugar, a little cinnamon finely powdered and the rind of a lemon grated; let them stand some time, turning them over frequently; beat two eggs very light, add one quarter of a pound of flour, a tablespoonful of melted butter, and as much cold water as will make a thin batter; drip the apples on a sieve, mix them with the batter, take one slice with a spoonful of butter to each fritter, fry them quick, of a light brown, drain them well, put them in a dish, sprinkling sugar over each, and glaze them nicely. (Randolph, *Virginia Housewife,* 155–56)

~ Jane's recipe contains only the bare bones by way of ingredients and instructions. Apparently an experienced cook was expected to know the rest.

| *Contemporary Recipe #1* | *Contemporary Recipe #2* |
| --- | --- |
| **Sturgeon soused to keep a long time**<br>Having drawn your Sturgeon, cut down your Sturgeon on the Back in Equal Sides and Rands; then wash it from the Blood with Water and Salt, then boil it in Water, Vinegar and Salt till it be tender, then lay it in some place to cool, when cold, barrel it up close with the Liquor it was boiled in. (Hall, *Queen's Royal Cookery,* 116) | ——— |
| **To Pickle Beat roots & Turnips**<br>Boyle your Beat Root in water & Salt, a pint of vineger, a little Cochineal, when they are half boyl'd put in ye Turnips being pare'd, when they boil'd take them off the fire & keep them in this pickle. (E. Kidder, *E. Kidder's Receipts* [1720], K.1) | ——— |
| **4. Carrot Pudding**<br>Take a large Carrot, boil it tender; then set it by to be cold, and grate it through a hair Sieve very fine; then put in half a pound of melted Butter; beaten together, with eight Eggs; leave out half the Whites, with two or three spoonfuls of Sack, or Orange-flower - water, half a Pint of good thick Cream, a Nutmeg, grated Bread, and a little Salt: Make it the thickeness of the Orange-Pudding, and the same baking; sweeten it to your Taste with fine Sugar, make Puff-paste, grate Sugar over it, and send it. (Howard, *England's Newest Way* [1710], 2–3) | ——— |
| **Fritters the English Way:**<br>Take a Pint of Canary, the like quantity of Ale, and a little Ale-Yest; the Yolks and Whites of nine Eggs beaten first very well by themselves, and then with the rest add a pound of fine Flower, and a little Ginger. Let the Butter stand a while, and then put in Apples thin sliced, and fry them with Beef-suet clarified, or a little Butter: take them out, and strew them over with fine Sugar; then Sprinkle them with Rose or Cinnamon-water. (Salmon, *Family Dictionary,* 109) | **To make Good Fritters.**<br>Mix half a pint of good Cream very thick with Flower, beat six Eggs, leaving out four Whites, and to the Eggs, put six spoonfuls of Sack and strain them into the Batter; put in a little grated Nutmeg, Ginger, and Cinamon, all very fine, also a little Salt; then put in another half pint of Cream, and beat the Batter near an Hour: pare and slice your Apples thin, dip every Piece in the Batter, and throw them in a Panfull of boiling Lard. (Several Hands, *Collection* [1714], 98) |

*"Jane Randolph her Cookery Book, 1743"*

**Shugar Cakes the best way**

Take 1 lb. 3 qrs. of good butter Well washd in rose water A pound of flower a pound of D R Shugar Beat & Sifted 10 Egs Leave out 1/2 the whites a whole Nutmeg grated mix the Butter & shugar first then half the flower then the Egs and Nutmeg then the rest of the flower put Currants in some Carraways in some, & Some plain Bake þm in Little pans

Pr Mrs. Herbert

*Comments*

**To make Sugar Cakes**

Take a Pound of the best Flowr well Dryed, a Pound and half of Fresh butter You must wash the butter in Orange Flower or Rose water, when well washed then beat the Butter a full Hour and half take twelve Eggs and the whites of Six of them half a Nutmeg Grated, the Eggs beaten well and Strained~then mix the Sugar it must be a Pound of Double Refined, beat very fine and Sifted mix the butter and Sugar, then half the Flower, then the Eggs and Nutmeg and then the Rest of the Flower. you must put Currents in Some. Carraway Seeds in Some. and Some Plain as you Please, Bake it in Lattin Pans Flowered, a quick Oven a Quarter of an Hour bakes them

By Mrs. Herbert (The Compiler [1744], Manuscript cookbook, 87)

**Apple Pudding**

Take as much pulp of appl[e] as will make a pudding 6 Egs, Leave out 1/2 the Whits, two Large sponfulls of grated Napls. Biskit & Shugar to yr. Tast the rind of an orrange or Lemon Boil'd tender, and Beaten In a morter Then mix it all together in a morter, With a 1/4 of a pound fresh Butter, put it in a dish with a past at top & Botto[m] & Bake not to mch

**French Rouls**

Take a pound of flower a Little yest a little Bit of Butter mix it Lightly with new milk from the cow lay it by the fire a while to rise cover'd with a cloth make them up in rouls flower them well & Bake them in a Quick Oven

**French Rolls.**

Sift a quart of flour, add a little salt, a spoonful of yeast, two eggs well beaten, and half a pint of milk, knead it and set it to rise; next morning, work in an ounce of butter, make the dough into small rolls, and bake them. The top crust should not be hard. (Randolph, *Virginia Housewife,* 170)

~ Mary's idea of French rolls is an obvious descendant of Jane's version, which in turn was based on these publications.

**Almonds Cheese Cakes**

Take half a pound of Blanch'd almonds Beat with Oat flower or rose water half a pound of Shugar 6 yolks of Eggs a Quarter of a pound fresh butter Bake them in little pans with puff paste under them

*Contemporary Recipe #1*

———

**An Apple Pudding**

Take as much Pulp of boil'd Pippins as you think will make your Pudding, and six Eggs well beaten, (leave out half the Whites,) two large spoonfuls of *Naples* Bisket finely grated, Sugar it to your Palate; take the Rind of an Orange or Lemon boil'd tender, and beaten in a Mortar; then mix all well together in a Mortar with a Quarter of a Pound of fresh Butter, and put it in your Dish, with Paste a - Top and Bottom. Let it not be done much. (R. Smith, *Court Cookery* [1725], 183)

**To make French Rolls**

Take a pound of the finest Flower, a little Yest, and a little sweet Butter, temper them lightly with new Milk warm from the Cow; then lay your Paste a while before the Fire, cover'd up in a Cloth, and make it up into Rolls, or Loaves, flower it well, and bake them in a very quick Oven. (R. Smith, *Court Cookery* [1723], 2:38)

**Another Way.**

To a Pound and half of Cheese-curd, put ten Ounces of Butter, beat them together 'till all looks like Butter; then beat a quarter of a Pound of Almonds with Orange-flower Water, and put to the Curds; add a Pound of Sugar, eight Eggs, leaving out half the Whites, a little Cream, and a little beaten Mace: Beat these all together for a quarter of an hour, and bake them in Puff-Crust in a quick Oven. (Nott, *Cook's and Confectioner's Dictionary,* #80)

*Contemporary Recipe #2*

———

**An Apple-Pudding to Bake, very good.**

Take twelve fair large Pippins, coddle them over the Fire very slowly, that they do not crack; when they are soft, peel and core them, and pulp them through a Cullender: Add to this three spoonfuls of Orange-flower-Water, ten Eggs well beat and strained half a pound of very good Butter melted; make it very sweet, the Apples require it: Add Candy'd Orange, Lemon, or Citron-peel: Put a Sheet of Puff-paste into a Dish, and pour in your Pudding; bake it with Care: 'Tis done in half an Hour. (Several Hands, *Collection* [1714], 51–52)

———

———

*"Jane Randolph her Cookery Book, 1743"* *Comments*

**To Keep Quinces all the year**

Boil the cores & pairings a little then wipe some Whole Quinces & put them in, and Boil them tender then put them in a pot, then bruse the cores & pairings & boil them to a Jealy cool it & put it on the Quinces put a weight upon them to keep them under

———

**To Pickle Walnuts**

Take young walnuts put them into a pot of water almost boiling hot in which let them Stand Seven days, then take them out & put them into a pot of boiling water let them boil a Quarter of an hour, wipe them & put them Into as much vinagar as will Cover them 2 Inches then add cloves ginger mace Nutmeg pepper crack't Mustard Seed, 10: or 12: cloves of garlick as much shallot, digest all in cold pickle for 9: or 10: Days put in the nuts & keep them close tied Down

———

**Gelly of hearts Horn**

Take hearts horn half a pound Boil it leasurely in Spring water close cover'd in a pipkin 5: or: 6 hours till it Jealy Strain it through a fine Jealy bag- then put it into a less pipkin with the juce of 8 or 9 lemons a pound 1/2 D. R. Shugar let it boil a little then put it up in your iealy glaces

———

| *Contemporary Recipe #1* | *Contemporary Recipe #2* |
| --- | --- |
| **To preserve quinces**<br>To preserue Quinces: first pare your Quinces and take out the cores and boile the cores and parings all together in faire water, and when they beginne to be soft, take them out and straine your liquor, and put the waight of your Quinces in sugar, and boile the Quinces in the sirrup till they be tender: then take the vp and boile your sirrup till it be thicke: If you will haue your Quinces red, couer in the boiling, and if you will haue them white doe not couer them. (Markham, *English House-Wife,* 123) | ——— |
| **To Pickle Walnuts like Mangoes**<br>Take green Walnuts before the Shell is grown to any hardness in them, pick them from the Stalks and put them into cold Water, and set them on a gentle Fire, till the the outward Skin begins to Peel off; then take coarse Cloths and wipe it off, then put them into a Tub or Pot, and put Water and Salt to them, changing once a day, for ten or twelve days, till the bitterness and discolouring of the Water be gone: Then take a good quantity of Mustard- seed, and beat it with Vinegar till it becomes coarse Mustard, some Cloves of Garlick, and some Ginger, and a little beaten Cloves and Mace; make a hole in each Nut, and put in a little of this, then take White-wine and White-wine Vinegar and boil it together, and as your are going to take it off the Fire, put in Pepper, Ginger, Cloves, Mace, and some of the Mustard and Garlick, according to your Discretion; then put the Nuts into it boiling hot, then put them into a Jar Glass or a well glazed Pot, and keep them under then Liquor close ty'd down, with Leather for your use[.] (Hall, *Queen's Royal Cookery,* 23–24) | ——— |
| **Hart's horn Jelly**<br>Take half a pound of Hart's horn, boil it in fair Spring-water leisurely, close covered, and in a well-glaxed Pipkin that will contain a Gallon, boil it till a spoonful will stand stiff, being cold, then strain it through a fine thick Canvas or fine Boultering, and put it again into another lesser Pipkin, with the Juice of eight or nine good large Limons, a pound and half of double refined Sugar, and boil it again a little while, then put it in a Gally Pot, or small Glasses, or cast it into Molds, or any Fashions of other Jellies; it is held by the Physicians for a special Cordial.<br>Or take half a pound of Hart's horn grated, and a good Capon, being finely cleansed and soaked from from the Blood, and the Fat taken of, truss it,and boil it in a Pot or Pipkin with the Hart's horn, in fair Spring-water, the same things as the former. (Hall, *Queen's Royal Cookery,* 159) | ——— |

*"Jane Randolph her Cookery Book, 1743"* — *Comments*

**Apple Pudding**

Take 7 Eggs well beaten well with Sugar, then put in a pint Cream, & half a pint new milk, then put in as much flower as will make Stiff enough for Fritters, then put in two double handfuls of Apples slic'd very thin in small peices or large which you please.

N B If your Apples are very sower twill take [mch?] more Sugar than any other Pudding.

———

**Almond Pudding**

Beat half a pound of almond with ~~oatmeal~~ [Spring?] [Tasting?] water, Grate 3 or 4 Biskets in 1/2 a pound of Butter, 3 or 4 Spoonfulls of Sack & Eggs Leave out 1/2 their whites a Quart of Cream Sugar to yr. Tast, Lay puffe Paste in the Bottom

Finis

———

**Cutlets Veal**

[Missing]

**Veal Cutlets**

Cut them from the fillet, put them in a stew pan with a piece of nice pork, a clove of garlic, a bundle of thyme and parsley, pepper and salt, cover them with water and let them stew ten or fifteen minutes, lay them on a dish, and when cold cover them well with the crumb of stale bread finely grated, mixed with the leaves of parsley chopped very small, some pepper, salt and grated nutmeg; press these on the veal with a knife, and when a little dried, turn it and do the same to the other side; put a good quantity of lard in a pan, when it boils lay the cutlets in carefully that the crumbs may not fall, fry them a little brown, lay them on a strainer to drain off the grease, do the same with the crumbs that have fallen in the pan; while this is doing simmer the water they were boiled in to half a pint, strain it and thicken it with four ounces of butter and a little browned flour; add a gill of wine and one of mushroom catsup, put in the cutlets and crumbs, and stew till tender; add forcemeat balls. (Randolph, *Virginia Housewife,* 252)

~ Perhaps Jane's recipe resembled the one published by Several Hands in 1714 or was an older version of her descendant Mary Randolph's two recipes for veal cutlets.

*Contemporary Recipe #1*

**An Almond-Pudding**

Beat half a pound of good sweet Almonds with Orange-flower-water, grated Biskets, three or four, as they are for size, half a pound of Butter, and four large spoonfuls of sack, eight Eggs, leaving out half the Whites, and a quart of Cream, with Sugar to your Taste; put a Puff-paste at the bottom of the Dish; and Garnish the edge with Paste, so pour it in and bake it: Those that love not, Orange-flower-Water, may put a grated Nutmeg instead of it, and beat the Almonds with fair Water, for fear of Oiling. (Several Hands, *Collection* [1714], 58)

**To make Veal-Cutlets**

Cut as many Slices of a Leg of Veal as will make a handsome Dish, beat them with your Rolling-pin, lay them singly in a large Dish, and grate Nutmeg all over them, and strew them with Salt, lard some with Bacon, and pour the Yolks of three Eggs, well beaten over all; make them all moist with the Egg, and fry them of a fine colour in clarify'd Butter, put fresh Frying to every Dish, When they are all nicely fry'd, put some Gravy into the Pan, and the Juice of a Lemon, with Butter and Flower shook in; toss up all 'till 'tis thick, and pour it over the Cutlets; garnish with bits of Bacon fry'd, and Forc'd-meat-Balls. If it be a Cow-calf, fill the Udder in fat with the Forc'd-meat, and roast it finely for the middle. Make your gravy for the Sauce of the Bones and Skins you do not use; a Bit of Beef, Sweet- herbs, Spice, and White-wine, to make it look Pale. (Several Hands, *Collection* [1714], 16–17)

*Contemporary Recipe #2*

**An Almond Pudding**

Blanch and pound half a pound of *Jordan* Almonds with four grated Biskets and three quarters of a pound of Butter, Sack and Orange-flower-Water, then mix it with a Quart of Cream boil'd and mix'd with eight Eggs, sweet Spice and Sugar, cover the Dish with Puff-paste, pour in the Butter, and bake it. (Carter, *Compleat City,* 165)

**Veal Cutlets From the Fillet Or Leg.**

Cut off the flank and take the bone out, then take slices the size of the fillet and half an inch thick, beat two yelks of eggs light, and have some grated bread mixed with pepper, salt, pounded nutmeg and chopped parsley; beat the slices a little, lay them on a board and wash the upper side with the egg, cover it thick with the bread crumbs, press them on with a knife, and let them stand to dry a little, that they may not fall off in frying, then turn them gently, put egg and crumbs on in the same manner, put them into a pan of boiling lard, and fry them a light brown; have some good gravy ready, season it with a teaspoonful of curry powder, a large one of wine, and one of lemon pickle, thicken with butter and brown flour, drain every drop of lard from the cutlets, lay them in the gravey, and stew them fifteen or twenty minutes; serve them up garnished with lemon cut in thin slices. (Randolph, *Virginia Housewife,* 45–46)

*"Jane Randolph her Cookery Book, 1743"*

*Comments*

**Sauce for Boiled Chickens**
(Missing)

~ Perhaps her recipe was a forerunner to the sauce named in Mary Randolph's index for boiled chickens. The title, however, was somewhat different, as shown on the right.

**To make White Sauce for Fowls.**
Take a scrag of veal, the necks of fowls, or any bits of mutton or veal you have, put them in a sauce pan with a blade or two of mace, a few black pepper corns, one anchovy, a head of celery, a bunch of sweet herbs, a slice of the end of a lemon, put in a quart of water, cover it close, let it boil till it is reduced to half a pint, strain it, and thicken it with a quarter of a pound of butter mixed with flour, boil it five or six minutes, put in two spoonsful of pickled mushrooms, mix the yelks of two eggs with a tea cup full of good cream and a little nutmeg, put it in the sauce, keep shaking it over the fire but don't let it boil. (Randolph, *Virginia House-wife,* 84)

**Black Pudding**
To make these the best & far exeeding way Boil the Umbles of a hog tender, take some of the Lights with the heart & all the flesh above them taking out the Sinews & mincing the rest very small do the like by the Liver - add grated Nutmeg 4 or 5 Yolks of Eggs a pint of sweet Cream 1/4 of a pint of Canary, Sugar Cloves, Mace & Cinnamon finely powder'd a few Carriaway seeds & a little Rose Water a pretty Quantity of Hogs fat & some Salt Roul it up abt. two hours—Before your put into the Guts & then Put into them after you have rinsed them in Rose Water

~ **Umbles** are the "edible inward parts of an animal, usually a deer" (*OED,* 11:20). **Lights** refers to lungs of animals such as sheep, pigs, and bullocks (*OED,* 6:280).

**Pigg Collar'd**
Take a fat Pigg Cut of his Head chine it down the Back, Bone it and Gris=tle it, Lay it in Spring Water for one Night the next Morning Dry it in a Cloth cut each side asunder season it with Sack, Bruised Pepper Nutmeg Sliced a Little beaten Mace & some Small Quantity of shred Sage Lemon peal & sweet herbs Rowl them up hard in a Cloth & boil it in Sower Drink with. mint Water & Bran strain out the Brane Skim of all the Fat & when Cold put the Collars in again.

**To Collier a Pig**
Take a ffat pig Cut of the head & Chine him down the back & take out all the bones & Grisells but take care you dont Cut the skin then lay it in Spring Water one night the next day dry it in A Cloth & Cut Each side in halves Season it with Nutmeg Salt & alittle beaten Mace alittle whole pepper alittle Sage rosemary & Lemon Peel then Rowle up hard in a Cloth & boyl them in bran & Water whole Pepper Salt & abay leaf or 2 & when they are tender take them up & tye them very tite & hang them up tell they are cold Season the head the Same way tye it up in A Cloth and the sow-cen drink in brann Milk & Water Strain out the brann & Scum of the fat let the Collars be Cold then put them in. (The Compiler [1744], Manuscript cookbook, 84)

~ Even though this recipe was copied only a year after the completion of Jane's manuscript, it is apparent that Jane's version is not only more brief but also older in language. The Compiler (1744) probably copied her recipe from one of many plagiarized versions in print.

| *Contemporary Recipe #1* | *Contemporary Recipe #2* |
| --- | --- |
| **Mushroom-Sauce for White Fowls boiled.** TAKE Half a Pint of Cream, and a Quarter of a Pound of Butter, stir them together one Way, till it is thick; then add a Spoonful of Mushroom Pickle, picked Mushrooms, or fresh, if you have them. Garnish only with Lemon. (Glasse, *Art of Cookery,* 35) | —— |
| **Black-Puddings:** To make these the best, and far exceeding the common way, Boil the Umbles of a Hog, tender, take some of the Lights with the Heart, and all the Flesh about them, taking out the Sinews, and mincing the rest very small; do the like by the Liver: add grated Nutmeg, four or five Yolks of Eggs, a pint of sweet Cream, a quarter of a pint of Canary, Sugar, Cloves, Mace and Cinnamon finely poudered, a few Carraway seeds, and a little Rose-Water, a pretty quantity of Hogs-fat, and some Salt: roll it up about two Hours before your put it into the Guts, and then put it into them after you have rinsed them in Rose-water. (Salmon, *Family Dictionary,* 33) | —— |
| **163. To Collar a Pig** Take a fat Pig, Cut of his Head, chine him down the Back, and take out all the bones and Gristles, take care you don't cut the Skin; then lay it in spring-water one Night, the next Morning dry it in a Cloth, and cut each side asunder; season it with Salt, whole Pepper, Nutmeg, and a little beaten Mace, a little Sage Rosemary, and limon-peel; rowl them up hard in a Cloth, and the sousen drink is Bran, and skim off all the Fat, and let your Collars be cold before you put them in. (Howard, *England's Newest Way* [1710], 86) | —— |

*"Jane Randolph her Cookery Book, 1743"* | *Comments*

**Cakes Excellent**

Take 3 lb very fine flower well dry'd by the fire & put to it, 1 1/2 lb of Loaf Sugar sifted in a very fine Sieve and dry'd three: lb of Currants well wash'd & dry'd in a Cloth & set by the Fire when your flower is well mixt wth. the Sugar & Currants you must put into it a pound & half of melted Butter 10 Spoonfulls of Cream wth. the Yolks of 3 new laid Eggs beat wth. it one Nutmeg & if you please 3 Spoonfull of Sack When you have wrought your Paste well you must put it in a Cloth & set it in a Dish before the Fire till it be thorough Warm, Then make them up in little Cakes & prick them full of Little holes You must Bake them in a quick Oven inclos'd Afterwards ice them over with Sugar the Cakes should be abt. the Bigness of a Hand: Breadth and thin of the size of a Sugr. Cake sold at Barnet.

~ **Barnet** is a suburb in London.

**Cakes very fine**

Take fine flower 4 lb sweet Cream a pint Butter 3/4 of a pound 10 Yolks of Eggs without the Whites a pint of Ale Yest Cloves, Mace Nutmeg of each in fine Powder 1/4 of an Ounce 2 oz: Damask rose Water Ambergrise dis=solv'd 10 Grains; Currants prick'd & Wash'd 1 1/2 lb Raisins of the Sun ston'ed & cut small 1 pound Kneed all these together very well and letting it lie & hour or two, then make it into Cakes. Bake 'em in an Oven not too hot not shutting up it's Mouth there let them be till they are sufficiently bak'd when you draw them have in Readiness D. L. S. wet in Damask rose Water & beaten in a Porringer till it is Clear in which dipp.g a Tuft of Feathers wet Cakes all over & set 'em in the Oven again this do 3 or 4 Times Letting it dry every Time So will their Tops be like Ice. NB Nothing is to be put in hot in the Kneeding but Butter and that is to be gently melted into wch. your Salt for the Seasoning.

~ **Porringer**, a dialectic word, refers to "a small basin or similar vessel of metal, earthenware, or wood, from which soup, broth, porridge," and "children's food, etc. is eaten" (*OED,* 7:1135).

**Cakes of Curds**

Take Cheese Curds or Wild Curds a quart 2 Yolks wth. 4 whites of Eggs white Loaf Sugar in Powder 4 ounces a Small Nutmeg grated, mix wth a little flower make a soft or dropping Paste Drop it like Frittars into a frying pan in which is boiling Butter.

———

*Contemporary Recipe #1*

**To make Excellent small Cakes.**

Take three pound of very fine Flour dry'd by the Fire, and put to it a pound and a half of Loaf-Sugar sifted in a very fine Sieve, and dried, three pound of Currans well washed and dryed in a Cloth, and set by the Fire, when your Flour is well mixed with the Sugar and Currans, you must put in a pound and a half of unmelted Butter, ten spoonfuls of Cream, with the Yolks of three new-laid Eggs beat with it, one Nutmeg, and if you please, three spoonfuls of Sack; when you have wrought your Paste well, you must put it in a Cloth, and set it in a Dish before the Fire, till it be thorough warm, then make them up in little Cakes, and prick them full of Holes; you must bake them in a quick Oven unclosed. (Hall, *Queen's Royal Cookery,* 141)

**How to make fine Cakes**

Take one quarter of a Peck of the finest Flower you can get, one Pint of sweet Cream, three quarters of a pound of Butter, 10 Yelks of Eggs without the Whites, a good Dish of Yest about a Pint, season it with Salt, a pennyworth of Cloves and Mace, with a little Nutmeg beaten altogether, half a quarter of a Pint of Rosewater, with a little Musk or Ambergrease dissolv'd in it, one pound and half of the best Currants well pick'd and washed in warm Water, one pound of the best Raisins of the Sun ston'd and shred very small, then knead all these things together very well, and then let it lye an hour in the Dough, then make up your Cake; let not your Oven be too hot, nor shut the Mouth of it, but be stirring your Cake now and then, let it not stand in the Oven a full Hour; when you draw your Cakes, have ready some of the best double Refin'd Sugar wet in Rose-water, and beaten in a Porringer until it be clear, then take a tuft of Silk or Feathers dipp'd in it, and wet your Cake all over, then set it in the Oven again, do this 3 or 4 times, but let it dry on every time, and that will make it like Ice, there must be nothing put in hot in the kneading but the butter, and that must be gently melted, not clarified, you must put your Salt in the melted butter[.] (*Pastry-Cook's Vade Mecum,* 16–17)

**To make Curd-Cakes**

Take a pint of Curds, four Eggs, take out two of the whites, put in some sugar, a little Nutmeg, and a little flour, stir them well together, and drop them in, and fry them with a little Butter. (Kent, *Gentlewoman's Delight,* 15)

*Contemporary Recipe #2*

———

———

**51. To make Curd-Cakes**

Take a pint of Curds, four Eggs, leaving two of the Whites out, add Sugar, and grated Nutmeg, with a little Flour, Mix them together, and drop them like Fritters in a Frying-pan in which Butter is hot. (Howard, *England's Newest Way* [1710], 124)

| *"Jane Randolph her Cookery Book, 1743"* | *Comments* |
|---|---|
| **Oat Cakes**<br>Take fine oat Flower | ~ This recipe was never completed. The following example might give an idea about what was missing. |
| **Wiggs to Make**<br>Take 2 lb flower, and a qr. of Butter, a qr. of Sugar a little spice, carraway Seeds, make them light with Cream & Yest let them stand by the fire to rise, then will bake very soon. | ——— |
| **A Cake to eat with Butter.**<br>Take 2 lb: flower, and 1/2 l b Butter, some Spice & Salt, a qtr. of a lb. Sugar, 1/2 lb Raisons, ston'd, 1/2 lb Currants, 1/2 a pt: yest, & 4 eggs, make it up with warm milk. an hour & 1/2 will bake it for Breakfast. | ——— |
| **Percimon Beer**<br>Take a tub with a fals bottom, and fill it up, with pircimmons, and warm water, mas'd together Just thin enough to drop like Molasses, it will be two or three days a dropping, then put some of it into water, mix: with hops according to the strength you woull have it, and boile it well, then work it with Yest. | ~ This beverage has Native American roots. |
| **Thomas Edwardses Receipt to keep Sturgeon**<br>You must wash & scrap it very clean, then take ot the bones, and grisle, then boile it in Salt and water, scum it all the while tis boiling when tis Colld enoug, lay it on clean straw to drain, then take some vinegar, and the liquor it was boild in, an equal guant[i]ty boil it together with pepper and Salt, let it cool and settle, when cold, wipe the sturgeon, and put it into the Souce, put the oil on it and cover it close | ——— |

*Contemporary Recipe #1*

**To make Oat Cakes.**
The Iron or Stone you bake them on, must be plac'd at some distance above the Fire. Mix Oat flour with a little Water, and a little new Ale-yeast, making your Dough pretty stiff; then roll them out into Cakes, and lay them on your Baking-stone, or Iron, let the Fire under them be gentle, they will be bak'd in about a quarter of an Hour; when they are done, roll them on the Edges, that they may be bak'd likewise; and turn them on the other side just to flat them, if you turn them too soon it will prevent them rising. (Nott, *Cook's and Confectioner's Dictionary*, #1)

**To make Wigs.**
Take two pounds of Flour, and a quarter of a pound of Butter, as much Sugar, a Nutmeg grated, a little Cloves and Mace, and a quarter of an ounce of Carraway-seeds, Cream and Yeast as much as will make it up into a pretty light Paste; make them up, and set them by the fire to rise till the Oven be ready; they will quickly be baked. (E. Smith, *Compleat Housewife* [1729], 127)

**An ordinary Cake to eat with Butter.**
Take two pounds of Flour, and rub into it half a pound of Butter; then put it some Spice, a little Salt, a quarter and half of Sugar, half a pound of Raisins stoned, and half a pound of Currants; make these into a Cake, with half a pint of Ale-Yeast, and four Eggs, and as much warm Milk as your see convenient; mix it well together, an hour and half will bake it. This Cake is good to eat with Butter for Breakfasts. (E. Smith, *Compleat Housewife* [1729], 124)

———

———

*Contemporary Recipe #2*

———

———

———

———

———

*"Jane Randolph her Cookery Book, 1743"* — *Comments*

**For a Scald**

Take a ps: fat Bacon and dip it in Tar, the stick it up before the fire and put, smething under it to save the driping, baste the Bacon with what drops out= first, and then let it drop till the Bacon is dry, then save the dripping, put some-Rum into it, and anoint the Head.

———

**Chocolate to make up.**

You must wash the Nuts very clean, the rost then to get the huls off, then roul them on the stone till tis a fine past. yu must mix a few of the best huls with it, to make it froth.

~ Of all the chocolate recipes seen in various publications, this version was the most labor-intensive.

**Harts Horn Drink**

To 2 oz: of Burnt Harts Horn put 2 qts. Water, a bit of Cinnamon, boil it half away, with a crust of Bread then Strain it off on a Brown Toast which must be taken out after Standing a little while:

———

**To make an Orange Pudding**

Take the Peel of six Oranges, peel'd very fine from the White, then boil them very tender, sifting it once or twice; so when it is boild tender, beat them in a Morter very fine, then take a Quarter of a Pound of Naples Bisket, boil them up in Some Cream, and rub it thro' your Cullender; then put your Peel to it, with the Yolks of six Eggs, and four White. Season it with a Nutmeg Salt & Sugar, if then be any wanting, put in Some Morrow minc'd very fine So Sheat a pan & bake it

———

**To make a Pudding Cake**

Take a Pound of Sewet minc'd very fine and as much Flower; four Eggs, and a Peice of Butter, mix these together; season with Nutmeg, Sugar, Cinnamond, a Little Rose Water and Salt, Make into a paste with Cream make it up like a Cake. So butter your Dish, and bake it

———

**To make a Seed Cake**

Take a Pound & a halfe of Flower dry'd, & a Pound of Butter, worke the Butter very well into a Pound of the Flower; take Seven eggs, and nine spoonfuls of Ale yest three Spoon =fuls of Rose Water a Quarter of a Pint of Sack put the Liquors together & Strain them into half a Pound of flower; it will be Like Batter. & it must be well beaten together and set it before the Fire to rise when it is well risen pour it into the flower that was mix'd with the Butter, & work it very thro' with your Hands: And last of all, mix in a Pound of very good

———

| *Contemporary Recipe #1* | *Contemporary Recipe #2* |
|---|---|
| — | — |
| **(Chocolate)** *Chocolate* is made with *Chocolate,* Milk, Eggs, White-wine, Rose-water, and Mace or Cinnamon, which the party fancies, they bring all boiled together over a gentle fire two ounces of *Chocolate,* eight eggs, half a pound of Sugar, a pint of White-wine, an ounce of Mace or Cinamon, and half a pound of Sugar answering in this case a gallon of milk. (Shirley, *Accomplished Ladies Rich Closet,* 20) | — |
| — | — |
| **Orange Pudding** Take the Peel of Six Oranges, peel'd thin from the White, boil them very tender, shifting the Water once or twice; when they are boil'd, beat them fine in a Mortar, then take a quarter of a pound of *Naples* Bisket, boil them up in Cream, and rub it thro' a Cullender; then put your Peel to it, with the Yolks of six Eggs, and the Whites of three; season it to your Taste with Nutmeg, Salt and Sugar; and then bake it (R. Smith, *Court Cookery* [1723], 2:20) | — |
| **To make a Pudding-Cake** Take a Pound of Sewet minc'd very fine, and as much Flower, four Eggs, and a Piece of Butter; mix these well together; season with Nutmeg, Sugar, Cinnamon, a little Rose-Water and Salt. Make it into a Paste with Cream; make it up like a Cake. So butter your Dish, and bake it. (Lamb, *Royal Cookery,* 106) | — |
| **To make a Seed Cake** Take a Pound and a Half of Flower dry'd, and a Pound of Butter, work the Butter very well into a Pound of the Flower; take seven Eggs, and nine Spoonfuls of Ale-Yest three Spoonfuls of Rose-water, a Quarter of a Pint of Sack; put the Liquors together, and strain them into half a Pound of Flower; it will be like Batter, and it must be well beat together, and set it before the Fire to rise, and when it is well risen, pour it into the Flower that was mix'd with the Butter, & work it very well thro' with your Hand: And, last of all, mix in a | — |

*"Jane Randolph her Cookery Book, 1743"* | *Comments*

Carway Comfit Bake it in a Hoop and try with a knife when it is enough a little time bakes it Put into the Flower two Oz. of Sugar & Salt

**The Seed Cake alter'd**

Take 3 lb. Flower, dry'd, a pound of butter, worke the Butter well into one half of the Flour, & a little Spice then take fourteen eggs, eighteen Spoonfuls yest, Three Spoonfuls rosewater, a quarter of p[int] Sack, or Madearea Wine made Sweet, Put these Liquors together, and Strain them into the rest of the Flour, it will be like Batter, and must be wel[l] beaten together and set before the fire to rise. when tis very light, pour it into the flour th[at] was mix'd with the Butter. work it all through your Hands and last of all install of Carraway Comfits mix in one pound powder Sugar, and Two pound currants & half a pound Ston'd Ria[sins].

~ The last **butter** should be batter here.

**Cherrys**

To 12 lb Cherrys a qt of Currant Juice 2 lb Sugar let it have a Boil or 2 cover close you may Scald them Every day drain them & dry in and Stove or oven.

~ Fortunately for us, Jane (Bolling) Randolph took unusual pains to state that this particular cherry recipe came from "Mr. Sylvanus Bevin Apothecary Plow Court Lombard Street London."

**Wafers**

Take a qt of thick Cream half a pound fine Sugar a cup of rose water as much fine flour as will make it thin Batter make your Iron hot put a Spoonful on it they will be presently done.

**Horne Wafers**

Take half a pound of flower five Ounces of Double Refin'd Sugar mix them first with Milk and put in two Eggs and when they are well beaten I mean mix'd together then thin it with Cream but don't let your Cream be to thick You may season them with Sack or Orainge flower Water and Spice of Chocolat as you think fit and keep them warm before the fire or Else they will fall flat and Eat very Tuff and not Crisp. (The Compiler [1744], Manuscript cookbook, 26)

~ Even though this recipe was copied a year after Jane (Bolling) Randolph completed her manuscript, it is a good example of obvious differences in language and technique.

**A Receipt to make Ink**

To a pint of Rain Water put one ounce of Galls & half an ounce of Gum arraback half an Oz. Coperas Bruise them together & put them in a Bottl[e] Let it be in a Warm place till it be fit to use.

~ **Galls,** excrescences produced by trees, especially oak, by the action of insects, are used in the manufacture of ink and tannin as well as medicine (*OED,* 4:20). **Gum arraback,** or **gum arabic,** is a substance "exuded by certain species of *Acacia*" that is "soluble in water" (*OED,* 4:423). **Coperas** in this context referred to green sulphates derived from iron that were used in making ink as well as dyeing and tanning (*OED,* 3:974).

*Contemporary Recipe #1*

*Contemporary Recipe #2*

Pound of very good Carway-Comfits. Bake it in a Hoop, and try with a Knife when it is enough, a little time bakes it. Put into the Flower two Ounces of Sugar and a little Salt. (Lamb, *Royal Cookery,* 84)

———

**Another Way to make a Seed Cake**

Take three pound of dry'd Flour, two pound of Butter, work the Butter very well into two pound of the Flour; take fourteen Eggs, and six Spoonfuls of Rose-water, half a pint of Sack, and eighteen Spoonfuls of Ale-Yeast; mix the Liquors all together, and strain them into the remaining pound of Flour: It will be like Batter, and you must beat it well together and set it before the Fire to rise, and when it is risen well, pour in four Ounces of Sugar and a little Salt, and work it well with your Hands; then put in two pound of Carraway comfits, put it into a Hoop and bake it; a little time bakes it, and you may try with a Knife when it is enough. (Nott, *Cook's and Confectioner's Dictionary,* #14)

———

———

**Wafers**

Dry your Flower, and make it into a thick Batter with Cream, put in Mace very fine beat, a little Sugar to your Taste; Butter your Irons, and let them be hot, then put in a Tea- spoonful of the Batter; so bake them with care, and roll them off the Iron, on a small Stick. (Several Hands, *Collection* [1714], 87)

———

**To Make good Ink**

Take 4 unces of Galls beaten fine, put them into a bottle of of strong beer 4 days, shaking the Bottle 2 or 3 times a day, then put in two ounces of Coperas & one ounce of Gum Araback. When it is too thick fill it up with strong or small beer. (Blencowe, *Receipt Book,* 13)

**To make Ink.**

Get one pound of the best Galls, half a pound of Copperas, a quarter of a pound of Gum-arabick, a quarter of a pound of white Sugar-candy; bruise the Galls, and beat your other Ingredients fine, and infuse them all in three quarts of White-wine or Rain-water, and let them stand hot by the fire three or four days; then put all into a new Pipkin, set it on a slow fire, so as not to boil; keep it frequently stirring, and let it stand five or six hours till one quarter is consumed, and when cold strain it thro' a clean coarse piece of Linnen; bottle it and keep it for use. (E. Smith, *Compleat Housewife* [1729], 260)

*"Jane Randolph her Cookery Book, 1743"*

*Comments*

**Mrs. Chiswel's Receipt for a Cake, very good**

To half a peck Flour put 2 lb Butter, 1 1/4 lb Sugar, 1/2 an oz: Nutmegs, 1/2 an oz: Mace, 1/4 an oz: Cloves 1/4 an oz: Cinnamon, 16 Eggs, 1/2 the Whites, a pt Cream, 1/2 pt. Sack a qt. Yest, & 5: lb Currants. Let it stand all Night to rise

~ Elizabeth Randolph married Col. John Chiswell of Scotchtown in 1736 ("Notes and Queries," *Virginia Magazine,* 87). Elizabeth Chiswell was described as "a most amiable lady: From her door the needy were never sent empty away" (*Virginia Gazette,* 8 March 1776). There was also Mrs. Esther Chiswell, who dined with William Byrd and Dr. Charles Barrett in 1709. In 1732, after more than 20 years, William Byrd was distressed to discover her former prettiness entirely gone and replaced with "very deep furrows in her fair skin" (Byrd, *Secret Diary,* 99). He gallantly added that she was "one of those absolute Rarities, a very good old Woman," and he was "very handsomely entertain'd" (Byrd, *Writings,* 343).

**Ginger Bread**

Take some Gum dragon Steep'd in rose Water G[o—] Double R Sugar some Almonds Blanch'd in cold Wate[r] Beat rose water kneed them all together on Moulds & Search'd Sugar

~ These gingerbread recipes were already a bit old-fashioned with their flavorings and use of comfits.

**Ginger Bread**

One pound Flour 3/4 lb sugar 3/4 of an oz Ginger Carraway Comfits & Annis seeds of each 1/4 of an oz 2 Oz & half of butter four yolks of Eggs 4 spoonfull sack 6 spoonfull of yest Orange Lemon & Citron peal to your liking it makes a light paste & must be bak'd in Pans.

———

**Shrubb**

To a Gallon of the best Brandy One doz: of Lemons and slice them infuse them Peal and all in the Brandy for five Days. then take out the Lemonds, and squeeze them as hard as you can in the Brandy then strain the Brandy add to it..two..Quts: Rhenish and if you'd have your Shrubb small add to it a pint Spring water, Three Pounds Dou: Refine sugar so bottle it for Use

for to make Shrubb for Punch one pint of Juice one pound Sugar to every Gallon of Spirits, the best way to preserve

———

**Firn the Virtues of it.**

Take the Root, & open it, in which you'd find a soft pith like Cotten you must Boil it in little Water & lay it on. Tis a Salve for every Sore

Harry Morris

~ This appears to be a personal recipe donated by Mr. Morris since nothing resembling it has been found in published works before or after 1744.

*Contemporary Recipe #1*

**A great Cake**

Take 5 or 6 pounds of currants, pick't, wash'd, & dried, & plump'd if you please, & set them before the fire that they may be warme. Take 5 pound of flower, putt it into a pan. Take sixteen eggs, putt away half ye whites, & beat them very well, & strain them & a pint of ale yeest, stirring together a pint of cream & a pound and half of butter, & putt them together that ye cream may warm ye yeeste & eggs; & with a warm liquor wett ye flower, & when it is mix'd cover it with a warm cloth, & sett it before ye fire, in a pan that you wett it in; & so let it stand, stirring it sometimes that it may be equally warm till ye oven be hott.

Take half an unce f mace & two good nutmegs, & cinamon or what spice you like best, & half a pound of sugar; & mix it all together, when ye oven is hott, with ye currants as they are warmed, putting it to ye dough, & when it is well mix'd have a large stronge paper, & butter it, & lett it be doubled with a paper hoope. Itt may be bak'd in an hour. (Blencowe, *Receipt Book,* 3)

———

———

**To make an excellent Liquor called Shrub**

Take two quarts of the best Brandy, five Limons sliced very thin, the Kernels picked clean out, stop it close in any Glass-Jar, or any close thing for 4 or 5 days; then strain out your Limons, and add to your Liquor one quart of White-wine, three half pints of Water, two pounds of Loaf-Sugar finely beaten, stir the Sugar in till it be melted, then put it in Bottles, but be sure do not fill the Bottle two full, put it in a cool place. (*Pastry-Cook's Vade Mecum,* 65–66)

———

*Contemporary Recipe #2*

———

———

———

**To make Shrub**

TAKE brandy two quarts, the juice of five lemons, and the peels of two lemons, half a Nutmeg; mix them together in a large bottle, stopt close, and let them stand three days then put in three pints of White wine, a pound and a half of sugar; mix and strain it twice through a flannel, and bottle it up for use. (Atkyns, *Family Magazine,* 1:88)

———

*"Jane Randolph her Cookery Book, 1743"*

**Sturgeon to keep.**

Cut out all the grissle, & then Salt it well, let it lie all Night then put it in some Brine to cleane it: then Boil it in good Venigar, whole pepper,- & a few Cloves. let it settle well, & clarifie the Oil, to put on the top.

*Comments*

**To Pickle Sturgeon.**

The best sturgeons are the small ones, about four feet long without the head, and the best part is the one next to the tail. After the sturgeon is split through the back bone, take a piece with the skin on, which is essential to its appearance and goodness, cut off the gristle, scrape th skin well, wash it, and salt it; let it lie twenty-four hours, wipe off the salt, roll it and tie it around with twine, put it on in a good deal of cold water, let it boil till you can run a straw easily into the skin, take it up, pull off the large scales, and when cold, put it in a pot, and cover it with one part winegar and two of salt and water; keep it closely stopped, and when served, garnish with green fennel. (Randolph, *Virginia Housewife,* 104)

~ Again, Jane's version gives the briefest possible information, but all the key elements are included. Mary Randolph may well have been familiar with all three of Jane's recipes for preserving or keeping sturgeon.

**Spot of grease in Silk.**

Take a little Pipe Stem Powder'd fine, & lay it on the Spot, cover it with Brown Paper & put a hot Iron on it. the Pipe Stem, will defend ye Paper from leav[ing a stain?]

~ The author has not yet been able to locate any recipe that utilized clay pipe stems to absorb grease. However, one following recipe operated along a similar principle through the use of bone.

**To make Spring Beer**

Take 10 gallns spring water, put in two handfuls inner Bar[k] of Sassafras, two of horse readish, the like quantity of Asparagus Roots, Cinque foil, wormwood, Elderbuds, or roots, four han[d]fuls Watercress, a like quantity of Spruce Pine tops boil it well, sweeten up the Musc: Sugar, strain it off, cool & turn it up as usual when tis clear, drink it Morning & Evening.

~ **Cinque foil** alludes to a plant, *Potentilla reptans,* which grows five leaflets and it also applies to other, similar plants (*OED,* 2:25).

**French Bread, or Rouls, for Oisters-**

Take 1 qt.: Flour three Eggs, a bit Butter, a little Saqk, make it up with warm Milk, very light, & Bake them in little patty-pans.—You must stew the oisters very nice, then scoop all the crum out of the Roles, & fil the hole with the stew'd Oisters, & put on the bit You cut off. Pour some melted Butter over the top, & Just set them in the Oven after they are drawn, to crisp them

**To Make Oyster Loaves.**

Take little round loaves, cut off the top, scrape out all the crumbs, then put the oysters into a stew pan with the crumbs that came out of the loaves, a little water, and a good lump of butter; stew them together ten or fifteen minutes, then put in a spoonful of good cream, fill your loaves, lay the bit of crust carefully on again, set them in the oven to crisp. Three are enough for a side dish. (Randolph, *Virginia Housewife,* 78)

*Contemporary Recipe #1*

*Contemporary Recipe #2*

**To take spots of oil or grease out of Satin, Silks, Stuff, or Woollen.**

BURN the bones of sheeps trotters, reduce them to a fine powder, lay it on fine paper, on both sides of the spots, and place upon the upper part a spoon, in which is a lighted coal that may heat pretty well through, and the heat will cause the powder to suck out the grease; then rub it over with a piece of fine white-bread to cleane it : if it does not sufficiently at once, repeat it twice or thrice, and it will not fail your expectation. (Atkyns, *Family Magazine,* 1:101)

**To make Oyster Loaves.**

TAKE several *French* Rolls, cut Holes on the top, about the bigness of a Half-Crown; scoop out all the Crumb, but do not break the Crust. Stew Oysters in their own Liquor, with a little White-wine, Salt, crackt Pepper, Nutmeg, and a Blade or two of Mace: Scum them, and thicken the Liquor with a bit of Butter roll'd up in flour: Then fill up the Rolls with these and lay on the Pieces you cut out; dip them into scalding Milk or

*"Jane Randolph her Cookery Book, 1743"*

*Comments*

Although modernized, this recipe maintained the basic elements of the recipe at left. Compare Mary's recipe to "Oysters Loves" in Anonymous (1700)'s collection. The very elaborateness and age of Anonymous (1700)'s recipe stands out.

**Lemon Pudding.**

Grate the Peal of three Lemons, then beat them in a Morter with a little Loaf Sugar, to keep their colour; then beat the Yolks of 14 Eggs very well, as much Sugar as will sweeten it last of all, put in half a pound of clear melted Butter - & Bake it, with a Puff Paste under it, & cross Bars on the top

N B Put in the Juice of a Lemon or Two.

**Lemon Pudding.**

Grate the rind from six fresh lemons, squeeze the juice from three, and strain in it; beat the yelks of sixteen eggs very light; put to them sixteen table-spoonful of powdered loaf sugar, not heaped up; add the grated rind and the juice, with flour crackers finely pounded; beat it till light, put a puff paste in your dish, pour the pudding in, and bake it in a moderate oven; it must not be very brown. (Randolph, *Virginia Housewife,* 150)

In spite of Mary's addition of four crackers, the main outline of Jane's pudding is still preserved.

**To keep Quinces all the Year**

Take the worst of your Quinces, & chop them small, Boil them in Water, till tis very strong, then let it stand to be cold; & then put in the fairest Quinces you can get. Tie them down with Leather. Let no Air get to them.

———

**Preserve Quinces.**

Put an equal Qantity of Sugar to your Quinces, To 6: lb Quinces, put one qt: Water, Clarifie it - with the white of an Egg, & tie up some of the Seeds in a bit of Muslin, to coalour it. Coddle your Quinces first.

———

**Quince Marmalade.**

After your Quinces are coddled, pare, & Core them, take the same quantity of Sugar & Quinces, Twelve Spoonfuls of Pippin Water, Put them over a gentil Fire, stiring them till the Sugar is desolv'd–then cover þm up close till your Quinces turn Red. put the Seeds in a bit of Muslin Rag, & let them stew till they are fit to break for the Marmalade, let them have a boil or Two, before you take them up.

**Quince Marmalade.**

Boil the quinces in water until soft, let them cool, and rub all the pulp thorugh a sieve; put two pounds of it to one of sugar, pound a little cochineal, sift it through fine muslin, and mix it with the quince to give a colour; pick out the seeds, tie them in a muslin bag, and boil them with the marmalade; when it is a thick jelly, take out the seeds and put it in pots. (Randolph, *Virginia Housewife,* 196)

This is a good evolutionary example of a recipe from one generation to the next. Some familiar elements are retained while new elements are adopted.

| *Contemporary Recipe #1* | *Contemporary Recipe #2* |
|---|---|
| Cream; put them into a Mazarene-dish, pour melted Butter over them; set them in an Oven moderately hot, till they are crisp, and serve them up. (Nott, *Cook's and Confectioner's Dictionary,* #16) | |
| **A Lemon Pudding.** TAKE two clear Lemons, grate off the outside rinds; then grate two Naples-biskets, and mix with your grated Peel, and add to it three quarters of a pound of fine Sugar, twelve yolks, and six whites of Eggs, well beat, and three quarters of a pound of Butter melted, and half a pint of thick Cream; mix these well together; put a Sheet of Paste at the bottom of the Dish; and just as the Oven is ready, put your Stuff in the Dish; sift a little double-refined Sugar over it before you put it in the Oven; an hour will bake it. (E. Smith, *Compleat Housewife* [1729], 82) | ——— |
| **To keep Quinces raw all the year** Take some of the worst Quinces and cut them into small pieces, and Coares and Parings, boyle them in water, and put to a Gallon of water, some three spoonfuls of Salt, as much Honey; boyle these together till they are very strong, and when it is cold, put it into half a pint of Vinegar in a wooden Vessel or Earthen Pot; and take then as many of your best Quinces as will go into your Liquor, then stop them up very close that no Aire get into them, and they will keep all the yeare. (W. M., *Compleat Cook,* 27) | ——— |
| **Marmalade White:** Take six pound of Quinces, pare and core them, and then boil 'em to a Pulp, put to it two pound of sugar, moistened well with the Juice of Quinces; boil them gently together it first till the Liquor be swelled out of the Quinces, and the Sugar dissolved, and all come into a convenient thickness, and so put it up for your use. (Salmon, *Family Dictionary,* 199) | ——— |
| ——— | ——— |

*"Jane Randolph her Cookery Book, 1743"*

**Preserve Peaches**

Pare your Peaches, & strew Sugar over them, to Five lb Peaches put Four pound Sugar, boil them very quick, Scum them all the time, & when they are tender, take them out of the Sirrup, & boil the Liquor to a Jelly.

**Bitter Wine**

Put the following Ingredients into 2 qts. Wine Vizt: 4 penny weig[h] Rhubarb, a Handful Cardus, a little Gentian Root, a little Orring Ro[ot] 2 Penny weigh common Snake Root, & a Handful Wormwood Let it stand 24 Hours.

**For a Rhumatism**

Take a quanty of Sassafras Roots & put it into an O—— A[?] first cut it to peices, & after drawing it off [but?] there will be an Oil, in it, of waich anoint the Joints, Drink the Leequer & wash with it, first, & then anoint with the Oyl.

**For the Bite of a Dog**

Take of grey ground Liverwort; in Powder, one dram; of Elicamplane Powder one dram; of black Helebore Root, in fine Powder, twenty grains; of native or factitious Cinnabar, well levigated, ten grains. mix them together for one Dose, to be taken on an empty Stomach the first Morning, if possible, after the Bite (fasting a few Hours after it) in a glass of Wine; or Wine and Water.

This Medicine is such a powerful Alterative, that, if taken in forty eight Hours after the Bite (Temperance

*Comments*

**To Preserve Clingstone Peaches**

Get the finest yellow clingstones, pare them and lay them in a bowl, have their weight of sugar pounded, and sprinkle over them as they are put in; let them stand two or three hours, put them together with the sugar into the pan, add a little water, and let the peaches remain till thoroughly scalded, take them out with the ladle, draining off the syrup; should there not be enough to cover the peaches, add more water, boil it and skim it, return the fruit, and do them gently till quite clear. Have some stones cracked, blanch the kernels, and preserve them with the peaches. (Randolph, *Virginia Housewife,* 192–93)

**Clingstones Sliced**

Pare the peaches and cut them in as large slices as possible, have their weight in sugar, and preserve them as the others. (Randolph, *Virginia Housewife,* 193)

~ Presumably, Jane meant her peaches to be whole, but they may have been sliced. Mary's version carefully spelled out every step of the process for any housewife to read, but the principles were the same. She added her own personal touch with the addition of kernels.

———

———

~ This medical cure obviously came from some publication. In the eighteenth century such "mad-dog" recipes became all the rage. **Hellebore** is the name given by the ancients to certain plants (*Helleborus officinalis*) with poisonous and medical properties and especially reputed as specifics for mental disease (*OED,* 5:204). **Factitious** refers to something "artificial" or something "made by or resulting from art"; mercury could be extracted from native cinnabar and then **levigated** (reduced to a fine and smooth powder) (*OED,* 4:13). Could this also be the case of extracting

*Contemporary Recipe #1*

*Contemporary Recipe #2*

**8. To preserve Peaches**

Heat water scalding hot first, then scald your Peaches till you may pull off the skin, which done, boil your Rosewater and Sugar till it be somewhat thi[c]k: then put in your Peaches one by one, st[r]owing the Sugar on them; and as the fire melteth, cast on more four or five times, letting them boyl with a soft fire till they be tender, keeping them covered as long as they seethe, then take them out, and put them up for use. (M. B., *Ladies Cabinet,* 5)

———

**A good Bitter Wine**

Take two quarts of strong White-wine, Infuse in it one dram of Rhubarb, a dram and half of Gentian-root, Roman Wormwood, tops of Carduus, Centory, Camomile- flowers, of each three drams, Yellow peep of Oranges, half an ounce; Nutmegs, Mace, and Cloves, of each one dram: Infuse all these two Days and Nights; strain and Drink a glass Fasting, and an Hour before Dinner, and Supper: Add Filings of Steel (if 'tis proper) two ounces[.] (Several Hands, *Collection* [1714], 186–87)

———

——— ———

——— ———

*"Jane Randolph her Cookery Book, 1743"*

Strictly observed) it will not only resist and correct, but soon expel the Poison. Innumerable Experiments have been tried with the greatest Success, not only upon the Human Species, but upon Dogs and other Animals; when those that took it did well, and those who took it not in a short time died raving mad. Tho' it may appear to some a Remedy of no consequence, as most things do when once made public, it is, notwithstanding found by Experience (if given in due time) to be as infallible a Preservative in the above mention'd case, as Mercury is in raising a Salivation, or the peruvian Bark in curing a regular Intermittion

NB The wound may be dressed and healed after the common Manner, with some proper Digestive.

*Comments*

some substance imitating cinnabar? Also known as **Jesuits bark, Peruvian bark** was derived from the cinchona tree, the source of quinine, and was "ground into powder and taken as a febrifuge" (*OED,* 7:672). **Dr. Richard Meade** (1673–1754), a royal physician of Oxford, England, who served Queen Anne and her successors, was an avid book collector who left more than ten thousand books at his death (*Dictionary of National Biography,* 32:181–83). His recipe for the bite of a mad dog became very popular.

**For Obstructions, & Shortness of Breath.**

Put Two Spoonfuls of fil'd Steel into a qt. of Red Wine & drink a Wine Glass full Morning; & Evening, keeping your Feet in warm Water half an Hour at least every time you Drink the Wine.

~ Many recipes were available for "shortness of breath," but not all of them contained filed steel as an ingredient. The following example parallels this one.

**[Title Missing]**

Take a Quantity of Ground Oatmeal Roast it make it as you do Coffee this is Extremly Good for a Vomiting. Sweaten it with the Surrup of Quinces made thus. Take the Juce of Quinces put to it Double Refine Sugar till it will take no more when it is Settled Then poor it of into Bottles

Prescrib'd by Mr. John Watson of Suffolk.

———

**Mrs. Lanhorns way to Bottle Cherrys**

Fill the Bottles, cork, & lash them down [with?] Pack thread, then put them in a Kettle [of] cold Water, & let them stand till they be[gin?] to simmer, then take them off & let them stand till the Water is cold, then Rosin the Corks, & put them in a Cellar.

———

**Mr. Hinters Receipt, to to harden F——**

After tis Fried up, you must melt it down again & stir it, till tis almost cold, or alm[ost?] as thick as Honey. This will make it flinty[?].

———

**The old Talors Receit for a Purging.**

Make a strong Decoction of the inner Bark of sweet Gum, from the Northside of ye: Tree. Drink a quarter of a pt: fasting, as much at Noon, & at Night for two, or three Days, & after that: drink it now, & then as you woud Small Beer.

———

*Contemporary Recipe #1*

**The Infalible Powder for Shortness of Breath, especially in Young Ladies.**

Take of Carraway and Aniseed, each one Ounce, Liquorice half an Ounce, one large Nutmeg, one Ounce of prepared Steel, and two Ounces of double refin'd Sugar; reduce all to a very fine Powder, and take as much as will lie on a Shilling, in the Morning, fasting, and at five in the afternoon, using Exercise. (Several Hands, *Collection* [1734], 177–78)

———

———

———

———

*Contemporary Recipe #2*

———

———

———

———

———

*"Jane Randolph her Cookery Book, 1743"*

*Comments*

**[Title Missing]**

Take 7 lb Flower 3 lb Butter 1 1/2 Sugar 1/2 an oz: Nutmegs Cloves & Mace 3/4: lbs Sweetmeats 8 lb. Fruit 1 pint & 1/2 Cream 1 pint Yest 1/2 a pint M Wine sweetened 2 doz. Eggs Mix the yest & Spice in the Flour first & then the Eggs &c.

~ This appears to be some kind of cake studded with fruit.

**Philadelphia Receipt. for. a Fever, & Ague-**

Take 2 oz Bark, 1 oz: Snake Root, 1 oz: Salt of Tartar, 1/2 oz: Camomile Flower, put them into a half Gallon Bottle, fill'd with Jamaica Spirit, & set it into a Kettle of Water, over a moderate Fire, & let the Ingreetients infuse three Days, the Water being kept rather warmer, then Blood, - Dose for a grown Person, half a Jill, 3 or 4 times between the Fitts. for a Child of a Year old a Tea Spoonful mix'd with Balm Tea; The Ingredients by adding more Spirit to them, make a good preventing Bitter.

———

**Baran's Receipt for a Rumatism.**

Put 4 oz: of Gumgoacum into a quart of Rum, let it stand three weeks in a warm place; shaking the Bottle twice a Day, then take a Tea Spoonful Mor$^{ng}$. & Evening.

~ **Gumgoacum,** or **gum guaiacum,** "a resin obtained from a tree native to the West Indies" and "warmer parts of America (e.g., *Guaiacum officinale*)," is a drug that supposedly was effective in medicine, including the treatment of scrofula (*OED,* 4:476).

**For the Rheumatism**

Take of Cochineal & English Safforn bruised in a Mortar of each a Dram: put the same in a bottle & pour these to a Quart of French, or Peach Brandy. In ten Days it will be fit for use but the Cochineal & Saffron may remain in the Bottle 'till the Brandy is all used. Let the Patient at Night going to Bed, take one spoon ful of the above Infusion; bathing the part affected with some of it warmed over a Fire: wrapping the Part in Flannel; but of the Disorder should be violent, he may take two spoonfls. Care should be taken in pouring it out that it may not be thick.

A W

———

**Eye Water, by Mrs. Farquer.**

Take as much calcin'd white Vitriol as will lie on a Shilling, pour on it a quart of boiling Water - Then add a quarter of a pint of Hungary Water. this is first to be us'd clear, then shake it up when you set it by. you may also add a little white sugar - Candy in it - NB you are to put one drop in the Eye at a time, three times a Day,

~ **Vitriol** is a native or artificial sulphate of metal in used in the arts or medicinally, especially sulphate of iron (*OED,* 12:265). **Hungary water** is a rectified spirit of wine infused with rosemary flowers and distilled (*OED,* 5:458).

*Contemporary Recipe #1*

*Contemporary Recipe #2*

*"Jane Randolph her Cookery Book, 1743"*

**A Receipt for a Purging**

Take half an oz: of Kipscacuanna, decoct it in one equal quantity of Clarit, & Water. let it boil from a qrt to less than a pint. Strain it, & add one Spoonful of Oil. give it in a Glister. If the Patient be very weak, or a Child, you must infuse less, of the Root, a Dram being a full Quanty for a Man - J Coupland.

**Doctor Jemmisons Diet Drink -**

Take 1/2 an oz: Sassaperrella, & as much China Root, one oz: Harts Horn Shavings, & Sixty grains sweet Fennel Seeds. Boil them from a quart, to a pint.

**An Electuary or a hurt in ye: Breath**

Mix two spoonfuls of Lucatellus Balsom, two spoonfuls St: Johnswort, & two spoonfuls Spermaceti groun up with a little Sugar & 2 Tea spoonfuls Balson Capevi

**Potatoe Custeard very good**

To a quart of Potatoe Pulp, put a quart of good top of Milk, Six Eggs 2 spoonfuls Rose Water, half a Nutmeg, sweeten it to your Taste. then bake it in good Paste.

*Comments*

~ **Kipscacuanna** is a variation of **ipscacuanna**, better known today as ipecacuanha or ipecac. The American version is identified among scientific circles as *Euphorbia Ipecauanha.* It was primarily used for emetic and purgative purposes (*OED*, 5:472).

~ Dr. Jemmison was Dr. Alexander Jameson who lived at Williamsburg and then at Flowerdew Hundred. In an advertisement in the *Virginia Gazette* (19 December 1755), he notified the public that his apothecary shop, now kept by Robert Artbuthnot, contained "Drugs and Medicines of all Kinds." He later moved to Blandford, Prince George County, where he died in 1766 (*Virginia Gazette,* 18 June 1766).

A diet drink was a form of laxative beverage. **Sassaperella,** now spelled **sarsaparilla,** is a plant of the order *Smilaceae* that is indigenous in the tropical region from Mexico to Peru and Jamaica (*OED*, 9:113). **China root** (*Smilax China L.*) is "the thick, fleshy root-stock of a shrubby climbing plant" similar to sarsaparilla; it was said to "possess great medical virtues" (*OED*, 2:351).

~ An **electuary** is a medical "conserve or paste, consisting of a powder or other ingredient mixed with honey, preserve, or syrup of some kind" (*OED*, 3:80). **Saint-John's-wort** is the "common English name" given to "plants of the genus *Hypericum,* includes a number of herbs and shrubs (*OED*, 5:502, 593). **Spermaceti,** which in its "purified state" looks like a soft, white, scaly mass, is found primarily in the "head of the sperm whale"; it was valued in medicine among other things (*OED*, 9:578). **Capevi** is actually copaiba, a balsam or resinous juice of aromatic odor and acrid taste from South American trees of the genus *Copaifera* (*OED*, 2:967).

*Contemporary Recipe #1*

*Contemporary Recipe #2*

**Potatoe-Pudding baked. From Mr. Shepherd of Windmill Street.**

Boil some fair Potatoes till they are tender; then, when they are made clean, bruise them in a Marble Mortar, till they become a Paste, with some Mace powder'd, some Sugar, and the Pulp of Oranges, with a Naples Biscuit or two grated in, and a large carrot grated. Add to these some Orange-Flower-Water; and when all these are well mix'd, put to them some butter'd Eggs, with some slices of Butter laid upon your Pudding, when it is put into the Dish, or Pan. A little baking will serve for it; and when it is enough, serve it hot, with a garnish of sliced Lemon or Orange. Some will put this into a Paste, but not cover it. (Bradley, *Complete Body of Husbandry,* 168)

| *"Jane Randolph her Cookery Book, 1743"* | *Comments* |
|---|---|

**Hartshorn Flummery**

You must have a quart of stiff Jelly ready, & then Just melt it: & put to it, half a pt: white Wine, a pint of new thick cream, & four spoonfuls O F Water scald your cream; & let it be cold before you mix it: sweeten it to your tast, & beat it all one way an hour, & half at least then wet your cups & pour it in. let it stand a day before you use it.

———

**Oat Meal Flumery.**

Put three large handfuls of fine oatmeal into two quarts water, let it stand a day & a night; then pour off the water, & put on the same quantity of fresh water. then strain it through a sifter, & boil it till tis as thick as a hasty Pudding. stir it all the while to make it smooth: before you set it - on the fire you must put in one spoonful L Sugar, & of O F or R water. when boild enough put it into cups, or shallow dishes.

———

**Ratafia Cacks.**

Take 8 oz: Apricot kernels, or bitter Almonds beaten fine with O F water, mix them with the whites of three eggs well beaten, two: lb single R sugar work all together into a paste, lay it in little round - bits on tin plates well flour'd.

———

*Contemporary Recipe #1*

**To make Hartshorn Flummery**

Boil half a Pound of Shaving of Hartshorn in three Pints of Water till it comes to a Pint; then strain it through a Sieve into a Bason, and set it by to cool; then set it over the Fire, let it just melt, and put to it half a Pint of thick Cream, scalded and grown cold again; a quarter of a Pint of White-wine, and two spoonfuls of Orange-Flower-Water; sweeten it with Sugar, and beat it for an Hour and half, or it will not mix well, nor look well; dip the Cups in Water before your pour in your Flummery, or else it will not turn out well, let it stand two Days before you use it; when you serve it, turn it out of the Cups, and stick blanch'd Almonds cut in Slices, all over the Tops; you may eat it either with Wine or Cream. (Nott, *Cook's and Confectioner's Dictionary,* #24)

———

**To make Ratafia Cacks**

Take eight ounces of Apricock-Kernels, or if they cannot be had, Bitter-Almonds will do as well, blanch them, and beat them very fine with a little Orange-flower-water, mix them with the Whites of three Eggs well beaten, and put to them two pounds of single-refin'd Sugar finely beaten and sifted; work all together, and 'twill be like a Paste; then lay it in little round Bits on Tin-plates flower'd, set them in an Oven that is not too hot, and they will puff up and be soon baked[.] (Several Hands, *Collection* [1714], 96)

*Contemporary Recipe #2*

———

———

———

Appendix

# WILL OF JANE RANDOLPH

Will of Jane Randolph, of "Curles." In the name of God Amen I Jane Randolph of Curles, in the County of Henrico, being of Sound Mind and Memory, do constitute and appoint this my last will & Testament, in manner and form following. Imprimis, I give & bequeath unto my Son Richard Randolph, one silver Salver; four large silver salt-cellars; one Counterpane of the largest size, & one fringed counterpane of the best sort: Item: I devise unto my Son Ryland, one silver Tankard; two small silver waiters; one large silver spoon, one Counterpane of the largest size, and one fringed counterpane of the best sort. Item; I devise unto my son John, one flat silver Candle Stick & snuffers; one dozen large silver Table spoons with the crest on them, ten silver sweet meat spoons, & two old silver Table spoons now about the House; with all the old Tea-spoons: one counterpane of the smallest size, a silk Quilt, the black Trunk in the Chamber, and two small Counterpanes of the worst sort; Item, I give to my Daughter-in-law Anne Randolph, The silver chased Milk Pot & the Coral and whereas by my late Husbands will, my Sons Brett, Ryland & John were entitled to sundry Slaves therein named, with their future increase which he lent me during my Life & were directed by my said Husband to be equally divided between them; three of which slaves to-wit, Jenny the Daughter of Joan, Hannah, & Ester the Daughter of Cato, were by me put into the possession of my said son Brett and by him sold to my son John; I do allot these following, Jenny, Stump, Seneca, & Jemmy the son of Bob; part of the said devised slaves, to be his share. I give unto my son Ryland & his Heirs old Jenny, old Dinah, Nelly, Ben, Sue the daughter of Jenny, York, Hannebal, & Pompey, Billy & Jenny the children of Sue. Item; I give unto my son John & his heirs,—Jack, Isaac, Bounshire [?], George & Cato, Joan & her son Thompson, and Jenny the Daughter of Chillis, and Nelly, Bob & Jenny the children of Sue. Item, I give unto my Daughter Elizabeth, the sum of sixty Pounds currency, My Gold Watch, Seal, Chain, and all appurtenances; the Mahogoney Press which stands in my Room; The chest which stands under the Window in the store Room & everything in it, except a pr. of cotton cards. I lent to my Niece Jane Eldridge, during her natural life, my negro woman Sally, with her sons Jemmy & nat, & her future increase. But my will is, that if my said Niece should marry, and have Issue then I give the said Slaves to my said niece in fee. But if this contingency should not happen, & my said niece should not marry, & have Issue, then I give the said slaves Sally, & her Children, unto my daughter Elizabeth & her Heirs. I give unto my Niece Jane Eldridge my black Walnut Press. Item. I give unto my Daughter Elizabeth. my Post Charriot. Item; I give all the Pewter & Copper furniture to my three sons Richard, Ryland & John and the eldest surviving son of my deceased son Brett to be equally divided among them by my Executors. Item; I give unto my Son Richard, the

Mahogony Scritoire in the little Hall. Item, I give unto my son Ryland my Picture of his Father's hanging in my Room and the Picture of my son Brett drawn in Crayons; also the large Mahogony Table in the Dining Room; and the small Mahogony Spring Table. Item, I give unto my Son John the Picture of Sr. John Randolph and the black Walnut Scrutiore in the Chamber. Item, I give unto the eldest surviving son of my deceased Son Brett, the Picture in the Chamber. Item, I give unto my three Sons, Richard, Ryland, & John & the eldest surviving son of my deceased son Brett, eight Feather Beds, to be equally divided among them by my executors I also give unto my said three sons & Grandson, to be equally divided all the cash I may leave, after my Debts, & legacies are paid. I leave all my effects not before disposed of in trust to my Sons Richard & Ryland, to be divided agreeable to Memorandum committed to their care. And I do appoint my sons Richard & Ryland, with Coll. Archibald Cary, my Executors. In witness whereof, I have hereto set my Hand & Seal & published this my last will & Testament this second day of March, one Thousand seven Hundred & sixty-six. But I first direct farther that there be no appraisement of my estate. Signed, sealed and published in presence of us Elizabeth Gay, Anne Murray. Jane Ralph [*sic*] (Black Wax Seal Arms.)

Henrico County Miscellaneous Court Records, Deeds, Wills, Etc., 1758–1769, pp. 1995–98

# NOTES

**Introduction**

Epigraphs are from Samuel Pepys, *The Diary of Samuel Pepys,* ed. R. C. Latham and W. Matthews (Berkeley: University of California Press), 4:14; Pepys, *Diary,* 1:218; and Robert Hunter, *Quebec to Carolina in 1785–1786: Being the Travel Diary and Observations of Robert Hunter Jr., a Young Merchant of London* (San Marino, Calif.: Huntington Library), 206–7. *The Diary of Samuel Pepys* is cited by permission of the University of California Press. Copyright © 1972–1986 The Master, Fellows and Scholars of Magdalen College, Cambridge, Robert Latham, and the Executors of William Matthews.

1. Henrico County Miscellaneous Court Records, 1738–46, 1069.

2. Theodore H. Price and Charlotte P. Price, "Notes on the Price Family, Cool Water, Hanover County, Virginia, Maternal Ancestry and Descent in Two Lines to the Year 1906," #26867, 6, Library of Virginia, Richmond, Va.,; William E. Barrett, "Reverend Robert Barrett Professor College of William and Mary in Virginia in 1737 and His Grandson Anderson Barret of Richmond (1773–1857)," bound manuscript, Library of Virginia, Richmond, Virginia.

3. Marion E. Briggs, letter to author, 28 January 1993.

4. Benedict Arnold to Sir Henry Clinton, 12 May 1781, in Lieutenant-General (Banastre) Tarleton, *A History of the Campaigns of 1780 and 1781, in the Southern Provinces of North America* (London: T. Cadell, 1787), 337. Benedict mentioned the destruction of Col. Cary's flour mills, etc., on 30 April 1781.

5. Maggs Brothers, *Notes on Autographs* No. 1 (London: Corner Press, 1934). Manuscripts Division, Library of Congress, Washington, D.C.

6. Sandra Oliver, conversation with author, Boston, November 1997.

7. Dr. Thomas B. King, conversation with author, Richmond, Va., 24 March 1998.

8. Josef Konvitz, "Identity, Self-Expression and the American Cook," *The Centennial Review* (spring 1975): 85–88.

9. [The Compiler (1744)], Manuscript cookbook, early eighteenth century, Va. Hist., VA., M. Mfm. 5A., Museum of Early Southern Decorative Arts, Winston-Salem, N.C.; hereafter cited as [The Compiler (1744)], "Manuscript cookbook." Notation on title page states: "Found in the House of Doctor Lumkins [sic], Mechanicsville, King William Co. [sic], Virginia."

10. [The Compiler (1744)]. "Manuscript cookbook," 88; and Elizabeth Tucker Coalter, Cookbook of Elizabeth Tucker Coalter, c. 1808, 174, Tucker-Coleman Collections, Special Collections, Swem Library, College of William and Mary.

11. L. Daniel Mouer, "Chesapeake Creoles: The Creation of Folk Culture in Colonial Virginia," in *The Archaeology of 17th-Century Virginia,* eds. Theodore R. Reinhart and Dennis J. Pogue, Special Publication/Archaeological Society of Virginia, no. 30 (Richmond, Va.: Archaeological Society of Virginia, 1993), 110–11, 118–23.

## Part One

**Tidewater Society in Colonial Virginia**

Epigraphs are from Pepys, *Diary,* 2:175; Henrico County Record Book No. 1, Deeds & Wills, 1677–92 [transcript], 115 and Henrico County Miscellaneous Court Records: Wills, Deeds, Etc. 1727–37, 891–92; William Byrd to Perry and Lane, 25 February 1683, in William Maxwell, ed., *The Virginia Register and Literary Advertiser* 1, no. 2: 63; Byrd, *The Secret Diary of William Byrd of Westover,*

*1709–1712,* eds. Louis B. Wright and Marion Tinling (Richmond, Va.: The Dietz Press, 1941), 206, 411, 230; Byrd, *Secret Diary,* 232; and Byrd, *Secret Diary,* 234–35, 410.

1. Louis B. Wright, *The First Gentlemen of Virginia; Intellectual Qualities of the Early Colonial Ruling Class* (San Marino, Calif.: The Huntington Library, 1940), 47–48; Rhys Isaac, *The Transformation of Virginia, 1740–1790* (Chapel Hill: University of North Carolina Press, 1982), 20, 111.

2. Wright, *First Gentlemen,* 48.

3. Ibid., 43–44; Anne Firor Scott and Suzanne D. Lebsock, *Virginia Women: The First Two Hundred Years* (Williamsburg, Va.: Colonial Williamsburg Foundation, 1988), 19.

4. Wright, *First Gentlemen,* 39.

5. Gerald Steffan Cowden, "The Randolphs of Turkey Island: A Prosopography of the First Three Generations, 1650–1806" (Ph.D. diss., College of William and Mary, 1980), 47.

6. Wright, *First Gentlemen,* 38–39, 47.

7. Cowden, "Randolphs," 47, 51.

8. Richard Bushman, preface to *The Refinement of America: Persons, Houses, Cities* (New York: Alfred A. Knopf, 1992), xii.

9. York County Deeds Orders Wills, Etc. No. 1, 1633–94, 182–86; Henrico County Deeds & Wills, Etc., 1688–97, 350–51, 706.

10. L. Daniel Mouer, "Reading 'Jane Randolph Her Book,'" in *Digging Sites and Telling Stories: Essays in Interpretive Historical Archaeology* (New York: Plenum Publishing), 274.

11. Wright, *First Gentlemen,* 2, 37.

12. François Durand, *A Huguenot Exile in Virginia,* ed. Gilbert Chinard (New York: Press of the Pioneers, 1934), 110.

13. Wright, *First Gentlemen,* 39, 44, 47; Isaac, *Transformation,* 34–38, 40–42.

14. Carole Shammas, "English-Born and Creole Elites in Turn-of-Century Virginia" in *The Chesapeake in the Seventeenth Century,* eds. Thad W. Tate and David L. Ammerman (Chapel Hill: University of North Carolina Press), 285.

15. Robert Beverley, *The History and Present State of Virginia* (Chapel Hill: University of North Carolina Press, 1947), 4:291.

16. Janet Ervin, ed., *The White House Cookbook* (Chicago: Follett Publishing Company, 1964), 330.

17. Cowden, "Randolphs," 434.

18. Isaac, *Transformation,* 133–35.

19. Daniel Blake Smith, *Inside the Great House: Planter Family Life in Eighteenth-Century Chesapeake Society* (Ithaca, N.Y.: Cornell University Press, 1980), 62, 105, 107; Lorena S. Walsh, "The Experiences and Status of Women in the Chesapeake, 1750–1775," in *The Web of Southern Social Relations: Women, Family, and Education,* eds. Walter J. Fraser Jr., R. Frank Saunders, and Jon L. Wakelyn (Athens: University of Georgia Press, 1985), 7–8.

20. Henrico County Order Book 1694–99, 284.

21. Cowden, "Randolphs," 65.

22. Henrico County Wills and Deeds 1748–50, C*, 112.

23. Hunter, *Quebec to Carolina,* 219.

24. Smith, *Inside the Great House,* 62–65; Walsh, "Experiences," 6–7.

25. Walsh, "Experiences," 9.

26. Smith, *Inside the Great House,* 62–65; Walsh, "Experiences," 8.

27. Surry County, Virginia Deeds 1752–58, Deed Book 9, 79–81.

28. Goochland County Deed Book 5, 1745–49, 74.

29. Sally Cary Fairfax, "Diary of a Little Colonial Girl," *Virginia Magazine of History and Biography* 11 (October 1903): 214.

**Men's Public Sphere in the Chesapeake**

Epigraphs come from Pepys, *Diary,* 1:113; Pepys, *Diary,* 1:324; Pepys, *Diary,* 7:35; William Maxwell, ed., "Letters came now this March, 1648, relate further," *Virginia Historical Register and Literary Advertiser,* 2, no. 2: 75; Byrd, *Secret Diary,* 74; Byrd, *Secret Diary,* 234; and Robert Rose, *The Diary of Robert*

*Rose: A View of Virginia by a Scottish Colonial Parson 1746–1751,* ed. Ralph E. Hall (Verona, Va.: McClure Press, 1977), 58, 41.

1. Isaac, *Transformation,* 32–33.
2. Bushman, *Refinement,* xii.
3. Isaac, *Transformation,* 34.
4. Shammas, "English-Born" 283.
5. Mary Douglas and Baron Isherwood, *The World of Goods* (New York: W. W. Norton & Company, 1987), 5.
6. Jane Carson, *Colonial Virginia Cookery* (Williamsburg, Va. : Colonial Williamsburg Foundation, 1985), 12.
7. Pepys, *Diary,* 2:68.
8. Pepys, *Diary,* 1:320, 2:4.
9. Pepys, *Diary,* 1:29; 3:3, 3:285–86; 8:104.
10. Pepys, *Diary,* 7:67–68.
11. Byrd, letter to Charles, Earl of Orrery, 5 July 1726. "Virginia Council Journals 1726–1753," *Virginia Magazine of History and Biography* 32 (January 1924): 27.
12. George Washington Greene, *The Life of Nathanael Greene, Major-General in the Army of the Revolution* (1871; reprint, Freeport, N.Y.: Books for Libraries Press), 507.
13. Bushman, preface to *Refinement,* xiv; Collins, "Women and the Production of Status Cultures," in *Cultivating Differences: Symbolic Boundaries and the Making of Inequality,* eds. Michèle Lamont and Marcel Fournier. (Chicago, Ill.: University of Chicago Press, 1992), 213.

**Women's Private Sphere: The English and Colonial Virginia Prescription**

Epigraphs from Pepys, *Diary,* 1:3, 1:291; Pepys, *Diary,* 7:420, 5:62; Byrd, *Secret Diary,* 42, 216, 537; and Barry to his daughter Susan, 1 Aug. 1824, in William T. Barry Letters (#2569), The Albert and Shirley Small Special Collections Library, University of Virginia Library, Richmond, Va.

1. Sir Hugh Platt, preface to *Delights for Ladies* (1609; reprint, London: Crosby Lockwood & Son Ltd, 1948), li–lii.
2. Gervase Markham, *The English Hus-wife* (London: I[John] B[eale], 1615), title page.
3. Stephen Mennell, *All Manners of Food* (Oxford: Basil Blackwell, Ltd., 1985), 85.
4. Platt, *Delights,* xlviii.
5. Ibid., xlvii–xlix.
6. Gervase Markham, *The English Housewife* (1615; reprint, ed. Michael Best Kingston: McGill-Queen's University, 1986), xlv.
7. Hannah Woolley, *The Gentlewoman's Companion* (London: Printed for B. Harris, 1675), 111.
8. Sarah Harrison, preface to *The House-Keeper's Pocket-Book and Compleat Family Cook* (London, 1733), ix–x.
9. Pepys, *Diary,* 9:20.
10. Walsh, "Women's Networks in the Colonial Chesapeake, 1750–1775" (paper presented at the annual meeting of the Organization of American Historians in Cincinnati, Ohio, 1983; a copy is found at the Colonial Williamsburg Foundation, Williamsburg, Va.), 6, 8, 33–34; Allan Kulikoff, *Tobacco and Slaves: The Development of Southern Cultures in the Chesapeake, 1680–1800* (Chapel Hill: University of North Carolina Press, 1986), 177.
11. Beth Norton, "The Evolution of White Women's Experience in Early America," *American Historical Review* 89 (June 1984): 609.
12. Julia Cherry Spruill, *Women's Life and Work in the Southern Colonies* (New York: Russell & Russell, 1969), 208.
13. Pepys, *Diary,* 2:21.
14. Henrico County Deeds, Wills, Etc., 1688–97, 628.
15. Woolley, *Gentlewoman's Companion,* 12; Barbara Welter, "The Cult of True Womanhood: 1820–1860" in *The American Family in Social-Historical Perspective,* ed. Michael Gordon (New York: St. Martin's Press, 1973), 227.

16. Spruill, *Women's Life,* 214; *The Lady's Companion or, An Infallible Guide to the Fair Sex,* 4th ed. (London, n.p., 1743), 32; Mary Sumner Benson, *Women in Eighteenth-Century America* (New York: Columbia University Press, 1935) 58; Woolley, *Gentlewoman's Companion,* 33, 43, 47.

17. Charles Carter, preface to *The Compleat City and Country Cook: or, Accomplish'd Housewife* (London: Printed for A. Bettesworth & C. Hitch & C. Davis, 1732), viii.

18. Henrico County Record Book No. 1, Deeds & Wills, 1677–92 [transcript], 79.

19. Woolley, *Gentlewoman's Companion,* 11.

20. R. G., *The Accomplish'd Female Instructor, or, A Very Useful Companion for Ladies, Gentlewomen, and Others* (London: John Shirley, 1704), 3.

21. Spruill, *Women's Life,* 214; *The Lady's Companion,* 32.

22. Woolley, *The Accomplish'd Lady's Delight in Preserving, Physick, Beautifying and Cookery* (London: Printed for B. Harris, 1675), pt.1, pp. 33, 43–44.

23. Ibid.

24. Hunter, *Quebec to Carolina,* 208.

25. Benson, *Women in Eighteenth-Century,* 19–20.

26. Smith, *Inside the Great House,* 59.

27. Platt, *Delights for Ladies,* xliii.

28. Markham, *The English Housewife,* xxvii, liii.

29. Jane (Bolling) Randolph, Jane Randolph her Cookery Book, 1743, Mss. 5:5 1507:1, (copy), Virginia Historical Society, Richmond, Va.; hereafter cited as Randolph, "Jane Randolph her Cookery Book."

30. Spruill, *Women's Life,* 232.

31. Woolley, *Gentlewoman's Companion,* B2.

32. Byrd, *Secret Diary,* 118.

33. Pepys, *Diary,* 7:14.

34. Princess Anne County Deed Book #17, 1780–82, 75.

35. Archibald Cary to Frances Bland Randolph, 18 Nov. 1775, Tucker-Coleman Papers, Special Collections, Swem Library, College of William and Mary, Williamsburg, Va.

36. Markham, *The English Housewife,* xxxix.

37. Markham, *The English Hus-Wife,* 69.

38. Pepys, *Diary,* 8:4.

39. Woolley, *Gentlewoman's Companion,* 9.

40. Rebecca Price, *The Compleat Cook* (1681; reprint, comp. Madeleine Masson, London: Rutledge & Kegan Paul, 1948), 13.

41. Sandra L. Oliver, *Saltwater Foodways: New Englanders and Their Food, at Sea and Ashore, in the Nineteenth Century* (Mystic, Conn.: Mystic Seaport Museum, 1995), n. 6.

42. Pepys, *Diary,* 2:170, 4:221.

43. Markham, *The English Housewife,* lii.

44. Woolley, *Gentlewoman's Companion,* 111–12.

45. Byrd, *Secret Diary,* 72.

46. Mouer, "Reading," 283.

47. Byrd, *Secret Diary,* 48.

48. Suzanne D. Lebsock, *"A Share of Honor": Virginia Women, 1600–1945* (Richmond, Va.: W. M. Brown & Son, 1984), 21; Smith, *Inside the Great House,* 59; Walsh, "Women's Networks," 7.

49. Philip Vickers Fithian, *The Journal and Letters of Philip Vickers Fithian, 1773–1774: A Plantation Tutor of the Old Dominion,* ed. Hunter Dickinson Farrish (Williamsburg, Va.: Colonial Williamsburg, 1965), 48.

50. Byrd, *Secret Diary,* 174, 461, 5, 315.

51. Pepys, *Diary,* 2:237, 4:13, 5:291.

52. Ibid., 1:54, 4:121, 5:349.

53. Landon Carter, *The Diary of Landon Carter of Sabine Hall, 1752–1778,* ed. Jack P. Greene (Charlottesville: University Press of Virginia, 1965), 1:574.

54. Byrd, *Secret Diary,* 22.
55. Pepys, *Diary,* 3:81, 4:287.
56. Fairfax, "Colonial Girl," 215.
57. Pepys, *Diary,* 4:289.
58. Carson, preface to *Colonial Virginia Cookery,* xix.
59. Catherine Clinton, *The Plantation Mistress* (New York: Pantheon Books, 1982), 112–13.

**Women's Public Sphere in the Chesapeake**

Epigraphs from Charles Francis Adams[, ed.], *Familiar Letters of John Adams and His Wife Abigail Adams, During the Revolution* (Freeport, N.Y.: Books for Libraries Press), 286–87; Adams cited in Linda K. Kerber, *Women of the Republic: Intellect and Ideology in Revolutionary America* (Chapel Hill: University of North Carolina Press, 1980), 35; and Byrd, *Secret Diary,* 235.

1. Linda K. Kerber, "Separate Spheres, Female Worlds, Women's Place: The Rhetoric of Women's History," *Journal of American History* 75 (June 1988): 17; Smith, *Inside the Great House,* 59; Kulikoff, *Tobacco,* 166.
2. Kerber, "Separate Spheres," 19.
3. Ibid., 19; Isaac, *Transformation,* 135.
4. Lebsock, *"A Share of Honor,"* 21; Mary Beth Norton, *Liberty's Daughter* (Boston: Little, Brown and Company, 1980), 596; Kulikoff, *Tobacco,* 166.
5. Walsh, "Women's Networks," 4; Kulikoff, *Tobacco,* 177; Scott and Lebsock, *Virginia Women,* 1.
6. Cowden, "Randolphs," 50–51.
7. Henrico County Deeds, Wills, Etc., 1688–97, 223.
8. Lebsock, *"A Share of Honor,"* 22; Walsh, "Experiences," 1, 11; Norton, "The Evolution," 601; Kulikoff, *Tobacco,* 30–31.
9. Byrd, *Another Secret Diary,* 169 n 119.
10. Walsh, "Women's Networks," 15.
11. Pepys, *Diary,* 4:262; 5:113.
12. Byrd, *Secret Diary,* 296.
13. Lebsock, *"A Share of Honor,"* 22.
14. Virginia Land Office, *Patents,* Book I: 42.
15. Virginia Ferrar to Lady Berkeley, 10 Aug. 1650, Colonial Virginia Records, no. 692, (microfilm #575). Library of Virginia, Richmond, Va.
16. Kulikoff, *Tobacco,* 33.
17. Walsh, "Women's Networks," 1.
18. Walsh, "Women's Networks," 4; Walsh, "Experiences," 3–5.
19. Walsh, "Women's Networks," 4; Norton, "The Evolution," 597; Kulikoff, *Tobacco,* 177.
20. Norton, "The Evolution," 597.
21. Ibid., 597, 600; Scott and Lebsock, *Virginia Women,* 8.
22. Scott and Lebsock, *Virginia Women,* 15–16; Walsh, "Experiences," 1–2, 6; Norton, "The Evolution," 597–98; Smith, *Inside the Great House,* 70.
23. Walsh, "Experiences," 6; Walsh, "Women's Network," 4.
24. Kulikoff, *Tobacco,* 167; Scott and Lebsock, *Virginia Women,* 23.
25. Walsh, "Women's Networks," 15.
26. Lebsock, *"A Share of Honor,"* 21–22.
27. Norton, *Liberty's Daughter,* xiii.
28. Lebsock, *"A Share of Honor,"* 21; Walsh, "Experiences," 4.
29. Smith, *Inside the Great House,* 62.
30. Byrd, *Secret Diary,* 461.
31. York County Deeds, Orders, Wills, Etc., No. 1, 1633–94, 296.
32. Spruill, *Women's Life,* 233.
33. Herbert R. Paschal, ed., "George Bancroft's 'Lost Notes' on the General Court Records of the Seventeenth Century Virginia," *Virginia Magazine of History and Biography* 9 (July 1983): 356.

34. "Heroines of Virginia," *William and Mary Quarterly* 1st ser., 15 (July 1906): 41.

35. Ann Cotton, "An Account of Our Late Troubles in Virginia," in *Force's Historical Tracts,* ed. Peter Force (New York: Peter Smith, 1947), 1:10.

36. "Marriage of Dr. Blair and Sarah Harrison," in "Papers Relating to the Administration of Governor Nicholson and to the Founding of William and Mary College," *Virginia Magazine of History and Biography* 7 (January 1900): 278.

37. Lebsock, *"A Share of Honor,"* 24.

38. Richard Beale Davis, "The Devil in Virginia in the Seventeenth Century," *Virginia Magazine of History and Biography* 65 (April 1957): 147; Lebsock, *"A Share of Honor,"* 25.

39. Walsh, "Experiences," 1, 15; Smith, *Inside the Great House,* 151, 177.

40. Norton, "The Evolution," 613.

41. Walsh, "Experiences," 10; Norton, "The Evolution," 603.

42. Walsh, "Women's Networks," 2–3, 6.

43. Walsh, "Women's Networks," 15; Walsh, "Experiences," 6.

44. Walsh, "Women's Networks," 1, 3; Kulikoff, *Tobacco,* 603.

45. Walsh, "Women's Networks," 8.

46. Norton, *Liberty's Daughters,* 190.

47. Judith Randolph to Martha Jefferson, 12 February 1785, Nicholas Philip Trist Papers, #2104, Southern Historical Collections, Wilson Library, University of North Carolina at Chapel Hill.

48. Walsh, "Women's Networks," 10; Walsh, "Experiences," 10; Norton, "The Evolution," 609.

49. Norton, "The Evolution," 605.

50. Scott and Lebsock, *Virginia Women,* 25.

51. "Proceedings of Visitors of William and Mary College, 1716," *Virginia Magazine of History and Biography* 4 (October 1896): 174.

52. Joanne Bowen, conversation with author, Williamsburg, Va., spring 1993.

53. Norton, "The Evolution," 616, 619.

54. Kerber, *Women of the Republic,* 35.

55. Norton, "The Evolution," 616, 619.

56. Christianna Hill, "History of Mrs. Mary Randolph of Virginia," microfilm #258269, (typescript), Mormon Archives, Salt Lake City, Utah.

57. Charles E. Claghorn, *Women Patriots of the American Revolution: A Biographical Dictionary* (Metuchen, N.J.: The Scarecrow Press, Inc., 1991), 420.

58. *Virginia Gazette,* 27 July 1769, 2.

59. *Virginia Gazette,* Postscript, 3 November 1774, 1.

60. Ibid.; Norton, *Liberty's Daughters,* 161; "Ladies of the Association," *William and Mary Quarterly* 1st ser., 8 (July 1899): 36.

61. Kerber, *Women of the Republic,* 33.

62. Norton, *Liberty's Daughters,* 163.

63. Abigail Adams, letter to John Adams, 31 March 1776, and John Adams to Abigail Adams, 14 April 1776, in L. H. Butterfield, Marc Friedlaender, and Mary-Jo Kline, eds., *The Book of Abigail and John: Selected Letters of the Adams Family, 1762–1784* (Cambridge: Harvard University Press, 1975), 121, 123.

64. Lebsock, *"A Share of Honor,"* 59.

65. Clinton, *Plantation Mistress,* 193–96.

66. Rose Wilder Lane, *Woman's Day Book of American Needlework* (New York: Simon and Schuster, 1963), 82.

67. Amelia Simmons, *American Cookery* (1796; reprint [Grand Rapids,] Mich.: William B. Eerdmans Publishing Co., 1965), 43–44.

68. Margaret Woolfolk, "Patriotic Desserts," *Early American Life* 23, no. 3 (1992): 37.

69. Ibid.; Fannie Merritt Farmer, *The Original Boston Cooking-School Cookbook 1896* (New York: Weathervane Books), 510; Ervin, *White House Cookbook,* 323.

70. Mary Randolph, *The Virginia Housewife* (1824, reprint, ed. Karen Hess, Columbia: University of South Carolina Press, 1984), 159.

71. C. W. Andrews, *Memoir of Mrs. Anne R. Page* (Philadelphia: Herman Hooker), 57.

72. Samuel Mordecai, *Richmond in By-Gone Days* (Richmond, Va.: The Dietz Press, 1860), 130.

73. Sterling P. Anderson Jr., "'Queen Molly' and *The Virginia Housewife*," *Virginia Cavalcade* 20 (spring 1971): 33, 34.

74. William H. Safford, *The Blennerhassett Papers* (Cincinnati, Ohio: Moore, Wilstach & Baldwin), 457–58.

75. Eliza Leslie, *Miss Leslie's New Cookery Book* (Philadelphia: T. B. Peterson & Brothers, 1857), 344.

76. Carson, *Colonial Virginian Cookery,* xxxii; Anderson, "Queen Molly," 30.

77. Neil November, "Hospitality Betrayed," *Richmond Times Dispatch Magazine,* no date/page. Clipping, Valentine Museum, Richmond, Va.

78. Norton, *Liberty's Daughters,* xiii.

79. Lebsock, *"A Share of Honor,"* 26.

80. Ibid., 22.

## Status and the Cookbook Authors

Epigraphs from Pepys, *Diary,* 4:4; Pepys, *Diary,* 1:263, 1:75, 4:360, 3:3, 4:302, 6:21, 4:221; Byrd, *Secret Diary,* 114; Byrd, *Secret Diary,* 403, 404; Byrd, *Secret Diary,* 204; Byrd, *Secret Diary,* 558; and epitaph in William S. Nicholson, *Historic Homes and Churches of Virginia's Eastern Shore* (Accomac, Va.: Atlantic Publications, 1984), 1:170.

1. Randall Collins, "Women and the Production of Status Cultures" in *Cultivating Differences: Symbolic Boundaries and the Making of Inequality,* ed. Michèle Lamont and Marcel Fournier (Chicago: University of Chicago Press, 1992), 213.

2. Walsh, "Women's Networks," 18–19, 28.

3. Collins, "Women," 219.

4. Walsh, "Women's Networks," 219–20.

5. Norton, "The Evolution," 597, 617.

6. Scott and Lebsock, *Virginia Women,* 12.

7. Smith, *Inside the Great House,* 68.

8. William Byrd, *Another Secret Diary of William Byrd of Westover, 1739–1741,* ed. Marion Tinling (Richmond, Va.: The Dietz Press, 1942), 144 n; Jonathan Daniels, *The Randolphs of Virginia* (Garden City, N.Y.: Doubleday & Company, 1972), genealogical tables.

9. Lorna Sass, *Dinner with Tom Jones: Eighteenth-Century Cookery Adapted for the Modern Kitchen* (New York: Metropolitan Museum of Art, 1977), 18.

10. Randolph, *The Virginia Housewife,* 246–50.

11. Harriot Pinckney Horry, *A Colonial Plantation Cookbook,* ed. Richard J. Hooker (Columbia: University of South Carolina Press), 10–11.

12. Carson, preface to *Colonial Virginia Cookery,* xxi.

13. Randolph, *The Virginia Housewife,* 34, 78, 90, 103–4, 123, 157.

14. Mary Banister, Cookbook of Mary Burton Augusta (Bolling) Banister, 1818–1821, MSS. 1C6458c, #10, 63–64, in Cocke Family Papers 1742–1976, Virginia Historical Society, Richmond, Va.

15. Konvitz, "Identity," 88.

16. Ibid.

## Virginia's Cultural Boom

Epigraphs from Pepys, *Diary,* 3:14; Pepys, *Diary,* 5:266; Pepys, *Diary,* 5:7; Pepys, *Diary,* 4:17–18; Henrico County Record Book No. 1, Deeds & Wills, 1677–92, 249; "Appraisement of the Estate of Philip Ludwell Esqr. Dec'd.," *Virginia Magazine of History and Biography* 20 (October 1913): 406–16.

1. Bushman, *Refinement,* 5.

2. Bushman, *Refinement,* xvi–xvii.
3. Ibid., xvii.
4. Ibid., xii–xiv, xv, xvi, xviii, xix, 5, 8–9, 28.
5. Ibid., xix.
6. Ibid., xii, 8, xix.
7. Ibid., 95.
8. Jane (Bolling) Randolph, letter to John Randolph, 26 April 1765, MSS 2 R1551 al, Virginia Historical Society, Richmond, Va.
9. Richard Randolph, letter to Thomas Jefferson, 10 January 1809, in Tucker-Coleman Papers, Special Collections, Swem Library, College of William and Mary, Williamsburg, Va.
10. Bushman, *Refinement,* 10.
11. Ibid., 90.
12. Turner, letter to Sally Randolph, 29 September 1797, in William Bolling Papers, 1724–99, Rare Book, Manuscript and Special Collections Library, Duke University, Durham, N.C.
13. Bushman, preface to *Refinement,* xiv.
14. Ibid., xvii.

### The Architectural Setting

Epigraphs from Pepys, *Diary,* 6:222; Byrd, *Secret Diary,* 203, 206, 535; Byrd, *Secret Diary,* 232, 314; Byrd, *Secret Diary,* 233, 233.

1. Bushman, *Refinement,* 104–5.
2. L. Daniel Mouer, conversation with author, Richmond, Va., 18 October 1996.
3. Mouer, conversation with author, Richmond, Va., 26 May 1998.
4. Mouer, "Reading," 268, 272–73.
5. Bushman, *Refinement,* 101.
6. Mouer, "Reading," 269.
7. Mouer, conversation with author, Richmond, Va., 26 May 1998.
8. Ibid.
9. Bushman, *Refinement,* 101, 114, 120, 126.
10. Henry K. Glassie, *Folk Housing in Middle Virginia* (Knoxville: University of Tennessee Press, 1975), 136.
11. Bushman, *Refinement,* 100–101
12. Ibid., 27.
13. Hunter, *Quebec to Carolina,* 209, 245.
14. Bushman, *Refinement,* 9, 15.
15. Ibid., 16, 121.
16. Ibid., 15.
17. Ibid., 47; and Fithian, *Journal and Letters.*
18. Bushman, *Refinement,* 129.
19. Ibid.

### The Kitchen

Epigraphs from Pepys, *Diary,* 3:132, 2:106; Pepys, *Diary,* 10:510, 10:184; Robert Carter, Inventory of Robert Carter, November 1733(?), MSS 1C248a20, Carter Family Papers 1651–1861, Section 10. Virginia Historical Society, Richmond, Va.; Byrd, *Secret Diary,* 316, 347.

1. Mouer, "Reading," 272.
2. Ibid., 273.
3. Ibid.
4. Ibid., 273, 280.
5. Ibid., 273.
6. Ibid., 274.
7. Ibid., 289.

8. Ibid., 275.
9. Ibid., 275–76.

### The Dining Room Stage

Epigraphs from Pepys, *Diary,* 1:290, 3:251, 7:71, 5:358, 7:9–10, 7:426, 7:151; Pepys, *Diary,* 1:261, 1:269, 3:225, 4:6; Pepys, *Diary,* 9:402, 7:398; Fithian, *Journal and Letters,* 90; Hunter, *Quebec to Carolina,* 229–30.

1. Barbara Carson, preface to *Ambitious Appetites: Dining, Behaviour, and Patterns of Consumption in Federal Washington* (Washington, D.C.: American Institute of Architects Press), vi.
2. Louise C. Beldon, "The Colonial Dessert Table," *Antiques* 108 (December 1975): 156–63.
3. Nancy Carter Crump, *Hearthside Cooking* (McLean, Va.: EPM Publications), 35.
4. Jack Goody, *Cooking, Cuisine, and Class: A Study in Comparative Sociology* (Cambridge: Cambridge University Press), 139.
5. Pepys, *Diary,* 8:4.
6. York County Deeds, Orders, Wills, Etc., No. 1, 1633–94, 182–86; Henrico County Record Book No. 1, Deeds & Wills, 1677–92, 155, 236; Henrico County Deeds, Wills, Etc., 1688–97, 350–51, 706.
7. William FitzHugh, "Letters of William FitzHugh," *Virginia Magazine of History and Biography* 2 (June 1895): 269.
8. Benjamin Franklin, *The Autobiography of Benjamin Franklin,* ed. Leonard E. Labaree (New Haven: Yale University Press, 1964), 145.
9. Bushman, *Refinement,* 184.
10. Pepys, *Diary,* 2:8.
11. Bushman, *Refinement,* 74.
12. Randolph, *The Virginia Housewife,* 24.
13. Bushman, *Refinement,* 74.
14. Byrd, *Secret Diary,* 402.
15. Hunter, *Quebec to Carolina,* 211.
16. Byrd, *Secret Diary,* 59.
17. Woolley, *Accomplish'd Lady,* A2.
18. François Pierre de La Varenne, *The French Cook Prescribing the Way of Making Ready of All Sorts of Meats, Fish and Flesh, with the Proper Sauces* (London: n.p., 1653), A3.
19. Vincent La Chapelle, preface to *The Modern Cook* (London: Author, 1736), I.
20. Pepys, *Diary,* 4:354.
21. François Massialot, *The Court and Country Cook* (London: n.p.,), 9.
22. Pepys, *Diary,* 9:425–26.
23. Byrd, *Secret Diary,* 87.
24. Ibid., 69.
25. From Alicia Middleton to her son, 27 February 1828, in Middleton Papers, #5087, Southern Historical Collection, Wilson Library, University of North Carolina at Chapel Hill.
26. Marie Kimball, *Thomas Jefferson's Cook Book* (Richmond, Va.: Garrett and Massie), 24.
27. Ervin, *White House Cookbook,* 323.
28. Irving Brant, *James Madison* Vol. 6 (Indianapolis, Ind.: Bobbs-Merrill, 1961), 27.
29. A. K. Adams, ed., *The Home Book of Humorous Quotations* (New York: Dodd, Mead & Company), 105, part 7. Attributed to Voltaire.
30. Ervin, *White House Cookbook,* 322. Attributed to Dolley Madison.

### Dining Room Decorum

Horace epigraph in Elizabeth Hill and Martha Starr, *Candles & Parsley: When Company Comes* (Washington, D.C.: Starhill Press, 1989), n.p.; Pepys, *Diary,* 4:14; Pepys, *Diary,* 3:132; Byrd, *Secret Diary,* 320; Byrd, *Secret Diary,* 325, 201, 230; Greene, *Life of Nathanael Greene,* 506; Fithian, *Journal and Letters,* 111 and in Bushman, *Refinement,* 54.

1. Bushman, *Refinement,* 57.

2. Goody, *Cooking,* 140.

3. Carson, *Ambitious Appetites,* 25; Henry Miller, "An Archaeological Perspective on the Evolution of Diet in the Colonial Chesapeake, 1620–1745," in *Colonial Chesapeake Society,* eds. Lois Green Carr, Philip D. Morgan, and Jean B. Russo (Chapel Hill: University of North Carolina Press, 1988), 189.

4. Barbara Ketcham Wheaton, *Savoring the Past: The French Kitchen and Table from 1300 to 1789* (Philadelphia: University of Pennsylvania Press, 1983), 138.

5. Carson, *Ambitious Appetites,* 48.

6. Pepys, *Diary,* 9:115.

7. Jane Carson, *Plantation Housekeeping in Colonial Virginia* (Williamsburg, Va.: Colonial Williamsburg Foundation, 1974), 59–60.

8. Carson, *Plantation Housekeeping,* 61.

9. Carson, *Colonial Virginia Cookery,* 5.

10. Carson, *Ambitious Appetites,* 83.

11. Ibid., 48.

12. Randolph, *The Virginia Housewife,* 27.

13. R. G., *Accomplish'd Female Instructor,* 23.

14. Woolley, *Gentlewomen's Companion,* 65, 69–71.

15. Pepys, *Diary,* 8:483.

16. Ibid., 3:62.

17. Ibid., 4:242–43.

18. Ibid., 7:278.

19. Byrd, *Secret Diary,* 110.

20. Carter, Diary, Nov. 25, 1770, in Sabine Hall Papers, #1959, The Albert and Shirley Small Special Collections Library, University of Virginia Library.

21. Hunter, *Quebec to Carolina,* 208.

22. Pepys, *Diary,* 3:22.

23. Carter, *Diary of Landon Carter,* 2:937; Fithian, *Journal and Letters,* 62, 64.

24. Sass, *Dinner,* 42–43.

25. Goody, *Cooking,* 136.

26. Spruill, *Women's Life,* 70 n. 24.

27. Woolley, *Gentlewomen's Companion,* 65.

28. Several Best Masters, *The Genteel Housekeepers Pastime: Or, the Mode of Carving at the Table Represented in a Pack of Playing Cards* (London: n.p., 1693), A4–A5.

29. Ibid., A1.

30. Byrd, *Secret Diary,* 309.

31. Randolph, *The Virginia Housewife,* 27.

32. Julianne Belote, *The Compleat American Housewife 1776* (Concord, Calif.: Nitty Gritty Productions, 1974), 172.

**All Things French**

Epigraphs from *The English Lady's Catechism; Shewing The Pride and Vaniety of our English Quality, in relieving Foreigners before their own Country Folks* (London, 1756), 6; Pepys, *Diary,* 8:211; Pepys, *Diary,* 3:400–401, 5:115; Pepys, *Diary,* 4:189; Byrd, *Secret Diary,* 132, 351–52, 325; Pepys, *Diary,* 195.

1. Philippa Pullar, *Consuming Passions: Being an Historic Inquiry into Certain English Appetites* (Boston: Little, Brown and Company, 1970), 129–30, 253.

2. Mennell, *All Manners,* 89.

3. Esther B. Aresty, preface to *The Exquisite Table: A History of French Cuisine* (New York: Bobbs-Merrill, 1980), xi–xii, 16, 20.

4. Wheaton, *Savoring the Past,* 138.

5. Aresty, *Exquisite Table,* 23.

6. Ibid., 11–12.

7. Christopher Driver and Michelle Berriedale-Johnson, *Pepys at Table: Seventeenth Century Recipes for the Modern Cook* (Berkeley, Los Angeles: University of California Press, 1984), 12.
8. Pepys, *Diary,* 4:341.
9. Robert May, *The Accomplisht Cook* (London: R. W., 1660), n.p.
10. Adams, *Home Book,* 689, part 15; attributed to Jonathan Swift in his "Advice to the Servants."
11. Aresty, *Exquisite Table,* 14.
12. Catherine Frances Frere, *A Proper Newe Booke of Cokerye* (Cambridge: W. Heffer & Sons, 1913), 52.
13. [Anonymous (1700)], Unidentified cookbook, c. 1700, MSS 5:5 Un 3:4, Virginia Historical Society, Richmond, Va.; hereafter cited as Anonymous (1700), "Unidentified cookbook."
14. [The Compiler (1744)], "Manuscript cookbook," 14–15, 31, 34–35, 57–58, 61–62, 65–68, 76, 81, 85.

**Religious Aspects of Foods**

Epigraphs from Pepys, *Diary,* 1:78; Pepys, *Diary,* 2:60, 6:117; Pepys, *Diary,* 2:112; Pepys, *Diary,* 5:200, 8:202; Pepys, *Diary,* 5:117, 4:104, 6:66; Pepys, *Diary,* 4:354; Byrd, *Secret Diary,* 549, 188; Henrico County Record Book No. 1, Deeds & Wills, 1677–92 (transcript), 258.

1. Kent Bailey and Ransom B. True, *A Guide to Seventeenth-Century Virginia Court Handwriting,* Research Bulletin 1 (Richmond, Va.: Association for the Preservation of Virginia Antiquities, 1980), 25.
2. Ibid.
3. Pepys, *Diary,* 2:52.
4. Carson, *Colonial Virginia Cookery,* 74; Anonymous (1700), "Unidentified cookbook."
5. Frances Phipps, *Colonial Kitchens, Their Furnishings, and Their Gardens* (New York: Hawthorne Book, 1972), 292.
6. C. Anne Wilson, *Food & Drink in Britain* (New York: Barnes & Noble, 1974), 266.
7. Anonymous (1700), "Unidentified cookbook."
8. Philip Alexander Bruce, *Social Life of Virginia in the Seventeenth Century* (Richmond, Va.: Whittet & Shepperson, Printers, 1907), 218.
9. Ibid., 219.
10. "Funeral Charges for Elizabeth Sindrey," *South Carolina Historical Magazine* 82 (January 1981): 83.
11. Pepys, *Diary,* 5:90.
12. Bruce, *Social Life,* 220–21.
13. Byrd, *Secret Diary,* 165, 342.
14. "Funeral Charges," 84.
15. York County Records, Vol. 1675–84, 485.
16. York County Records, Vol. 1675–84, 165.

**The Dinner Table**

Epigraphs from Pepys, *Diary,* 3:293, 3:54; Pepys, *Diary,* 2:22; Pepys, *Diary,* 4:95;Byrd, *Secret Diary,* 200, 4; Byrd, *Secret Diary,* 233; Fithian, *Journal,* 141; and cited in Virginia D. Cox and Willie T. Weathers, *Old Houses of King and Queen County, Virginia* ([King and Queen Courthouse, Va.]: King and Queen Historical Society, 1973), 239.

1. Carson, *Colonial Virginia Cookery,* 83.
2. Sass, *Dinner,* 42
3. Ibid., 9, 42.
4. Thomas H. Wolf, "Once Upon a Time a Cookbook Was a Recipe for Excess," *Smithsonian* 22, no. 8 (1991): 126.
5. John Shirley, *The Accomplished Ladies Rich Closet of Rareties . . . Maides Delightful Companion* (N.p.: Printed for N. Bodington, 1690), 52.
6. Richard Bradley, *A Complete Body of Husbandry . . . Adorn'd with Cuts* (London: Printed for James Woodman, and David Lyon, 1727), 20.

7. Patricia Storace, "Repasts Past," *House and Garden,* 158, no. 6 (1986): 68.

8. R. G., *Accomplish'd Female Instructor,* 107.

9. Pepys, *Diary,* 3:4.

10. Hannah Glasse, *The Art of Cookery Made Plain and Easy* (1747; reprint, London: Prospect Books, 1983), 288.

11. [The Compiler (1744)], "Manuscript cookbook," 75.

12. Pepys, *Diary,* 8:371.

13. Byrd, *Secret Diary,* 194.

14. Mary Douglas, "A Distinctive Anthropological Perspective" in *Constructive Drinking,* edited by Mary Douglas (New York: Cambridge University Press), 8 and Joseph Gusfield, "Passage to Play: Rituals of Drinking Time in American Society" in *Constructive Drinking,* 80–81.

15. Pepys, *Diary,* 1:223; 5:18.

16. Carson, *Colonial Virginia Cooking,* 117.

17. Anonymous (1700), "Unidentified cookbook."

18. Carson, *Colonial Virginia Cooking,* 122.

19. Carson, *Ambitious Appetites,* vi.

20. Thomas E. Buckley, "The Duties of a Wife: Bishop James Madison to His Daughter, 1811." *Virginia Magazine of History and Biography* 91 (January 1983): 98–104.

## Part Two

### Meats—One

Epigraphs from Pepys, Diary, 2:160, 3:3, 8:1, 9:48, 4:247, 6:222; Smith cited in Lyon G. Tyler, *Narratives of Early Virginia, 1606–1625* (New York: C. Scribner's Sons, 1907; reprint, New York: Barnes & Noble, 1952), 163; Henrico County Deeds, Wills, Etc., 1688–97, 375; William Byrd, "Letter to Gov. Robert Hunter?, 26 July 1711," in *The Correspondence of The Three William Byrds of Westover, Virginia, 1684–1776* (Charlottesville: University Press of Virginia), 1:283–84; Rose, *The Diary,* 43, 95; Byrd, *Secret Diary,* 578, 392–93, 292.

1. Wheaton, *Savoring the Past,* 10.

2. Fernand Braudel, *Capitalism and Material Life, 1400–1800* (New York: Harper and Row, 1973), 130, 132; Driver and Berriedale-Johnson, *Pepys at Table,* 23; J. C. Drummond and Anne Wilbraham, *The Englishman's Food: A History of Five Centuries of English Diet* (London: Jonathan Cape, 1969), 97, 117.

3. Thomas Tusser, *Five Hundred Points of Good Husbandry* (London: J. M., 1663), 55.

4. Attributed to Richard Leveridge, "The Roast Beef of Old England" (stanza 1), in John Bartlett, ed., *Bartlett's Familiar Quotations* (Boston: Little, Brown and Company, 1955), 5, part 298.

5. Drummond and Wilbraham, *Englishman's Food,* 108.

6. Pepys, *Diary,* 2:207.

7. Miller, "An Archaeological Perspective," 101–2, 106–7; Drummond and Wilbraham, *Englishman's Food,* 101; Mennell, *All Manners,* 40, 56.

8. Karen Hess, ed., *Martha Washington's Booke of Cookery* (New York: Columbia University Press, 1981), 14; Drummond and Wilbraham, *Englishman's Food,* 98–99.

9. Pepys, *Diary,* 7:218.

10. Barrie Kavasch, preface to *Native Harvests* (New York: Random House, 1977), xvii; Clara Kidwell, "Native American Foods" in *Spirit of the Harvest,* eds. Beverly Cox and Martin Jacobs (New York: Stewart, Tabori & Change, 1991), 12.

11. Kavasch, *Native Harvests,* 89.

12. Phipps, *Colonial Kitchens,* 103.

13. Kavasch, *Native Harvests,* 28.

14. Mouer, "Chesapeake Creoles," 122

15. Randolph, *The Virginia Housewife,* 17–19.

16. Sally Smith Booth, *Hung, Strung & Potted* (New York: Clarkson N. Potter, 1971), 5.

17. Joanne Bowen, "Foodways in Eighteenth-Century Chesapeake," unpublished paper, at the Colonial Williamsburg Foundation, Williamsburg, Va., 1993, 14; Miller, "An Archaeological Perspective," 182–83; Booth, *Hung,* 69.

18. Anonymous (1700), "Unidentified cookbook"; Randolph, "Jane Randolph her Cookery Book"; [The Compiler (1744)], "Manuscript cookbook," 65.

19. Randolph, *The Virginia Housewife,* 88, 93–94, 108, 110, and 112–13.

20. John Hammond, "Leah and Rachel, or, The Two Fruitful Sisters Virginia and Maryland," in *Force's Historical Tracts,* edited by Peter Force (New York: Peter Smith, 1947), 3:2.

21. Crump, *Hearthside Cooking,* 117.

22. Howard C. Rice Jr., comp., *The American Campaigns of Rochambeau's Army, 1780, 1781, 1782, 1783,* eds. and trans. Howard C. Rice Jr. and Anne S. K. Brown, vol. 1 (Princeton, N.J.: Princeton University Press, 1972), 68.

23. York County Deeds, Orders, Wills, Etc., No. 1, 1633–94, 31.

24. York County Deeds #2, 1645–49, 374, 390–93.

25. Lyman Carrier, *Agriculture in Virginia, 1607–1699* (Williamsburg, Va.: Virginia 350th Anniversary Celebration Corporation, 1957), 29.

26. "A Perfect Description of Virginia 1648" in *The Virginia Historical Register and Literary Advertiser,* ed. William Maxwell (Richmond, Va.: Macfarlane & Fergusson, 1973), 2:62.

27. Henrico County Record Book No. 1, Deeds & Wills, 1677–92 (transcript), 313–14, 376, 110.

28. Ibid., 126.

29. Hammond, "Leah and Rachel," 13.

30. Ibid., 19.

31. Henrico County Record Book No. 1, Deeds & Wills, 1677–92 (transcript), 126.

32. Hammond, "Leah and Rachel," 13.

33. Durand, *A Huguenot Exile,* 123.

34. Pepys, *Diary,* 1:26.

35. Randolph, "Jane Randolph her Cookery Book."

36. William Byrd, *William Byrd's Natural History of Virginia; or, The Newly Discovered Eden,* eds. and trans. Richmond Croom Beatty and William J. Mulloy (Richmond, Va.: The Dietz Press, 1940), 19–20, 88–89.

37. Hammond, "Leah and Rachel," 13.

38. Pepys, *Diary,* 1:189.

39. Durand, *A Huguenot Exile,* 42.

40. Pehr Kalm, *Peter Kalm's Travels in North America* (New York: Wilson-Erickson, 1937), 370.

41. Joseph Doddridge, *Note on the Settlement and Indian Wars of the Western Parks of Virginia and Pennsylvania from 1763 to 1783* (Pittsburgh, Pa.), 88; and Beverley, *History,* 292.

42. Miller, "An Archaeological Perspective," 176, 186, 188–95; Bowen, Foodways, 5–10, 13–14, 16–18, 20.

43. Sandra Oliver, conversation with author, Boston, November 1997. Mouer also noted this in "Reading," 299.

44. Braudel, *Capitalism,* 127.

45. Lawrence Butler, "Letters from Lawrence Butler, of Westmoreland County, Virginia to Mrs. Anna F. Cradock, Cumley House, near Harbrough, Leicestershire, England," *Virginia Magazine of History and Biography* 40 (July 1932): 266–67; Carson, *Ambitious Appetites,* 108.

**Meats—Two**

Epigraphs from Byrd, *Secret Diary,* 499; and Ann Cary Randolph, letter to Thomas Jefferson, 4 July 1806, in Edgehill-Randolph Papers, #962, The Albert and Shirley Small Special Collections Library, University of Virginia Library.

1. Hess, *Martha Washington's,* 8.

2. [The Compiler (1744)], "Manuscript cookbook," 56–57.

3. Rabisha, *The Whole Body of Cookery Dissected, Taught . . . Dutch &c.* (London: Printed for E. Calvert by R. W., 1661), 45.

4. [The Compiler (1744)], "Manuscript cookbook," 62–63, 65–66, 69, 75, 84.

5. Sass, *Dinner,* 198; *Webster's Third International Dictionary* (Springfield, Mass.: G. & C. Merriam Company), 269.

6. Hess, *Martha Washington's,* 72.

7. *The Oxford English Dictionary* (Oxford: At the Clarendon Press, 1933) 1:1064.

8. John Murrell, *A Delightful Daily Exercise for Ladies and Gentlewomen* (London: Printed for Tho. Dewe, 1621), B21.

9. Alain Outlaw, *Governor's Land: Archaeology of Early Seventeenth-Century Virginia Settlements* (Charlottesville: Published for the Dept. of Historic Resources by the University Press of Virginia, 1990), 55–56, 174.

10. Platt, *Delights for Ladies,* #13.

11. Frere, *A Proper New Booke,* in notes after p. xlii; Harrison, *House-Keeper's Pocket-Book,* 47.

12. Harrison, *House-Keeper's Pocket-Book,* 47; Katharine E. Harbury, "Virginia's Cooking Dynasty: Women's Spheres and Culinary Arts" (master's thesis, College of William and Mary, 1994), 85–86.

13. Pepys, *Diary,* 2:228; Pullar, *Consuming Passions,* 136.

14. Roger Goodburn, letter to author, 12 Jan. 1993.

15. Yeadon, "To Market, To Market: On the Prowl around London's Smithfield," *Washington Post,* 17 December 1995, E8.

16. *OED,* 2:305

17. Anonymous (1700), "Unidentified cookbook."

18. Mrs. Ernest Goodburn, letter to author, Mechanicsville, Va., 12 January 1993.

19. [The Compiler (1744)], "Manuscript cookbook," 63.

20. Randolph, *The Virginia Housewife,* 43, 66, 85.

21. Ibid., 81–83, 189.

22. See, for example, Miller, "An Archaeological Perspective."

23. Wilson, *Food & Drink,* 313–14.

24. Randolph, *The Virginia Housewife,* 66–67.

25. Bowen, conversation with author, Williamsburg, Va., spring 1993.

26. Randolph, "Jane Randolph her Cookery Book."

27. Randolph, *The Virginia Housewife,* 62–65.

28. Hess, *Martha Washingtion's,* 26

29. Wilson, *Food & Drink,* 314.

30. Randolph, "Jane Randolph her Cookery Book."

31. Wilson, *Food & Drink,* 293–94; Joyce M. Hawkins and Robert Allen, eds., *The Oxford Encyclopedic Dictionary* (Oxford: Oxford University Press, 1991), 1283; Randolph, *The Virginia Housewife,* 185, 267.

32. Anne C. Moore, "The Cook's Oracle: Cookbooks at the American Antiquarian Society," *The Journal of Gastronomy* 5 (winter 1989–90): 24.

33. Randolph, *The Virginia Housewife,* 17–19.

34. Ibid., 85–86, 188, 253.

35. Anonymous (1700), "Unidentified cookbook."

36. Randolph, "Jane Randolph her Cookery Book."

37. [The Compiler (1744)], "Manuscript cookbook," 67.

38. Randolph, *The Virginia Housewife,* 87–88.

**Seafood**

Epigraphs from Pepys, *Diary,* 1:56, 1:88, 9:228, 7:281; Pepys, *Diary,* 7:316, 3:96; Pepys, *Diary,* 3:53; Pepys, *Diary,* 3:71; Pepys, *Diary,* 3:55; Byrd, *Secret Diary,* 543, 177; Byrd, *Secret Diary,* 565, 101, 73; Fithian, *Journal,* 171.

1. Mennell, *All Manners,* 40, 56; Wheaton, *Savoring the Past,* 10–11.

2. Braudel, *Capitalism,* 145.
3. Pepys, *Diary,* 1:113; 2:73.
4. Wheaton, *Savoring the Past,* 12.
5. Pepys, *Diary,* 3:81; 4:232.
6. Ibid., 3:120.
7. Ibid., 1:74.
8. Ibid., 1:161–62.
9. Maxwell, ed., "Letters," 62.
10. Hammond, "Leah and Rachel," 13.
11. Beverley, *History,* 147.
12. Carter, *Diary of Landon Carter,* 861, 1062.
13. Byrd, *Secret Diary,* 113; Rose, *The Diary,* 33.
14. Henrico County Order Book & Wills, 1678–93, 368.
15. "Wyatt Manuscripts," *William and Mary Quarterly* 2d ser., 8 (January 1928): 50.
16. Anonymous (1700), "Unidentified cookbook."
17. Booth, *Hung,* 108.
18. Byrd, *Secret Diary,* 73.
19. Mouer, "Reading," 294.
20. Ibid.
21. Randolph, "Jane Randolph her Cookery Book."
22. [The Compiler (1744)], "Manuscript cookbook," 16, 56, 71–73
23. Randolph, *The Virginia Housewife,* 71–72.
24. Ibid., 73–74.
25. Anonymous (1700), "Unidentified cookbook."
26. Randolph, *The Virginia Housewife,* 40
27. Ibid., 76.
28. Ibid., 77–78, 99.
29. Ibid.
30. Several Hands, *A Collection of Above Three Hundred Receipts in Cookery, Physick and Surgery* (London: Printed for Richard Wilkin, 1714).

**Condiments**

Epigraphs from Pepys, *Diary,* 6:300; Pepys, *Diary,* 6:240; Pepys, *Diary,* 7:6; Byrd, *Secret Diary,* 525; Pepys, *Diary,* 1:250; and Byrd, letter to Charles, Earl of Orrery, 364.

1. Wilson, *Food & Drink,* 296.
2. Richard Weiss, "Health Hypothesis Curries Favor in Evolution of Spice" *Washington Post,* 2 March 1998, A3.
3. Hess, *Martha Washington's,* 10.
4. Randolph, "Jane Randolph her Cookery Book."
5. Jennifer Stead, *Food and Cooking in 18th Century Britain* (Birmingham, U.K.: English Heritage, 1985), 19; Wilson, *Food & Drink,* 296, 300.
6. Carter, *Diary of Landon Carter,* 2:608.
7. Pepys, *Diary,* 2:225.
8. Ibid., 9:443
9. Ibid., 1:308; Byrd, *Secret Diary,* 500.
10. Randolph, *The Virginia Housewife,* 25, 56, 63, 92–93, 108–14.
11. Pepys, *Diary,* 3:114; Braudel, *Capitalism,* 156.
12. Wilson, *Food & Drink,* 297, 356.

**Corn and Other Grains**

Benét quote from Elizabeth Rozin, *Blue Corn and Chocolate* (New York: Alfred A. Knopf, 1992), 3; Pepys, *Diary,* 9:498; Smith cited in Tyler, *Narratives,* 38; "Some Grievances of Rappahannock," *Journal of House of Burgesses 1659/60–1693* (Richmond, Va.: Virginia State Library), 105–6; Rose, *The Diary,* 53; Byrd, *Secret Diary,* 223, Byrd, *Another Secret Diary,* 79, and Byrd, *Secret Diary,* 221; and Byrd, *Secret Diary,* 380, 189, 60.

1. Scott and Lebsock, *Virginia Women,* 3.
2. York County Deeds, Orders, Wills, Etc., No. 1, 1633–94, 31, 182–86; York County Deeds #2, 1645–49, 873–74; Henrico County Record Book No. 1, Deeds & Wills, 1677–92 (transcript), 86–87.
3. John Lawson, *History of North Carolina* (1714; reprint, Richmond, Va.: Garrett & Massie, 1937), 76.
4. Maxwell, ed., "Letters," 63.
5. Byrd, *William Byrd's Natural History,* 20–21.
6. Kidwell, "The Southeast" in *Spirit of the Harvest,* eds. Beverly Cox and Mary Jacobs (New York: Stewart, Tabori & Chang, 1991), 16.
7. John Bartram, *Travels in Pensilvania and Canada* (1751; reprint, Ann Arbor: University Microfilms, 1966), 71.
8. Fithian, *Journal,* 55.
9. Mennell, *All Manners,* 303.
10. Hess, *Martha's Washington's,* 4; Wilson, *Food & Drink,* 255–56; Drummond and Wilbraham, *Englishman's Food,* 43, 106.
11. Beverley, *History,* 292.
12. Randolph, *The Virginia Housewife,* 100, 138–39, 153–54, 157, 171–72.
13. Maxwell, ed., "Letters," 74
14. Hess, preface to *The Carolina Rice Kitchen: The African Connection* (Columbia: University of South Carolina), xi, 3, 15.
15. Ibid., 2, 5.
16. Ibid., xiii.
17. Quoted in ibid, 11.
18. Ibid, 11.
19. Ibid., 28.
20. [The Compiler (1744)], "Manuscript cookbook," 18.
21. Hess, *Carolina Rice Kitchen.*
22. Hess in Randolph, *The Virginia Housewife,* 273.
23. Ibid., 260.
24. Ibid., 259–60.
25. Elizabeth David, *English Bread and Yeast Cookery* (New York: The Viking Press, 1977), 334.
26. Ibid., 332.
27. Ibid., 332–33.
28. Ibid., 331.
29. [The Compiler (1744)], "Manuscript cookbook," 34–35, 57–58.
30. Randolph, *The Virginia Housewife,* 260.
31. Ibid., 146, 173, 183, 239, 274; [The Compiler (1744)], "Manuscript cookbook," 18.

**Dairy Products**

Tusser, *Five Hundred Points,* 128; Lewis Carroll, "Your Old Father William," St. 7, in *Alice's Adventures in Wonderland,* quoted in John Bartlett, ed., *Bartlett's Familiar Quotations,* 517; Pepys, *Diary,* 2:24, 4:29; Pepys, *Diary,* 1:6–7, 6:224, 8:435; Pepys, *Diary,* 8:381–82; Pepys, *Diary,* 8:339; Carter, *Diary of Landon Carter,* 2:1048; Byrd, *Secret Diary,* 62, 114.

1. Drummond and Wilbraham, *Englishman's Food,* 49; Wilson, *Food & Drink,* 155–64.
2. York County Deeds, Orders, Wills, Etc., No. 1, 1633–94, 182–86; York County Deeds #2, 1645–49, 156, 873–74; Henrico County Record Book No. 1, Deeds & Wills, 1677–92 (transcript), 86–87.
3. Braudel, *Capitalism,* 144; Wilson, *Food & Drink,* 256.
4. Pepys, *Diary,* 1:221–22.

5. Rose, *The Diary,* 95.

6. Hess, *Martha Washington's,* 9.

7. [The Compiler (1744)], "Manuscript cookbook," 25.

8. Clayton, "John Clayton of James City: Afterwards of Crofton, Yorkshire," *William and Mary Quarterly* 2d ser., 1 (April 1921): 115.

9. [The Compiler (1744)], "Manuscript cookbook," 58.

10. *OED,* 5:632.

11. [The Compiler (1744)], "Manuscript cookbook," 89; Tucker Coalter, Cookbook of Elizabeth Tucker Coalter, c. 1808, 15–16, Tucker-Coleman Collections, Special Collections, Swem Library, College of William and Mary.

12. Randolph, *The Virginia Housewife,* 55.

13. [The Compiler (1744)], "Manuscript cookbook," 17.

14. Randolph, *The Virginia Housewife,* 178, 180–81.

15. Ibid., 178, 181.

16. Ibid., 175.

17. Ibid., 148.

18. [The Compiler (1744)], "Manuscript cookbook," 17–21, 47–48, 50–51.

**Vegetables**

Epigraphs from Pepys, *Diary,* 1:139, 3:87; Pepys, *Diary,* 9:202; Pepys, *Diary,* 7:104, 1:6; Pepys, *Diary,* 1:64; Byrd, *Secret Diary,* 292, 38, 346, 358; Thomas Jefferson, *Notes on Virginia* (New York: Harper & Row Publishers, 1964), 145–46; Byrd, *Secret Diary,* 404 and Byrd, *Secret Diary,* 545; William Byrd, "Letter to John Custis from London, 19 Oct. 1717," in *The Correspondence of the Three William Byrds,* 1:307.

1. Bowen, conversation with the author, Williamsburg, Va., spring 1993.

2. Sass, *Dinner,* 13; Mennell, *All Manners,* 303; Drummond and Wilbraham, *Englishman's Food,* 125.

3. Peter Brears, *Food and Cooking in 17th Century Britain* (Birmingham, U.K.: English Heritage), 9; Wilson, *Food & Drink,* 348.

4. Pepys, *Diary,* 4:285.

5. Drummond and Wilbraham, *Englishman's Food,* 125; Driver and Berriedale-Johnson, *Pepys at Table,* 10; and Maryellen Spencer, "Food in Seventeenth-Century Tidewater Virginia: A Method for Studying Historical Cuisines" (Ph.D. diss., Virginia Polytechnic Institute and State University, 1982), 86–87.

6. Dale Brown, *American Cooking* (New York: Time-Life Books, 1968), 40.

7. Spencer, "Food," 87.

8. Kalm, *Peter Kalm's Travels,* 19; Anonymous (1700), "Unidentified cookbook."

9. Elizabeth B. Pryor, "Exotic Vegetables in the Colonial Chesapeake," in *The National Colonial Farm Research Report No. 18* (Accokeek, Md.: Accokeek Foundation, 1983), 43.

10. Mouer, "Reading," 286.

11. Pepys, *Diary,* 3:69.

12. Ibid., 8:173.

13. Ibid., 4:189.

14. Ibid., 9:511.

15. Maxwell, ed., "Letters," 62–63.

16. Byrd, *William Byrd's Natural History,* 22–23.

17. Bowen, conversation with author, Williamsburg, Va., spring 1993.

18. Fithian, *Journal,* 78–79.

19. Rose, *The Diary,* 35, 52, 55.

20. Ibid., 8.

21. Crump, *Hearthside Cooking,* 33.

22. Byrd, *William Byrd's Natural History,* 22; Beverley, *History,* 141–45.

23. Carter, *Diary of Landon Carter,* 2:626.

24. Marjorie Fleming Warner, "The Earliest American Book on Kitchen Gardening" in *Annual Report of the American Historical Association for The Year 1919* (Washington, D.C.: Government Printing Office, 1919), 1:433–35.
25. Belote, *Compleat American,* 85.
26. Phipps, *Colonial Kitchens,* 128, 181–82.
27. Randolph, *The Virginia Housewife,* xxxiii.

**Fruits**

Epigraphs from Pepys, *Diary,* 4:5; Pepys, *Diary,* 4:13, 4:219, 4:261; Martha W. Hiden, ed., "Accompts of the Tristram and Jane," *Virginia Magazine of History and Biography* 62 (October 1954), 425–26; Byrd, *Secret Diary,* 73, 192; Byrd, *Secret Diary,* 180, 217, 231, 405, 408; Byrd, *Secret Diary,* 406, 219; Fithian, *Journal,* 110, 132.

1. Beverley, *History,* 293, 314.
2. Fithian, *Journal,* 90.
3. Henrico County Record Book No. 1, Deeds & Wills, 1677–92 (transcript), 104.
4. Byrd, *William Byrd's Natural History,* 33.
5. Beverley, *History,* 129–34.
6. Brears, *Food and Cooking,* 9.
7. Pepys, *Diary,* 9:477.
8. Byrd, *Secret Diary,* 185, 193, 199.
9. Ibid., 190.
10. Pepys, *Diary,* 2:185–86.
11. Byrd, *Secret Diary,* 214.
12. Anonymous (1700), "Unidentified cookbook."
13. [The Compiler (1744)], "Manuscript cookbook," 8.
14. Pepys, *Diary,* 6:322, 4:13.
15. Ibid., 7:67.
16. Frere, *A Proper Newe Booke,* xxxii.
17. Anonymous (1700), "Unidentified cookbook"; Randolph, "Jane Randolph her Cookery Book."
18. Randolph, *The Virginia Housewife,* 198–99.
19. [The Compiler (1744)], "Manuscript cookbook," 1, 3, 8, 24.
20. *OED,* 11:24.

**Sugar**

Epigraphs from Pepys, *Diary,* 4:363, 3:143; Richard Ligon, *A True & Exact History of the Island of Barbadoes* (1673; facsimile, London: Frank Cass, 1970), 85; Henry R. McIlwaine, ed., "Minutes of the Council and General Court 1622–1629," *Virginia Magazine of History and Biography* 29 (January 1921): 51; Hiden, "Accompts," 84–85; William Byrd, "Letters of William Byrd First [letter of 23 January 1690]," *Virginia Magazine of History and Biography* 27 (October 1919): 280; William Byrd, letter to Messrs. Sadler & Thomas, Merchants in Barbadoes pr Wells, 10 February 1685, ed. William Maxwell, in *The Virginia Historical Register,* 2:206; William Byrd, "William Byrd to Mr. Hutchinson of New England, 1 Aug. 1690," *Virginia Magazine of History and Biography* 26 (July 1918): 258.

1. David, *English Bread,* 138–39.
2. Frances Carnahan, "Discoveries," *Early American Life* 23 (October 1992): 3.
3. David, *English Bread,* 138–39.
4. Pepys, *Diary,* 3:91.
5. Ibid., 1:95; 4:290, 4:361.
6. Sidney W. Mintz, "Time, Sugar and Sweetness," *Marxist Perspectives* 2 (winter 1979/80), 56–72.
7. David, *English Bread,* 139.
8. Booth, *Hung,* 3, 54.
9. David, *English Bread,* 141–42.
10. Ibid., 142.

11. Randolph, "Jane Randolph her Cookery Book."
12. Markham, *The English Housewife,* xxxvi.
13. Virginia T. Elverson and Mary Ann McLanahan, *A Cookery Legacy* (New York: Walker and Company, 1975), 28.
14. Fairfax, "Colonial Girl," 214.
15. Rose, *The Diary,* 49.
16. Wilson, *Food & Drink,* 302.
17. David, *English Bread,* 139–40.
18. Ibid., 142.

**The Crowning Glory**

Epigraphs from Pepys, *Diary,* 4:243, 4:251, 1:9; Pepys, *Diary,* 3:293, 7:420; Pepys, *Diary,* 9:460–61, 9:13; William Byrd, "Letter to Sr. ———, 20 May 1690," *Virginia Magazine of History and Biography* 26 (April 1918): 126; Byrd, *Secret Diary,* 87, 201, 222, 221; Byrd, *Another Secret Diary,* 107; Fairfax, "Colonial Girl," 212.

1. R. H., *A Closet for Ladies and Gentlewomen: The Preserving, Conserving, and Candying* (London: Printed for R. M., 1651), 19–20.
2. Dawson, *The Treasury of Hidden Secrets, Commonly Called, The Goodhuswives Closet of Provision, for the Health of Her Houshold* (London: Jane Bell, 1653), #27.
3. W. M., *The Compleat Cook Expertly Prescribing the Most Ready Wayes . . . Making of Pastry* (London: Printed for Nath. Brook, 1659), 3–4.
4. John Murrell, *A Daily Exercise for Ladies and Gentlewomen* (London: Printed for the Widow Helme, 1617), #53.
5. Ibid., #57.
6. Patrick Lamb, *Royal Cookery; or, the Complete Court-Cook* (London: Printed for Abel Roper, 1710), inserts between 14–15 and 26–27.
7. Ibid., 1.
8. Anonymous (1700), "Unidentified cookbook."
9. [The Compiler (1744)], "Manuscript cookbook," 14–15, 21, 26, 76.
10. Randle Holme, *The Academy of Armory, or, A Storehouse of Armory and Blazon* (Chester: Printed for the author, 1688), bk. 3, ch. 3, p. 80.
11. David, *English Bread,* 144–46, 485–86.
12. Ibid., 136–37.
13. Kimball, *Thomas Jefferson's Cook Book,* 10.
14. David, *English Bread,* 444.
15. Nancy Carter Crump, conversation with author, Petersburg, Va., spring 1992; La Chapelle, *The Modern Cook,* 2:316. He mentioned "syringed fritters."
16. Cooper, *The Art of Cookery, Refin'd and Augmented* (London: J. G., 1654), 154–55.
17. Murrell, *A Delightful Daily Exercise,* pt. 2, B51; Dawson, *Treasury,* ch. 4.
18. Anonymous (1700), "Unidentified cookbook"; Randolph, "Jane Randolph her Cookery Book."
19. Randolph, *The Virginia Housewife,* 184–85.
20. Ibid., 165–66.

**Beverages**

Epigraphs from Pepys, *Diary,* 7:175, 3:154; Pepys, *Diary,* 1:321; Pepys, *Diary,* 1:296, 3:89; Pepys, *Diary,* 7:208, 7:115, 1:72, 5:76; Byrd, *Secret Diary,* 358, 585; Rose, *The Diary,* 94, 105; Byrd, *Secret Diary,* 121, 4–5; Fithian, *Journal,* 195–96; Fithian, *Journal,* 141; Fithian, *Journal,* 54.

1. Rose, *The Diary,* 76.
2. Pepys, *Diary,* 7:207.
3. York County Deeds, Orders, Wills, Etc., No. 1, 1633–94, 85–86, 182–86; York County Deeds #2, 1645–49, 156, 185–86.
4. Byrd, *Secret Diary,* 293–95.

5. Ibid., 181.
6. Drummond and Wilbraham, *Englishman's Food,* 112–13; Driver and Berriedale-Johnson, *Pepys at Table,* 21.
7. Drummond and Wilbraham, *Englishman's Food,* 114.
8. Pepys, *Diary,* 3:220.
9. Ibid., 7:207.
10. Ibid., 2:125, 2:212, 1:29.
11. Ibid., 4:18.
12. Ibid., 4:346.
13. Ibid., 6:151.
14. Ibid., 1:253.
15. Ibid., 3:226–27.
16. Ibid., 5:329; Drummond and Wilbraham, *Englishman's Food,* 116–17.
17. Drummond and Wilbraham, *Englishman's Food,* 116.
18. Driver and Berriedale-Johnson, *Pepys at Table,* 19–21; Drummond and Wilbraham, *Englishman's Food,* 116, 203.
19. Hiden, "Accompts," 425.
20. Hugh Jones, *The Present State of Virginia* (1748–49; reprint, ed. Richard L. Morton, Chapel Hill: University of North Carolina Press, 1956), 86.
21. Crump, *Hearthside Cooking,* 77.
22. Kalm, *Peter Kalm's Travels,* 189–90, 370.
23. Byrd, *Secret Diary,* 200.
24. Ibid., 249–50.
25. Fairfax, "Colonial Girl," 213.
26. Booth, *Hung,* 204–5; Spencer, "Food," 87–88.
27. McIlwaine, "Minutes," 64.
28. Byrd, *Secret Diary,* 190.
29. Ibid., 69.
30. Henrico County Order Book, 1694–1701, 270.
31. Mouer, "Reading," 281 and Mouer, conversation with author, Richmond, Va., January 1998.
32. Mouer, "Reading," 281.
33. Beverley, *History,* 293.
34. York County Deeds, Orders, Wills, Etc., No. 1, 1633–94, 182–86.
35. Stanley Baron, *Brewed in America: A History of Beer and Ale in the United States* (Boston: Little, Brown and Company, 1962), 32.
36. Ibid., 143.
37. Carter, *Diary of Landon Carter,* 2:1118.
38. Maxwell, ed., "Letter," 74.
39. Henrico County Record Book No. 1, Deeds & Wills, 1677–92 (transcript), 193.
40. Byrd, *Secret Diary,* 192.
41. Ibid., 561.
42. Randolph, *The Virginia Housewife,* 142.
43. Byrd, *Secret Diary,* 405.
44. Fithian, *Journal,* 175.
45. Booth, *Hung,* 208.
46. Rose, *The Diary,* 4.
47. Crump, *Hearthside Cooking,* 77; Spruill, *Women's Life,* 67; Baron, *Brewed in America,* 31.
48. Kalm, *Peter Kalm's,* 181–82; Waverly Root and Richard De Rochmont, *Eating in America: A History* (New York: Morrow, 1976), 361.
49. Pepys, *Diary,* 7:218.
50. Maxwell, ed., "Letter," 76.

**Tobacco**

Epigraphs from Henrico County Record Book No. 1, Deeds & Wills, 1677–92 (transcript) 110; Henrico County Record Book No. 1, Deeds & Wills, 1677–92 (transcript) 110; Henrico County Record Book No. 1, Deeds & Wills, 1677–92 (transcript) 110; Rose, *The Diary,* 158 n. 150; Hiden, "Accompts," 433; Rose, *The Diary,* 33; Byrd, *Secret Diary,* 58; Byrd, *Secret Diary,* 207, 208–9.

1. Pepys, *Diary,* 6:120, and 6:120 n. 2.
2. Carrier, *Agriculture,* 19.
3. Melvin Herndon, *Tobacco in Colonial Virginia, 'The Sovereign Remedy'* (Williamsburg, Va.: Virginia 350th Anniversary Celebration Corporation, 1957), 46–49.
4. Carrier, *Agriculture,* 19.
5. Ibid., 20.
6. York County Deeds, Orders, Wills, Etc., No. 1, 1633–94, 302.
7. Herndon, *Tobacco,* 50.
8. York County Deeds, Orders, Wills, Etc., No. 1, 1633–94, 296.
9. Thomas P. Hughes, *Medicine in Virginia, 1607–1699* (Williamsburg, Va.: Virginia 350th Anniversary Celebration Corporation, 1957), 46.
10. Ibid., 46.
11. Randolph, "Jane Randolph her Cookery Book."
12. Mouer, "Reading," 286, 289.
13. Smith, *Inside the Great House,* 76.

**Medicines**

Epigraphs from Pepys, *Diary,* 4:329, 5:118, 7:75; Henrico County Order Book & Wills, 1678–93, 321; Rose, *The Diary,* 11, 60; Byrd, *Secret Diary,* 209, 315, 325, 327, 332, 333; Hunter, *Quebec to Carolina,* 258; and Currie's letter to Thomas Jefferson of 9 July 1786, in *The Papers of Thomas Jefferson,* ed. Julian P. Boyd (Princeton, N.J.: Princeton University Press, 1950–2000), 10:109.

1. Hughes, *Medicine,* 2.
2. Ibid., 3.
3. Fithian, *Journal,* 107.
4. Samuel Johnson, *A Dictionary of the English Language . . . and an English Grammar* (London: Printed for Longman, Hurst, Rees, Orme, and Brown, 1818), s.v. "Receipt."
5. John Partridge, preface to *The Treasurie of Commodious Conceits, & Hidden Secrets* (London: Richarde Jones, 1573), lrvii; William Vaughan, *Directions for Health, both Naturall and Artificiall . . . modern as ancient* (London: T. S., 1617), 272–74; Murrell, *A Delightful Daily Exercise,* pt. 2, B69; Platt, *A Closet for Ladies and Gentlewomen, or, The Art of Preserving, Conserving, and Candying* (London: T. Purfoot, 1611), 102.
6. E. Smith, *The Compleat Housewife: or, Accomplished Gentlewoman's Companion* (London: Printed for J. Pemberton, 1729), 223–24; M. B., *The Ladies Cabinet Enlarged and Opened: Containing Many Rare Secrets, and Rich Ornaments of several kindes, and different uses* (London: T. M., printed for M. M. G. Bedell and T. Collins, 1654), 139.
7. Randolph, "Jane Randolph her Cookery Book."
8. York County Deeds, Wills, Etc., 1657–62, 25 [415].
9. Byrd, *Secret Diary,* 293.
10. Ibid., 213.
11. Pepys, *Diary,* 4:202.
12. Byrd, *Secret Diary,* 4.
13. Hughes, *Medicine,* 3–4.
14. Ibid., 4.
15. Ibid., 3–4 and illustration facing 15.
16. Pepys, *Diary,* 6:67.
17. Byrd, *Secret Diary,* 191.

18. Phipps, *Colonial Kitchens,* 205–6.
19. Hughes, *Medicine,* 32.
20. Ibid., 9, 11.
21. Ibid., 45.
22. Rose, *The Diary,* 14.
23. Byrd, *Secret Diary,* 401.
24. Henrico County Deeds, Wills, Etc., 1688–97, 455.
25. Carter, *Diary of Landon Carter,* 2:636–37.
26. See the chapters "Women's Private Sphere: The English and Colonial Virginia Prescription" and "Women's Public Sphere in the Chesapeake" for further discussions of domestic training.
27. Byrd, *Secret Diary,* 208.
28. Ibid., 538.
29. Pepys, *Diary,* 6:163.
30. *OED,* 2:560.
31. Ibid., 1:360
32. Ibid., 3:281.
33. Pepys, *Diary,* 9:265.
34. *OED,* 3:281.
35. Dr. Helen Rountree, letter to author, 5 November 1992.
36. Carter, *Diary of Landon Carter,* 1:216.
37. Byrd, *Secret Diary,* 196.
38. Ibid., 121, 181.
39. Pepys, *Diary,* 8:340.

**Conclusions**

Epigraphs from *Virginia Gazette Day Book* 1764–65, June 1764, 66; *Virginia Gazette,* 18 July 1746, 4.
1. Spruill, *Women's Life,* 65.
2. Carol C. Mukhopadhyay and Patricia J. Higgins, "Anthropological Studies of Women's Status Revisited: 1977–1988," *Annual Review of Anthropology* 17 (1988): 465–66.
3. Susannah Clay, letter to Clement Clay, 24 January 1833, in Clay Collection, Rare Book, Manuscript & Special Collections Library, Duke University, Durham, N.C.
4. Fairfax, "Colonial Girl," 215.
5. Konvitz, "Identity," 85, 89.
6. Ibid., 88.
7. Ibid.
8. Mouer, "Reading," 271.

## Part Three

Epigraphs from Byrd, *Secret Diary,* 37; Byrd, *Secret Diary,* 99; Byrd, *Secret Diary,* 72; Byrd, *Another Secret Diary,* 19; Byrd, *Another Secret Diary,* 91; Byrd, *Another Secret Diary,* 103; Byrd, *Another Secret Diary,* 143–44; Rose, *The Diary,* 84, 61; Rose, *The Diary,* 84; Byrd, *Secret Diary,* 178; Washington cited in Julianne Belote, *The Compleat American Housewife 1776* (Concord, Calif.: Nitty Gritty Productions, 1974), 178.

# BIBLIOGRAPHY

## Manuscripts

[Anonymous (1700)]. Unidentified cookbook, c. 1700. MSS 5:5 Un 3:4. Virginia Historical Society, Richmond.

[Anonymous (c. 1720)]. Handwritten notes in the back of Edward Kidder's *E. Kidder's Receipts of Pastry, and Cookery* (1720[? 1740] ed.), Library of Congress, Washington, D.C.

Banister, Mary Burton Augusta (Bolling). Cookbook of Mary Burton Augusta (Bolling) Banister, 1818–21. MSS 1C6458c, #10, 63–64. Cocke Family Papers, 1742–1976. Virginia Historical Society, Richmond.

Carter, Landon. Diary, 25 November 1770. Sabine Hall Papers #1959. The Albert and Shirley Small Special Collections Library, University of Virginia Library, Charlottesville.

Carter, Robert. Inventory of Robert Carter, November 1733(?). MSS 1C248a20. Carter Family Papers 1651–1861, Sec. 10. Virginia Historical Society, Richmond.

[The Compiler (1744)]. Manuscript cookbook, early eighteenth century. Va. Hist., VA. M. Mfm. 5A. Museum of Early Southern Decorative Arts, Winston-Salem, N.C.

Randolph, Jane (Bolling). Jane Randolph her Cookery Book, 1743. MSS 5:5 1507:1 (copy). Virginia Historical Society, Richmond.

Tucker Coalter, Elizabeth. Cookbook of Elizabeth Tucker Coalter, c. 1808. Tucker-Coleman Collections, Box 27, #40 T79. Special Collections. Earl Gregg Swem Library, College of William and Mary, Williamsburg, Va.

## Unpublished Papers

Barrett, William E. "Reverend Robert Barrett Professor College of William and Mary in Virginia in 1737 and His Grandson Anderson Barrett of Richmond (1773–1857)." Library of Virginia, Richmond.

Bowen, Joanne. "Foodways in Eighteenth-Century Chesapeake." Colonial Williamsburg Foundation, Williamsburg, Va., 1993.

Hill, Mrs. Christianna. "History of Mrs. Mary Randolph of Virginia." Microfilm #258269 (typescript). Mormon Archives, Salt Lake City, Utah, n.d.

Price, Theodore H., and Charlotte P. Price. "Notes on the Price Family, Cool Water, Hanover County, Virginia, Maternal Ancestry and Descent in Two Lines to the Year 1906." Library of Virginia, Richmond.

Walsh, Lorena S. "Women's Networks in the Colonial Chesapeake." Paper presented at the annual meeting of the Organization of American Historians in Cincinnati, Ohio, 1983. Colonial Williamsburg Foundation, Williamsburg, Va., has a copy of this paper in its archives.

## Correspondence

Barry, W. T. Letter to Susan (last name unknown), 1 August 1824. William T. Barry Letters (#2569), The Albert and Shirley Small Special Collections Library, University of Virginia Library, Charlottesville.

Cary, Archibald. Letter to Frances Bland Randolph, 18 November 1775. Tucker-Coleman Papers. Special Collections. Swem Library, College of William and Mary, Williamsburg, Va.

Clay, Susannah. Letter to Clement Clay, 24 January 1833. Clay Collection. Rare Book, Manuscript & Special Collections Library, Duke University, Durham, N.C.

Ferrar, Virginia. Letter to Lady Berkeley, 10 August 1650. Colonial Virginia Records, No. 692, microfilm #575. Library of Virginia, Richmond.

Middleton, Alicia. Letter to her son, 27 February 1828. Nathaniel Russell Middleton Papers (#507). Southern Historical Collection. Wilson Library, University of North Carolina at Chapel Hill.

Randolph, Ann Cary. Letter to Thomas Jefferson, 4 July 1806. Thomas Jefferson Papers. The Albert and Shirley Small Special Collections Library, University of Virginia Library, Charlottesville.

Randolph, Jane (Bolling). Letter to John Randolph, 26 April 1765. MSS 2 R1551 a1. Virginia Historical Society, Richmond.

Randolph, Judith. Letter to Martha Jefferson, 12 February 1785. Nicholas Philip Trist Papers (#2104). Southern Historical Collections. University of North Carolina at Chapel Hill.

Randolph, Richard. Letters to Thomas Jefferson, 10 and 21 January 1809. Tucker-Coleman Collections. Special Collections. Swem Library, College of William and Mary, Williamsburg, Va.

Turner, Jane. Letter to Sally Randolph, 29 September 1797. William Bolling Correspondence Papers, 1724–99. Rare Book, Manuscript & Special Collections Library, Duke University, Durham, N.C.

## Personal Communications

Bowen, Joanne. Conversation with author, Williamsburg, Va., 1993.

Briggs, Marion E. Letter to author, 28 January 1993.

Crump, Nancy Carter. Conversation with author, Petersburg, Va., 1992.

Goodburn, Mrs. Ernest. Letter to author, 12 January 1993.

Goodburn, Mr. Roger, Esq. Letter to author, 12 January 1993.

King, Dr. Thomas B. Conversation with author, Richmond, Va., 24 March 1998.

Mouer, Dr. L. Daniel. Conversations with author, Richmond, Va., 18 October 1996, January 1998, and 26 May 1998.

Oliver, Sandra. Conversation with author, Boston, Mass., November 1997.

Rountree, Dr. Helen. Letter to author, 5 November 1992.

Shepard, E. Lee. Conversation with author, Richmond, Va., spring 1993.

## Newspapers and Newspaper Articles

November, Neil. "Hospitality Betrayed." *Richmond Times-Dispatch Magazine.* Clipping, n.d. Valentine Museum, Richmond, Va.

*Virginia Gazette,* 9 June 1738; 18 July 1746; 19 December 1755; 18 June 1766; 27 July 1769; 21 March 1771; 3 November 1774; 8 March 1776

*Virginia Gazette Daybook 1764–1765,* June 1764

Weiss, Richard. "Health Hypothesis Curries Favor in Evolution of Spice." *Washington Post,* 2 March 1998, A3.

Yeadon, David. "To Market, To Market: On the Prowl around London's Smithfield." *Washington Post,* 17 December 1995, E1, E7–8.

## Virginia Records

Goochland County Deed Book #5, 1745–49

Henrico County Deeds, Wills, Etc., 1688–97

Henrico County Miscellaneous Court Records: Deeds, Wills, Etc., 1727–37; 1738–46; 1758–69

Henrico County Order Book & Wills, 1678–93

Henrico County Order Book, 1694–1701

Henrico County Record Book No. 1, Deeds & Wills, 1677–92 (transcript)

Henrico County Records Book No. 3, [Orders] (transcript)

Henrico County Wills and Deeds, 1748–50 C*

Princess Anne County Deed Book #17, 1780–82

Surry County Deeds, 1752–58, Deed Book 9
Surry County Deeds, Wills, Etc., No. 1, 1652–72
Virginia Land Office, Patent Book 1
York County Deeds #2, 1645–49
York County Deeds, Orders, Wills, Etc., No. 1, 1633–94
York County Deeds, Wills, Etc., 1657–62
York County Records, Vol. 1675–84

## Periodicals

Anderson, Sterling P., Jr. "'Queen Molly' and *The Virginia Housewife*." *Virginia Cavalcade* 20 (spring 1971): 34.

"Appraisement of the Estate of Philip Ludwell Esqr. Decd." *Virginia Magazine of History and Biography* 21 (October 1913): 395–416.

Belden, Louise C. "The Colonial Dessert Table." *Antiques* 108 (December 1975): 156–63.

Buckley, Thomas E. "The Duties of a Wife: Bishop James Madison to His Daughter, 1811." *Virginia Magazine of History and Biography* 91 (January 1983): 98–104.

Butler, Lawrence. "Letters from Lawrence Butler, of Westmoreland County, Virginia, to Mrs. Anna F. Cradock, Cumley House, near Harbrough, Leicestershire, England." *Virginia Magazine of History and Biography* 40 (July 1932): 266–67.

Byrd, William. 'Letter to Charles, Earl of Orrery, 5 July 1726.' In "Virginia Council Journals 1726–1758." *Virginia Magazine of History and Biography* 32 (October 1924): 396.

———. "Letter to Messrs. Sadler and Thomas, 10 February 1685." In *The Virginia Historical Register, and Literary Advertiser,* edited by William Maxwell, 2:206. Richmond, Va.:Macfarlane & Fergusson, 1973.

———. "Letter to Sir ———, 29 May 1690." *Virginia Magazine of History and Biography* 26 (April 1918): 126.

———. "Letters of William Byrd, First." Letter dated 23 January 1690. *Virginia Magazine of History and Biography* 27 (July and October 1919): 126, 280, respectively.

———. "Letters of William Byrd, First." Letter dated 29 May 1690. *Virginia Magazine of History and Biography,* 26 (April 1918): 126.

———. "William Byrd to Mr. Hutchinson of New England, 1 Aug. 1690." *Virginia Magazine of History and Biography,* 26 (July 1918): 258.

Carnahan, Frances. "Discoveries." *Early American Life* 23 (October 1992): 2–3.

Clayton, John. "John Clayton of James City, Afterwards of Crofton, Yorkshire." *William and Mary Quarterly,* 2d ser., 1 (April 1921): 115.

Cotton, Ann. "An Account of Our Late Troubles in Virginia." In *Force's Historical Tracts,* edited by Peter Force, 1:10. New York: Peter Smith, 1947.

Davis, Richard Beale. "The Devil in Virginia in the Seventeenth Century." *Virginia Magazine of History and Biography* 65 (April 1957): 146.

Fairfax, Sally Cary. "Diary of a Little Colonial Girl." *Virginia Magazine of History and Biography* 11 (October 1903): 212–15.

FitzHugh, William. "Letters of William FitzHugh." *Virginia Magazine of History and Biography* 2 (June 1895): 269.

"Funeral Charges for Elizabeth Sindrey." *South Carolina Historical Magazine* 82 (January 1981): 81–84.

Hammond, John. "Leah and Rachel, or, The Two Fruitful Sisters Virginia and Maryland." In *Force's Historical Tracts,* edited by Peter Force, 3:15. New York: Peter Smith, 1947.

"Heroines of Virginia." *William and Mary Quarterly,* 1st ser., 15 (July 1906): 39–41.

Hiden, Martha W., ed. "Accompts of the Tristram and Jane." *Virginia Magazine of History and Biography,* 62 (October 1954): 425–26, 433.

Kerber, Linda K. "Separate Spheres, Female Worlds, Women's Place: The Rhetoric of Women's History." *Journal of American History* 75 (June 1988): 9–39.

Konvitz, Josef. "Identity, Self-Expression and the American Cook." *Centennial Review* 19 (spring 1975): 85–88.

"Ladies of the Association." *William and Mary Quarterly,* 1st ser., 8 (July 1899): 36.

'Marriage of Dr. Blair and Sarah Harrison.' In "Papers Relating to the Administration of Governor Nicholson and to the Founding of William and Mary College." *Virginia Magazine of History and Biography* 7 (January 1900): 278.

McIlwaine, Henry R. "Minutes of the Council and General Court of Colonial Virginia, 1622–1629." *Virginia Magazine of History and Biography* 29 (January 1921): 51.

Mintz, Sidney W. "Time, Sugar and Sweetness." *Marxist Perspectives* 2 (winter 1979/80): 56–72.

Moore, Anne C. "The Cook's Oracle: Cookbooks at the American Antiquarian Society." *Journal of Gastronomy* 5 (winter 1989–90).

Mukhopadhyay, Carol C., and Patricia J. Higgins. "Anthropological Studies of Women's Status Revisited: 1977–1988." In *Annual Review of Anthropology* 17 (1988): 461–95.

Norton, Mary Beth. "The Evolution of White Women's Experience in Early America." *American Historical Review* 89 (June 1984): 593–619.

"Notes and Queries." *Virginia Magazine of History and Biography* 33 (January 1925): 87.

Paschal, Herbert R., ed. "George Bancroft's 'Lost Notes' on the General Court Records of the Seventeenth Century Virginia." *Virginia Magazine of History and Biography* 91 (July 1983): 348–62.

"Proceedings of the Visitors at William and Mary College, 1716." *Virginia Magazine of History and Biography* 4 (October 1896): 174.

"Some Grievances of Rappahannock." *Journal of House of Burgesses 1659/60–1695.* Richmond: Virginia State Library, 1914, 386.

Storace, Patricia. "Repasts Past." *House & Garden* 158, no. 6 (1986): 62–72.

Warner, Majorie Fleming. "The Earliest American Book on Kitchen Gardening." In *Annual Report of the American Historical Association for the Year 1919,* vol. 1, 433–34. Washington, D.C.: Government Printing Office, 1919.

Wolf, Thomas H. "Once Upon a Time a Cookbook Was a Recipe for Excess." *Smithsonian* 22, no. 8 (1991): 118–31.

Woolfolk, Margaret. "Patriotic Desserts." *Early American Life* 23, no. 3 (1992): 36–39.

"Wyatt Manuscripts." *William and Mary Quarterly,* 2d ser., 8 (January 1928): 485.

## Books and Parts of Books

Adams, A. K., ed. *The Home Book of Humorous Quotations.* New York: Dodd, Mead & Company, 1969.

Adams, Charles Francis[, ed.]. *Familiar Letters of John Adams and His Wife Abigail Adams, during the Revolution.* 1875. Reprint, Freeport, N.Y.: Books for Libraries Press, 1970.

Andrews, Rev. C. W. *Memoir of Mrs. Anne R. Page.* Philadelphia: Herman Hooker, 1844.

Aresty, Esther B. *The Exquisite Table: A History of French Cuisine.* New York: Bobbs-Merrill Company, 1980.

Atkyns, Arabella. *The Family Magazine: In Two Parts . . . Prolonging of Life.* London: Printed for J. Osborn, 1741.

B., M. [Lord Ruthven]. *The Ladies Cabinet Enlarged and Opened: Containing Many Rare Secrets, and Rich Ornaments of several kindes, and different uses.* London: T. M., printed for M. M. G. Bedell and T. Collins, 1654.

Bailey, Kent P., and Ransom B. True. *A Guide to Seventeenth-Century Virginia Court Handwriting.* Research Bulletin 1. Richmond, Va.: Association for the Preservation of Virginia Antiquities, 1980.

Baron, Stanley. *Brewed in America: A History of Beer and Ale in the United States.* Boston: Little, Brown and Company, 1962.

Bartlett, John, ed. *Bartlett's Familiar Quotations.* 13th ed. Boston: Little, Brown and Company, 1955.

Bartram, John. *Travels in Pensilvania and Canada.* 1751. Reprint, Ann Arbor, Mich.: University Microfilms, 1966.

Bayard, Tania. *A Medieval Home Companion: Housekeeping in the Fourteenth Century.* New York: Harper Perennial, 1992.
Belote, Julianne. *The Compleat American Housewife 1776.* Concord, Calif.: Nitty Gritty Productions, 1974.
Benson, Mary Sumner. *Women in Eighteenth-Century America.* New York: Columbia University Press, 1935.
Beverley, Robert. *The History and Present State of Virginia.* 1705. Reprint, Chapel Hill: University of North Carolina Press, 1947.
Blencowe, Mrs. Ann. *The Receipt Book of Mrs. Ann Blencowe A.D. 1694.* 1694. Reprint, Cottonport, La.: Polyanthos, 1972.
Booth, Sally Smith. *Hung, Strung & Potted.* New York: Clarkson N. Potter, 1971.
Boyd, Julian P., ed. *The Papers of Thomas Jefferson.* 28 vols. Princeton, N.J.: Princeton University Press, 1950–2000.
Bradley, Richard. *A Complete Body of Husbandry . . . Adorn'd with Cuts.* London: Printed for James Woodman, and David Lyon, 1727.
———. *The Country Housewife and Lady's Director.* 1736. Reprint, London, 1980.
Brant, Irving. *James Madison.* Vol. 6. Indianapolis, Ind.: Bobbs-Merrill, 1961.
Braudel, Fernand. *Capitalism and Material Life, 1400–1800.* New York: Harper and Row, 1973.
Brears, Peter. *Food and Cooking in 17th Century Britain.* Birmingham, U.K.: English Heritage, 1985.
Brown, Dale. *American Cooking.* New York: Time-Life Books, 1968.
Bruce, Philip Alexander. *Social Life of Virginia in the Seventeenth Century.* Richmond, Va.: Whittet & Shepperson, Printers, 1907.
Bucher, Ward, ed. *Dictionary of Building Preservation.* New York: John Wiley and Sons, 1996.
Bushman, Richard. *The Refinement of America: Persons, Houses, Cities.* New York: Alfred A. Knopf, 1992.
Butterfield, L. H., Marc Friedlaender, and Mary-Jo Kline, eds. *The Book of Abigail and John: Selected Letters of the Adams Family, 1762–1782.* Cambridge: Harvard University Press, 1975.
Byrd, William. *Another Secret Diary of William Byrd of Westover, 1739–1741.* Edited by Marion Tinling. Richmond, Va.: The Dietz Press, 1942.
———. *The Correspondence of the Three William Byrds of Westover, Virginia, 1684–1776.* Edited by Marion Tinling. Vol. 1. Charlottesville: University Press of Virginia, 1977.
———. *The Secret Diary of William Byrd of Westover, 1709–1712.* Edited by Louis B. Wright and Marion Tinling. Richmond, Va.: The Dietz Press, 1941.
———. *William Byrd's Natural History of Virginia, or The Newly Discovered Eden.* Edited and translated by Richard Croom Beatty and William J. Molloy. Richmond, Va.: The Dietz Press, 1940.
———. *The Writings of "Colonel William Byrd of Westover in Virginia, Esqr."* Edited by John Spencer Bassett. New York: Doubleday Page (De Vinne), 1901.
Carrier, Lyman. *Agriculture in Virginia, 1607–1699.* Williamsburg, Va.: Virginia 350th Anniversary Celebration Corporation, 1957.
Carson, Barbara. *Ambitious Appetites: Dining, Behavior, and Patterns of Consumption in Federal Washington.* Washington, D.C.: American Institute of Architects Press, 1990.
Carson, Jane. *Colonial Virginia Cookery.* Williamsburg, Va.: Colonial Williamsburg Foundation, 1985.
———. *Plantation Housekeeping in Colonial Virginia.* Williamsburg, Va.: Colonial Williamsburg Foundation, 1974.
Carter, Charles. *The Compleat City and Country Cook: or, Accomplish'd Housewife.* London: Printed for A. Bettesworth & C. Hitch & C. Davis, 1732.
Carter, Landon. *The Diary of Landon Carter of Sabine Hall, 1752–1778.* Edited by Jack P. Greene. 2 vols. Charlottesville: University Press of Virginia, 1965.
Claghorn, Charles E. *Women Patriots of the American Revolution: A Biographical Dictionary.* Metuchen, N.J.: Scarecrow Press, 1991.
Clinton, Catherine. *The Plantation Mistress.* New York: Pantheon Books, 1982.

Collins, Randall. "Women and the Production of Status Cultures." In *Cultivating Differences: Symbolic Boundaries and the Making of Inequality,* edited by Michèle Lamont and Marcel Fournier. Chicago, Ill.: University of Chicago Press, 1992.

Cooper, Joseph. *The Art of Cookery, Refin'd and Augmented.* London: J. G., 1654.

Cowden, Gerald Steffan. "The Randolphs of Turkey Island: A Prosopography of the First Three Generations, 1650–1806." Ph.D. diss., College of William and Mary, 1980.

Cox, Virginia D., and Willie T. Weathers. *Old Houses of King and Queen County, Virginia.* [King and Queen Court House, Va.]: King and Queen Historical Society, 1973.

Cromwell, Elizabeth. *The Court & Kitchen of Elizabeth, Commonly Joan Cromwel, The Wife of the Late Usurper . . . for General Satisfaction.* London: Tho. Milbourn, 1664.

Crump, Nancy Carter. *Hearthside Cooking.* McLean, Va.: EPM Publications, 1986.

Daniels, Jonathan. *The Randolphs of Virginia.* Garden City, N.Y.: Doubleday & Company, 1972.

David, Elizabeth. *English Bread and Yeast Cookery.* New York: Viking Press, 1977.

Dawson, Thomas. *The Treasury of Hidden Secrets, Commonly Called, The Goodhuswives Closet of Provision, for the Health of Her Houshold.* London: Jane Bell, 1653.

*Dictionary of National Biography,* 1937–38 ed., s.v. "Butler, Dr. William," 6:542; "Meade, Richard," 13:181–83; and "Steevens, Richard," 18:1035–36.

Digby, Sir Kenelm. *Choice and Experimental Receipts in Physick and Chirurgery . . . to Her Majesty the Queen Mother.* London: Printed for the author, and are to be sold by H. Brome at the Star in Litle-Britain, 1668.

———. *Choice and Experimental Receipts in Physick and Chirurgery . . . to Her Majesty the Queen Mother.* London: Printed for the author, 1669.

———. *The Closet of the Eminently Learned Sir Kenelm Digby Kt. Opened . . . Candying, &c.* London: E. C. & A. C., 1671.

Doddridge, Joseph. *Notes on the Settlement and Indian Wars of the Western Parks of Virginia and Pennsylvania from 1763 to 1783.* Pittsburgh, Pa., 1912.

Dorman, John Frederick. *Adventure of Purse and Person 1607–1624/5.* Richmond, Va.: Order of First Families of Virginia through The Dietz Press, 1987.

Douglas, Mary. "Distinctive Anthropological Perspective." In *Constructive Drinking,* edited by Mary Douglas. New York: Cambridge University Press, 1987.

Douglas, Mary, and Baron Isherwood. *The World of Goods.* New York: W. W. Norton & Company, 1979.

Driver, Christopher, and Michelle Berriedale-Johnson. *Pepys at Table: Seventeenth Century Recipes for the Modern Cook.* Berkeley and Los Angeles: University of California Press, 1984.

Drummond, J. C., and Anne Wilbraham. *The Englishman's Food: A History of Five Centuries of English Diet.* London: Jonathan Cape, 1969.

Durand, François. *A Huguenot Exile in Virginia.* 1686–87. Reprint, edited by Gilbert Chinard, New York: Press of the Pioneers, 1934.

Elverson, Virginia T., and Mary Ann McLanahan. *A Cooking Legacy.* New York: Walker and Company, 1975.

*The English Lady's Catechism; Shewing The Pride and Variety of our English Quality, in relieving Foreigners before their own Country Folks.* London, 1756.

Ervin, Janet Halliday, ed. *The White House Cookbook.* Chicago: Follett Publishing Company, 1964.

Evelyn, John. *John Evelyn, Cook: The Manuscript Receipt Book of John Evelyn.* Edited by Christopher Driver. Totnes, U.K.: Prospect Books, 1997.

Fairfax Family. *Arcana Fairfaxiana Manuscripta.* Edited by George Weddell. Newcastle-on-Tyne, U.K.: Mawson, Swan, & Morgan, 1890.

Farmer, Fannie Merritt. *The Original Boston Cooking-School Cookbook.* New York: Weathervane Books, 1896.

Fithian, Philip Vickers. *The Journal and Letters of Philip Vickers Fithian, 1773–1774: A Plantation Tutor of the Old Dominion.* Edited by Hunter Dickinson Farrish. Williamsburg, Va.: Colonial Williamsburg, 1965.

———. *Journal and Letters 1767–1774.* Edited by John Rogers Williams. Princeton, N.J.: University Library, 1900.

Franklin, Benjamin. *The Autobiography of Benjamin Franklin.* Edited by Leonard E. Labaree. New Haven: Yale University Press, 1964.

Frere, Catherine Frances. *A Proper Newe Booke of Cokerye.* Cambridge, U.K.: W. Heffer & Sons, 1913.

G., R. *The Accomplish'd Female Instructor, or, A Very Useful Companion for Ladies, Gentlewomen, and Others.* London: John Shirley, 1704.

Glasse, Hannah. *The Art of Cookery Made Plain and Easy.* 1747. Reprint, London: Prospect Books, 1983.

Glassie, Henry H. *Folk Housing in Middle Virginia.* Knoxville: University of Tennessee Press, 1975.

Goffman, Erving. *The Presentation of Self in Everyday Life.* Woodstock, N.Y.: Overlook Press, 1973.

Goody, Jack. *Cooking, Cuisine, and Class: A Study in Comparative Sociology.* Cambridge: Cambridge University Press, 1982.

Greene, George Washington. *The Life of Nathanael Green, Major-General in the Army of the Revolution.* 1871. Reprint, New York: Books for Libraries Press, 1972.

Gusfield, Joseph. "Passage to Play: Rituals of Drinking Time in American Society." In *Constructive Drinking,* edited by Mary Douglas. New York: Cambridge University Press, 1987.

H., R. *A Closet for Ladies and Gentlewomen: The Art of Preserving, Conserving, and Candying.* London: Printed by R. M., 1651.

Hall, T. *The Queen's Royal Cookery.* London: Printed for C. Bat & A. Bettesworth, 1709.

Harbury, Katharine E. "Colonial Virginia's Cooking Dynasty: Women's Spheres and Culinary Arts." Master's thesis, College of William and Mary, 1994.

Harrison, Sarah. *The House-keeper's Pocket-Book and Compleat Family Cook.* London, 1733.

Herndon, Melvin. *Tobacco in Colonial Virginia, 'The Sovereign Remedy.'* Williamsburg, Va.: Virginia 350th Anniversary Celebration Corporation, 1957.

Hess, Karen. *The Carolina Rice Kitchen: The African Connection.* Columbia: University of South Carolina, 1992.

———, ed. *Martha Washington's Booke of Cookery.* New York: Columbia University Press, 1981.

Hill, Elizabeth, and Martha Starr. *Candles & Parsley: When Company Comes.* Washington, D.C.: Starrhill Press, 1989.

Holme, Randle. *The Academy of Armory, or, A Storehouse of Armory and Blazon.* Chester: Printed for the author, 1688.

Horry, Harriot Pinckney. *A Colonial Plantation Cookbook.* 1815. Reprint, edited by Richard J. Hooker, Columbia: University of South Carolina Press, 1984.

Howard, Henry. *England's Newest Way in All Sorts of Cookery, Pastry, and All Pickles That Are Fit to Be Used.* London: Printed for Chr. Coningsby, 1710.

———. *England's Newest Way in All Sorts of Cookery, Pastry, and All Pickles That Are Fit to Be Used.* London: Printed for J. Knapton, R. Kanplock, et al., 1726.

Hughes, Thomas P. *Medicine in Virginia, 1607–1699.* Williamsburg, Va.: Virginia 350th Anniversary Celebration Corporation, 1957.

Hunter, Robert. *Quebec to Carolina in 1785–1786: Being the Travel Diary and Observations of Robert Hunter Jr., a Young Merchant of London.* San Marino, Calif.: Huntington Library, 1943.

Isaac, Rhys. *The Transformation of Virginia, 1740–1790.* Chapel Hill: University of North Carolina Press, 1982.

Jefferson, Thomas. *Notes on the State of Virginia.* 1861. Reprint, New York: Harper & Row, 1964.

Jenner, Thomas. *A Book of Fruits & Flowers.* 1653. Reprint, edited by C. Anne Wilson, London: Prospect Books, 1984.

Johnson, Samuel. *A Dictionary of the English Language . . . and an English Grammar.* London: Printed for Longman, Hurst, Rees, Orme, and Brown, 1818.

Jones, Hugh. *The Present State of Virginia.* 1724. Reprint, edited by Richard L. Morton, Chapel Hill: University of North Carolina Press, 1956.

Kalm, Pehr. *Peter Kalm's Travels in North America.* 1748–49. Reprint, edited by Adolph B. Benson, New York: Wilson-Erickson, 1937.

Kavasch, Barrie. *Native Harvests.* New York: Random House, 1977.

Kent, Elizabeth (Talbot) Grey, Countess of. *A Choice Manual of Rare and Select Secrets in Physick and Chyrurgery . . . As Also Most Exquisite Ways of Preserving, Conserving, Candying, &c.* Part 2, *A True Gentlewomans Delight,* with separate title page and pagination is bound with part 1. London: Published by W. I. Gent, printed by G. D., 1653.

———. *A True Gentlewomans Delight. See* Kent, Elizabeth (Talbot) Grey, Countess of. *A Choice Manual of Rare and Select Secrets in Physick and Chyrurgery . . .*

Kerber, Linda K. *Women of the Republic: Intellect and Ideology in Revolutionary America.* Chapel Hill: University of North Carolina Press, 1980.

Kidder, Edward. *E. Kidder's Receipts of Pastry, and Cookery.* London, 1720[? 1740].

———. *E. Kidder's Receipts of Pastry, and Cookery.* London: Holborn, 1740.

Kidwell, Clara Sue. "Native American Foods." In *Spirit of the Harvest,* edited by Beverly Cox and Martin Jacobs. New York: Stewart, Tabori & Chang, 1991.

———. "The Southeast." In *Spirit of the Harvest,* edited by Beverly Cox and Martin Jacobs. New York: Stewart, Tabori & Chang, 1991.

Kimball, Marie. *Thomas Jefferson's Cook Book.* Richmond, Va.: Garrett & Massie, 1938.

Kulikoff, Allan. *Tobacco and Slaves: The Development of Southern Cultures in the Chesapeake, 1680–1800.* Chapel Hill: University of North Carolina Press, 1986.

La Chapelle, Vincent. *The Modern Cook.* London: Author, 1736.

*The Lady's Companion, or, An Infallible Guide to the Fair Sex.* 4th ed. Vols. 1 and 2. London, 1743.

Lamb, Patrick. *Royal Cookery; or, the Complete Court-Cook.* London: Printed for Abel Roper, 1710.

Lane, Rose Wilder. *Woman's Day Book of American Needlework.* New York: Simon and Schuster, 1963.

La Varenne, François Pierre de. *The French Cook Prescribing the Way of Making Ready of All Sorts of Meats, Fish and Flesh, with the Proper Sauces.* London, 1653.

Lawson, John. *History of North Carolina.* 1714. Reprint, Richmond, Va.: Garrett and Massie, 1937.

Lebsock, Suzanne D. *"A Share of Honor": Virginia Women, 1600–1945.* Richmond, Va.: W. M. Brown & Son, 1984.

Leslie, Eliza. *Miss Leslie's New Cookery Book.* Philadelphia: T. B. Peterson & Brothers, 1857.

Ligon, Richard, Gent. *A True & Exact History of the Island of Barbadoes.* London: Printed by Peter Parker, 1673 [facsimile reprint, London: Frank Cass, 1970].

M., G. [Markham, Gervase]. *The English House-Wife, Containing . . . to an Household.* London: B. Alsop, 1649.

M., W. *The Compleat Cook Expertly Prescribing the Most Ready Wayes . . . Making of Pastry.* London: Printed for Nath. Brook, 1659.

———. *The Queen's Closet Opened. Incomparable Secrets in Physick, Chirurgery, Preserving, Candying, and Cookery.* Part 2, *A Queen's Delight: or, The Art of Preserving, Conserving and Candying,* with separate title page and pagination is bound with part 1. London: E. Tyler and R. Holt, 1671.

———. *A Queen's Delight.* See M., W. *The Queen's Closet Opened. Incomparable Secrets in Physick, Chirurgery, Preserving, Candying, and Cookery.*

Maggs Bros. *Notes on Autographs.* No. 1. London: Corner Press, 1934.

Markham, Gervase. *The English House-Wife.* London: B. Alsop, 1638.

———. *The English Housewife.* 1615. Reprint, edited by Michael Best, Kingston: McGill-Queen's University, 1986.

———. *The English Hus-Wife.* London: I[John] B[eale], 1615.

Massialot, François. *The Court and Country Cook.* London, 1702.

Maxwell, William, ed. *The Virginia Historical Register, and Literary Advertiser.* Vols. 1–2. 1848–49. Reprint, Richmond, Va.: Macfarlane & Fergusson, 1973.

May, Robert. *The Accomplisht Cook, or, The Art and Mystery of Cookery.* London: R. W., 1660.

McIlwaine, Henry R., ed. *Minutes of the Council and General Court of Colonial Virginia.* Richmond: Virginia State Library, 1979.

Mendes, Helen. *The African Heritage Cookbook.* New York: Macmillan, 1971.

Mennell, Stephen. *All Manners of Food.* Oxford, U.K.: Basil Blackwell, Ltd., 1985.

Middleton, John. *Five Hundred New Receipts in Cookery . . . by All Good Housewives*. London: Printed for Thomas Astley, 1734.

Miller, Henry. "An Archaeological Perspective on the Evolution of Diet in the Colonial Chesapeake, 1620–1745." In *Colonial Chesapeake Society*, edited by Lois Green Carr, Philip D. Morgan, and Jean B. Russo. Chapel Hill: University of North Carolina Press, 1988.

Moffett [Muffett], Thomas. *Health's Improvement*. London: Published by T. Newcomb for Samuel Thomson, 1655.

Moore, Henrietta. *Feminism and Anthropology*. Minneapolis: University of Minnesota Press, 1988.

Mordecai, Samuel. *Richmond in By-Gone Days*. Richmond, Va.: The Dietz Press, 1860.

Moss, Kay, and Kathryn Hoffman. *The Backcountry Housewife: A Study of Eighteenth Century Foods*. Vol. 1. Gastonia, N.C.: Schiele Museum, 1985.

Mouer, L. Daniel. "Chesapeake Creoles: The Creation of Folk Culture in Colonial Virginia." In *The Archaeology of 17th-Century Virginia*, edited by Theodore R. Reinhart and Dennis J. Pogue. Special Publication/Archaeological Society of Virginia, no. 30. Richmond, Va.: Archaeological Society of Virginia, 1993.

———. "Reading 'Jane Randolph Her Book.'" In *Digging Sites and Telling Stories: Essays in Interpretive Historical Archaeology*. New York: Plenum Publishing, 1998.

Murrell, John. *A Booke of Cookerie* (1621). See Murrell, John. *A Delightful Daily Exercise for Ladies and Gentlewomen*.

———. *A Daily Exercise for Ladies and Gentlewomen*. London: Printed for Widow Helme, 1617.

———. *A Delightful Daily Exercise for Ladies and Gentlewomen*. Part 2, *A Booke of Cookerie: Containing . . . Dutch Fashions. . .* , with separate title page and pagination is bound with part 1. London: Printed for Tho. Dewe, 1621.

———. *A New Booke of Cookerie*. London: Printed for J. Browne, 1617.

Nicholson, William S. *Historic Homes and Churches of Virginia's Eastern Shore*. Accomac, Va.: Atlantic Publications, 1984.

Norton, Mary Beth. *Liberty's Daughter*. Boston: Little, Brown and Company, 1980.

Nott, John. *The Cook's and Confectioner's Dictionary: or, the Accomplish'd Housewives Companion*. 2d ed. London: Printed for C. Rivington, 1724.

Oliver, Sandra L. *Saltwater Foodways: New Englanders and Their Food, at Sea and Ashore, in the Nineteenth Century*. Mystic, Conn.: Mystic Seaport Museum, 1995.

Outlaw, Alain. *Governor's Land: Archaeology of Early Seventeenth-Century Virginia Settlements*. Charlottesville: Published for the Dept. of Historic Resources by the University Press of Virginia, 1990.

Partridge, John. *The Treasurie of Commodious Conceits, & Hidden Secrets*. London: Richarde Jones, 1573.

*The Pastry-Cook's Vade-Mecum: or a Pocket Companion for Cooks, Housekeepers, Country Gentlewomen &c*. London: Printed for Abel Roper, 1705.

Pepys, Samuel. *The Diary of Samuel Pepys*. 10 vols. Reprint, edited by R. C. Latham and W. Matthews, Berkeley: University of California Press, 1970–83.

Phipps, Frances. *Colonial Kitchens, Their Furnishings, and Their Gardens*. New York: Hawthorne Books, 1972.

Platt, Sir Hugh. *A Closet for Ladies and Gentlewomen, or, The Art of Preserving, Conserving, and Candying*. London: T. Purfoot, 1611.

———. *Delights for Ladies*. 1609. Reprint, London: Crosby Lockwood & Son Ltd., 1948.

Price, Rebecca. *The Compleat Cook*. 1681. Reprint, compiled by Medeleine Masson, London: Routledge & Kegan Paul, 1948.

Pryor, Elizabeth B. "Exotic Vegetables in the Colonial Chesapeake." In *The National Colonial Farm Research Report No. 18*. Accokeek, Md.: Accokeek Foundation, 1983.

Pullar, Philippa. *Consuming Passions: Being an Historic Inquiry into Certain English Appetites*. Boston: Little, Brown and Company, 1970.

Rabisha, William. *The Whole Body of Cookery Dissected, Taught . . . Dutch &c*. London: Printed for Giles Calvert by R. W., 1661.

———. *The Whole Body of Cookery Dissected, Taught . . . Dutch &c.* London: Printed for E. Calvert, 1673.

Randolph, Mary. *The Virginia Housewife.* 1824. Reprint, edited by Karen Hess, Columbia: University of South Carolina Press. 1984.

Rice, Howard C., Jr., comp. *The American Campaigns of Rochambeau's Army, 1780, 1781, 1782, 1783.* Edited and translated by Howard C. Rice Jr. and Anne S. K. Brown. Vol. 1. Princeton, N.J.: Princeton University Press, 1972.

Root, Waverly, and Richard De Rochmont. *Eating in America: A History.* New York: Morrow, 1976.

Rose, Robert. *The Diary of Robert Rose: A View of Virginia by a Scottish Colonial Parson 1746–1751.* Edited by Ralph E. Hall. Verona, Va.: McClure Press, 1977.

Rozin, Elizabeth. *Blue Corn and Chocolate.* New York: Alfred A. Knopf, 1992.

Safford, William H. *The Blennerhassett Papers.* Cincinnati, Ohio: Moore, Wilstach, & Baldwin, 1864.

Salmon, William. *The Family Dictionary: Or, Household Companion.* 2d ed. London: Printed for H. Rhodes, 1696.

Sass, Lorna. *Dinner with Tom Jones: Eighteenth-Century Cookery Adapted for the Modern Kitchen.* New York: Metropolitan Museum of Art, 1977.

Scott, Anne Firor, and Suzanne D. Lebsock. *Virginia Women: The First Two Hundred Years.* Williamsburg, Va.: Colonial Williamsburg Foundation, 1988.

Several Best Masters. *The Genteel Housekeepers Pastime: Or, the Mode of Carving at the Table Represented in a Pack of Playing Cards.* London, 1693.

Several Hands. *A Collection of Above Three Hundred Receipts in Cookery, Physick and Surgery.* 2 vols. London: Printed for Richard Wilkin, 1714.

———. *A Collection of Above Three Hundred Receipts in Cookery, Physick and Surgery.* London: Printed for Mary Kettilby, 1724.

———. *A Collection of Above Three Hundred Receipts in Cookery, Physick and Surgery.* London: Printed for executrix of Mary Kettilby, 1734.

Shammas, Carole. "English-Born and Creole Elites in Turn-of-Century Virginia." In *The Chesapeake in the Seventeenth Century,* edited by Thad W. Tate and David L. Ammerman. Chapel Hill: University of North Carolina Press, 1979.

Shirley, John. *The Accomplished Ladies Rich Closet of Rareties . . . Maides Delightful Companion.* N.p.: Printed for N. Bodington, 1690.

Simmons, Amelia. *American Cookery.* 1796. Reprint, [Grand Rapids,] Mich.: William B. Eerdmans Publishing Co., 1965.

Skelly, Carole. *Dictionary of Herbs, Spices, Seasonings, and Natural Flavorings.* New York: Garland Publishers, 1994.

Smith, Daniel Blake. *Inside the Great House: Planter Family Life in Eighteenth-Century Chesapeake Society.* Ithaca, N.Y.: Cornell University Press, 1980.

Smith, E. *The Compleat Housewife: or, Accomplished Gentlewoman's Companion.* 3d ed. London: Printed for J Pemberton, 1729.

———. *The Compleat Housewife: or, Accomplished Gentlewoman's Companion.* London: Printed for R. Ware, S. Birt, T. Longman, C. Hitch, J Hodges [and 4 others in London], 1753.

Smith, Robert. *Court Cookery, or, The Compleat English Cook.* Vols. 1–2. London: Printed for T. Wotton, 1723.

———. *Court Cookery, or, The Compleat English Cook.* Vols. 1–2. London: Printed for T. Wotton, 1724.

Spencer, Maryellen. "Food in Seventeenth-Century Tidewater Virginia: A Method for Studying Historical Cuisines." Ph.D. diss., Virginia Polytechnic Institute and State University, 1982.

Spruill, Julia Cherry. *Women's Life and Work in the Southern Colonies.* New York: Russell & Russell, 1969.

Stead, Jennifer. *Food and Cooking in 18th Century Britain.* Birmingham, U.K.: English Heritage, 1985.

Tarleton, Lieutenant-Colonel (Banastre). *A History of the Campaigns of 1780 and 1781, in the Southern Provinces of North America.* London: Printed for T. Caddell, in the Strand, 1787.

Tryon, Thomas. *The Way to Get Wealth.* 2d ed. London, 1702.

Tusser, Thomas. *Five Hundred Points of Good Husbandry.* London: J. M., 1663.

Tyler, Lyon G., *Narratives of Early Virginia 1606–1625.* New York: C. Scribner's Sons, 1907; New York: Barnes & Noble, 1952.

Vaughan, William. *Directions for Health, both Naturall and Artificiall . . . modern as ancient.* London: T. S., 1617.

Walsh, Lorena S. "The Experiences and Status of Women in the Chesapeake 1750–1775." In *The Web of Southern Social Relations: Women, Family, and Education,* edited by Walter J. Fraser Jr., R. Frank Saunders, and Jon L. Wakelyn. Athens: University of Georgia Press, 1985.

Welter, Barbara. "The Cult of True Womanhood: 1820–1860." In *The American Family in Social-Historical Perspective,* edited by Michael Gordon. New York: St. Martin's Press, 1973.

Wheaton, Barbara Ketcham. *Savoring the Past: The French Kitchen and Table from 1300 to 1789.* Philadelphia: University of Pennsylvania Press, 1983.

Wilkins, Patricia, ed. *America's Heritage Quilts.* Des Moines, Iowa: Meredith Corporation, 1991.

Wilson, C. Anne. *Food & Drink in Britain.* New York: Barnes & Noble, 1974.

Woolley, Hannah. *The Accomplish'd Lady's Delight in Preserving, Physick, Beautifying and Cookery.* London: Printed for B. Harris, 1675. Part 3, *The Compleat Cook's Guide,* with separate title page and pagination is bound with part 1.

———. *The Compleat Cook's Guide.* See Woolley, Hannah. *The Accomplish'd Lady's Delight in Preserving, Physick, Beautifying and Cookery.*

———. *The Gentlewoman's Companion . . . from Their Childhood Down to Old Age.* London: A. Maxwell, 1675.

Wright, Louis B. *The First Gentlemen of Virginia; Intellectual Qualities of the Early Colonial Ruling Class.* San Marino, Calif.: The Huntington Library, 1940.

Y-Worth, W. *Chymicus Rationalis: Or, The Fundamental Grounds of the Chymical Art.* London: Printed for Thomas Salusbury, 1692.

*The Young Lady's Companion in cookery . . . candying.* London: Printed for A. Bettesworth and C. Hitch, J. Hazard, W. Bickerton and C. Corbett, and R. Willock, 1734.

# INDEX TO PARTS ONE AND TWO

This index covers only Parts 1 and 2 of this book. For an index to the recipes that appear in Part 3, please see pages 469–479. Page numbers *in italic* refer to illustrations.

# INDEX TO THE RECIPES

This index covers only part 3 of this book, and it includes three types of entries:

(1) *Recipes by title* from the two featured cookbooks [one by Anonymous (1700) and the other by Mary (Bolling) Randolph]: These recipes are listed under general recipe categories (such as breads, cakes, meat recipes, sweets, et cetera) shown in **bold type**. Please note that the *contemporary recipes* by other cookbook authors have not been indexed, as they can be found on the same or facing page, to the right of the featured recipes.

(2) *Main ingredient/s* in each featured recipe (where applicable).

(3) *Special terms* that appear in the "Comments" column next to the featured recipes.